Reading Latin

GRAMMAR AND EXERCISES
Second edition

Reading Latin, first published in 1986, is a bestselling Latin course designed to help mature beginners read classical Latin fluently and intelligently, primarily in the context of classical culture, but with some medieval Latin too. It does this in three ways: it encourages the reading of continuous texts from the start without compromising grammatical rigour; it offers generous help with translation at every stage; and it integrates the learning of classical Latin with an appreciation of the influence of the Latin language upon English and European culture from antiquity to the present.

The *Text and Vocabulary*, richly illustrated, consists at the start of carefully graded adaptations from original classical Latin texts. The adaptations are gradually phased out until unadulterated prose and verse can be read. The accompanying *Grammar and Exercises* volume supplies all the grammatical help needed to do this, together with a range of reinforcing exercises for each section, including English into Latin for those who want it. It also contains a full and detailed reference grammar at the back. For each section, a selection of Latin epigrams, mottoes, quotations, everyday Latin, word-derivations, examples of medieval Latin and discussions of the influence of Latin upon English illustrate the language's impact on Western culture.

Reading Latin is principally designed for college/university and adult beginners, but also for those in the final years of school. It is also ideal for those people who may have learned Latin many years ago, and wish to renew their acquaintance with the language. The revised optional *Independent Study Guide* will provide a great deal of help to the student learning without a teacher.

The second edition has been fully revised and updated, with revisions to the early chapters in the *Text* volume including a new one on stories from early Roman history, and extensively redesigned to make it easier and clearer to navigate. The vocabulary has been moved into the same volume as the text and placed alongside it.

PETER JONES was Senior Lecturer in Classics at the University of Newcastle upon Tyne until his retirement. He has written many books for the student of Latin and Greek, most recently *Reading Ovid* (Cambridge, 2007), *Reading Virgil* (Cambridge, 2011) and (with Keith Sidwell) the *Reading Latin* textbook series.

KEITH SIDWELL is Emeritus Professor of Latin and Greek, University College Cork and Adjunct Professor in the Department of Classics and Religion at the University of Calgary. He has written on Greek drama, later Greek literature and Neo-Latin writing: his books include *Lucian: Chattering Courtesans and Other Sardonic Sketches* (2004) and *Aristophanes the Democrat* (Cambridge, 2009). As well as co-authoring the *Reading Latin* series with Peter Jones, he is the author of *Reading Medieval Latin* (Cambridge, 1995).

SENATVS
POPVLVSQVE ROMANVS
IMP CAESARI DIVI F AVGVSTO
COS VIII DEDIT CLVPEVM
VIRTVTIS CLEMENTIAE
IVSTITIAE PIETATIS ERGA
DEOS PATRIAMQVE

Marble copy of the *Clupeus Virtutis* of Augustus, found at Arles (see p. xvi)

Reading Latin
Grammar and Exercises

Second edition

Peter Jones
and Keith Sidwell

CAMBRIDGE
UNIVERSITY PRESS

CAMBRIDGE
UNIVERSITY PRESS

University Printing House, Cambridge CB2 8BS, United Kingdom

Cambridge University Press is part of the University of Cambridge.

It furthers the University's mission by disseminating knowledge in the pursuit of education, learning and research at the highest international levels of excellence.

www.cambridge.org
Information on this title: www.cambridge.org/9781107632264

First edition © Cambridge University Press 1986
This second edition © Peter Jones and Keith Sidwell 2016

First edition published 1986
Second edition published 2016

Printed in the United Kingdom by Clays, St Ives plc

A catalogue record for this publication is available from the British Library

ISBN 978-1-107-63226-4 Paperback

Contents

This list gives the contents of the Grammar and Exercises in detail, by section number, but only general headings for the Reference Grammar. For detailed references to the latter see Index of Grammar, pp. 447–58.

Preface

ūsus magister est optimus
    (Cicero, *Rab. Post.* 4.9)

Winston Churchill on his introduction to Latin at his prep school

I was taken into a Form Room and told to sit at a desk. All the other boys were out of doors, and I was alone with the Form Master. He produced a thin greeny-brown covered book filled with words in different types of print.

'You have never done any Latin before, have you?' he said.

'No, sir.'

'This is a Latin grammar.' He opened it at a well-thumbed page. 'You must learn this,' he said, pointing to a number of words in a frame of lines. 'I will come back in half an hour and see what you know.'

Behold me then on a gloomy evening, with an aching heart, seated in front of the First Declension.

    Mensa – a table
    Mensa – O table
    Mensam – a table
    Mensae – of a table
    Mensae – to or for a table
    Mensa – by, with or from a table

What on earth did it mean? Where was the sense in it? It seemed absolute rigmarole to me. However, there was one thing I could always do: I could learn by heart. And I thereupon proceeded, as far as my private sorrows would allow, to memorise the acrostic-looking task which had been set me.

In due course the Master returned.

'Have you learnt it?' he asked.

'I think I can *say* it, sir,' I replied; and I gabbled it off.

He seemed so satisfied with this that I was emboldened to ask a question.

'What does it mean, sir?'

'It means what it says. Mensa, a table. Mensa is a noun of the First Declension. There are five declensions. You have learnt the singular of the First Declension.'

'But,' I repeated,' what does it mean?'

'Mensa means a table,' he answered.

'Then why does mensa also mean O table,' I enquired, 'and what does O table mean?'

'Mensa, O table, is the vocative case,' he replied.

'But why O table?' I persisted in genuine curiosity.

'O table – you would use that in addressing a table, in invoking a table.' And then seeing he was not carrying me with him, 'You would use it in speaking to a table.'

'But I never do,' I blurted out in honest amazement.

'If you are impertinent, you will be punished, and punished, let me tell you, very severely,' was his conclusive rejoinder.

Such was my first introduction to the classics from which, I have been told, many of our cleverest men have derived so much solace and profit.

Winston Churchill, *My Early Life*

Notes to Grammar and Exercises

This volume accompanies *Reading Latin* (*Text and Vocabulary*) (Cambridge 2016) and is to be used in conjunction with it. For an introduction to the *Reading Latin* course – its aims, methodology and future development – and our acknowledgements of all the help we have received in its production, please refer to the Introduction of the *Text and Vocabulary* volume.

1 All dates are BC, unless otherwise specified.

2 In the Running Grammar for each section, it is extremely important to note that the exercises should be regarded as a pool out of which the teacher/students should choose what to do, and whether in or out of class. Some of the simpler exercises we have split into necessary and optional sections, but this principle has been extended to other exercises marked EITHER/OR throughout.

3 On pp. 281–396 there is a full Reference Grammar, based on the Running Grammar explanations, but in many cases adding further information to that given in the running explanations.

4 On pp. 397–408 there is an Appendix on the Latin language.

5 On pp. 409–30 there is the Total Latin–English Learning Vocabulary, and on pp. 431–46 an English–Latin Vocabulary for those doing the English–Latin sentence and prose exercises.

6 In cross-references, superior figures appended to a section number indicate *Notes*, e.g. **144**[4]. If the reference is in the form '**150.1**', the last digit indicates a numbered sub-section.

7 The case which follows an adjective or a verb is usually indicated by e.g. '(+ acc.)'. But occasionally it will be phrased e.g. 'X (acc.)', indicating the Latin word X is in the accusative.

8 In places where standard beginners' texts print *v* (i.e. consonantal *u*), we have in accordance with early MS practice printed *u*. But in some later Latin texts we have reverted to *v*, which is commonly found in early printed books.

9 Bold numbers in page-heads, e.g. **15**, refer to sections of the Running Grammar.

Peter Jones
Newcastle upon Tyne

Keith Sidwell
Emeritus Professor of Latin and Greek, University College Cork
and Adjunct Professor, Department of Classics and Religion, University of
Calgary

Abbreviations

For the meaning of these terms, see Glossary, pp. xvi–xxiv

abl.(ative)

abs.(olute)

acc.(usative)

act.(ive)

adj.(ective)

adv.(erb)

cf. (= *cōnfer* (Latin), 'compare')

comp.(arative)

conj.(ugation, ugated)

dat.(ive)

decl.(ension)

dep.(onent)

dir.(ect)

f.(eminine)

fut.(ure)

gen.(itive)

imper.(ative)

impf. (= imperfect)

indecl.(inable)

ind.(icative)

indir.(ect)

inf.(initive)

intrans.(itive)

irr.(egular)

lit.(erally)

m.(asculine)

neg.(ative)

n.(euter)

nom.(inative)

part.(iciple)

pass.(ive)

perf.(ect)

pl.(ural)

plupf. (= pluperfect)

p.p. (= principal part)

prep.(osition)

pres.(ent)

prim.(ary)

pron.(oun)

q.(uestion)

rel.(ative)

s.(ingular)

sc. (= *scīlicet* (Latin), 'presumably')

sec.(ondary)

seq.(uence)

sp.(eech)

subj.(unctive)

sup.(erlative)

trans.(itive)

tr.(anslate)

vb (= verb)

voc.(ative)

1st, 2nd, 3rd refer to persons of the verb, i.e.

1st s.	= I
2nd s.	= you (s.)
3rd s.	= he, she, it
1st pl.	= we
2nd pl.	= you (pl.)
3rd pl.	= they

1f., 2m. etc. refer to declension and gender of nouns

Pronunciation

'English' refers throughout to the standard or 'received' pronunciation of southern British English unless otherwise qualified.

a as English 'c*up*', or '*a*ha' (cf. '*ca*t', or Italian or French '*a*-')

ā as English 'f*a*ther' (roughly)

ae as in English 'h*igh*' (roughly)

au as in English 'h*ow*'

b as English

c as English 'c' in '*c*at' (not '*c*ider', '*c*ello')

ch as English 'pa*ck-h*orse'

d as English

e as in English 'p*e*t'

ē as in 'fian*cée*' (French pronunciation)

ei as in English 'd*ay*'

eu 'e-oo' (cf. Cockney 'b*el*t')

f as English

g as English '*g*ot'; but 'gn' = 'ngn' as in 'ha*ngn*ail'

h as English

i as in English 'd*i*p'

ī as in English 'd*ee*p'

i consonant (sometimes written as a 'j'); as English '*you*'

k as English

l as English

m as English at the beginning and in the middle of words (cf. '*m*at', 'ca*m*p'); a final 'm' expresses nasalisation of the preceding vowel (cf. French 'parfu*m*')

n as English

o as in English 'p*o*t'

ō as in French 'b*eau*'

oe as in English 'b*oy*'; but note *poēta* is pronounced po-*ē*-ta (short 'o')

p as English

ph as English

qu as in English '*qu*ick'

r as Scottish 'rolled' 'r'

s as 's' in English 'sing' (never as in 'roses')

t as 't' in English '*t*in' (cleanly pronounced, with no 'h' sound)

th as in English 'po*t-h*ouse'

u as in English 'p*u*t'

ū as in English 'f*oo*l'

u (pronounced as a consonant) as English 'w' (sometimes written as 'v')

x as English

y as French 'u'

z as English

Rules of word stress (accent)

1 A word of two syllables is stressed on the first syllable, e.g. *ámō, ámās.*

2 A word of more than two syllables is stressed on the penultimate (i.e. second syllable from the end) if that syllable is heavy, e.g. *astū́tus, audiúntur* (see pp. 273–4 for the terms 'heavy', 'light').

3 In all other cases, words of more than two syllables are stressed on the antepenultimate (i.e. third syllable from the end), e.g. *amábitis, pulchérrimus.*

4 Words of one syllable (monosyllables) always have the stress, e.g. *nóx.* But prepositions *before* a noun are not accented, e.g. *ad hóminem.*

5 Some words, e.g. *-que, -ne* and *-ue,* which are appended to the word which precedes them, cause the stress to fall on the last syllable of that word, e.g *uírum* but *uirúmque.*

For a clear account of classical Latin pronunciation see W. S. Allen, *Vox Latina* (2nd edition, Cambridge 1975). Today, the pronunciation of church Latin is basically Italian.

Illustration

Frontispiece The *Clupeus Virtutis* of Augustus. Marble copy of the gold original set up in the senate house (*cūria*):

SENATVS POPVLVSQVE ROMANVS IMP(ERATORI) CAESARI DIVI F(ILIO) AVGVSTO CO(N)S(VLI) VIII DEDIT CLVPEVM VIRTVTIS CLEMENTIAE IVSTITIAE PIETATIS ERGA DEOS PATRIAMQVE

The Senate and the Roman People gave to the emperor Caesar Augustus son of the god, consul for the eighth time, a shield of [= honouring him for his] Virtue, Clemency, Justice [and] Piety in relation to the gods and the fatherland

Arles, Musée Lapidaire, Photo: The Bridgeman Art Library

Glossary of Grammatical Terms

This short glossary explains the most important terminology used in Latin grammar, with examples in English. To make it as practically useful as possible, we provide simple definitions with down-to-earth examples of each term. Students should bear in mind, however, that (1) there is only a limited 'fit' between English grammar and Latin grammar, and (2) brevity and simplicity may not do full justice to grammatical terms, which are notoriously difficult to define. So this index should be regarded as a simplified guide to the subject, for use when you forget the definition of a term used in the grammar, or to refresh your memory of grammatical terms before you begin the course.

Before beginning the course, you should be familiar and feel comfortable with the following terms: noun, adjective, pronoun, conjunction, preposition, verb, person, number, tense, gender, case, singular, plural.

ablative: a grammatical case of the noun and pronoun, often meaning 'by', 'with' or 'from' the (pro)noun in question. Functions defined at Reference Grammar **L**.

accidence: the part of grammar which deals with variable forms of words, e.g. declensions, conjugations.

accusative: name of a case of the noun, pronoun or adjective. Function defined at Reference Grammar **L**.

active: a verb is active when the subject is doing the action, e.g. 'she (subject) *runs*', 'Thomas Aquinas (subject) *reads* his book.'

adjective: word which defines the quality of a noun or pronoun by describing it, e.g. '*steep* hill', '*red* house', '*clever* me'. There are also adjectival clauses, for which see *relative clause*. Possessive adjectives are 'my', 'your', 'our', 'his', 'her', 'their'. In Latin adjectives must agree with nouns or pronouns in case, number and gender.

adverb: word which defines the quality of a verb by showing how the action of the verb is carried out, e.g. 'she ran *quickly*', 'she works *enthusiastically*'. *Adverbial clauses* do the same job, e.g. 'she ran *as quickly as she was able*'. Adverbs in Latin are indeclinable.

agree(ment): an adjective agrees with a noun when it adopts the same case, number and gender as the noun. E.g. if a noun is nominative singular masculine, an adjective which is to describe it must also be nominative singular masculine.

apposition: nouns or noun-plus-adjective phrases which add further information about a noun already mentioned are said to be 'in apposition' to it, e.g. 'the house, a red-brick building, was placed on the side of a hill' – here 'a red-brick building' is 'in apposition' to 'the house'.

article: the definite article is the word 'the', the indefinite article the word 'a'.

aspect: whether the action of the verb is seen as a simple statement, as continuing, habitual, complete, or as a description of a state of affairs, e.g. 'I run', 'I am running' (or, in English, emphasised 'I *do* run') are all present *tense* but all differ in aspect. See also *tense*.

auxiliary (verb): in 'she will love', 'she does love', 'she has loved', the verbs 'will', 'does' and 'have' are auxiliary verbs, brought in to help the verb 'love' (*auxilium* = help), defining its tense and aspect. 'May', 'might', 'would', 'should' are auxiliaries indicating the mood of the verb to which they are attached. Latin uses auxiliary verbs only in the perfect, pluperfect and future perfect deponent and passive.

case: form of the noun, pronoun or adjective which defines the relationship between that word and the rest of the sentence, e.g. a Latin word adopting the form which shows that it is in the nominative case (e.g. *serua*) might show that the word is the subject of its clause; a Latin word adopting the form which shows that it is in the accusative case (e.g. *seruam*) might show that it is the object of the sentence. There are six cases in Latin: nominative, vocative, accusative, genitive, dative and ablative. Most have more than one function.

causal clause: clause expressing the reason why something has happened or will happen, e.g. clauses beginning 'because …', 'since …'

clause: part of a sentence containing a subject and a finite verb, e.g. main clause 'she had finished', 'she hated it', 'she may succeed'; subordinate clause 'when she had finished', 'which she hated', 'so that she may succeed'. Cf. *phrase.* See *adjective, adverb, noun.*

comparative: form of adjective or adverb which implies a comparison, e.g. 'hotter', 'better', 'more slowly'.

complement: when a subject is said *to be* something, or *to be called, to be thought*, or *to seem* something, the 'something' is the complement of the verb, e.g. 'she is *intelligent*', 'it seems *OK*', 'she is thought to be *a promising scholar*'.

concessive clause: clause introduced by the word 'although', e.g. '*although it is raining*, we shall go to the shops'.

conditional clause: clause introduced by the word 'if', e.g. '*If it rains today*, I shall not go to the shops', or sometimes 'should' e.g. '*should* it rain today…' The technical term for the 'if' clause is *protasis*, and for the main clause *apodosis* ('pay-off').

conjugation (conjugate): the parts of a verb are its conjugation, e.g. the conjugation of 'I love' in the present indicative active is 'I love, you love, he/she/it loves, we love, you love, they love'.

conjunction: word which links words, clauses, phrases or sentences, e.g. '*When* the light was out *and* she went up to have dinner, the burglar entered *and* took the piano. *But* he was not unseen ...' Co-ordinating conjunctions link together units (e.g. clauses, sentences, phrases) of equal grammatical value, e.g. 'He went *and* stood *and* laughed out loud; *but* she sulked *and* stalked off *and* had a drink.' Subordinating conjunctions, words like 'when', 'although', 'if', 'because', 'since', 'after', introduce units of different grammatical value compared with the main clause. See *main verb*.

consecutive clause: see *result clause*.

consonant: a sound or letter which is not a vowel, e.g. 'b', 'c', 'd', 'f', 'g' 'h' etc. Note that 'y' is a consonant in 'yak' but a vowel in 'my'.

dative: a grammatical case of the noun and pronoun, often meaning 'to' or 'for' the (pro)noun in question, e.g. 'Helena gave a book *to Toby.*' For function, see Reference Grammar **L**.

declension (decline): the forms of a noun, pronoun or adjective. To decline a noun is to list all its forms in their conventional order in both singular and plural. This is nominative, vocative, accusative, genitive, dative, ablative in the UK.

deponent: a verb whose dictionary form (1st person singular) ends in *-or* e.g. *minor, hortor, sequor* etc., and whose meaning is always *active*.

diphthong: see *vowel*.

direct object: a direct object is the noun, pronoun or noun-phrase directly affected by the action of the verb, e.g. 'she hits *the ball*', 'they love *books*', 'they love *to read books*', 'we say *we are the greatest*'. Cf. *indirect object*.

direct speech: speech which is quoted verbatim, in the exact words of the speaker, e.g. 'Give me that book'. Cf. *indirect speech*.

final clause: a subordinate clause which expresses the idea '(in order) (not) to', i.e. it expresses the idea of an end (Latin *finis*), goal or purpose. E.g. '*in order to* swim the river, she took off her shoes', '*to* cross the railway, use the bridge', 'close the gate *to stop* the horse getting out'.

finite (verb): a verb which has a defined number and person, e.g. 'she runs' (third person, singular). Contrast 'to run', 'running', which are examples of the non-finite verb. Cf. *infinitive*.

future perfect tense: a verb form of the type 'I shall have —ed', e.g. 'I shall have tried', 'you will have gone', 'he will have spoken'.

future tense: a verb form of the type 'I shall/will —', e.g. 'I shall go', 'you will be', 'they will run'. It denotes a state or action that will take place in the future.

gender: whether a noun, pronoun or adjective is masculine, feminine or neuter.

genitive: a grammatical case of the noun or pronoun, often meaning 'of', e.g. 'the pen of my aunt', 'Charlotte's friends', 'love of her'. Function defined at Reference Grammar **L**.

historic sequence (also called 'secondary sequence'): when the main verb of a sentence is in a past tense ('I have —ed' counts as a present tense and therefore is in 'primary sequence').

imperative: the mood of a verb used to give a simple command, e.g. 'run!'

imperfect tense: the past tense verb form indicating continuing or repeated action in the past, e.g. 'I was —ing', 'I used to —', 'I kept on —ing.'

indeclinable: used of a word which has only one form, however it is used (e.g. 'sheep' in English, used for both singular and plural).

indicative: the mood of a verb which states something as a fact, not as a wish or command or something imagined, e.g. 'she runs'. Compare 'run!', 'may she run!', 'if she were to run' etc.

indirect object: term used e.g. for the person *to whom* something is given or said, e.g. 'she said *to him*', 'give it *to me*'; 'she told *the man* to give *her* the book'. The verb indirectly affects the indirect object. Cf. *direct object*.

indirect speech: words or thoughts which are reported, not, as in direct speech, stated exactly as the speaker said or thought them, e.g. direct command 'let me go', indirect command 'she told them to let her go'; direct statement 'he has gone', indirect statement 'he said that he had gone'; direct question 'Where am I?', indirect question 'she wondered where she was'. Any verb, noun or adjective that denotes a type of speaking or thinking can introduce indirect speech, e.g. 'The question *why she was so talented* often crossed his mind.'

infinitive: verb form prefixed in English by 'to', e.g. 'to run', 'to have walked', 'to be about to jump' etc.

inflection: the different endings that a word takes to express its grammatical meaning in a sentence, e.g. '*she* (subject) sent *her* (object) to the library'; 'they *say*', 'she *says*', 'we *said*', indicating tense.

interrogative: a word used for asking a question, e.g. 'who?' is an interrogative pronoun, 'which' is an interrogative adjective in 'which book?'

intransitive (verb): a verb is intransitive when it does not require a direct object to complete its meaning, e.g. 'I stand', 'I sit'. In English such words can be used transitively as well, when they adopt a different meaning, e.g. 'I sit (= take) an exam'; 'I cannot stand (= endure) that man.'

jussive (subjunctive): related to giving orders. The form of the jussive subjunctive in English is 'let him/them/me/us do X', e.g. 'let's go', 'let them eat cake'.

locative case: the grammatical case of a noun used to indicate where something is at. It is used in Latin with names of towns and one-town islands, e.g. 'at Rome', 'on Malta'.

main verb: the main verb(s) of a sentence is (are) the verb(s) left when all other verbs have been cut out (e.g. infinitives, participles, verbs in subordinating clauses), e.g. '(Although being something of a bibliophile) (*who loved nothing more than a good read) (if she could get one), she *sold* her books (when the examinations were over) and *lived* in misery the rest of her life with her friends (who were totally illiterate).' Main verbs – 'sold' and 'lived'.

mood: whether a verb is indicative, subjunctive or imperative, e.g. 'you are coming' is indicative mood, 'suppose you were to come' subjunctive mood, and 'come!' imperative mood.

morphology: study of the different structures, forms and variations of a word. For example, noun 'farm', plural 'farms', verb '[he] farms', past tense '[he] farmed', participle 'I saw him farming', agent-noun 'farmer'.

nominative: a grammatical case of a noun or pronoun, usually the 'subject' of a sentence. For function, see **6.2, 4**; and **L**.

noun: name of a person ('woman', 'child'), place ('London'), thing ('table', 'chair', 'mountain') or abstraction ('virtue', 'courage', 'thought', 'quality').

noun clauses are clauses which do the job of a noun in the sentence, e.g. all indirect speech (e.g. 'he says words' – 'words' = noun, object; 'he says this, *that she is divine*' – 'that she is divine' = noun clause, object); constructions following 'I fear that/lest, I doubt that, I prevent X from' and 'it happened that …'

number: whether something is singular or plural; 'table' and 'he' are singular, 'tables' and 'they' are plural.

object: see *direct object.*

participle: a form of the verb with the qualities and functions of an adjective, e.g. 'a *running* sore', 'a woman *thinking*…' In Latin there are present participles active (meaning ' —ing'), future participles active (meaning 'about to —; on the point of —ing'), and perfect participles active (meaning 'having —ed') and passive (meaning 'having been —ed').

passive: a verb is passive when the subject is not doing the action, but having the action done to it. The same *action* may be described in both the active and the passive 'voice', e.g. 'she hit the ball' (active), 'the ball was hit by her' (passive); 'we visited Rome' (active), 'Rome was visited by us' (passive).

perfect tense: verb form of the type 'I —ed', 'I have —ed', 'I did —', expressing a simple action in the past, e.g. 'I walked', 'we did walk' or the present result of an action completed in the past, e.g. 'I have walked' (and therefore am tired).

person: the persons are expressed by the pronouns 'I', 'we' (first person singular and plural); 'you' (second person singular and plural); 'he'/'she'/'it', 'they' (third person singular and plural).

phrase: part of a sentence not having a finite verb, often introduced by a preposition, e.g. 'in the house' (prepositional phrase); '*going to work*, he —' (participle phrase); 'I wish *to do it*' (infinitive phrase).

pluperfect tense: a tense of verb of the type 'I had —ed', e.g. 'I had walked', 'they had gone'. It expresses the idea of a state or action achieved or completed in the past.

plural: more than one, e.g. 'tables' is plural, 'table' is singular.

predicate: what is said about the subject of a sentence, e.g. 'The man (subject) wore blue socks' (predicate).

predicative: to predicate something of a person is to say something new about them. So when adjectives (including participles) and nouns say something about a person or thing, they are being used 'predicatively'. In English, predicative adjectives and participles usually come *after* the nouns they go with, e.g. 'I saw the man *working*', 'the woman went away *happy*', 'Caesar became *consul*', 'she is a *a big help* to them' (the last two are predicative nouns). Contrast 'I saw the working man', 'the happy woman went away', in which the adjectives describe what is already understood or acknowledged, adding nothing new (such adjectives are called 'attributive').

prefix: a small addition to the front of a word, which alters the basic meaning, e.g. fix, *re*fix, *pre*fix; *ex*port, *im*port, *re*port, *de*port, *trans*port, *sup*port.

preposition: word or phrase coming before a noun or pronoun denoting its relation to the (pro)noun in space, time or logic, e.g. '*into* the house', '*from* the pot', '*from* the hill', '*with* my friend', '*by* train'. Such expressions are called 'prepositional phrases'.

present tense: the tense of the verb of the type 'I —', 'I am —ing', 'I do —', e.g. 'I love', 'I am loving', 'I do love.' It indicates an occurrence in present time.

primary sequence: when the main verb of a sentence is present or future, or perfect in the form 'I have —ed.'

principal parts: (in Latin) the four parts of an active verb (present indicative, present infinitive, perfect indicative and perfect participle) from which all other parts are formed; deponent verbs have only three such parts (present indicative, present infinitive and perfect participle).

pronoun: this refers to a noun, without naming it, e.g. 'he' (as against 'the man', or 'Caesar'), 'they' (as against 'the women', or 'the Mitfords'), 'we', 'you', 'who', 'which'.

question (direct): a sentence ending in '?' See also *indirect speech*.

reflexive: a pronoun or adjective is reflexive when it refers to (i.e. is the same person or thing as) the subject of the clause in which it stands, e.g. 'they warmed *themselves* by the fire', 'when they had checked *their* equipment, the leader gave them (*not* reflexive, since 'leader' is the subject) orders'.

regular: a 'regular' verb, noun or adjective follows the predictable pattern of the type of conjugation or declension to which it belongs, without deviation, e.g. 'I bake', 'I shall bake', 'I baked', 'I have baked'. Contrast 'I am', 'I shall be', 'I was', 'I have been'.

relative clause: a clause introduced by a relative pronoun such as 'who', 'which', 'what', 'whose', 'whom', 'that'. The relative pronoun refers back to ('picks up') a previous noun or pronoun (sometimes it refers forward to it) and the whole clause helps to describe or define the noun or pronoun referred to (hence it is an adjectival clause). Examples would be 'the book *which I am reading* is rubbish', 'she presented the man *whom she had brought*', '*Who* dreads, yet undismayed / Dares face his terror … *Him* let Saint Thomas guide.'

reported speech: see *indirect speech.*

result clause: a clause which expresses the result or consequence of an action. It takes the form 'so… that / as to…' e.g. 'they were *so* forgetful *that they left* (or '*as to leave*') *all their money behind*'.

secondary sequence: see *historic sequence.*

semi-deponent: a verb which takes active forms in present, future and imperfect tenses, but deponent forms in perfect, future perfect and pluperfect.

sequence: see *primary sequence* and *historic sequence.*

singular: expresses *one* of something, e.g. 'table' is singular, 'tables' is plural; 'he' (singular), 'they' (plural).

statement: an utterance presented as a fact, e.g. 'I am carrying this pot.' Cf. the question 'Am I carrying this pot?', or the command 'Carry this pot!'

subject: the subject of a sentence is, in the case of active verbs, the person/ thing doing the action or being in the state (e.g. '*Gloria* hits out'; '*Gloria* is champion'); in the case of passive verbs, the subject is the person or thing on the receiving end of, or affected by, the action, e.g. '*the ball* was hit by Gloria'.

subjunctive: the mood of the verb used in certain main and subordinate clauses in Latin and English, often expressing wishes or possibilities or commands, e.g. 'may I win!', 'let him think!', 'she left in order that she *might* catch the bus', 'if I were a rich man'.

subordinating clause (sub-clause): any clause which is not the main one (see *adverb, causal clause, concessive clause, conditional clause, final clause, infinitive, noun, participle, relative clause, result clause, temporal clause*). Cf. *phrase.* Also see *main verb.*

suffix: a small addition to the end of a word which changes its meaning and makes a new word, e.g. 'act', 'act*or*', 'act*ion*', 'act*ive*'.

superlative: the form of an adjective or adverb which expresses its highest or very high degree, e.g. 'the *fastest* horse', 'he jumped *very high*', 'she worked *extremely hard*'.

syllable: a vowel or a vowel + consonant combination, pronounced without interruption as a word or part of a word, e.g. 'the' (one syllable), 'horses' (two syllables), 'Calgary' (three syllables), 'antidisestablishmentarianism' (eleven – or is it twelve? – syllables). A Latin syllable could be a vowel/diphthong, a consonant + vowel/diphthong, or consonant + vowel/diphthong + consonant, e.g. *Athenis* 'in Athens' has three syllables – *A-the-nis*.

syntax: the branch of grammar which deals with the constructions of a sentence (e.g. indirect speech, result clauses, temporal clauses, participle phrases etc.).

temporal clause: a clause expressing the time *when* something happened in relation to the rest of the sentence, e.g. 'when …', 'after …', 'while …', 'before …', 'as soon as …'.

tense: the grammatical term for the time at which the action of a verb is meant to take place. See under *present tense, future tense, imperfect tense, perfect tense, future perfect tense, pluperfect tense.*

transitive (verb): a verb which takes a direct object to complete its meaning, e.g. 'I put *the book* on the table', 'I make *a chart*'. It is very difficult to think of a context in which 'I put' and 'I make' could make a sentence *on their own*. This is not the case with *intransitive* verbs, e.g. 'I sit.'

verb: a word expressing action, event or state, e.g. 'run', 'jump', 'stand', 'think', 'be', 'say'. (See under *active* and *passive*.) Every complete sentence has at least one.

vocative: the case of the noun or pronoun used when addressing someone (e.g. 'you too, <u>Brutus</u>?', '*et tū, <u>Brūte</u>?*').

voice: a grammatical function of a verb, i.e. whether it is active ('I love') or passive ('I am loved').

vowel: 'a', 'e', 'i', 'o', 'u' and 'y'. Diphthongs are two vowels pronounced as a single syllable (e.g. 'ou' as in 'bough', 'au' as in 'taut'). English (like Latin) pronounces vowels short and long, e.g. 'h<u>a</u>t' and 'c<u>a</u>rt'.

Grammar and exercises for Sections 1–6

Section 1 Introduction

Notes

1 All vowels are pronounced *short* unless marked with a ‾ over them. So observe different vowel length of '*i*' in e.g. *fīlia*, etc. It may be helpful, but is not essential, to mark macra in your exercises.

2 ′ above a vowel indicates *stress*. Stress marks are included in all tables and throughout the Reference Grammar.

3 You should learn the Learning Vocabulary for each section *before* attempting the exercises. Please see *Text and Vocabulary*, pp. xiv–xv for suggested methodology.

Grammar and exercises for Introduction – *familia Eucliōnis*

1

sum: 'I am'

1st person singular	*(1st s.)*	su-m	'I am'
2nd person singular	*(2nd s.)*	es	'you are'
3rd person singular	*(3rd s.)*	es-t	'he/she/it is/there is'
1st person plural	*(1st pl.)*	sú-mus	'we are'
2nd person plural	*(2nd pl.)*	és-tis	'you (*pl.*) are'
3rd person plural	*(3rd pl.)*	su-nt	'they/there are'

Notes

1 *sum* is the most common verb in Latin.

2 Whereas English takes two words to express 'I am', Latin takes *one*. This is because the *endings* of the verb – *-m, -s, -t, -mus, -tis, -nt* – indicate the person doing the action. Thus in full:

$$-m \quad = \quad I^1$$
$$-s \quad = \quad you~(s.)$$
$$-t \quad = \quad he,~she,~it,~there$$
$$-mus \quad = \quad we$$
$$-tis \quad = \quad you~(pl.)$$
$$-nt \quad = \quad they,~there$$

1. In other verbs *-ō* = I.

3 *sum* is irregular because, as you can see, the stem changes from *su-* to *es-*. If it is any consolation, all verbs meaning 'to be' are irregular, e.g. English 'I *am*', 'you *are*', 'he *is*'; French (deriving from Latin) 'je *suis*', 'tu *es*', 'il *est*' etc.

4 In the 3rd s. and 3rd pl., *est* and *sunt* mean only 'is' and 'are' if the subject is named, e.g. *senex est* = 'he is an old man'; *Ecliō senex est* = 'Euclio is an old man'; *seruae sunt* = 'they are slave-women'; *omnēs seruae sunt* = 'all are slave-women'.

5 Note the following points about word-order in sentences with *sum*:

  (a) Where subject and complement are stated

      (i)   the unemphatic order is: subject complement *sum*, e.g.

          Ecliō senex est 'Euclio is an old man.'

      (ii) other orders place emphasis on the first word, e.g.

          senex est Ecliō (complement *sum* subject)

          senex Ecliō est (complement subject *sum*)

          Both mean 'An old man, that's what Euclio is.'

NB The order 'subject *sum* complement' emphasises the subject.

      (iii) The verb *sum* may come first and is then emphatic, e.g.

          est enim Ecliō auārus (*sum* subject complement) 'For Euclio *is* (in fact) a miser.'

  (b)   Where the subject is not stated in Latin, the usual order is: complement *sum*, e.g.

      Staphyla est 'It's Staphyla.'

  (c)   *est/sunt* at the beginning of a sentence commonly indicate the *existence* of something, and are often best translated 'there is/there are', e.g.,

      est locus. . . 'there is a place …'

  In such sentences, more information will be expected, e.g. 'there is a place, where roses grow', 'there are people, who like Latin'.

NB In (a) (i) and (ii) and (b) observe how complement + *sum* usually stick together to form the predicate, e.g.

      Ecliō senex-est
      senex-est Ecliō

sum is likely to go closely with the word preceding it, except where the order has been altered for special emphasis (as in e.g. *senex Ecliō est*).

EXERCISES

Morphology

1 *Translate into Latin*: you (*s.*) are; there are; he is; there is; you (*pl.*) are; they are; it is; I am; she is.

2 *Change s. to pl. and vice versa*: sum; sunt; estis; est; sumus; es.

Reading exercise

Using Note 5 in the grammar section, give the correct translation of these sentences:

(a) familia est.

(b) serua Staphyla est.

(c) est enim aula aurī plēna (aula, *pot*; aurī plēna, *full of gold*).

(d) coquus est seruus (coquus, *cook*; seruus, *slave*).

(e) Phaedra fīlia est.

(f) in aedibus sunt Eucliō, Phaedra et serua (in aedibus, *in the house*).

(g) auārus est senex (auārus, *miser*; senex, *old man*).

(h) est prope flūmen paruus ager (prope flūmen, *near the river*; paruus, *small*; ager, *field*).

English–Latin

Translate the Latin sentences into English. Then translate the English sentences into Latin, using the pattern of the Latin ones to help you arrange the word-order correctly.

(a) sunt in familiā Eucliō, Phaedra, Staphyla.
   There is in the household a slave-girl.

(b) Eucliō et Phaedra in aedibus sunt.
   The slave-girl is in the house.

(c) Eucliō sum.
   You (*s.*) are a slave.

(d) fīlia Eucliōnis Phaedra est.
   Euclio's slave is Staphyla.

(e) quis es?
   I am Euclio.

(f) quī estis?
   We are Euclio and Phaedra.

Section 1A

Grammar and exercises for 1A

(Please see *Text and Vocabulary*, pp. xiv–xv for a suggested methodology. Most importantly, make a SELECTION from the exercises.)

2 **Present indicative active (1st conjugation): *amō* 'I love', 'I am loving', 'I do love'**

1st s.	ám-ō	'I love', 'I am loving', 'I do love'
2nd s.	ámā-s	'you (*s.*) love' *etc.*
3rd s.	áma-t	'he/she/it loves'
1st pl.	amā́-mus	'we love'
2nd pl.	amā́-tis	'you (*pl.*) love'
3rd pl.	áma-nt	'they love'

3 **Present indicative active (2nd conjugation): *habeō* 'I have', 'I am having', 'I do have'**

1st s.	hábe-ō	'I have', 'I am having', 'I do have'
2nd s.	hábē-s	'you (*s.*) have' *etc.*
3rd s.	hábe-t	'he/she/it has'
1st pl.	habḗ-mus	'we have'
2nd pl.	habḗ-tis	'you (*pl.*) have'
3rd pl.	hábe-nt	'they have'

Notes

1 All verbs called '1st conjugation' conjugate in the present like *am-ō*, e.g. *habit-ō* 'I live', *intr-ō* 'I enter', *uoc-ō* 'I call', *clām-ō* 'I shout', *par-ō* 'I prepare', *cēl-ō* 'I hide'.

   All verbs called '2nd conjugation', which all end in *-eō*, conjugate like *habe-ō*, e.g. *time-ō* 'I fear'.

2 Observe that these regular verbs are built up out of a *stem + endings.* The stem gives the *meaning* of the verb (*ama-* 'love', *habe-* 'have'), the endings give the *person*, i.e.:

-ō   'I' (*cf.* su-m)

-s   'you (*s.*)'

-t   'he/she/it; there'

-mus   'we'

-tis   'you (*pl.*)'

-nt   'they/there'

3   Observe that the 'key' vowel of 1st conjugation verbs is *A* (*amA-*), of 2nd conjugation is *E* (*habE-*). The only exception is the 1st s. *amō* 'I love', though this was originally *amaō*.

4   **Terminology**

Conjugation means 'the setting out of a verb in all its persons' as illustrated in **2** and **3**. Thus to conjugate a verb means to set it out as at **2** and **3**.

Indicative means that the action is being presented as a fact (though it need not be actually true), e.g.

'I speak to you' (fact, true)

'The pig flies past the window' (presented as a fact, but not true!)

Active means the subject is performing the action, e.g. '*Euclio* runs'; '*Staphyla* sees the daughter'.

Tense means the time at which the action is taking place. Thus 'present' means 'present tense', i.e. the action is happening in the present, e.g. 'I am running'. Cf. future tense 'I will run' etc.

5   **Meaning**

The present indicative active of e.g. *amō* has three meanings, i.e. 'I love', 'I am loving', 'I do love'. Each of these three 'aspects' (as they are called) of the present tense represents the actions in a slightly different way. 'I love' is the plainest statement of fact, 'I am loving' gives a more vivid, 'close-up', continuous picture (you can see it actually going on), 'I do love' is emphatic. You must select *by context* which meaning suits best. Remember, however, that in general the emphatic meaning is indicated in Latin by the verb being put first in the sentence.

EXERCISES

Morphology

1   *Conjugate*: cēlō; timeō; portō; habeō (*optional*: habitō; clāmō; intrō; uocō; sum).

2   *Translate, then change pl. to s. and vice versa*: clāmās; habent; intrat; uocō; sumus; portāmus; timēs; habētis; est; timet; uocant; cēlātis; timēmus; habeō; sunt.

3   *Translate into Latin*: you (*pl.*) have; I do hide; we are carrying; they call; you (*s.*) are afraid of; she is dwelling; there are; it has; there enters; she is.

6   The cases in Latin: terminology and meaning

The terms 'nominative', 'vocative', 'accusative', 'genitive', 'dative' and 'ablative' are the technical terms for the six so-called 'cases' of Latin nouns and adjectives. The cases will be referred to as nom., voc., acc., gen., dat. and abl. after Section 1B. When laid out in this form the cases are called a 'declension'. 'Declining' a noun means to go through all its cases. *The different forms of the cases are of absolutely vital importance in Latin and must be learned by heart till you know them to perfection.*

The reason is as follows. In English, we determine the meaning of a sentence by the order in which the words come. The sentence 'Man bites dog' means something quite different from 'Dog bites man', for no other reason than that the words come in a different order. A Roman would have been bewildered by this, because in Latin word-order does not determine the grammatical functions of the words in the sentence (though it plays its part in emphasis): what is vital is the *form* the words take. In 'daughter calls the slave', 'daughter' is the subject of the sentence, and 'slave' the object. A Roman used the *nominative* form to indicate a subject, and the *accusative* form to indicate an object. Thus when he wrote or said the word for daughter, *filia*, he indicated not only what the word meant, but also its function in the sentence – in this case, subject; likewise, when he said 'slave', *seruum*, the form he used would tell him that slave was the object of the sentence. Thus, hearing *filia seruum*, a Roman would conclude at once that a daughter was doing something to a slave. Had the Roman heard *filiam seruus*, he would have concluded that a slave, *seruus*, which is here in the nominative case, was doing something to a daughter, *filiam*, here in the accusative case.

So a Roman could write those words in any order he liked – 'calls slave daughter'/'daughter slave calls'/'calls daughter slave' and so on, because if the slave was in the nominative and daughter the accusative, it would mean 'The slave calls the daughter'. WORD-ORDER IN LATIN IS OF SECONDARY IMPORTANCE since its function relates not to grammar or syntax so much as to emphasis, contrast and style. To English speakers word-order is, of course, the critical indicator of meaning. In Latin, grammar or syntax is indicated by WORD FORM. WORD FORM IS VITAL.

We can note here that English has a residual case system left, e.g. 'I like beer', not 'me like beer'; 'he loves me', not 'him loves I'; and cf. he, him / she, her, hers / they, them, theirs. It is, however, noticeable that even this system is increasingly breaking down. One regularly hears people saying e.g. 'Charlotte went to the match with Toby and I.' Traditional usage would favour 'with Toby and [with] me'; one would never say 'he went to the match with I' – would one?

1 *Noun*: the name of something (real or abstract), e.g. 'house', 'door', 'idea', 'intelligence', 'Helena'.

2 *Nominative case*: the most important functions are (i) as subject of a sentence, and (ii) as complement after the verb 'to be'. Nominative means 'naming' (*nōminō* 'I name'). In Latin, the subject of a sentence is 'in the verb', e.g.

> *habeō* means 'I have'
>
> *habet* means 'he/she/it has'

If one wants to 'name' the subject, it goes into the nominative case, e.g.

> *habeō serua* 'I (the slave) have'
>
> *habet serua* 'she (the slave) has', 'the slave has'
>
> *habet uir* 'he (the man) has', 'the man has'

3 *Vocative case*: used when addressing someone or something, e.g. 'O (male) slave', *'[o] serue'*, 'O table', *'[o] mēnsa'*, though the young Winston Churchill, faced with this for the first time, pointed out that he never actually did address a table (see pp. ix–x). In nearly all instances the form of the vocative is the same as that of the nominative.

4 *Accusative case*: the most important function is as direct object of a verb. The accusative case denotes the person or thing on the receiving end of the action, e.g. 'the man bites <u>the dog</u>'. One may also look at it as limiting or defining the extent of the action, e.g. 'the man bites' (what does he bite? A bullet? A jam sandwich? A table? No –) 'the dog'. So the accusative case can also limit or define the extent of a description, e.g. *nūdus <u>pedēs</u>* 'naked <u>in respect of</u> the feet', 'with naked feet'.

NB The verb 'to be' is NEVER followed by a direct object in the accusative, but frequently by a 'complement', in the NOMINATIVE, e.g. 'Phaedra is the <u>daughter</u>' *Phaedra <u>fīlia</u> est.* This is perfectly reasonable, since 'daughter' obviously describes Phaedra. They are both the same person, and will be in the same case.

5 *Genitive case*: this case expresses various senses of the English 'of'. Its root is the same as *genitor*, 'author', 'originator', 'father'. Thus it denotes the idea 'belonging to' (possession), e.g. 'slave *of Euclio*', and origin, e.g. 'son *of Euclio*'. Cf. English 'dog's dinner' (= 'dinner of dog') and 'dogs' dinner' (= 'dinner of the dogs'), where *dog*'s and *dogs*' are genitive forms.

> *Dative and ablative cases*: these will be used only in very limited ways in the *Text* at the moment, but you must learn their forms now as they are crucially important and will appear in exercise work.

6 *Word-order*: the usual word-order in English for a simple sentence consisting of subject, verb and object is: (i) subject (ii) verb (iii) object, e.g. 'The man (subj.) bites (verb) the dog (obj.).'

> In Latin the usual order is (i) subject (ii) object (iii) verb. See **1**⁵ above and Reference Grammar **W** for a full discussion.

7   Singular and plural; masculine, feminine and neuter

As well as having 'case', nouns can be either singular (s.), when there will be one of the persons or things named, or plural (pl.), when there will be more than one. This feature is called the 'number' of a noun. Nouns also possess 'gender', i.e. are masculine (m.), feminine (f.) or neuter (n.).

8   **1st declension nouns: *seru-a ae* 1 feminine (f.) 'slave-woman'**

The pattern which nouns follow is called 'declension'. Nouns 'decline'.

	case	*s.*	
nominative	(*nom.*)	séru-a	'slave-woman'
vocative	(*voc.*)	séru-a	'O slave-woman'
accusative	(*acc.*)	séru-am	'slave-woman'
genitive	(*gen.*)	séru-ae (-āī)	'of the slave-woman'
dative	(*dat.*)	séru-ae	'to/for the slave-woman'
ablative	(*abl.*)	séru-ā	'by/with/from the slave-woman'

	case	*pl.*	
nominative	(*nom.*)	séru-ae	'slave-women'
vocative	(*voc.*)	séru-ae	'O slave-women'
accusative	(*acc.*)	séru-ās	'slave-women'
genitive	(*gen.*)	seru-árum	'of the slave-women'
dative	(*dat.*)	séru-īs	'to/for the slave-women'
ablative	(*abl.*)	séru-īs	'by/with/from the slave-women'

Notes

1 Latin never uses a word corresponding to 'the' and only in special circumstances to 'a'. So *serua* can mean 'slave-woman', 'the slave-woman' or 'a slave-woman'. The same applies to all nouns in Latin.

2 All 1st decl. nouns end in -*a* in the nominative s. This is called the 'ending', the rest of the noun is called the 'stem'. So the stem of *serua* is *seru*-, the ending -*a*. The same applies to all 1st decl. nouns. Cf. *fīli-a, famili-a, Phaedr-a, Staphyl-a, aul-a, corōn-a, scaen-a.*

3 Most 1st decl. nouns are f. in gender (common exceptions are e.g. *agricol-a* 'farmer', *naut-a* 'sailor', both m.).

4 Note ambiguities:

   (a) *seru-ae* can be genitive s., dative s., or nominative/vocative pl.

   (b) *seru-a* is nominative/vocative s., but *seru-ā* = ablative s. (not ambiguous if you note vowel length carefully: -*a* nominative / -*ā* ablative)

   (c) *seru-īs* can be dative or ablative pl.

5 Nouns of this declension you should have learned are: *famili-a* 'household', *fīli-a* 'daughter', *Phaedr-a* 'Phaedra', *seru-a* 'slave-woman', *Staphyl-a* 'Staphyla', *aul-a* 'pot', *corōn-a* 'garland', *scaen-a* 'stage', 'scene'.

9   **2nd declension nouns: *seru-us ī* 2 masculine (m.) 'male slave'**

	s.		pl.	
nominative	séru-us	'male slave'	séru-ī	'male slaves'
vocative	séru-e	'O male slave'	séru-ī	'O male slaves'
accusative	séru-um	'male slave'	séru-ōs	'male slaves'
genitive	séru-ī	'of the male slave'	seru-órum	'of the male slaves'
dative	séru-ō	'to/for the male slave'	séru-īs	'to/for the male slaves'
ablative	séru-ō	'by/with/from the male slave'	séru-īs	'by/with/from the male slaves'

Notes

1 The vocative case, used when addressing people (e.g. 'hello, Brutus'), ends in *-e* in the 2nd decl. m., e.g. 'you too, Brutus?' *et tū, Brūt̠e?* (see **17A** for full discussion).

2 Observe ambiguities:

   (a) *seru-ō* can be dative or ablative s.

   (b) *seru-īs* can be dative or ablative pl.

   (c) *seru-ī* can be genitive s. or nominative vocative pl.

   (d) Watch *-um* endings of accusative s. and genitive pl.

3 The other noun of this decl. you should have learned is *coqu-us* 'cook'.

4 **Important translation note**: the suggested meanings for the dative and ablative cases in particular are to be treated with some caution. But one must start somewhere, and this does give an overview of some of the English uses.

EXERCISES

1 *Decline*: coquus; aula (*optional*: seruus, familia, corōna, scaena).

2 *Name the case or cases of each of these words*: seruārum; coquō; corōnam; seruōs; scaenae; fīliā; coquus; seruī; coquum; fīliae; scaenās; seruō; coquōrum; aula; seruīs.

3 *Translate each sentence, then change noun(s) and verb to pl. or s. as appropriate. E.g.* coquus seruam uocat: *the cook calls the slave-girl*, coquī seruās uocant.

   (a) sum seruus.

   (b) aulam portō.

   (c) corōnās habent.

   (d) serua timet seruum.

11

(e) seruās uocātis.

(f) seruae aulās portant.

(g) cēlāmus aulās.

(h) seruās cēlant coquī.

(i) familia corōnam habet.

(j) uocat seruus seruam.

10   **Prepositions**

Prepositions (*prae-positus* 'in front-placed') are the little words *placed in front* of nouns, e.g. *in* 'into', *ad* 'towards' etc. Learn the following important prepositions.

in, ad + *accusative*

> *in* 'into', 'onto', e.g. *in scaenam intrat* 'he enters onto (i.e. right onto) the stage'
>
> *ad* 'to(wards)', e.g. *ad scaenam aulam portat* 'he carries the pot towards (not necessarily onto) the stage'

Observe that the accusative denotes direction *towards which* something moves. Compare the next preposition.

in + *ablative*

> *in* 'in', 'on', e.g. *in scaenā est* 'he is on the stage'

Observe that *in* + ablative denotes position *at/on/in*.

Note

It is crucial to distinguish between *in* followed by the accusative and *in* followed by the ablative

EXERCISE

Write the Latin for: onto the stage; in the pot; onto the garlands; into the pots; in the household; towards the slave-woman; in the slaves; towards the daughter.

Translation hint

In order to develop reading skills, it is extremely important that Latin words be taken in the order in which they appear in a sentence, but that judgment about the final meaning of the sentence be suspended until all the necessary clues have been provided. Take, for example, the following sentences:

(a) *aulam igitur clam sub terrā cēlō*

One should approach it as follows:

> *aulam* 'pot': *-am* = accusative case, so something is happening to it
>
> *igitur* 'therefore' (fixed)
>
> *clam* 'secretly' (fixed)
>
> *sub* 'underneath' (fixed)
>
> *terrā* 'earth', so probably 'underneath the earth'
>
> *cēlō* something to do with 'hide', person ending *-ō*, so 'I hide'.

That gives us subject and verb; *aulam* must be object, so 'I hide the pot under the earth'. Add 'therefore' and 'secretly' in the most apt place.

(b) *in scaenam intrant seruus et serua et nūptiās parant*

> *in* 'in' or 'into', depending on case of following noun
>
> *scaenam* = plural, so 'house'. accusative, so 'onto the stage'
>
> *intrant* = something to do with entering, *-ant* = 'they', so 'they enter'
>
> *seruus* = something to do with a slave. But *-us* shows subject, so the slave must be doing something. Can he be 'entering'? But *intrant* is plural, 'they enter'. Oh dear!
>
> *et* 'and'. Ah. Perhaps another subject is about to appear.
>
> *serua* 'slave-woman', *-a* ending shows subject. Excellent: 'The slave and the slave-woman [they] are entering into the house.'
>
> *et* 'and'. More people entering? Or another clause?
>
> *nūptiās* 'marriage-rites', *-ās* shows object. So something is being done to the marriage-rites.
>
> *parant*: something about preparing, *-ant* shows 'they'. So 'they prepare the marriage-rites'. Since the two slaves of the earlier clause are in the nominative, they must presumably be subject of *parant* too. So 'The slave and slave-woman [they] enter onto the stage and [they] prepare the marriage-rites.'

What you have done here is to *read* the sentence. Reformulating it into normal English is to *translate* it, a further step beyond the analytical understanding of the Latin. The technique outlined above is the best way to approach a Latin sentence. A number of the exercises will encourage you to do this kind of analysis.

READ
VS
TRANS-
LATE

Reading exercises

1 *Read each of these sentences, then, without translating, say what the subject of the second verb is (in Latin). Finally, translate each sentence into English.*

(a) seruus in scaenam intrat. corōnās portat.

(b) coquī in scaerā sunt. seruās uocant.

13

(c) est in familiā Eucliōnis serua. Staphyla est.

(d) in scaenam intrat Dēmaenetus. aulam aurī plēnam habet.

(e) coquus et serua clāmant; seruum enim timent.

2 *Take each word as it comes and define its job in the sentence (e.g.* Dēmaenetus coquum... *– Demaenetus is subject, so Demaenetus is doing something,* coquum *is object, so Demaenetus is doing something to a cook). Then add an appropriate verb in the right form (e.g. Demaenetus calls a cook –* Dēmaenetus coquum uocat).

(a) aulam seruus ...

(b) serua corōnam, aulam seruus ...[1]

(c) seruās seruī ...

(d) familia coquōs ...

(e) Lar seruōs ...

(f) aurum ego ...

(g) Eucliō familiam ...

(h) aulās aurī plēnās et corōnās seruae ...

1. The verb must be s.

EITHER

3 *With the help of the running vocabulary for* **1A**, *work through the Latin passage* 'Dēmaenetus ...', *following these steps*:

(a) *As you meet each word, ask*

(i) *its meaning*

(ii) *its job in the sentence (i.e. subject or object? part of a phrase?), e.g.*

Dēmaenetus coquōs et tībīcinās uidet.

Dēmaenetus *'Demaenetus', subject*; coquōs *'cooks', object*; et *'and' almost certainly joining something to* coquōs; tībīcinās *'pipe-girls', object – part of a phrase* coquōs et tībīcinās; uidet *'(he) sees', verb*: '*Demaenetus the cooks and pipe-girls (he) sees.*'

(b) *Next produce a version in good English, e.g. 'Demaenetus sees the cooks and pipe-girls.'*

(c) *When you have worked through the whole passage, go back to the Latin and read the piece aloud, taking care to phrase correctly, thinking through the meaning as you read.*

Dēmaenetus coquōs et tībīcinās uidet. ad nūptiās fīliae ueniunt. in aedīs[1]
Dēmaenetī intrant et nūptiās parant. nunc aedēs Dēmaenetī coquōrum et
tībīcinārum plēnae sunt. Dēmaenetus autem timet. aulam enim aurī plēnam habet.
nam sī aula Dēmaenetī in aedibus est aurī plēna, fūrēs ualdē timet Dēmaenetus.
aulam Dēmaenetus cēlat. nunc aurum saluum est, nunc saluus Dēmaenetus, nunc
salua aula. Lar enim aulam habet plēnam aurī. nunc prope Larem Dēmaenetī   5
aula sub terrā latet. nunc igitur ad Larem appropinquat Dēmaenetus et supplicat.
'ō Lar, ego Dēmaenetus tē uocō. ō tūtēla meae familiae, aulam ad tē aurī plēnam
portō. fīliae nūptiae sunt hodiē. ego autem fūrēs timeō. nam aedēs meae fūrum
plēnae sunt. tē ōrō et obsecrō, aulam Dēmaenetī aurī plēnam seruā.'

1 aedīs *house* (acc.)

2 aedēs *house* (nom.); *agrees with* plēnae

3 aedibus *house* (abl.)

4 fūrēs *of thieves* (acc.)

5 fūram *of thieves* (gen.)

OR

English–Latin

*Translate the Latin sentences into English. Then translate the English sentences
into Latin, using the pattern of the Latin ones to help you arrange the word-order
correctly.*

(a) coquus aulam Dēmaenetī portat.
    The slave has the cooks' garlands.

(b) tū clāmās, ego autem aulās portō.
    The slave girl is afraid. Therefore *I* am calling the cook.

(c) cūr scaena plēna est seruōrum?
    Why is the household full of cooks?

(d) ego Lar tē uocō. cūr mē timēs?
    (It is) I, Phaedra (who)[1] enter. Why are you (*pl.*) hiding the pot?

(e) sī aurum habet, Dēmaenetus timet.
    If they hide the pot, the slaves are afraid.

(f) corōnās et aulās portant seruī.
    (It is)[1] a cook and a slave-girl Demaenetus is summoning.

1 Put stressed words first in the sentence.

15

Grammar and exercises for 1B

11   **3rd declension nouns (consonant stem): *fūr fūr-is* 3m. 'thief'**

	s.		pl.	
nominative	fūr	'thief'	fū́r-ēs	'thieves'
vocative	fūr	'thief'	fū́r-ēs	'O thieves'
accusative	fū́r-em	'thief'	fū́r-ēs	'thieves'
genitive	fū́r-is	'of the thief'	fū́r-um	'of thieves'
dative	fū́r-ī	'to/for the thief'	fū́r-ibus	'to/for thieves'
ablative	fū́r-e	'by/with/from the thief'	fū́r-ibus	'by/with/from thieves'

Note

This is the standard pattern of endings for 3rd decl. nouns whose stems end in a consonant. There are, however, slight changes of pattern in nouns whose stem ends in the vowel -*i*- (the so-called '*i*-stem' nouns) as follows. See **H3 notes**.

12   **3rd declension nouns (*i*-stem) *aedis aed-is* 3f. 'room', 'temple'; in plural 'temples', 'house'**

	s.	
nominative	aéd-is	'room', 'temple'
vocative	aéd-is	'O room', 'O temple'
accusative	aéd-em	'room', 'temple'
genitive	aéd-is	'of the room', 'of the temple'
dative	aéd-ī	'to/for the room/temple'
ablative	aéd-e (aéd-ī)	'by/with/from the room/temple'

	pl.	
nominative	aéd-ēs	'temples'/'house'
vocative	aéd-ēs	'O temples'/'O house'
accusative	aéd-īs (-ēs)	'temples'/'house'
genitive	aéd-ium	'of temples'/'of the house'
dative	aéd-ibus	'to/for temples/the house'
ablative	aéd-ibus	'by/with/from temples/the house'

Notes

1 *aed-is* in the s. means 'room', 'temple'; in the pl. usually 'house'.

2 Observe accusative pl. in *-īs*, genitive pl. in *-ium*, and alternative ablative s. in *-ī*. This dominance of *-i-* is the mark of *i*-stem nouns of the third declension. In fact originally *all* the cases would have had the *-i-*, since it is part of the stem. The s. of *turris* 3f. 'tower', which keeps the old forms even in classical Latin, will demonstrate this: *turri-s, turri-s, turri-m, turri-s, turrī, turrī.*

Some hints on typical consonant stems are given below, but for practical reasons we present all endings as for consonant stems, i.e. *aed-is*, not (the technically correct) *aedi-s.*

13 Stems and endings of 3rd declension nouns

1 3rd decl. nouns have a great variety of endings in the nominative s. What unites them all is that their genitive s. has the same ending, e.g. *Eucliō Eucliōn-is, senex sen-is.* You must therefore learn both the decl. and the genitive s. as well as the gender of these 3rd decl. nouns, i.e. not *aedis* 'temple', pl. 'house', but *aedis aed-is* 3f. 'temple', pl. 'house'.

2 The genitive s. is doubly important, because it gives you the STEM OF THE NOUN to which the endings are added to make the declension. Thus when you have learned *senex sen-is* 3m., you know that the stem is *sen-*. IT IS THE GENITIVE S. WHICH GIVES YOU THIS.

3 You also need to be able to work back from the stem to the nominative s. in order to find the word in a dictionary. E.g. if you see *pācem* in the text, you MUST be able to deduce that the nominative s. is *pāx*, otherwise you will not be able to look the word up. Observe the following common patterns of CONSONANT STEMS:

(a) stems ending in *-l-* or *-r-* keep *l* and *r* in the nominative, e.g.

> *cōnsul-is*→nominative *cōnsul* 'consul'
> *fūr-is*→nominative *fūr* 'thief'

(b) stems ending in *-d-* or *-t-* end in *-s* in the nominative, e.g.

> *ped-is*→nominative *pēs* 'foot'
> *dōt-is*→nominative *dōs* 'dowry'

(c) stems ending in *-c-* or *-g-* end in *-x* in the nominative, e.g.

> *rēg-is*→nominative *rēx* 'king'
> *duc-is*→nominative *dux* 'general'

(d) stems ending in *-iōn-* or *-ōn-* end in *-iō* or *-ō* in the nominative, e.g.

> *Scīpiōn-is*→nominative *Scīpiō* 'Scipio'
> *praedōn-is*→nominative *praedō* 'pirate'

EXERCISES

1 *Decline*: Eucliō (*s.*), fūr (*optional*: honor, Lar, aedis).

2 *Name the case of each of these words*: Eucliōnis, fūrem, aedium, honōrēs, Lar, senum, aedīs, honōrem, fūr, Laris.

3 *Translate each sentence, then change noun(s) and verb(s) to s. or pl. as appropriate, e.g.* fūrem seruus timet – *the slave is afraid of a thief* – fūrēs seruī timent.

(a) deinde thēsaurum senis fūr uidet.

(b) Lar honōrem nōn habet.

(c) senem igitur deus nōn cūrat.

(d) quārē tamen supplicātis, senēs?

(e) unguentum senex tandem possidet.

(f) in aedibus senex nunc habitat.

(g) fūr aulam aurī plēnam semper amat.

(h) honōrem tamen nōn habet fūr.

(i) quārē in aedīs nōn intrās, senex?

(j) seruam clam amat senex.

14   **1st/2nd declension adjectives: *mult-us a um* 'much', 'many'**

	s.		
	m.	*f.*	*n.*
nominative	múlt-us	múlt-a	múlt-um
vocative	múlt-e	múlt-a	múlt-um
accusative	múlt-um	múlt-am	múlt-um
genitive	múlt-ī	múlt-ae	múlt-ī
dative	múlt-ō	múlt-ae	múlt-ō
ablative	múlt-ō	múlt-ā	múlt-ō
	pl.		
	m.	*f.*	*n.*
nominative	múlt-ī	múlt-ae	múlt-a
vocative	múlt-ī	múlt-ae	múlt-a
accusative	múlt-ōs	múlt-ās	múlt-a
genitive	mult-órum	mult-árum	mult-órum
dative	múlt-īs	múlt-īs	múlt-īs
ablative	múlt-īs	múlt-īs	múlt-īs

Notes

1 Adjectives (from *adiectus* 'added to') give additional information about a noun,
  e.g. *fast* horse, *steep* hill (adjectives are often called 'describing words').

2 Since nouns can be m., f. or n., adjectives need to have m., f. and n. forms
  so that they can 'AGREE' grammatically with the noun they describe. So
  adjectives must agree with nouns in *gender.*

3 Adjectives must also 'AGREE' with nouns in *number*, s. or pl.

4 Finally, they must 'AGREE' with nouns in *case* (nominative, accusative,
  genitive, dative or ablative). A noun in the accusative can be described only by
  an adjective in the accusative.

5 In summary, if a noun is to be described by an adjective in Latin, the adjective
  will have to agree with it in *gender, number and case*. Here are three examples:

  (a) 'I see *many* temples' – 'temples' are the object, and pl.; the word we shall
      use in Latin is *aedīs*, which is f. So if 'many' is to agree with 'temples', it
      will need to be accusative pl. and f. Answer: *multās aedīs*. Note that the
      endings of the accusative pl. adjective *mult-ās* and noun *aed-īs* are not the
      same. This is because they decline differently.

  (b) 'He shows *much* respect' – 'respect' is object, s. The word we shall use,
      honor honōr-is, is m. So 'much' will have to be accusative s. m. Answer:
      multum honōrem. Note *mult-um honōr-em* and see (a) above.

  (c) 'I hear the voice of *many* slaves' – 'slaves' is genitive, and pl.; the word we
      shall use, *serua*, is f. So 'many' will be genitive pl. f. Answer: *multārum
      seruārum.*

6 It is worth emphasising here that an adjective does not necessarily describe a
  noun it is standing next to. It describes a noun it *agrees with* in case, number
  and gender, e.g.

  (a) *multum fīlia seruat thēsaurum. multum* = accusative s. m.; *fīlia* =
      nominative s. f; *thēsaurum* = accusative s. m., i.e. 'It's <u>much treasure</u> the
      daughter keeps.'

  (b) *nūllum fūrum cōnsilium placet. nūllum* = accusative s. m. or
      nominative/accusative s. n.; *fūrum* = genitive pl.; *cōnsilium* =
      nominative/accusative s. n., i.e. '<u>No scheme</u> of thieves is pleasing.'

  multus usually precedes its noun, e.g. *multī seruī* 'many slaves'. When it
  follows its noun it is emphatic, e.g. *seruōs multōs habeō* 'I've got *loads* of
  slaves.'

7 Adjectives can be used on their own as nouns, when *gender* will indicate
  meaning, e.g. *bonus* (m.) 'a good man', *bonum* (n.) 'a good thing'.

15   **2nd declension neuter nouns: *somni-um ī* 2n. 'dream'**

	s.		pl.	
nominative	sómni-um	'dream'	sómni-a	'dreams'
vocative	sómni-um	'O dream'	sómni-a	'O dreams'
accusative	sómni-um	'dream'	sómni-a	'dreams'
genitive	sómnī *or* sómni-ī	'of the dream'	somni-órum	'of dreams'
dative	sómni-ō	'to/for the dream'	sómni-īs	'to/for dreams'
ablative	sómni-ō	'by/with/from the dream'	sómni-īs	'by/with/from dreams'

Notes

1 There is only one neuter noun type of the 2nd decl.; they all end in *-um* in nominative s. Cf. *aur-um* 'gold', *unguent-um* 'ointment'.

2 As with other neuters, the nominative and accusative s. and pl. are the same (see **26**).

3 Do not confuse the neuter nominative s. forms with the accusative s. of 2nd decl. m. nouns like *seru-us* (*seru-um*) or genitive pl. of 3rd decl., nouns like *aedis* (*aedium*). Be sure that you learn nouns like *somnium* as type 2 *neuter*.

4 As with all neuters, there is a danger of confusing the pl. forms in *-a* with 1st decl. f. nouns like *serua*.

5 Note the genitive s. *somnī* or *somniī*. Nouns of the 2nd decl. ending in *-ius* (e.g. *fīlius* 'son') usually have genitive s. in *-ī* (e.g. *fīlī*) and nominative pl. always in *-iī* (e.g. *fīliī*).

6 2nd decl. neuter nouns share the same endings as the 2nd decl. m. nouns in the genitive, dative and ablative, both s. and pl. (cf. *seruus* **9**).

EXERCISES

1 *Here to learn is a list of 2nd decl. n. nouns like* somnium:

       exiti-um ī 2n. 'death', 'destruction'
       ingeni-um ī 2n. 'talent', 'ability'
       perīcul-um ī 2n. 'danger'

2 *Pick out the genitive pls. from the following list. Say what nouns they come from, with what meaning (e.g.* perīculōrum = *genitive pl. of* perīcul-um ī *'danger'*): honōrum, ingenium, aedibus, fūrum, exitiō, seruum, unguentōrum, aurum, senum, thēsaurīs.

3 *Pick out, and give the meanings of, the pl. nouns in the following list:* scaena, serua, ingenia, familia, cūra, unguentīs, fīliā, somnia, corōna, perīcula.

16   **2nd declension noun (irregular): *de-us ī* 2m. 'god'**

	s.	pl.
nominative	dé-us	dī
vocative	dé-us	dī
accusative	dé-um	déōs
genitive	dé-ī	de-órum (dé-um)
dative	dé-ō	dīs
ablative	dé-ō	dīs

17A   **Vocatives**

The vocative case (*uocō* 'I call') is used when addressing a person. Its form is the same as the nominative in all nouns, except 2nd decl. m., where -*us* of nominative s. becomes -*e* (e.g. O *Dēmaenete* 'Demaenetus!', *serue* 'O slave') and the -*ius* of nominative s. becomes -*ī* (e.g. *filius* 'son'; *filī* 'O son').

NB The vocative s. of *meus* 'my' is not *mee* (!) but *mī*, e.g. *mī filī* 'O my son'.

17B   **Apposition**

Consider this sentence:

> *sum Dēmaenetus, Eucliōnis auus* 'I am Demaenetus, Euclio's grandfather.'

The phrase *Eucliōnis auus* gives more information about Demaenetus. It is said to be 'in apposition' to *Dēmaenetus* (from *adpositus* 'placed near'). Note that *auus*, the main piece of information, is the same case as *Dēmaenetus*.

Note

Appositional phrases may be added to a noun in any case, e.g. *sum seruus Dēmaenetī* <u>*senis*</u> 'I am the slave of Demaenetus <u>the old man</u>'. *senis* (genitive) is in apposition to *Dēmaenetī* (genitive).

EXERCISES

1   *Attach the correct form of* multus *to these nouns (in ambiguous cases, give all possible alternatives)*: cūrās, aurum, fūrēs, senem, honōris, aedem, seruōrum, senum, aedīs, corōnae (*optional*: seruum, unguenta, aedis, familiam, aedium, honor, aedēs).

2   *Pair the given form of* multus *with the nouns with which it can agree*:

> multus: senex, cūra, Larem, familiae, seruus
>
> multī: honor, aedēs, Laris, senēs, seruī

multīs: honōribus, aedīs, cūram, seruum, deum, senibus, aurum

multās: senis, honōrēs, aedīs, cūram, familiās

multae: seruae, aedī, cūram, senēs, dī

multa: aedēs, unguenta, senem, cūra, corōnārum

(*optional*:

multōs: aedīs, unguentum, cūrās, seruōs, fūrēs

multō: aurum, Larem, cūram, honōrī, aedem

multōrum: aedium, unguentōrum, seruum, senum, deōrum, corōnārum

multārum: fūrum, aurum, honōrem, seruārum, aedium)

3 *Translate into Latin*: many slave-girls (*nominative*); of much respect; of many garlands; much gold; many an old man (*accusative*); of many thieves; many old men (*accusative*).

Optional exercises

1 *Identify the case (or cases, where ambiguities exist) of the following words, say what they mean, and then turn s. into pl. and pl. into s.*: seruae, honōrī, thēsaurīs, familiā, deum, fīliā, dīs, corōna, senum.

2 *Give the declension and case of each of the following words*: thēsaurum, honōrum, deōrum, seruārum, aedium.

3 *Case work*

(a) *Group the following words by case (i.e. list all nominatives, accusatives, genitives etc.). When you have done that, identify s. and pl. within each group*: Eucliōnem, senī, thēsaurō, fīliae, familia, deī, corōna, scaenās, dī, aedēs, honōribus, seruārum, multīs.

(b) *Identify the following noun forms by showing*:

what case they are

whether s. or pl.

their nominative s. form, genitive s. form and gender

their meaning

e.g. senem *is accusative s. of* senex sen-is, *m.* 'old man'. *Remember ambiguities!*

(i) *3rd decl.*: aedēs, patris, senibus, honōrum, senem, aedibus, honōrī, sene, aedium, honōris, senēs, aedīs

(ii) *1st decl. f.*: Phaedrae, aulārum, corōnās, scaenā, cūrīs, fīliārum, familiae, Staphylam, seruīs, aulam, corōnae, scaenās

(iii) *2nd decl. m.*: seruī, coquus, thēsaurum, seruīs, coquī, seruō, deōs, thēsaurīs, coquō, deī

(iv) *Various declensions*: sene, seruīs, patris, coquīs, honōrī, aedīs, aulārum, honōrum, deum, seruārum

Reading exercise

In each of these sentences, the verb comes first or second. Say in each case whether the subject is s. or pl., then, moving on, say in order as they come whether the following words are subjects or objects of the verb. Next, translate into English. Finally read out the sentences in Latin with the correct phrasing.

(a) clāmant seruī, senex, seruae.

(b) dat igitur honōrem multum Phaedra.

(c) nunc possidet Lar aedīs.

(d) amant dī multum honōrem.

(e) dat aurum multās cūrās.

(f) habitant quoque in aedibus seruī.

(g) est aurum in aulā multum.

(h) timent autem fūrēs multī senēs.

(i) quārē intrant senex et seruus in scaenam?

(j) tandem explicat Lar cūrās senis.

Quotations

Translate these sentences with the help of the appended vocabulary:

(a) *nūlla potentia longa est.* (Ovid)

(b) *uīta nec bonum nec malum est.* (Seneca: see **14.7**)

(c) *nōbilitās sōla est atque ūnica uirtūs.* (Juvenal)

(d) *longa est uīta sī plēna est.* (Seneca)

(e) *fortūna caeca est.* (Cicero)

potenti-a ae 1f. power
long-us a um long, long-lived
uīt-a ae 1f. life
nec ... nec neither ... nor
bon-us a um good
mal-us a um bad
nōbilitās nōbilitāt-is 3f. nobility

sōl-us a um only
atque and
ūnic-us a um unique, unparalleled
uirtūs uirtūt-is 3f. goodness
fortūn-a ae 1f. fortune
caec-us a um blind

23

EITHER

Reading exercise / Test exercise

Read through this passage, as for Reading exercise no. 3 in **1A**, *p. 15. For an adjective, say (i) what it belongs with (if it follows its noun), and (ii) what sort of noun you will expect with it (if it precedes). Use the running vocabulary of* **1B** *for any words you do not know. At the end, after translating the passage, read it out in Latin, correctly phrased.*

Lar in scaenam intrat. deus est Eucliōnis familiae. seruat Lar sub terrā thēsaurum Dēmaenetī. multus in aulā thēsaurus est. ignōrat autem dē thēsaurō Eucliō, quod Larem nōn cūrat. nam nūllum dat unguentum, nūllās corōnās, honōrem nūllum. Phaedram autem, senis auārī fīliam, Lar amat. dat enim Eucliōnis fīlia multum unguentum, multās corōnās, multum honōrem. Lar igitur Dēmaenetī aulam, 5 quod bona est Eucliōnis fīlia, Eucliōnī dat. Eucliō autem aulam, quod auārus est, sub terrā iterum collocat. nam fūrēs ualdē timet Eucliō! cūrās habet multās! uexat thēsaurus senem auārum et anxium. plēnae enim fūrum sunt dīuitum hominum aedēs.

OR

English–Latin

Translate the Latin sentences into English. Then translate the English sentences into Latin, using the pattern of the Latin ones to help you arrange the word-order correctly.

(a) Lar igitur Eucliōnem, quod honōrem nōn dat, nōn amat.
   The gods therefore care for Phaedra, my son, because she cares for the Lar.

(b) senex autem cūrās habet multās, quod aurum habet multum.
   The slaves however are carrying many garlands, because they are bestowing much respect.

(c) Eucliōnis aedēs fūrum sunt plēnae, quod aulam aurī plēnam habet senex.
   The temple of the gods is full of gold, because the daughters of the rich give pots full of gold.

(d) ego multum unguentum, corōnās multās, multum honōrem habeō.
   You (s.) have much worry and much treasure.

(e) tē, Dēmaenete, nōn amō.
   I'm not carrying *gold*, my son.

(f) clāmant seruī, supplicant seruae, timet senex.
   The daughter is praying, the old men shouting and the slave-girls are afraid.

Dēliciae Latīnae

These sections, which will occur at the end of Grammar and Exercise sections, will consist of a mixture of hints on word-building, word exercises and Latin words and phrases in everyday use. The title means 'Latin delights'. Extra reading in the form of short passages of (mostly) real Latin, accompanied by notes and glossary, is appended, section by section, in Part Four of the *Text and Vocabulary* volume.

Derivations

The Roman Empire extended over modern Italy, Spain, Portugal and France, all of the languages of which are descended directly from Latin. Britain was part of the Roman Empire, but it was overrun by Anglo-Saxons in the years following the end of Roman rule, so that there was no major Latin influence on the language at this stage – Anglo-Saxon was the predominant tongue. Latin was, however, still the language of the Church in Britain, so all interaction was not wholly lost. (Bede (*Baeda*), the eighth-century monk from Jarrow near Newcastle upon Tyne, wrote his history of the English church in Latin.) The turning point for the English language came in 1066 when the Norman Duke William (the Conqueror) took England. French-speaking kings ruled England for some 300 years (till Agincourt, 1415), when English again became the official language of royalty. The Latin-based French language became incorporated into Middle English, adding enormous richness to it, e.g. Middle English gives us 'kingly', French/Latin adds 'regal', 'royal', 'sovereign'. It is largely through French that English has the Latin component that it does. (On all this, see pp. 397–408.)

Consequently, Latin is very useful to anyone who wants to learn the Romance languages (i.e. languages descended from the language of the Romans), and vice versa knowledge of Romance languages can help you to understand Latin. Five hints:

(a) Identify the stem of the Latin word as well as its nominative s. form, e.g. *senex* gives us 'senile' (from the Latin adjective *senīlis*, formed from *sen-*, the stem of *senex*).

(b) Many English words ending in *-ion* come from Latin via French.

(c) Many English words ending in *-ate*, *-ance*, *-ent*, *-ence* come from Latin, again via French.

(d) English derivatives have 'j' and 'v' where the Latin words from which they come have *i* and *u* used as consonants (i.e. before or between vowels). So *Iānuārius* produces 'January' and *uideō* produces 'video'. The reverse process will help you to see whether a word has a Latin root, e.g. 'juvenile' comes from Latin *iuuenīlis*.

(e) When Latin was written entirely in capitals, it used V to represent the sounds that we know as the vowel *u*, either long as in FVR 'thief' or short

as in BONVS 'good'; and the 'glide' or semi-vowel *w* as in VOCO
'I call'. Thus classical and late Latin had only one sign for the vowel
and semi-vowel, and that sign was V. When minuscules (lower-case letters)
were introduced (*c.* fourth century AD), V in both its pronunciations
became *u*. But many writers (and, much later, printers) of 'standard' Latin
then decided to distinguish between the vowel and semi-vowel, and chose
u for the vowel and *v* for the semi-vowel, thus distinguishing between e.g.
bonus and *voco* – and *v* at that time was pronounced as in English 'vein'.
That was how the unclassical lower-case intruder *v* slipped into the Latin
alphabet, bringing with it a non-classical sound as well. This explains why
we use *u* throughout. As a matter of interest, the letter indicating pure 'w'
does appear in Latin around the first century AD as VV (e.g. the German
name VVITILDES).

It is worth noting that these are letters relevant only to the writing of Latin.
At this early stage the Latin alphabet had no relevance to the writing of
Anglo-Saxon (the basis of English), which used a runic alphabet till about
the eighth century AD. Anglo-Saxon then gradually adopted the Latin
alphabet, the source of the English alphabet we have today, even more so
after the Norman invasion of 1066. The Church, of course, was writing in
Latin throughout this period!

Note

English has taken some of its Latin-based words direct from Latin rather than
through an intermediary language such as French, e.g. 'wine' from *uīnum*, 'wall'
from *uallum* (see Appendix p. 406). Other English words look similar to Latin
not because they have been taken from Latin, but because both English and
Latin share a common linguistic ancestor, Indo-European, the vocabulary of
which is preserved in different ways in the various derivative tongues. Thus the
Indo-European word for 'two', which can be reconstructed as **duō*, emerges in
English as *two*, German *zwei*, Sanskrit *dvau* and Latin *duo* (whence French *deux*,
Italian *due*, Spanish *dos*).

Word-building

(a) Stems

The stem of one word gives the clue to the meaning of many other words, e.g.
seru- in the form *seru-us* or *seru-a* means 'slave'; as a verb, with a verb-ending,
seruiō, it means 'I am a slave to'.

> *coqu-* in the noun form *coquus* = 'a/the cook'; in the verb form
> *coquō* = 'I cook'
>
> *aed-* in the form *aedēs* = 'a/the house'; with the suffix *-ficō* (= 'make'):
> *aedificō* = 'I build'; in the form *aedīlis*, it means 'aedile', a Roman state
> official originally with a particular responsibility for building

(b) Prefixes

A 'prefix' (*prae* 'in front *of*', *fixus* 'fixed', cf. 'preposition', p. 12) is a word fixed in front of another. Most prepositions (see **10**), e.g. *in* 'into', 'in', 'on', *ad* 'towards' etc., can also be used as prefixes, and as such slightly alter the meaning of the 'root' word to which they are fixed, e.g.:

> root word *sum* 'I am': *adsum* 'I am near'; *īnsum* 'I am in'
>
> root word *portō* 'I carry': *importō* 'I carry in'; *apportō* 'I carry to'
> (observe that *inp-* becomes *imp-* and *adp-* becomes *app-*)

Note the following prepositions which are commonly used as prefixes:

> *cum* (*con-*) 'with'
>
> *prae* 'before, in front of, at the head of'
>
> *post* 'after'

EXERCISE

Split the following Latin words up into prefix and root, and say what they might mean: conuocō, inhabitō, inuocō, praeuideō, comportō, praesum, posthabeō.

(c) Verb-stems different from the present stem

As you will soon discover, Latin verbs have a number of different 'stems'. So far you have learnt the present stem, e.g. *uoc-ō* 'I call'. But most 1st conjugation verbs have another stem in *-āt-* i.e. *uoc-āt-* (which you will come to later). This stem was very fruitful in forming other Latin words, and so French words, and so English words, particularly those in *-ate* or *-ation*. Thus *vocation, convocation, invocation, invocate* etc.

EXERCISE

Give an English word in -ate or -ation from the following Latin words, and say what it means: supplicō, explicō, importō, dō, habitō.

   uideō *has another stem,* uīs-, *and* possideō *has* possess-, *giving us what English nouns, by the addition of what letters?*

Word exercises

1 *Give English words connected with the following Latin words*: familia, corōna, scaena, timeō, deus, multus, uideō.

2 *With what Latin words are the following connected?* pecuniary, honorific, amatory, thesaurus, porter, clamorous, filial, edifice (*Latin* ae *becomes* e), unguent, furtive, servile, nullify.

Everyday Latin

We use Latin words and phrases every day of our lives:

> a.m. = *ante merīdiem*. What does *ante* mean?
>
> p.m. = *post merīdiem*. What does *post* mean? What is a *post mortem?* What is a *post scrīptum?*
>
> *iānua* = 'door'. *Iānus* (Janus) was a Roman god who had two faces, so that he could look out and in like a door and, like the month January, forward to the new year and back to the old
>
> *tandem* = 'at length', just like the bicycle made for two (introduced originally as a learned joke; the Latin word was never used of space)
>
> *uōx* (= 'voice') *populī*, *uōx deī* – meaning? Cf. *agnus* ('lamb') *deī*

Frequently in English we give Latin words their correct Latin plurals, e.g. we talk of termini, pl. of the Latin *terminus*. What would you say of someone who gave the plural of 'ignoramus' as 'ignorami' (*ignōr-ō* 1)?

Consider the following plurals: *data* ('given things'), *agenda* ('things to be done'), *media* ('things in the middle'). They are neuter plurals, declining like *multus*, directly from Latin. What are their singular forms? Those who know Latin gain much pleasure, and suffer much pain, in noticing the inconsistency with which English speakers treat Latin plurals, e.g. 'the data *is* significant'. But should Latin rules control the English language? (Do not write on both sides of the paper at once.)

NOTE: From now on the cases will be shown in their shortened form, nom., voc., acc., gen., dat., abl.

Section 1C

Grammar and exercises for 1C

18 **Present imperative active, 1st and 2nd conjugation**

	1st conj.		*2nd conj.*	
2nd s.	ámā	'love!'	hábē	'have!'
2nd pl.	amá-te	'love!'	habē-te	'have!'

Notes

1 These forms express a command/order ('imperative') in Latin.

2 The understood subject is 'you' (s. or pl.).

3 The s. form is the bare stem of the verb; the pl. adds -*te*.

EXERCISES

1 *Construct and translate the s. and pl. imperatives of these verbs*: timeō, rogō, taceō, cōgitō, moneō, cūrō, possideō (*optional*: habeō, stō, explicō, cēlo, amō, uideō, maneō).

2 *Translate into English*: dā corōnam!; portā aquam!; in aedibus manēte!; tacē!; thēsaurum seruā!; monēte fīliam!

3 *Translate into Latin*: see! (*pl.*); ask Euclio! (*s.*); be quiet! (*pl.*); hide the pot! (*pl.*).

19 ***eō* 'I go', 'I come' (irregular): present indicative active**

1st s.	é-ō	'I go', 'I come', 'I am going/coming', 'I do go/come'
2nd s.	ī-s	'you (*s.*) go', 'you (*s.*) come', 'you (*s.*) are going/coming'
3rd s.	i-t	'he/she/it goes/comes/is going/coming'
1st pl.	í-mus	'we go', 'we come', 'we are going/coming'
2nd pl.	í-tis	'you (*pl.*) go', 'you (*pl.*) come', 'you (*pl.*) are going/coming'
3rd pl.	é-u-nt	'they go', 'they come', 'they are going/coming'

Imperatives		
2nd s.	ī	'go!' etc.
2nd pl.	í-te	'go!' etc.

Notes

1 The stem of the verb is simply *i-* (as shown by the imperative s.).

2 There are many compound words based on *eō*, e.g. *adeō* 'I approach', 'I go up to' (cf. *ad* 'towards', 'near'); see Learning Vocabulary for **1C**.

EXERCISES

1 *Translate into English and then turn s. into pl. and vice versa*: ī, eunt, ītis, eō, it, īmus, exītis, abīmus, abītis, redeunt, redītis, īte, redeō, exeunt.

2 *Translate into Latin*: we are going away; they return; go away! (*s.*); you (*pl.*) are approaching; she is coming out; I am going; go back! (*pl.*); you (*s.*) go.

20   **1st and 2nd declension adjectives: *meus, tuus***

me-us a um 'my', 'mine', and *tu-us a um* 'your(s)' decline exactly like *mult-us a um*, and agree with their nouns in the same way. Observe that *tu-us* means 'your(s)' when you are *one* person.

NB The vocative of *meus* is *mī* (cf. **17A**), e.g. *mī fīlī* 'O my son'.

21   **1st and 2nd declension adjectives: *miser miser-a miser-um***

	s.		
	m.	*f.*	*n.*
nom.	míser	míser-a	míser-um
voc.	míser	míser-a	míser-um
acc.	míser-um	míser-am	míser-um
gen.	míser-ī	míser-ae	míser-ī
dat.	míser-ō	míser-ae	míser-ō
abl.	míser-ō	míser-ā	míser-ō

	pl.		
	m.	*f.*	*n.*
nom.	míser-ī	míser-ae	míser-a
voc.	míser-ī	míser-ae	míser-a
acc.	míser-ōs	míser-ās	míser-a
gen.	miser-órum	miser-árum	miser-órum
dat.		← míser-īs →	
abl.		← míser-īs →	

Notes

1 All the endings of *miser* are the same as those of *mult-us*, on the stem *miser-*, except for the nom. and voc. m. s.

2 Arrows indicate that the form shown is the same for all genders. For learning purposes, say '*míser-īs* throughout' or repeat the word three times.

EXERCISES

1 *Add the appropriate forms of* meus *and* tuus *to the following nouns (see* **20**) *and say what case they are*: igne, aedīs, honōris, familiā, oculōrum, dominō, aquae, Eucliōnem, senex.

2 Optional. *Add the appropriate form of* miser *to the following nouns and say what case they are*: Eucliōnī, Phaedrā, deus, fīliam, aedibus, dominī, seruārum, coquīs, senum.

22   **Personal pronouns: *ego* 'I' and *tū* 'you'**

nom.	égo	'I'	tū	'you'
acc.	mē		tē	
gen.	méī		túī	
dat.	míhi (mī)		tíbi	
abl.	mē		tē	

Notes

1 *tū* is used when one person is being referred to (cf. *tuus*).

2 When 'I' or 'you' are subject of a verb, we have seen that Latin does not need to express them separately, since the verb itself indicates the person by its personal endings *-ō, -s, -t* etc. But Latin does use *ego, tū* when the speaker wants to stress the identity of the person talking or draw a specific contrast between one person and another. E.g.:

    (a) *ego Eucliōnem amō, tū Phaedram* 'I like Euclio, whereas *you* like Phaedra.'

    (b) *ego deum cūrō* '*I* am the person who cares for the god.'

    It is a matter of emphasis, especially when a contrast is involved.

3 *meī* and *tuī* are 'objective' genitives, i.e. 'of me', 'of you' means 'directed at me/you'. For example, *amor tuī* means 'love of/for you' in the sense 'love directed at you'. The idea 'belonging to me/you' is performed by the adjectives *meus, tuus*, e.g. *pater meus* = 'my father', i.e. 'the father belonging to me'.

EXERCISE

*In these sentences, most adjectives are not directly next to the noun they qualify.
Read through each sentence, predicting the gender, number and case of the
noun you await (where the adjective comes first) and indicating when the
adjective is 'solved'. Then translate, bringing out the force of the word-order.*

(a) malus igitur senex nōn multum habet honōrem.

(b) meā est tuus ignis in aulā.

(c) meīs tamen in aedibus multī habitant patrēs.

(d) malōs enim senēs Lar nōn amat meus.

(e) meusne tuum seruat pater ignem? (-ne = ?)

23   **Prepositions**

Note that *ā, ab* '(away) from' and *ē, ex* 'out of', 'from' take the ablative (cf. *in*
+ abl. at **10**).
NB *ab* and *ex* are the forms used before following vowels, e.g. *ab aulā, ex igne*
but *ā scaenā*.

EXERCISE

Translate into Latin: out of the water; into the eye; away from the fire; towards
the masters; away from the house; onto the stage (*optional*: out of the pot; towards the thieves; from the old men; into the house).

Reading exercises

1 *Take the Latin as it comes and, as you translate, say what each word is doing
in the sentence, taking care to ascribe adjectives to the correct nouns (if they
follow them) or to predict the number, gender and case of the noun (if the
adjective precedes). Then select a suitable verb in the correct person from the
list below and translate into correct English.*

(a) uīcīnum senex miser ...

(b) dominus enim meus tuum ignem ...

(c) neque ego meum neque tū tuum seruum ... [1]

(d) deinde mē seruī malī ...

(e) seruōs malōs uīcīnus meus ...

(f) aulam, mī domine, serua mala ...

(g) fūrem miserum ego quoque ...

(h) ignem tū, ego aquam ... [2]

(i) oculōs meōs serua tua semper …

(j) quārē aurum et unguentum et corōnās Eucliō miser numquam …?

portō, cēlō, vexō, rogō, timeō, moneō, seruō, habeō, uerberō, uocō

1. Verb 2nd s.
2. Verb 1st s.

2 Practice in English

Analyse noun-functions, adjectives and verbs:

(a)   Close up the casement, draw the blind
      Shut out that stealing moon,
      She wears too much the guise she wore
      Before our lutes were strewn
      With years-deep dust, and names we read
      On a white stone were hewn.

                                          (Thomas Hardy)

(b)   Hail, native language, that by sinews weak
      Didst move my first endeavouring tongue to speak,
      And mad'st imperfect words with childish trips,
      Half unpronounced, slide through my infant lips …

                                                  (Milton)

(c)   Know then thyself, presume not God to scan;
      The proper study of Mankind is Man.

                                                   (Pope)

3 Quotations

Translate:

(a) *sōla pecūnia rēgnat.* (Petronius)

(b) *uēritās numquam perit.* (Seneca)

(c) *semper auārus eget.* (Horace)

(d) *nōn dēterret sapientem mors.* (Cicero)

(e) *in fugā foeda mors est, in uictōriā glōriōsa.* (Cicero)

---

sōl-us a um alone
pecūni-a ae 1f. money
rēgnō 1 I rule, am king
uēritās uēritāt-is 3f. truth
pereō (conjugates like *eō*) I die

auār-us ī 2m. miser
egeō 2 I am in need
dēterreō 2 I frighten off, deter
sapiēns sapient-is 3m. wise man

foed-us a um disgraceful
fug-a ae 1f. rout, flight
mors mort-is 3f. death
uictōri-a ae 1f. victory
glōriōs-us a um glorious

EITHER

Reading exercise / Test exercise

Read the following passage carefully, translating each word as it comes and analysing its function. Identify word-groups and anticipate, as far as you can, what is to come. When you have done this, translate into correct English. Finally read out the passage in Latin with the correct phrasing, thinking out the meaning as you read. Use the running vocabulary of 1C.

EUCLIŌ (*clāmat*) exī! exī ex aedibus, serua.

(*serua in scaenam intrat*)

SERVA quid est, mī domine? quārē tū mē ex aedibus uocās? (*Eucliō seruam uerberat*) ō mē miseram. ut dominus meus mē uexat. nunc enim mē uerberat. sed tū, mī domine, quārē mē uerberās?   5

EUC. ō mē miserum. tacē, ut mala es! ut mē miserum uexās! manē istīc, Staphyla, manē! stā! moneō tē.

(*in aedīs intrat Eucliō*)

SER. ō mē miseram. ut miser dominus meus est!

(*Eucliō ex aedibus in scaenam intrat*)   10

EUC. saluum est. tū tamen quārē istīc stās? quārē in aedīs nōn īs? abī! intrā in aedīs! occlūde iānuam!

(*serua in aedīs intrat*)

nunc abeō ad praetōrem, quod pauper sum. ut inuītus eō! sed sī hīc maneō, uīcīnī meī 'hem' inquiunt 'senex miser multum habet aurum.'   15

OR

English–Latin

Translate the Latin sentences into English. Then translate the English sentences into Latin, using the pattern of the Latin ones to help you arrange the word-order correctly.

(a) Staphyla, abī et aquam portā!
    Slave-women, go out and ask for fire!

(b) tū autem, mī domine, quārē cūrās malās habēs?
    But why do you, my Euclio, love a wretched slave-woman?

(c) ut aurum multum senēs uexat miserōs!
    How the evil old man beats his unhappy slaves!

(d) ō mē miseram! ut oculī meī mē uexant!
    O dear me! How wretched an old man I am!

(e) malōs dominōs miserī seruī habent.
     (It is) a wretched old man the unhappy daughter loves.

(f) malōrum seruōrum oculī dominī miserī cūrās nōn uident.
     The eyes of a bad slave-woman do not see the worry of the unhappy daughter.

Dēliciae Latīnae

Word-building

Prefixes

in- can = 'into', 'in' (e.g. *ineō* 'I go in', *īnsum* 'I am in'), but it can equally well
    be a negative, e.g. *īnsānus = in + sānus* 'not sane', 'mad'

ē-, *ex-* usually means 'out of', 'out', e.g. *exit* 'he goes out', *exstinguō* 'I put out',
    expellō 'I push out'

ā-, *ab-* = 'away (from)', e.g. *abeō* 'I go away'

re- (only used as a prefix) = 'back', 'again', e.g. *redit* 'he returns'. (Observe
    that *re-* becomes *red-* before vowels.)

EXERCISES

1 *Give the Latin derivation (prefix and root) of the following English words:*
   cogitate, excogitate, instate, reinstate, reverberate, export, revoke, abrogate,
   reserve, explicate (*plicō* 'fold').

2 *Give English words, with meanings, formed from the following stems:* māns-
   (maneō); monit- (moneō). *Use prefixes as necessary.*

Word exercises

1 *What do the following English words mean?* vexatious, admonish, aquatic,
   dominant, impecunious, inexplicable.

2 *Give English words from:* ignis, oculus, maneō, malus, saluus.

Everyday Latin

> *notā bene* (NB) 'note well!' What conjugation is *notō*?
>
> *vidē*[1] *infrā* (or simply *vidē*, abbreviated *v.*) 'see below'
>
> *adeste, fidēlēs* 'be present, faithful!' 'O come, all ye faithful'
>
> *exit* '(s)he goes out'; *exeunt* 'they go out'

1. See n. 8 on p. xi

Grammar and exercises for 1D

24   **Present indicative active (3rd conjugation): *dīc-ō* 'I speak', 'I say'**

1st s.	dī́c-ō	'I say'
2nd s.	dī́c-i-s	'you (*s.*) say'
3rd s.	dī́c-i-t	'he/she/it says'
1st pl.	dī́c-i-mus	'we say'
2nd pl.	dī́c-i-tis	'you (*pl.*) say'
3rd pl.	dī́c-u-nt	'they say'
	Imperatives	
2nd s.	dīc	'say!' (*irregular*)
2nd pl.	dī́c-i-te	'say!'

Notes

1 Note the key vowel in the 3rd conj. – the short *-i-* throughout. This *-i-* is *not* part of the stem in the way that *-e-* in *habeō* (stem *habe-*) was.

2 Observe that the 3rd pl. is *dīc-u-nt*.

3 A similar verb to this is *dūcō* 'I lead', 'I take'. Imperative *dūc*, *dūcite*.

4 Normal imperatives of 3rd conj. verbs end in *-e*, *-ite* (see **36**). Note that the vowels in these endings are all short. Cf. imperatives of *audiō* in **25**.

25   **Present indicative active (4th conjugation): *audiō* 'I hear', 'I listen to'**

1st s.	aúdi-ō	'I hear'
2nd s.	aúdī-s	'you (*s.*) hear'
3rd s.	aúdi-t	'he/she/it hears'
1st pl.	audī́-mus	'we hear'
2nd pl.	audī́-tis	'you (*pl.*) hear'
3rd pl.	aúdi-u-nt	'they hear'
	Imperatives	
2nd s.	aúdī	'listen!'
2nd pl.	audī́-te	'listen!'

Notes

1 The key vowel in the 4th conj. is -*i*- which follows the same pattern of long and short as the -*e*- of the 2nd conj., and is, like that, part of the stem. So -*i*- appears throughout (contrast the -*i*- in *dīcō*).

2 Observe the 3rd pl. in -*i-unt*; cf. *dīc-unt*.

EXERCISES

1 *Translate into Latin*: she says; they are leading; we hear; we say; you (*pl.*) hear; speak! (*s.*); listen! (*pl.*); lead! (*pl.*), you (*s.*) are saying; he hears; they are listening.

2 *Identify the conjugation (1st, 2nd, 3rd or 4th) of the following verbs and translate them:* cūrō, cēlat, habētis, dūcunt, rogās, possidēmus, audiō (*optional:* iubētis, supplicō, clāmāmus).

3 *Translate and turn s. into pl. and vice versa:* dīcitis, audiunt, supplicāmus, audīs, dīcō, dūcimus, audīmus, clāmant, tacēs (*optional:* rogat, dīcit, cōgitō, manētis, amātis, dūcunt, moneō, uocās, dūcis).

26   ### 3rd declension nouns: *nōmen nōmin-is* 3n. 'name'

	s.	*pl.*
nom.	nṓmen	nṓmin-a
voc.	nṓmen	nṓmin-a
acc.	nṓmen	nṓmin-a
gen.	nṓmin-is	nṓmin-um
dat.	nṓmin-ī	nōmín-ibus
abl.	nṓmin-e	nōmín-ibus

Notes

1 All n. nouns have the same forms for the nom. and acc. in both s. and pl. (-*a*); cf. **15**. Only the context will tell you whether they are subject or object. Note that if the verb is singular then a neuter pl. in -*a* must be the object; if the verb is plural, then neuter s. must be the object.

2 All 3rd decl. nouns in -*men* are neuter, and follow the pattern *of nōmen*.

3 *nōmen* is a consonant-stem noun. There are also 3rd decl. n. *i*-stems. You will meet these later.

27   1st/2nd declension adjectives: *pulcher pulchr-a pulchr-um* 'beautiful', 'handsome'

	s.		
	m.	f.	n.
nom.	púlcher	púlchr-a	púlchr-um
voc.	púlcher	púlchr-a	púlchr-um
acc.	púlchr-um	púlchr-am	púlchr-um
gen.	púlchr-ī	púlchr-ae	púlchr-ī
dat.	púlchr-ō	púlchr-ae	púlchr-ō
abl.	púlchr-ō	púlchr-ā	púlchr-ō

	pl.		
	m.	f.	n.
nom.	púlchr-ī	púlchr-ae	púlchr-a
voc.	púlchr-ī	púlchr-ae	púlchr-a
acc.	púlchr-ōs	púlchr-ās	púlchr-a
gen.	pulchr-órum	pulchr-árum	pulchr-órum
dat.	← púlchr-īs →		
abl.	← púlchr-īs →		

Note

We have already met *miser*, which, apart from the nom. s. m., declines like *multus* on the stem *miser-* (**21**). *pulcher* is identical, except that it declines on the stem *pulchr-*.

28   2nd declension nouns: *puer puer-ī* 2m. 'boy', *uir uir-ī* 2m. 'man', *culter cultr-ī* 2m. 'knife'

puer puer-ī 2m. 'boy'[1]

	s.	pl.
nom.	púer	púer-ī
voc.	púer	púer-ī
acc.	púer-um	púer-ōs
gen.	púer-ī	puer-órum
dat.	púer-ō	púer-īs
abl.	púer-ō	púer-īs

uir uir-ī 2m. 'man'[1]

	s.	pl.
nom.	uir	uír-ī
voc.	uir	uír-ī
acc.	uír-um	uír-ōs
gen.	uír-ī	uir-órum (uír-um – see **16**)
dat.	uír-ō	uír-īs
abl.	uír-ō	uír-īs

1. These nouns decline exactly like *seru-us* on the stems *puer-* and *uir-*. Only nom. s. m. is different. Cf. *miser* (**21**).

culter cultr-ī 2m. 'knife'[1]

	s.	*pl.*
nom.	cúlter	cúltr-ī
voc.	cúlter	cúltr-ī
acc.	cúltr-um	cúltr-ōs
gen.	cúltr-ī	cultr-órum
dat.	cúltr-ō	cúltr-īs
abl.	cúltr-ō	cúltr-īs

1 This noun declines exactly like *seru-us* on the stem *cultr-*. Only nom. s. m. is different.
Cf. *pulcher* (**27**).

EXERCISES

1 *Give the correct form of the adjectives* magnus, miser, pulcher *for these cases of* nōmen: nōmen, nōminis, nōmine, nōmina, nōminum.

2 *Give the correct form of* pulcher *and* miser *to describe each of these nouns (e.g.* senem *acc. s. m., so* senem pulchrum): uxōrum, sorōribus, uirō, uxōris, fēminae, frātrī, aedīs, Larem, seruā, aedēs, fēminīs, dominī, seruōs.

Optional exercise

Add the appropriate form of miser, *then of* pulcher, *to the following words and translate (e.g.* Eucliōnem = *acc. s. m.* – miserum/pulchrum *'unhappy/handsome Euclio'*): sorōre, dīuitis, uir, uxōrī, fēminae, puellīs, fīliī, uīcīnō, Larem, frātrum, seruā.

29 **Interrogative pronoun/adjective: *quis/quī, quis/quae, quid/quod* 'who?', 'which?', 'what?'**

		s.			*pl.*		
		m.	*f.*	*n.*	*m.*	*f.*	*n.*
nom.	*pron.*	quis	quis	quid	quī	quae	quae
	adj.	quī	quae	quod			
acc.	*pron.*	quem	quam	quid	quōs	quās	quae
	adj.			quod			
gen.			← cúius →		quórum	quárum	quórum
dat.			← cui →			← quíbus (quīs) →	
abl.		quō	quā	quō		← quíbus (quīs) →	

Notes

1 'Interrogative' means 'asking a question'.

2 Observe that the endings are a mixture of 2nd and 3rd declension. You will meet this again (it is called the 'pronominal' declension).

3 Adjective and pronoun are identical except for nom. s. and the acc. s. n.

4 For the pronoun use, cf. '<u>who</u> is calling?' *quis uocat?* '<u>what</u> do I see?' *quid uideō?*; for the adjective '<u>what</u> man is it?' *quī (quis) uir est?*, '<u>what</u> gold do I see?' *quod aurum uideō?*

EXERCISES

1 *Translate into Latin the underlined words with the appropriate form of* quis *or* quī + *noun. You will need to ask whether the question word is a pronoun or an adjective, and then define its case.*

(a) <u>Whose</u> (*s. m.*) are these books?

(b) <u>Which women</u> do we see?

(c) <u>What</u> is this?

(d) <u>What name</u> is this?

(e) <u>Whom</u> (*m. s.*) do you hate most?

(f) <u>What woman's</u> are these?

(g) <u>Whom</u> (*f. s.*) should we persecute?

(h) <u>Which man</u> is guilty?

30   *domus* 'house', 'home'

domus used with prepositions means 'house'. But when it means 'home' it is used without the preposition in the following ways: *domum* '(to) home'; *domī* 'at home'; *domō* 'from home'. Cf. *aedēs* 'house': *in aedīs* 'into the house', *in aedibus* 'in the house'.

31   *satis* 'enough', *nimis* 'too much', 'too many'

Both these words control nouns in the gen. case (the so-called 'partitive' genitive indicating *part of* a whole), e.g. *satis pecūniae* 'enough (of) money', *nimis honōris* 'too much (of) respect'. *satis* and *nimis* are fixed in form.

32   *-que*

-que means 'and' and either (i) links the noun it is joined to with the previous word, e.g. *seruum patremque* 'slave <u>and</u> father', or (ii) in poetry indicates that a list is coming, e.g. *seruumque patremque sorōremque* '<u>both</u> slave <u>and</u> father <u>and</u> sister'.

EXERCISES

1 *In each of these sentences, there is one adjective which precedes and does not stand next to the noun it qualifies. Read through each sentence, predicting the gender, number and case of the noun awaited, noting when the adjective is 'solved'. Then translate.*

(a) nōn multam possident pecūniam optimae uxōrēs.

(b) multī meās sorōrēs amant fīliī.

(c) seruōs miserōs optimī nōn uexant senēs.

(d) malī frātrēs pulchrās uerberant sorōrēs.

(e) multī fēminās pulchrās domum dūcunt senēs.

   Before doing Exercises 2 and 3, revise carefully the ablative forms of nouns of the 1st, 2nd and 3rd declensions.

2 *Translate into English*: in aedīs; in aulā; ad Larem; ab ignibus; in aquam; ex aulīs; in aedibus; in aquā; ā dominō; ex oculīs (*optional*: ad dominum; in scaenam; in nōmine; ā seruā; in aulam; in scaenā).

3 *Translate into Latin*: in the house (*use* aedēs); towards the girl; towards the brothers; away from the wife; onto the stage; in the house; out of water; away from the fires (*optional*: in the waters; from the stage; into the family; in the eye; towards the masters; out of the household).

4 *Translate*: nimis corōnārum; satis seruōrum; nimis aquae; satis nōminum; nimis sorōrum; satis ignis.

Reading exercises

1 *Observe the following*:

> ego tē uxōrem habeō = *I regard you as a wife.*
>
> ego tē pauperem faciō = *I make you poor / a poor man* (*NB* faciō *conjugates like* audiō, *but* -i- *is short throughout*).

   Supply a part of habeō *or* faciō *which will make sense of the following combinations and translate. Then read out in Latin, phrasing correctly.*

(a) tandem uir mē fīlium …

(b) Eucliō uīcīnum dīuitem …

(c) Eucliōnem pauperem …

(d) Megadōrus fīliam Eucliōnis uxōrem …

(e) ego autem dīuitēs miserōs …

(f) dominus malōs seruōs miserōs …

2 Practice in English

Analyse the following passage in terms of subject, object; genitive usages; adjectives; prepositions.

Zeus, as he had promised, has Apollo remove the body of Sarpedon, 'the breathless hero', from the battlefield.

> Apollo bows, and from Mount Ida's Height
> Swift to the Field precipitates his Flight;
> Thence, from the War, the breathless Hero bore,
> Veil'd in a Cloud, to silver Simois' shore:
> There bath'd his honourable wounds, and drest   5
> His manly Members in th' Immortal Vest,
> And with Perfumes of Sweet Ambrosial Dews,
> Restores his Freshness, and his Form renews.
> Then Sleep and Death, two twins of winged Race,
> Of matchless swiftness, but of silent Pace,   10
> Received Sarpedon, at the Gods' command,
> And in a Moment reach'd the Lycian land;
> The Corps amidst his weeping Friends they laid,
> Where endless Honours wait the Sacred Shade.

(Pope, translation of *Iliad* XVI)

Quotations

Translate:

(a) *uir bonus est quis?* (Horace)

(b) *quis nōn paupertātem extimēscit?* (Cicero)

(c) *quis bene cēlat amōrem?* (Ovid)

(d) *quid est beāta uīta? sēcūritās et perpetua tranquillitās.* (Seneca)

(e) *mors quid est? aut fīnis aut trānsitus.* (Seneca)

(f) *immodica īra gignit īnsāniam.* (Seneca)

(g) *uītam regit fortūna, nōn sapientia.* (Cicero)

bon-us a um good	*mors mort-is* 3f. death
paupertās paupertāt-is 3f. poverty	*aut ... aut* either ... or
extimēscō 3 I am greatly afraid of	*fīn-is fīn-is* 3m. end
bene well	*trānsit-us* (nom.) transition
amor amōr-is 3m. love	*immodic-us a um* immoderate
beāt-us a um happy, blessed	*īr-a ae* 1f. anger
uīt-a ae 1f. life	*gignō* 3 I beget, cause
sēcūritās sēcūritāt-is 3f. freedom	*īnsāni-a ae* 1f. madness
from worry	*regō* 3 I rule, direct
perpetu-us a um perpetual, continuous	*fortūn-a ae* 1f. fortune
tranquillitās tranquillitāt-is 3f. peace	*sapienti-a ae* 1f. wisdom

EITHER

Reading exercise / Test exercise

*Read the following passage carefully, translating in order of the words and analysing the function of each one, defining word-groups, and anticipating, as far as you can, what is to come. Then translate into correct English. Finally, read the passage aloud with the correct phrasing, thinking through the meaning as you read. Use the running vocabulary of **1D**.*

Megadōrum, uirum dīuitem et Eucliōnis uīcīnum, soror Eunomia ex aedibus uocat. Eunomia enim anxia (*worried*) est, quod Megadōrus uxōrem nōn habet. Megadōrus autem uxōrem nōn uult (*wants*). nam uxōrēs uirōs dīuitēs pauperēs faciunt. habet satis aurī Megadōrus et fēminās pulchrās nōn amat. ut enim pulchra fēmina est, ita uirum uexat. ut uir dīues est, ita uxor uirum pauperem   5
facit. Eunomiam autem sorōrem optimam Megadōrus habet. ut igitur postulat (*demands*) soror, ita facit frāter. Phaedram enim, Eucliōnis fīliam, puellam optimam habet. ut tamen pauper Eucliō est, ita dōtem habet Phaedra nūllam. Megadōrus autem dōtem nōn uult (*wants*). nam sī dīuitēs uxōrēs sunt magnamque habent dōtem, magnus est post nūptiās sūmptus, nimis dant uirī pecūniae.   10

OR

English–Latin

Translate the Latin sentences into English. Then translate the English sentences into Latin, using the pattern of the Latin ones to help you arrange the word-order correctly.

(a) ut ego soror optima sum, ita tū frāter optimus.
    Just as Phaedra is an excellent daughter, so Euclio is an excellent father.

(b) dominus meus frātrem uirum optimum habet.
    I consider beautiful women (to be) bad wives.

(c) quid nōmen uxōris est tuae?
    Who is the brother of my neighbour?

(d) uir pauper uxōrem pauperem domum dūcit.
    The best husbands marry beautiful wives.

(e) fēminae in aedibus stant.
    The girls are going into the water.

(f) satis ego aurī habeō, satis pecūniae.
    The rich man has too much money and too much worry.

43

Dēliciae Latīnae

Word exercises

1 *What do the following English words mean?* sorority, uxorious, fraternal, virile, optimise, pauper, pulchritude, duke (*also*: il duce; duchy; duchess; doge; ducat [*coin bearing the duke*'s *image*]), audio-visual, magnify.

2 *Derive English words from the following Latin*: nōmen, domī, pecūnia, fēmina, ualē, satis.

Everyday Latin

Where would one write *ex librīs* (*liber, libr-* 'book')?

What sort of statement comes *ex cathedrā*? (*Cathedra* is a special papal seat – originally the bishop's seat in his church, hence 'cathedral'.)

Christ told the story of Dives and Lazarus. Who was Dives? (See Luke 16:19ff.)

Often things seem to go on *ad īnfīnītum* – explain. What is the force of the *in-* prefix?

in vīnō vēritās (= 'truth'). Where is truth found?

To 'ad lib' is to talk *ad libitum*, i.e. to whatever extent you want (*libet* 'it is pleasing, desirable').

ad nauseam – to what point?

deus ex māchinā. Māchina is a stage crane. Explain how the phrase comes to refer to a miraculous ending to an event.

per ardua ad astra (Royal Air Force motto) 'Through the heights / through difficulties …' – where?

Word-building

dūcō has another stem, *duct-*. Use the 'pool' of prefixes (pp. 27, 35) and your knowledge of common endings to produce at least ten English derivatives, with meanings.

See how large a score you can make with *audiō, audīt-* and *dīcō, dict-* in the same way.

Section 1E

Grammar and exercises for 1E

33   **Present indicative active (3rd/4th conjugation): *capiō* 'I capture'**

1st s.	cápi-ō	'I capture'
2nd s.	cápi-s	'you (*s.*) capture'
3rd s.	cápi-t	'he/she/it captures'
1st pl.	cápi-mus	'we capture'
2nd pl.	cápi-tis	'you (*pl.*) capture'
3rd pl.	cápi-u-nt	'they capture'

Notes

1 There are a number of verbs which draw their forms from both 3rd and 4th conjugations. You have met *faciō*, 'I make, do'.

2 *capiō* appears to be straight 4th conjugation in the pres. ind. act., but observe a difference. True, it keeps the -*i*- all the way through, but the -*i*- remains *short* as in the 3rd conj.

34   ***uolō* 'I wish', 'I want' (irregular): present indicative active**

1st s.	uól-ō	'I wish', 'I want'
2nd s.	uī-s	'you (*s.*) wish', 'you (*s.*) want'
3rd s.	uul-t (uol-t)	'he/she/it wishes/wants'
1st pl.	uól-u-mus	'we wish/want'
2nd pl.	uúl-tis (uól-tis)	'you (*pl.*) wish/want'
3rd pl.	uól-u-nt	'they wish/want'

Note

The stem of *uolō* is irregular but observe that the personal endings are regular, i.e. -*o*, -*s*, -*t* etc.

35   ***ferō* 'I bear', 'I carry, 'I lead' (irregular): present indicative active**

1st s.	fér-ō	'I bear'
2nd s.	fer-s	'you (*s.*) bear'
3rd s.	fer-t	'he/she/it bears'
1st pl.	fér-i-mus	'we bear'
2nd pl.	fér-tis	'you (*pl.*) bear'
3rd pl.	fér-u-nt	'they bear'

Note

It is the absence of *-i-* between stem and ending in 2nd, 3rd s. and 2nd pl. that makes this irregular.

36 **Present imperatives active (all conjugations)**

	1		*2*		*3*		*4*		*3/4*	
2 s.	ámā	'love!'	hábē	'have!'	pósc-e	'ask!'	aúdī	'hear!'	cáp-e	'take!'
2 pl.	amā́-te		habḗ –te		pósc-ite		audī́-te		cápi-te	

Notes

1 We use *poscō* for 3rd conj. as *dīco* has an irregular imperative. *capiō* 'I take', 'I capture' should be learnt now, as it will exemplify 3rd/4th conj. throughout.

2 Note the similarity of 3rd and 3rd/4th conj. imperative forms. Despite the presence of the *-i-* in *capiō*, the imperative form in the s. is still *cap-e*.

37 **Irregular imperatives**

	Sum	*eō*	*dīcō*	*dūcō*	*ferō*	*faciō*
2 s.	es 'be!'	ī 'go!'	dīc 'say!'	dūc 'lead!'	fer 'bring!'	fac 'do!', 'make!'
2 pl.	és-te	ī́-te	dī́c-i-te	dū́c-i-te	fér-te	fáci-te

Notes

1 Herewith a mnemonic to help you remember four of the irregular imperatives: '*dīc* had a *dūc* with *fer* on its back, and that's a *fac*'. Purists will prefer to emphasise the long vowels.

2 Observe the lack of *-i-* in *ferte* (cf. *fertis* at **35**).

EXERCISES

1 *Translate into Latin*: you (*s.*) make; hear! (*pl.*); they carry; bring! (*s.*, *two verbs*); she wishes; we do; he bears; go! (*pl.*); you (*s.*) want; demand! (*s.*); I do; take (*s.*) the dowry! (*optional*: we make; you (*s.*) endure; you (*pl.*) bring; you (*pl.*) wish; love (*s.*) your father!).

2 *Translate the following, then change s. to pl. and vice versa*: facimus; fert; uult; ferunt; dīc; ferte; uolumus; est; eunt; facis; dūcite; īte; capite (*optional*: fac; uīs; es; habent; dīcit; audīte; faciunt; fers).

38   **3rd declension nouns: *onus oner-is* 3n. 'load', 'burden'**

	s.	*pl.*
nom.	ónus	óner-a
voc.	ónus	óner-a
acc.	ónus	óner-a
gen.	óner-is	óner-um
dat.	óner-ī	onér-ibus
abl.	óner-e	onér-ibus

Note

All 3rd decl. nouns in *-us*, *-eris* are n. (cf. *nōmen* **26**). Observe that, as usual, the nom. and acc. forms are the same; and that, like *nōmen*, the nom. and acc. pl. end in *-a*. It is vital to know the full categorisation (i.e. *onus oner-is* 3n.) of nouns like *onus*; otherwise you might mistake *onus* for a m. noun or *onera* for a f. noun. *onus* is a consonant-stem noun.

EXERCISES

1 *Give the correct form of* multus *for these cases of* onus: onus, oneris, onere, onera, oneribus.

2 *Find the words which agree with the given form of* pulcher:

        pulchrō: oneris, scelere, dominī, facinus, deī, dī
        pulchra: fēmina, facinora, scelera, seruae, senex
        pulchrum: opus, seruum, fēminam, senēs, Larem, scelus, facinoris
        pulchrōrum: nōminum, seruārum, deōrum, senum, scelerum

39   **Questions in *-ne?***

-ne attached to the FIRST word of a sentence turns a statement into a question, e.g. *puerum amās* 'you love the boy' – *amāsne puerum?* 'do you love the boy?'

NB Emphasis is placed on the first word in such questions. *puerumne amās?* means 'is it *the boy* you love?'

EXERCISE

Read out these sentences in Latin, correctly phrased. Then translate. Next turn each into a question, putting the word to be questioned first, and adding -ne *to it. Translate and read out the Latin again.*

(a) est bona puella.

(b) īmus ad aedīs Eucliōnis.

(c) fert bene onus serua.

(d) optimum cōnsilium habent.

(e) Eucliō fīliam statim prōmittit.

(f) Megadōrus satis pecūniae habet.

(g) soror frātrem bene audit.

(h) scaenam uidētis.

(i) Eucliō honōrem numquam dat.

(j) uxōrēs nimis aurī semper habent.

40   *quid* + **genitive**

We have already met *satis* + gen. 'enough (of)', and *nimis* + gen. 'too much (of)'; *quid* + gen. = 'what (of)?', e.g. *quid cōnsilī est?* 'what (of) plan is there?' *quid negōtī est?* 'what (of) trouble is there?' 'what's the problem?' This is another example of the so-called 'partitive' genitive (cf. **31**).

> **EXERCISES**

1 *Translate*: in aedīs; ē dōte; in animō; ad hominēs; ab aquā; ex ignibus; domī; ē perīculō; in exitium; ad aquās; in perīculum.

2 *Translate these sentences*:

(a) ubi est Megadōrus? quid cōnsilī habet?

(b) uxōremne pulchram uult uir dīues? quid negōtī est?

(c) tē igitur bonum habeō.

(d) seruī in aedibus nimis faciunt scelerum, nimis facinorum malōrum.

(e) quid oneris fers? quo īs?

Reading exercises

1 *Read through each of these pairs of sentences. In each case (1) say whether the subject of the second sentence is m., f. or n., (2) say to what or whom the second sentence refers, (3) translate the sentences, (4) read aloud in Latin, correctly phrased.*

(a) Megadōrus fīliam Eucliōnis sine dōte domum dūcit. optimus igitur homo est.

(b) Megadōrus domī hodiē neque nūptiās parat neque coquōs uocat. malum est.

(c) Eunomia soror Megadōrī est. bona fēmina est.

(d) Eunomia frātrem habet. nōn dubium est.

(e) Eucliō fīliam amat. malus nōn est.

(f) Eucliō timet. nōn dubium est.

(g) Staphyla cōnsilium Eucliōnis audit. malum est.

(h) Staphyla in aedīs redit. cūrae enim plēna est.

2 Practice in English

Analyse the following piece, stating, as you read, subject, verb, object, adjective.

> But anxious Cares the pensive Nymph oppress'd,
> And secret Passions labour'd in her Breast.
> Not youthful Kings in Battle seiz'd alive,
> Not scornful Virgins who their Charms survive,
> Not ardent Lovers robb'd of all their Bliss,   5
> Not ancient Ladies when refused a Kiss,
> Not Tyrants fierce that unrepenting die,
> Not Cynthia when her Mantle's pinned awry,
> E'er felt such Rage, Resentment and Despair,
> As thou, sad Virgin! for thy ravish'd Hair.   10
>
> (Pope, *Rape of the Lock*)

3 Quotations

Translate:

(a) *festīnā lentē.* (Suetonius)

(b) *uirtūs sōla uītam efficit beātam.* (Cicero)

(c) *nihil inuītus facit sapiēns.* (Seneca)

(d) *auctor opus laudat.* (Ovid)

(e) *nihil in uulgō modicum.* (Tacitus)

(f) *neque bonum est uoluptās neque malum.* (Aulus Gellius)

festīnō 1 I hurry, hasten	*inuīt-us a um* unwilling(ly)
lentē slowly	*sapiēns sapient-is* 3m. wise man
uirtūs uirtūt-is 3f. goodness	*auctor auctōr-is* 3m. author
sōl-us a um alone, only	*opus oper-is* 3n. work
uīt-a ae 1f. life	*laudō* 1 I praise
efficiō 3/4 I make X (acc.) Y (acc.)	*uulg-us ī* 2n. crowd, mob
beāt-us a um happy, blessed	*modic-us a um* moderate
nihil nothing	*uoluptās uoluptāt-is* 3f. pleasure

EITHER

Reading exercise / Test exercise

Read carefully through this passage, translating in the order of the words, analysing the function of each and the groupings of the words, and anticipating the direction of the sentences. Translate into correct English. Then read aloud the passage with correct phrasing, thinking through the meaning as you read. Use the running vocabulary of 1E.

Megadōrus Eucliōnem uīcīnum uidet. ā forō abit Eucliō. anxius est. nam animus Eucliōnis, quod aurum nōn uidet, domī est, Eucliō ipse (*himself*) forīs (*outside*). Eucliōnem blandē salūtat Megadōrus, homo dīues pauperem. timet autem Eucliō, quod Megadōrus uir dīues est. perspicuum est. Megadōrus thēsaurum Eucliōnis uult. nōn dubium est. Eucliō in aedīs it, uidet aurum, saluum est. ex aedibus igitur   5
exit. Megadōrus fīliam Eucliōnis uxōrem poscit. fīliam prōmittit Eucliō, sed sine dōte. pauper enim est. dōtem igitur habet nūllam. Megadōrus dōtem uult nūllam. bonus est et dīues satis. nūptiae hodiē sunt. coquum igitur uocat Megadōrus in aedīs. timet autem Staphyla, quod Phaedra ē Lycōnidē grauida est. Megadōrus uxōrem domum dūcit grauidam. malum est.   10

OR

English–Latin

Translate the Latin sentences into English. Then translate the English sentences into Latin, using the pattern of the Latin ones to help you arrange the word-order correctly.

(a) irrīdēsne mē, homo malus uirum optimum?
     Is he, a rich man, pouring scorn on Euclio, a poor man?

(b) malum est. Megadōrus enim fīliam Eucliōnis uxōrem facit.
     There's no doubt. The old man considers the girl his daughter.

(c) redīte ad Larem, seruī! corōnās ferte multās!
     Go into the house, slave-woman! Bring your burdens!

(d) quid cōnsilī est? Megadōrusne dōtem uult? malum est.
     What's up? Do you want money? There's no doubt (of that).

(e) quō abīs? īsne in aedīs? nūptiāsne parās hodiē? optimum est.
     What do they want? Are they going home? Are they carrying loads?
     They're good lads.

(f) bonum habē animum, Megadōre! nam cōnsilium bonum est.
     Cheer up, master. The deed's a very good one.

Dēliciae Latīnae

Word-building

trāns means 'across'. Sometimes it appears as *trā-*, e.g. *trādō* 'I hand over', 'I hand across (the ages)' – whence 'tradition'.

prō means 'in front of, 'on behalf of', 'for'.

Learn three important stems:

mittō has another stem *miss-* (thus *prō* + *mittō* 'send ahead', 'send in advance'
    gives 'promise').

faciō has another stem *fact-*. When *faciō* has a prefix, it becomes *-ficiō*, stem
    fect-, e.g. *prae* + *faciō* becomes *praeficiō*, stem *praefect-*. Add -ant/-ent to
    your list of suffixes, e.g. efficient.

ferō has another stem *lāt-*.

EXERCISE

*Using the pool of prefixes and suffixes you have built up so far (pp. 27, 35, 44),
construct English words from the stems of* mittō *(miss-),* faciō *(fact-),* ferō *(lāt-)
and* dūcō *(duct-). Say how the English word gets its meaning. The final list
should be on the long side.*

Word exercise

1 *Give the meaning and Latin connection of these English words*: nuptial,
   animate, hominid (-id = 'son of'), voluntary, onus, fact.

2 *Observe how fruitful the* fer- *stem is in English. Give the meanings of*:
   igniferous, auriferous.

3 *What sort of people are those who are asinine and bovine?*

4 *Note that* ae- *in Latin becomes* e- *in medieval Latin and so, often, in English,
   e.g.* aequus – 'equal'.

Everyday Latin

Cf. = *cōnfer* 'compare!' (*cum* + *ferō* 'bring together').

A 'recipe' in English is an imperative – *recipe*! 'take!', from *recipiō*. This is a
useful way of remembering 3/4 imperatives.

A common neuter noun in *-us* in Latin is *corpus*. Remember it is neuter; and
remember the stem is *corpor-* with the help of this quotation: *mēns sāna in
corpore sānō* 'a healthy mind in a healthy body' (Juvenal *c.* AD 100, Roman
satirist, telling us what all men should pray for). Cf. corporeal, incorporate,
corporation. Equally helpful may be the important legal principle *habeās corpus*
'you must have the body', i.e. the accuser must present the defendant in person
for examination in court (see **157** for the grammar of *habeās*).

Grammar and exercises for 1F

41   **Present infinitive active 'to –' (= second principal part): all conjugations**

1	2	3	4	3/4
'to love'	'to have'	'to say'	'to hear'	'to capture'
amā́-re	habḗ-re	dī́c-e-re	audī́-re	cáp-e-re

Notes

1 The infinitive commonly means 'to —', e.g. *amāre* 'to love'. It is, in fact, an indeclinable noun based on a verb (derivation = *in* 'no', *fīnis* 'ending'). Consider how 'I like *a run*' ('run', noun, object) means virtually the same as 'I like *to run*' ('to run' noun, object). It completes verbs such as *volō* 'I wish to', e.g. *amāre volō* 'I wish to love'.

2 Note the long vowel in conjs. 1, 2 and 4, and the loss of -*i*- in the 3rd/4th conj. infinitive.

3 The infinitive is known as the second principal part (the first principal part being the dictionary form, i.e. *amō, habeō, dīcō, audiō, capiō*). At the moment it is important to learn because, in conjunction with the first principal part, it tells you infallibly what conjugation the verb is. Thus:

1st p.p.	2nd p.p.	
-ō	-āre	= 1st conjugation
-eō	-ēre	= 2nd conjugation
-ō	-ere	= 3rd conjugation
-iō	-īre	= 4th conjugation
-iō	-ere	= 3rd/4th conjugation

42   **Irregular infinitives: *sum, eō, uolō, ferō***

Learn the following irregular infinitives:

sum – és-se 'to be'

eō – ī́-re 'to go'

uolō – uél-le 'to wish'

ferō – fér-re 'to bear'

EXERCISE

Give the infinitive of these verbs and translate: habeō, explicō, cēlō, inueniō, maneō, redeō, dūcō, dīcō, poscō, stō, rogō, fugiō, āmittō, auferō, faciō, sum (*optional*: uerberō, coquō, dormiō, seruō, uolō).

43   **Personal pronouns: *ego* 'I', *nōs* 'we'; *tū* 'you' (*s.*), *uōs* you (*pl.*)**

nom.	égo	'I'	nōs	'we'	tū	'you'	uōs	'you'
acc.	mē		nōs		tē		uōs	
gen.	méī		nóstrum ⎫		túī		uéstrum ⎫	
			nóstrī ⎭				uéstrī ⎭	
dat.	míhi (mī)		nṓbīs		tíbi		uṓbīs	
abl.	mē		nṓbīs		tē		uṓbīs	

Notes

1 You have already met the s. forms *ego*, *tū* (**22**). Here are their plurals, *nōs*, *uōs*. Note the gen. pl. forms.

2 *nostrum*, *uestrum* are the so-called 'partitive' genitives (**31**), e.g. *multī nostrum* 'many of us', *nostrī*, *uestrī* are 'objective' genitives (see **22³**), e.g. *memor nostrī* 'mindful of us', i.e. X remembers us (direct object, hence 'objective' genitive).

44   **3rd declension adjectives: *omn-is e* 'all', 'every'**

	S.		pl.	
	m./f.	*n.*	*m./f.*	*n.*
nom.	ómni-s	ómn-e	ómn-ēs	ómn-ia
voc.	ómni-s	ómn-e	ómn-ēs	ómn-ia
acc.	ómn-em	ómn-e	ómn-īs (omn-ēs)	ómn-ia
gen.	← ómn-is →		← ómn-ium →	
dat.	← ómn-ī →		← ómn-ibus →	
abl.	← ómn-ī →		← ómn-ibus →	

Notes

1 Just as with 2nd decl. adjectives like *mult-us a um*, 3rd decl. adjectives must agree in *gender*, *number and case* with the nouns they describe (**14**).

2 M. and f. forms are the same as each other in s. and pl. – a useful saving of labour for the learner.

3 Generally, 3rd decl. adjectives are *i*-stems (cf. **12**) and have:

  abl. s. in *-ī*, acc. pl. in *-īs*, n. pl. in *-ia*, gen. pl. in *-ium*

  Contrast 3rd decl. consonant-stem *nouns*, which have:

  abl. s. in *-e*, acc. pl. in *-ēs*, n. pl. in *-a*, gen. pl. in *-um*

4 Similar to *omnis*: *trīst-is e* 'sad'; *facil-is e* 'easy'; *difficil-is e* 'difficult'.

45   **3rd declension adjectives: *ingēns ingēns* (*ingent-*) 'huge'**

	s.		pl.	
	m./f.	*n.*	*m./f.*	*n.*
nom.	íngēns	íngēns	ingént-ēs	ingént-ia
voc.	íngēns	íngēns	ingént-ēs	ingént-ia
acc.	ingént-em	íngēns	ingént-īs (ingént-ēs)	ingént-ia
gen.	← ingént-is →		← ingént-ium →	
dat.	← ingént-ī →		← ingént-ibus →	
abl.	← ingént-ī →		← ingént-ibus →	

Note

Observe the stem change of this common type of adjective in *-ēns* and note that its n. s. form is the same as the m./f. form in the nom. Otherwise, its endings are identical to those of *omnis*.

46   **3rd declension adjectives: *audāx audāx* (*audāc-*) 'bold', 'courageous'**

	s.		pl.	
	m/f.	*n.*	*m./f.*	*n.*
nom.	aúdāx	aúdāx	audā́c-ēs	audā́c-ia
voc.	aúdāx	aúdāx	audā́c-ēs	audā́c-ia
acc.	audā́c-em	aúdāx	audā́c-īs (audā́c-ēs)	audā́c-ia
gen.	← audā́c-is →		← audā́c-ium →	
dat.	← audā́c-ī →		← audā́c-ibus →	
abl.	← audā́c-ī →		← audā́c-ibus →	

Note

This very common 3rd decl. adjective type ends in *-x* in the nom., and has its stem in *-c-*. *audāx* follows the pattern of *ingēns* in the relationship between the nom. s. m. and n. forms. Other endings identical with *omnis, ingēns*.

EXERCISES

1 *Decline in full*: puer audāx; omnis aqua; ingēns perīculum.

2 *Construct a grid consisting of 7 columns with headings as follows*:

NOUN   CASE   NUMBER   GENDER   omnis   ingēns   audāx

Under the heading NOUN *write the following list of nouns down the column*: seruae, thēsaurī, oculōs, dominus, nōminibus, cōnsilium, cēnā, turbārum, cīuī, pecūniās, puellā, perīculō, ignis, animīs.

Leave plenty of space between each noun. In the next three columns, define exactly the case, number and gender of each of the nouns. In the last three columns make omnis, ingēns *and* audāx *agree with the noun. Where the form of the noun indicates different possible cases, write down all the possibilities. E.g.*

NOUN	CASE	NUMBER	GENDER	omnis	ingēns	audāx
fīliae	gen.	s.	f.	omnis	ingentis	audācis
	dat.	s.	f.	omnī	ingentī	audācī
	nom.	pl.	f.	omnēs	ingentēs	audācēs

3 *Determine which of the nouns is in agreement with the given adjective (the answer may be one or more than one)*:

ingentem – nōminum, cōnsilium, deum, seruārum
audāx – puellā, cōnsilium, homo, dominus, ingenia
omnium – oculum, coquōrum, perīculum, honōrem
trīstēs – animōs, dominī, fīliae, familiam, aedīs
facilia – aqua, serua, puella, familia, scelera
difficilī – coquō, frāter, sorōris, dominus, fīliā, turba, exitiō

47   *dīues dīuit-is* 'wealthy', 'a wealthy man'; *pauper pauper-is* 'poor', 'a poor man'

	s.		*pl.*	
	m/f.	*n.*	*m./f.*	*n.*
nom.	dī́ues	dī́ues	dī́uit-ēs	dī́uit-a
voc.	dī́ues	dī́ues	dī́uit-ēs	dī́uit-a
acc.	dī́uit-em	dī́ues	dī́uit-ēs	dī́uit-a
gen.	← dī́uit-is →		← dī́uit-um →	
dat.	← dī́uit-ī →		← dīuít-ibus →	
abl.	← dī́uit-e →		← dīuít-ibus →	

	s.		*pl.*	
	m./f.	*n.*	*m./f.*	*n.*
nom.	paúper	paúper	paúper-ēs	paúper-a
voc.	paúper	paúper	paúper-ēs	paúper-a
acc.	paúper-em	paúper	paúper-ēs	paúper-a
gen.	← paúper-is →		← paúper-um →	
dat.	← paúper-ī →		← paupér-ibus →	
abl.	← paúper-e →		← paupér-ibus →	

These decline like 3rd decl. consonant-stem nouns (abl. in -*e*, gen. pl. in -*um*) but the same forms are also used as adjectives. Contrast the *i*-stem *omnis, ingēns, audāx* **44–6**.

When used as adjectives these mean 'wealthy' or 'poor'. But they can be used *on their own*, when they act as *nouns*, and mean 'a wealthy person', 'a poor person', e.g. *Eucliō dīuitēs amat* 'Euclio adores the rich/rich people' (noun); but *Eucliō homo pauper est* 'Euclio is a poor man' (adjective).

The same principle applies to all adjectives in Latin. When used on their own, they can stand as nouns. In such circumstances, it is very important to pay close attention to the *gender* of the adjective, e.g. *multī* (pl.) on its own would mean 'many men'; *multae* 'many women'; *multa* 'many things', *omnēs* could mean 'all men' or 'all women'; but *omnia* would mean 'all things', 'everything'.

EXERCISE

Translate into English:

(a) multae neque dormiunt neque cēnam coquunt.

(b) bona aufert.

(c) omnia scīre uultis.

(d) pulchrī pulchrās amant.

(e) omnēs pecūniam habēre uolunt.

(f) multī fugiunt, multī autem stant.

(g) pauperem dīues nōn amat.

(h) omnēs bonī cīuīs cūrant.

(i) malī mala cōgitant.

(j) pecūnia omnīs uexat.

Reading exercises

1 *Say, as you translate in the order of the words, what the functions of the words
and the word-groups are in these incomplete sentences. Complete them* (*with
a form of* uolō) *and translate into correct English. Then read them aloud,
phrasing them correctly.*

(a) ubi pauper cēnam ingentem habēre …?

(b) quō tū inīre …?

(c) cūrās dīuitis ferre omnis pauper …

(d) amāre puellās pulchrās et aurum dominī auferre nōs seruī …

(e) facile ferre onus cīuēs omnēs …

(f) uōs apud Eucliōnem cēnam coquere numquam …

2 **Practice in English**

Analyse these examples, in the order of the words, determining subject, object,
verb, infinitive.

(a) The intellect of man is forced to choose
     Perfection of the life, or of the work. (Yeats)

(b) To err is human, to forgive divine. (Pope)

(c) And that same prayer doth teach us all to render
     The deeds of mercy. (Shakespeare)

(d) We'll teach you to drink deep. (Shakespeare)

(e) To make dictionaries is dull work. (Johnson)

(f) Love looks not with the eyes but with the mind,
     And therefore is wing'd Cupid painted blind. (Shakespeare)

3 **Quotations**

Translate:

(a) *aeuum omne et breue et fragile est.* (Pliny)

(b) *senectūs īnsānābilis morbus est.* (Seneca)

(c) *īra furor breuis est.* (Horace)

(d) *ratiōnāle animal est homo.* (Seneca)

(e) *facilis est ad beātam uītam uia.* (Seneca)

(f) *difficile est saturam nōn scrībere.* (Juvenal)

(g) *difficile est longum subitō dēpōnere amōrem.* (Catullus)

(h) *nātūram quidem mūtāre difficile est.* (Seneca)

(i) *uarium et mūtābile semper / fēmina.* (Virgil)

(j) *turpe senex mīles, turpe senīlis amor.* (Ovid)

aeu-um ī 2n. age

breu-is e short

fragil-is e brittle, frail

senectūs senectūt-is 3f. old age

īnsānābil-is e incurable

morb-us ī 2m. disease

īr-a ae 1f. anger

furor furōr-is 3m. madness

ratiōnāl-is e possessing reason

animal animal-is 3n. animal

beāt-us a um happy, blessed

uīt-a ae 1f. life

ui-a ae 1f. road, way

difficil-is e difficult

satur-a ae 1f. satire

scrībō 3 I write

long-us a um long, long-lasting

subitō suddenly

dēpōnō 3 I lay aside

amor amor-is 3m. love

nātur-a ae 1f. nature

quidem indeed (emphasises preceding word)

mūtō 1 I change, alter

uari-us a um variable

mūtābil-is e changeable

turp-is e disgraceful

mīles mīlit-is 3m. soldier

senīl-is e in an old man

EITHER

Reading exercise / Test exercise

Read this passage, translating in word-order, defining the function of each word and anticipating the construction. Translate into correct English. Then read the passage aloud in Latin, phrasing correctly, thinking through the meaning as you read. Use the running vocabulary of IF.

Megadōrus nūptiās facere uult. coquōs igitur uocat multōs ad aedīs. coquōrum opus est cēnam coquere ingentem. uxōrem domum dūcit Megadōrus Phaedram, Eucliōnis fīliam. sed coquī Eucliōnem uirum pauperem habent et trīstem. nam nīl āmittere uult. follem enim ingentem, ubi dormīre uult, in ōs impōnit. ita animam, dum dormit, nōn āmittit. apud tōnsōrem praesegmina, quod nihil uult 5 āmittere, colligit omnia et domum fert. aquam dare nōn uult. ignem dare, quod āmittere timet, nōn uult. uir trīstis est. coquī igitur in aedīs inīre Megadōrī, uirī dīuitis et facilis, uolunt. perīculum autem in aedibus Megadōrī multum est, uāsa argentea ingentia, uestēs multae, multum aurum. sī quid seruī āmittunt, coquōs fūrēs putant (*think*) et comprehendere uolunt. apud Eucliōnem autem coquī saluī 10 sunt. uāsa enim argentea ex aedibus auferre Eucliōnis facile nōn est, quod uāsa nūlla habet!

OR

English–Latin

Translate the Latin sentences into English. Then translate the English sentences into Latin, using the pattern of the Latin ones to help you arrange the word-order correctly.

(a) quārē in aedīs Megadōrī, uirī dīuitis, onus ferre uultis?
   Do you want to cook dinner in a poor man's, Euclio's, house?

(b) cīuēs omnēs ē perīculō exīre uolunt.
   Resolute slaves want to escape from the house.

(c) ingentem enim āmittere pecūniam quis uult?
   What woman doesn't want to find a bold slave?

(d) dīuitēs ubi nūptiās faciunt, coquōs in aedīs uocant.
   When they want a large dinner, masters ask for a good cook.

(e) omnēs coquī cultrōs portant ingentīs.
   A beautiful woman draws (*ferō*) a big crowd.

(f) apud tamen pauperem cēna trīstis est.
   At a rich man's house dinners are excellent.

Dēliciae Latīnae

Word-building

ā/ab appears as *au* as a prefix to *ferō*, i.e. *auferō* 'I take away'.

   in means 'into', 'upon' in *inueniō* 'I come upon', 'I find'.
Observe the interesting combination of elements in *negōtium* 'business'. The
   word is built up of *nec(g)-* 'not' + *ōtium* 'leisure'.

EXERCISES

1 *Give the meaning and Latin connection of*: civilised, nihilistic, cook,
   dormitory, fugitive, negotiate, initial, invention, science, emit.

2 *Give English words from the Latin*: facilis, audāx, omnis (*dat. pl.*), āridus,
   lapis (*NB stem*), tōnsor.

Word study

uestis means 'clothes' (*uestiō* 'I dress'), so English 'vest'. *uestiārium* 'dressing
room' emerges in English as 'vestry', *inuestīre* 'to put clothes on', 'surround'
gives 'investiture' and 'invest' (clothing one's money with yet more?), *trāns*
'across' + *uest-* yields 'transvestite', one who crosses over to the clothes of the
opposite sex, or simply one who disguises him/herself: hence 'travesty'. *dī-*
(indicating separation) + *uest-* gives 'divest', 'take clothes off'.

   Do not confuse with 'vestige', from *uestīgium* 'footprint', 'trace': hence e.g.
'investigate', which means 'following on someone's tracks'.

Grammar and exercises for 1G

48   **The dative case: usage and meaning**

Summary of dative forms

	1st/2nd decl.			3rd decl.
	m.	*f.*	*n.*	*m./f./n.*
s.	-ō	-ae	-ō	-ī
pl.	-īs	-īs	-īs	-ibus

1   The dative is in one sense only the 'giving' case (the word derives from *dō* 'I give', which has another stem *dat-*). That is, if I give something *to* a person, the person who receives it is in the dative case, e.g. <u>*mihi*</u> *aulam dat* 'he gives <u>me</u> the pot / the pot <u>to me</u>' (known as the indirect object). But equally, it is the 'losing' case too, since if I take something *from* a person, the person goes into the dative case, e.g. <u>*hominī*</u> *aulam auferō* 'I take the pot <u>from the man</u>'. So one can say that the dative is the case defining the gainer or the loser, the one *advantaged* or *disadvantaged*.

2   Another 'advantage' sense is that of possession, expressed by *sum* + dative, e.g. *est* <u>*mihi*</u> *pecūnia* 'there is money <u>to me</u>', 'I have money'.

3   Another common usage of the dative is to denote the person spoken to (also, in some sense, a gainer – a gainer of the words you have spoken), e.g. <u>*fēminae*</u> *dīcit multa* 'he says many things <u>to the woman</u>' (indirect object again).

'To' (i.e. 'to the advantage of') and 'from' (i.e. 'to the disadvantage of), and sometimes 'for', will translate the dative best for the time being. But you should note that the usages and meanings of the dative are very wide, and that when they are all gathered together the common idea behind them all seems to be that the person in the dative is somehow *involved or interested* in *the action of the verb*: that action has some consequences for the person, sometimes specific, sometimes quite vague. So when you come across a dative, ask first 'How is the person in the dative case affected by the verb, or other word, that controls it?'

Distinguish between 'to' and 'from' indicating primarily *motion* (when Latin uses *ad, ex, ab*) and the dative usages (indicating gain or loss) outlined above.

EXERCISES

1 *Form the dative s. and pl. of these noun + adjective phrases*: senex miser;
puella audāx; puer ingēns; onus multum; cōnsilium audāx (*optional*: soror
optima; nōmen meum; culter tuus; seruus omnis).

2 *Pick out the datives in this list*: cūram, animō, fāna, uirtūtī, audāciae, hominis,
animōs, dīuitibus, uxor, onerī, pecūniam, fīliīs, aquae, dominō, ignibus,
uīcīnum, dīs, honōrēs, fēminīs, corōnae, cōnsiliō.

3 *Give the Latin for*: to the huge slaves; for me; to the unhappy old man's
disadvantage; to the wicked wives; for us; belonging to you (*s.*) (*optional*: to
the advantage of the best citizen; belonging to the bold slave-girl; to the good
father's disadvantage; for every boy).

4 *Translate these sentences*:

    (a) deinde Lar familiae aulam Eucliōnī dat aurī plēnam.

    (b) senex miser tamen aurum omne fānō crēdit.

    (c) sed seruus audāx senī miserō aurum auferre uult.

    (d) Eucliō autem ita seruō clāmat malō: 'quid tibi negōtī est in fānō? quid mihi
aufers?'

    (e) seruus igitur timet et Eucliōnī aurum nōn aufert.

    (f) Eucliō autem ā fānō aulam aufert, quod nunc deō aurum crēdere nōn uult.

49   **Ablative of description**

The ablative is used to *describe the qualities* people or things have which enable
them to act as they do. This is the ablative of description, e.g. *uir summā uirtūte*
'a man with/of great courage', *iuuenis nūllā continentiā* 'a young man with/of
no self-control'. Translate such ablatives as 'with' first time round, then adjust to
produce a smooth English version.

EXERCISES

1 *Form the ablative s. and pl. of these noun + adjective phrases*: senex miser;
puella audāx; puer ingēns; onus multum; cōnsilium audāx (*optional*: soror
optima; nōmen meum; culter tuus; seruus omnis).

2 *Pick out the ablatives in this list*: cūrā, animō, fānum, uirtūtis, audāciīs, homine,
animī, dīuitī, uxōre, pecūnia, fīliīs, aquam, dominō, ignibus, uīcīnōs, deus,
honōribus, fēminā, corōnīs, cōnsiliō, scelere.

3 *Give the Latin for*: in the shrine; away from the woman; out of the waters; in a
crime; out of the mind; in the plans; out of the fires (*optional*: away from worry;
out of the pots; in the household; away from a brother; out of the names).

4 *Translate these sentences*:

   (a) Eucliō uir est summā continentiā.

   (a) Lycōnidēs iuuenis summā pulchritūdine est, nūllā continentiā.

   (b) animō aequō es, mī fīlī.

   (c) tū serua es summā audāciā, summā pulchritūdine, continentiā nūllā.

   (d) animō bonō sum, quod fīliam meam summā uirtūte puellam habeō.

Reading exercise

1 *Read through these sentences carefully. As you translate, in the order of the words, define the function of each word (making certain that you phrase the words correctly). When you meet a dative, if you have not yet had any clue to help define its function closely (e.g. a verb like* crēdō, reddō), *register dative as 'affecting X' and proceed until the precise meaning emerges, e.g.*:

> crēdō ('*I entrust*' – *you expect an object + a dative*) tibi (*dative* – '*to you*', *solved by* crēdō) aurum (*object* – '*the gold*', *already anticipated*)
>
> aurum ('*gold*' – *subject or object*) tibi (*dative* – *with some effect on you; not solved yet* – *we expect a verb*) auferō ('*I take away*' – aurum *object*, tibi '*from you*', *solved by meaning of* auferō).

   (a) senī miserō seruus audāx multa dīcit mala.

   (b) unguentum et corōnās et aurum mihi ostende.

   (c) uxōrī meae domī nimis cūrārum est.

   (d) quārē tū mihi meum aurum nōn reddis?

   (e) ego tibi, quod uīcīnus es bonus, meam fīliam prōmittō.

   (f) uxōrēs pulchrae dīuitibus, quod coquīs pecūniam multam dare uolunt, aurum semper auferunt.

   (g) tibi multōs seruōs pecūniamque multam dō.

   (h) seruō audācī et seruae pulchrae numquam crēdō.

   (i) uirō dīuitī, quod mihi dōs nūlla est, fīliam meam prōmittere uolō.

   (j) nōbīs corōna, unguentum uōbīs domī est.

2 Quotations

Translate:
   (a) *fortīs fortūna iuuat.* (Terence)

   (b) *nēmo est in amōre fidēlis.* (Propertius)

(c) *omnis ars nātūrae imitātiō est.* (Seneca)

(d) *patet omnibus uēritās.* (Seneca)

(e) *omnī aetātī mors est commūnis.* (Cicero)

(f) *magna dī cūrant, parua neglegunt.* (Cicero)

(g) *Britannī capillō sunt prōmissō, atque omnī parte corporis rāsā, praeter caput et labrum superius.* (Caesar)

fort-is e brave
fortūn-a ae 1f. fortune
iuuō 1 I help
nēmo (nom.) no one
amor amōr-is 3m. love
fidēl-is e faithful
ars art-is 3f. art
nātūr-a ae 1f. nature
imitātiō imitātiōn-is 3f. imitation
pateō 2 I lie open
uēritās uēritāt-is 3f. truth
aetās aetāt-is 3f. age
mors mort-is 3f. death
commūn-is e common (to: + dat.)

paru-us a um small
neglegō 3 I neglect, do not bother with
Britann-ī ōrum 2m. pl. Britons
capill-us ī 2m. hair
prōmiss-us a um long
atque and
pars part-is 3f. part
corpus corpor-is 3n. body
rās-us a um shaved
praeter (+ acc.) except
caput capit-is 3n. head
labr-um ī 2n. lip
superius upper (n. s.)

EITHER

Reading exercise / Test exercise

Read the following passage carefully, defining, as you translate, in word-order, the functions of the words and word-groups, and anticipating the following parts of the sentence. When you have done this, translate. Finally, read out the passage, phrasing correctly, thinking through the meaning as you read. Use the running vocabulary of 1G.

est Eucliōnī aula aurī plēna. Eucliō aulam ex aedibus portat. timet enim ualdē. omnibus enim bonīs fūrēs omne aurum auferre semper uolunt. uult igitur in fānō aulam cēlāre. ubi aurum in fānō cēlat Eucliō, Strobīlus uidet. ē fānō exit Eucliō. bonō animō est, quod nunc fūrem timet nūllum. Strobīlus autem ut lumbrīcus in fānum inrēpit. nam aulam Eucliōnī miserō auferre uult. sed seruum audācem   5 uidet Eucliō. seruō audācī mala multa dīcit et aurum poscit. seruus autem senī aurum reddere nōn uult, quod aurum nōn habet. Eucliōnī manum dextram seruus ostendit. deinde senī miserō ostendit laeuam. Eucliō autem manum tertiam rogat. seruus Eucliōnem īnsānum habet et exit; aulam Eucliō ā fānō aufert et alterī (*dat. s. m.*) locō clam crēdit.   10

OR

English–Latin

Translate the Latin sentences into English. Then translate the English sentences into Latin, using the pattern of the Latin ones to help you arrange the word-order correctly.

(a) Eucliō uir summā uirtūtē est.
     Phaedra is an extremely beautiful girl.

(b) bonō animō es et dā mihi pecūniam.
     Be calm (*s.*) and take the gold from the slave.

(c) senex miser hominī malō aulam aurī plēnam crēdit.
     All the old men are returning the pots full of money to the good citizens.

(d) uōs autem quārē senī aurum nōn redditis?
     But why are you taking the young man's garland from him?

(e) quid tibi negōtī est in aedibus senis miserī?
     What business have you (*pl.*) in the shrine of my household god?

(f) est mihi pater optimus, uir summā continentiā.
     I've an excellent son, a young man of the highest qualities.

Dēliciae Latīnae

Word-building

(*a*) *Prefixes*

sub- (sometimes appears as *su-*, *sus-*) 'under', 'from under'

dē- 'down from'

per- 'through', 'thoroughly', 'very'

EXERCISE

Divide each of the following words into its compound parts and suggest a meaning for each: ēuocō, circumdūcō, perfacilis, trānsmittō, redeō, prōuideō, efferō, praeficiō, āmittō, reddō, subdūcō, ēdūcō, subeō, permultus, anteferō, trādō, perficiō, circumdō, dēdūcō, referō, dēuocō, summittō, perstō.

(*b*) *Noun formation*

Many nouns are formed from verbs or adjectives. This is often done by placing a suffix (*sub-fīxus* 'fixed on under', i.e. at the end) onto the verb or adjective stem. This suffix frequently gives a clue to the meaning of the noun, e.g.

-*sor* or -*tor* (gen. s. -*ōris* m.) means 'the person who', e.g. *amātor* 'lover'

-*or* (gen. s. -*ōris* m.) means 'activity', 'state' or 'condition', e.g. *amor* 'the state of loving', 'love'

-*iō*, -*tiō*, -*siō* (gen. s. -*iōnis* f.) means 'action or result of an action', e.g. *cōgitātiō* 'the act of thinking', 'thought'

-*ium* n. means 'action or result of an action', e.g. *aedificium* 'the result of making a house', 'a building'

-*men* (gen. s. -*minis* n.) means 'means, or result of an action', e.g. *nōmen* 'means of knowing', 'name'

EXERCISES

1 *Give the meaning of the following nouns*: audītor, cūrātor, uexātiō, inuentiō, cōnsilium, dictiō, turbātor, prōmissiō, maleficium, beneficium, habitātiō.

2 *Form the genitive singular of*: uexātiō, dictiō, habitātiō, inuentiō, audītor, turbātor.

50   **Future indicative active: 'I shall —' (all conjugations)**

	1	2	3
	'I shall love'	'I shall have'	'I shall say'
1st s.	amá-b-ō	habé-b-ō	díc-a-m
2nd s.	amá-bi-s	habé-bi-s	díc-ē-s
3rd s.	amá-bi-t	habé-bi-t	díc-e-t
1st pl.	amá-bi-mus	habé-bi-mus	díc-é-mus
2nd pl.	amá-bi-tis	habé-bi-tis	díc-é-tis
3rd pl.	amá-bu-nt	habé-bu-nt	díc-e-nt

	4	3/4
	'I shall hear'	'I shall capture'
1st s.	aúdi-a-m	cápi-a-m
2nd s.	aúdi-ē-s	cápi-ē-s
3rd s.	aúdi-e-t	cápi-e-t
1st pl.	audi-é-mus	capi-é-mus
2nd pl.	audi-é-tis	capi-é-tis
3rd pl.	aúdi-e-nt	cápi-e-nt

Notes

1 The following rhythmic chant may help you to memorise future forms: '*-bō -bis -bit* in 1 and 2, and *-am -ēs -et* in 3 and 4'.

2 Note that in 1st and 2nd conjs., the endings *-bō -bis -bit* etc. follow the pattern of 3rd conj. present, i.e. *dūc-ō -is -it* etc. In 3rd and 4th conjs. the new 1st s. ending in *-am* needs to be learned.

51   **Irregular futures: *sum → erō; eō → ībō***

	'I shall be' etc.	'I shall go' etc.
1st s.	ér-ō	í-b-ō
2nd s.	ér-i-s	í-bi-s
3rd s.	ér-i-t	í-bi-t
1st pl.	ér-i-mus	í-bi-mus
2nd pl.	ér-i-tis	í-bi-tis
3rd pl.	ér-u-nt	í-bu-nt

Notes

1   The future of *sum* was originally *es-ō*. The *s* became *r* between vowels, hence *erō*.

2   *ferō* is regular in the future – *fer-am -ēs -et* etc.

EXERCISES

1   *Translate these futures, change s. to pl. and vice versa, and say to what conjugation each regular verb belongs*: ībis, erunt, cēlābunt, perget, āmittēs, habēbimus, dēcipient, iubēbit, crēdet, capiētis, facient, uinciētis (*optional*: dormiet, fugiēs, habitābitis, clāmābit, timēbis, uidēbimus, poscēmus, prōmittam, ostendent, tacēbitis, amābunt).

2   *Give the corresponding future form of each of these presents, then translate*: crēdunt, salūtat, fers, estis, it, rogō, cūrant, pergis (*optional*: uincīs, capiō, sunt, dēcipimus, scītis, possidēs, exeō, portō, tangunt, reddis, irrīdēmus, dat).

3   *Form and translate 3rd s. and 3rd pl. of the future of the following verbs*: dō, clāmō, maneō, taceō, dūcō, poscō, dormiō, uinciō, capiō, fugiō, sum, redeō (*optional*: uocō, moneō, habeō, prōmittō, dīcō, sciō, inueniō, dēcipiō, faciō).

4   *Translate into Latin*: they will be; you (*pl.*) will return; you (*s.*) will hear; they will call; I shall make; we will speak; you (*pl.*) will be silent; he will lead; we will capture (*optional*: they will deceive; you (*s.*) will continue; I shall keep; you (*pl.*) will cook; she will see).

5   *Pick out the futures in this list and translate*: eritis, eunt, ferunt, dūcent, uident, dīcis, possidēs, dūcēs, amābunt, capiētis, facimus, fugiēmus, timēmus, mittēs, manēs, pergitis, dēcipiēs.

52   **Three irregular verbs: *possum, nōlō, mālō***

Present indicative

	'I can', 'I am able'	'I am unwilling', 'I do not want', 'I refuse'	'I prefer'
1st s.	pós-sum	nṓl-ō	mā́l-ō
2nd s.	pót-es	nōn uīs	mā́-uīs
3rd s.	pót-est	nōn uult	mā́-uult
1st pl.	pós-sumus	nṓl-u-mus	mā́l-u-mus
2nd pl.	pot-éstis	nōn uúltis	mā-uúltis
3rd pl.	pós-sunt	nṓl-u-nt	mā́l-u-nt
Infinitive	pós-se	nṓl-le	mā́l-le

Notes

1 *possum* is a combination of the stem *pot-* meaning 'power', 'capacity' + *sum*. Where *t* and *s* meet, the result is *-ss*, e.g. *potsum→possum*.

2 *nōlō, mālō* are based on *uolō*. *nōlō* is a combination of *nē* + *uolō*. *mālō* is a combination of *magis* (*ma-*) 'more' + *uolō* 'I want (to do X) more (than Y)'.

3 All three verbs control an infinitive, as they do in English, e.g. 'I am unwilling *to*', 'I am able *to*', 'I prefer *to*'. Note that *mālō* often controls two infinitives, separated by *quam* 'than', e.g. *mālō amāre quam pugnāre* 'I prefer to have love affairs rather than to fight'. The construction often has acc. nouns rather than infinitives, e.g. *mālō pecūniam quam uirtūtem* 'I prefer money rather than courage'.

4 The futures of *nōlō, mālō, uolō* are quite regular – interestingly, note that *nōlam, mālam, mālēs* are not actually found in surviving classical literature; the future of *possum* is again a combination of *pot* + the future of *sum*:

Future indicative

	'I shall be able'	'I shall wish'	'I shall refuse'	'I shall prefer'
1st s.	pót-erō	uól-a-m	(nṓl-a-m)	(mā́l-a-m)
2nd s.	pót-eris	uól-ē-s	nṓl-ē-s	(mā́l-ē-s)
3rd s.	pót-erit	uól-e-t	nṓl-e-t	mā́l-e-t
1st pl.	pot-érimus	uol-ḗ-mus	nōl-ḗ-mus	māl-ḗ-mus
2nd pl.	pot-éritis	uol-ḗ-tis	nōl-ḗ-tis	māl-ḗ-tis
3rd pl.	pót-erunt	uól-e-nt	nṓl-e-nt	mā́l-e-nt

EXERCISES

1 *Translate into Latin*: you (*s.*) wish; we prefer; they refuse; he can; we will prefer; you (*pl.*) do not wish; you (*s.*) are able; they will refuse (*optional*: he will wish; they can; we will be able; you (*s.*) prefer; we can; I shall be able).

2 *Translate and convert presents into futures, futures into presents*: est, possunt, uolēs, mālent, nōn uīs, erimus, nōlumus (*optional*: erunt, uult, poterit, nōlet, māuultis, uīs, potes).

Adjectives in *-er*: noster, uester; celer; ācer

1st/2nd declension adjectives: noster, uester

noster 'our(s)' and *uester* 'your(s)' decline like *pulcher pulchr-a um* (**27**). The difference between *uester* and *tuus* is that *uester* means 'your(s)' when 'you' are more than one person (cf. **20**).

3rd declension adjectives ending in -er (e.g. *celer celer-is celer-e* 'swift', 'fast')

	s.			*pl.*	
	m.	*f.*	*n.*	*m./f.*	*n.*
nom.	céler	céler-is	céler-e	céler-ēs	celér-ia
voc.	céler	céler-is	céler-e	céler-ēs	celér-ia
acc.	céler-em	céler-em	céler-e	céler-īs (-ēs)	celér-ia
gen.	← celér-is →			← celér-ium →	
dat.	← céler-ī →			← celér-ibus →	
abl.	← céler-ī →			← celér-ibus →	

Notes

1 3rd decl. adjectives ending in *-er* decline virtually identically with *omnis*, but do show a difference between the nom. s. m. (*celer*) and f. (*celeris*). They are *i*-stems (cf. **12**). It is easy to confuse these with 2nd decl. adjectives like *miser, pulcher*. Advice: learn the declension of *-er* adjectives!

2 Note that, while *celer* keeps the *-er* throughout the declension (cf. *miser* of the lst/2nd decl.), some *-er* adjectives drop the '*e*' (cf. *pulcher* of the lst/2nd decl.), e.g. *ācer*:

ācer ācris ācre 'keen', 'sharp'

	s.			pl.	
	m.	*f.*	*n.*	*m./f.*	*n.*
nom.	ácer	ácr-is	ácr-e	ácr-ēs	ácr-ia
voc.	ácer	ácr-is	ácr-e	ácr-ēs	ácr-ia
acc.	ácr-em	ácr-em	ácr-e	ácr-īs (-ēs)	ácr-ia
gen.	← ácr-is →			← ácr-ium →	
dat.	← ácr-ī →			← ácr-ibus →	
abl.	← ácr-ī →			← ácr-ibus →	

54   Cardinal numerals 1–10, 100–1,000

			s.		
			m.	*f.*	*n.*
1	I	*nom.*	ún-us	ún-a	ún-um
		acc.	ún-um	ún-am	ún-um
		gen.		←ūn-íus→	
		dat.		←ún-ī→	
		abl.	ún-ō	ún-ā	ún-ō

Plural ún-ī ún-ae ún-a (*like pl. of* multus)

			m.	*f.*	*n.*
2	II	*nom.*	dú-o	dú-ae	dú-o
		acc.	dú-ōs (dú-o)	dú-ās	dú-o
		gen.	du-ŏrum	du-ắrum	du-ŏrum
		dat./abl.	du-ŏbus	du-ắbus	du-ŏbus
			m./f.	*n.*	
3	III	*nom.*	tr-ēs	tr-ía	
		acc.	tr-ēs (tr-īs)	tr-ía	
		gen.	← tr-íum →		
		dat.	← tr-íbus →		
		abl.	← tr-íbus →		
4	IV/IIII	quáttuor			
5	V	quínque			
6	VI	sex			
7	VII	séptem			
8	VIII	óctō			
9	IX/VIIII	nóuem			
10	X	décem			

100	C	céntum
200	CC	ducént-ī ae a (*like pl. of* multus)
300	CCC	trecént-ī ae a
400	CD	quadringént-ī ae a
500	D	quīngént-ī ae a
1,000	M	mílle (*indecl. adj.*), *pl.* mília *gen.* mílium *dat./abl*
		mílibus (*see Note*)

Note

Normally, *mīlle* is used as an adjective and *mīlia* as a noun, e.g.

        mīlle mīlitēs = one thousand soldiers

        duo mīlia mīlitum = two thousand(s) (of) soldiers

        tria mīlia mīlitum = three thousand(s) (of) soldiers etc.

55   **4th declension nouns: *manus man-ūs* 4f. 'hand'**

	s.	pl.
nom.	mánu-s	mánū-s
voc.	mánu-s	mánū-s
acc.	mánu-m	mánū-s
gen.	mánū-s	mánu-um
dat.	mánu-ī	máni-bus
abl.	mánū	máni-bus

Notes

1 1 Most 4th decl. nouns are m. (*manus* is one of the few exceptions).

2 It is obviously very easy to confuse these with 2nd decl. nouns such as *thēsaurus*, so it is vital to learn the nom. and gen. s. together.

3 Care is needed with the *-ūs* ending, which might be gen. s., nom. or acc. pl. Note that the form *manus* can only be nom. (or voc.) s.

56   **4th declension noun (irregular): *domus dom-ūs* 'house' 4f.**

	s.	pl.
nom.	dómu-s	dómū-s
voc.	dómu-s	dómū-s
acc.	dómu-m	dómū-s (dómō-s)
gen.	dómū-s (dom-ī)	dom-ṓrum (dómu-um)
dat.	dómu-ī (dóm-ō)	dóm-ibus
abl.	dóm-ō	dóm-ibus

Notes

1 See **30** above for *domum*, *domī* and *domō* meanings.

2 *domus* has a mixture of 2nd and 4th decl. forms.

EXERCISES

1 *Give the Latin for*: beautiful hand; large hand; my hand; swift hand. *Now decline noun and adjective together in all cases, s. and pl.*

2 *Pick out datives and ablatives from this list* (*note where the form is ambiguous*): uiā, mendācēs, oppida, lūnam, nocte, manuī, celerī exercitū, officiō difficilī, scelere audācī, rēgēs bonōs, sōlī, ducentīs, continentiae tuae, uictōriam meam, Iouī magnō.

3 *Translate into Latin*: (*i*) *in the genitive*: one road, three victories, eight armies; (*ii*) *in the dative*: a thousand armies, three thousand towns, seven moons (*iii*) *in the accusative*: one word, three nights, two hands.

57 **3rd declension monosyllables**

If a 3rd decl. noun is a *monosyllable* with *two consonants at the end of the stem*, it is an *i*-stem noun, with gen. pl. in -*ium*, e.g.

> *nox no<u>ct</u>-is*, gen. pl. *noct<u>ium</u>*
> Contrast *dōs dō<u>t</u>-is*, gen. pl. *dō<u>t</u><u>um</u>*

Cf. the normal rule for consonant stems at **11**.

EXERCISES

1 *Translate these sentences*:

(a) dum Amphitruō, uir fortis, cum exercitū manet, Iuppiter, deus mendāx, hīc cum Alcumēnā clam dormiet.

(b) ecce! quid uīs mē facere? mālō enim seruum dēcipere.

(c) quia longa atque nigra erit nox, exercitus nihil facere poterit.

(d) seruus meus, uir audāx et ācer, officium in oppidō faciet; uōs uestrum facere mālam.

(e) dā mihi manum tuam; ecce, ego tibi meam dabō. bene.

(f) dum tacet nox, Iuppiter, rēx deōrum, Alcumēnae domum clam intrābit ac iterum iterumque amābit.

(g) quid negōtī est? cūr sīc mē tangis? cūr sīc manūs meās uincīs? abī! tē mē capere nōlō.

(h) sī Amphitruō mox cum exercitibus in oppidum redībit, uictōriam omnibus nūntiāre uolet.

(i) uictōria autem nōn difficilis sed celeris erit, sī exercitum nostrum Amphitruō dūcet; uir enim magnā sapientiā est ac uirtūte.

(j) Alcumēna, fēmina summā continentiā, Iouī, deō mendācī, crēdet, quia Amphitruōnis similis erit.

Reading exercises

Infinitives may add a simple idea to verbs like *possum, uolō, nōlō, mālō* etc.; e.g. *uidēre possum* = I can see; *īre uolō* = I want to go.

They may also introduce more complex ideas, since *uolō* commands an object (e.g. I want X [direct obj.] e.g. *my wife to go*), in which case 'my wife' will be in the acc. E.g. *uxōrem meam iterum uidēre uolō* = I want to see my wife again; *in aedīs inīre possum* = I can go into the house. The limits of the infinitive phrase are marked by the underlining.

In the case of *uolō, nōlō, mālō, iubeō*, the verb itself may also have an object, which becomes attached to the infinitive phrase: e.g. *tē* (obj.) *uxōrem meam iterum uidēre uolō* = I want you (obj.) to see my wife again.

mālō is more complex still, since it often outlines a preference between two things, which are compared by *quam* = 'than', e.g. *lūnam uidēre quam sōlem mālō* = I prefer to see the moon than [to see] the sun.

1 *In the following sentences, translate in word-order and make explicit the boundaries of the infinitive phrase. Mark which word in the phrase is the object of the introductory verb, not of the infinitive.*

(a) Alcumēna Amphitruōnem domī manēre quam exercitum dūcere mālet.

(b) seruum hominem esse magnā sapientiā nōlō.

(c) tē tuum officium quam mē facere meum rēx mālet.

(d) rēgem quam seruum in oppidō nūntiāre uictōriam cīuēs mālent.

(e) uxōrēs uirōs amāre iubeō.

2 *Now read out the sentences above in Latin, phrasing so as to avoid any possible ambiguities. How would you read sentence (e) in response to these two questions?*

(a) What do you tell husbands to do?

(b) What do you tell wives to do?

3 *Here are some disembodied infinitive phrases. Translate in word-order, then add a part of* uolō, nōlō, mālō *or* iubeō *to complete the sense. Translate into correct English. Finally, read out the Latin correctly phrased.*

(a) tē mihi crēdere …

(b) noctem longam ac nigram esse …

(c) oppidum capere atque uictōriam nūntiāre …

(d) uxōrem mē amāre meam …

(e) tē exercitum dūcere …

(f) hominēs ex oppidō exīre audācīs …

(g) Iouem iterum dēcipere Alcumēnam …

(h) fīlium tē in oppidum dūcere, domum fīliam …

4 *In English, the following is normal: 'I want to have the gold. Give **it** to me.'*
But in Latin this would be: aurum habēre uolō. dā mihi (no equivalent of 'it').
  Say in each of the following pairs of sentences which pronoun English inserts and Latin omits.

(a) uidērene oppidum potestis? capite!

(b) seruus domō iterum exit. dēcipe!

(c) Alcumēna domī manēbit. amā!

(d) uōs officīum uestrum facere iubeō. facite!

5 Quotations

Translate:

(a) *ūsus magister est optimus.* (Cicero)

(b) *sed quis custōdiet ipsōs custōdēs?* (Juvenal)

(c) *ācta deōs numquam mortālia fallunt.* (Ovid)

(d) *īrācundia leōnēs adiuuat, pauor ceruōs, accipitrem impetus, columbam fuga.* (Seneca)

(e) *potest ex casā uir magnus exīre, potest ex dēfōrmī humilīque corpusculō fōrmōsus animus et magnus.* (Seneca)

(f) *beātus esse sine uirtūte nēmo potest.* (Cicero)

(g) *sine imperiō nec domus ūlla nec cīuitās stāre potest.* (Cicero)

ūs-us ūs 4m. experience	*ceru-us ī* 2m. stag
magister magistr-ī 2m. teacher	*accipiter accipitr-is* 3m. hawk
optim-us a um best	*impet-us ūs* 4m. vehemence; attack
custōdiō 4 I guard	*columb-a ae* 1f. dove
ipsōs (acc. pl. m.) themselves	*fug-a ae* 1f. flight
custōs custōd-is 3m. guard (Juvenal is saying that wives are so sex-mad that if you put a guard over them, they will seduce the guards.)	*cas-a ae* 1f. cottage, hovel
	dēfōrm-is e ugly, misshapen
	humil-is e humble, lowly
	corpuscul-um ī 2n. little body
āct-um ī 2n. deed	*fōrmōs-us a um* beautiful
mortāl-is e of human beings	*beāt-us a um* happy, blessed
fallō 3 I deceive, escape the notice of	*nēmo* (nom.) no one
īrācundi-a ae 1f. rage	*imperi-um ī* 2n. control, authority
leō leōn-is 3m. lion	*ūll-us a um* any
pauor pauōr-is 3m. panic, fear	*cīuitās cīuitāt-is* 3f. state

EITHER

Reading exercise / Test exercise

Read carefully this passage, translating in the order of the words and defining the function of each word and phrase and anticipating the direction of the sense. Then translate into correct English. Finally, read aloud the passage, phrasing correctly, thinking out the meaning as you read. If you have learned the vocabulary, you should be able to do this without further help.

Mercurius, deus mendāx, domum Alcumēnae cum patre Ioue, rēge et hominum et deōrum, adībit. amat enim Iuppiter Alcumēnam, fēminam pulchram, uxōrem Amphitruōnis, uirī fortis. Iuppiter igitur cum Alcumēna per noctem longam dormīre uolet. Alcumēna tamen uxor est summā continentiā, atque Amphitruōnem bene amat. sī cōnsilia Iouis sciet, domō rēgem deōrum exīre iubēbit. difficile igitur   5
Iouī opus erit. sed Mercurius, deus summā audāciā, semper multa cōnsilia scit. imāginem igitur Sōsiae Mercurius capiet, Amphitruōnis Iouem capere iubēbit. sīc domum Alcumēnae intrābunt duo deī, alter Sōsiae similis, alter Amphitruōnis. et Iuppiter noctem faciet longam et nigram. mox in oppidum reueniet Sōsia, seruus ācer sed stultus. uolet uictōriam exercitūs Amphitruōnis Alcumēnae nūntiāre, sed   10
nōn poterit. Mercurius enim seruum domum intrāre nōlet.

OR

English–Latin

Translate the Latin sentences into English. Then translate the English sentences into Latin, using the pattern of the Latin ones to help you arrange the word-order correctly.

(a) Alcumēnam Iouem domum dūcere nōlle iubēbō.
     Jupiter will want Mercury to deceive the stupid slave again.

(b) uictōriam celerem dominī seruus nūntiāre uolet.
     I shall refuse to make love to the wife of a brave king.

(c) manum meam tibi dabō, sī tū dabis tuam mihi.
     We will lead our army into your city if you refuse to lead your army out of ours.

(d) uir summā uirtūte est, uxor summā continentiā.
     The slave is not a fellow of much wisdom but of great boldness.

(e) rēgem dēcipere difficile erit, sed nōn seruum.
     It is stupid to want to lead the army but not capture the town.

Dēliciae Latīnae

Word-building

dē + abl. = 'about', 'concerning', 'down from'.

dē- as a prefix to verbs = 'away', 'down', e.g. *dēscendō* 'I go down' (see above p. 64), cf. *spērō* 'I hope', *dēspērō* 'I lose hope'. Sometimes it intensifies the word, e.g. *capiō* 'I catch', *dēcipiō* 'I catch out' (from which comes our 'deceive').

If the simple verb has a short *ă* or *ĕ* as its first vowel, e.g. *căpiō*, that vowel will usually change to an *ĭ* after a prefix, e.g.

$$căpiō \longrightarrow dēcĭpiō$$
$$făciō \longrightarrow perfĭciō$$

Word exercise

Give the meaning and Latin connection of: lunatic, official, difficult, nocturnal, solar, manual, mendacious, credible, a posse, beneficial, reiterate, viaduct, accelerate, acrid.

Everyday Latin

What does it mean to go to one place *via* another?
What is one's *alter ego*?

Word study

alter

alter means 'one, or the other, of two people'; so *alternō* 'I change', so 'alter'. *ad* + *alter* + *ō* gives us 'adultery', i.e. moving from one state to another, so changing a lot, so corrupting. The word 'adult' derives from *adultus*, past participle of *adolēscō* 'I grow up'. An 'adolescent' is 'one growing up', and 'adult' is 'one having grown up'.

possum

As we saw, this word is a combination of *pot* + *sum*. The *pot-* root means 'ability', 'power', so *possum* means 'I am able', 'I can', the infinitive of which is *posse* 'to be able'. Hence 'possibility', 'possible', 'impossible' etc.

A sheriff's posse derives from medieval Latin *posse comitātūs* 'the power of the county', i.e. a force with legal authority. The *pot-* root yields Latin *potentia* 'power', hence 'potential', 'potency' and the negative 'impotence'. With *omni-* 'all', we have 'omnipotence'.

domus

aedēs, one Latin word for 'house', is in fact a plural form, the s. *aedis* meaning 'room'. *domus* gives us Latin *dominus* 'master of the house' and our 'dome', 'domestic', 'domicile', 'dominie' ('schoolmaster', a Scottish usage no longer common) and 'dominate' (= be master over), 'domineer' and 'dominion'. By another route, *dominus* became the Spanish *don* (whence university dons); and *domina* became Italian *donna*, whence *Madonna* 'my lady'. There is also a connection with dominoes, but it is not all clear how this came about. See what your dictionary makes of it.

But what does the phrase *dulce domum* mean? *dulcis* means 'sweet, delightful, welcome'. But can it agree with *domum* to mean 'home [is] welcome', or perhaps 'home, sweet home'? No: *dulce* is neuter, *domum* is acc. s. f. But the motto was made up by a schoolboy *c.* 1800 at Winchester, an ancient boarding school, so he may have thought it did. On the other hand, he may have got it right: *dulce* is also the adverb form, 'sweetly', and *domum* means 'to home' – 'sweetly homewards', the cry of boarders down the centuries.

Grammar and exercises for 2B

58   **Present deponent (all conjugations): indicative, imperative, infinitive**

	1	*2*	*3*
	'I threaten'	*'I promise'*	*'I speak'*
Indicative			
1st s.	mín-o-r	pollíce-o-r	lóqu-o-r
2nd s.	minā́-ris (-re)	pollicḗ-ris (-re)	lóqu-e-ris (-re)
3rd s.	minā́-tur	pollicḗ-tur	lóqu-i-tur
1st pl.	minā́-mur	pollicḗ-mur	lóqu-i-mur
2nd pl.	minā́-minī	pollicḗ-minī	loqu-í-minī
3rd pl.	minā́-ntur	pollicḗ-ntur	loqu-ú-ntur
Imperative			
2nd s.	minā́-re	pollicḗ-re	lóqu-e-re
2nd pl.	minā́-minī	pollicḗ-minī	loqu-í-minī
Infinitive	minā́-rī	pollicḗ-rī	lóqu-ī

	4	*3/4*
	'I lie'	*'I advance'*
Indicative		
1st s.	ménti-o-r	prōgrédi-o-r
2nd s.	mentī́-ris (-re)	prōgréd-e-ris (-re)
3rd s.	mentī́-tur	prōgrédi-tur
1st pl.	mentī́-mur	prōgrédi-mur
2nd pl.	mentī́-minī	prōgredí-minī
3rd pl.	menti-ú-ntur	prōgredi-ú-ntur
Imperative		
2nd s.	mentī́-re	prōgréd-e-re
2nd pl.	mentī́-minī	prōgredí-minī
Infinitive	mentī́-rī	prógred-ī

Notes

1 So far you have met verbs only in their 'active' forms. But there is another class of verb, called 'deponent'. It is this class you are now meeting for the first time. Deponents are identified by the different personal endings they take.

2 The personal endings of active verbs are, as we know, *-ō, -s, -t, -mus, -tis, -nt*. The personal endings of deponent verbs are *-r, -ris (-re), -tur, -mur, -minī, -ntur*. These new personal endings are of the highest importance as they are more widely used than just with deponents (as you will see). Consequently, if you learn them now, you will be saving yourself a great deal of learning in the future.

3 Given the new personal endings, deponent verbs are constructed exactly as active verbs are, i.e. stem with its key vowel + personal endings, e.g.

>   1st conj.: *mina-* + endings (cf. *amō*).
>
>   2nd conj.: *pollice-* + endings (cf. *habeō*).
>
>   3rd conj.: *loqu-* + *-i-* + endings. (cf. *dīcō*; *loquuntur*, cf. *dīcunt*. The really difficult one here is the 2nd s.: *loqueris*, cf. *dīcis*. It will help to remember that the vowel in the ending is always short in both *dīcō* and *loquor*.)
>
>   4th conj.: *menti-* + endings (cf. *audiō*)
>
>   3rd/4th conj.: *prōgredi-* + endings, except for 2nd s., where the *-i-* of the stem alters to *-e-* (as in 3rd conj.). Note that the *-i-* remains short (contrast 4th conj. *mentīris*, *mentītur* etc.).

4 Imperatives present a problem, in that the s. and pl. imperatives can be identical in form with the indicatives. For example, *mināminī* may mean 'you threaten' or 'threaten!' (pl.), and *mināre* could mean 'you threaten' or 'threaten!' (s.). The context will tell you which is right.

5 Do not confuse s. deponent forms in *-āre, -ere, -ēre* and *-īre* with active infinitives such as *amāre* etc.

6 The most difficult infinitive is the 3rd and 3rd/4th conj. infinitive, which ends in plain *-ī*, e.g. *loqu-ī, prōgred-ī*. All the rest end in stem + key vowel + *-rī*.

EXERCISES

1 *Translate and convert s. to pl. and vice versa (be sure to give both versions of the 2nd s.):* precātur, mentīris, pollicēmur, sequuntur, mināris, loquiminī, mentior, opīnāre, prōgrediminī, loqueris, pollicēre, mināmur (*optional:* recordor, ēgreditur, oblīuīscuntur, sequeris, precāre, opīnāmur, adgrederis, loquitur, mentiuntur, prōgrediuntur, mināmur).

2 *Give the Latin for (two versions of the 2nd s.):* we threaten; he promises; they forget; you (*pl.*) remember; you (*s.*) speak; I am following; advance! (*s.*); beg!

(s.); talk! (pl.); promise! (s.) (optional: we are thinking; they advance; he comes out; she threatens; remember! (pl.); we are lying; they speak; you (pl.) promise; talk! (s.); you (s.) follow).

3 *Say whether each of the following is an infinitive or an imperative and translate*: amāre, mināre, pollicēre, sequere, uocāre, habēre, loquī, audī, inuenīre, prōgredī, dormī, mentīrī, precāre, opīnārī, inuenī, dūcere, loquere, inīre, iubēre, prōgredere.

4 *Give the meaning, infinitive and s. imperative of the following verbs*: agō, pugnō, minor, loquor, audiō, dūcō, mittō, precor, fugiō, cognōscō (*optional*: opīnor, prōgredior, caueō, sequor, maneō, polliceor).

59   ***nōlī* + infinitive**

nōlī (pl. *nōlīte*), the imperative of *nōlō*, means in Latin 'don't!', and is followed by the infinitive (lit. 'do not wish to!', 'refuse to!'). E.g. *nōlī/nōlīte clāmāre* 'don't shout!', *nōlī/nōlīte loquī* 'don't speak!'

> ### EXERCISE

Translate into Latin: don't (s.) follow; don't (pl.) threaten me; don't (s.) complete the task; don't (pl.) send the ambassador; don't (s.) reply; don't (pl.) lead the army (*optional*: don't (s.) advance; don't (pl.) mention; don't (s.) do the business today; don't (pl.) fight).

60   **5th declension nouns: *rēs re-ī* 5f. 'thing', 'matter', 'business', 'affair'**

	s.	pl.
nom.	rē-s	rē-s
voc.	rē-s	rē-s
acc.	re-m	rē-s
gen.	ré-ī	ré-rum
dat.	ré-ī	ré-bus
abl.	rē	ré-bus

Note

Most 5th decl. nouns are f. But *diēs* 'day' is normally m. (it is f. when it denotes a specific day, e.g. a birthday, date of a letter).

EXERCISE

Decline in full: omnis rēs; pulcher diēs; mea rēs; trīstis diēs.

61   3rd declension n. noun: *caput capit-is* 'head'

	s.	pl.
nom.	cáput	cápit-a
voc.	cáput	cápit-a
acc.	cáput	cápit-a
gen.	cápit-is	cápit-um
dat.	cápit-ī	capít-ibus
abl.	cápit-e	capít-ibus

Note

Given the gen. s. *capit-is*, this noun follows the normal pattern of 3rd decl. n. nouns like e.g. *nōmen* (**26**).

62   Special lst/2nd declension adjectives: *nūll-us a um* 'no(ne)', 'not any'; *alter alter-a um* 'one' (of two), 'the one … the other'

	s.			pl.		
	m.	f.	n.	m.	f.	n.
nom.	nū́ll-us	nū́ll-a	nū́ll-um	nū́ll-ī	nū́ll-ae	nū́ll-a
acc.	nū́ll-um	nū́ll-am	nū́ll-um	nū́ll-ōs	nū́ll-ās	nū́ll-a
gen.	←——— nūll-ī́us ———→			nūll-ṓrum	nūll-ṓrum	nūll-ṓrum
dat.	←——— nū́ll-ī ———→			←——— nū́ll-īs ———→		
abl.	nū́ll-ō	nū́ll-ā	nū́ll-ō	←——— nū́ll-īs ———→		

	s.			pl.		
	m.	f.	n.	m.	f.	n.
nom.	álter	álter-a	álter-um	álter-ī	álter-ae	álter-a
acc.	álter-um	álter-am	álter-um	álter-ōs	álter-ās	álter-a
gen.	←——— alter-íus ———→			alter-ṓrum	alter-ā́rum	alter-ṓrum
dat.	←——— álter-ī ———→			←——— álter-īs ———→		
abl.	álter-ō	álter-ā	álter-ō	←——— álter-īs ———→		

Note

Both these adjectives are entirely regular except that the gen. s. ends in -*īus*, e.g. *nūllīus, alterīus*, and the dat. s. in -*ī*; cf. *quis* gen. s. *cuius* dat. s. *cui*, *ūnus* gen. s. *ūnīus* dat. s. *ūnī*.

EXERCISES

1 *Translate into English*:

(a) *Mercurius*: nōlī mihi minārī, serue stulte. *Sōsia*: at, ut rēs est, sīc tibi loquor.

(b) seruus, nūllīus sapientiae plēnus, nīl nisi capita rērum recordātur.

(c) lēgatī hostīs adloquuntur; deinde ad castra regrediuntur atque uerba hostium ducī nostrō nūntiant.

(d) hostēs nostrōrum ē proeliō in oppidum fugiunt; at nostrī sequuntur et pugnant.

(e) dux exercitum adloquitur et praedam ingentem uirīs omnibus pollicētur.

(f) opus in agrō hostium perficite, uirī! uōs progredī iubeō et hostīs sequī; pergite, et multam praedam ē proeliō adipīsciminī!

(g) rēs omnīs cognōsce; tē enim recordārī quam oblīuīscī mālam.

(h) ut pollicēris, sīc rem esse uolō.

(i) cauē, serue. nūllīus reī oblīuīscere; at recordāre omnia ac loquere nūllī.

(j) quid opīnāminī, lēgātī? ecce, lēgātus hostium, uir saeuus, mihi minātur, deinde mentītur, tum dēcipit.

Reading exercises

1 *When a sentence contains more than one clause, there are, in the conjunctions and other small words within previous clauses, signposts marking the direction of the sense. You have met* ita ... *leading up to* ut (*or vice versa*) *and in* **2B** (Text) *you saw* tam ... quam = '*as ... as*' *and* tantī ... quantī = '*worth as much ... as*'. *Ambiguities in the conjunction are often resolved in advance by markers, e.g.* tum, ubi ... *shows* ubi *to mean 'when' rather than 'where'. More generally, you will know from seeing* sī, *that the sentence is conditional ('if* X, *then* Y') *and* quod/quia *give the reason for something in another clause.*

Translate only the 'signposts' (markers like tum, tam *etc. and conjunctions like* sī, quod *etc.: these are in bold below) and say what the basic structure of each of these sentences is. When you have done this, translate (in word-order first, then into correct English). Finally read aloud, phrasing correctly, thinking through the meaning as you read.*

(a) **tum,** ut opīnor, rem omnem, lēgāte, cognōscēs, **sī** scīre uolēs, **ubi** hostēs ē proeliō fugient.

(b) **ut** tu mihi rem dīcis, **sīc** ego, **quia** tibi crēdō, opīnor.

(c) **quod** tē rēs omnīs scīre uolō, **ita** iubeō tē ē castrīs in hostium agrum progredī et uidēre, **sī** oculōs habēs, omnem praedam.

(d) **sīc** proelium Alcumēnae nūntiābō **ut** rem diēī omnem recordor, **sī** audīre uolet.

2   Quotations

Translate:

(a) *crēdula rēs amor est.* (Ovid)

(b) *rēs est magna tacēre.* (Martial)

(c) *uitia erunt dōnec hominēs.* (Tacitus)

(d) *rēs hūmānae fragilēs cadūcaeque sunt.* (Cicero)

(e) *dulce et decōrum est prō patriā morī.* (Horace)

(f) *et facere et patī fortia Rōmānum est.* (Livy)

crēdul-us a um confiding, unsuspecting	*decōr-us a um* fitting, seemly, honourable
amor amōr-is 3m. love	*prō* (+ abl.) for, on behalf of
uiti-um ī 2n. fault, crime	*patri-a ae* 1f. native land
dōnec while, as long as (sc. there are)	*morior* 3/4 dep. I die
hūmān-us a um human	*patior* 3/4 dep. I suffer, endure
fragil-is e brittle, frail	*fort-is e* brave
cadūc-us a um perishable	*Rōmān-us a um* Roman
dulc-is e sweet	

EITHER

Reading exercise / Test exercise

Read this passage carefully, translating in word-order. Define the function of each word as you go, grouping them into the correct phrases and anticipating the direction of the sense. Then translate into correct English. Finally, read aloud, with the correct phrasing, thinking out the meaning as you read. You should be able to do this unseen.

quia hostēs praedam ingentem terrā in nostrā capiunt, Amphitruō ulcīscī uult. cum exercitū igitur ē castrīs in hostium agrum proficīscitur. Amphitruō, uir summā uirtūte, per lēgātōs hostīs praedam reddere iubet; at hostēs, uirī saeuī, multa exercituī nostrō minantur: 'cauēte! nōlīte manēre in terrā nostrā! nōlīte nōs adloquī! nōlīte pugnāre! mālētis enim statim abīre quam in agrō manēre, 5 quia capiēmus uōs omnīs et seruōs faciēmus! nūllam uictōriam cīuibus uestrīs nūntiāre poteritis, hominēs miserī! abīte! nōlīte redīre!' Amphitruō deōs precātur ac exercitum hortātur et in proelium dūcit. longum est proelium exercituī atque saeuum. tandem uictōriam magnam adipīscuntur nostrī uirī. lēgātī hostium miserī ex oppidō proficīscuntur et in castra nostra cum praedā multā et multā pecūniā 10 ineunt. rēs omnīs nōbīs dant et redeunt.

OR

English–Latin

Translate the Latin sentences into English. Then translate the English sentences into Latin, using the pattern of the Latin ones to help you arrange the word-order correctly.

(a) nōlīte mē adloquī, hominēs.
   Don't threaten the army, ambassador.

(b) ubi dīcere uīs, rem in animō habē; uerba mox sequuntur.
   As you recall the matter, remember one thing: do not lie.

(c) ego tibi nōn minor, sed ita loquor ut rēs est.
   We are not lying, but telling you how the matter stands.

(d) sequiminī mē, uirī, in proelium, atque omnia oblīuīsciminī.
   Follow me, my son, into the field and pray to the gods.

Dēliciae Latīnae

Word-building

sub + abl./acc. = 'under', 'close up to'.

   sub- as a prefix (sometimes appearing as *su-* or *sus-*) attaches the same meaning to the verb, e.g. *sub + capiō = suscipiō* 'undertake'; *sub + sequor = subsequor* 'follow closely'. Cf. submarine, subcutaneous etc. See above p. 64.

Word exercise

Give the meanings and Latin connection of: perfect, capital, opinion, loquacious, progressive, stultify, oblivious, record (*cor cordis* heart), hostile, pugnacious, response, action, cognition, aggression, nullify.

Everyday Latin

In logic, what does a *nōn sequitur* not do?

   secundus 'second' is connected with *sequor*. It is, after all, what follows the first. Since a following wind was favourable to sailors, *secundus* also means 'favourable'.

   Letters often say '*re* your bill for drinks now outstanding at …' This, the abl. of *rēs* , means 'in the matter of'. Something *ad rem* is 'to the point', 'relevant to the matter in hand' (also a motto of the Wright family).

   If you see (*sic*), it indicates that what has just been written is intentionally written (*sic*) like that. Often used *de haut en bas*, to suggest the bottomless ignorance of the riter (*sic*).

Word study

ambulō

ambulō means 'I walk', 'take a turn'. Hence 'amble', and 'preamble', the introductory stroll round a subject (*prae* 'in front of). The French had an *hôpital ambulant*, i.e. 'touring hospital', 'field hospital', whence our 'ambulance'. 'Perambulate' means 'walk through or over' (*per* 'through'); hence the English derivation 'perambulator', which *should* mean 'one who walks over'. It is tempting to think that 'ramble' comes from *re + ambulō*, but this is disputed.

diēs

The Latin adjective *dīus* means 'divine', 'of the sky' and 'luminous'. It connects with *deus* 'god' (cf. Greek '*Zeus*'), whence *dīuus*, *dīuīnus*, the goddess *Diāna*, English 'divine'. It also connects with *diēs* 'day' – so 'light' and 'god' appear to be closely connected semantically. (Cf. John 1:4: 'In Him was life and the life was the light of men'; 1 John 1:5: 'God is light and in Him there is no darkness at all.') *Iuppiter* is cognate with Greek *Zeu pater* 'O Zeus father'. Observe that Jupiter also appears in Latin as *diēspiter* (connected with *diēs + pater* 'father of day'), and that the gen. s. of *Iuppiter* is *Iouis*, in primitive Latin *Diouis*. Both *diēspiter* and *Diouis* bring us back to the *di-* root again. *Iou-* gives us 'jovial' (from the astrological influence of the planet Jupiter). There is also a connection between *Zeus*, *deus* and the Old English god of war *Tīw*, whence Tuesday!

    diēs helps to give us 'dismal' (*diēs malī* 'unlucky days'), and 'diary' (*diārium* 'ration for the day'). From *diēs* Latin got the adjective *diurnus* 'daily', giving English 'diurnal' and (through French) 'journal'. Note that in France and Italy, Thursday is named after Jupiter (Fr. *jeudi*, It. *gióvedi*).

Grammar and exercises for 2C

63   *hic haec hoc* 'this', 'this person', 'this thing', 'the latter', pl. 'these'

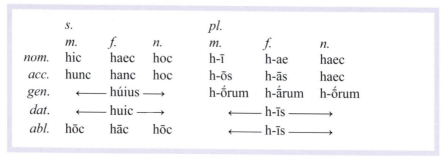

	s.			pl.		
	m.	*f.*	*n.*	*m.*	*f.*	*n.*
nom.	hic	haec	hoc	h-ī	h-ae	haec
acc.	hunc	hanc	hoc	h-ōs	h-ās	haec
gen.	←—— húius ——→			h-ṓrum	h-ā́rum	h-ṓrum
dat.	←—— huic ——→			←——— h-īs ———→		
abl.	hōc	hāc	hōc	←——— h-īs ———→		

Notes

1 Describing a noun, *hic* means 'this' (pl. 'these'); on its own, it will mean 'this man', 'this woman', 'this thing', depending on gender and context. Often 'he', 'she', 'it' will suffice.

2 Its forms seem to be irregular, but note the *-ius* of the gen. s. (cf. *nūllus, alter* **62** and *quis* **29**), and the pl., except for *haec*, is just like *multus* on the stem *h-*.

3 NB *hinc* 'from here'; *hīc* '(at) here'; *hūc* '(to) here'.

64   *ille illa illud* 'that', 'that person', 'that thing', 'the former', pl. 'those'

	s.			pl.		
	m.	*f.*	*n.*	*m.*	*f.*	*n.*
nom.	íll-e	íll-a	íll-ud	íll-ī	íll-ae	íll-a
acc.	íll-um	ill-am	íll-ud	íll-ōs	íll-ās	íll-a
gen.	←—— ill-íus ——→			ill-ṓrum	ill-ā́rum	ill-ṓrum
dat.	←—— íll-ī ——→			←——— íll-īs ———→		
abl.	íll-ō	íll-ā	íll-ō	←——— íll-īs ———→		

Notes

1 On its own, *ille* means 'that man', 'that woman', 'that thing', depending on gender and context; describing a noun, it means 'that', 'those'. Often it best translates as 'he', 'she', 'it'.

2 The forms at first glance seem irregular, but on closer inspection you will see that, apart from *ille, illud, illīus, illī* (cf. *nūllīus, nūllī; cuius, cui; alterīus, alterī*) they are simply the stem *ill-* with 2nd decl. adjective endings like *multus*.

3 From *ille* came French *le, la* and Italian *il, la*.

4 NB *illinc* 'from there'; *illīc* '(at) there'; *illūc* '(to) there'. Cf. **63**[3].

5 *ille … hic* are often used in contrast to mean 'the former' (i.e. the first mentioned, *that one* over there, further away) and 'the latter' (i.e. the second item just mentioned, *this one* right here).

6 Ambiguities: note that *illī* can be dat. s. m. f. or n. or nom. pl. m. But *illae* can be only nom. pl. f., because gen. and dat. s. are *illīus, illī*.

EXERCISES

1 *Decline in all cases*: hic seruus; ille mīles; haec serua; illud perīculum; hoc uerbum; illa mulier.

2 *Give the case or cases of the following phrases*: huius patris; hāc fīliā; hae uxōrēs; huic animō; hoc onus; hīs cenīs (*optional*: hunc diem; hārum noctium; hōs seruōs; haec cōnsilia; hōc capite; huius perīculī); illō uerbō; illud opus; illōs diēs; illīs sceleribus; illī manuī (*optional*: illam turbam; illa soror; illīus ignis; illī familiae; illōs honōrēs; illīus rēī; illa domus; illā rē).

3 *Give the Latin for*: this soldier (*acc.*); to that old man; this girl's; those plans (*nom./acc.*); these dangers (*nom./acc.*); that woman's.

4 *Give the case of the following phrases, where the noun could be ambiguous, but where the form of* hic *or* ille *solves the problem*: hī thēsaurī; illīus thēsaurī; illās sorōrēs; hae sorōrēs; illa rēs; hās rēs; illae rēs; huius manūs; illae manūs; hae manūs; illās mulierēs; hae mulierēs; illī puerō; hōc puerō; illae fēminae; huic fēminae; illīus fēminae; hic diēs; illōs diēs; hī diēs.

5 *Join* hic *or* ille *to the word(s) with which it agrees, and translate*:

huius: seruus, amīcī, mulierēs, lūnae

illum: cōnsilium, opus, puerum, diērum, frātrem, rem

illā: uxōre, nox, manū, officia

hoc: mīles, officium, nōmen, cīuem, aurum

haec: aedēs, corōna, opera, manus, negōtia, rēs

illōs: cīuīs, senem, facinus, deōs, domus

6 *Translate*: cum hīs mulieribus; in illō capite; ad hanc rem; per illam turbam; ex illō perīculō.

87

7 *Give the Latin for*: onto this stage; with that woman; through these fires; with those brothers; in this eye; into that town; through these dangers.

Reading exercises

1 *Translate in word-order, defining which is subject (if one is quoted), which is object etc. in these incomplete sentences, then supply a verb to complete them and translate into correct English. Finally read out the sentences in Latin with correct phrasing, thinking through the meaning as you read.*

(a) ille mīles hanc mulierem huic iuuenī crēdere …

(b) illum huius senis seruum …

(c) hoc aurum illī mīlitī hic seruus …

(d) cum hāc muliere illum iuuenem hic mīles mox …

(e) huic ille fēminae hanc pecūniam omnem dare …

2 Quotations

(a) *ūna salūs uictīs nūllam spērāre salūtem.* (Virgil)

(b) *praeterita mūtāre nōn possumus.* (Cicero)

(c) *nītimur in uetitum semper cupimusque negāta.* (Ovid)

(d) *semel ēmissum uolat irreuocābile uerbum.* (Horace)

salūs salūt-is 3f. salvation, source of safety
uict-ī ōrum 2m. pl. the conquered
spērō 1 I hope for
praeterit-a ōrum 2n. pl. the past
mūtō 1 I change
nītor 3 dep. I strive towards (*in* + acc.)
uetit-um ī 2n. the forbidden

cupiō 3/4 I yearn for
negāt-a ōrum 2n. pl. things (we have been) denied
semel once
ēmiss-us a um spoken, sent forth
uolō 1 I fly
irreuocābil-is e beyond recall, irrevocable

EITHER

Reading exercise / Test exercise

Read this passage carefully, translating in word-order as usual. Translate into correct English; then, finally, read the passage aloud in Latin, phrasing correctly, thinking through the meaning as you read.

mē pater meus, rēx deōrum, officium magnum perficere iubet. quandō patrem meum cūrō, omnia faciam ut iubet. dum enim hic Alcumēnam, Amphitruōnis mulierem, dēcipit, ego hunc seruum illīus domum intrāre nōn sinam. meā enim audāciā seruum stultum īrātum faciam, et fōrmā meā dēcipiam. nam mihi homo ille nūllā sapientiā uidētur esse. mē igitur similem fōrmae illīus faciam, et illum   5
domum adgredī nōn sinam. Sōsia haud mihi crēdet, quandō illī dīcam 'plānē nōn tū Sōsia es, sed ego!' īrātus erit homo ille stultus et 'mentīris' dīcet. 'fōrma tua similis meī est, ut arbitror, at ego Sōsia sum, nōn tū. abī, homo sceleste!' ego tamen 'quam nescius est hic seruus, sī mē scelestum arbitrātur. nam sī ego scelestus sum, Sōsia ille scelestus est – nam ego Sōsia, at tū homo nihilī!'   10

OR

English–Latin

1 *Translate these sentences into Latin, taking care to choose a word-order which gives the correct emphasis (see Reference Grammar **W**):*

(a) This soldier loves *that* man's daughter.

(b) *This* young man's father seems to be ignorant.

(c) *Those* women I consider as enemies.

(d) *This* is a great duty for good citizens.

(e) *That* soldier wants to defend this woman.

(f) It's the character of these women I consider wicked.

(*Remember 'it's the' is just a way English has of emphasising something; Latin puts the emphatic words early in the sentence.*)

OR

2 *Translate this passage (after rereading the text of 2C):*

Clearly, this slave will achieve nothing. He wants to enter into [his] master's house, and to announce that man's victory. But none of these things (='none these things') will that ignorant and stupid man be able to do. For I shall make my shape seem similar to that man's, and my character similar as well. In this way (use abl.) I shall defend this house, while my master makes love to the wife of that Amphitruo. That man's slave will clearly be angry, but I shall not allow that man to enter or even approach [his] master's house. How bold and lying and wicked am I! How unhappy that stupid slave will be!

Dēliciae Latīnae

Word-building

Suffixes

Verbs often receive a change in their meaning from a suffix (or 'infix') which becomes part of their stem, e.g.:

-sc- indicates the beginning of an action. So *cognōscō* means 'I begin to know', 'I get to know'; *pacīscor* 'I begin/attempt to make a treaty'. All *-scō* verbs are 3rd conjugation.

-it- denotes repetition. So *clāmitō* ='I keep on shouting'. All verbs in *-itō* are 1st conjugation.

EXERCISE

Give the meaning of these words and their connections with Latin: military; (*French*) le, la; (*Italian*) il, la; conative; arbitrate; morals.

Everyday Latin

ad hoc 'for, directed at, this one occasion', i.e. unplanned.

post hoc, ergō propter hoc 'after this, therefore because of this'. A famous logical trap into which it is only too easy for politicians and others to fall. After you learned Latin you became a drunken layabout; therefore it was because you learned Latin that … etc.

Word study

plānus

This means 'flat', 'level', so 'clear', 'obvious' in Latin. This becomes English 'plane', a level surface, and the tool which makes a surface level. Through French, we have English 'plain', a level surface, and plainsong (as opposed to measured music, i.e. Gregorian chant as opposed to polyphony). In Italian *plānus* emerges as *piano*, 'flat', hence in music 'softly'. Combined with Italian *forte* 'loud' (cf. Latin *fortis* 'brave', 'strong'), it yields 'pianoforte', which can play both soft and loud. 'Explain' comes from *explānō* 'flatten', 'spread out', literally and before the mind.

Do not confuse with the '-plain' of e.g. 'complain', which derives (again through French) from Latin *plangō*, 'mourn', 'lament' (cf. 'plangent', 'plaintiff').

Grammar and exercises for 2D

65   **Perfect indicative active: 'I —ed', 'I have —ed'**

	1 '*I loved*', '*I have loved*'	*2* '*I had*', '*I have had*'	*3* '*I said*', '*I have said*'
1st s.	amā́-u-ī	háb-u-ī	dī́x-ī
2nd s.	amā-u-ístī (amā́stī)	hab-u-ístī	dīx-ístī (dī́xtī)
3rd s.	amā́-u-i-t	háb-u-i-t	dī́x-i-t
1st pl.	amā́-u-i-mus	hab-ú-i-mus	dī́x-i-mus
2nd pl.	amā-u-ís-tis (amā́stis)	hab-u-ís-tis	dīx-ís-tis
3rd pl.	amā-u-éru-nt (amāuére/amā́runt)	hab-u-éru-nt (habuére)	dīx-éru-nt (dīxére)

	4 '*I heard*', '*I have heard*'	*3/4* '*I captured*', '*I have captured*'
1st s.	audī́-u-ī	cḗp-ī
2nd s.	audī-u-ístī (audiístī/audī́stī)	cēp-ístī
3rd s.	audī́-u-i-t	cḗp-i-t
1st pl.	audī́-u-i-mus	cḗp-i-mus
2nd pl.	audī-u-ís-tis (audī́stis)	cēp-ís-tis
3rd pl.	audī-u-éru-nt (audīuére/audiérunt/audiére)	cēp-éru-nt (cēpére)

Notes

1 The perfect tense (*perfectus* 'completed', 'finished') has three basic meanings:

   (a) (by far the most common): completed action in past time, e.g. *amāuī* 'I loved'.

   (b) action in the past seen from the point of view of the present, e.g. *amāuī* 'I have loved'.

   (c) present state arising from past action, e.g. *periī* 'I am done for' (i.e. 'I have perished and therefore am (now) done for').

Cf. Cicero's announcement that the conspirators involved with Catiline had been executed – *uīxērunt* 'they have lived', i.e. 'they are dead'. Generally speaking, the choice will be between (a) and (b), according to context.

2 Formation of the perfect tense:

(a) The key to perfect active in conjugations 1, 2 and 4 is the *-u-* + endings. The perfect active for 1st and 4th conj. is formed by adding *-uī* to the stem, e.g. *amā-uī, audī-uī.* 2nd conj. verbs, e.g. *habeō,* often drop the *-e* of the stem and replace it with *-uī,* thus *habuī.* They can also add *uī* to the *stem,* e.g. *dēleō dēlēre dēlēuī*; and there are several other irregular types (see **66** below, under 2nd conj.).

Third conj. verbs are unpredictable (see Note 4).

(b) Note, however, that in 1st and 4th conjugations, *-ui-/-ue-/-u-* is sometimes dropped giving e.g. *amāstī* for *amāuistī, audiit* for *audīuit* etc. See the bracketed forms in the chart.

3 BUT: *all* perfect actives have personal endings in:

> *-ī*
>
> *-istī*
>
> *-it*
>
> *-imus*
>
> *-istis*
>
> *-ērunt (-ēre)*

Note that, apart from 1st and 2nd s., the personal endings (*-t, -mus, -tis, -nt*) are the normal active ones. Note variations on *-ērunt*: it can be *-ēre,* e.g. *amāuērunt* or *amāuēre* (do not confuse with infinitives, e.g. *habēre* – which would be *habuērunt* or *habuēre* in the perfect – and 2nd s. deponents, e.g. *pollicēre*).

4 The perfect active stems of 3rd and 3rd/4th conjugation verbs, and some irregular 1st, 2nd and 3rd conj. verbs, are not as neatly predictable as those of the other conjugations, but certain patterns do emerge, e.g.

(a) adding *-sī* to the stem, like:

> *maneō* 2 *mānsī* 'I stayed'
>
> *irrīdeō* 2 *irrīsī* 'I laughed at'
>
> *iubeō* 2 *iussī* 'I ordered'
>
> *mittō mīsī* 'I sent'

Note the effect on e.g.:

> *dūcō dūxī* 'I led'
>
> *dīcō dīxī* 'I said'
>
> *uinciō* 4 *uīnxī* 'I bound'

(b) doubling up ('reduplicating') the initial consonant and adding a vowel, like:

> *dō* 1 *dedī* 'I gave'
>
> *tangō tetigī* 'I touched'
>
> *poscō poposcī* 'I demanded'

(c) lengthening the vowel in the stem:

> *inueniō* 4 *inuēnī* 'I found'
>
> *fugiō fūgī* 'I fled'

Contrast, therefore, *inuēnit* (perf.) and *inuenit* (pres.). It is important to learn the correct vowel length. One does this best by reading out loud.

(d) changing the vowel in the stem:

> *faciō fēcī* 'I made', 'I did'
>
> *agō ēgī* 'I did', 'I drove'
>
> *capiō cēpī* 'I took'

(e) no change in the stem at all. (In these cases e.g. *dēfendit* could be present or perfect. Only the context will tell you which.)

> *dēfendō dēfendī* 'I defended'
>
> compounds of *-cendō -cendī*
>
> verbs in *-uō -uī*, e.g. *soluō soluī* 'I released'

(f) stems ending in *l, m, n, r* ('liquids', 'nasals') add *-uī*, e.g.

> *uolō uoluī* 'I wished'
>
> *aperiō* 4 *aperuī* 'I opened'

66   **Irregular verbs**

Irregular verbs learned to date are:

1   *dō dare dedī* 'I give'
         stō stāre stetī 'I stand'

2   *caueō cauēre cāuī* 'I am wary', 'I look out'
         dēleō dēlēre dēlēuī 'I destroy'
         irrīdeō irrīdēre irrīsī 'I laugh at'
         iubeō iubēre iussī 'I order'
         maneō manēre mānsī 'I remain'
         possideō possidēre possēdī 'I possess'
         respondeō respondēre respondī 'I reply'
         uideō uidēre uīdī 'I see'

3   *agō agere ēgī* 'I do', 'I act'
         āmittō see *mittō*
         cognōscō cognōscere cognōuī 'I get to know'
         coquō coquere coxī 'I cook'
         crēdō crēdere crēdidī 'I believe', 'I trust'
         dēfendō dēfendere dēfendī 'I defend'
         dīcō dīcere dīxī 'I say'
         dūcō dūcere dūxī 'I lead'
         gerō gerere gessī 'I do', 'I act' ('I wage')

mittō mittere mīsī 'I send'; *ā-* 'I lose'

opprimō opprimere oppressī 'I surprise'; 'I catch'; 'I crush'

ostendō ostendere ostendī 'I show'

pergō pergere perrēxī 'I carry on'

poscō poscere poposcī 'I demand'

reddō reddere reddidī 'I give back'

soluō soluere soluī 'I release'

tangō tangere tetigī 'I touch'

uincō uincere uīcī 'I conquer'

4   *inueniō inuenīre inuēnī* 'I find'

uinciō uincīre uīnxī 'I bind'

3/4   *capiō capere cēpī* 'I capture'

dēcipiō dēcipere dēcēpī 'I deceive'

faciō facere fēcī 'I do', 'I make'

fugiō fugere fūgī 'I flee'

perficiō perficere perfēcī 'I complete'

Note in particular:

adsum 'I am present': see *sum*

auferō auferre abstulī 'I take away', 'I remove'

eō īre iī or *īuī* 'I go' (not really irregular, as the stem is *-i*)

mālō mālle māluī 'I prefer'

nōlō nōlle nōluī 'I do not want'

sum esse fuī 'I am'

uolō uelle uoluī 'I wish'

EXERCISES

1 *Form and then conjugate the perfect of these verbs*: clāmō, uideō, uincō, uinciō, abeō, sum, dō, capiō, ferō, faciō (*optional*: castīgō, salūtō, dēfendō, sinō, mālō, nōlō, dormiō, redeō).

2 *Translate each of these perfects. Change s. to pl. and vice versa*: dēlēuistī, gessērunt, uīcit, adfuistis, soluī, pugnāuimus, abiīstis (*optional*: amāuit, habuērunt, dēfendistī, necāuērunt, audīuī, cēpistis).

3 *What verbs are these perfects from? Translate them*: dedistī, crēdidit, fuit, dēbuistis, mānsī, oppressimus, tetigit, āmīsistī, dīximus, exiit (*optional*: uīdit, mīsī, habitāuimus, timuistī, possēdistis, rogāuērunt, stetī, monuit, inuēnērunt, iniīstī, abstulimus, reddidī, potuit, uoluī, māluērunt, cāuistis, perfēcimus, ēgit).

4 *Give the Latin for*: I have given; we fought; you (*s.*) destroyed; he has loved; they were present; you (*pl.*) conquered; I went out; they have killed; he replied; you (*s.*) have acted; we completed; you (*pl.*) carried.

5 *Give present, future and perfect 3rd s. and pl. of these verbs*: dormiō, pugnō, dēleō, gerō, sum, auferō, redeō, dēcipiō.

6 *Translate the following verbs, saying which tense, or tenses, each is*: stābit, dedērunt, crēdet, aderis, uīcistī, pugnābunt, soluunt, dēlent, gerent, mānsī, inuēnistis, perficiēs, habēs, monuistis, dēfendit, fūgit, soluit.

67   **Ablatives: phrases of time**

We have met two uses of the ablative to date: with prepositions (esp. of place, e.g. 'in', 'at', 'from'), and descriptive ('a man <u>of great arrogance</u>') (cf. **10, 23, 49**).

    The ablative case is also used to show the time *at which* or *within which* something took place (cf. locational use), e.g. *illō tempore* 'at that time'; *prīmā hōrā* 'at the first hour'; *decem diēbus* '(with)in ten days'.

> **EXERCISE**

Translate these sentences:

(a) Amphitruō, sine dubiō īrātus, uerba uxōris audīuit et illam iterum castigāuit; illa ergō tacita nōn fuit, sed subitō respondit.

(b) Alcumēna domī uirum, ut dēbuit, salūtāuit; post, grātiās multās ēgit, quod aulam auream possēdit.

(c) ante lūcem Amphitruō domum rediit et uxōrī 'domī iam adsum' inquit. 'nam hostēs hāc nocte exercitus meus dēlēuit.'

(d) hōc tempore noctis omnēs dormīre dēbent; uērum Alcumēna cum Ioue uoluptātem habuit.

(e) illā hōrā in urbem rediit Sōsia et omnia dē Mercuriō mendācī dīxit.

(f) 'immō' inquit Amphitruō 'tibi illā nocte pateram auream nōn dedī; quārē tū nōn mihi crēdidistī? nōlō tē mendācem esse suspicārī; uērum sī iam mentīris, ego tē castigābō.'

Reading exercises

1 *Recognising the function of an ablative phrase is not always easy. So far you have met three types: (a) descriptive, e.g.* uir summō ingeniō *'a very intelligent man', (b) prepositional, e.g.* cum illā muliere *'with that woman', (c) time when or within which, e.g.* hōc tempore *'at this time',* ūnā hōrā *'(with)in one hour'. Translate the following phrases and say to which category they belong*: uir summā audāciā; illō tempore; hāc nocte; dē tuō perīculō; tacitā nocte; ā senibus miserīs; seruus multā audāciā; mēcum; hōrīs multīs; magnō post tempore; fēmina summā uirtūte; ē castrīs; illō noctis tempore; cum meā uxōre; diēbus decem.

Quotations

2 *Translate these sentences*:

(a) *dēfēnsor culpae dīcit mihi 'fēcimus et nōs / haec iuuenēs.'* (Juvenal)

(b) *dīc mihi, quid fēcī, nisi nōn sapienter amāuī?* (Ovid)

(c) *fuimus Trōes: fuit Īlium.* (Virgil)

(d) *lūsistī satis, ēdistī satis atque bibistī; / tempus abīre tibi est.* (Horace)

(e) *nātūra sēmina nōbīs scientiae dedit; scientiam nōn dedit.* (Seneca)

dēfēnsor defensōr-is 3m. defender	*lūdō* 3 *lūsī* I play, have fun
culp-a ae 1f. fault	*ēdō ēsse ēdī* I eat
nisi except that	*bibō* 3 *bibī* I drink
sapienter wisely	*nātūr-a ae* 1f. nature
Trōs Trō-is 3m. Trojan	*sēmen sēmin-is* 3n. seed
Īli-um ī 2n. Troy	*scienti-a ae* 1f. knowledge

EITHER

Reading exercise / Test exercise

Read this passage carefully, translating in word-order. You will need to stop to group the ablative phrases and decide their function. Often the words in the phrase will not be next to one another. Attempt as you read to classify ablative adjectives and hold them in your mind without attempting to translate fully until the noun solves them. Translate into correct English, then read aloud in Latin, phrasing correctly, thinking through the meaning as you read.

Atrīdae longō post tempore Īlium cēpērunt. decimō enim annō urbem Trōiam tandem expugnāuērunt. nam illō tempore rēgēs in urbem equum mīsērunt ligneum. Epēus, uir sapientiā magnā, equum illum aedificāuit. mīlitēs in equō fuērunt armātī, summā audāciā uirī. hī ex equō illā exiērunt nocte et urbem mox dēlēuērunt. sīc illō diē Trōia urbs ūnā periit hōrā.   5

OR

English–Latin

1 *Translate into Latin. Consult Reference Grammar **W** on word-order.*

(a) At this time of day the young man went away, silently, into the house.

(b) Why are you suspecting me? You did not believe me when I said 'You gave me that golden pot.'

(c) Truly I was not present afterwards, when your army waged war against the city and conquered it.

(d) On that night therefore we suddenly destroyed the camp of the enemy and captured the town.

(e) At this hour you ought not to have feared* the angry soldiers.

(f) The army has seen the signal and departed from the camp; soon, without doubt, it will wage war against the enemy.

*put 'ought' in the perfect and use the present infinitive of 'fear'

OR

2 *Translate this passage (after rereading the text of 2D):*

AMPHITRUO: Why do you stand there silent, my wife? What have I said?

ALCUMENA: You have rebuked me, husband; but in truth I have done nothing. Tell me: am I a woman of no self-control?

AMPH.: But you said 'This night you were [present] at home with me.' So I say: are you lying? Did you see me that night?

ALC.: You suspect me to be lying, but without doubt I did see you. Why were you not able to believe me?

AMPH: Because at that hour I was not [present] at home with you, but waged war against the enemy.

Dēliciae Latīnae

Word-building

Further suffixes

The following suffixes commonly form abstract nouns, 'the quality of', 'the condition of':

> -ia (gen. s. -iae f.), e.g. *audācia* 'boldness'
>
> -tās (gen. s. -tātis f.), e.g. *uoluptās* 'agreeable experience, pleasure'
>
> -tūs (gen. s. -tūtis f.), e.g. *seruitūs* 'slavery'
>
> -tūdō (gen. s. -tūdinis f.), e.g. *multitūdō* 'manyness', 'crowd', 'plenty'

EXERCISES

1 *Derive and give the meaning of the following nouns*: iuuentūs, scientia, timor, uirtūs, pulchritūdō, paupertās, praedictiō, facilitās, malefactor, clāmor, cīuitās.

2 *Form the gen. s. of*: uirtūs, pulchritūdō, paupertās, facilitās, timor.

3 *What are the nominatives of the following nouns, none of which you have met?*
   Scīpiōnis, Cicerōnis, longitūdinem, uictōrēs, cupiditātī, ēruptiōne, iuuentūtis,
   lībertātem, explōratōrum.

4 *Can you guess the meaning of any of the nouns in 3?*

Adjective formation

Here is a list of common suffixes which form adjectives:

-*ilis* ⎫
         ⎬ 'able to be', e.g. *ductilis* 'leadable', *mōbilis* 'mobile'
-*bilis* ⎭

-*idus* 'in a condition of', e.g. *timidus* 'being in a condition of fear',
   'afraid'

-*ōsus* 'full of', e.g. *perīculōsus* 'full of danger', 'dangerous'

-*eus* 'made of', e.g. *aureus* 'made of gold', 'golden'

The following list of suffixes may best be covered by the meaning 'pertaining
to': -*ālis*, -*ānus*, -*āris*, -*ārius*, -*icus*, -*īlis*, -*īnus*, -*īuus*, -*ius*, e.g. *Rōm-ānus*
'pertaining to Rome', *Lat-īnus* 'pertaining to Latium', *seru-īlis* 'pertaining to
slaves', 'servile', *patr-ius* 'pertaining to one's father', 'paternal', 'ancestral' etc.

EXERCISE

*Analyse the following adjectives etymologically, and reach a conclusion about
their meaning*: familiāris, facilis, audībilis, incrēdibilis, fertilis, scaenicus,
fūrtīuus, senīlis, honōrābilis, oculeus (*used of monsters*), aquārius, pecūniōsus,
uirīlis, uxōrius, domesticus, nōminātīuus, dōtālis, animōsus, cīuīlis, iuuenīlis.

Everyday Latin

Remember three important perfects with reference to Julius Caesar's famous
words that he wrote on a placard at a huge triumph in Rome in 46 celebrating one
of his quickest victories (at Zela in Asia Minor in 47):

uēnī, uīdī, uīcī 'I came, I saw, I conquered'

On tombstones *fl.* = *floruit* '(s)he flourished' and *ob.* = *obiit* '(s)he died' (cf.
'obituary') – both perfect tense.

Word exercise

Give the Latin connection of the following words: predatory, temporary, urbane,
tacit, pugnacious, delete, debt, solve, ante-chamber, grateful, signal, voluptuous.

Word study

sinecure (*cūra*, *cūrō*)

This derives from *sine* + *cūra*, 'without the care', and *cūra*, through French, came to mean 'cure' in Middle English. In ecclesiastical language, *cūra* became the 'cure of souls', whence 'curate', one who cures souls (cf. French *curé*). So a 'sinecure' was a church office which paid a salary but did not involve the cure of souls. 'Secure' comes from *sē-* ('without') + *cūra*, 'without anxiety or care'; and *sēcūrus* became *seür* in Old French, whence English 'sure'. Late Latin *excūrō* 'I clean off' (classical Latin 'I take great care') becomes, by a circuitous route, 'scour'! 'Curious' comes from *cūra* too. Latin *cūriōsus* means 'full of cares', 'anxious about', and so also 'inquisitive': hence 'curiosity', and in abbreviated form 'curio'. 'Accurate' comes from *ad* + *cūrō* 'give care to'.

aequus and *equus*

Since classical *ae-* became *e-* in medieval Latin, the derivations of these two words are easily confused! *aequus* 'even', 'equal' gives all the 'equality' words (and through French 'egalitarian'). 'Equations', of course, are supposed to balance and the 'equator' equates, i.e. makes equal, the two halves of the earth. 'Equitable' means 'fair', and its negative gives 'iniquity'; *adaequāre* means 'I make truly level' (i.e. 'at a suitable level'), so 'adequate'. 'Equilibrium' is 'even balance' (*lībra* 'scales'), 'equanimity' is the state of a balanced *animus* or 'mind', and an 'equinox' occurs when night equals day.

Do not confuse with *equus* 'horse' (cf. *eques* 'cavalryman'), giving us 'equine', 'equestrianism' etc.

exercitus

An *exercitus* is a trained, controlled force. Latin *arceō* (*-erceō* in compounds) means 'keep close, confine; control, govern', and *ex-erceō* 'govern/train by practice', hence 'exercise'. *co-erceō* (= *cum* + *arceō*) means 'restrain within bounds', whence 'coerce'. *arca*, 'box', 'coffer', comes from the same root as *arceō*; *arcānus* means 'boxed in', 'closed in', whence 'arcane', meaning 'secret'.

Grammar and exercises for 2E

68   **Future indicative deponent (all conjugations)**

	1 'I shall threaten'	*2* 'I shall promise'	*3* 'I shall speak'
1st s.	miná-bo-r	pollicé-bo-r	lóqu-a-r
2nd s.	miná-be-ris (miná-be-re)	pollicé-be-ris (pollicé-be-re)	loqu-é-ris (loqu-é-re)
3rd s.	miná-bi-tur	pollicé-bi-tur	loqu-é-tur
1st pl.	miná-bi-mur	pollicé-bi-mur	loqu-é-mur
2nd pl.	miná-bí-minī	pollicē-bí-minī	loqu-é-minī
3rd pl.	miná-bú-ntur	pollicē-bú-ntur	loqu-é-ntur

	4 'I shall lie'	*3/4* 'I shall advance'
1st s.	ménti-a-r	prōgrédi-a-r
2nd s.	menti-é-ris (menti-é-re)	prōgredi-é-ris (progredi-é-re)
3rd s.	menti-é-tur	prōgredi-é-tur
1st pl.	menti-é-mur	prōgredi-é-mur
2nd pl.	menti-é-minī	prōgredi-é-minī
3rd pl.	menti-é-ntur	prōgredi-é-ntur

Notes

1 We noticed the close relationship between present deponent and present active forms at **58**. There is an equally close relationship between future deponent and future active forms (for which see **50**).

2 While in the 3rd and 4th conjs. the *-am, -ēs, -et* of the active becomes regularly *-ar, -ēris (-ēre), -ētur*, in the 1st and 2nd conjs., the active *-bō, bis, -bit* becomes *-bor, -beris (-bere), -bitur*. Cf. 3rd conj. presents (*loqu<u>or</u>, loqu-<u>eris</u>, loqu-<u>itur</u>*). Note in both the change of vowel *-i-* to *-e-* in 2nd s.

3 Observe the vowel length of the 2nd s. future of *loquor – loquēris*. Contrast the 2nd s. present – *loqueris*.

EXERCISES

1 *Conjugate the future of*: opīnor, cōnspicor, uideor, īrāscor, oblīuīscor, mentior, ēgredior, patior (*optional*: minor, precor, recordor, sequor, ingredior, suspicor).

2 *Translate and turn s. to pl. and vice versa*: opīnābor, mentiēris, precābitur, uidēbiminī, loquēris, pollicēbimur (*optional*: ingrediar, sequētur, uidēberis, cōnspicābuntur).

3 *Give the Latin for*: you (*s.*) will pray; she will threaten; they will seem; you (*pl.*) will talk; I shall advance; we shall think; they will try; he will follow.

4 *Turn the following presents into their future equivalents and translate*: minātur, precantur, opīnor, uidēminī, cōnspicātur, sequitur, loquuntur (*optional*: īrāsceris, mentīris, ēgredior, prōgrediminī, precāmur, patimur).

5 *Turn these futures into their present equivalents and translate*: arbitrāberis, cōnābitur, patientur, loquēminī, sequēmur, adgrediēris, morābor, opīnābimur, prōgrediēminī, uidēbitur, mentiar.

6 *Name the tenses of these verbs*: dedit, cōnāberis, mentītur, uidēbitur, fēcērunt, amant, dēlent, dīcent, loquēris, tulistī (*optional*: fert, erit, īrāscar, fuistis, timet, dūcet, potest, mānsī).

69   Genitive of value

The genitive case is used to express the value put on a person or thing, e.g. *homo nihilī* 'a man of nothing' i.e. 'of no value', 'worth nothing'; *tantī es quantī fungus* 'you are of such (value) as a mushroom' (lit. 'you are of such value as of what value (is) a mushroom').

EXERCISES

1 *Translate these sentences*:
  (a) propter Iouem Amphitruōnī Alcumēna nīl nisi mulier nihilī esse uidēbitur.
  (b) nisi mē iterum amplexāberis, tē nōn amplexābor hāc nocte.
  (c) quamquam Alcumēna uxor magnā fuit continentiā, Amphitruō illī nōn crēdidit.
  (d) sī longa uīta tua erit, malum longum accipiēs.
  (e) nihil cōnspicāberis nisi intrō ad uxōrem ingredī audēbis.

(f) quamquam īrātus fuī propter Iouis dolum, grātiās uxōrī meae agere mālam propter fīliōs ambō, alterum meī, Iouis alterum.

(g) quid est? uōcemne Iouis audīre possum? o mē miserum! fugiam, quia mē cōnspicābitur et īrāscētur.

2 Quotations

(a) *humilēs labōrant, ubi potentēs dissident.* (Phaedrus)

(b) *dīuīna nātūra dedit agrōs, ars hūmāna aedificāuit urbīs.* (Varro)

(c) *meminī enim, meminī neque umquam oblīuīscar noctis illīus.* (Cicero)

(d) *hīc, ubi nunc Rōma est, orbis caput, arbor et herbae*
      et paucae pecudēs et casa rāra fuit. (Ovid)

(e) *religiō peperit scelerōsa atque impia facta.* (Lucretius)

(f) *nēmo repente fuit turpissimus.* (Juvenal)

humil-is humil-is 3m. lowly person	*herb-a ae* 1f. grass
labōrō 1 I have a hard time	*pauc-ī ae a* a few
potēns potent-is 3m. powerful man	*pecus pecud-is* 3f. cattle
dissideō 2 I disagree	*cas-a ae* 1f. cottage, hovel
dīuīn-us a um divine	*rārus a um* few and far between,
nātūr-a ae 1f. nature	scattered
ager agr-ī 2m. field	*rēligiō rēligiōn-is* 3f. religion
ars, art-is 3f. art, skill	*pariō* 3/4 *peperī* I bring forth, cause
hūmān-us a um human	*scelerōs-us a um* wicked
aedificō 1 I build	*impi-us a um* impious
meminī I remember	*fact-um ī* 2n. deed
umquam ever	*nēmo* no one
oblīuīscor 3 dep. (+ gen.) I forget	*repente* suddenly
Rōm-a ae 1f. Rome	*turpissimus* (nom. m.) an utter
orb-is orb-is 3m. world	scoundrel
arbor arbor-is 3f. tree	

EITHER

Reading exercise / Test exercise

Below are given a number of main clauses ((a) – (f)) and a pool containing an equal number of subordinate clauses or phrases to complete them ((i) – (vi)). Read and translate each main clause, then, on the basis of sense, choose the subordinate clause which best fulfils your expectations.

(a) tibi haud crēdam …

(b) similis meī nōn es …

(c) hodie tē hominem nihilī arbitrābor …

(d) nolī mihi īrāscī …

(e) mālō tibi crēdere …

(f) uītam mihi trīstem faciēs, mī uxor …

(i) … quamquam mē sollicitās propter dolōs tuōs.

(ii) … nisi grātiās mihi agēs.

(iii)… quamquam sine dubiō uir summā uirtūte es.

(iv)… nisi mē tibi īrāscī uīs.

(v) … nisi mē tē amplexārī patiēris.

(vi)… quamquam similis esse uidēris.

OR

English–Latin

Translate into Latin:

(a) If you do not believe me, I shall be angry.

(b) Nothing bothers me except a lying wife.

(c) That man will seem to me to be worth as much as a wicked slave.

(d) I shall not embrace my wife, unless she dares [use future] to send that man from the house.

(e) At this time I can hear no voice but [= *nisi*] yours.

(f) Although death will not be bad [i.e. 'a bad thing'], all men prefer to pass [use *agō*] a long life.

OR

Read the text of 2E again carefully, then translate this passage:

AMPHITRUO: What shall I do? Although I love her and want to believe her, my wife is lying. She is a woman of no worth.

ALCUMENA: You must believe me, Amphitruo. Do not rebuke or threaten me. A wife never ought to lie to [her] husband.

AMPH.: Do not say that again! I shall grow angry; for this night, when I was not present with you, that man came to our house. Do you have two husbands?

ALC.: Be quiet! You are my husband and there is no other; and you came to our house! There can be no one like you!

AMPH.: You be quiet too! If I find [use future] that other husband, I promise this: his [of him] life will not be long. On account of [his] crimes, I shall send him to death!

Dēliciae Latīnae

Word exercise

Give the meaning and Latin connections of: vital, malicious, vociferous, castigate, solicitous, patience, mortal, accept, ingress.

Word-building

English suffixes

Note the common anglicisation of Latin suffixes (via French):

English	Latin	
-ry	*-ris, -rius, -ria*	
-an	*-ānus*	
-ious	*-ius*	'pertaining to'
-ic	*-icus*	
-ive	*-īuus*	
-able	*-ābilis*	'able to be'
-ible	*-ibilis*	
-ion	*-iō*	'action or result of action'
-ate, -ite	*-ātus, -itus*	
-ty	*-tās*	'quality, condition of'
-nce	*-ntia*	
-tude	*-tūdo*	

EXERCISE

Say what you can about the derivation and meaning of the following English words:

Adjectives: inaudible, irrevocable, military, captive, laudable, urban, scenic, nuptial, impecunious, filial, visible.

Nouns: fraternity, sorority, submission, nomination, audition, vicinity, admonition, station, visibility, vision, mission, longitude, instance (= *īnstō* I urge), arrogance (= *adrogō* I claim), fugitive.

Word study

forum

The *forum* was the legal and business centre of a town. *forum* yields the adjective *forēnsis* 'connected with the legal and business centre', hence English 'forensic', 'connected with the law'. *forestis* is a late Latin adjective often connected with *silua* 'a wood out of doors', whence 'forest'. From *forāneus* through Middle English *foreine* and Old French *forain* we eventually get 'foreign'.

70   *is ea id*: 'that', 'those', 'that person', 'he', 'she', 'it'

	s.			pl.		
	m.	f.	n.	m.	f.	n.
nom.	is	é-a	id	é-ī[1]	é-ae	é-a
acc.	é-um	é-am	id	é-ōs	é-ās	é-a
gen.	←— é-ius —→			é-órum	e-árum	e-órum
dat.	←— é-ī —→			←— é-īs[2] —→		
abl.	é-ō	é-ā	é-ō	←— é-īs[2] —→		

1. *éī* (nom. pl.) often becomes *īī*.
2. *éīs* often becomes *īīs*.

Notes

1 This word works in the same way as *hic, ille*. On its own, it means 'that man', 'that woman', 'that thing'; 'he', 'she', 'it' depending on gender and context; describing a noun it means 'that'. The difference between *is* and *ille* is that *is* = 'the one mentioned', while *ille* = 'that one over there I'm pointing to' or 'the former one as opposed to this one'.

In summary: *hic* = 'this one here', *ille* = 'that one there' and *is* = 'the one mentioned', cf. **64**[5].

2 Apart from *is, id, eius, eī* (cf. *illud huius, illīus, illī*), the word declines exactly like *mult-us a um* on the stem *e-*. This shows up most regularly in the pl.

71   **Accusative of time: 'throughout', 'for', 'during'**

Time 'for' or 'throughout' is expressed either by *per* + acc., or the plain acc. without any preposition at all; e.g. *per eam noctem* or *eam noctem* 'through that night', 'for that night'. Distinguish between the accusative and the plain ablative (**67**), which expresses time when or within which, e.g. *eā nocte* 'within that night', 'in that night'.

The accusative in time phrases may be graphically represented as a line ——; the ablative as a dot or as a point *within* a circle ⊙.

EXERCISES

1 *Decline in all cases s. and pl.*: id bellum; ea urbs; is pāstor.

2 *What case(s) and number are the following phrases in?* eius rēgis; eī exercitūs; eī uxōrī; iīs bellīs; eam uxōrem; eōrum nōminum; ea moenia; ea nox; eum annum; eōs mīlitēs.

3 *Give the Latin (using* is) *for*: (through) those days; that victory (acc. s.); of that war; for those kings; those shepherds (acc.); that war (nom./acc.); to that goddess; those customs (nom.); his; to them; hers; to him; to her; on that night.

4 *Say with which of the words in each line the given part of* is *agrees (where there is ambiguity, explain the alternatives)*:

>   eī: mīlitem, uirī, fēminae, exercituī, arbitrō, patrēs
>
>   eae: uxōrī, deae, noctis, uiās, rēs
>
>   ea: bella, Ītalia, uirtūs, sōl, urbs, capita, manus
>
>   eius: operis, arbitrī, reī, exercitūs, mōrēs, aedis
>
>   eīs: mīlitēs, signīs, gentibus, bellīs, uirīs, mōribus

5 *Translate*: in eō oppidō; propter eam uirtūtem; apud eōs; eō tempore; per eam uiam; cum eā; eā nocte; in eam urbem; eās hōrās; ad eōs mīlitēs; eam noctem; multōs diēs; eō annō; id tempus.

6 *Give the Latin for (using* is): with those women; at that hour; at his house; onto that stage; in those cities; because of those dangers; on those nights; on account of that war; over those hours.

7 *Replace the English word in these sentences with the appropriate form of* hic, ille *or* is, *and translate*:

(a) (These) fēminae pulchrae sunt.

(b) uidēsne (those) mīlitēs?

(c) satis (of that) bellī est.

(d) (That man's) caput ingēns est.

(e) turba (of those) mulierum ingreditur.

72   Comparative adjectives: *asper-ior ius* 'harsher'

Comparative adjectives carry the meanings 'more …', 'rather …', '—er', 'quite …', 'too …'; e.g. *asperior* 'harsher', 'quite harsh', 'rather harsh'.

Basic rule: look for the stem + *-ior-* and in the neuter s. + *-ius*.

	s.		*pl.*	
	m./f.	*n.*	*m./f*	*n.*
nom.	asper-ior	asper-ius	asper-iór-es	asper-iór-a
voc.	asper-ior	asper-ius	asper-iór-es	asper-iór-a
acc.	asper-iór-em	asper-ius	asper-iór-es	asper-iór-a
gen.	← asper-iór-is→		← asper-iór-um →	
dat.	← asper-iór-ī→		← asper-iór-ibus→	
abl.	← asper-iór-e→		← asper-iór-ibus→	

Notes

1 To form the comparative, take the gen. s. of the positive adjective, remove the ending (leaving you with the stem) and add the endings for the comparative as indicated above. E.g. *longus long-ī – longior*; *ingēns ingent-is – ingentior*; *audāx audāc-is – audācior*; *breuis breu-is – breuior*.

2 Comparatives have consonant stems. This accounts for abl. in *-e*, n. pl. in *-a*, gen. pl. in *-um*. Note *-ius* in nom. and acc. n. s.

3 The original ending of the comparative was *-ios* (which became the neuter *-ius*). Then the *s* of *ios* became *r* between vowels: so *longio*r*em,* not *longiosem*. For the original ending of the comparative, cf. Reference Grammar **E5 note 1** and **H3(d) note**.

4 Note the Latin for 'than', used very frequently with comparatives – *quam*. The thing being compared in the *quam* clause adopts the same case as the thing it is being compared with, e.g. 'Phaedra is more lovely than Euclio' – *Phaedra* (nom.) *pulchrior est quam Euclio* (nom.); 'I hold you more foolish than him' – *habeō tē stultiōrem quam illum*.

73   Superlative adjectives: *īrātissim-us a um* 'angriest'

Superlative adjectives carry the meanings '—est', 'most...' 'very...', 'extremely ...'; e.g. *īrātissimus* 'angriest', 'very angry', 'extremely angry'. Basic rule: look for *-ISSIM-* or *-ERRIM-*.

	s.		
	m.	*f.*	*n.*
nom.	īrāt-íssim-us	īrāt-íssim-a	īrāt-íssim-um
voc.	īrāt-íssim-e	īrāt-íssim-a	īrāt-íssim-um
acc.	īrāt-íssim-um	īrāt-íssim-am	īrāt-íssim-um
gen.	īrāt-íssim-ī	īrāt-íssim-ae	īrāt-íssim-ī
dat.	īrāt-íssim-ō	īrāt-íssim-ae	īrāt-íssim-ō
abl.	īrāt-íssim-ō	īrāt-íssim-ā	īrāt-íssim-ō

	pl.		
	m.	*f.*	*n.*
nom.	īrāt-íssim-ī	īrāt-íssim-ae	īrāt-íssim-a
voc.	īrāt-íssim-ī	īrāt-íssim-ae	īrāt-íssim-a
acc.	īrāt-íssim-ōs	īrāt-íssim-ās	īrāt-íssim-a
gen.	īrāt-issim-órum	īrāt-issim-árum	īrāt-issim-órum
dat.	← īrāt-íssim-īs →		
abl.	← īrāt-íssim-īs →		

Notes

1 These superlatives are again based on the gen. s. stem of the positive adjective, to which the endings *-issimus a um* (older spelling *-issumus*) are added, declining exactly like *multus*, e.g. *ingēns ingent-is → ingentissim-us a um*.

2 Adjectives ending in *-er* like *pulcher, celer, miser, asper* form their comparatives regularly (based on the stem of the gen. s.) but have superlatives in *-errimus a um*, e.g. *pulcher* (*pulchr-ī*) comp. *pulchrior*, sup. *pulcherrimus*; *celer* (*celer-is*) comp. *celerior*, sup. *celerrimus*; *miser* (*miser-ī*) comp. *miserior*, sup. *miserrimus*; *asper* (*asper-is*) comp. *asperior*, sup. *asperrimus*.

3 Two common irregular adjectives are *facilis, similis* (and their opposites *difficilis, dissimilis*). These have regular comparatives (*facilior, similior*), but irregular superlatives *facillimus, simillimus*. See Reference Grammar **J3**.

EXERCISE

Add the appropriate forms of both comparative and superlative degrees of the given adjective to the nouns:

> longus: diem, nocte
>
> celer: mīlitēs, oculō
>
> ingēns: aedēs, familiam
>
> pulcher: manūs, mulierum
>
> stultus: cōnsilia, hominī, operum
>
> asper: bellīs, annōrum, gentī

74   **Irregular comparatives and superlatives: *bonus, malus, multus, magnus, paruus***

bon-us a um	melior (meliōr-is)	optim-us a um	'good', 'better', 'best' (*cf. ameliorate, optimise*)
mal-us a um	pēior (pēiōr-is)	pessim-us a um	'bad', 'worse', worst' (*cf. pejorative, pessimist*)
mult-us a um	plūs (plūr-is)	plūrim-us a um	'much', 'more', 'most' (*cf. plus (+)*)
magn-us a um	māior (māiōr-is)	maxim-us a um	'big', 'bigger', 'biggest' (*cf. major, maximise*)
paru-us a um	minor (minōr-is)	minim-us a um	'small'/'few', 'smaller'/'fewer'/'less', 'smallest'/'fewest'/'least' (*cf. minor, minimise*)

These decline quite regularly (see *longior longissimus*) except for *plūs*:

	s.	pl.	
	(*plūs plūr-is* 3n., noun)	(*plūr-ēs plūr-a*, 3rd decl. adj.)	
	m./f./n.	m./f.	n.
nom.	plūs	plŭr-ēs	plŭr-a
acc.	plūs	plŭr-īs (plūrēs)	plŭr-a
gen.	plŭr-is	← plŭr-ium →	
dat.	—	← plŭr-ibus →	
abl.	plŭr-e	← plŭr-ibus →	

Notes

1 Note: abl. s. in *-e*, n. pl. in *-a*; and then gen. pl. in *-ium*. *plūs* is consonant stem, but *plūrēs* is *i*-stem (cf. **12**).

2 To express 'more of', Romans used in the s. *plūs* (the noun) + gen., and in the pl. the adjective *plūrēs*. So to express 'more ...' in the s., *plūs* + *gen.* 'more *of...*' is used (cf. *satis, nimis, quid?*), e.g. *plūs pecūni̱ae* 'more (of) money'. In the pl., *plūrēs* the adjective agrees with its noun, e.g. *plūrēs hominēs* 'more men'.

EXERCISES

Construct comparative and superlative of the following adjectives, giving their meanings when you have done so: ācer, fortis, bonus, niger, similis, magnus, celer, paruus, scelestus, stultus, malus, trīstis, facilis, multus, ingēns.

Reading exercises

1 *Read (translating in word-order) each of these incomplete sentences (all containing a comparative idea) and choose from the pool below them the correct phrase to complete them. Then translate into correct English.*

(a) noctem numquam uīdī longiōrem ...

(b) hic pāstor pulchrior est ...

(c) eī arbitrō aurī plūs dabō ...

(d) is uir māiōre uirtūte est ...

(e) seruum stultissimum mālō ...

(f) numquam bellum māius gerere poterō ...

(g) mīlitēs numquam fuērunt fortiōrēs ...

(h) fēminamne deae similiōrem umquam uīdistis ...?

(i) deāsne pulchriōrēs umquam cōnspicābor ...?

quam hic; quam hoc; quam hanc; quam huic; quam eās; quam illī; quam ille; quam mendācem; quam illam.

2   Quotations

(a) *posteriōrēs cōgitātiōnēs, ut aiunt, sapientiōrēs solent esse.* (Cicero)

(b) *nōn faciunt meliōrem equum aureī frēnī.* (Seneca)

(c) *uideō meliōra probōque, dēteriōra sequor.* (Ovid)

(d) *nūlla seruitūs turpior est quam uoluntāria.* (Seneca)

(e) *amā ratiōnem: huius tē amor contrā dūrissima armābit.* (Seneca)

poster-ior ius later	*seruitūs seruitūt-is* 3f. slavery
cōgitātiō cōgitātiōn-is 3f. thought	*turp-is e* base, degrading
aiō I say	*uoluntāri-us a um* voluntary, willing
sapiēns sapient-is wise	*ratiō ratiōn-is* 3f. reason
soleō 2 I am accustomed	*amor amōr-is* 3m. love
frēn-ī ōrum 2m. pl. bridle	*contrā* (+ acc.) against
probō 1 I approve	*dūr-us a um* hard, difficult
dēter-ior ius worse	*armō* 1 I arm, equip

EITHER

Reading exercise / Test exercise

Read this passage carefully, translating in word-order, defining the functions of words and the groups to which they belong, and stating at each point what you anticipate on the basis of the information you already have. Then translate into correct English. Finally, read out in Latin, phrasing correctly, thinking through the meaning as you read. Use the running vocabulary of **3A**.

ubi deae Iūnō, Venus, Minerua iūdicium Iouis dē pulchritūdine rogāuērunt, Iuppiter id eīs dare nōluit. nam eī omnēs pulcherrimae esse uidentur. 'Venus', dīxit eīs 'pulchrior nōn est quam Minerua, nec Iūnō pulchrior quam Venus et Minerua. sed iuuenis est, Paris nōmine. is pulchritūdinem uestram melius iūdicāre poterit quam ego.'   5

    deae igitur cum Mercuriō Īlium uēnērunt, ubi Paris domum habuit. Mercurius pāstōrī eī dīxit 'quis deārum hārum pulcherrima est? quis eārum plūs pulchritūdinis praestat?' respondit pāstor 'nōlī mē rogāre. omnēs pulcherrimae esse uidentur. eam deam nōn pulchriōrem habeō quam hanc aut illam.'

    Paris, quamquam deās iūdicāre nōn uult, cum eīs tamen loquitur. Iūnō eī 'tē 10 māiōrem faciam et plūs pecūniae tibi dabō.' Minerua eī 'tē fortiōrem faciam et in omnibus rēbus meliōrem.' Sed Venus eī 'tibi dabō uxōrem, Helenam, fēminam pulchriōrem quam omnīs mulierēs.'

    tum Paris Venerem pulcherrimam deārum iūdicāuit et mox Helenam, uxōrem futūram, domō dūxit.   15

OR

English–Latin

Translate into Latin:

(a) This victory was greater than that (one).

(b) In those years because of a rather stupid king, many very brave soldiers fought a very long war.

(c) There is nothing better than the duty of the best citizens.

(d) The wisdom of the gods is greater than (that) of men. (Miss out the second 'that'.)

(e) My brother is more like my father than me.

(f) Nothing is worse than this trouble.

OR

Read the text of **3A(ii)** *again, then translate this passage into Latin:*

Aeneas left Troy and came to Carthage. Carthage was a very rich city. But the gods wanted a better fate for him. He left Carthage and came to Italy, where he founded a city destined to be greater and more ferocious than Carthage. For many years he reigned in that city. Later his son put up the walls of a larger city. He reigned for thirty years. Then after three hundred years, Romulus founded the city of Rome, the greatest of all.

Dēliciae Latīnae

Word exercise

Give the Latin connections of: bellicose, judicial, regnal, pastoral, asperity, relinquish, equine, meditate, brevity.

Everyday Latin

The *ego* (and *superego*) and the *id* were terms used by Sigmund Freud to denote respectively the conscious and subconscious self

i.e. = *id est* 'that is'

An argument *ā fortiōrī* (alternative later form for the classical *fortiōre*) is one 'from a stronger case', e.g. 'Hercules cannot pick up this rock; *ā fortiōrī* a baby will not be able to.'

Other useful comparatives are *posterior* ('further behind'), *superior* ('higher'), *iūnior* ('younger' from *iuuenis*, cf. English 'junior'), *senior* ('older' from *senex*).

ē plūribus ūnum 'from rather many, one' – the motto on the Great
    Seal of the United States

An important principle of law is *dē minimīs nōn cūrat lēx* –
    meaning?

Preferring bad apples

Nineteenth-century Latin textbooks often used mnemonics to help pupils learn
difficult material. *mālō mālō malō malō* ('I prefer [to be] in an apple-tree
[than] a wicked person in trouble') was used by Benjamin Britten in his opera
The Turn of the Screw, for Miles' song: '*mālō* I would rather be, *mālō* in an
apple tree, *malō* than a naughty boy, *malō* in adversity'. The four words are all
spelled the same way, but the first two both have two long first vowels, while
the second two have short first vowels. By remembering this little verse, you
can distinguish between the words for 'I prefer' (*mālō*) and apple/apple-tree
(*mālum/mālus*, both of which have ablative in -*ō*) on the one side, and the words
for 'bad' (*malus*) and 'evil' (*malum*) on the other. The ablatives used here are (1)
mālō 'in an apple-tree' and *malō* 'in adversity': locative ablative (see Reference
Grammar **100A(2)**); (2) *malō* 'than a naughty boy': ablative of comparison (see
Reference Grammar **100B(1)**).

Word study

summus

summus means 'the top', 'highest point' and gives us 'to sum', i.e. calculate the
total of, since the Romans added columns of figures from the bottom up, till they
reached the *summa līnea* 'the top line'. Hence a 'sum', especially of money.
summārius is an accountant, one who does the sums, or sums up, whence English
'summary'. A 'summit' is the highest point of a hill. A 'consummation' is the
complete (*con-*) summing up, so a completion or achievement.

Do not confuse with 'summon' – from *submoneō* 'warn secretly' – or words
like 'consume', 'assume' from *sūmō* 'take up', 'take upon oneself', 'spend'.

fortis

fortis means 'strong' or 'brave'. The English 'force' derives ultimately from the n.
pl. of *fortis*, i.e. *fortia*. English derivatives include 'fort', 'fortify' and 'fortitude'.
They also include 'comfort' ('strengthen together' or 'strengthen considerably')
and 'effort' (through Old French *esfors*, 'forcing oneself out' (*es-* = Latin *ex-*)).

Grammar and exercises for 3B

75   **Perfect indicative deponent: 'I —ed', 'I have —ed'**

	1 'I threatened' / 'I have threatened'	*2* 'I promised' / 'I have promised'	*3* 'I spoke' / 'I have spoken'
1st s.	minất-us a um sum	pollícit-us a um sum	locū́t-us a um sum
2nd s.	minất-us a um es	pollícit-us a um es	locū́t-us a um es
3rd s.	minất-us a um est	pollícit-us a um est	locū́t-us a um est
1st pl.	minất-ī ae a súmus	pollícit-ī ae a súmus	locū́t-ī ae a súmus
2nd pl.	minất-ī ae a éstis	pollícit-ī ae a éstis	locū́t-ī ae a éstis
3rd pl.	minất-ī ae a sunt	pollícit-ī ae a sunt	locū́t-ī ae a sunt

	4 'I lied' / 'I have lied'	*3/4* 'I advanced' / 'I have advanced'
1st s.	mentī́t-us a um sum	prōgréss-us a um sum
2nd s.	mentī́t-us a um es	prōgréss-us a um es
3rd s.	mentī́t-us a um est	prōgréss-us a um est
1st pl.	mentī́t-ī ae a súmus	prōgréss-ī ae a súmus
2nd pl.	mentī́t-ī ae a éstis	prōgréss-ī ae a éstis
3rd pl.	mentī́t-ī ae a sunt	prōgréss-ī ae a sunt

Notes

1 *Formation of perfect stem*

(a) The perfect stem of the deponent is regularly formed by adding *-t-us a um* to the stem of the verb. Thus:

> 1st conj.: *minā-t-us a um*
>
> 2nd conj.: *pollici-t-us a um* (note that *-e* changes to *-i*)
>
> 4th conj.: *mentī-t-us a um*

Standing on its own, it forms the perfect participle and means 'having —ed' (see **77**), e.g. *minātus* 'having threatened' etc.

(b) You have now met the three 'principal parts' of deponent verbs, i.e. the present indicative active (e.g. *minor*), the infinitive (e.g. *minārī*) and the perfect (e.g. *minātus*). Of regular deponent verbs, the principal parts are formed as follows:

> 1: *minor minārī minātus*
>
> 2: *polliceor pollicērī pollicitus*
>
> 4: *mentior mentīrī mentītus*

These are the bases for forming *all parts of the deponent*, and must be learned from now on.

(c) As we found with non-deponent verbs, however, 3rd and 3rd/4th conj. deponent verbs are unpredictable in their formation of the perfect stem. Perfect stems of these verbs are formed in *-t-us a um* and *-s-us a um*. Here are the three 'principal parts' of the *irregular* deponents you have met so far (including one 2nd decl. verb):

> in *-s-us a um*

2   *uideor uidērī uīsus* 'I seem'

> 3/4   (*ad-*)
> (*ē-*)
> (*in-*)   } *gredior gredī gressus* 'I go', 'I come'
> (*prō-*)

patior patī passus 'I endure', 'I undergo', 'I suffer'

> in *-t-us a um*

3   (*ad-*)*loquor loquī locūtus* 'I speak (to)'

> *sequor sequī secūtus* 'I follow'
>
> *oblīuīscor oblīuīscī oblītus* 'I forget'
>
> *īrāscor īrāscī īrātus* 'I get angry'
>
> *adipīscor adipīscī adeptus* 'I gain', 'I get'
>
> *proficīscor proficīscī profectus* 'I set out'

2 *Formation of deponent perfect indicative*

To form the perfect indicative deponent, the perfect stem ending in *-us -a -um* (which means on its own 'having —ed') is combined with the appropriate part of *sum es est sumus estis sunt*, e.g. *locūtus sum* (lit.) 'I am (in a state of) having spoken', 'I spoke', 'I have spoken', 'I did speak'. Since the perfect stem ending in *-us a um* acts as an adjective, it must *agree with the subject*, e.g.:

> 'I (= a woman) spoke' *locūta sum*
>
> 'they (= the men) promised' *pollicitī sunt*
>
> 'the boy lied' *puer mentītus est*
>
> 'you (= the women) set out' *profectae estis*

The perfect stem in *-us a um* will be in the *nominative*, since it is agreeing with the subject of the sentence.

3 *Meaning*

The meaning, literally 'I am (in a state of) having —ed', can be treated as identical with 'I —ed', 'I have —ed' and (in certain cases) 'I am —' – a present state which results from a past action.

76   Semi-deponents: *audeō* and *fīō*

A number of verbs, called 'semi-deponents', adopt *active forms* in some tenses, and *deponent forms* in others. Of the tenses you have met so far, present and future forms of such verbs are active in form; the perfects, however, are deponent in form. Thus:

***audeō* 'I dare'; *audēre* 'to dare' (no perfect active stem); *ausus* 'having dared'**

	Present	*Future*	*Perfect*
1st s.	aúde-ō 'I dare'	audé-b-ō 'I shall dare'	aús-us a um sum 'I dared' *etc.*
2nd s.	aúdē-s	audé-bi-s	aús-us a um es
3rd s.	aúde-t	audé-bi-t	aús-us a um est
1st pl.	audé-mus	audé-bi-mus	aús-ī ae a súmus
2nd pl.	audé-tis	audé-bi-tis	aús-ī ae a éstis
3rd pl.	aúde-nt	audé-bu-nt	aús-ī ae a sunt

***fīō* 'I become', 'I am made', 'I happen'; *fierī* 'to become, be made' (no perfect active stem); *factus* 'having become', 'having been made'**

	Present	*Future*	*Perfect*
1st s.	fī-ō 'I become' *etc.*	fī-a-m 'I shall become' *etc.*	fáct-us a um sum 'I became' *etc.*
2nd s.	fī-s	fī-ē-s	fáct-us a um es
3rd s.	fī-t	fī-e-t	fáct-us a um est
1st pl.	—[1]	fī-é-mus	fáct-ī ae a súmus
2nd pl.	—[1]	fī-é-tis	fáct-ī ae a éstis
3rd pl.	fī-u-nt	fī-e-nt	fáct-ī ae a sunt

1. *fīmus* and *fītis* are not found.

116

EXERCISES

1   *Form and conjugate the perfect of*: meditor, cōnor, uideor, oblīuīscor, proficīscor, mentior, prōgredior, patior (*optional*: cōnspicor, adipīscor, polliceor, hortor, sequor, recordor, ēgredior, īrāscor).

2   *Translate each perfect then change s. to pl. and vice versa*: locūtus sum; uīsum est; recordāta est; mentītī sumus; ingressae sunt, pollicita es; secūta sunt; adeptus est (*optional*: īrāta est; oblītus sum; passa es; profectus est; meditātī estis; arbitrātī sunt; suspicātae sunt).

3   *Say what verbs these perfects come from and translate*: uīsus est; adepta est; oblītus sum; ingressae sumus; locūtī estis; profectī sunt; factum est.

4   *Give the Latin for*: she has threatened; they (*m.*) set out; I (*m.*) have encouraged; you (*s. f.*) seemed; we (*f.*) forgot; he promised; it happened; you (*pl. m.*) have lied.

5   *Give 3rd s. and pl. present, future and perfect of these verbs and translate*: īrāscor, minor, polliceor, mentior, patior (*optional*: proficīscor, ingredior, uideor, fīō, recordor).

77   ### Perfect participles deponent: 'having —ed'

A participle is an *adjective* which derives from a *verb* and shares the nature of both ('participle' derives from *pars* and *capiō* 'take a share/part in').

In English, it tends to be formed in '—ing' or 'having —ed', e.g. 'I saw the man <u>running</u>', 'the men, <u>having departed</u>, reached home'.

The perfect stem of deponent verbs ending in -*us a um* is the *perfect participle* and means 'having —ed', e.g. *minātus* 'having threatened', *locūtus* 'having spoken', *ēgressus* 'having gone out'.

These perfect participles decline like *mult-us a um* and, like any adjectives, agree with the person described as 'having —ed', e.g. 'Rhea Silvia, <u>having spoken</u>, goes out' *Rhea Siluia <u>locūta</u> ēgreditur*, 'Romulus and Remus, <u>having spoken</u>, go out' *Rōmulus Remusque <u>locūtī</u> ēgrediuntur*, 'I see the boys <u>having-gone-out</u> / the boys <u>when they have gone out</u>' *puerōs <u>ēgressōs</u> uideō*.

Participles are on the whole used predicatively, i.e. they say what people *do* rather than *describe* or *define* people. Thus *Rhea locūta ēgreditur* should be translated 'Rhea – after speaking / having spoken / when she has spoken / speaks and – goes out'. It is not accurate to translate it 'the woman *who has spoken* goes out'. See 'predicative', p. xxii. See further Reference Grammar **C4** note 2.

EXERCISE

Give the meaning of these words and say from what verb each comes: locūtus, profectus, adeptus, īrātus, nātus, cōnātus, precātus, ortus, suspicātus, pollicitus, ēgressus, factus (*optional*: arbitrātus, opīnātus, mentītus, secūtus, passus, hortātus, uīsus, adgressus).

78   **Translating participles**

Deponent participles can, of course, control their own little clauses (and sometimes not so little), in the same way that infinitives do. Observe how infinitives and some direct objects in the following sentences depend on the participle, not on the main verb:

> *custōdēs fugere cōnātōs necāuimus* 'we killed the guards
>   having-tried to escape', '... the men after they had tried to
>   escape' (*fugere* depends on *cōnātōs*)
>
> *mulierēs hoc locūtās nōn amō* 'I do not like the women having-said /
>   since they said this'
>
> *mīlitēs, multa minātī, ēgrediuntur* 'the soldiers, having threatened
>   much, depart'

Observe the way in which the participles in such complex sentences gravitate towards the end of their clause, in the same way that main verbs and infinitives tend to. Often this results in a pleasing 'bracketing' effect rather like an equation, especially when the participle has a direct object, e.g. 'The priest, seeing the horse galloping down the street, gave chase.' A typical Latin order for this would be: 'The priest (nom.), the horse (acc.) down the street galloping (acc.) seeing (nom.), gave chase.'

EXERCISES

1 *Translate these sentences*:
   (a) Rōmulus rēgnum adeptus est.
   (b) Rōmulus et Remus, cīuīs adlocūtī, deum Martem inuocāuērunt.
   (c) uirgō grauida facta est.
   (d) uirginēs, ad urbem adgressae, coniugēs factae sunt.
   (e) spectāculum magnum in urbe factum est.
   (f) fundāmenta urbis Rōmae, custōdem adepta, salua fuērunt.

2 *Translate these sentences*:
   (a) Rōmulus, custōdem adlocūtus, fundāmenta urbis seruāre iussit.
   (b) frāter Rōmulī, mūrōs minimōs cōnspicātus, irrīsit.
   (c) custōs frātrem Rōmulī fundāmenta minima cōnspicātum secūtus est.
   (d) is frātrī mūrōs cōnspicātō hoc dīxit: 'nōlī fundāmenta trānsīre.'

(e) ille autem custōdis hoc locūtī uerba irrīsit et, ad fundāmenta adgressus, trānsīre stultē ausus est.

(f) custōs igitur, uerba Rōmulī secūtus, frātrem eius hoc stultē ausum, interfēcit.

Practice in English

Select subject, verb, adjective and participle in these sentences:

(a) She writhed about, convulsed with scarlet pain. (Keats)

(b) Naked she lay, clasped in my longing arms. (Rochester)

(c) I saw three ships go sailing by on Christmas day. (*Do you place 'on Christmas day' with the 'I saw' clause or the 'go sailing by' clause?*)

(d) … Know you not,
Being mechanical, you ought not walk
Upon a labouring day…?
(Shakespeare)

(e) See! from the Brake the whirring Pheasant springs,
And mounts exulting on triumphant Wings:
Short is his Joy; he feels the fiery Wound,
Flutters in Blood, and panting beats the Ground.
(Pope)

79   Regular and irregular adverbs

A common way of forming adverbs in English is to add '-ly' to an adjective (e.g. 'slow-ly','quick-ly', 'passionate-ly'). In Latin, adverbs (which never change their form) are also regularly formed from adjectives, as follows:

Adverbs based on 1st/2nd declension adjectives: add *-ē* to the stem, e.g. *stultus – stultē* 'foolishly'; *miser – miserē* 'unhappily'; *pulcher – pulchrē* 'beautifully'. A very few end in *-ter*.

Adverbs based on 3rd declension adjectives: add *-(i)ter* to the stem, e.g. *fortis – fortiter* 'bravely'; *audāx – audācter* 'boldly'; *celer – celeriter* 'swiftly'. But note an important exception: *facile* 'easily'.

Here are some irregularly formed adverbs:

> *bonus – bene* 'well'
>
> *paruus – paulum* '(a) little', 'slightly'
>
> *multus – multum* 'much'
>
> *magnus – magnopere* 'greatly' (= *magnō* + *opere*)

NB *longē* (regularly formed from *longus* 'long') 'far'.

EXERCISES

1 *Identify and translate the adverbs in this list*: hōrum, uariē, audācter, mulier, malum, multae, male, līberī, bene, omne, laetē, magnopere, multum, scelere, pater, celeriter, pulchrē, proelium, paulum, benīgnē.

2 *Form adverbs from these adjectives and translate*: stultus, bonus, fortis, benīgnus, longus, similis, saeuus, laetus, magnus, celer, multus, miser, uarius.

3 *The Roman literary critic Quintilian here lists the sorts of styles an orator will need to develop to suit all occasions. Translate*:

dicet ... grauiter, seuērē, ācriter, uehementer, concitātē, cōpiōsē, amārē, cōmiter, remissē, subtīliter, blandē, lēniter, dulciter, breuiter, urbānē.

grauis serious	*remissus* gentle
seuērus stern	*subtīlis* precise
concitātus passionate	*blandus* flattering
amārus bitter	*lēnis* kind
cōmis affable	*urbānus* witty

80 *sē; su-us a um*

So far you have met *ego* 'I' (pl. *nōs* 'we'), *tu* (pl. *uōs* 'you') and their possessive forms *meus* 'mine', *tuus* 'your(s)', *noster* 'our(s)', *uester* 'your(s)'. But we have not yet fully grappled with the reflexive forms for 'him, her, it, them' and their possessive forms 'his, her(s), its, their(s)'.

Latin makes an important distinction between reflexive usage of such words (which means that the 'him, her' etc. being referred to is the same person as the subject of the clause) and non-reflexive (when the 'him, her' etc. being referred to is not the same person as the subject of the clause).

When Latin uses a form of *sē*, the 'him, her, it, them' being referred to is the same person as the subject of the verb of the particular clause.

Likewise, when Latin uses a form of *su-us a um*, the person referred to in the 'his, her(s), their(s)' is the same as the subject of the verb, e.g.:

> *Siluia sē adloquitur* 'Silvia addresses (*sē* must = Silvia) herself.'
>
> *Siluia eam adloquitur* 'Silvia addresses (*eam* cannot be Silvia) her (i.e. someone else).'
>
> *Rōmulus lēgātōs suōs mīsit* 'Romulus sent (*suōs* must refer to Romulus) his own (i.e. no one else's) officials.'
>
> *Rōmulus lēgātōs eius mīsit* 'Romulus sent (*eius* must refer to someone else) his [someone else's] officials.'

sē declined

	s./pl.
nom.	—
acc.	sē
gen.	súī
dat.	síbi
abl.	sē

NB The forms are the same for s. and pl. and all genders. Reference to the subject of the verb will tell you whether to translate s. or pl., m., f. or n.

su-us a um

This possessive adjective 'his', 'hers', 'its', 'theirs' declines like *mult-us a um*.

EXERCISE

Translate into English:
(a) Rōmulus, sē adlocūtus, 'sī Rōmānī' inquit 'coniugēs sibi habēre uolunt, cōnsilium prō eīs capere dēbēbimus.'
(b) is igitur in urbe suā spectāculum fēcit.
(c) ad eius spectāculum multae mulierēs sē ferre uoluērunt.
(d) Rōmulus sibi dīxit: 'nunc uirī Rōmānī coniugēs sibi rapere poterunt.'
(e) ubi tempus eius spectāculī uēnit, Rōmānī uirginēs celeriter rapuērunt et eās coniugēs suās fēcērunt.

Reading exercises

1 *As you translate in word-order, determine the limits of the participle phrase in each of these sentences and say what function it has in the sentence (i.e. agreeing with and describing subject, object, indirect object etc.) Then translate into correct English, finally returning to the Latin to read it out correctly phrased. E.g.* hanc praedam adeptī domum regressī sunt. *Participle phrase:* hanc ... adeptī: *agreeing with subject.* 'When they had obtained this booty, they returned home'. *Read out with a comma pause after* adeptī.

(a) Amūlius Martis fīliōs magnopere ueritus necāre uoluit.
(b) rēx paulum morātus eōs in flūmen mīsit.
(c) puerōs autem in flūmen ingressōs deus flūminis seruāuit.
(d) pāstor Rōmulum et Remum ē flūmine ēgressōs domum suum dūxit.
(e) geminī uirī factī Amūlium occīdērunt.

121

2 *Read these participle phrases, translating in word-order, and decide their*
   function in the sentence (NB there are no ablatives). Then pair each with the
   correct ending from the list below. Finally, having translated into correct
   English, read aloud in Latin, phrasing correctly, and thinking through the
   meaning as you read.

   (a) puerīs in flūmen ingressīs …

   (b) lēgātos haec uerba locūtōs …

   (c) geminōrum ē flūmine profectōrum …

   (d) eīs mulieribus patrēs domum secūtīs …

   (e) Remum ad mūrōs nouae urbis trānsīre ausum …

           (i) Rōmulus minātus est.

           (ii) Amūlius mortem minātus est.

           (iii) Celer necāuit.

           (iv) uītam pāstor seruāuit.

           (v) mīlitēs secūtī sunt.

3 Quotations

(a) *nōn uīuere bonum est, sed bene uīuere.* (Seneca)

(b) *nēmo togam sūmit nisi mortuus.* (Juvenal)

(c) *multōrum opēs praepotentium exclūdunt amīcitiās fidēlīs: nōn enim*
     sōlum ipsa fortūna caeca est, sed eōs etiam plērumque efficit caecōs quōs
     complexa est. (Cicero)

uīuō 3 I live	*nōn sōlum … sed etiam* not only … but also
tog-a ae 1f. toga	*ipsa* herself (nom. s. f.)
sūmō 3 I put on	*fortūn-a ae* 1f. fortune
morior 3/4 dep. *mortuus* I die	*caec-us a um* blind
op-ēs op-um 3f. pl. wealth	*plērumque* generally
praepotēns praepotent-is 3m. very powerful man	*efficiō* 3/4 I make X (acc.) Y (acc.)
exclūdō 3 I exclude, prevent	*quōs* (acc. pl. m.) whom
amīciti-a ae 1f. friendship	*complector* 3 dep. *complexus* I embrace
fidēl-is e loyal, faithful	

EITHER

Reading exercise / Test exercise

Read this passage carefully, translating in word-order, determining as you go
the function of the words met and the groups in which they should be phrased and

stating what each new item makes you anticipate. Translate into correct English, then read aloud in Latin, phrasing correctly, thinking through the meaning as you read.

Rōmulus in lūcum omnīs inuītāuit. multōs hominēs in lūcum ingressōs Rōmulus cīuīs Rōmānōs fēcit. sed nūllae mulierēs domō profectae in lūcum sē tulērunt. lēgātī ex urbe prōgressī aliās urbēs coniugēs rogāuērunt. nūlla autem urbs benīgnē lēgātīs ex urbe nouā profectīs respondit. Rōmulus igitur paulum meditātus ad spectāculum uīcīnōs uocāuit. Rōmam multae uirginēs gentis Sabīnae profectae   5
sunt. sed ubi tempus spectāculī uēnit, uirginēs Rōmam ingressās iuuenēs Rōmanī celeriter et audācter rapuērunt. nam cōnūbium adeptī līberōs ex mulieribus Sabīnīs habēre uoluērunt. patrēs tamen uirginum Sabīnārum, multum minātī, Rōmānīs maximē īrātī sunt. sed uirginēs, cōnūbium passae, coniugēs Rōmānōrum factae sunt. sīc ex maximō malō grātia maxima orta est.   10

OR

English–Latin

In both these exercises, use participles and participial phrases rather than subordinate clauses.

Translate into Latin:

(a) Having grown very angry, the king threatened the twins.

(b) But when the boys had entered the river, a shepherd saved them.

(c) Romulus and Remus, having spoken boldly to the Roman citizens, dared to build the foundations of a new city.

(d) Romulus threatened death to citizens if they had dared to cross the new foundations.

(e) Remus, having seen the very small walls of the future Rome, became bold.

(f) When Remus tried to cross the walls, the guardian killed him.

OR

*Read through the text of **3B** again and then translate this passage:*

Many men betook themselves to the grove. But no woman dared to come to that grove. Romulus, after thinking for a short time, sent ambassadors to the neighbouring cities. These ambassadors, after speaking for a long time, asked the neighbours for marriages. The neighbours, however, fearing the future power of the Romans, did not respond kindly. But the Romans invited their neighbours to a show. When many unmarried girls had entered the city, the Roman youths boldly snatched them away and married them.

Dēliciae Latīnae

Word-building

The prefix *dī-* or *dis-* (or *dif-*) means 'apart', 'asunder', 'not' (occasionally 'exceedingly'), e.g.

> *distō* 1 'I stand apart' (cf. 'distant')
>
> *dissideō* 'I sit apart' (i.e. disagree) (cf. 'dissident')
>
> *differō* 'I scatter', 'I differ'

sē- as a prefix means 'apart', 'without', e.g. *sēcūrus* 'free from worry', *sēdūcō* 'I lead aside, astray', *sēditiō* 'a going (*eō*, *it-*) apart', *sēdulus* 'aside from tricks' (*dolus* 'trick'), *sēcrētus* 'separated apart' (cf. English 'secret' – something set apart; hence 'a secretary' deals with confidentialities). This *sē-* has nothing to do with *sē* reflexive.

Word exercise

Give the meaning and discuss the Latin connections of: various, spectacle, edifice, custodian, fundamental, mural, martial, nascent, puerile, transit, amorous, benign, celerity, conjugal, *ex gratia* payment, image, populate, fratricide, suicide (last two words: -cid- comes from a simple form of the verb *caedō* 'I kill').

Everyday Latin

> *per sē* 'through itself', 'because of its own nature'

Word study

castrum

castrum in the s. means a fortified post or settlement, in the pl. a camp. The '-caster', '-cester', '-chester' endings to the names of towns indicate 'camp' e.g. Lancaster, Worcester, Manchester and Chester. *castrum* has a diminutive *castellum*, whence 'castle' and in French *château* (a French circumflex accent often indicates a 'hidden' *s*; cf. Latin *fenestra* 'window', French *fenêtre*). Newcastle upon Tyne was so called because it had a *Novum Castellum* built by William Rufus in 1080.

castrum may be akin to *castrō*, 'I cut', i.e. *castrum* = 'a place cut off', 'entrenchment'. If so, *castrum* and English 'castrate' have similar origins!

sequor

sequor 'I follow' has a present participle *sequēns* 'following' and perfect participle *secūtus* 'having followed'. From these we get 'sequel' and 'sequence' and through the French *suivre* a 'suit', hence 'suitor', one who pursues a marriage partner, and 'sue', to chase someone at law. 'Pursue' derives from *prōsequor* (French *poursuivre*). *cōnsequor* 'I follow all together', gives 'consecutive' and 'consequence', *exsequor* 'I follow out' gives 'execute' in the sense of 'carry out' or 'judicially put to death'. *obsequor* 'I follow on account of / in accordance with the wishes of' gives 'obsequious', while *persequor* 'I follow thoroughly' gives 'persecute'. *subsequor* 'I follow under', hence to succeed (as in a list), gives 'subsequent'.

Grammar and exercises for 3C

81 **Future participles, active and deponent: 'about to / on the point of –ing'**

Future participles of both deponent *and* active verbs are always active in *meaning*. They mean 'about to —', 'on the point of —ing', 'intending to —', and are formed by adding *-ūrus a um* to the stem of the perfect participle, e.g. *minātūrus* 'about to threaten', *amātūrus* 'about to love' etc. As with deponent perfect participles, these forms are *adjectives* and must agree in person, number and gender with the person 'about to ...', e.g. *locūtūra* (fem.) *est* 'she is about to speak'; *ēgressūrī sunt* 'they are about to go out'; *eōs prōgressūrōs uideō* 'I see them on the point of advancing'. Note the clue to form in the word 'fut<u>ur</u>e' – giving you *-ūr-us*.

82 **The 4th principal part (perfect participle) of active verbs**

You have already met three principal parts of active verbs, i.e. the dictionary form, the present infinitive and the perfect indicative (e.g. *amō, amāre, amāuī*; *habeō, habēre, habuī* etc.). The perfect participle of 1st, 2nd and 4th conjugation verbs is formed as follows:

Regular principal parts

	Present indicative	Present infinitive	Perfect indicative	Perfect participle passive
1st conj.	ámō	amáre	amā́uī	amā́-t-us a um
2nd conj.	hábeō	habḗre	hábuī	hábi-t-us a um
4th conj.	aúdiō	audī́re	audī́uī	audī́-t-us a um

Notes

1 As you can see, the perfect participle is regularly formed by adding *-t-us a um* to the stem: *amā-t-us, audī-t-us* etc. Note *habi-t-us* (*-e-* changes to *-i-*). Thus the future participles of the three regular conjugations will be *amāt-ūr-us a um, habit-ūr-us a um, audīt-ūr-us a um*.

2 The meaning of this participle on its own is 'having been —ed', e.g. *amātus* 'having been loved'. Cf. **77** for deponent and semi-deponent participles, which, as we have seen, mean 'having —ed'. The perfect participle meaning 'having been —ed' will not be met properly till **119**.

EXERCISES

1 *Translate these future participles and say what verb each is from*: intrātūrus, clāmātūrus, factūrus, interfectūrus, habitūrus, relictūrus, monitūrus, mānsūrus, audītūrus, mentītūrus, ēgressūrus, ductūrus, captūrus (*optional*: suspicātūrus, reditūrus, locūtūrus, datūrus, rogātūrus, precātūrus, dictūrus, dēfēnsūrus, raptūrus, trānsitūrus, dēlētūrus, solūtūrus, passūrus).

2 *Say which in this list are future participles and which past*: raptūrō, locūtae, āctūrīs, inuentūrī, secūtās, ēgressūra, acceptūrōrum, futūra, morātūrum, gestūrum, nūntiātūrōs, suspicātus, uictūram, hortātōs, relictī.

3 *Give the Latin for*: about to go; on the point of making; intending to defend; about to give back; on the point of snatching; about to place; about to see; intending to kill; intending to found.

83   **Unpredictable principal parts**

The principal parts of all 3rd and 3rd/4th conj. verbs are best treated as unpredictable, and need to be learned. Note, however, that stem + *-tus* (sometimes + *-sus*) is one pattern, e.g. *dīc-ō dic-tus*. Here are the full principal parts of the active verbs of these conjugations which you have learned so far, plus four new and important verbs (*legō* 'I read', *moueō* 'I move', *praesum* (+ dat.) 'I am in charge of', *scrībō* 'I write'), plus those of irregular 1st, 2nd and 4th conj. verbs. Note that where the verb is intransitive, the so-called 'supine' ending in *-um* (**118** note 2) is given. A hyphen will be used for verbs lacking a supine.

The verbs are listed alphabetically, and the section where you learned the word originally is also given for ease of reference. We have included here some verbs learned in section **3D**.

Present	Infinitive	Perfect	4th p.p.	Meaning
abeō	*abīre*	*abiī*	*abitum*	I go away, leave **1C**
accipiō	*accipere*	*accēpī*	*acceptus*	I receive, welcome, learn, obtain **2E**
adeō	*adīre*	*adiī*	*aditum*	I approach, go to **1C**
adgredior	*adgredī*		*adgressus*	I approach **2B**
adipīscor	*adipīscī*		*adeptus*	I gain, get **2B**
adloquor	*adloquī*		*adlocūtus*	I address, talk to **2B**
adsum	*adesse*	*adfuī*	*adfutūrus*	I am present with (+ dat.) **(2D) (3D(iv))**
agō	*agere*	*ēgī*	*āctus*	I do, act **2B**
āmitt-ō	*āmittere*	*āmīsī*	*āmissus*	I lose **1F**
audeō	*audēre*		*ausus*	I dare **2E**
auferō	*auferre*	*abstulī*	*ablātus*	I take away **1F**
capiō	*capere*	*cēpī*	*captus*	I take, capture **2A**

caueō	*cauēre*	*cāuī*	*cautum*	I am wary **2B**
cognōscō	*cognōscere*	*cognōuī*	*cognitus*	I get to know, examine **2B**
cond-ō	*condere*	*condidī*	*conditus*	I found **3A(ii)**
coqu-ō	*coquere*	*coxī*	*coctus*	I cook **1F**
crēdō	*crēdere*	*crēdidī*	*crēditus*	I believe (+ dat.); I entrust X (acc.) to Y (dat.) **1G**
dēcipiō	*dēcipere*	*dēcēpī*	*dēceptus*	I deceive **2A**
dēdō	*dēdere*	*dēdidī*	*dēditus*	I surrender **3D(v)**
dēdūcō	*dēdūcere*	*dēdūxī*	*dēductus*	I lead away, down **2B**
dēfendō	*dêfendere*	*dēfendī*	*dēfēnsus*	I defend **2C**
dēleō	*dēlēre*	*dēlēuī*	*dēlētus*	I destroy **2D**
dīcō	*dīcere*	*dīxī*	*dictus*	I speak, say **1D**
dō	*dare*	*dedī*	*datus*	I give **1B**
dūcō	*dūcere*	*dūxī*	*ductus*	I lead **1D**
ēgredior	*ēgredī*		*ēgressus*	I go/come out **2B**
eō	*īre*	*iī*	*itum*	I go, come **1C**
exeō	*exīre*	*exiī*	*exitum*	I go out, leave **1C**
faciō	*facere*	*fēcī*	*factus*	I make, do **1E**
ferō	*ferre*	*tulī*	*lātus*	I bear, lead **1E**
fīō	*fierī*		*factus*	I become, am done, am made **2D**
fugiō	*fugere*	*fūgī*	*fugitum*	I escape, run off, flee **1F**
gerō	*gerere*	*gessī*	*gestus*	I do, conduct **2D**
ine-ō	*inīre*	*iniī*	*initum*	I enter, go in **1F**
ingredior	*ingredī*		*ingressus*	I enter **2E**
inquam		*inquiī*		I say (*inquam inquis inquit*, 3 pl. *inquiunt*) **2D**
īnspiciō	*īnspicere*	*īnspexī*	*īnspectus*	I look into; inspect, examine **2B**
interficiō	*interficere*	*interfēcī*	*interfectus*	I kill, murder **3B(i)**
inueniō	*inuenīre*	*inuēnī*	*inuentus*	I find **1F**
īrāscor	*īrāscī*		*īrātus*	I grow angry **2C**
irrīdeō	*irrīdēre*	*irrīsī*	*irrīsus*	I laugh at, mock **1E**
iubeō	*iubēre*	*iussī*	*iussus*	I order, command, tell **1D**
legō	*legere*	*lēgī*	*lēctus*	I read
loquor	*loquī*		*locūtus*	I talk, speak, say **2B**
maneō	*manēre*	*mānsī*	*mānsum*	I remain, wait **1C**
mittō	*mittere*	*mīsī*	*missus*	I send **1F**
morior	*morī*		*mortuus*	I die **3C(ii)**
moueō	*mouēre*	*mōuī*	*mōtus*	I move
nāscor	*nāscī*		*nātus*	I am born **3B(i)**
oblīuīscor	*oblīuīscī*		*oblītus*	I forget **2A**

obstō	*obstāre*	*obstitī*	*(obstātum)*	I stand in the way of, obstruct, hinder (+dat.) **3D(iv)**
occido	*occidere*	*occidī*	*occāsum*	I fall down; die **1E**
occīdō	*occīdere*	*occīdī*	*occīsus*	I kill **3A(ii)**
opprimō	*opprimere*	*oppressī*	*oppressus*	I surprise, catch; crush **2C**; press down (on) **3C(ii)**
orior	*orīrī*		*ortus*	I arise, begin **3B(ii)**
ostendō	*ostendere*	*ostendī*	*ostēnsus* (or *ostentus*)	I show, reveal **1G**
patior	*patī*		*passus*	I endure, suffer; allow **2E**
pereō	*perīre*	*periī*	*peritum*	I perish **1E**
perficiō	*perficere*	*perfēcī*	*perfectus*	I finish, complete; carry out **2B**
pergō	*pergere*	*perrēxī*	*perrēctum*	I proceed, continue **2A**
pōnō	*pōnere*	*posuī*	*positus*	I set up, place **3A(ii)**
poscō	*poscere*	*poposcī*	-	I demand **1E**
possideō	*possidēre*	*possēdī*	*possessus*	I have, hold, possess **1B**
praesum	*praedesse*	*praefuī*	*praefutūrus*	I am in charge of (+ dat.)
proficīscor	*proficīscī*		*profectus*	I set out **2B**
prōgredior	*prōgredī*		*prōgressus*	I advance **2B**
prōmittō	*prōmittere*	*prōmīsī*	*prōmissus*	I promise **1E**
prōtegō	*prōtegere*	*prōtexī*	*prōtectus*	I protect **3D(v)**
rapiō	*rapere*	*rapuī*	*raptus*	I seize, snatch away **3B(ii)**
reddō	*reddere*	*reddidī*	*redditus*	I return, give back **1G**
redeō	*redīre*	*rediī*	*reditum*	I return **1C**
relinquō	*relinquere*	*relīquī*	*relictus*	I leave, abandon **3A(ii)**
respondeō	*respondēre*	*respondī*	*respōnsum*	I reply **2B**
scrībō	*scrībere*	*scrīpsī*	*scrīptus*	I write
sequor	*sequī*		*secūtus*	I follow **2B**
sinō	*sinere*	*sīuī*	*situs*	I allow, permit **2C**
soluō	*soluere*	*soluī*	*solūtus*	I release, undo **2D**
stō	*stāre*	*stetī*	*stātum*	I stand **1C**
tangō	*tangere*	*tetigī*	*tāctus*	I touch, lay hands on **1G**
teneō	*tenēre*	*tenuī*	*tentus*	I hold **3C(iii)**
trānseō	*trānsīre*	*trānsiī*	*trānsitus*	I cross **3B(i)**
ueniō	*uenīre*	*uēnī*	*uentum*	I come **3A(i)**
uideō	*uidēre*	*uīdī*	*uīsus*	I see **1B**
uideor	*uidērī*		*uīsus*	I seem **2C**
uinciō	*uincīre*	*uīnxī*	*uīnctus*	I bind **2A**
uincō	*uincere*	*uīcī*	*uictus*	I conquer **2D**
uīuō	*uīuere*	*uīxī*	*uīctum*	I live **3C(i)**

129

Notes

1 Dictionaries show all 4th principal parts ending in -*um* (called the 'supine', see **118**[2]). We show them differently in order to distinguish transitive verbs, whose 4th principal part means 'having been -ed', from intransitive verbs, which have only impersonal passive forms in the perfect tenses (**160**).

2 As you attempt to learn these vital 4th principal parts, you will not fail to notice how extraordinarily fruitful they have been in the formation of English words. You will find that you can frequently form an English word by adding '-ion', '-ive', '-ure' and '-or' to the stem of the perfect participle (cf. **82**[2] and p. 134): try the list above. For formation of the future participle see **81** and **82** above.

EXERCISES

1 *Give the full principal parts and meanings of*: legō, occīdō, praesum, pōnō, relinquō, uīuō, scrībō, moueō, interficiō, rapiō (*optional*: teneō, redeō, accipiō, dīcō, auferō, adipīscor, soluō, tangō, dō, uincō).

2 *Identify the verb from which the following forms derive* (*by citing the 1st p. s. present active*) *and translate* (*see* **82**[2] *for the meaning of the perfect participle passive*): acceptus, tulit, ēgimus, lātus, posuistis, oppressus, tetigistī, uīnctus, scrīpsērunt, mōuimus (*optional*: gessistis, īnspexit, rapuērunt, adeptus, cāuistī, dīximus, nātī sunt, lēctus, periistis, solūtus).

84   **Ablative of instrument or means: 'by means of', 'with'**

We have identified three areas of usage for the ablative:

(a) Locative, e.g. 'in', 'at', 'on', 'within' of place and time (cf. **10**, **67**).

(b) Separation (cf. *aufero – ablātus* 'I take away'), e.g. *ex*, *ab* + abl. (cf. **23**).

(c) The ablative of description, e.g. 'a woman of/with great courage' (cf. **49**).

We now meet the 'instrumental' usage of the ablative for the first time. This shows the instrument *with which* or means *by which* an action is carried out, e.g. *mē manibus suīs oppressit* 'he has crushed me with his hands', i.e. 'using his hands as the instrument'; *Rōmam equīs prōgressī sunt* 'they advanced to Rome on horses', i.e. 'with their horses as their instruments'.

EXERCISES

1 *Translate*:

(a) mulierem manibus suīs oppressit homo pessimus.

(b) uirī Rōmam equīs celeribus prōgressī sunt.

(c) gladiō uictor hostem illō tempore occīdit.

(d) neque minīs neque precibus neque pretiō cīuium animōs capiēs.

(e) hostis ferrō mortuus est.

(f) omnīs aliās uxōrēs Lucrētia pudīcitiā uīcit.

2 *Translate*:

(a) nūntius ille in aedīs intrātūrus est.

(b) ego uirum noxium manibus meīs interfectūrus sum.

(c) uxor mea in diēs plūs lānae factūra est.

(d) Tarquinius Lucrētiam libīdine suā occīsūrus est.

(e) rēgis fīlius amōrem sine uoluptāte adeptūrus est.

(f) nam Brūtus impiger mortem miseram eī minātūrus est.

85 **nōnne?** 'doesn't ... ?'

nōnne? asks a question in such a way that the speaker is fishing for the answer 'yes'. The best formula for translation is 'doesn't X happen?' (or 'X does happen, doesn't it?'); 'surely?' is also a safe translation. E.g.

> *nōnne eam amō?* 'don't I love her?', 'I do love her, don't I?',
> 'surely I love her?'

86 **īdem** 'the same' and **nēmo** 'no one'

	s.			pl		
	m.	*f.*	*n.*	*m.*	*f.*	*n.*
nom.	í-dem	éa-dem	í-dem	eí-dem[1]	eaé-dem	éa-dem
acc.	eún-dem	eán-dem	í-dem	eós-dem	eás-dem	éa-dem
gen.	← eiús-dem →			eōrún-dem	eārún-dem	eōrún-dem
dat.	← eí-dem →			← eís-dem[2] →		
abl.	eó-dem	eá-dem	eó-dem	← eís-dem[2] →		

1. *īdem* also found.
2. *īsdem* also found.

Note

This declines like *is ea id* + *-dem* (but NB *īdem*, where one might expect *isdem*, *iddem*). Note that where the forms of *is* end in *-m*, the *-m* becomes an *-n-* before the *-d-* of *-dem*, e.g. *eum-dem → eun-dem*; *eārum-dem → eārun-dem*.

nēmo 3 _m/f._

nom.	nḗmo
acc.	nḗmin-em
gen.	nūll-ī́us (nḗmin-is)
dat.	nḗmin-ī
abl.	nū́ll-ō (nḗmin-e)

NB A number of nouns in Latin can be m. or f., dependent on context.

87   Comparative and superlative adverbs: 'more –ly', 'most –ly'

Comparative and superlative adverbs are formed from the comparative and superlative adjectives. Comparative adverbs are the equivalent of the neuter s., superlatives add _-e_ to the stem.

	foolish(ly)	_more foolish(ly)_	_most foolish(ly)_
Adjective	stúlt-us	stúlt-<u>ior</u>	stultíssim-<u>us</u>
Adverb	stúlt-<u>ē</u>	stúlt-<u>ius</u> (_n._)	stultíssim-<u>ē</u>
	quick(ly)	_more quick(ly)_	_most quick(ly)_
Adjective	céler	celér-<u>ior</u>	celérrim-<u>us</u>
Adverb	celér-<u>iter</u>	celér-<u>ius</u> (_n._)	celérrim-<u>ē</u>

Irregular comparative and superlative adverbs

NB Most of these are irregular only in as far as the corresponding adjective has irregular comparative and superlative forms. If you already know the adjective forms, most of these adverbs are formed quite regularly from the adjective:

béne	'well'	mélius	'better'	óptimē	'best'
mále	'badly'	péius	'worse'	péssimē	'worst', 'very badly'
paúlum	'a little'	mínus	'less'	mínimē	'very little'; 'no'
múltum	'much'	plūs	'more'	plū́rimum	'most'; 'a lot'
magnópere	'greatly'	mágis	'more'	máximē	'very much'; 'most'; 'yes'

EXERCISES

1 _Form and translate the comparative and superlative adverbs of_: stultē, bene, maestē, benīgnē, pulchrē, celeriter, audācter, dīligenter (_optional_: seuērē, pūtidē, multum, paulum, plānē, magnopere, male, facile, miserē).

2 *Identify and translate the comparative and superlative adverbs in this list*: facillimē, malum, scelere, illīus, asperius, uērō, optimē, stultē, opere, magnopere, fortius, alterīus, nimis, magis, minimē, hodiē, pulcherrimē.

3 *Translate each of these phrases*: uir summā uirtūte; summā uirtūte; mulier summā pudīcitiā; pudīcitiā summā; manibus suīs; hōc annō; eādem fōrmā; meīs pugnīs; eōdem tempore.

4 *Give the Latin for*: on the same day; a wife of the utmost chastity; with the greatest courage; with my sword; in the same year; with the same sword; a man of great lust; with threats and prayers.

Quotations

(a) *omne futūrum incertum est.* (Seneca)

(b) *inter peritūra uīuimus.* (Seneca)

(c) *dē futūrīs rēbus semper difficile est dīcere.* (Cicero)

(d) *uirtūs eadem in homine ac deō est.* (Cicero)

(e) *fit uia uī.* (Virgil)

incert-us a um uncertain   *uīuō* 3 I live
inter (+ acc.) among   *uīs* f. force, violence (abl *uī*)
pereō perīre periī peritum I die

EITHER

Reading exercise / Test exercise

Read this passage, translating in word-order, defining the function of each word and phrase-group. Translate into correct English. Finally, read aloud the Latin, correctly phrased, thinking through the meaning as you read.

dum in castrīs cēnant coniūnx Lucrētiae et aliī iuuenēs Rōmānī, dē uxōribus suīs forte loquuntur et dē pudīcitiā eārum. 'nēmō uxōrem meam pudīcitiā uictūra est', inquit Collātīnus. 'sī Rōmam prōgrediēmur, mox oculīs nostrīs melius quam uerbīs cognitūrī sumus.' iuuenēs equīs celerrimīs domum ueniunt, ubi aliās coniugēs in epulīs inueniunt. Lucrētia autem, ut semper impigra, dīligentissimē 5
cum seruīs lānam facit. 'nōnne uictor sum?' inquit coniūnx, 'nōnne uxor dīligentissimē uīuit? nōnne Lucrētia fēmina summā pudīcitiā est? ' sed Collātīnus, nescius futūrī, uerbīs suīs mortem coniugī suae fert. nam mala libīdō eādem diē animum Sextī Tarquiniī capit. 'nōnne mē Lucrētia amātūra est?' sēcum inquit. 'nisi mē amātūra est, nōnne eam ferrō et minīs eam captūrus sum?' Tarquinius 10
domum Lucrētiae it et cōnsilium pessimum pessimē perficit.

OR

English–Latin

1 *Translate into Latin, using future participles where possible*:

(a) No one intends to kill this man with a sword.

(b) I am going to die by the same sword.

(c) I intend to live as a victor.

(d) I intend to threaten her with death.[1]

(e) I intend to deceive Lucretia with kind words.

(f) I shall do nothing more easily, nothing better, nothing more quickly.

1. = 'threaten death (acc.) to her (dat.)'

OR

2 *Read the text of 3C(iii) again, then translate this passage:*

Lucretia sent the same sad message to her spouse and her father. 'Come quickly to Rome. Harmful things have been done. I intend to wait in my bedroom.' When they found Lucretia, she said 'The lust of Sextus Tarquinius will bring death to me. No one will go on living without her chastity because of Lucretia.' Having said this, with a sword she killed herself. Brutus on the same day threatened the king with death. That same day brought destruction to the kings of Rome.

Dēliciae Latīnae

Word-building

(a) Suffixes

-fex -fic-is as a suffix is connected with *faciō* 'I make', 'I do' and commonly expresses occupation. So *carnufex* = *carō* (*carn-*) 'meat' + *-fex*, 'meat-maker', 'executioner', 'scoundrel'; *artifex* = *ars* (*art-*) 'skill', 'craft' + *-fex*, 'craftsman'; *aurifex* = *aurum* + *-fex*, 'goldsmith'.

Nero said of himself on his death-bed *quālis artifex pereō* 'What an (*quālis*) artist perishes in me!'

(b) Perfect participle

The perfect participle (see **82**) is an enormously fruitful source of vocabulary. Many English words are formed by the addition of '-ion', '-ure', '-ive', '-or' to that stem, e.g. 'production', 'diction', 'factor', 'missive', 'capture', 'perfection', 'action' etc., etc. Consequently, you can use these words to help you determine what the perfect participle is. For example, what is the perfect participle of *scrībō*? *scrībitus*? No English word 'scribition'. But there is a word 'inscription'. Chances are, therefore, that the perfect participle is *scrīptus*. Likewise, for Latin-into-English translation, a word like *prōgressūrus* reminds one of 'progression', i.e. going forward.

-ūr-a ae 1f. added to the stem of the 4th principal part generates abstract nouns denoting:

> action: *scrīptūra* 'writing' (*scrībō* 'I write')
>
> result: *nātūra* 'birth', 'nature' (*nāscor* 'I am born')
>
> occupation: *mercātūra* 'trade' (*mercor* 'I sell, trade)

Word exercise

Give the meaning and Latin connection of these words: form, pedestrian, ameliorate, pejorative, interrogate, station, mansion, vision, retention, possession, position, verify, gesture, solution, concoction, elation, future, status, amateur.

Everyday Latin

> *placebo* 'I shall please satisfy' = the harmless pill or coloured water given to pacify hypochondriac patients

> *id.* = *idem* 'the same' (usually, 'the same author')

> *ibid.* = *ibidem* 'the same place in the same author already cited'

> Those on their way to die in the gladiatorial arena saluted the emperor with the words *auē* ('hail'), *Caesar, moritūrī tē salūtant.*

> *auē atque uale* 'hail and farewell', 'hello and goodbye' (common on tombstones)

> One's *magnum opus* is one's 'great work' – usually referring to a book.

The following phrases will help you remember the difference between *in* + acc. and *in* + abl.:

> *in locō parentis* 'in the position of a parent'

> *in camerā* 'in private', 'in secret' (*camera* = vaulted room, the origin of our 'chamber'. The term refers to legal judgments made privately by a judge in his rooms.)

> *in propriā persōnā* '(speaking) in one's own person'

> *in absentiā* 'in one's absence'

> *in flagrante dēlictō* '(caught) in flagrant (open) sin (crime)', i.e. taken in the act, caught red-handed

> *in memoriam* 'to the memory'

> *in mediās rēs* '(plunged) into the middle of the action'

Word study

pēs

pēs ped-is means 'foot', and is akin to Greek *pous pod-os* 'foot' – cf. 'octopus' ('eight feet'), 'podium', 'antipodes' ('people with their feet opposite'), 'tripod' ('three-feet'). The adjective *pedālis* gives 'pedal' and *pedester* gives 'pedestrian', 'of the feet', hence 'lowly', 'earth-bound', 'using one's feet'; *pedō* is late Latin for 'foot-soldier', whence English 'pawn', via Old French *pion*.

expediō

expediō means 'I free [my] feet', whence 'expedient', meaning 'advantageous' and to 'expedite', meaning 'get things moving'. Conversely, 'impede' comes from

135

impediō 'I put feet in shackles'; so *impedīmentum* 'hindrance', *impedicō* 'I tangle someone's feet in a *pedica* ('foot-trap')' gives Middle French *empechier* and English 'impeach', meaning 'charge with an official crime'. Less obviously, *repudium*, meaning 'back-footing', yields 'repudiate'. Piedmont is the area at the foot of the mountains (*mōns mont-is*). Most fascinating of all, 'pedigree', a register of descent or lineage, comes from *pēs* + *dē* + *grūs*, Middle French *pié de grue* 'foot of a crane', the three-line mark like a bird's foot (⅄) which is used to show family succession.

Section 3D

Grammar and exercises for 3D

88   **Datives**

So far the dative case has been used to indicate the person advantaged[1] or disadvantaged by an action (*mī aurum dedit* 'he gave the gold to me', *mihi aurum abstulit* 'he took the gold from me'; this sense includes the possessor also, e.g. *est mihi pecūnia* 'I have money'), and to indicate the person spoken to (*mihi dīxit* 'he spoke to me'). But, as was said at the time, the range of the dative is far wider than that, and its root meaning seems to be that the person is in some way interested or involved in the action of the verb, and when faced by a dative one should ask 'In what way is the person in the dative affected by the verb?'

1. Q. What is an omnibus? A. A vehicle 'for everyone' – 'to everyone's advantage'.

Possessive dative: further notes

Remember the two ways of expressing the idea of possession in Latin:

(a) *habeō* or *teneō* + acc. 'I have', e.g. *seruum habeō* 'I have a slave.'

(b) *est/sunt* + person possessing in the dative (lit. 'there is/are to X…'), e.g. *est mihi seruus* 'there is a slave to me', 'I have a slave'; *sunt Amphitruōnī multī seruī* 'there are to Amphitruo many slaves', 'Amphitruo has many slaves.'

Note the idiom *nōmen Mercuriō est mihi* 'the name to me is Mercury', i.e. 'my name is Mercury'. Observe that *Mercuriō* agrees with *mihi* (see **17B**).

Verbs which take the dative

All the following verbs take the dative:

>   *adsum* 'I am present with', 'I am close to', 'assist': *sociīs adest* 'he is present with his friends', 'he helps his friends'
>
>   *crēdō* 'I have belief in', 'I trust': *eīs crēdit* 'he believes them'. (Cf. the meaning 'I entrust': *crēdō* X (acc.) to Y (dat.), e.g. *deō aurum crēdit* 'he entrusts the gold to the god'.)
>
>   *imperō* 'I give orders': *mulier nōbīs imperat* 'the woman gives us orders' (NB *iubeō* takes the acc. + inf., e.g. *seruam exīre iubet* 'he orders the slave to go out'.)

obstō 'I hinder' 'I stand in the way of: *hic mīlitibus obstat* 'he hinders the soldiers'

licet[1] 'it is permitted': *uōbīs licet* 'it is permitted to you', 'you are allowed'

placet[1] 'it pleases': *cīuibus placet* 'it is pleasing to the citizens', 'the citizens agree/vote' (cf. *placet / nōn placet* as voting procedure at some universities)

minor 'I make a threat against': *dominus seruō minātur* 'the master threatens the slave'

pāreō 'I obey': *seruus dominō pāret* 'the slave obeys his master'

seruiō 'I serve': *seruus dominō seruit* 'the slave serves his master'

supplicō 'I implore', 'I bow to': *dīs omnibus supplicat* 'he implores all the gods'

1. For these 'impersonal verbs' see further **159** and Reference Grammar **F2**.

Non-personal uses of the dative

The dative case is used in certain circumstances to denote the purpose for which something is done, e.g.

pecūniam dōtī dat 'he gives money for/as a dowry'

mihi auxiliō it 'he comes for a help to me', i.e. 'to help me'

Similar to this is the so-called predicative dative, where datives of purpose are used with the verb 'to be', e.g.

mīlitēs salūtī sunt cīuibus 'the soldiers are for a salvation to the citizens', 'the soldiers save the citizens', 'the soldiers are a salvation to the citizens'[1]

auxiliō erimus oppidō 'we shall be for a help to the town', 'we shall help the town'[1]

A variety of this is the predicative dative, where double datives are virtually compulsory:

cordī sum 'I am beloved by X (dat.)'

impedīmentō sum 'I am a hindrance to X (dat.)'

odiō sum 'I am a source of hatred to X (dat.)', 'I am hated by X (dat.)'

uoluptātī sum 'I am a source of pleasure to X (dat.)'

ūsuī sum 'I am useful to X (dat.)'

1. Notice the double datives here: one dative is the dative of purpose, the other the dative of the person involved in or affected by that purpose.

Note

For further information see Reference Grammar **L(e)**.

Revision exercises

1 *Give the meaning, and then form the dative s. and pl., of the following nouns*:

1st/2nd decl.: familia, oculus, cōnsilium, animus, cēna, bellum, deus, turba, uictōria, oppidum, praeda, amīcus, puer (*optional*: officium, lūna, serua, fōrma, lēgātus, grātia, ōtium, proelium, cūra, auxilium). *3rd–5th decl.*: pater, honor, aedēs, frāter, soror, uxor, onus, homo, cīuis, manus, diēs, nox, opus, caput, corpus, senātus, pars (*optional*: rēs, mīles, scelus, uōx, urbs, rēx, exercitus, hostis, equitēs, mōs, uoluptās, cōnsul, iūs).

2 *Give the meaning, and then form the dative s. and pl., of the following adjectives*:

1st/2nd decl. (*m.f.n. forms in the s., one form for the pl.*): multus, miser, malus, meus, tuus, noster, uester (*optional*: bonus, summus, longus, alter,[1] nūllus,[1] īrātus, optimus, pessimus)

3rd decl. and others (*one form for both dative s. and pl.*): omnis, trīstis, ingēns, breuis, audāx, hic (*optional*: facilis, fortis, ille, melior, is, pēior, māior)

1. These are irregular in genitive and dative s. See **62**.

3 *Principal parts*

Give meaning and principal parts of: dō, stō, iubeō, possideō, sum, eō, ferō, uolō, dīcō, dūcō, capiō, gerō, ueniō, uincō.

Give meaning and all three principal parts of: adipīscor, adgredior, loquor, sequor, proficīscor, hortor, polliceor, mentior, cōnspicor, arbitror, cōnor.

Reading exercises

1 *Put the bracketed noun/pronoun in the correct case and translate the sentence* (*NB not every example requires the dative*).

(a) (ego) licet ex aedibus exīre.

(b) (Rōmānī) Hannibal minātus est.

(c) (hic) imperātor Rōmānus obstitit.

(d) (tu) nōn crēdō.

(e) (uxor) uir maximē amat.

(f) (uōs) is seruus bene seruīuit.

(g) (pater) fīlius bonus semper pāret.

(h) (cēna) coquus nōbīs nunc parat.

(i) (exercitus) imperātor pessimē imperat.

(j) (tū) aedīs inīre iubeō.

2 *Translate*:

(a) equitēs Rōmānī Hannibalī impedīmentō sunt.

(b) Hannibal patrī cordī fuit.

(c) cīuis hic malus omnibus bonīs odiō est.

(d) Hannibal mīlitibus suīs semper salūtī fuit.

(e) urbī huic ego auxiliō erō.

(f) hoc officium mihi uolupātī est.

(g) hoc tibi officiō est.

3 *Translate* (*refer back to* **48.2** *and* **88.1** *for possessive dative*):

(a) fuit mihi fīlius bonus.

(b) uxōrī meae dōs maxima est.

(c) cīuibus nostrīs nūllum auxilium fuit.

(d) nēminī seruus amīcus est.

(e) sunt eīs fīlius et fīlia.

4 Quotations

Translate:

(a) *doctō hominī et ērudītō uīuere est cōgitāre.* (Cicero)

(b) *inuia uirtūtī nūlla est uia.* (Ovid)

(c) *iniūria sapientī nōn potest fierī.* (Seneca)

(d) *hominēs amplius oculīs quam auribus crēdunt.* (Seneca)

(e) *omne tulit pūnctum quī miscuit ūtile dulcī.* (Horace)

doct-us a um learned	*auris aur-is* 3f. ear
ērudīt-us a um educated	*pūnct-um ī* 2n. vote
uīuō 3 I live	*quī* (nom. s. m.) the man (writer) who
inui-us a um impassable	*misceō* 2 I mix X (acc.) with Y (dat.)
iniūri-a ae 1f. harm, injury	*ūtil-is e* useful; profitable
sapiēns sapient-is wise	*dulc-is e* sweet, pleasurable,
amplius more	entertaining

EITHER

Reading exercise / Test exercise

Datives (or ablatives) placed early in a sentence are often difficult to tackle, until you come to the verb (or something else which solves the intransigent case). You must 'hold' the dative in these circumstances until you have information which will solve it. Read this passage and, as you translate it in word-order, say which are the datives and where the construction becomes clear. E.g.

ille mihi pecūniam multam auferre uult

At mihi *there is no clue as to whether the idea is possession, advantage/ disadvantage or indirect object. So hold it as 'in relation to me', 'affecting me'. When you reach* auferre, *you can see that it is likely to be disadvantage, since that verb construes with accusative and dative meaning 'take something away from someone'.*

Note that mihi, tibi *and* sibi *are often to be found as second word in their clauses, however far away the verb is.*

etiam post uictōriam Rōmānīs Hannibal odiō et impedīmentō fuit. nam eī rēx Prūsiās aedificium dedit, ubi sē tenuit. hoc aedificium Hannibalī diū salūtī fuit. tum lēgātī ex Prūsiae rēgnō Rōmam uēnērunt et dum cum Rōmānīs amīcē loquuntur, forte eīs dīxērunt 'Hannibal in rēgnō Prūsiae est.' ad rēgem mox Rōmānī lēgātōs mīsērunt et eum Hannibalem rogant. eīs rēx sīc respondit 'mihi crēdite, Rōmānī,   5 Hannibalem diūtius prōtegere nōlō. sed uōbīs eum dēdere nōn possum. aedificium autem ubi sē tenet facile inuentūrī estis.' lēgātī Rōmānī celeriter domum Hannibalis uēnērunt et uītae eius minātī sunt. Hannibal autem, quod fugere nōn potuit, manū suā sē interfēcit.

OR

English–Latin

Translate into Latin:

(a) His friend was a great hindrance to Hannibal.

(b) The consul is hated by the citizens of Rome.

(c) I am allowed to give orders to my soldiers.

(d) Long dinners were not of great pleasure to Hannibal.

(e) A bad citizen is hated by everyone.

(f) A good slave serves his master well.

(g) I am permitted to protect my friends.

(h) The general has decided to hinder the enemy.

(i) You (s.) must leave that building very quickly.

(j) Good soldiers are a very great help to their commander.

OR

*Read the text of **3D(i)** again and then translate this passage*:

When Hannibal was a boy, he gave an oath to his father Hasdrubal. This oath was not friendly to the Romans. Indeed, the oath was destined to threaten the walls of Rome. While his father prayed to the gods, Hannibal said 'I shall never be a friend to the citizens of Rome.' No one could have disbelieved his intention. War was always Hannibal's pleasure. And Rome was always hated by him.

Dēliciae Latīnae

Word-building

Prefix

You have already met *prae-* as a prefix = 'before', 'in front of', e.g. *praeeō* 'I go in front', 'I go ahead'; *praesum* 'I am in front of, 'I am in charge'; but *prae-* can also mean 'extremely', 'very', e.g. *praealtus* 'very high'.

Word exercise

Give the meaning and Latin connection of: amicable, mentality, preparation, supplicate, equal, subservient, corporal, jurisdiction, virtue, consular, necessary, edifice, impediment, odious, partition, protection, Senate, licence.

Note that 'parent' comes from *pariō parere* 'I procure, give birth to', not *pāreō* 'I obey'.

Everyday Latin

'Let there be sung *Non Nobis and Te Deum*' (Shakespeare, *Henry V*, IV.8.122: Henry V after the battle of Agincourt). *Non Nobis* is Psalm 115 (Vulgate, part of Ps. 113), which begins *nōn nōbis, Domine, nōn nōbis, sed nōminī tuō dā glōriam* (*glōri-a ae* 1f. 'glory'). *Te Deum* is the beginning of the canticle *tē deum laudāmus* (*laudō* 1 'I praise').

> *cui bonō?* 'to whom (is it) for a benefit?' 'to whose advantage is it?' (NOT 'what use is it?').

> *urbī et orbī* 'to the city and the world'. The papal pronouncement made from the Vatican at Easter to the crowds below.

Word study

auxilium

The root of *auxilium* 'help' is *augeo* 'I enlarge', 'I increase', with its perfect participle *auctus*. Hence 'auction', an increasing, and 'author', originally an *auctor* 'increaser', hence 'founder', and so 'authority' etc. An augment is an increase, and *aug-silium* 'an increase (in forces)', 'an auxiliary' – hence 'help'. More strangely still, *augur* probably means 'one who predicts increase, i.e. success', so 'augury', 'inaugurate' (= 'give a start to', 'consecrate'); *augustus* signifies either 'consecrated by the augurs' or 'undertaken under favourable auspices'. This was the name given to Octavius Caesar in 27, who, as Augustus, was the first Roman emperor and gave his name to the month August. Note the following place-names which originate from the name Augustus: Val d'Aosta (Augusta Praetoria), Autun (Augustodunum), Zaragoza (Saragossa) = Caesar-augusta.

Grammar and exercises for 4A

89 **Imperfect indicative active: 'I was —ing', 'I used to —', 'I began to —',
'I tried to —'**

	1	2	3
	'I was loving'	'I was having'	'I was saying'
1st s.	amā́-ba-m	habḗ-ba-m	dīc-ḗ-ba-m
2nd s.	amā́-bā-s	habḗ-bā-s	dīc-ḗ-bā-s
3rd s.	amā́-ba-t	habḗ-ba-t	dīc-ḗ-ba-t
1st pl.	amā-bā́-mus	habē-bā́-mus	dīc-ē-bā́-mus
2nd pl.	amā-bā́-tis	habē-bā́-tis	dīc-ē-bā́-tis
3rd pl.	amā́-ba-nt	habḗ-ba-nt	dīc-ḗ-ba-nt

	4	3/4
	'I was hearing'	'I was capturing'
1st s.	audi-ḗ-ba-m	capi-ḗ-ba-m
2nd s.	audi-ḗ-bā-s	capi-ḗ-bā-s
3rd s.	audi-ḗ-ba-t	capi-ḗ-ba-t
1st pl.	audi-ē-bā́-mus	capi-ē-bā́-mus
2nd pl.	audi-ē-bā́-tis	capi-ē-bā́-tis
3rd pl.	audi-ḗ-ba-nt	capi-ḗ-ba-nt

Notes

1 Imperfect ind. act. is formed by taking the present stem (+ key vowel -*ē*- in
3rd, 4th and 3rd/4th conj.) and adding -*bam*, -*bās*, -*bat*, -*bāmus*, -*bātis*, -*bant*.

2 Note the regular personal endings: -*m*, -*s*, -*t*, -*mus*, -*tis*, -*nt*.

3 The imperfect conjugation is based on the stem of the present tense. So its
basic meaning is 'I was in the process of —ing', cf. present 'I <u>am</u> in the
process of —ing.' The action, which is uncompleted (*imperfectus*
'uncompleted', cf. *perfectus* 'completed'), is depicted as continuing, or being
repeated, or beginning or being attempted. Thus the most common translations
for the imperfect are:

$$\left.\begin{array}{l}\text{'I was —ing'}\\\text{'I used to —'}\end{array}\right\}\text{(continuing, repeated)}$$

'I began to —' ('inceptive' imperfect, cf. *incipiō inceptus* 'begin')

'I tried to —' ('conative' imperfect, cf. *cōnor cōnātus* 'try')

Since English does not always distinguish between completed and uncompleted actions, it will often be possible to translate the imperfect as a simple past tense, e.g. *uidēbātur* 'it seemed'; compare *hī concurrērunt* (perf.) *et templum expugnābant* (impf.) 'they made a charge and began attacking the temple'.

4 Learn the following irregulars:

sum →	*1st s.*	ér-a-m '*I was*' etc.	eō →	*1st s.*	ī́-ba-m '*I was going*' etc.
	2nd s.	ér-ā-s		*2nd s.*	ī́-bā-s
	3rd s.	ér-a-t		*3rd s.*	ī́-ba-t
	1st pl.	er-ā́-mus		*1st pl.*	ī-bā́-mus
	2nd pl.	er-ā́-tis		*2nd pl.*	ī-bā́-tis
	3rd pl.	ér-a-nt		*3rd pl.*	ī́-ba-nt

possum →	*1st s.*	pót-eram '*I was able*', '*I could*' etc.
	2nd s.	pót-erās
	3rd s.	pót-erat
	1st pl.	pot-erā́mus
	2nd pl.	pot-erā́tis
	3rd pl.	pót-erant

5 *uolō* (*uolēbam*), *nōlō* (*nōlēbam*) and *mālō* (*mālēbam*) are all regular.

6 Semi-deponents (see **76**) take the *active* form of the imperfect, i.e. *audē-bam* 'I was daring', *fīē-bam* 'I was being made.' In summary, semi-deponents have ACTIVE forms in the present, future and imperfect (*audeō, audēbō, audēbam*) and DEPONENT forms in the perfect (*ausus sum*).

90   **Imperfect indicative deponent**

	1 'I was threatening'	*2* 'I was promising'	*3* 'I was speaking'
1st s.	minā́-ba-r	pollicḗ-ba-r	loqu-é-ba-r
2nd s.	minā-bā́-ris (-re)	pollicē-bā́-ris (-re)	loqu-ē-bā́-ris (-re)
3rd s.	minā-bā́-tur	pollicē-bā́-tur	loqu-e-bā́-tur
1st pl.	minā-bā́-mur	pollicē-bā́-mur	loqu-ē-bā́-mur
2nd pl.	minā-bā́-minī	pollicē-bā́-minī	loqu-ē-bā́-minī
3rd pl.	minā-bá-ntur	pollicē-bá-ntur	loqu-ē-bá-ntur

	4	3/4
	'I was lying'	*'I was advancing'*
1st s.	menti-ḗ-ba-r	prōgredi-ḗ-ba-r
2nd s.	menti-ē-bā́-ris (-re)	prōgredi-ē-bā́-ris (-re)
3rd s.	menti-ē-bā́-tur	prōgredi-ē-bā́-tur
1st pl.	menti-ē-bā́-mur	prōgredi-ē-bā́-mur
2nd pl.	menti-ē-bā́-minī	prōgredi-ē-bā́-minī
3rd pl.	menti-ē-bá-ntur	prōgredi-ē-bá-ntur

Notes

1 The imperfect ind. dep. is formed by taking the present stem (+ key vowel -*ē*-
  in 3rd, 4th and 3rd/4th conjugations) and adding -*bar* -*bāris* (or -*bāre*) -*bātur*
  -*bāmur* -*bāminī* -*bantur.*

2 Note the regular personal endings for the deponent: -*r* -*ris* (or -*re*) -*tur* -*mur*
  -*minī* -*ntur.*

3 For meaning, see **89**[3].

EXERCISES

Morphology

1. *Form and conjugate the imperfect, giving the meaning of 1st person singular
   imperfect, of*: uideor, expugnō, fīō, peruenio, sum, cōnor, iubeō, dūcō, īrāscor,
   faciō (*optional*: legō, eō, affirmō, soleō, moror, proficīscor, adgredior, ferō, nōlō,
   sentiō).

2. *Translate each verb, then change s. to pl. and vice versa*: tenēbās, loquēbantur,
   praeerat, minābāminī, imperābam, ueniēbātis, audēbant, oblīuīscēbāris,
   audiēbat, patiēbāmur, auferēbāmus, sequēbar (*optional*: negābam, pollicēbāris,
   pōnēbat, adipīscēbantur, tollēbātis, īrāscēbātur, faciēbās, mentiēbar, putābāmus,
   cōnspicābāminī, uetābant, arbitrābāmur).

3. *Give the Latin for*: I used to think; he was abandoning; they were throwing;
   we used to follow; you (*s.*) were reporting; she was going out; they were
   accustomed; you (*pl.*) were; we were stating strongly (*optional*: he used to find;
   they were daring; you (*s.*) were speaking; they used to lie; I was encouraging;
   you (*pl.*) were setting out; we were removing; I was asserting).

4. *Give 3rd s. and pl. of the following verbs in present, future, imperfect and
   perfect*: sentiō, minor, uetō, tollō, eō, sum, audeō, adipīscor, uideor, teneō,
   adgredior, mentior, accūsō, colō (*optional*: loquor, negō, soleō, taceō, reperiō,
   proficīscor, peruenio, dēferō, sequor, faciō).

5. *Locate and translate the imperfects in this list, stating the tense of each of the other verbs*: loquar, sentiēbat, amābit, negābat, solēbunt, audēbant, pōnam, tollēbātis, relīquit, habēbit, tacēbant, opīnāberis, arbitrābāris, expugnant, repellēbās, iūdicābātis, coniēcistis (*optional*: dormiēbātis, iubēbitis, sequēbātur, hortābimur, uolēbās, sciētis, prōmittis, habuistis, inueniēbāmus, inībimus, coquēbat, āmittis, crēdēbant, recordābitur).

91   *iste ista istud* 'that (of yours)'

iste declines as follows:

	s.			pl.		
	m.	f.	n.	m.	f.	n.
nom.	íst-e	íst-a	íst-ud	íst-ī	íst-ae	íst-a
acc.	íst-um	íst-am	íst-ud	íst-ōs	íst-ās	íst-a
gen.	←——— ist-íus ———→			ist-órum	ist-árum	ist-órum
dat.	←——— íst-ī ———→			←——— íst-īs ———→		
abl.	íst-ō	íst-ā	íst-ō	←——— íst-īs ———→		

Notes

1 *iste* declines exactly like *ille* **64**. Cf. *is* **70**. *iste* also has a neuter s. in -*d*, a gen. s. in -*īus* and dat. s. in -*ī*.

2 While *iste* means 'that of yours' (2nd p.), *hic* suggests 'this here/of mine' and *ille* 'that there/of his or hers'. So *iste* is frequently used contemptuously of an opponent in a lawsuit, and is so used of Verres by Cicero throughout his Verrine speeches.

EXERCISES

1 *Say with which of the nouns in each line the given form of* iste *agrees*:

> istīus: seruī, fēminae, templī, manūs, rēī, custōdis, impetūs
> istā: lēge, uirginem, seruī, sacerdōte, negōtiō
> istī: seruī, uirtūtī, manuī, negōtiō, mīlitēs
> ista: fēmina, clāmor, rēs, simulācra, puellā

2 *Make* iste *agree with these nouns*: seruī (*2 possibilities*), negōtiō (*2 possibilities*), uirtūtī, custōdibus, manūs (*3 possibilities*).

92   *quīdam, quaedam, quoddam* 'a', 'a certain'

	s.			
	m.	f.	n.	
nom.	quí-dam	quaé-dam	quód-dam	(quid-dam)
acc.	quén-dam	quán-dam	quód-dam	(quid-dam)
gen.	← cuiús-dam →			
dat.	← cuí-dam →			
abl.	quṓ-dam	quā́-dam	quṓ-dam	

	pl.		
	m.	f.	n.
nom.	quī́-dam	quaé-dam	quaé-dam
acc.	quṓs-dam	quā́s-dam	quaé-dam
gen.	quōrún-dam	quārún-dam	quōrún-dam
dat.	←——— quibús-dam ———→		
abl.	←——— quibús-dam ———→		

Notes

1 The forms correspond with those of *quī* 'who?' (**29**) + *-dam*.

2 *quīdam* is the nearest classical Latin ever got to an indefinite article, 'a', 'a certain'.

EXERCISES

1 *Translate and identify the case of*: seruōrum quōrundam; custōdī cuidam; signa quaedam; clāmōrēs quōsdam; dolō quōdam; iūdicibus quibusdam.

2 *Say with which of the nouns in each line the given form of* quīdam *agrees*:

cuiusdam: seruā, templī, sacerdōtis, custōdum, manūs, impetū
quaedam: fēmina, rēs, negōtia, mīlitēs, lēgēs, loca
quīdam: custōs, nūntius, puerī, mīlitēs, magistrātūs, iūdicēs

93   *num* 'surely... not'

You have already met *nōnne*, which means 'doesn't?' 'surely?' ('it *is* the case, isn't it?') (**85**), e.g. *nōnne seruī templum intrāuērunt?* 'the slaves *have* entered the temple, haven't they?'

num puts the opposite emphasis, i.e. 'surely something is *not* the case?', 'it *isn't* the case, is it?', e.g.

num peiōra audīuistis? 'surely you have *not* heard worse things?', 'you *haven't* heard worse things, have you?'

num seruī effūgērunt? 'surely the slaves haven't run away?', 'the slaves *haven't* run away, have they?'

nōnne ('surely X *is* the case?') is used to ask a question in such a way that the speaker is inviting the listener to answer 'yes, it is the case'.

num ('surely X *isn't* the case?') is used to ask a question in such a way that the speaker is inviting the listener to answer 'no, it is not the case'.

94   **Forming the infinitive in Latin**

You have already met present infinitives (cf. **41, 58**), but here is a revision table:

	1	2	3	4	3/4
Active	-āre	-ēre	-ere	-īre	-ere
Deponent	-ārī	-ērī	-ī	-īrī	-ī

Below are the other infinitive (active and deponent) tables.

95   **Perfect infinitive active: 'to have —ed'**

1		2	3
'to have loved'		*'to have had'*	*'to have said'*
amāu-ísse (*or* amásse)		habu-ísse	dīx-ísse

4	3/4
'to have heard'	*'to have captured'*
audīu-ísse (*or* audiísse *or* audísse)	cēp-ísse

Notes

1 Perfect infins. act. are formed by taking the stem of the 3rd p.p. and adding *-isse*.

2 Note how *-ui-* can be dropped, giving e.g. *amásse* (*amāuisse*) 'to have loved', *dēlésse* (*dēlēuisse*) 'to have destroyed', *nósse* (*nōuisse*) 'to have got to know', 'to know' (from *nōscō* 3 *nōuī*) and especially *audísse*.

96   **Perfect infinitive deponent: 'to have —ed'**

1	2
'to have threatened'	*'to have promised'*
minát-us a um ésse	pollícit-us a um ésse

3	4	3/4
'to have said'	*'to have lied'*	*'to have advanced'*
locút-us a um ésse	mentít-us a um ésse	prōgréss-us a um ésse

Notes

1 The perfect inf. dep. is formed by combining the perfect participle with the inf. of the verb 'to be', *esse*.

2 The perfect participle acts as an adjective and must agree with the person doing the action, e.g.

> 'he seems to have lied' *uidētur mentītus esse*

> 'the girls seem to have spoken' *puellae uidentur locūtae esse*

97 Future infinitives active and deponent: 'to be about to—'

	1	2	3
Active	*'to be about to love'* amātúr-us a um ésse	*'to be about to have'* habitúr-us a um ésse	*'to be about to say'* dictúr-us a um ésse
Deponent	*'to be about to threaten'* minātúr-us a um ésse	*'to be about to promise'* pollicitúr-us a um ésse	*'to be about to speak'* locūtúr-us a um ésse

	4	3/4
Active	*'to be about to hear'* audītúr-us a um ésse	*'to be about to capture'* captúr-us a um ésse
Deponent	*'to be about to lie'* mentītúr-us a um ésse	*'to be about to advance'* prōgressúr-us a um ésse

Notes

1 The future infinitives active and deponent are formed in exactly the same way, i.e. combining the future participle with *esse* (cf. perfect deponent infinitives **96**).

2 The future participle acts as an adjective and will agree with the person 'about to —', e.g.

> 'he seems to be about to speak' *uidētur dictūrus esse*

> 'she seemed to be about to listen' *uidēbātur āudītūra esse*

3 The future infinitive of 'to be' is either (regular) *futūrus esse* or the fixed form *fore*.

4 Verbs which have no future participle have no future infinitive. Among these are: *uolō, mālō, nōlō, possum*. Note that *uīsūrus esse* means 'to be about to see' (never 'seem'), *factūrus esse* means 'to be about to make/do' (never 'become').

EXERCISES

1 *Form the present, perfect and future infinitives of*: sum, accūsō, expugnō, cōnfirmō, iubeō, dūcō, tollō, coniciō, ēgredior, mentior, ueniō, eō (*optional*: sentiō, audeō, ferō, nōlō (*no future infinitive*), adipīscor, cōnor, faciō, patior, dō, colō).

2 *State the tense of these infinitives and say which verbs they come from*: passūrus esse, loquī, amāuisse, sentīre, habitūrus esse, sustulisse, minātus esse, uelle, itūrus esse, expugnāre, secūtus esse, poscere, posuisse, adeptus esse, iūdicāsse, repertūrus esse, dēferre.

3 *Give the Latin for*: to seem; to have forbidden; to be about to think; to report; to have found; to be about to remove; to follow; to have remembered; to be about to lie; to promise; to have spoken; to be about to forget (*optional*: to have driven back; to be about to worship; to throw; to be about to confirm).

4 *Pick out the infinitives and say what tense each is, stating also what part of the verb the others are*: solitus es, dētulistis, cōnfirmāuēre, affirmāre, sequere, coluisse, putā, hortātus esse, reperīre, mentīre, accūsātūrus esse, ausus est, repellere, loquere, expugnāuisse, audītūrus esse, dēferēbat, iudicātūrus esse.

98 **Indirect (or reported) statements: the accusative and infinitive**

Observe the following utterances:

(a) *dīcit Verrem uenīre* 'he says Verres to be coming', i.e. 'that Verres *is coming*'

(b) *dīxit Verrem uenīre* 'he said Verres to be coming', i.e. 'that Verres *was coming*'

(c) *dīcit Verrem uēnisse* 'he says Verres to have come', i.e. 'that Verres *has come*'

(d) *dīxit Verrem uēnisse* 'he said Verres to have come', i.e. 'that Verres *had come*'

(e) *dīcit Verrem uentūrum esse* 'he says Verres to be about to come', i.e. 'that Verres *will come*'

(f) *dīxit Verrem uentūrum esse* 'he said Verres to be about to come', i.e. 'that Verres *would come*'

In all these cases, where English uses a 'that' clause, Latin (i) dispenses with the equivalent of 'that', (ii) puts the subject of the clause in the accusative, and (iii) puts the verb in the infinitive.

This is Latin's way of *reporting* a statement (the *direct* statement of (a) above being 'Verres is coming', of (c) 'Verres has come' etc.).

Note that the tense of the inf. reflects the tense of the *original, direct utterance*.

So be on the lookout for verbs of *saying, thinking, knowing, reporting, announcing* followed by the *accusative and infinitive*. Translate such sentences literally first, and then adjust to the English 'that' form.

Notes

1   English has a parallel construction, e.g. 'he knows *me to be* wise', or 'he knows that I am wise'.

2   Latin uses the reflexive (*sē, suus*) to refer in the 'that' clause to the *subject of the main verb*, e.g.

> *Caesar dīxit <u>sē</u> peruēnisse* 'Caesar said that <u>he</u> (= <u>Caesar</u>) had arrived'
>
> *Caesar dīxit <u>eum</u> peruēnisse* 'Caesar said that <u>he</u> (= <u>someone else</u>) had arrived'

3   Observe the correct English form when the main verb is past, e.g.

> *Caesar dīxit Rōmam sē uentūrum esse* 'Caesar said himself to be about to come to Rome', i.e. 'Caesar said that he would come to Rome'
>
> *Caesar dīxit Rōmam sē uēnisse* 'Caesar said himself to have come to Rome', i.e. 'Caesar said that he had come to Rome'
>
> *Caesar dīxit Rōmam sē uenīre* 'Caesar said himself to be coming to Rome' i.e. 'Caesar said that he was coming to Rome'

4   Note that the normal position for *sē* is second word in its sentence or clause (see examples in note 3 above). If it comes first word in its clause, or first word after a natural break in the sense, it is usually emphatic, e.g. *Caesar mihi heri dīxit sē Rōmam uentūrum esse* 'Caesar said to me yesterday | that as for himself *he* would come to Rome.' This rule applies to all pronouns.

5   The accusative and infinitive construction is so common in Latin that Latin will sometimes use it *with* an introductory *noun* (*implying* speech) e.g. *nūntium accēpī seruōs templum intrāuisse* 'I received a message (saying) that the slaves had entered the temple.' Very often, several indirect statements (sometimes a whole speech) follow one another with no repetition of the introductory word(s). So remember always to start your final translation of a Latin accusative and infinitive with the English word THAT, e.g.

> *dīxit seruōs templum intrāuisse; custōdēs effūgisse; seruōs simulācrum commouēre* 'he said THAT the slaves had entered the temple; THAT the guards had fled; THAT the slaves were shifting the statue'

151

99   *nego¯* 'I say (that) … not', 'I deny'

Latin generally does not use *dīcō* + negative to express the idea 'I say that …
not', but prefers *negō*, e.g.

> *negat seruōs templum intrāuisse* 'he says that the slaves <u>did not</u> enter
> the temple' (lit. 'he denies the slaves to have entered the temple')

EXERCISES

1 *Translate these sentences*:

(a) Cicerō affirmat Agrigentīnōs Herculis simulācrum habēre.

(b) Agrigentīnī Verrem praetōrem bonum fuisse negābant.

(c) fama erat seruōs istīus in templum ingressōs esse et signum sustulisse.

(d) nūntium quendam haec omnia nūntiāuisse Agrigentīnīs Cicerō dīxit.

(e) ego putō istum semper uōbīs mentītūrum esse.

(f) opīnābatur Cicerō nēminem umquam scelera pēiōra quam istum factūrum
esse.

(g) Verrēs seruōs in templa mittēbat, cīuibus aurum uī auferēbat, scelera omnia
amplexābātur.

(h) Verrem seruī cuiusdam nōmen dēlātūrum esse audiō.

(i) Verrēs, quod nōlēbat in crimine esse, amīcum quendam mentīrī iussit.

(j) Verrem sciō innocentīs accūsāre solitum esse.

(k) num facinora scelestiōra umquam audīuistis, iūdicēs?

(l) nōnne Verrēs homo est scelestissimus?

(m) Agrigentīnōs in Verris seruōs impetum fēcisse audīuī.

Reading exercises

1 *Begin each of these accusative and infinitive phrases with* dīcit *and* dīxit
*and translate the 'that' clause accordingly. Note that in some cases there is
ambiguity, e.g.:*

eum fīliam amāre

(a) eum: '*that he*' *or* '*that him*' (*i.e. someone other than the subject of the
introductory verb*)

(b) fīliam: '*the daughter*' (*subject or object of* amāre)

(c) amāre: (*present in the orginal direct utterance*) '*loves*',

i.e. '*that he loves the daughter*' *or* '*that the daughter loves him*' *or, if the main
verb is past,* '*that he loved the daughter*' *or* '*that the daughter loved him*'

(a) seruōs templum expugnātūrōs esse.

(b) Verrem seruōs ad templum mīsisse.

(c) Assōrīnōs Chrȳsam colere.

(d) Verrem mē accūsātūrum esse.

(e) simulācra sē amāre.

(f) Scīpiōnem hominem summā hūmānitāte fuisse.

(g) omnia sē cōnspicātās esse.

(h) istum nocte ex urbe ēgressūrum esse.

(i) clāmōrem magnum factum esse.

(j) eum domum īre.

2 Quotations

Translate:

(a) *ratiō docet esse deōs.* (Cicero)

(b) *ēuentus docuit fortīs fortūnam iuuāre.* (Livy)

(c) *homo sum: hūmānī nīl ā mē aliēnum putō.* (Terence)

(d) *Dēmocritum aiunt numquam sine rīsū in pūblicō fuisse.* (Seneca)

(e) *spērat adulēscēns diū sē uīctūrum* [sc. *esse*]. (Cicero)

(f) *glōria uarium et uolūbile quiddam est.* (Seneca)

(g) *nūper mē cuiusdam amīcī languor admonuit, optimōs esse nōs dum īnfirmī sumus. quem enim īnfirmum aut auāritia aut libīdō sollicitat?* (Pliny)

(h) *hīc, ubi nunc Rōma est, incaedua silua uirēbat, / tantaque rēs paucīs pāscua būbus erat.* (Ovid)

ratiō ratiōn-is 3f. reason
doceō 2 I teach, inform
ēuent-us ūs 4m. outcome; event
fortūn-a ae 1f. fortune
iuuō 1 I help
hūmānī nīl nothing (of) human
aliēn-us a um of no concern to X
    (*ā* + abl.)
Dēmocrit-us ī 2m. Democritus (Greek
    philosopher)
aiō I say
rīs-us ūs 4m. laughter, laughing
in pūblicō in public
spērō 1 I hope
adulēscēns adulēscent-is 3m. youth
diū for a long time
uīuō 3 *uīxī uīctum* I live

glōri-a ae 1f. fame, renown
uari-us a um fickle, inconstant
uolūbil-is e unstable, liable change
nūper recently
languor languōr-is 3m. illness
admoneō 2 I remind
īnfirm-us a um weak, feeble
auāriti-a ae 1f. avarice, greed
libīdō libīdin-is 3f. lust
Rōm-a ae 1f. Rome
incaedu-us a um uncut, untilled
silu-a ae 1f. wood
uireō 2 I am green (with foliage)
pauc-ī ae a a few
pāscu-a ōrum 2n. pl. pasture
bōs bou-is 3m. or f. ox, cow; (pl.)
    cattle (dat. and abl. *būbus*)

153

EITHER

Reading exercise / Test exercise

audiō apud Catinēnsīs esse Cereris sacrārium. in sacrārium illud uirīs intrāre nōn licēre omnēs sciunt. fāma est mulierēs et uirginēs ibi sacra cōnficere solēre. in eō sacrāriō fuisse signum Cereris perantīquum multī affirmant. hoc signum seruōs Verris Cicerō dīxit nocte ex illō locō sustulisse; omnibus rem atrōcissimam uīsam esse. Verrem deinde iussisse amīcum quendam aliquem reperīre et accūsāre   5
Cicerō dīxit; nam eum in crīmine esse nōlle. Cicerō amīcum affirmāuit seruī cuiusdam nōmen dētulisse, seruum accūsāuisse, in eum fictōs dedisse testīs, senātum autem Catinēnsium sacerdōtēs uocāuisse et dē omnibus rēbus rogāuisse. sacerdōtēs dīxit Cicerō omnia omnīs cōnspicātās esse, senātum seruum innocen-tem esse dīxisse. iūdicēs numquam pēiōra audīuisse scelera arbitrābātur Cicerō,   10
mox autem pēiōra audītūrōs esse.

aliquem someone (acc. m. s.)

OR

English–Latin

Translate into Latin:

(a) I think that Verres did this.

(b) Cicero said that the slaves entered the temple.

(c) Many citizens used to come to the city, do business, then return home.

(d) Verres' friend reported the name of a certain slave.

(e) We all know that the defendant is a scoundrel.

(f) Surely you don't think that the slaves took away the statue?

(g) Cicero was an excellent man, used gladly to defend his friends, and[1] never forgot the crimes of our enemies.

(h) Cicero thinks the judges will never hear of a worse crime.

OR

Read the text of **4A(iv)** *again, then translate this passage*:

The Syracusans have a law concerning the priesthood of Jupiter. Cicero says that this law enjoins the Syracusans to elect three men; that the Syracusans must then cast lots; that one of the three men becomes priest. He states that Verres wanted to give the priesthood to a friend, called Theomnastus, that the Syracusans refused, but[1] that Verres by a trick achieved his object.

1. No need to translate.

Dēliciae Latīnae

Word-building

Prefixes

per-, rather like *prae-*, often intensifies the meaning of the word to which it is added, e.g. *antīquus* 'old', *perantīquus* 'very old'.

Note the way the following prefixes may change in response to the consonant to which they are attached (this is called assimilation):

> *ad-* + *capiō* = *accipiō*[1] 'I receive'
>
> *ad-* + *firmō* = *affirmō*[2] 'I assert'
>
> *ad-* + *loquor* = *alloquor* 'I address'
>
> *ad-* + *propinquō* = *appropinquō* 'I draw near'
>
> *ad-* + *tulī* = *attulī* 'I have brought (to)'
>
> *ad-* + *rapiō* = *arripiō* 'I seize'
>
> *con-* + *locō* = *collocō* 'I place'
>
> *con-* + *pellō* (3 'I drive') = *compellō* 'I compel'
>
> *con-* + *rapiō* = *corripiō* 'I snatch up'
>
> *con-* + *moueō* = *commoueō* 'I move'
>
> *inter-* + *legō* = *intellegō* 'I understand'
>
> *sub-* + *capiō* = *suscipiō* 'I undertake'
>
> *sub-* + *cēdō* = *succēdō* 'I go under'
>
> *sub-* + *gerō* = *suggerō* 'I supply'
>
> *sub-* + *rapiō* = *surripiō* 'I steal'
>
> *sub-* + *tulī* = *sustulī* 'I filched'

1. Observe how a short *a* (*capiō*) becomes *i* (*accipiō*) when a prefix is added. Cf. *rapiō→arripiō* etc.
2. It is common for the prefixes *ad-* and *con-* to be printed without assimilation, e.g. *adloquor*, *conlocō*. With assimilation, they appear as *all-* and *coll-*. Dictionaries differ in their practice. The prefix *con-* (= *cum*) can express joint action, conlaboration (*sic*), simultaneity, partnership, intensity or completeness.

Suffixes: revision

-c(u)lum, *-crum* added to a verb stem give neuter nouns, e.g. *simulō* 'I copy', 'I pretend' + *-crum* = *simulācrum* 'image', 'statue'; *pō-tus* 'drink' + *-culum* = *pōculum* 'drink', 'cup'; *uehō* 'carry' + *-culum* = *uehiculum* 'carriage'. Such words are usually instruments for carrying out the action.

-io, -iōnis 3f. added to the stem of the perfect participle gives an abstract noun, e.g. *legō lēct-us* 'I read'→ *lēctiō* 'reading'; *audiō audīt-us* 'I hear'→ *audītiō* 'hearing' etc. Cf. *sessiō, mōtiō, accūsātiō* etc. Such words show an action, or its result.

Word exercises

Give the meaning and connection with Latin of: clamour, custodial, temple, repulsion, renunciation (*NB* nūntiō *becomes* nūnciō *in medieval Latin*), total, pugnacious, convention, sign, cult, relic, sensibility, sacerdotal, conjecture, putative, veto, legal, amicable, defamation, impetuous, judicial, triumvirate.

Grammar and exercises for 4B

100A   **The ablative case: summary of forms and usages to date**

Here is a summary of the forms of the ablative:

	1st/2nd decl.			3rd decl.	4th decl.	5th decl.
	m.	*f.*	*n.*	*m./f./n.*		
s.	-ō	-ā	-ō	-e/ī	-ū	-ē
pl.	-īs	-īs	-īs	-ibus	-ibus	-ēbus

Notes

1 If you pay attention to the length of the vowels in the ending, you will cut out some of the possible confusions, e.g. *-is* = nom. s. (e.g. *cīu-is*) or gen. s. (e.g. *urb-is*) of 3rd decl., while the dat./abl. pl. of the 1st/2nd decl. is *-īs* (e.g. *seru-īs*). Confusion may result, however, from the acc. pl. form of 3rd decl. *-i-* stems, which is *-īs* (e.g. *cīu-īs*).

2 Watch out for the long *-ā* of 1st decl. abl. s. (e.g. *seru-ā*) and do not confuse it with the short *-a* of the 1st decl. nom. s. (e.g. *seru-a*) and the 2nd/3rd decl. n. plurals (e.g. *cōnsilia, scelera, ingentia*).

3 The *-ō* of the 2nd decl. can be dat. *or* abl. (e.g. *seru-ō*).

4 The *-e* of the 3rd decl. (e.g. *urb-e*) should not be confused with the *-e* of the nom. acc. s. n. of adjectives (e.g. *trīst-e*).

5 The *-ī* of the 3rd decl. adjectives (e.g. *trīst-ī*) and one noun-type (*mare*, which you will meet in **127**) should not be confused with 2nd decl. *-ī* in the gen. s. (*seru-ī*) and nom. pl. (*seru-ī*).

None of these problems will arise if you make sure you know to which declension belong the nouns and adjectives that you learn.

The ablative: survey of uses

Basically, the ablative has three functions:

(a) the 'true' ablative (*ablātus* from *auferō* – 'I take away'), the point *from which* the action, literally or figuratively, moves, e.g. *ē templō, ā fānō* (**10, 23**)

(b) the 'locative' ablative, i.e. the point in *time or space where or when* something takes place, e.g. *in templō, illō tempore, decem annīs* (**10, 23, 67**)

(c) the 'instrumental-accompanying' ablative, i.e. the means/instrument *by which* the action is carried out, or the people, qualities or circumstances *which accompany* the action (in English, often 'by' or 'with'), e.g. *uir summā uirtūte* (qualities which accompany the action, **49**) and *pugnīs mē uerberat* (means/instrument by which the action takes place, **84**).

The ablative often seems a difficult case because it appears to have so many uses, but if you remember these three basic functions you will see how (what appear to be) separate uses slip into place.

100B   **Further uses of the ablative**

1 Under 'true' ablative: the ablative of comparison (the standard *from which* comparisons can be made), e.g.

> 'this town is more famous than all others' *hoc oppidum clārius est omnibus aliīs* ('all the others' are the starting point *from which* comparisons are made)

Observe that there is no equivalent of 'than' in this construction. Contrast the construction using *quam* which you have met at **72⁴**, where the two things compared are put in the same case, e.g. *hoc oppidum clārius est quam omnia alia.*

2 Under 'instrumental-accompanying' ablative: the ablative of attendant circumstances, 'together with', e.g. *peruēnit cum magnā calamitāte cīuitātis* 'he came with great disaster for the state', 'he came and the circumstances in which he came led to great disaster'. *cum* + abl. is frequent, but sometimes *cum* is omitted and the plain ablative used.

3 Under 'instrumental-accompanying' ablative: the ablative of manner, which shows *how* something is done. This can again be constructed with *cum* or not, e.g.

> *summā celeritāte peruēnit* ⎫
> *summā cum celeritāte peruēnit* ⎬ 'he arrived with great speed'

4 Under 'instrumental-accompanying' ablative, the ablative after *ūtor* 3 dep. *ūsus* 'I use', and *fruor* 3 dep. *frūctus* 'I enjoy', e.g. *hīs uerbīs ūsī* 'using these words'.

5 Under 'instrumental-accompanying' ablative: the ablative expressing measure of difference, e.g.

> *Verrēs multō turpior est quam comitēs suī* 'Verres is much (i.e. by a great amount) viler than his companions'
>
> *sōl multīs partibus māior est quam terra* 'The sun is many times (lit. 'by many parts') larger than the earth' (Cicero)

101 **Genitive of description**

The genitive case is often used for description (cf. the ablative of description at **49**), e.g.

> *eum fīliam habēre <u>eximiae pulchritūdinis</u>* 'that he had a daughter <u>of outstanding beauty</u>'

Cf. English idiom. Note that an *adjective* always accompanies the noun in this usage.

EXERCISES

1 *Revision of ablative forms*:

(a) *Give the ablative s. and pl. of these noun + adjective phrases*: comes clārus; calamitās magna; conuīuium Graecum; amīcus nōbilis; magistrātus innocēns; fōrma turpis; rēs Rōmāna

(b) *Pick out the ablatives in this list*: praetōrī, comitibus, Asiā, cōnsulis, conuīuiīs, laetitia, sermōne, cupiditātem, uī, amīcō, diēbus, homine turpī, uirō nōbilī, manū celerī

(c) *In each list, with which nouns will the adjective go?*

> ingentī: nūntius, puella, templō, uirgine, cūrā
>
> audācibus: uirum, fēminīs, sacerdōtibus, amicus
>
> solā: uirō, agrō, fēmina, uirtūte
>
> magnīs: puerīs, comitis, manibus, cōnsilia
>
> tantō: cupiditāte, proeliō, sceleribus, praetōre
>
> longiōre: noctī, perīculō, sermōnis, clāmor, uiā

2 *Translate these sentences*:

(a) uir multō melior omnibus aliīs erat.

(b) negāuit sē summā uī hominem cecīdisse.

(c) iste saxīs iānuam cecīdit.

(d) Cicerō Agrigentīnōs affirmāuit uirōs esse magnae uirtūtis.

(e) praetōrēs, uirī summā grauitāte, conuīuiīs nōn fruuntur.

(f) Lampsacēnī mōre Graecō rēs suās gerēbant.

(g) mālunt Graecī ōtiō et pāce uītam dēgere (= *to pass*) quam bellō et calamitātibus.

(h) Cicerō Verrem cēterīs praetōribus pēiōrem esse putābat.

(i) Verris seruōs fāma erat summā uī ūsōs esse.

(j) eō tempore Iānitor ad Verrem summā celeritāte uēnit et eum multīs uerbīs retinēre cōnābātur.

102   **Pronoun/adjectives: *alius* 'other', 'another', 'different' and *aliqui(s)*
'someone' 'some'**

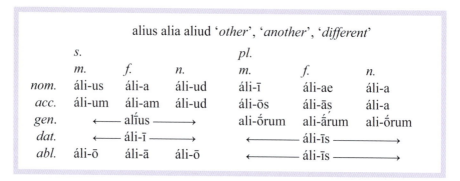

alius alia aliud *'other'*, *'another'*, *'different'*

	s.			pl.		
	m.	f.	n.	m.	f.	n.
nom.	áli-us	áli-a	áli-ud	áli-ī	áli-ae	áli-a
acc.	áli-um	áli-am	áli-ud	áli-ōs	áli-ās	áli-a
gen.	←———— alíus ————→			ali-ṓrum	ali-ā́rum	ali-ṓrum
dat.	←——— áli-ī ———→			←————— áli-īs ————→		
abl.	áli-ō	áli-ā	áli-ō	←————— áli-īs ————→		

Notes

1 Observe the idiom <u>*alius ex aliā*</u> *parte* '<u>different</u> men from <u>different</u> places'.
This idiom can appear with the parts of *alius* in any case, e.g. *alius aliud
laudat* or *aliī alia laudant* 'different people praise different things', or with
other indefinite words, e.g. *alius alibī* 'different people in different places'. It
is equally possible to translate the first example as 'one person from one place,
one from another'.

2 Note also *aliī ... aliī* 'some ... others' (sometimes *aliī ... pars* or *pars ... pars*).

3 Note *aliās* 'at another time', *alibī* 'in another place' and *aliēn-us a um*
'belonging to another' (and the English 'alias', 'alibi' and 'alien').

aliquis aliqua aliquid 'someone' and aliquī(s) aliqua aliquod 'some'

	aliquis *'someone'*			aliquī *'some' (adj.)*		
	m.	f.	n.	m.	f.	n.
nom.	áli-quis	áli-qua	áli-quid	áli-quī(s)	áli-qua	áli-quod
acc.	áli-quem	áli-quam	áli-quid	áli-quem	áli-quam	áli-quod
gen.	←———— ali-cúius ———→			←———— ali-cúius ———→		
dat.	←——— áli-cui ———→			←——— áli-cui ———→		
abl.	áli-quō	áli-quā	áli-quō	áli-quō	áli-quā	áli-quō

Notes

1 Note other *ali-* indefinites: *aliquandō* 'at some time', *alicubī* 'somewhere',
aliquantō 'to some extent', *aliquot* 'some', 'several'.

2 The pl. is the same as for *ali-* + *-quī* (see **29**), except that the n. pl. is *aliqua*.

3 Note *aliquid* + gen. = 'some', e.g. *aliquid artificī* 'some (of) skill'. Cf. **31** *satis,
nimis*.

EXERCISES

1 *With which nouns do the adjectives go?*

        alīus: hospitis, comes, cōnsulī, calamitātis, praetōrēs

        aliī: Lampsacēnō, sermōnēs, Rōmānōs, conuīuī, iānuae

        alia: calamitāte, conuīuia, cōnsule, uirgō, cupiditātibus

        aliā: iānua, conuīuiō, sermōnī, cōnsul, calamitāte

        aliqua: sermō, iānuae, mulier, uerba, amīcōs

        aliquā: cōnsule, fēmina, rē, conuīuia, seruā

2 *Translate*:

(a) alius aliud dīcit.

(b) aliī Lampsacēnī, aliī Agrigentīnī erant.

(c) aliī alibī in oppidum impetum faciunt.

(d) aliī ex agrīs, pars ex oppidō concurrērunt.

(e) dīcet aliquis aliquid.

(f) at quis appellat? magistrātus aliquī? nēmo. (Cicero)

(g) Catilīna, dubitās … abīre in aliquās terrās? (Cicero)

(h) Verrēs cum aliquō comite domō exiit.

appellō 1 I call
dubitō 1 I hesitate

103 ***ipse ipsa ipsum* 'very', 'actual', 'self'**

	s.			*pl.*		
	m.	*f.*	*n.*	*m.*	*f.*	*n.*
nom.	íps-e	íps-a	íps-um	íps-ī	íps-ae	íps-a
acc.	íps-um	íps-am	íps-um	íps-ōs	íps-ās	íps-a
gen.	←——— ips-íus ———→			ips-órum	ips-árum	ips-órum
dat.	←——— íps-ī ———→			←——— íps-īs ———→		
abl.	íps-ō	íps-ā	íps-ō	←——— íps-īs ———→		

Notes

1 Gen./dat. s. are normal for pronouns, cf. *huius, illīus, istīus, eius, cuius* (also *nūllīus, ūllīus, ūnīus, tōtīus, sōlīus*) *illī, istī, eī, cui* (also *nūllī, ūllī, ūnī, tōtī, sōlī*). For nom. s. m. cf. *ille* and *iste*; other forms are like *mult-us a um*.

2 *ipse* is an emphatic and intensive adjective, e.g.

> *retinēte uōs ipsōs* 'restrain your*selves*' (*nos.* is *acc.*, *ipsōs* 'selves'
>   agrees with it);
> *ipse hoc faciō* 'It is actually I *myself* who am doing this'

Compare the phrase *ipsō factō* 'by the actual/very act'. *ipse* can be translated
'self', 'very', 'actual', e.g. *id ipsum mihi placet* 'that's the *very* thing I like'. It
can stand on its own as a noun, e.g. *ipsī* 'the men themselves'. Compare English
'I did it *of my own accord*', 'the *very* person who wrote the law broke it'.

EXERCISES

1 *With which nouns do the parts of* ipse *agree?*

> ipsī: calamitātī, cōnsulēs, conuīuiō, templī, nūntiī
> ipsa: grauitās, cupiditāte, signa, fāmā, simulācra
> ipsā: laetitia, sermōne, grauitāte, conuīuia, celeritās

2 *Translate*: ipsī uoluēre; signum ipsum; ipsae clāmārunt; cōnsiliō ipsō;
ipsī hominī pepercērunt (*two possibilities; after translating, read aloud,
distinguishing by your phrasing which is which*); ipsa laetitia; obsecrārunt ipsī
ōrāruntque; nōlī ipsam retinēre.

Reading exercises

1 *Pick out the ablative phrases in Exercise 2 p. 159 above. Write your translation
next to each. Then say what each phrase adds to the sentence (you may use the
formal categories, but it is more important that you try to define their function
in your own way first). E.g.*

> mōre Graecō bibērunt: '*they drank in the Greek way*'
> mōre Graecō: *this tells us the* way *they drank; ablative of manner.*

*Do not be surprised if occasionally you find it difficult to be precise or if a phrase
may fit more than one category.*

2 Quotations

Translate:

(a) *tranquillō animō esse potest nēmo.* (Cicero)

(b) *sapiēns uincit uirtūte fortūnam.* (Seneca)

(c) *heu, Fortūna, quis est crūdēlior in nōs tē deus?* (Horace)

(d) *is maximē dīuitiīs fruitur quī minimē dīuitiīs indiget.* (Seneca)

(e) *heu, quam difficile est crīmen nōn prōdere uultū.* (Ovid)

(f) *uīlius argentum est aurō, uirtūtibus aurum.* (Horace)

(g) *honesta mors turpī uītā potior.* (Tacitus)

162

(h) *ex Āfricā semper aliquid nouī.* (Pliny)

(i) *hominis tōta uīta nihil aliud quam ad mortem iter est.* (Seneca)

(j) *aliud aliī nātūra iter ostendit.* (Sallust)

tranquill-us a um calm	*prōdō* 3 I betray, reveal
sapiēns sapient-is wise	*uult-us ūs* 4m. face, expression
fortūn-a ae 1f. fortune (*Fortūna* = the goddess Fortune)	*uīl-is e* cheap
	argent-um ī 2n. silver
crūdēl-is e cruel	*honest-us a um* honourable
dīuiti-ae ārum 1f. pl. riches	*potior* preferable, better
quī (nom. s. m.) who	*Āfric-a ae* 1f. Africa
indigeō 2 (+ abl.) I want, need	*nou-us a um* new
heu alas!	*iter itiner-is* 3n. journey; route
crīmen crīmin-is 3n. offence, crime	*nātūr-a ae* 1f. nature

EITHER

Reading exercise / Test exercise

in Hellēspontō oppidum esse scītis, iūdicēs, cēterīs oppidīs Asiae clārius et nōbilius, nōmine Lampsacum. Lampsacēnōs ipsōs affirmō hominēs esse quiētōs. illī mōre Graecō uītam dēgunt (= *spend*). mālunt enim ōtiō ūtī et pāce quam bellō et calamitātibus uītam dēgere. iste Lampsacum tempore quōdam peruēnit. ad Iānitōrem, uirum summae grauitātis, Lampsacēnī eum dēdūxērunt. iste autem   5
mox sē ad Philodāmum quondam migrātūrum esse dīcēbat; Philodāmus enim domī habēbat fīliam pulcherrimam. Verrem scītis, iūdicēs, fēminās pulchrās semper omnibus modīs et omnibus temporibus uehementer sequī. Iānitor sē Verrem offendisse aliquō modō opīnātus est atque istum summā retinēre uī coepit. Verrēs igitur Rubrium ad Philodāmum mīsit, cōnsiliō ūsus pessimō,   10
quod Philodāmus uir erat magnae apud Lampsacēnōs exīstimātiōnis et praetōrēs cōnsulēsque recipere solēbat, nōn amīcōs eōrum. sed Verrēs Philodāmum per uim Rubrium dēdūcere iussit. Philodāmus autem, quod inuītus uidērī nōluit, conuīuium parāuit, Rubrium comitēs inuītāre omnīs iussit. illī summā celeritāte uēnērunt; discubuēre; prīmō Graecō bibērunt mōre, mox pōculīs māiōribus.   15
conuīuium sermōnibus celebrābant hōc tempore et laetitiā. mox autem Rubrius, 'Philodāme,' inquit, 'fīliam uocā tuam.' sed ille, uir grauitāte summā, īrāscēbātur. mulierēs in conuīuiō cum uirīs accumbere oportēre negāuit. clāmor factus est maximus per aedīs. Lampsacēnī, ubi tumultum audiuēre, nocte celeritāte summā ad Philodāmī aedīs conueniēbant. postrīdiē (= *next day*) autem ad Verris   20
hospitium (= *lodging*) profectī sunt. ferrō iānuam et saxīs caedere coepērunt, eōdem tempore ignī circumdare. Verrī autem Lampsacēnī pepercērunt, quod cīuēs quīdam Rōmānī eīs hoc melius fore dīxērunt quam praetōrem necāre Rōmānum.

OR

English–Latin

Translate into Latin:

(a) Verres was more wicked than Rubrius.

(b) The people of Lampsacum used to enjoy peace and leisure.

(c) Philodamus was a man of great seriousness,[1] Verres a man of great lust.[1]

(d) The cooks were getting the party ready amid conversation and merriment.

(e) Verres and his friends were drinking in the Greek way.

(f) The people of Lampsacum were beating the door with their fists and at the same time shouting at the top of their voices.[2]

1. Translate each phrase in two different ways.
2. Use abl. s. of *summa uōx*.

OR

Reread the text of **4B(iii)**, *then translate this passage into Latin*:

Philodamus was a man of great seriousness, but[1] nevertheless always much more hospitable than others. He invited Rubrius and his friends to a party. They all came very quickly. They were drinking amid conversations and merriment. But suddenly Rubrius ordered Philodamus to call his daughter. Philodamus said that he would not call her. Then there was a scene.

1. Leave this out; just translate 'nevertheless'.

Dēliciae Latīnae

Word-building: revision

Suffixes

Abstract nouns are formed with the suffixes *-i-um -ī* 2n. and *-i-ēs -ē-ī* 5f., e.g.

> *artifici-um ī* 2n. trick
>
> *cōnsili-um ī* 2n. plan
>
> *conuīui-um ī* 2n. feast
>
> *perniciēs perniciē-ī* 5f. destruction

Word exercise

Give the meaning and Latin connections of: calamity, hospitable, clarity, turpitude, cupidity, use, vim, negligence, reception, gravity, sermon, convenient, intellect, oration, retention, bibulous, celerity, usufruct, concurrent.

Everyday Latin

(a) Some ablative usages

>   AD = *annō Dominī* 'in the year (abl. of time) of our Lord'
>
>   *bonā fidē* 'in good faith' (in situations where trust is being assured)
>
>   *in tōtō* 'in the whole', 'entirely'
>
>   *s.p.* (attached to an epitaph) = *suā pecūniā* '(buried) at his own exense'
>
>   *mōre suō* 'after his own manner', '(he did it) his way'
>
>   *prīmā faciē* 'at first sight', 'apparently' (used in legal contexts)

(b) Uses of *ipse*

>   *ipsō factō* 'by the very fact itself'
>
>   *ipsissima uerba* 'the very words themselves' (note the superlative of *ipse*)
>
>   An *ipse dīxit* lit. 'he himself said it', i.e. an authoritarian assertion, dogmatic statement

(c) Uses of *inter*

>   *inter alia* 'among other things'
>
>   *inter aliōs* 'among other persons'
>
>   *inter sē* 'among/between themselves'
>
>   *inter vīvōs* lit. 'between living people', i.e. 'from one living person to another'
>
>   *inter nōs* 'between ourselves'
>
>   *inter pōcula* lit. 'between cups', i.e. 'over a glass'

Section 4C

Grammar and exercises for 4C

104   **Pluperfect indicative active: 'I had —ed'**

	1 *'I had loved'*	*2* *'I had had'*	*3* *'I had said'*
1st s.	amáu-era-m (*or* amáram *etc.*)	habú-era-m	díx-era-m
2nd s.	amáu-erā-s	habú-erā-s	díx-erā-s
3rd s.	amáu-era-t	habú-era-t	díx-era-t
1st pl.	amāu-erá-mus	habu-erá-mus	díx-erá-mus
2nd pl.	amāu-erá-tis	habu-erá-tis	díx-erá-tis
3rd pl.	amáu-era-nt	habú-era-nt	díx-era-nt

	4 *'I had heard'*	*3/4* *'I had captured'*
1st s.	audíu-era-m (*or* audíeram *etc.*)	cép-era-m
2nd s.	audíu-erā-s	cép-erā-s
3rd s.	audíu-era-t	cép-era-t
1st pl.	audīu-erá-mus	cēp-erá-mus
2nd pl.	audīu-erá-tis	cēp-erá-tis
3rd pl.	audíu-era-nt	cép-era-nt

Notes

1   The pluperfect (*plūs quam perfectum* 'more than finished') means 'had —ed', and pushes the merely 'finished' (*perfectum*) perfect even further back into the past. In other words, the action of the pluperfect occurs before that of the perfect.

2   It is formed by taking the stem of the 3rd p.p. and adding:

> -*eram*
>
> -*erās*
>
> -*erat*
>
> -*erāmus*
>
> -*erātis*
>
> -*erant*

Note that the normal active personal endings are used (*-m, -s, -t, -mus, -tis, -nt*).

3 As we have observed elsewhere (**65**), the *-ue-* and *-u-* can be dropped, giving e.g. *amā-ram amā-rās* etc. and *audi-eram audi-erās* etc.

4 Whereas in Latin *ubi* 'when' and *postquam* 'after' are generally followed by the perfect tense, English usually translates with the pluperfect, e.g.

> *ubi Verrēs haec f̄ecit, domum rediit* 'when Verres <u>had done</u> this, he went home'

105   **Pluperfect indicative deponent: 'I had —ed'**

	1	*2*	*3*
	'*I had threatened*'	'*I had promised*'	'*I had spoken*'
1st s.	minát-us a um éram	pollícit-us a um éram	locút-us a um éram
2nd s.	minát-us a um érās	pollícit-us a um érās	locút-us a um érās
3rd s.	minát-us a um érat	pollícit-us a um érat	locút-us a um érat
1st pl.	minát-ī ae a erámus	pollícit-ī ae a erámus	locút-ī ae a erámus
2nd pl.	minát-ī ae a erátis	pollícit-ī ae a erátis	locút-ī ae a erátis
3rd pl.	minát-ī ae a érant	pollícit-ī ae a érant	locút-ī ae a érant

	4	*3/4*
	'*I had lied*'	'*I had advanced*'
1st s.	mentít-us a um éram	prōgréss-us a um éram
2nd s.	mentít-us a um érās	prōgréss-us a um érās
3rd s.	mentít-us a um érat	prōgréss-us a um érat
1st pl.	mentít-ī ae a erámus	prōgréss-ī ae a erámus
2nd pl.	mentít-ī ae a erátis	prōgréss-ī ae a erátis
3rd pl.	mentít-ī ae a érant	prōgréss-ī ae a érant

Note

The deponent pluperfect is formed by taking the perfect participle in *-us -a -um* as appropriate, and adding the imperfect of *sum*, i.e. *eram erās* etc. The perfect participle acts as an adjective and will agree with the subject of the verb (see on perfect deponents, **75**).

EXERCISES

1 *Form and conjugate the pluperfect indicative of these verbs* (*give the meaning of 1st s. pluperfect*): cōnor, excōgitō, uideor, moneō, ūtor, faciō, absum, colligō, commoueō (*optional*: cōnstituō, reuocō, nōlō, ferō, fruor, cupiō, recipiō, proficīscor, coepī).

2 *Translate each verb, then change s. to pl. and vice versa*: ōrāuerātis,
cōnspicātus erās, commōuerat, hortātae erant, peperceram, recordāta
erat, recēperāmus, amplexus eram, cecīderās, oblītī erāmus, neglēxerant,
prōgressī erātis (*optional*: āfuerant, cōnātus eram, circumierās, suspicāta erat,
reuocāuerātis, passī erant, excōgitāuerat, ausa erās, cōnstituerāmus, precātae
erātis, cognōueram, uīsī erāmus).

3 *Give the Latin for*: I had decided; you (*s. m.*) had suffered; they had called back;
they (*f.*) had remembered; he had become acquainted with; she had obtained;
we had devised; you (*pl. m.*) had embraced; we had collected; you (*s.*) had
disturbed (*optional*: he had cut; you (*s. m.*) had spoken; we had besought;
they (*f.*) had set out; you (*pl.*) had run together; she had gone out; they had
understood; we (*m.*) had forgotten).

4 *Give 3rd s. and pl. of the following verbs in present, future, imperfect, perfect
and pluperfect indicative*: reuocō, teneō, arbitror, uideor, neglegō, sentiō,
ūtor, patior, fīō, nōlō, sum, colligō, cōnstituō (*optional*: circumeō, commoueō,
cognōscō, adgredior, faciō, precor, mentior, fruor, cupiō, absum, polliceor).

5 *Locate and translate the pluperfects in this list, stating the tense of each of
the other verbs*: excōgitābam, reuocāuerat, passus est, collēgerās, circumībit,
commouet, perlēgerant, cognōscet, cōnātus erās, āfuērunt, fuerātis, recēpit,
ēgressī erant, ingressa est, pōnit, ūtētur, cecīderāmus (*optional*: obsecrāuērunt,
ōrāuerās, suspicātus sum, amplectar, hortātus erat, dēdūcēbātis, cupīueram,
precābimur, pollicita es, oblītus eram, fruēmur, secūtī erant, audēbis, audiēbam,
ausus erās).

106   **The relative pronoun *quī quae quod* 'who', 'which'**

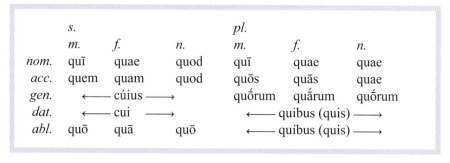

	s.			*pl.*		
	m.	*f.*	*n.*	*m.*	*f.*	*n.*
nom.	quī	quae	quod	quī	quae	quae
acc.	quem	quam	quod	quōs	quās	quae
gen.	←——— cúius ———→			quórum	quárum	quórum
dat.	←— cui —→			←——— quibus (quis) ———→		
abl.	quō	quā	quō	←——— quíbus (quis) ———→		

Notes

1 The forms of *quī* relative are identical with those of the interrogative adjective
quī 'who?', 'what?' (**29**).

168

Punctuation will normally tell you whether you are dealing with a form of the interrogative.

2 The function of a relative is *adjectival*: it is to identify or describe a noun. It does this by means of a complete subordinate clause, i.e. a clause with a finite verb of its own, e.g.

(a) 'I see the cat <u>which is sitting on the mat</u>': 'which … mat' is the relative clause, describing 'cat'.

(b) 'the barge <u>(which) she sat in</u>, like a burnished throne, burned in the water': relative clause '(which) she sat in' describing barge. Note how English can omit the relative. Latin *never* does.

(c) '… the oars were silver,
<u>Which to the tune of flutes kept stroke</u>, and made
The water <u>which they beat</u> to follow faster'
(*Antony and Cleopatra* II.ii, describing Cleopatra's barge)
'which… stroke': relative clause describing 'oars'; 'which… beat': relative clause describing 'water'.

3 'Antecedent' (*antecēdō* 'I go before') is the technical term for the word which the relative refers back to, e.g. 'I dropped the books which I was carrying' ('books' = antecedent); 'the cups which belonged to Diodorus went to Verres' ('cups' = antecedent).

4 The relative takes its gender (m. f. or n.) and its number (s. or pl.) from the antecedent. When you come across a relative in Latin, you must check that it is the same *gender* and *number* as the word you think is its antecedent. The *case* of the antecedent is irrelevant.

5 The relative takes its case *not* from the antecedent, but from its function inside the relative clause. Consider the following sentences:

(a) 'Verres hated Diodorus, who wanted to keep his own property'

'who' is m. and s., because the antecedent is Diodorus. But while Diodorus is object of 'hated' (in Latin *Diodōrum*), 'who' is subject of 'wanted' (since Diodorus, the person meant by 'who', 'wanted to keep his own property'). The relative form will therefore be m., s. and nom., i.e. *quī*:

Verrēs ōderat Diodōrum, quī sua seruāre uolēbat.

(b) 'Diodorus, whom Verres hated, was afraid'

'whom' will be m. and s., since it refers back to Diodorus, but will be accusative in case, since it is the object of 'Verres hated' ('Verres hated <u>Diodorus</u>', the person represented by 'whom'). Note the use of 'whom' as direct object of the verb of the relative clause in English:

Diodōrus, quem Verrēs ōderat, timēbat.

(c) Now determine the case of the relative for the examples in note 3 above.

107   The connecting relative

A relative at the start of the sentence, referring *back* to something or somebody in the *previous* sentence, is best translated by English 'this', 'he', 'she', 'it', e.g.

> *hominēs audīuī. quōs ubi audīuī...* 'I heard the men. Which (men) when I heard ...' i.e. 'when I heard these men / them'.

Note in particular the *order of words*. The relative comes first, to emphasise that it is picking something up from the previous sentence, even though it may belong to an *ubi* 'when' or *postquam* 'after' clause. Cf.

> *ad amīcum litterās mīsit. quās ubi ille perlēgit ...* 'he sent a letter to a friend. When that man had read <u>it</u> ...' (Latin word-order 'which when that man had read ...').

Because the relative pronoun is used to connect sentences, the pedant may often add 'and' or 'but'. So, in the above, 'And/but when ...'

EXERCISES

1 *Translate these sentences and locate the antecedent of* quī *in each*:

(a) Diodōrus parua pōcula, quae Mentōr fēcerat, habēbat.

(b) litterae, quās scrīpserat, mox in Siciliam peruēnērunt.

(c) uirōs, quī sē Rōmae esse affirmāuerant, reuocābat.

(d) rēs scelesta est quam excōgitāuistī.

(e) Diodōrus, quem Verrēs pōcula quaedam pulcherrima habēre sciēbat, abierat.

(f) Diodōrus genere nōbilī nātus erat, quod clārum numquam factum erat.

2 *Say which noun is the antecedent of the given relative*:

> quae: poculīs, annum, praetōrēs, templum
>
> quem: fēminam, mulieris, uirōs, seruus
>
> cuius: litterās, hominum, genus, prōuinciās
>
> quī: fīliō, ratiōne, cupiditātī, lēgēs
>
> quibus: senātū, fāna, uirtūtis, amīcum

3 *Translate these* ubi *clauses (see **104**[4]), which all begin with a connecting relative (**107**). E.g.* quem ubi uīdit ... *'and when he had seen him ...'*

(a) quod ubi audīuit ...

(b) quae ubi nārrāuit ...

(c) quās ubi reuocāuērunt ...

(d) quōs ubi cōnspicātī sunt ...

(e) cui ubi minātus est ...

108   **More uses of the ablative**

1 Under 'true' ablative: 'ablative of origin, or source' ('from'):

> *nātus genere nōbīlī* 'born from a good family'

2 Under 'instrumental-accompanying' ablative: 'ablative of cause', showing why an action was carried out ('out of', 'because of', 'from'):

> *timōre hoc fēcit* 'he did this from fear' (i.e. because of his fear)
>
> *Verrēs hominem argentī cupiditāte accūsāuit* 'Verres accused the man out of desire for silver'

109   **Ablative absolute**

If you come across a noun *in the ablative* in agreement with another noun or adjective (especially a participle) *in the ablative*, for the moment regard it as an ablative of attendant circumstances and translate 'with', 'what with', or 'in the circumstances of', e.g.

> *Verre praetōre* '[what] with Verres (as) praetor', 'in the circumstances of Verres (as) praetor'
>
> *tē praetōre* '[what] with you (as) praetor', 'in the circumstances of you (as) praetor'
>
> *mē amīcō* '[what] with me (as) friend', 'in the circumstances of me (as) friend'

You can then retranslate to make a better English phrase or clause which points up the circumstances more clearly, e.g.

> *Metellō et Afrāniō cōnsulibus* '[what] with Metellus and Afranius as consuls' → 'in the consulship of Metellus and Afranius', 'when Metellus and Afranius were consuls'

(This expression is used to date events: the year indicated here is 60, where Horace dated the origin of the civil wars.)

The term ablative absolute (*absolūtus* 'released') is used because the phrase has no obvious *grammatical* connection with the rest of the sentence.

110   **Locative**

Names of towns and one-town islands (e.g. *Melita* = 'the town of Malta') do *not* use a preposition to express 'in(to)', 'towards', 'at' and 'from'. In this way they follow the example of *domus*, which you have already met, for which *domum* = to home, *domī* = at home, *domō* = from home.

Such words use the *accusative* to express 'to', e.g. *Rōmam* 'to Rome'; *Carthāginem* 'to Carthage'.

They use the *ablative* to express 'from', e.g. *Rōmā* 'from Rome'; *Carthāgine* 'from Carthage'.

They use the *locative* to express 'at'. Here are the locative endings:

1st decl. s. *-ae* ⎱
2nd decl. s. *-ī* ⎰ = gen. s.   pl. *-īs* ⎱
3rd decl. s. *-ī*   = dat. s.   pl. *-īs* ⎰ =abl. pl.
                                  pl. *-ibus* ⎰

Some examples:

      'at Rome' *Rōmae*

      'at/from Athens' (pl.) *Athēnīs*

      'at Carthage' *Carthāginī*

Notes

1 With a few words (denoting place or district), the ablative *without* a preposition is used to express 'at' or 'in', e.g. *eō locō* 'in that place'. Note the common phrase *terrā marīque* 'on land and sea'.

2 'To/from the *vicinity* of a town' is expressed by *ad/ab*, e.g. *ad Rōmam* 'to the vicinity of Rome'; *ā Rōmā* 'from the vicinity of Rome'.

3 In addition to place-names, a few common nouns also have locative forms (cf. *domī*). Note *rūrī* (from *rūs* 3n.) 'in the country'; *humī* (*humus* 2f.) 'on the ground'; *bellī* (*bellum* 2n.) 'in war'; *mīlitiae* (*mīlitia* 1f.) 'in war', 'on military service'; *animī* (*animus* 2m.) 'in the mind'.

EXERCISES

1 *Translate these phrases and sentences*:

(a) uirgō fāmae optimae.

(b) Cicerōne et Antōniō cōnsulibus (*the year 63*).

(c) mē duce.

(d) uirginēs nātae genere nōbilī.

(e) audāciā et cupiditāte aurum sustulit.

(f) Rōmā.

(g) domī.

(h) Lilybaeō.

(i) tōtā prōuinciā.

(j) praetōribus absentibus.

2 *Give the Latin for (NB the previous exercise will help)*:

(a) A man of great courage (*2 ways*).

(b) In Verres' praetorship.

(c) Under your (*s.*) leadership.

(d) A boy born of a noble family.

(e) He acted thus from lust.

(f) At Rome.

(g) From home.

(h) To Lilybaeum.

(i) In the whole of Sicily.

(j) In the absence of the rest.

3 Quotations

Translate:

(a) *quī multum habet, plūs cupit*. (Seneca)

(b) *nōn quī parum habet, sed quī plūs cupit pauper est*. (Seneca)

(c) *dīmidium factī quī coepit habet*. (Horace)

(d) *nihil ēripit fortūna nisi quod dedit*. (Seneca)

(e) *quae fuit dūrum patī, meminisse dulce est*. (Seneca)

(f) *nūper erat medicus, nunc est uespillo Diaulus:*

    quod uespillo facit, fēcerat et medicus. (Martial)

quī he who	*dūr-us a um* hard
parum too little	*meminī* (perf.) I remember
dīmidi-um ī 2n. half	*dulc-is e* sweet, pleasant
fact-um ī 2n. deed	*nūper* recently
ēripiō 3/4 I snatch away	*medic-us ī* 2m. doctor
fortūn-a ae 1f. fortune	*Diaul-us ī* 2m. Diaulus
quod and *quae* what	*uespillo uespillōn-is* 3m. undertaker

EITHER

Reading exercise / Test exercise

Diodōrum Melitēnsem, quī multō ante Melitā ēgressus erat et illō tempore Lilybaeī habitābat, iste cupiditāte suā ā prōuinciā reppulit. ille apud Lilybītānōs, quī eum summā uirtūte uirum esse cognōuerant, uir multī honōris fuerat. sed Verre praetōre, domō caruit prope triennium propter pōcula quaedam pulchra quae habēbat. istī enim comitēs, quōs sēcum, ubi ad prōuinciam peruēnit, dūxerat, Diodōrum haec 5 pōcula habēre nūntiāuerant; quod ubi cognōuit, cupiditāte īnflammātus iste ad sē Diodōrum uocāuerat et pōcula poposcerat. Diodōrus autem, quī pōcula āmittere nōlēbat, ea Melitae esse apud propinquum quondam affirmāuerat. sed ubi Verrēs ad propinquum illum litterās, in quibus pōcula rogābat, scrīpsit, ille ea paucīs illīs diēbus Lilybaeum mīsisse dīxerat. intereā Diodōrus Lilybaeō abierat. 10

OR

English–Latin

Translate into Latin:

(a) Diodorus, who possessed many beautiful cups, had gone away from Lilybaeum to Rome.

(b) In Verres' praetorship, in the whole province men were able to devise wicked crimes.

(c) Verres, who was born of a noble family, always acted from lust, rather than from courage.

(d) The friends, whom Verres had brought with him to the province, were scoundrels.

OR

*Reread the text of **4C(ii)**, then translate this passage into Latin:*

When Verres heard this,[1] from madness he decided to accuse Diodorus in his absence.[2] In the whole province the matter was well known. The story was that Verres through greed for silver had accused an innocent man in his absence.[2] Diodorus, who was at this time in Rome, told his patrons everything which he had heard. When Verres' father learned this,[1] he sent a letter to him. In this[1] letter[3] he said that everyone throughout the city knew that Verres was a scoundrel. When Verres had read this,[1] he held back his lust, from fear, rather than from shame.

1. Use a part of *quī* at the beginning of the sentence.
2. Use *absēns, absentis* agreeing with 'Diodorus', 'man'.
3. Place 'in' after part of *quī* and before 'letter'.

Dēliciae Latīnae

Word-building

Suffixes

-ēnsis frequently makes an adjective out of a place-name, e.g. *Melita* (Malta) → *Melitēnsis*; *Londinium* → *Londiniēnsis*; *Cantabrigia* (Cambridge) → *Cantabrigiēnsis* etc.

   -ānus can also serve this function, e.g. *Rōma* → *Rōmānus* 'Roman', but has a wider range too, e.g. *mōns mont*-is 'mountain'→ *montānus* 'from the mountains'.

Revision

-i-a ae 1f. forms an abstract noun, e.g. *īnsānus* 'mad' → *īnsānia* 'madness'; *miser* 'wretched' → *miseria* 'wretchedness'.

  -or (or *-ōs*) *-ōr-is* 3m. forms abstract nouns of condition, e.g. *furor* 'madness', *amor* 'love', *timor* 'fear', *honor* (or *honōs*) 'respect' etc.

Word exercises

Give the meaning and Latin connections of: generation, literal (*note change of spelling in medieval Latin from* litterae *to* literae), ante-natal, mode, rational, primary, constitution, revoke, circuit, circumlocution, conservation, commotion, collection.

Everyday Latin

(a) **Relative usages**

  quī facit per alium facit per sē 'he who acts through another is himself responsible' (lit. 'acts through himself)

  quī tacet cōnsentit 'he who keeps silence consents'

  q.v. = quod vidē 'which see', 'see this'

  q.e.d. = quod erat dēmōnstrandum 'which was to-be-proved' (and now has been)

  quod ubīque, quod semper, quod ab omnibus 'that which everywhere, that which always, that which by all (sc. has been believed)' – definition of orthodoxy by St Vincent of Lérins

  sine quā nōn 'without which not', i.e. an absolute essential

  status quo (*ante*) 'the position in which ([things were] before)'

(b) **Ablative absolute usages**

  cēterīs paribus '(with) other things (being) equal'

  vīvā vōce 'with living voice'

  mē iūdice 'with me being judge', 'in my opinion'

(c) **Others**

  etc. = et cētera 'and the rest'

  The Classical degree at Oxford is called *lit. hum. = literae hūmāniōrēs* 'humane letters' (lit. 'more human literature' as opposed to theology, originally)

Grammar and exercises for 4D

111   **The passive**

The active 'voice' (as it is called) usually indicates that the subject is doing something, e.g. 'Tom hits the ball.' The passive voice is used to say exactly the same thing, only another way round, this time with the subject *having something done to it* (cf. *passus* 'having undergone, suffered' from *patior*), e.g. 'The ball *is hit* by Tom.' The subject 'ball' here is not doing anything – it is having something done to it *by Tom*, who is called (when he functions like this in a sentence) 'the agent', lit. 'the doer', 'person doing' (from *agō*).

Below (**112–18**) are the forms of the passive, with meanings, of all four conjugations, in present, future, imperfect, perfect and pluperfect indicative, the present, perfect and future infinitive, and the present imperative. It should not be too long before you recognise that the *forms* of the passive and the *forms* of the deponent are ABSOLUTELY IDENTICAL. Consequently, THERE ARE VIRTUALLY NO NEW FORMS TO LEARN HERE.

But remember: the meaning of an *active* verb in Latin is changed when it takes on the passive forms: *amō* 'I love' becomes *amor* 'I am loved.' A deponent verb simply has passive *looking* forms and no other. So *sequor* (deponent) means 'I follow.' It has no forms which can make it mean 'I am followed.'

Notes

1 The *forms* of the passive are identical with those of deponent. But while deponent verbs, with a few, rare exceptions, have only an active *meaning* (e.g. *sequor* 'I follow' (you cannot say 'I am being followed' using *sequor*)), active verbs will have an active meaning when they use active forms, and a passive meaning when they use passive forms, e.g. *amō* 'I love', *amor* 'I am loved'.

2 'By' a *person* in Latin is expressed by *ā/ab* + abl.; 'by'/'with' a *thing* is expressed by the plain ablative (ablative of instrument – see **100A(c)**), e.g.

> 'The boat was captured <u>by Tadius</u>' *nāuis <u>ā Tadiō</u> capta est*

> 'They were being hit <u>by/with an axe</u> (i.e. executed)' *feriēbantur <u>secūrī</u>*

If a person is seen as a tool, or is unwillingly involved, *ā/ab* can be dropped, e.g.

> *seruō paene cōnstrīctus* 'almost strangled by his slave'

a seruō would mean the slave meant it.

3 *uideor* 'I seem' is actually the *passive* of *uideō* and not a real deponent verb. It can also, therefore, mean 'I am seen'; *uīsūrus* is fut. participle of *uideō*, and means 'about to see' (never 'about to seem').

4 *fīō fierī factus sum* is the passive of *faciō*, meaning 'I am made' (as well as 'I become', 'I happen').

112   **Present indicative passive (all conjugations): 'I am being —ed'**

	1	*2*	*3*
	'I am (being) loved'	*'I am (being) held'*	*'I am (being) said'*
1st s.	ám-o-r	hábe-o-r	dī́c-o-r
2nd s.	amá-ris (-re)	habḗ-ris (-re)	dī́c-e-ris (-re)
3rd s.	amā́-tur	habḗ-tur	dī́c-i-tur
1st pl.	amā́-mur	habḗ-mur	dī́c-i-mur
2nd pl.	amā́-minī	habḗ-minī	dīc-ī́-minī
3rd pl.	amá-ntur	habé-ntur	dīc-ú-ntur

	4	*3/4*
	'I am (being) heard'	*'I am (being) captured'*
1st s.	aúdi-or	cápi-o-r
2nd s.	audī́-ris (-re)	cáp-e-ris (-re)
3rd s.	audī́-tur	cápi-tur
1st pl.	audī́-mur	cápi-mur
2nd pl.	audī́-minī	capī́-minī
3rd pl.	audi-ú-ntur	capi-ú-ntur

113   **Future indicative passive (all conjugations): 'I shall be —ed'**

	1	*2*	*3*
	'I shall be loved'	*'I shall be held'*	*'I shall he said'*
1st s.	amā́-bo-r	habḗ-bo-r	dī́c-a-r
2nd s.	amā́-be-ris (-re)	habḗ-be-ris (-re)	dīc-ḗ-ris (-re)
3rd s.	amā́-bi-tur	habḗ-bi-tur	dīc-ḗ-tur
1st pl.	amā́-bi-mur	habḗ-bi-mur	dīc-ḗ-mur
2nd pl.	amā-bí-minī	habē-bí-minī	dīc-ḗ-minī
3rd pl.	amā-bú-ntur	habē-bú-ntur	dīc-é-ntur

	4	*3/4*
	'I shall be heard'	*'I shall be captured'*
1st s.	aúdi-a-r	cápi-a-r
2nd s.	audi-ḗ-ris (-re)	capi-ḗ-ris (-re)
3rd s.	audi-ḗ-tur	capi-ḗ-tur
1st pl.	audi-ḗ-mur	capi-ḗ-mur
2nd pl.	audi-ḗ-minī	capi-ḗ-minī
3rd pl.	audi-é-ntur	capi-é-ntur

114   **Imperfect indicative passive (all conjugations): 'I was being —ed'**

	1	*2*	*3*
	'I was being loved'	'I was being held'	'I was being said'
1st s.	amā́-ba-r	habḗ-ba-r	dīc-ḗ-ba-r
2nd s.	amā-bā́-ris (-re)	habē-bā́-ris (-re)	dīc-ē-bā́-ris (-re)
3rd s.	amā-bā́-tur	habē-bā́-tur	dīc-ē-bā́-tur
1st pl.	āmā-bā́-mur	habē-bā́-mur	dīc-ē-bā́-mur
2nd pl.	amā-bā́-minī	habē-bā́-minī	dīc-ē-bā́-minī
3rd pl.	amā-bá-ntur	habē-bá-ntur	dīc-ē-bá-ntur

	4	*3/4*
	'I was being heard'	'I was being captured'
1st s.	audi-ḗ-ba-r	capi-ḗ-ba-r
2nd s.	audi-ē-bā́-ris (-re)	capi-ē-bā́-ris (-re)
3rd s.	audi-ē-bā́-tur	capi-ē-bā́-tur
1st pl.	audi-ē-bā́-mur	capi-ē-bā́-mur
2nd pl.	audi-ē-bā́-minī	capi-ē-bā́-minī
3rd pl.	audi-ē-bá-ntur	capi-ē-bá-ntur

115   **Perfect indicative passive (all conjugations): 'I was —ed', 'I have been —ed'**

	1	*2*	*3*
	'I was loved',	'I was held',	'I was said',
	'I have been loved'	'I have been held'	'I have been said'
1st s.	amā́t-us a um sum	hábit-us a um sum	díct-us a um sum
2nd s.	amā́t-us a um es	hábit-us a um es	díct-us a um es
3rd s.	amā́t-us a um est	hábit-us a um est	díct-us a um est
1st pl.	amā́t-ī ae a súmus	hábit-ī ae a súmus	díct-ī ae a súmus
2nd pl.	amā́t-ī ae a éstis	hábit-ī ae a éstis	díct-ī ae a éstis
3rd pl.	amā́t-ī ae a sunt	hábit-ī ae a sunt	díct-ī ae a sunt

	4	*3/4*
	'I was heard',	'I was captured',
	'I have been heard'	'I have been captured'
1st s.	audī́t-us a um sum	cápt-us a um sum
2nd s.	audī́t-us a um es	cápt-us a um es
3rd s.	audī́t-us a um est	cápt-us a um est
1st pl.	audī́t-ī ae a súmus	cápt-ī ae a súmus
2nd pl.	audī́t-ī ae a éstis	cápt-ī ae a éstis
3rd pl.	audī́t-ī ae a sunt	cápt-ī ae a sunt

Note

As with deponent verbs, the perfect participle acts as an *adjective* and will agree with the subject in gender, number and case.

116 **Pluperfect indicative passive (all conjugations): 'had been —ed'**

	1	2	3
	'I had been loved'	*'I had been held'*	*'I had been said'*
1st s.	amắt-us a um éram	hábit-us a um éram	díct-us a um éram
2nd s.	amắt-us a um érās	hábit-us a um érās	díct-us a um érās
3rd s.	amắt-us a um érat	hábit-us a um érat	díct-us a um érat
1st pl.	amắt-ī ae a erắmus	hábit-ī ae a erắmus	díct-ī ae a erắmus
2nd pl.	amắt-ī ae a erắtis	hábit-ī ae a erắtis	díct-ī ae a erắtis
3rd pl.	amắt-ī ae a érant	hábit-ī ae a érant	díct-ī ae a érant

	4	3/4
	'I had been heard'	*'I had been captured'*
1st s.	audít-us a um éram	cápt-us a um éram
2nd s.	audít-us a um érās	cápt-us a um érās
3rd s.	audít-us a um érat	cápt-us a um érat
1st pl.	audít-ī ae a erắmus	cápt-ī ae a erắmus
2nd pl.	audít-ī ae a erắtis	cápt-ī ae a erắtis
3rd pl.	audít-ī ae a érant	cápt-ī ae a érant

Note

See perfect passive (**115**) for agreement of perfect participle with the subject.

117 **Passive imperative (all conjugations): 'be —ed'**

	1	2	3	4	3/4
	'be loved!'	*'be held!'*	*'be said!'*	*'be heard!'*	*'be captured!'*
s.	amắ-re	habé-re	díc-e-re	audí-re	cáp-e-re
pl.	amắ-minī	habé-minī	dīc-í-minī	audí-minī	capí-minī

118 **Passive infinitive (all conjugations)**

Present 'to be —ed'

1	2	3	4	3/4
'to be loved'	*'to be held'*	*'to be said'*	*'to be heard'*	*'to be captured'*
amắ-rī	habé-rī	díc-ī	audí-rī	cáp-ī

Perfect 'to have been —ed'

1	2	3
'to have been loved'	*'to have been held'*	*'to have been said'*
amā́t-us a um ésse	hábit-us a um ésse	díct-us a um ésse

4	3/4	
'to have been heard'	*'to have been captured'*	
audī́t-us a um ésse	cápt-us a um ésse	

Form traditionally described as 'future infinitive passive': used only in indirect statement (acc. + inf.)

1	2	3
'that there is a movement to love'	*'that there is a movement to have'*	*'that there is a movement to say'*
amā́tum ī́rī	hábitum ī́rī	díctum ī́rī

4	3/4	
'that there is a movement to hear'	*'that there is a movement to capture'*	
audī́tum ī́rī	cáptum ī́rī	

Notes

1 *īrī* is the impersonal passive infinitive of *eō* 'I go', i.e. 'to be gone'. In the context of an acc. + inf. clause, this means 'that there is a movement'.

2 The forms *amātum*, *habitum* etc. are called 'supine'. Basically, the supine expresses purpose after a verb of motion, e.g. *amātum* 'to love', *audītum* 'to hear' etc. Cf. *cubitum it* 'he goes *to lie down*', *sessum it* 'he goes *to sit*', *Vārus mē uīsum dūxerat* 'Varus had brought me *to see*' (Catullus).

3 Consequently, the literal meaning of the so-called 'future infinitive passive' is 'that there is a movement to ...', e.g.

> *putant sē audītum īrī* 'they think that there is a movement to hear them', i.e. 'that they will be heard'

> *fēmina negat sē captum īrī* 'the woman denies that there is a movement towards capturing her', i.e. 'that she will be captured'. Notice *captum*, not *captam* – see next note.

4 The supine has a *fixed form* (ending *-um*). Its stem is the same as that of the 4th p.p. See **A7**.

EXERCISES

1 *Form and translate the 'future infinitive passive' of*: capiō, līberō, iubeō, auferō, reperiō.

2 *Translate these sentences*:

(a) Verrēs praedōnēs captum īrī dīxit.

(b) Verrēs cīuīs Rōmānōs negābat līberātum īrī.

(c) Verrēs Diodōrī pōcula ablātum īrī affirmat.

(d) Diodōrus pōcula ā Verre repertum īrī negat.

(e) Verrēs amīcōs dīxit pōcula reperīre iussum īrī.

(f) ībō uīsum sī domī est. (Terence)

(g) lūsum it Maecēnās, dormītum ego Vergiliusque. (Horace)

lūdō 3 supine *lūsum* I play

Maecēnās (nom.) Maecenas

Vergilius Virgil

119 **Past (perfect) participle passive**

The past (or perfect) participle of deponent verbs is *active* in meaning, e.g. *morātus* 'having delayed', *locūtus* 'having spoken' etc. (Cf. *locūtus sum* 'I have spoken'.)

   The past (or perfect) participle of all other verbs is *passive* in meaning, e.g. *amātus* 'having been loved', *audītus* 'having been heard', *factus* 'having been made', *captus* 'having been captured' etc. (Cf. *captus sum* 'I have been captured.') Like deponents, they act as 1/2 decl. adjectives (*amāt-us a um*) in agreeing with the person or thing 'having been —ed' and in describing action prior to the main verb. But they are most frequently used predicatively (see **77**), e.g. *mulieris amātae* 'of the woman having-been-captured', 'of the woman when she had been captured'; *lēgātī audītī* 'the ambassadors having-been-heard', 'the ambassadors after they had been heard'; *nāuis capta* 'the ship having-been-captured', 'the ship after it had been captured'.

   Here are whole sentences illustrating the point:

> *mīlitēs captī in carcerem dēductī sunt* '[once] the soldiers had been captured, they were taken off to prison'. (Here *captī* is nom. pl. m. to agree with 'soldiers', the subject of the sentence.)
>
> *custōdēs uīsōs secūtī sunt* 'they followed the having-been-seen guards (acc.)', 'they saw the guards and followed them'. (Here *uīsōs* is acc. pl. m. to agree with 'the guards', the object of the sentence.)
>
> *mihi captō auxilium dedit* 'he gave help to me having-been-captured', 'though I had been captured, he gave me help'. (*captō* is dat. s. m. to agree with *mihi*.)

Another common usage requires the participle + noun to be translated abstractly, e.g.

> *Hannibal uictus* Rōmānōs metū līberāuit 'the <u>defeat of Hannibal</u>
> (lit. 'the having-been-defeated Hannibal') freed the Romans from
> fear'.

Note that even when you are reading sentences using the perfect participle in this predicative way as each word comes (e.g. *mihi captō auxilium dedit* 'to me having-been-captured help he-gave'), you may need to reformulate the phrases into something more like real English in order to understand them fully (and will have to if you are producing a translation). Proceed by putting the perfect participle into a clause (most often subordinate, which may be causal ['since'], temporal ['when', 'once'] or concessive ['although']), e.g. *mihi captō* becomes 'once I had been captured'.

As noted above, however, an abstract noun can be the best substitute for the Latin perfect participle, as in e.g. *nāuis capta* 'the having-been-captured ship' = 'the capture of the ship'.

NB *ab urbe conditā* means 'from the city having-been-founded, i.e. 'after the foundation of the city' (meaning 'Rome'). Shortened, it gives *a.u.c.*, occasionally used by Roman writers to date events. Since Romans came to date their foundation from 753 BC, and subtracted *inclusively*, II a.u.c., 'two years after the foundation of Rome' = 752 BC.

EXERCISES

1 *Form the perfect participle passive of these verbs and translate them*: capiō, opprimō, sollicitō, tollō, interficiō, dō, accūsō, caedō, uincō, commoueō (*optional*: audiō, feriō, līberō, colligō, exspectō, cōnstituō, perlegō, ōrō, intellegō, parō).

2 *Translate the participles in this list. Say whether they are deponent or passive*: portātus, pollicitus, inuentus, hortātus, nūntiātus, coctus, mortuus, ūsus, datus, lātus, gestus, cognitus, cōnātus, secūtus, intellēctus, locūtus, prōmissus, uocātus, arbitrātus, seruātus, minātus, necātus, amplexus (*optional*: profectus, adeptus, repulsus, locūtus, occīsus, exspectātus, adlocūtus, mortuus, āctus, perfectus, secūtus, positus, cultus, solitus, relictus, ausus, uetitus, mentītus, uīsus, īrātus, passus).

EITHER

3 *Translate these sentences*:

(a) Verrēs nāuem pīrātārum cōnspicātus omnia quae in eō erant capere uolēbat.

(b) praefectī classis Rōmānae nāuem captam Verrī dedērunt.

(c) Verrēs sēcum multa locūtus pīrātās līberāre cōnstituerat.

(d) pīrātae fōrmōsissimī ā Verre captī domum suam missī sunt.

(e) pīrātārum ducem ā Verre līberātum nēmō posteā uīdit.

(f) Verrī praetōrī nāuis capta uictōria maxima uidēbātur.

OR

4 *Translate into Latin using perfect participles passive to translate 'when' and*
   'as' clauses:

(a) When they had captured the ship, the prefects gave it to Verres.

(b) After the ship had been seen, Verres hurried towards it.

(c) When the pirates had been captured Verres gave them orders.

(d) The capture of the ship seemed a very great victory to Verres.

(e) Verres' prefects killed the old pirates, using axes captured from the ship.

120   **Ablative absolute with passive participle**

You have already seen (**109**; see further below **122⁶**) how Latin likes to put a noun
with another noun, adjective or present participle in the ablative as a separate
phrase in a sentence, e.g. *Verre praetōre* 'with Verres as praetor', *Cleomenē ēbriō*
'with Cleomenes drunk', *Cleomenē pōtante* 'with Cleomenes drinking'.

The most common usage, however, is to put the noun with a *past participle*, e.g.

> *nāuibus captīs* '(with) the ships having been captured'
> *hominibus interfectīs* '(with) the men having been killed'

This style of ablative absolute construction is very common indeed in Latin.
Since it is not very common in English, it is best not to settle for a wholly literal
translation. Try the following suggestions:

> *signō uīsō, coniūrātōrēs fūgērunt* (lit.) 'With the signal having been
>   seen, the conspirators fled'

This can be translated as:

> 'Because/when/after they saw the signal, the conspirators fled'
> 'The conspirators saw the signal and fled'
> 'The signal was seen and the conspirators fled'
> 'After/when/because the signal was seen, the conspirators fled'

Notes

1 Sometimes 'although' will be the best translation for an abl. abs., e.g. *mīlitibus*
   captīs, Catilīna tamen pugnābat 'though the soldiers were taken, Catiline
   fought on'. As with *cum* = 'although' and *quī* = 'although', some word for
   'nevertheless' (*tamen, nihilōminus* etc.) will often be found, e.g. *exiguā parte*
   aestātis reliquā, Caesar tamen *in Britanniam proficīscī contendit* 'only a small

part of the summer remaining, Caesar *however* hastened to set out for Britain', i.e. '*although* only a small part of the summer remained, Caesar hastened to ...' (no need to translate *tamen*).

2 The construction is called 'absolute' (*absoluō absolūtus* 'having been released': note the passive past participle!) because the phrase does not appear to be integral to its clause, since it qualifies neither subject nor object – it seems to stand all alone, 'released' from its surroundings, e.g. '*this said*, I would still argue ...'; '*the curtain having risen*, the play began'.

3 Cf. *uice uersā* '(with) the position turned/changed'; *pollice uersō* '(with) the thumb turned' (*up* to indicate death, the evidence suggests).

EXERCISES

1 *Translate these ablative absolute phrases (at first use the pattern 'with X having been —ed'):*

(a) imāgine conuulsā.

(b) hīs rēbus nārrātīs.

(c) īnstructīs mīlitibus.

(d) exercitū quaesīto.

(e) sublātō signō.

(f) factīs cognitīs.

(g) hostibus oppressīs.

(h) rēgīnā aspectā.

(i) interfectīs sociīs.

(j) dōnīs petītīs.

2 *Translate these sentences. In (a) to (e) say whether the ablative absolute is better regarded as temporal ('when — had been —ed'), causal ('because — had been —ed'), concessive ('although — had been —ed') or conditional ('if – had been —ed').*

(a) dōnīs datīs dī dīligentius precēs nostrās audiēnt.

(b) proeliō commissō dux interfectus est.

(c) imāginibus sublātīs dī Verrem nōn interfēcērunt.

(d) seruīs ā Verre simulācra tollere iussīs cīuēs Siciliae Cicerōnem socium petēbant.

(e) religiōne sublātā omnia facta, scelera omnia commissa sunt.

(f) bene facta male locūta[1] male facta arbitror. (Ennius)

(g) nihil est simul inuentum et perfectum. (Cicero)

1. *locūta* 'spoken of', 'described'. (For passive usage of deponent past participle see Reference Grammar **C4** note 2.)

English–Latin

Translate these clauses into Latin, using ablative absolute with past participle:

(a) Once the statues had been removed …

(b) When the queen had been compelled …

(c) Although the base had been torn away …

(d) Because the allies had been drawn up …

(e) If gifts had been given …

(f) Had the dignity of the state been saved …

121   **Irregular *ferō*, transitive compounds of *eō* in the passive**

> fero: *present indicative passive*
> | | | |
> |---|---|---|
> | *1st s.* | fér-o-r | 'I am (being) carried' |
> | *2nd s.* | fér-ris | |
> | *3rd s.* | fér-tur | |
> | *1st pl.* | fér-i-mur | |
> | *2nd pl.* | fer-í-minī | |
> | *3rd pl.* | fer-ú-ntur | |

> *Present infinitive*
> fér-rī   'to be carried'

> fero: *imperative passive*
>
> | | | |
> |---|---|---|
> | *s.* | fér-re | |
> | *pl.* | fer-í-minī | 'be carried!' |

NB *ferō* is regular 3rd conj. in the formation of all its other tenses. Its principal parts are *ferō ferre tulī lātus.*

> adeo: *present indicative passive*
> | | | |
> |---|---|---|
> | *1st s.* | ád-eo-r | 'I am (being) approached' |
> | *2nd s.* | ad-í-ris (-re) | |
> | *3rd s.* | ad-í-tur | |
> | *1st pl.* | ad-í-mur | |
> | *2nd pl.* | ad-í-minī | |
> | *3rd pl.* | ad-eú-ntur | |

> adeo: *future indicative passive*
> ad-í-bo-r etc. 'I will be approached'

> adeo: *imperfective indicative passive*
> ad-í-ba-r etc. 'I was being approached'

> adeo: *perfect indicative passive*
> ád-it-us sum etc. 'I was / have been approached'

EXERCISES

1 *Form the passive parts of these verbs as specified in the bracket and translate. Conjugate imperatives and indicatives*: līberō (*pres.*), adiuuō (*impf.*), iubeō (*fut.*), uideō (*pres.*), ferō (*plupf.*), caedō (*perf.*), reuocō (*pres. inf.*), cōnfirmō (*perf. inf.*), recipiō (*pres.*), dīcō (*fut.*) (*optional*: commoueō (*imperative*), colligō (*pres.*), uideō (*perf. inf.*), recipiō (*pres. inf.*), sentiō (*pres.*), dēdūcō (*imperative*), accūsō (*plupf.*), relinquō (*impf.*), auferō (*perf.*), pōnō (*fut.*)).

2 *These verbs include both deponents and passives. Say which each is and translate*: secūta est, accūsātur, ablāta sunt, relictus est, portātur, loquitur, mentītus est, cōnspicābātur, arbitrābitur, cōnābitur, nārrābitur, nūntiātum est, uīsum est, ausum est (*optional*: fertur, adipīscitur, dīcitur, fruētur, colligētur, ōrābātur, opīnābātur, passus erat, iussus erat, amplexus est, caesus est, relinquī, sequī, dīcere, ūtere).

3 *Give the Latin for*: he will be captured; to be freed; they were being struck; it had been taken away; to have been called back; it has been read through.

4 *Transform these sentences from* active *to* passive, *e.g.* praedō nāuem inuēnit 'the pirate found the ship'; nāuis ā praedōne inuenta est '*the ship was found by the pirate*':

(a) Rōmānī hominēs dēfendēbant.

(b) tū numerum praedōnum cognōuistī.

(c) Verrēs pecūniam dedit.

(d) Verrēs cīuīs Rōmānōs secūrī ferit.

(e) ille nautās līberābit.

(f) Diodōrus pōcula abstulerat.

EITHER

Reading exercise / Test exercise

P. Caesētiō et P. Tadiō praefectīs, nāuem pīrātārum quandam captam esse Verrī nūntiātum est; plēnam esse eam nāuem iuuenum fōrmōsissimōrum, argentī, uestium. Verrēs nāuem Syrācūsās ā nautīs appellī iussit. tum exspectābātur ab omnibus supplicium. sed quamquam senēs statim necātī sunt, iuuenēs tamen fōrmōsī ab eō abductī et amīcīs datī sunt. nēmo praedōnēs līberātum īrī arbitrātus   5
erat. hoc tamen ā Verre factum est.

sed posteā facinus multō scelestius ab istō factum est. nam in locum praedōnum, quī līberātī erant, Verrēs cīuīs Rōmānōs substituere coepit, quī in carcerem anteā coniectī erant. quamquam illī ā multīs cognitī erant, secūrī tamen feriēbantur.

OR

English–Latin

Translate these sentences into Latin:

(a) The ship was found by Romans.

(b) Money was being given to Verres by the pirates.

(c) Young men are being sent to Rome.

(d) It had been announced that the ship had been captured and was being brought[1] to Syracuse.

(e) No one had realised that the pirates would be captured.

(f) Verres will be accused at Rome.

1. Use *appellō* 3.

OR

*Reread the text of **4D(ii)**, then translate this passage into Latin*:

The Syracusans had an account of the pirates who had been executed. This[1] account had been made[2] from the number of oars which had been taken. A large number of pirates was missing, because many had been set free by Verres. However, in the pirates' place Roman citizens were substituted. Verres claimed that they had been soldiers of Sertorius. Although they were known[3] by many Syracusans, they were killed with the axe.

1. Use connecting relative (*quī, quae, quod*).
2. Use *habeō*.
3. Use pluperfect of *cognōscō*.

187

Dēliciae Latīnae

Word-building

Suffixes

-cul-us a um and *-ol/ul-us a um* often indicate diminutives, which can be endearing or condemnatory, e.g.

> *mulier* 'woman' – *muliercula* 'silly woman'
>
> *homo* 'man' – *homunculus* 'little jerk'
>
> *Vērānius* – *Vērāniolus* 'dear Veranius'

Word exercises

Give the meaning and Latin connections of: class, decimate, juvenile, prefect, inebriated, adjacent, liberate, vest, nefarious, quotidian.

Everyday Latin

> *contrāria contrāriīs cūrantur* 'opposites are cured by opposites'
>
> *data et accepta* 'expenditures and receipts' (lit. 'things given and received')
>
> *Graecum est*: *nōn legitur* 'it is Greek: it is not read' (i.e. I can't read it. This is found beside Greek words in medieval MSS – when knowledge of the language was rare)
>
> *negātur* 'it is denied'
>
> *probātum est* 'it has been proved'

Grammar and exercises for 4E

122   **Present participles: '—ing', 'while —ing'**

Present participles of both active and deponent verbs are formed in the same way — with *-ns* added to the stem (+ key vowel *-e-* in 3rd, 4th and 3rd/4th conjugations). They are declined like *ingēns* (*ingent-*), e.g.

	s.		pl.	
	m./f.	*n.*	*m./f.*	*n*
nom.	ámā-ns	ámā-ns	amánt-ēs	amánt-ia
acc.	amánt-em	ámā-ns	amánt-īs (-ēs)	amánt-ia
gen.	← amánt-is →		← amánt-ium (-um) →	
dat.	← amánt-ī →		← amánt-ibus →	
abl.	← amánt-e (-ī) →		← amánt-ibus →	

So in conspectus we get:
Active

1	2	3	4	3/4
'loving'	'having'	'saying'	'hearing'	'capturing'
ámāns	hábēns	dícēns	aúdiēns	cápiēns
amánt-	habént-	dīcént-	audiént-	capiént-

Deponent

1	2	3	4	3/4
'threatening'	'promising'	'speaking'	'lying'	'advancing'
mínāns	póllicēns	lóquēns	méntiēns	prōgrédiēns
minánt-	pollicént-	loquént-	mentiént-	prōgrediént-

Notes

1   Observe that the very word 'present' is itself a participle form (*praesēns praesentis*) from *praesum* 'I preside'; so the word 'present' is in itself a clue to the form and meaning of present participles. (Cf. 'future', which gave the clue to the *-ūr-us* ending of future participles, **81**).

2   Present participles mean '—ing', and indicate that the action of the participle is going on at the same time as the verb of the clause.

3 As with future participles and deponent past participles, present participles act like adjectives in agreeing with the person 'doing' in gender, number and case. They are most often used predicatively. See **77**. They can also be used as nouns, e.g. *agēns* 'a person doing something', 'an active man/woman'; *amāns* 'a person loving', 'a lover' (see **138**)

4 The ablatives usually ends in *-e*, and the gen. pl. in *-ium*. The ablative s. ends in *-ī* when the verb is being used *adjectivally*. (Cf. English 'a charming man came here', 'I saw a man charming snakes': the first participle is being used adjectivally, the second with verbal force – predicatively. See **77**).

5 Note the irregular *iēns*, *eunt-is* 'going' (from *eō*).

6 Note that present participles are often used in the 'ablative absolute' construction (**109**, **120**), to mean 'while X is/was —ing', e.g. *Cleomene pōtante* 'while Cleomenes is/was drinking'. In the s., the ending is always *-e*.

EXERCISES

1 *Form the present participle of each of these verbs. Give also gen. s. and translate*: reuocō, incendō, accipiō, sentiō, iubeō, adipīscor, ēgredior, fruor, recordor, exeō (*optional*: loquor, intellegō, commoror, cōnflagrō, egeō, nītor, nāuigō, mentior, oblīuīscor, cōnor).

2 *Say with which noun(s) in each line the given present participle agrees*:

   īnspicientī: seruae, muliere, mīlitis, uirō

   accēdentem: imperātōrum, prīncipem, multitūdine, incendium

   nītente: Verrī, mulieris, seruā, imperātōrēs

   commorantum: populum, mulierum, manum

   cōnflagrantibus: moenibus, cibus, nāuīs, cēterīs

   circumiēns: Iouis, Cicerō, mulier, imperātōrēs

3 *Translate these sentences*:

   (a) Verrēs muliere nītēns in lītore stābat.

   (b) illīs rogantibus praedō respondit sē nāuīs fugientīs uīdisse.

   (c) nautīs cibō egentibus, Cleomenēs nihil fēcit.

   (d) Verre mulierem amante, nūntiātum est nāuem captam esse.

   (e) nāuem incendiō cōnflagrantem uidēre potes.

   (f) reliquōs paulō tardius sequentīs cōnspicātī sunt.

   (g) Syrācūsīs commorantēs praedōnēs moenia urbis uīdērunt.

   (h) Verrēs negāuit nāuīs sē ad portum accēdentīs uīdisse.

   (i) nūllus agentī[1] diēs longus est. (Seneca)

   (j) nīl difficile amantī. (Cicero)

   1. *agō* 3 I am busy.

4 *Translate into Latin (using ablative absolute with present participle), e.g. 'as the leader delayed'* principe commorante:

in Verres' absence; while the sailors were following; with the people watching; as the ships were burning; with Cleomenes delaying; although the crowd was encouraging the leader.

123   Pluperfect subjunctive active: 'had —ed'

The subjunctive (from *subiungō, subiūnctus* 'I subjoin') is the third 'mood' of the Latin verb (along with the indicative, for stating facts or perceived facts, and the imperative, for commands). In this section we introduce only one tense (the pluperfect) and only in clauses where its meaning is the same as the indicative ('had —ed'). A further meaning of this tense will be introduced later (**173**), and other tenses and usages of this new mood will loom large in the remainder of the course (**129–37, 143–7, 149–50, 155–8, 163, 165.2–172, 174, 179.3**).

	1	2	3
1st s.	amāu-ísse-m (*or* amássem *etc.*)	habu-ísse-m	dīx-ísse-m
2nd s.	amāu-íssē-s	habu-íssē-s	dīx-íssē-s
3rd s.	amāu-ísse-t	habu-ísse-t	dīx-ísse-t
1st pl.	amāu-issé-mus	habu-issé-mus	dīx-issé-mus
2nd pl.	amāu-issé-tis	habu-issé-tis	dīx-issé-tis
3rd pl.	amāu-ísse-nt	habu-ísse-nt	dīx-ísse-nt

	4	3/4
1st s.	audīu-ísse-m (*or* audíssem *etc.*)	cēp-ísse-m
2nd s.	audīu-íssē-s	cēp-íssē-s
3rd s.	audīu-ísse-t	cēp-ísse-t
1st pl.	audīu-issé-mus	cēp-issé-mus
2nd pl.	audīu-issé-tis	cēp-issé-tis
3rd pl.	audīu-ísse-nt	cēp-ísse-nt

Notes

1 Remember pluperfect subjunctive active as formed from the perfect infinitive active plus the normal personal endings (*-m, -s, -t, -mus, -tis, -nt*).

2 Observe how the *-ui-* can drop out (cf. **65, 104**[3]), e.g. *amā-ssem, dēlē-ssem* (=*dēlēuissem*) etc.

124 **Pluperfect subjunctive deponent: 'had –ed'**

	1	2	3
1st s.	mināt-us a um éssem	pollícit-us a um éssem	locūt-us a um éssem
2nd s.	mināt-us a um éssēs	pollícit-us a um éssēs	locūt-us a um éssēs
3rd s.	mināt-us a um ésset	pollícit-us a um ésset	locūt-us a um ésset
1st pl.	mināt-ī ae a essḗmus	pollícit-ī ae a essḗmus	locūt-ī ae a essḗmus
2nd pl.	mināt-ī ae a essḗtis	pollícit-ī ae a essḗtis	locūt-ī ae a essḗtis
3rd pl.	mināt-ī ae a éssent	pollícit-ī ae a éssent	locūt-ī ae a éssent
	4	3/4	
1st s.	mentīt-us a um éssem	progréss-us a um éssem	
2nd s.	mentīt-us a um éssēs	prōgréss-us a um éssēs	
3rd s.	mentīt-us a um ésset	prōgréss-us a um ésset	
1st pl.	mentīt-ī ae a essḗmus	prōgréss-ī ae a essḗmus	
2nd pl.	mentīt-ī ae a essḗtis	prōgréss-ī ae a essḗtis	
3rd pl.	mentīt-ī ae a éssent	prōgréss-ī ae a éssent	

Note

The pluperfect subjunctive deponent is formed from the perfect participle in *-us a um* (agreeing with the subject) and the auxiliary verb *essem essēs esset* etc. (imperfect subjunctive of *sum*).

125 **Pluperfect subjunctive passive: 'had been –ed'**

	1	2	3
1st s.	amāt-us a um éssem	hábit-us a um éssem	díct-us a um éssem
2nd s.	amāt-us a um éssēs	hábit-us a um éssēs	díct-us a um éssēs
3rd s.	amāt-us a um ésset	hábit-us a um ésset	díct-us a um ésset
1st pl.	amāt-ī ae a essḗmus	hábit-ī ae a essḗmus	dict-ī ae a essḗmus
2nd pl.	amāt-ī ae a essḗtis	hábit-ī ae a essḗtis	díct-ī ae a essḗtis
3rd pl.	amāt-ī ae a éssent	hábit-ī ae a éssent	díct-ī ae a éssent

	4	*3/4*
1st s.	audít-us a um éssem	cápt-us a um éssem
2nd s.	audít-us a um éssēs	cápt-us a um éssēs
3rd s.	audít-us a um ésset	cápt-us a um ésset
1st pl.	audít-ī ae a essḗmus	cápt-ī ae a essḗmus
2nd pl.	audít-ī ae a essḗtis	cápt-ī ae a essḗtis
3rd pl.	audít-ī ae a éssent	cápt-ī ae a éssent

Note

For formation of the pluperfect subjunctive passive, see note on plupf. deponent above, **124**.

126   *cum* + subjunctive: 'when', 'since', 'although'

cum followed by the pluperfect subjunctive has pluperfect force: 'when' or 'since' or 'although X had —ed'.

Here are two examples of *cum* + pluperfect subjunctive:

> *cum abiissent, laetus eram* 'when/since they had gone, I was delighted'

> *cum haec locūtī essent, abiērunt* 'when/since they had said this, they left'

Notes

1   Distinguish *cum* = 'with' (followed closely by an ablative) from *cum* = 'since', 'when', 'although'.

2   Remember *mēcum* 'with me', *tēcum* 'with you', *nōbīscum* 'with us' etc., and *quōcum, quibuscum* 'with whom'.

3   *cum* 'although' is often signposted by e.g. *tamen* or *nihilōminus* in the main clause, e.g. *cum sapiēns esset, stultē* <u>tamen</u> *sē gessit* 'though he was wise, <u>all the same</u> he acted foolishly' (see **132**[1] for the form *esset*).

4   It is common for conjunctions like *cum*, *sī* 'if', *ubi* 'when' etc. to drift towards the verb, i.e. away from the start of the sentence, e.g. *ad templum cum peruēnisset*, 'when he had reached the temple'. Be prepared for this when you translate.

EXERCISES

1 *Form and conjugate the pluperfect subjunctive of these verbs (form passive only where asked)*: egeō, cōnflagrō, commoror, sequor, accipiō (*passive*), incendō (*passive*), nītor, occīdō, sentiō, līberō (*passive*), accēdō (*optional*: dēsum, circumeō, nōlō, ferō (*passive*), recordor, audeō, cōnspicor, iaceō, cōnstituō (*passive*), excōgitō, nāuigō).

2 *Translate these sentences (taking care over the meaning of* cum = '*when, since, although*'):

(a) cum Cleomenēs fūgisset, cēterī secūtī sunt.

(b) cum praedōnēs celerrimē prōgressī essent, nāuēs Rōmānōrum postrēmae in perīculō prīncipēs erant.

(c) cum imperātor ad lītus celeriter accessisset, cēterī tamen tardius nāuigābant.

(d) Cleomenēs ad lītus cum nāue cum peruēnisset, sē domī cēlāuit.

(e) cēterī quoque, cum marī nūllō modō praedōnēs effugere potuissent, nāuīs relīquērunt.

(f) praedōnum dux nāuīs, cum captae essent, incendī iussit.

3 *Say which of these verbs are subjunctive, which indicative or infinitive*: eguit, cōnflagrāsset, tulerat, recordātus essēs, cōnstituisse, excōgitāuerās, accēpissent, captus esse, occīsī essent, cōnspicātī sunt (*optional*: iacuistī, commorātī sunt, secūta esset, fuisse, fūgissent, cēlāuerant, nāuigāssent, nōluistis, potuissēs, incēnsus esse).

127   **3rd declension neuter *i*-stem nouns in *-al*, *-ar*, *-re* and *-le*, e.g. *mare* *mar-is* 3n. 'sea'**

All these nouns decline in the same way, like *mare*:

	s.	*pl.*
nom.	máre	már-ia
voc.	máre	már-ia
acc.	máre	már-ia
gen.	már-is	már-ium (már-um *is found*)
dat.	már-ī	már-ibus
abl.	már-ī (máre is *found*)	már-ibus

The same endings are used for *animal* 'animal', *calcar* 'spur' and *cubīle* 'couch'.

Note

The abl. s. in -*ī*, nom. and acc. pl. in -*ia*, and gen. pl. in -*ium* are exactly like other neuter *i*-stems (see **44**). Cf. **12** and contrast **26**.

128   **Relative pronoun in the genitive**

cuius and *quōrum quārum quōrum* nearly always mean 'whose', 'of which' or 'of whom', e.g.

> *nāuis cuius imperātor erat Phȳlarchus* 'the ship the captain of
> which was Phylarchus'
> *hominēs quōrum argentum Verrēs cupīuit* 'the men whose silver
> Verres desired'

Note

This form is also found as a connecting relative (**107**), as in e.g. *quārum rērum grauium nūntius Syrācūsās peruēnit ad praetōrium*, lit. '*Of which* grave events a messenger came to the governor's residence in Syracuse ...' i.e. '*And* a messenger *bearing this serious news* came to the governor's residence in Syracuse ...').

EITHER

Reading exercise / Test exercise

*Here is a slightly cut (but otherwise unadapted) passage from the original text of **4E(ii)**. Read the passage, analysing explicitly your procedure as you go. End, after translation, with a reading aloud of the Latin.*

ita prīma Haluntīnōrum nāuis capitur, cui praeerat Haluntīnus homo nōbilis, Phȳlarchus, quem ab illīs praedōnibus Locrēnsēs[1] posteā pūblicē redēmērunt[2]... deinde Apollōniēnsis nāuis capitur, et eius praefectus Anthrōpinus occīditur. haec dum aguntur, intereā Cleomenēs iam ad Helōrī lītus peruēnerat; iam sēsē in terram ē nāuī ēiēcerat, quadrirēmemque[3] fluctuantem in salō [= marī] relīquerat.   5 reliquī praefectī nāuium, cum in terram imperātor exiisset, Cleomenem persecūtī[4] sunt. (Cicero, *In Verrem* II 5, 34.90–35.91)

1. *Locrēnsis Locrēns-is* 3m. person from Locri.
2. *redimō* 3 *redēmī* I ransom, buy back (thus English 'redeem').
3. *quadrirēmis quadrirēm-is* 3f. ship – with four banks of oars.
4. *per-* intensifies the simple verb *sequor.*

OR

English–Latin

Translate these sentences into Latin:

(a) The crowd caught sight of the ships as they were burning.

(b) When Cleomenes had disembarked, the rest of the ships' captains followed him.

(c) Cleomenes, whose wife was on the shore with Verres, left harbour with the ships following.

(d) Since they had not been able to escape the pirates by sea, the captains followed their leader and disembarked.

OR

Read the text of 4E(iii) again, then translate this passage:

When the ships had been set on fire, the pirates decided to go to Syracuse. They had heard that the harbour of the Syracusans was very beautiful and knew that they would never see it except in Verres' praetorship. When they had decided this,[1] they sailed to Syracuse. A pirate ship, in Verres' praetorship, while our ships were burning, came up to the actual harbour of the Syracusans. Ye gods! What a vile deed!

1. Use connecting relative (*quī quae quod*).

Dēliciae Latīnae

Word-building

Suffixes: revision

-bil-is e is the suffix often used to form adjectives with passive force, e.g. *amābilis* 'lovable', *crēdibilis* 'credible', 'which can be believed'. Cf. English '-ble'.

EXERCISE

Give the meaning of: stabilis, mōbilis, laudābilis, dūrābilis, nāuigābilis.

Present participles

Many English words are based on the present participle stem in *-ent* and *-ant*, and these frequently tell you what conj. the verb is. If *-ant*, the verbs are 1st conj., if *-ent*, 2nd/3rd conj., if *-ient*, 4th or 3rd/4th conj.

Discuss the origins of: gradient, intelligent, permanent, Vincent, inhabitant, tangent.

Some words, however, come through French, whose present participle always ends in *-ant.* So: descendant, defendant, tenant, attendant. But we sometimes use the French form as a noun, e.g. 'a depend*ant*', with the Latin as an adjective, 'dependent' (*dēpendeō* 2 I hang from).

Word exercises

1   *The following words all use the stem of a Latin noun you should know. Say what is the nom. s. of the noun in each case*: legal, pacify, military, ducal, capital, custodian.

2   *Give an English word derived from the stem of*: tempus, uōx, nōmen, opus, lītus,[1] prīnceps, multitūdō.

1. Clue: double the *-t-*.

Everyday Latin

Ablative absolutes and present participles

D.V. = Deō uolente '(with) God willing'

nem. con. = nēmine contrādīcente '(with) no one contradicting', 'unanimously'

A *locum* in medical parlance means someone who takes the place of a doctor who is away for whatever reason. Its origin is *locum tenēns* '(one) taking the place' (cf. French *lieu-tenant*, identical in formation).

et seq. = et sequēns 'and (the one) following', *et seqq. = et sequentēs* 'and (the ones) following'. Note how a double letter indicates the plural. Cf. *ex.* = example; *exx.* = examples.

timeō Danaōs, et dōna ferentīs 'I fear the Greeks even (though they are) bearing gifts' (Virgil, *Aeneid* 2, 49).

volentī nōn fit iniūria 'to one willing, injury does not happen' (i.e. no wrong is done to one who consents). An important legal principle at the heart of many cases, e.g. rape.

Grammar and exercises for 4F

129   Present subjunctive active

	1	2	3	4	3/4
1st s.	ám-e-m	hábe-a-m	dī́c-a-m	aúdi-a-m	cápi-a-m
2nd s.	ám-ē-s	hábe-ā-s	dī́c-ā-s	aúdi-ā-s	cápi-ā-s
3rd s.	ám-e-t	hábe-a-t	dī́c-a-t	aúdi-a-t	cápi-a-t
1st pl.	am-ḗ-mus	habe-ā́-mus	dīc-ā́-mus	audi-ā́-mus	capi-ā́-mus
2nd pl.	am-ḗ-tis	habe-ā́-tis	dīc-ā́-tis	audi-ā́-tis	capi-ā́-tis
3rd pl.	ám-e-nt	hábe-a-nt	dī́c-a-nt	aúdi-a-nt	cápi-a-nt

Notes

1   Observe the regular personal endings *-m -s -t -mus -tis -nt.*

2   The key vowel in conjs. 2–3/4 is *A* while in 1st conj. it is *E* (to distinguish it from the indicative). One could summarise the present subjunctive with the following chart:

1	2	3	4	3/4
E	EA	A	IA	IA

3   Note that the 1st s. forms of *dicam*, *audiam* and *capiam* in the *present subjunctive* are the same as those of the 1st s. forms of the *future indicative* of these conjugations.

4   Particular attention should be paid to the learning of which conjugation each verb belongs to, since the *subjunctive endings of 1st conj.* are almost identical to the *present indicative endings of 2nd conj.* (cf. *amem amēs amet* with *habeō habēs habet* etc.), while the *subjunctive endings of the 3rd conj.* are almost the same as those of the *indicative endings of the 1st conj.* (cf. *dīcam dīcās dīcat* with *amō amās amat* etc.).

5   Learn the following irregular subjunctives:

	sum	*possum*	*uolō*	*nōlō*	*mālō*
1st s.	s-i-m	pós-sim	uél-i-m	nól-i-m	mãl-i-m
2nd s.	s-ī-s	pós-sīs	uél-ī-s	nól-ī-s	mãl-ī-s
3rd s.	s-i-t	pós-sit	uél-i-t	nól-i-t	mãl-i-t
1st pl.	s-ī-mus	pos-sī́mus	uel-ī́-mus	nōl-ī́-mus	mál-ī́-mus
2nd pl.	s-ī-tis	pos-sī́tis	uel-ī́-tis	nōl-ī́-tis	mál-ī́-tis
3rd pl.	s-i-nt	pós-sint	uél-i-nt	nól-i-nt	mãl-i-nt

6   The subjunctive of *eō* is regular: *e-a-m, e-ā-s* etc.

130   Present subjunctive deponent

	1	*2*	*3*
1st s.	mín-e-r	pollíce-a-r	lóqu-a-r
2nd s.	min-ḗ-ris (-re)	pollice-ā́-ris (-re)	loqu-ā́-ris (-re)
3rd s.	min-ḗ-tur	pollice-ā́-tur	loqu-ā́-tur
1st pl.	min-ḗ-mur	pollice-ā́-mur	loqu-ā́-mur
2nd pl.	min-ḗ-minī	pollice-ā́-minī	loqu-ā́-minī
3rd pl.	min-é-ntur	pollice-á-ntur	loqu-á-ntur

	4	*3/4*
1st s.	ménti-a-r	prōgrédi-a-r
2nd s.	menti-ā́-ris (-re)	prōgredi-ā́-ris (-re)
3rd s.	menti-ā́-tur	prōgredi-ā́-tur
1st pl.	menti-ā́-mur	prōgredi-ā́-mur
2nd pl.	menti-ā́-minī	prōgredi-ā́-minī
3rd pl.	menti-á-ntur	prōgredi-á-ntur

Notes

1   Observe the regular personal endings *-r -ris (-re) -tur -mur -mint -ntur*.

2   For notes on regularities and ambiguities, see notes 2–4 on the active above.

131   Present subjunctive passive

	1	*2*	*3*
1st s.	ám-e-r	hábe-a-r	dī́c-a-r
2nd s.	am-ḗ-ris (-re)	habe-ā́-ris (-re)	dīc-ā́-ris (-re)
3rd s.	am-ḗ-tur	habe-ā́-tur	dīc-ā́-tur
1st pl.	am-ḗ-mur	habe-ā́-mur	dīc-ā́-mur
2nd pl.	am-ḗ-minī	habe-ā́-minī	dīc-ā́-minī
3rd pl.	am-é-ntur	habe-á-ntur	dīc-á-ntur

	4	3/4
1st s.	aúdi-a-r	cápi-a-r
2nd s.	audi-ā́-ris (-re)	capi-ā́-ris (-re)
3rd s.	audi-ā́-tur	capi-ā́-tur
1st pl.	audi-ā́-mur	capi-ā́-mur
2nd pl.	audi-ā́-minī	capi-ā́-minī
3rd pl.	audi-á-ntur	capi-á-ntur

Notes

1 See under deponent (**130** above) for notes.

132   Imperfect subjunctive active

	1	2	3	4	3/4
1st s.	amā́re-m	habére-m	dícere-m	audíre-m	cápere-m
2nd s.	amā́rē-s	habérē-s	dícerē-s	audírē-s	cáperē-s
3rd s.	amā́re-t	habére-t	dícere-t	audíre-t	cápere-t
1st pl.	amārḗ-mus	habērḗ-mus	dicerḗ-mus	audīrḗ-mus	caperḗ-mus
2nd pl.	amārḗ-tis	habērḗ-tis	dicerḗ-tis	audīrḗ-tis	caperḗ-tis
3rd s.	amā́re-nt	habére-nt	dícere-nt	audíre-nt	cápere-nt

Notes

1 Remember the imperfect subjunctive as formed from the present infinitive plus the personal endings. Thus *amāre-m amārē-s* etc. Even irregulars follow this rule, e.g. *sum → esse → essem*; *eō → īre → īrem*; *ferō → ferre → ferrem*; cf. *uellem, nōllem, māllem, possem*. Cf. pluperfect subjunctive active, **123**[1].

2 Note the alternative impf. subjunctive of *sum: fore-m, forē-s, fore-t* etc. (formed from the future inf. *fore*: see **97**[3]).

133   Imperfect subjunctive deponent

	1	2	3
1st s.	minā́re-r	pollicére-r	lóquere-r
2nd s.	minārḗ-ris (-re)	pollicērḗ-ris(-re)	loquerḗ-ris (-re)
3rd s.	minārḗ-tur	pollicērḗ-tur	loquerḗ-tur
1st pl.	minārḗ-mur	pollicērḗ-mur	loquerḗ-mur
2nd pl.	minārḗ-minī	pollicērḗ-minī	loquerḗ-minī
3rd pl.	minārḗ-ntur	pollicērḗ-ntur	loquerḗ-ntur

	4	*3/4*
1st s.	mentíre-r	prōgrédere-r
2nd s.	mentīrḗ-ris (-re)	prōgrederḗ-ris (-re)
3rd s.	mentīrḗ-tur	prōgrederḗ-tur
1st pl.	mentīrḗ-mur	prōgrederḗ-mur
2nd pl.	mentīrḗ-minī	prōgrederḗ-minī
3rd pl.	mentīré-ntur	prōgrederé-ntur

Note

The imperfect deponent subjunctive may be regarded as formed by taking a hypothetical ACTIVE infinitive, and adding the deponent personal endings, e.g. not *minārī* but *mināre* giving *mināre-r -ris -tur* etc. Likewise with *pollicērī* → *pollicēre-r*, *loquī* → *loquere-r*, *mentīrī* → *mentīre-r*, *prōgredī* → *prōgredere-r*.

134   Imperfect subjunctive passive

	1	*2*	*3*
1st s.	amáre-r	habére-r	dícere-r
2nd s.	amārḗ-ris (-re)	habērḗ-ris (-re)	dīcerḗ-ris (-re)
3rd s.	amārḗ-tur	habērḗ-tur	dīcerḗ-tur
1st pl.	amārḗ-mur	habērḗ-mur	dīcerḗ-mur
2nd pl.	amārḗ-minī	habērḗ-minī	dīcerḗ-minī
3rd pl.	amāré-ntur	habērḗ-ntur	dīceré-ntur

	4	*3/4*
1st s.	audíre-r	cápere-r
2nd s.	audīrḗ-ris (-re)	caperḗ-ris (-re)
3rd s.	audīrḗ-tur	caperḗ-tur
1st pl.	audīrḗ-mur	caperḗ-mur
2nd pl.	audīrḗ-minī	caperḗ-minī
3rd pl.	audīré-ntur	caperé-ntur

Note

For notes, see deponent (above).

135   **Summary of subjunctive forms**

Present subjunctive

Present stem + key vowel + personal endings. Key vowels: 1st conj. *E*, 2nd, 3rd, 4th, 3rd/4th *A*. Personal endings, active: *-m -s -t* etc.; deponent/passive: *-r -ris* (*-re*) *-tur* etc. Irregular: *sim, uēlim, nōlim, mālim, possim.*

Imperfect subjunctive

Active infinitive + personal endings (active: *-m -s -t* etc.; deponent/passive: *-r/-ris* (*-re*) *-tur* etc.)

Deponent verbs in the imperfect subjunctive are constructed on a hypothetical active infinitive, e.g.

> 1st conj.: *minārī* becomes *mināre-*
>
> 2nd conj.: *pollicērī* becomes *pollicēre-*
>
> 3rd conj.*: loquī* becomes *loquere-*
>
> 4th conj.: *mentīrī* becomes *mentīre-*
>
> 3rd/4th conj.: *prōgredī* becomes *prōgredere-*

Pluperfect subjunctive

Active: perfect infinitive active + personal endings (*-m, -s, -t* etc.).

Deponent/passive: perfect participle + *essem* etc.

EXERCISES

1 *Form and conjugate the present and imperfect subjunctive of these verbs* (*where '*(*passive*)*' is written, give active and passive; for other active verbs give only active tenses*): concidō, hortor, morior, sum, timeō, auferō (*passive*), reuocō (*passive*), nāuigō (*optional:* abiciō (*passive*), cōnor, egeō, uolō, dēsum, perlegō (*passive*), excōgitō, ūtor).

2 *Say which of these verbs is subjunctive, which indicative or infinitive* (*state tense of all verbs*): clāmet, amat, dormīret, auferret, cōnspicātus esse, cōnātī essent, dat, dīcētur, excōgitat, cūret, nescīrem, cupīuisse, loquitur, abstulisset, moneāris, accidat, aget, persuādet, perficiās (*optional:* commorātur, moriātur, placēret, redībat, rogāssent, conciderēmus, accūsētis, parcēmus, profūgisse, nītātur, proficīscitur, uocant, uincant, uincientur, uocāuissētis).

3 *Form 3rd s. of present, imperfect and pluperfect indicative and subjunctive of these verbs* (*where '*(*passive*)*' is written, give active and passive; for other active verbs give only active tenses*): agō (*passive*), perficiō, commoror, līberō (*passive*), iaceō, sequor, nōlō, accidit (*optional:* īnspiciō (*passive*), circumeō, mālō, ōrō, persuādeō, recordor, patior, caedō (*passive*)).

136   **Indirect (reported) commands: *ut/nē* + subjunctive**

Observe the following sentences:

(*a*) *Caesar imperat mīlitibus ut prōgrediantur* 'Caesar gives orders to the soldiers that they should advance' or 'to advance'.

(*b*) *eōs hortātus sum nē hoc facerent* 'I urged them that they should not do this' or 'not to do this'.

(*c*) *mihi persuādēbit ut sēcum prōfugiam* 'he will persuade me that I should flee with him' or 'to flee with him'.

To express these *reported* commands (the original command of (a) was 'Soldiers, advance!', of (b) 'Do not do this!' etc.), Latin commonly adopts the form 'that X should' (*ut* + subjunctive) or 'that-not X should' (*nē* + subjunctive).

English does use this construction with verbs like e.g. ordain (e.g. 'he ordained that I should go'), though English more commonly uses the straight 'to / not to' form: e.g. (a) above is most easily translated 'Caesar gives orders to the soldiers to advance.'

Translate literally to start with, then convert to normal English.

Which verbs take *ut/nē*?

> *hortor* + *ut/nē* 'I urge X (acc.) that he should / should not'
>
> *ōrō* + *ut/nē* 'I beg X (acc.) that he should / should not'
>
> *imperō* + *ut/nē* 'I give orders to X (dat.) that he should / should not'
>
> *persuādeō* + *ut/nē* 'I persuade X (dat.) that he should / should not'
>
> *petō* + *ut/nē* 'I beg *ā/ab* X (abl.) that he should / should not'
>
> *postulō* + *ut/nē* 'I demand *ā/ab* X (abl.) that he should / should not'
>
> *rogō* + *ut/nē* 'I ask X (acc.) that he should / should not'

moneō 'I advise', *obsecrō* 'I beseech', *precor* 'I pray' also take *ut/nē*.

Exceptions

iubeō 'I order' and *uetō* 'I forbid', 'tell X *not* to' both, like English, usually take a plain present infinitive. Compare:

> *iubeō tē abīre*
> *imperō tibi ut abeās* } 'I order you to go'
>
> *uetō uōs manēre*
> *imperō uōbis ne maneatis* } 'I tell you not to stay'

Notes

1   The tense of the subjunctive depends on the tense of the main verb of the sentence. The subjunctive will be *present* when the main verb is 'primary',

imperfect when it is 'secondary/historic'. This rule is called 'sequence of tenses' (see **A–G Intro.(a)**).

2 Any reference, inside the *ut/nē* clause, to the subject of the main verb will involve the use of a *reflexive* pronoun, e.g.

> *Caesar imperat nōbīs ut sibi pāreāmus* 'Caesar gives orders to us to obey him (= Caesar)'

3 Note that *nē quis* = 'that no one', *nē quid* = 'that nothing' = e.g.

> *imperat nē quis exeat* 'he orders that no one should go out'

Cf. *nē umquam* = 'that never', *nē ūllus* = 'not any', 'that no one', *nē usquam* = 'that nowhere'.

For the forms of *quis* (indefinite) see **14**.

EXERCISES

EITHER

1 *Translate these sentences* (*remember* ut + *indicative means 'as' or 'when' and that* ut *may be used without a verb to mean 'as'*):

(a) Verrēs Seruīliō persuāsit ut Lilybaeum adīret.

(b) Seruīlius, ut Lilybaeum peruēnit, ā līctōribus caesus est.

(c) Verrēs līctōribus imperāuerat ut uirum caederent.

(d) Seruīlius, ut cīuis Rōmānus, Verrem ōrat nē sē caedat nēue necet.

(e) ut Verrēs cīuīs Rōmānōs caedit, ita ipsum affirmō ā cīuibus Rōmānīs caesum īrī.

(f) Verrēs seruōs quōsdam hortātur nē Seruīliō parcant nēue ōrantī auxilium dent.

OR

2 *Translate the underlined words into Latin* (*using* ut/nē + *subjunctive*); *take care to get the correct sequence* (*see* **136¹**):

(a) Verres orders Servilius <u>to come to Lilybaeum</u>.

(b) I beg you (*pl.*) <u>not to go away</u>.

(c) Verres ordered the lictors <u>to beat Servilius</u>.

(d) In the end Verres persuaded Servilius <u>not to keep quiet</u>.

(e) How can I persuade you <u>to believe me?</u>

(f) I ordain[1] <u>that no one shall escape and that you</u> (*pl.*) <u>shall not go away.</u>

1. *dēcernō* 3.

137   *accidit, perficiō ut* + **subjunctive**

accidit ut (*nōn*) 'it happens that (not)', and *perficiō ut* (*nōn*) (and *nē*) 'I bring it about that (not)' are followed by the subjunctive. In primary sequence the subjunctive is *present*; in secondary, *imperfect*. The perfect subjunctive, which you will meet later later (**167–9**), is also found in this construction:

> *accidit ut perfugeret* 'it happened that he escaped' (= so-called 'result' clause – see **149**)

> *perficiam ut effugiam* 'I shall bring it about that I escape' (= so-called 'purpose' clause – see **150**).

EXERCISES

EITHER

1 *Translate these sentences* (*take care to check the tense of subjunctive in clauses introduced by* accidit, *since* accidit *may be present or perfect*):

(a) accidit ut Seruīlius dē Verris nēquitiā paulō līberius loquātur.

(b) Verrēs perfēcit ut Seruīlius Lilybaeum adīret.

(c) accidit ut Seruīlius, cum Lilybaeum peruēnisset, ā līctōribus caederētur.

(d) Gauius, cum in uinclīs Syrācūsīs esset, dīxit sē perfectūrum ut profugeret Messānamque peruenīret.

(e) Verrēs perficiet ut cīuēs Rōmānī necentur.

OR

2 *Prefix each of these statements with* perficiam ut (*following rules for primary sequence*) *and* accidit ut (*following rules for secondary sequence*). *You will thus need to change the verbs to present subjunctive* (*for* perficiam ut) *and imperfect* (*for* accidit ut). *Translate the new sentences*:

(a) Verrēs Lilybaeum adit.

(b) uir ā līctōribus caeditur.

(c) seruī eum ad terram abiciunt.

(d) uerberibus moritur.

(e) sociī Rōmam profugiunt.

138   **Present participle**

When a participle is used on its own, and in agreement with no other word, there are two ways in which it may be being used:

(a) As a noun 'a/the person —ing', e.g.

> *iacet corpus dormientis ut mortuī* 'The body of a person sleeping lies like (that) of a dead person' (Cicero)

> Cf. *moritūrī tē salūtant* 'men about to die salute you'

205

(b) Agreeing with a noun or pronoun which has been left out, referring to a person already mentioned, e.g.

> *haec dīcentis latus hastā transfixit* 'He pierced with a spear the side of (the man) as he was saying this' (Curtius). Note that 'the man' must be known to us already (he has just spoken *haec*).

139   Relative pronoun (dative and ablative)

1 *cui* and *quibus* (dat.) normally mean 'to whom, for whom', e.g.

> *puer cui pecūniam dedī* 'the boy to whom I gave the money'

But since the verb in the relative clause may control a dative, or require a dative of disadvantage etc., it will usually be necessary to 'hold' the relative pronoun until it is 'solved' by the construction, e.g.

> *nāuis cui praeerat Phŷlarchus* 'the ship of which Phylarchus was in charge' (because *praesum* 'I am in charge of' takes a dat.)
> *uir cui Verrēs pōcula abstulerat* 'the man from whom Verres had taken the cups' (because *auferō* has its meaning completed by a dative of disadvantage)

2 *quō/quā* and *quibus* (abl.) bear a very wide range of meanings, but 'by', 'with', 'in/at' and 'from' should all be kept in mind. It will often be necessary to 'hold' the abl. relative pronoun until 'solved' by the construction (as with the dat.), e.g.

> *incendium quō urbs incēnsa est* 'the fire by which the city was burned'
> *genus quō nātus erat* 'the family from which he was born'
> *celeritās quā nāuem cēpit* 'the speed with which he took the ship'

Bear in mind again that some verbs put *objects* in the abl., e.g.

> *cōnsilium quō ūsus sum* 'the plan which I used' ('which' is object of *ūtor*; *ūtor* takes the abl.)

3 *quō* very often means '(to) where'; *quā* can mean 'where'.

EITHER

Reading exercise / Test exercise

Gauius hic, quem dīcō, Cōnsānus, cum in illō numerō cīuium Rōmānōrum ab istō in uincla coniectus esset et nesciō quā ratiōne clam ē lautumiīs profūgisset Messānamque uēnisset, quī tam prope iam Ītaliam et moenia Rēgīnōrum, cīuium Rōmānōrum, uidēret, et ex illō metū mortis ac tenebrīs quasi lūce lībertātis et odōre aliquō lēgum recreātus reuīxisset, loquī Messānae et querī coepit sē cīuem Rōmānum in uincla coniectum, sibi rēctā iter esse Rōmam, Verrī sē praestō aduenientī futūrum. (Cicero, *In Verrem* II 5, 61.160 (original of **F(ii)**) 5

Cōnsān-us a um from Consa

nesciō quis (lit. 'I do not know who')
   some (or other)

quī + subj. = 'since he'

Ītali-a ae 1f. Italy

Rēgīn-ī ōrum 2m. pl. inhabitants of
   Rhegium (on the toe of Italy)

tenebr-ae ārum 1f. pl. darkness,
   shadows

quasi as if

lūx lūc-is 3f. light

lībertās lībertāt-is 3f. liberty

odor odōr-is 3m. smell, scent

recreāt-us a um renewed

reuīuō 3 reuīxī I revive, come back
   to life

Messānae: locative of *Messān-a ae*
   1f. Messana

queror 3 dep. I complain

coniectum: understand *esse*

rēctā directly

iter itiner-is 3n. way, route

praestō 'to face' (+ dat. + part of
   esse)

adueniō 4 I arrive

futūrum: understand *esse*

OR

English–Latin

*Read the text of **4F(ii)** again and translate this passage into Latin*:

Verres had thrown into chains a man whose name was Gavius.[1] This[2] Gavius had managed to escape and arrive at Messana.[3] He declared that he would accuse Verres at Rome. Verres, however, when he had heard this, ordered his slaves to capture the man. They[4] dragged him back as he was embarking[5] and took him to the magistrate. When Verres had arrived at Messana,[3] he gave orders that Gavius be stripped in the middle of the forum and beaten. The lictors did not spare the man[5] although he was begging and kept asserting[5] that he was a Roman citizen. In this way it happened that a Roman citizen was murdered by Verres.

1. Use dative with *sum*. Remember that the idiom is to put the name into dative also.
2. 'This': use connecting relative.
3. 'at Messana': use accusative, since movement towards is indicated, although English idiom is different.
4. 'They': change of subject; use part of *ille*.
5. 'him … as he was embarking': use present participle on its own; 'the man although he was begging and kept asserting': use present participles and join 'begging' to 'kept asserting' with *et* or *-que*.

Grammar and exercises for 4G

140   **Future perfect indicative active: 'I shall have —ed'**

	1 '*I shall have loved*'	*2* '*I shall have had*'	*3* '*I shall have said*'
1st s.	amā́u-er-ō (amā́rō *etc.*)	habú-er-ō	díx-er-ō
2nd s.	amā́u-eri-s	habú-eri-s	díx-eri-s
3rd s.	amā́u-eri-t	habú-eri-t	díx-eri-t
1st pl.	amāu-éri-mus	habu-éri-mus	dīx-éri-mus
2nd pl.	amāu-éri-tis	habu-éri-tis	dīx-éri-tis
3rd pl.	amā́u-eri-nt	habú-eri-nt	díx-eri-nt

	4 '*I shall have heard*'	*3/4* '*I shall have captured*'
1st s.	audī́u-er-ō (audíerō *etc.*)	cḗp-er-ō
2nd s.	audī́u-eri-s	cḗp-eri-s
3rd s.	audī́u-eri-t	cḗp-eri-t
1st pl.	audīu-éri-mus	cēp-éri-mus
2nd pl.	audīu-éri-tis	cēp-éri-tis
3rd pl.	audī́u-eri-nt	cḗp-eri-nt

Notes

1 The fut. perf. can be translated literally into English as 'I shall have —ed'. It marks a distinction, important in Latin, but hardly used in English, between two future events, one of which will already have occurred when the other is going to happen. In English, the idiomatic way to express the meaning of this tense is usually with the plain present or perfect with 'have'. E.g.

> *ubi cōnsulēs uocāuerō, sententiam dīcam* 'when I (shall) have called the consuls, I shall speak my mind'
>
> *nisi pūnītī erunt, rēī pūblicae nocēbō* 'unless they are (= shall have been) punished, I shall be hurting the republic'

2 The future perfect active is formed by taking the stem of the 3rd p.p. and adding *-erō -eris -erit -erimus -eritis -erint*. Note that the normal active personal endings (*-ō, -s, -t, -mus, -tis, -nt*) are used.

3 Note the alternative forms of 1st and 4th conj. *amārō* and *audierō*, where *-u-* has been dropped. This also occurs with some other verbs, e.g. *dēlērō* = *dēlēuerō*.

141 Future perfect indicative deponent: 'I shall have —ed'

	1 '*I shall have threatened*'	*2* '*I shall have promised*'	*3* '*I shall have spoken*'
1st s.	minát-us a um érō	pollícit-us a um érō	locút-us a um érō
2nd s.	minát-us a um éris	pollícit-us a um éris	locút-us a um éris
3rd s.	minát-us a um érit	pollícit-us a um érit	locút-us a um érit
1st pl.	minát-ī ae a érimus	pollícit-ī ae a érimus	locút-ī ae a érimus
2nd pl.	minát-ī ae a éritis	pollícit-ī ae a éritis	locút-ī ae a éritis
3rd pl.	minát-ī ae a érunt	pollícit-ī ae a érunt	locút-ī ae a érunt

	4 '*I shall have lied*'	*3/4* '*I shall have advanced*'
1st s.	mentít-us a um érō	prōgréss-us a um érō
2nd s.	mentít-us a um éris	prōgréss-us a um éris
3rd s.	mentít-us a um érit	prōgréss-us a um érit
1st pl.	mentít-ī ae a érimus	prōgréss-ī ae a érimus
2nd pl.	mentít-ī ae a éritis	prōgréss-ī ae a éritis
3rd pl.	mentít-ī ae a érunt	prōgréss-ī ae a érunt

Note

The future perfect deponent is formed by taking the stem of the perfect participle, adding the appropriate endings *-us -a um* etc. to agree with the subject, and adding *erō eris erit erimus eritis erunt*, the future of *sum*.

142 Future perfect indicative passive: 'I shall have been —ed'

	1 '*I shall have been loved*'	*2* '*I shall have been held*'	*3* '*I shall have been said*'
1st s.	amát-us a um érō	hábit-us a um érō	díct-us a um érō
2nd s.	amát-us a um éris	hábit-us a um éris	díct-us a um éris
3rd s.	amát-us a um érit	hábit-us a um érit	díct-us a um érit
1st pl.	amát-ī ae a érimus	hábit-ī ae a érimus	díct-ī ae a érimus
2nd pl.	amát-ī ae a éritis	hábit-ī ae a éritis	díct-ī ae a éritis
3rd pl.	amát-ī ae a érunt	hábit-ī ae a érunt	díct-ī ae a érunt

	4 'I shall have been heard'	3/4 'I shall have been captured'
1st s.	audít-us a um érō	cápt-us a um érō
2nd s.	audít-us a um éris	cápt-us a um éris
3rd s.	audít-us a um érit	cápt-us a um érit
1st pl.	audít-ī ae a érimus	cápt-ī ae a érimus
2nd pl.	audít-ī ae a éritis	cápt-ī ae a éritis
3rd pl.	audít-ī ae a érunt	cápt-ī ae a érunt

Note

For formation of the future perfect indicative passive, see note on future perfect
deponent (above) **141**.

EXERCISES

1 *Form and conjugate these verbs in the future perfect tense* (*where '(passive)'*
   is written, give active and *passive – give deponent and passive in m. form*).
   commoror, tollō, accūsō (*passive*), coniciō, egeō, relinquō (*passive*), morior,
   absum (*optional*: nītor, sentiō (*passive*), nōlō, adeō, cupiō (*passive*), ūtor, patior,
   iaceō).

2 *Translate these future perfects, then change s. to pl. or vice versa*: retinuerit,
   dēfueritis, parāta erit, seruātī erunt, putāuerint, cōnātus eris, conuēnerimus,
   biberō, aggressa erunt, potuerint (*optional*: posuerit, comparāuerimus,
   exspectātus erit, petīuerint, reuocāta erunt, recordātus eris, iacuerō, ōrātum erit,
   profectī eritis, frūcta erit).

3 *Give the Latin for*: I shall have abandoned; he will have accused; they (*m.*)
   will have thought; she will have been sought out; it will have seemed; you
   (*pl.*) will have spared; they (*n.*) will have been stripped; you (*s.*) will have
   desired (*optional*: it will have attacked; they (*f.*) will have delayed; I shall have
   run away; it will have been reported; she will have worshipped; we will have
   placed; you (*pl.*) will have besieged; they (*n.*) will have been read through).

4 *Locate and translate the future perfects in this list* (*say which tense the others*
   are): cupīueram, commorātī erunt, parāuerās, reperta eris, seruāuissent,
   recepta erit, imperāuistī, ūsī eritis, accessistis, uocāuerātis, iacuerō, līberāuerit,
   affirmāuimus, mortua esset, commōuerit, nīsus erō, sēnsistis, negāuērunt,
   inuītāuerint, prōfūgit, adierimus, aggressus esset, petīuerit, uīsum erat.

5 *Translate these sentences*:

(a) etiam sī pater ipse Verris iūdicāuerit, fīlium suum scelestum esse nōn negābit.

(b) Verrēs ubi cīuīs Rōmānōs secūrī percusserit, ab omnibus accūsābitur.

(c) sī quis sē cīuem Rōmānum esse affirmāuerit, praetōrem eum līberāre oportēbit.

(d) sī ad rēgna numquam anteā inuenta adgressī erimus, cīuitātis Rōmānae nōmen nōs etiam ibi prōteget.

(e) sī litterās ad Lūcium Raecium mīseris, ille Gauium cīuem Rōmānum esse cōnfirmābit.

(f) ubi uīxerimus, mortuī erimus.

143   The meanings of the subjunctive

Subjunctive means 'subordinated' (*subiungō subiūnctus* 'I join under'), and came to be used in clauses just because they were subordinate (e.g. *cum* + subjunctive, **126,** which always took the indicative in early Latin, and does occasionally in classical). But it does have a specific meaning of its own: to simplify, it indicates that the speaker wants an action to take place (because he thinks it should or because it is his desire that it should) or that the speaker thinks it possible that under certain conditions it *could* take place. (Sometimes, but rarely, it indicates that the speaker expects the action to take place, but this function is normally carried out by the future indicative.)

Observe how the subjunctives met so far fit into these categories: indirect commands ('he ordered him to go': *ut/nē* + subjunctive) use the subjunctive to express the speaker's *will* that something should happen; 'it happens that' (*accidit ut* (*nōn*) + subjunctive) uses the subjunctive to indicate that *conditions make it possible* for X to happen; 'I bring it about that' (*perficiō ut/nē* + subjunctive) often expresses the speaker's *intentions* that something should happen.

144   Conditionals with subjunctive verbs: 'if X were: … Y would'

Given the above functions of the subjunctive, it is not surprising that Latin uses the subjunctive in conditional sentences where the conditions stated are *unreal* or *unfulfilled*, i.e. they contain the words 'would' or 'should' in English. E.g.

> 'If I were rich, I would not (now) be working' (referring to present time)
> 'If I were to become rich, I would give all my money to the poor' (referring to future time)

Consider the Latin translations:

> *sī dīues essem, nōn labōrārem*
> *sī dīues fīam, omnem pecūniam pauperibus dem*

Observe that the imperfect subjunctive is used *in both clauses* where reference is to the present time, and the present subjunctive *in both clauses* where the reference is to the future time. Study the following examples and check this rule:

> *sī pater <u>adesset</u>, quid <u>dīceret</u>?* 'if father were (now) here, what
>   would he (now) be saying?'
> *sī Verrī <u>ignōscātis</u>, nēmō uōbīs <u>ignōscat</u>* 'if you were to pardon
>   Verres (some time in the future), no one would pardon
>   you'
> *sī <u>fugiant</u>, <u>sequāmur</u>* 'if they were to flee, we would follow'
> *sī <u>mentīrēris</u>, tē <u>caederem</u>* 'if you were (now) lying, I would (now)
>   be beating you'

So the basic rules are:

> *sī* + subjunctive (followed by a main clause with subjunctive verb)
>   indicates conditions with 'would' or 'should'
> *sī* + imperfect subjunctive (main clause verb in imperfect
>   subjunctive): 'if X were (now) the case, Y would (now) be the
>   case'
> *sī* + present subjunctive (main clause verb in present subjunctive)
>   'if X were to be (in the future) the case, Y would be the
>   case'

We say 'basic' rules, because Latin is flexible and can mix subjunctive and indicative in these clauses.

Notes

1 *sī quis* = 'if anyone', e.g. *sī quis exeat, puniātur* 'if anyone were to go out, he would be punished' (cf. on *nē quis* **136**[3] and **150**[2]; forms **14**).

2 *nisi* 'if not', 'unless' follows the same rules, e.g. *nisi pulcher essēs, tē nōn amārem* 'if you were not (now) so handsome, I would not (now) be in love with you', *nisi quis* = 'unless anyone', see note 1 above.

3 In some instances, the imperfect subjunctives refer to the *past*, e.g. *sī Raecius cognōsceret hominem, aliquid ... remitterēs* 'if Raecius had recognised the fellow, you would have remitted something'. The context will make clear when this meaning is appropriate. The more usual way Latin expresses 'would have —ed' is with the pluperfect subjunctive (see **173**).

4 Quite often, a statement includes only the main clause of a condition omitting the *sī* clause, e.g. *uidērēs* 'you would have seen', *uelim* 'I would like'.

EXERCISES

EITHER

1 *Translate these sentences*:

(a) sī Verris pater adesset, fīlium suum cīuitātī nostrae hostem esse iūdicāret. (*2 possibilities*)

(b) sī Verrī ignōscāmus, stultī sīmus.

(c) sī Verrēs mea pōcula postulet, ego sine morā ad eum litterās mittam.

(d) etiam animālia, sī haec audīrent, commouērentur. (*2 possibilities*)

(e) nisi tē cīuem Rōmānum esse clāmitēs, necēris.

(f) sī hoc praesidium habērēs, etiam hostēs tibi parcerent. (*2 possibilities*)

(g) sī esset prōuidentia, nūlla essent mala. (Gellius)

(h) uīna parant animum Venerī, nisi plūrima sūmās. (Ovid)

   prōuidenti-a ae 1f. foresight, providence

   uīn-um ī 2n. wine

   Venus Vener-is 3f. Venus; love-making

   sūmō 3 I take

OR

2 *Give the Latin for the following (remember reference to future 'were to' = present subjunctive, and 'would' also = present; 'were —ing', 'were (now)' = imperfect subjunctive; 'would have' also = imperfect subjunctive)*:

(a) If I were (now) a Roman citizen ...

(b) If he were to demand protection ...

(c) If there were not (now) a delay ...

(d) If our friends were to be moved ...

(e) If we were asking for protection ...

(f) If I were to keep shouting ...

(g) I would like to say ...

(h) I would have liked to ask ...

(i) I would have demanded ...

(j) I would be moved ...

145 Subjunctive in relative clauses

We have already met relative clauses with indicative verbs (**106**), which serve to identify the person or thing referred to (e.g. *Diodōrus, quem Verrēs ōderat, timēbat* 'Diodorus, whom Verres hated, was afraid'). When the verb in the relative clause is subjunctive (except within reported speech: see **147** below), other factors than mere factual identification are at play. Such relative + subjunctive clauses fall under one of three main headings (for a fourth, see **150**):

1 'Generic': where the relative clause refers to the type of person or thing, not to any specific one. The construction is especially common after (a) *est quī / sunt quī* 'there exists/exist the sort of person/people who', (b) *is quī* 'the sort of person who', e.g.

    (a) *sunt <u>quī sciant</u>* 'there are (those of the sort) <u>who know</u>'

    (b) *ea nōn est <u>quae</u> hoc <u>faciat</u>* 'she is not the one <u>who does</u> this' = 'not the sort of person who …'

Contrast the use of the indicative: e.g. *ea nōn est <u>quae</u> hoc <u>facit</u>* 'it is not she who is doing this'.

    Another term for such clauses is 'relative clauses of characteristics': the subjunctive may be classified as 'consecutive' (see **149**) or 'establishing conditions for possible action'.

2 Causal, i.e. the relative clause shows the *reason why* something is happening, e.g.

> *sānus tū nōn es quī mē fūrem uocēs* (Plautus) 'you are not sane who call me a thief' = 'because you call me a thief'

This usage is sometimes strongly 'signposted' by the addition of the fixed form *quippe* 'inasmuch as', e.g.

> *sōlis candor inlūstrior est quam ūllīus ignis, <u>quippe quī</u> inmēnsō mundō tam longē lātēque conlūceat* 'The brightness of the sun is more brilliant than that of any fire, <u>inasmuch as it</u> shines so far and wide in an immeasurable universe' (Cicero)

3 Concessive, i.e. the relative clause means 'although'. Words such as *tamen* may signpost this usage, e.g.

> *Verrēs, quī uīsus multīs diēbus nōn esset, tamen sē in cōnspectum dedit* 'Verres, who had not been seen for many days, nevertheless presented himself to view', i.e. 'Verres, *although* he …' (concessive).

146   *cum, quamuīs* + subjunctive

1 We have already met *cum* + pluperfect subjunctive meaning 'when', 'since',
   'although' 'X had —ed' (**126**). *cum* is also used with the imperfect subjunctive,
   to mean 'when', 'since', 'although' 'X was —ing', and with the present
   subjunctive, to mean 'since', 'although' 'X is —ing'. (NB NOT 'when'.)

2 *quamuīs* means 'although' (really 'however') and takes the subjunctive, e.g.
   quamuīs fortis <u>esset</u> ab hostibus fūgit 'although he was courageous, he fled
   from the enemy' (really 'however brave he might have been, he still fled from
   the enemy'; contrast *quamquam* 'although', which takes the indicative).

147   **Subjunctive in reported speech**

In reported speech subordinate clauses have their verb in the subjunctive. Since
this is simply a way of showing that the clause belongs in the indirect quotation,
the meaning is the same as the indicative, e.g.

> Direct: 'because I am handsome, everyone loves me' *<u>quod</u> pulcher
>   <u>sum</u>, omnēs mē amant*
>
> Indirect (past): 'he said that, because (as he said) he was handsome,
>   everyone loved him' *dīxit omnīs sē, <u>quod</u> pulcher <u>esset</u>, amāre*
>
> Indirect (present): 'he says that, because he is handsome, all love
>   him' *dīcit omnīs sē, <u>quod</u> pulcher <u>sit</u>, amāre*
>
> Cf. *Gauium… dīcis… clāmitāsse sē cīuem Rōmānum esse <u>quod</u>
>   moram mortī <u>quaereret</u>* 'you say that Gavius shouted continually
>   that he was a Roman citizen <u>because he was seeking</u> a delay to
>   his death'

Two important consequences of this rule are:

1 Certain distinctions in conditions and relative clauses will now *not* stand out,
   since everything becomes subjunctive, e.g. *dīcō seruum <u>quem cēperis</u> stultum
   esse* 'I say that the slave <u>whom you captured</u> is stupid' – the relative clause in
   the subjunctive does not imply 'when/although/since' (cf. **145**).

2 If a subordinate clause in reported speech has an *indicative* verb, it implies
   that this represents the *author's* view of the matter, e.g. *dīcō seruum <u>quī stultus
   est</u> mox fugitūrum esse* 'I say that the slave <u>who is stupid</u> [understood: 'in my
   opinion'] will soon run away'.

Note

Generally speaking, it will be obvious from context what tense in the original
statement is represented by the subjunctive. Here is a summary of the main rules
determining the tense of the subjunctive:

	Subjunctive used in 'reported' speech	
	Primary sequence	*Secondary sequence*
If the 'unreported' verb was originally present indicative	Present	Imperfect
If the 'unreported' verb was originally future indicative	*-ūrus* (i.e. fut. part.) + *sim* (sometimes present)	*-ūrus essem* (sometimes imperfect)
If the 'unreported' verb was originally past indicative	Perfect	Pluperfect

148　　Infinitives without *esse* in reported speech

In accusative and infinitive constructions, *esse* is often dropped, e.g.

> *dīxit sē moritūrum* (*esse*) 'he said that he would die'
>
> *dīxērunt urbem captam* (*esse*) 'they said that the city had been captured'
>
> *negat sē secūtūram* (*esse*) 'she says that she will not follow' (how do you know it is 'she'?)

Here are two examples from *Text*, **4G(i)**:

> *sī audīret ā tē cīuīs Rōmānōs secūrī percussōs* 'if he heard that Roman citizens had been executed by you'
>
> *arbitrātī … hanc rem sibi praesidiō futūram* 'thinking that this would be a protection for them'

EITHER

Reading exercise / Test exercise

*Here is part of the original of section **4F(ii)**. Gavius has just been arrested at Messana. Remember that Latin literature was composed to be read aloud. The final product of your study of each passage should be a well-phrased* recitatio *('reading aloud').*

itaque ad magistrātum Māmertīnum statim dēdūcitur Gauius, eōque ipsō diē cāsū Messānam Verrēs uēnit. rēs ad eum defertur, esse cīuem Rōmānum quī sē Syrācūsīs in lautumiīs fuisse quererētur; quem iam ingredientem in nāuem et Verrī nimis atrōciter minitantem ab sē retractum esse et adseruātum … agit hominibus grātiās et eōrum beneuolentiam ergā sē dīligentiamque conlaudat, ipse īnflammātus scelere et furōre in forum uēnit; ārdēbant oculī, tōtō ex ōre crūdēlitās ēminēbat … repente hominem prōripī atque in forō mediō nūdarī ac dēligārī et uirgās expedīrī iubet. clāmābat ille miser sē cīuem esse Rōmānum   5

mūnicipem Cōnsānum; meruisse cum L. Raeciō, splendidissimō equite
Rōmānō, quī Panhormī negōtiārētur, ex quo haec Verrēs scīre posset. tum iste,   10
sē comperīsse eum … in Siciliam ā ducibus fugitīuōrum esse missum … deinde
iubet undique hominem uehementissimē uerberārī. caedēbātur uirgīs in mediō
forō Messānae cīuis Rōmānus, iūdicēs, cum intereā nūllus gemitus, nūlla uōx
alia illīus miserī inter dolōrem crepitumque plāgārum audiēbātur nisi haec 'cīuis
Rōmānus sum.' hāc sē commemorātiōne cīuitātis omnia uerbera depulsūrum   15
cruciātumque ā corpore dēiectūrum arbitrābātur; is nōn modo hoc nōn perfēcit,
ut uirgārum uim dēprecārētur, sed cum implōrāret saepius ūsūrpāretque nōmen
cīuitātis, crux – crux, inquam – īnfēlīcī et aerumnōsō, quī numquam istam
pestem uīderat, comparābātur. (Cicero, *In Verrem* II 5, 62.160–2)

Māmertīn-us a um of Messana
cāsū by chance
esse cīuem … [acc. + inf. after
    dēfertur]
sē [hold: expect reflexive verb or acc.
    + inf.]
adseruō 1 I keep (in custody)
lautumi-ae ārum 1f. pl. stone-quarries
queror 3 dep. I complain
quem [connecting relative – who is
    the antecedent?]
Verrī [hold: it will be governed by
    minitantem]
minitor 1 dep. I threaten continually
    [*minor* + -*it*-]
sē [i.e. the people reporting to
    Verres]
retrahō 3 *retrāxī retractus* I drag
    back
[subject of *agit* is *Verres*]
beneuolenti-a ae 1f. good will
ergā (+ acc.) towards
dīligenti-a ae 1f. care
conlaud-ō 1 I praise
ārdeō 2 I burn (intrans.)
crūdēlitās crūdēlitāt-is 3f. cruelty
ēmineō 2 I stand out
prōripiō 3/4 I drag forward
dēligō 1 I bind

uirg-a ae 1f. rod
expediō 4 I get ready
ille miser [i.e. Gavius]
mūniceps mūnicip-is 3m. citizen of a
    mūnicipium (= free town)
Cōnsān-us a um of Consa
meruisse [acc. + inf. construction
    continues with *sē* still as
    subject]
mereō 2 I serve (in the army)
splendid-us a um distinguished
Panhorm-us ī 2f. Palermo [cf.   10
    Lilybaeī for case]
negōtior 1 dep. I do business
haec [hold]
iste [change of subject to Verres. The
    introductory verb for the acc. + inf.
    sē comperīsse is omitted – supply
    dīxit.]
comperiō 4 *comperī* I find out,
    learn
eum [i.e. Gavius]
fugitīu-us ī 2m. deserter
undique from all sides
gemit-us ūs 4m. groan [Note lack of *et*
    between *nūllus gemitus* and *nūlla
    uōx* (though they are to be taken
    together): this is called *asyndeton*:
    see p. 270(c).]

dolor dolōr-is 3m. pain

crepit-us ūs 4m. noise

plāg-a ae 1f. blow

sē [hold: it is part of an acc. + inf.
phrase (in unemphatic position:
see **98⁴**)]

15 *commemorātiō commemorātiōn-is* 3f.
mention

cīuitās cīuitāt-is 3f. (here) citizenship

dēpulsūrum [understand *esse*]

dēpellō 3 *dēpulī dēpulsus* I turn away,
prevent

cruciāt-us ūs 4m. torture [cf. *crux
cruc-is*]

corpus corpor-is 3n. body

dēiectūrum [understand *esse*]

dēiciō 3/4 *dēiēcī dēiectus* I drive
away

hoc [refers forward to the *ut* clause]

dēprecor 1 dep. I ward off (by earnest
prayer)

implōrō 1 I implore, beseech

ūsūrpō 1 I use

crux cruc-is 3f. cross

infēlīx īnfēlīc-is unfortunate [used as
noun here]

aerumnōs-us a um miserable [sc. 'man'
– used as noun here]

pestis pest-is 3f. curse, bane [refers to
crux]

OR

English–Latin

*Reread the text of **4G(ii)** and then translate this passage into Latin*:

Although[1] Gavius had named Raecius as his guarantor, you did not send a letter
to him. I would like[2] you to tell me, Verres, this. Why did you delay? Why did you
not send him a letter at once? Did not Gavius say,[3] 'If you were to[4] send a letter
to Raecius, he would[4] say that I am a Roman citizen. If he were[5] present, here,
he would[5] declare that I, whom you are accusing,[6] am innocent.' But you, Verres,
with the utmost disregard for Gavius, got a cross ready. If I were telling[5] this
story[7] to wild beasts, even they would[5] be moved.

1. *quamquam* + indicative, or *quamuīs* or *cum* + subjunctive.
2. Potential – use present subjunctive. See **144⁴**.
3. 'say': open inverted commas and start the next part before inserting *inquit*.
4. 'were to … would': present subjunctives.
5. 'were … would': use imperfect subjunctives.
6. Subordinate clause in indirect speech: use present subjunctive verb.
7. 'story': use n. s. or pl. of *hic*, or use *rēs*.

149   **Result (or 'consecutive') clauses: 'so ... that'**

Result clauses are expressed in Latin by an introductory word such as *tam, adeō, sīc, ita* (all 'so'), *tot* 'so many', *tantus* 'so big' picked up by *ut* 'that' (negative *ut nōn / numquam / nēmo / nūllus* etc.). The verb in the *ut* clause is in the subjunctive (present or perfect (to be met at **167–9**) in primary sequence, imperfect in secondary sequence).

Diagrammatically:

'so' word	that (not)
tam 'so'	
adeō 'to such an extent'	
sīc / *ita* 'in such a way'	*ut* (*nōn*) + verb in subjunctive
tantus 'so great'	
tot 'so many'	
tālis 'of such a kind'	

E.g.

> *tam ferōx est ut omnēs eum timeant* 'he is so fierce that everyone fears him'
>
> *tam pauper erat ut fīliae dōtem dare nōn posset* 'he was so poor that he was not able to give his daughter a dowry'
>
> *sīc ... Deus dīlēxit mundum, ut ... daret* 'God so loved the world that he gave ...' (John 3.16)

Cf. this example from *Text* **4H**:

> *tē, Mercurī, tantum dēspexit, ut imāginem tuam in domō et prīuātā palaestrā pōneret* 'You, Mercury, he despised so much that he placed your statue in his house and in a private wrestling-ground.'

Notes

1 These are often called 'consecutive' clauses – from *cōnsequor cōnsecūtus* 'I follow closely' – because the result follows closely on, is the consequence or result of, the action.

2 Compare this construction with *accidit ut* (**137**). Both establish the *conditions* that make the result *possible*, and so fall within the range of specific usages of the subjunctive (**143**), as do *est/sunt quī* 'he is / they are the sort to / who' and *is quī* 'the sort of person who' (**145.1**) and *perficiō ut* 'I bring it about that' (**137**).

3 Similar constructions are:

> *longē abest ut* + subjunctive 'he is far from —ing', e.g. *longē abest ut timeat* 'he is far from being afraid'

> *fierī potest ut* + subjunctive 'it can come about that', e.g. *fierī potest ut rem perficiat* 'it can happen that he will achieve his ends'

See also **145.1** for 'generic' relative clauses introduced e.g. by *is est quī* ('he is the sort of person who …'), which can also be classed as 'consecutive'.

EXERCISES

1 *Translate into English*:
   (a) Verrī religiō adeō dēest ut deōrum imāginēs ē fānīs conuellere audeat.
   (b) Verrem tantus furor cēperat ut etiam contrā deōs scelera committeret.
   (c) tam audāx erat ut simulācra religiōsissima domī suae pōneret.
   (d) dignitās reīpūblicae tālis est ut hominibus maximō auxiliō sit.
   (e) fierī poterat ut Verrēs ā iūdicibus Siciliā fugere cōgī posset.

2 *Translate into Latin the underlined words*:
   (a) So great (*s.f.*) is the dignity of the state that it forces men to obey the laws.
   (b) Verres was so criminal that he attacked the gods themselves.
   (c) Verres was inflamed to such an extent by his eagerness for gain that he removed sacred statues from the temples of the gods.
   (d) Verres is so vile, that he ought to be forced to leave Sicily.
   (e) May the gods regard this crime as such that Verres suffers the greatest penalty.

150 **Purpose (or 'final') clauses: 'in order that/to', 'to'**

Purpose (or 'final': *finis* 'end') clauses in Latin are expressed by *ut* ('in order that, in order to, to') or its negative *nē* ('lest', 'in order that … not', 'in order not to', 'not to'), followed by the subjunctive: present subjunctive in primary sequence, imperfect subjunctive in secondary sequence. E.g.

> *hoc facit ut benīgnus sit* 'he is doing this (in order) to be kind, '(in order) that he may be kind'

> *hoc fēcit nē miser esset* 'he did this (in order) not to be unhappy', 'lest he be unhappy', '(in order) that he might not be unhappy'

(Observe how English favours 'may' in primary sequence, and 'might' in secondary.)

Cf. this example from **4H**:

simulācrum tuum, Iuppiter Optime Maxime, iste Syrācūsīs sustulit,
ut domī suae tenēret 'Your statue, Jupiter Best and Greatest, that
fellow took from Syracuse, in order to keep it at his own house'
In particular, quī quae quod + subjunctive can also express purpose, especially
after a main verb of motion, e.g.

nūntiōs mīsit quī bellum cīuibus nūntiārent 'he sent messengers <u>who
were to announce</u>', '<u>who were to announce</u> war to the citizens'

cōnsilium perfēcit quō effugerent 'he put into practice a plan <u>by
which they might escape</u>', '<u>for them to escape by</u>'

locum petit unde (= ex quō) hostem aggrediātur 'he is looking for a
position <u>from which to attack the enemy</u>'

Cf. this example from **4H**:

fūrēs suōs Segestam mīsit, quī templum tuum compīlārent ... 'he sent
his thieves to Segesta <u>who would rob</u> your temple' '... <u>to rob</u>'

The construction falls within the scope of specific usages of the subjunctive.
It shows the speaker's *intention* that something should happen. Cf. *perficiō
ut* (**137**).

Notes

1 Any references to the subject of the main verb inside the *ut/nē* clause will be
reflexive, e.g.

'Verres said this in order that the citizens should fear him (= Verres)'
Verrēs haec dīxit ut cīuēs sē timērent

2 The Latin for 'in order that no one' is *nē quis* (lit. 'lest anyone'); 'in order that
nothing' is *nē quid* (lit. 'lest anything') etc., e.g.

'Euclio hides the gold in order that no one may see it' *Eucliō aurum
cēlat nē quis id uideat*

See **136**[3] for *nē quis* in indirect command, and **14** for forms.

EXERCISES

1 *Translate into English*:

   (a) Verrēs seruōs mīsit quī simulācrum Iouis Syrācūsīs tollerent.

   (b) Verrēs simulācrum Iouis abstulit ut domī suae tenēret.

   (c) iste Iūnōnis fāna nūdat ut omnia dōna possideat.

   (d) nocte mediā sociī Verris fānum aggressī sunt nē quis sibi obstāret.

   (e) seruī Verris simulācrum, quod ā uirō aspicī fās nōn est, auferunt ut uir
tandem deae imāginem uideat.

(f) scrībēbat Aelius ōrātiōnēs[1] quās aliī dīcerent. (Cicero)

(g) nihil tam absurdē[2] dīcī potest quod nōn dīcātur ab aliquō philosophōrum.[3] (Cicero)

1. *ōrātiō ōrātiōn-is* 3f. speech.
2. *absurdē* stupidly. (See **145.1** for the construction in this sentence.)
3. *philosoph-us* ī 2m. philosopher.

2 *Translate the underlined words into Latin (take care to get the right sequence of tenses – see* **150**):

(a) Verres is sending his friends to[1] take away the statue of Jupiter.

(b) The slaves came by night in order that no one would see them.[2]

(c) Verres ordered his men to bring the statue to him.[2]

(d) The citizens of Sicily hide their belongings so that Verres may not take them away.

(e) In order to be safe, the citizens must ensure Verres' condemnation.

1. Use *quī* + subjunctive.
2. 'him', 'them': use part of *sē*.

Reading: *ut*

You have now met *ut* as a conjunction in several different senses.

ut + indicative

(a) 'how!'

(b) 'as', 'when'

ut + subjunctive

(a) Indirect command (after e.g. *imperō*, *persuādeō* etc.) 'to ...'

(b) Result (after e.g. *tam*, *tantus*, *adeō* etc.) 'so ... that'

(c) Purpose 'in order that/to'.

(d) After *perficiō* 'I bring it about that', *accidit* 'it happens that'.

To solve *ut*, watch out for: (i) indicative or subjunctive? (ii) if subjunctive, a verb of commanding will suggest (a), a 'flag' such as *tam*, *tantus* will suggest (b), and a negative *ut nōn* will suggest (b) or (d), while the negative *nē* will suggest (a) or (c). E.g.

> *Verrēs seruīs imperat ut* ... 'Verres to the slaves gives orders that ...'

solves itself very quickly. But

> *Verrēs ut seruīs* ...

leaves doubts about *ut* and *seruīs*, so hold these words till solved.

NB *ut* is also found in the meaning 'as', qualifying a noun, e.g. *canem et fēlem ut deōs colunt* 'They worship the dog and the cat *as gods.*'

EXERCISE

Read these sentences, making explicit your steps in understanding, especially when you reach ut (*or equivalent*). *State the moment when you can solve* ut:

(a) eōs ut benīgnī essent hortābātur.

(b) Verrēs tam malus est ut deōrum fāna dōnīs nūdet.

(c) ut ego iubēbō, ita tū faciēs.

(d) hōrum contumēliās[1] sapiēns[2] ut iocōs accipit. (Seneca)

(e) Verrēs perfēcit ut imāginēs nōn redderentur.

(f) nē imāginēs redderentur, Verrēs Rōmam mīsit.

(g) ut fōrmōsum Iouis simulācrum est!

1 *contumēli-a ae* 1f. insult
2 *sapiēns* nom. s. m. wise man

151   **Gerundives: *-ndus -nda -ndum* 'to be —ed'**

The gerundive is an adjective based on a verb and declining like *mult-us a um*. Its meaning is passive, 'to be —ed', rather like a future passive participle. Note that this is virtually the only case where deponent verbs are *passive* in meaning (see **C4** note 2). Here is the formation:

1	2	3
'to be loved'	'to be had'	'to be said'
amá-nd-us a um	habé-nd-us a um	dīc-é-nd-us a um
'to be encouraged'	'to be promised'	'to be said'
hortánd-us a um[1]	pollicé-nd-us a um	loqu-é-nd-us a um

4	3/4
'to be heard'	'to be captured'
audi-é-nd-us a um	capi-é-nd-us a um
'to be started'	'to be attacked'
ordi-é-nd-us a um[1]	aggredi-é-nd-us a um[1]

1. The usual paradigm verbs *mentior* and *prōgredior*, being intransitive, have only neuter forms of the gerundive, so we have used transitive alternatives here. See **162**.

152   **Uses of the gerundive**

1   As an adjective meaning 'to be —ed', e.g.

> *suscēpit nōs ēdūcandōs* 'he took us <u>to be educated</u>'

A number of other verbs take this construction, e.g. *dō*, *petō*, *cūrō* etc., e.g.

> *Caesar pontem in Arare <u>faciendum cūrat</u>* 'Caesar <u>saw to the making</u> of a bridge over the Arar' (Caesar)

2   With nouns, especially *ad* + acc. to denote purpose, e.g.

> *ad conuellendās sēdēs* 'for the foundations to be torn away', i.e. 'for tearing away the foundations' / 'with a view to tearing away the foundations'

The ablatives *causā/grātiā* 'for the sake of' (which *follow* the phrase which they govern) are commonly used with a gerundive construction to express purpose, e.g.

> *templī uidendī causā* 'for the sake of the temple-to-be-seen', 'for the sake of seeing the temple', 'to see the temple'

(Cf. *honōris causā* (or *grātiā*) 'for honour's sake', 'as an honour'; e.g. = *exemplī grātiā* 'for (the sake of) an example')

NB Where awkwardness results from literal translation of the gerundive, turn the phrase into an *active* form in English, e.g. *ad mīlitēs necandōs* lit. 'with a view to the soldiers to be killed' → 'with a view to killing the soldiers'.

EXERCISES

1   *Form the gerundive of the following verbs and translate*: cogō, dēleō, habeō, pōnō, necō, dormiō, amplexor, uideō (*optional*: committō, īnstruō, seruō, relinquō, retineō, sequor, reperiō, hortor).

2   *Translate*:

(a) ad urbem dēlendam.

(b) dōnī dandī causā.

(c) dux hostīs interficiendōs suscēpit.

(d) ad rempūblicam dēfendendam.

(e) Cicerō Siciliae cīuīs seruandōs cūrat.

(f) ad manūs tenendās.

(g) ducis necandī grātiā.

(h) Cicerōnī cīuēs Siciliam dēfendendam dedērunt.

(i) ad imāginēs dēlendās.

(j) Verris accūsandī causā.

(k) ad dignitātem seruandam.

3 *Give the Latin for*:

   (a) To accuse Verres. (*Use* ad + *acc.*)

   (b) To defend Sicily. (*Use* causā *or* grātiā + *gen. after the phrase*)

   (c) To retain dignity. (*Use* ad + *acc.*)

   (d) For the sake of taking away the statue. (*Use* causā *or* grātiā + *gen. after
        the phrase*)

   (e) To force the citizens. (*Use* ad + *acc.*)

Grammar and exercises for 5A

153 **The historic infinitive**

In places where the narrative is drawn in rapid, broad strokes, especially where one action follows swiftly upon another, Latin can use the *present infinitive* where we would expect an indicative (usually imperfect indicative). The infinitive tells us what the verbal action is; subject is nominative, tense has to be gathered from the broad context. E.g.

> *intereā Catilīna Rōmae multa simul <u>agere</u>; īnsidiās <u>collocāre</u>, <u>parāre</u> incendia, loca <u>obsidēre</u>, ipse cum tēlō <u>esse</u>.*

> 'Meanwhile, Catiline <u>put</u> many schemes into operation simultaneously in Rome: he <u>set up</u> ambushes, <u>prepared</u> fires, <u>laid siege</u> to places, <u>went around</u> himself under arms.'

Note the atmosphere of busy activity, in which historic infinitives most commonly occur.

EXERCISE

Translate these sentences and say whether the infinitive is prolative (i.e. completes the meaning of a verb, e.g. nolō, possum *etc.), reporting speech (accusative and infinitive), or historic:*

(a) nōbilēs Catilīnae cōnsulātum mandāre nōluērunt.

(b) Fuluia multīs Catilīnam coniūrātiōnem parāre dīxerat.

(c) Catilīna in diēs plūra agitāre, arma collocāre, pecūniam ad Mānlium mittere.

(d) coniūrātiōnem sē facere negat Catilīna.

(e) Semprōnia uersūs facere, sermōne ūtī modestō.

(f) Cicerō Cornēlium et Varguntēium in aedīs suās intrāre uetuit.

154A **Ablative of respect: 'in point of'**

A common use of the ablative, especially in poetry, is to specify the *respect in which* something is the case, e.g.

> *numquam uictus est <u>uirtūte</u>* 'he was never conquered <u>in point of</u> / <u>in respect of</u> courage'

> *<u>litterīs Latīnīs</u> docta* 'learned <u>in point of</u> / <u>in respect of</u> Latin literature'

> *<u>genere</u> fortūnāta* 'lucky <u>in point of</u> / <u>in respect of</u> her birth'

EXERCISE

Translate these sentences; *pick out ablatives, distinguishing ablatives of respect from other usages*:

(a) Semprōnia, genere nōbilī nāta, litterīs Latīnīs docta erat.

(b) uir quīdam, Curius nōmine, eō tempōre Fuluiam amābat.

(c) nōn tōtā rē, sed temporibus errāstī.[1] (Cicero)

(d) eā nocte Cornēlius et Varguntēius Cicerōnis iānuā prohibitī sunt.

(e) Catilīna, quamuīs genere atque fōrmā fortūnātus esset, uir tamen minimā sapientiā fuit.

1. *errō* 1 I am wrong.

154B   *quī*

quī has different meanings. In differentiating between them, the first step will be to ask whether the verb is *indicative* or *subjunctive*.

quī + indicative

This is the descriptive relative 'who', 'which', 'what', 'that'.

quī + subjunctive

(a) Purpose (with verbs of motion)

(b) Consecutive (*est quī, is quī*) 'the sort of person who'

(c) Causal, 'since'

(d) Indirect speech, where it may = ordinary relative, unless context demands otherwise

(e) Concessive 'although', e.g. *uir quī fortis esset tamen effūgit* 'the man, who was brave, nevertheless fled', i.e. 'the man, although he was brave, fled'

EXERCISES

Read these sentences, using the information just outlined. State the moment when quī *is solved*:

(a) Catilīna Rōmam sociōs mittit, quī urbem incendant.

(b) Semprōnia, quae uirōs semper petēbat, mātrōna Rōmāna erat.

(c) Clūsīnī[1] lēgātōs Rōmam, quī auxilium ā senātū peterent, mīsēre. (Livy)

(d) multī arbitrābantur coniūrātiōnem uiam esse, quā aere aliēnō sē līberāre possent.

(e) fēminae etiam aliquot sē coniūrātiōnī adiūnxērunt, quae in aes aliēnum maximum conciderant.

(f) quī reī pūblicae sit hostis, fēlīx[2] esse nēmo potest. (Cicero)

(g) tē amō quī sīs tam fortis.

1. *Clūsīnī* 2m. pl. the people of Clusium.
2. *fēlīx fēlīc-is* 'fortunate'.

EITHER

Reading exercise / Test exercise

Catiline has just made a speech to his fellow conspirators, rousing them to action. Sallust describes their demand for a clear-cut goal and Catiline's promises of various rewards.

postquam accēpēre ea hominēs, quibus mala abundē omnia erant, sed neque rēs neque spēs bona ūlla, tametsī illīs quiēta mouēre magna mercēs uidēbatur, tamen postulāuēre plērīque ut prōpōneret condiciōnēs bellī et praemia. tum Catilīna pollicērī tabulās nouās, prōscrīptiōnem locuplētium, magistrātūs, sacerdōtia, rapīnās, alia omnia, quae bellum atque   5
libīdō uictōrum fert. (Sallust, *Catiline* 21.1–2, slightly adapted)

ea [refers back to Catiline's speech]

abundē plentifully

mala: n. pl. of *malus* 'misfortune', in contrast with *rēs* and *spēs bona*

spēs spē-ī 5f. hope

tametsī although

quiēt-us a um quiet, peaceful; quiēta movēre (subject) = 'create disorder'

mercēs mercēd-is 3f. reward

plērīque plēraeque plēraque   the majority

prōpōnō 3 I state

condiciō condiciōn-is 3f. term

praemi-um ī 2n. reward

Catilīna pollicērī [Note (1) case of *Catilīna*, (2) what part of the verb *pollicērī* is: refer, if necessary, to **153**.]

tabul-ae ārum 1f. pl. accounts [*tabulae nouae* implies the cancellation of existing debts]

prōscrīptiō prōscrīptiōn-is 3f. proscription (i.e. notice proclaiming someone an
    outlaw, and confiscation of his goods)

5 *locuplēs locuplēt-is* rich

    sacerdōti-um ī 2n. priesthood

    rapīn-a ae 1f. plunder, forcible seizure of property

    uictor uictōr-is 3m. victor

OR

English–Latin

*Reread the text of **5A(iii)**, then translate this passage*:

Although Catiline[1] had got ready the conspiracy, he nevertheless stood for the
consulship again. Meanwhile, he kept attempting to persuade his allies to attack
Cicero. Cicero, however, had made plans in order to escape the danger. Through
Fulvia and Curius he had managed to hear of Catiline's plans.

    Again the nobles were so afraid that they did not entrust the consulship to
Catiline. He then decided to wage war. He stationed his supporters in various
parts of Italy. Meanwhile at Rome he set[2] a trap for the consul, went around[2] with
a weapon, and[3] encouraged[2] his supporters to be brave.

1. Catiline is subject of both clauses, so place him before the conjunction.
2. Use historic infinitives.
3. Omit – use asyndeton (no connections: see p. 270(c)).

Grammar and exercises for 5B

155   **Purpose clauses: *quō* + comparative + subjunctive 'in order that … more'**

When a purpose clause contains a comparative (adverb or adjective), it is introduced NOT by *ut* but by *quō*, e.g.

> *hoc fēcit quō celerius peruenīret* 'he did this (<u>in order</u>) to arrive <u>more quickly</u>'

cf.

> *quō facilior aditus ad cōnsulem fieret* '<u>in order that</u> there might be <u>an easier</u> approach to the consul'

The verb in the *quō* clauses follows the normal rule, and will be either present or imperfect subjunctive. This construction is not difficult to spot, since it has three markers in a sentence: (i) *quō*, (ii) a comparative, (iii) verb in the subjunctive. Remember, when these clues are given, to translate *quō* by 'in order that/to'.

156   ***fore ut* + subjunctive: 'that it will/would come about that …'**

Latin often 'talks its way round' (the technical term for this is 'periphrasis') the so-called future infinitive passive (see **118**) by using *fore ut* + subjunctive, e.g.

> *dīxit sē captum īrī* 'he said <u>that he would be seized</u>' (lit. 'he said that there was a movement towards seizing him')

could also be expressed thus:

> *dīxit fore ut* (fixed form) *caperētur* lit. 'he said <u>that it would come about that</u> he would be seized'

Thus both *dīcit eōs remissum īrī* and *dīcit fore ut remittantur* mean 'he says <u>that they will be sent back</u>'.

So in reported speech, watch out for *fore ut* (*nōn*) + subjunctive, and translate literally 'that it will/would (not) come about that', then retranslate for smoother final effect.

NB *fore* is the same as *futūrum esse*, the future infinitive of *sum*, '[that] it will be the case [that *ut*]'.

EXERCISE

Translate these sentences:
(a) Catilīna sociīs suīs nūntiāuit fore ut incendium et caedēs in urbe fierent.
(b) Vmbrēnus Gabīnium uocāuit, quō facilius Allobrogibus uerbīs suīs persuādēret.

   (c) Allobrogēs, quippe quī praemia bellī magna fore arbitrārentur, rem diū
       cōnsīderābant.

   (d) sed lēgātī tandem sēnsērunt fore ut opibus cīuitātis Rōmānae facillimē
       uincerentur.

   (e) igitur Allobrogum lēgātī Cicerōnī omnia nārrāuērunt, quō māius auxilium
       cīuitātī suae ferrent.

English–Latin

Reread the text of 5B(i)–(ii), then translate this passage:

Umbrenus led the ambassadors of the Allobroges out of the forum into a certain person's house. Next he called Gabinius, a man of great weight, so as to persuade them more quickly. When Gabinius had been called,[1] Umbrenus persuaded the ambassadors to promise their aid. But they had not yet decided to join the conspiracy, inasmuch as they thought that they would be defeated[2] by the resources of the Roman state. Finally, they revealed the whole matter to Sanga. When Cicero had found out the plan[2] via Sanga, he instructed the Allobroges to feign enthusiasm, so that he might more easily capture the conspirators.

1. Use ablative absolute.
2. Use *fore ut* + subjunctive ('that it would turn out that ...').

Grammar and exercises for 5C

157   **Jussive subjunctives**

Jussive subjunctives (*iubeō iussus* 'ordered') are so called because the subjunctive in these cases acts as an imperative (cf. on the meanings of the subjunctive **143**). A subjunctive in this sense stands on its own as the main verb of a sentence. It is thus an 'independent' use. Note that English only has 2nd person imperatives ('make it so!', 'stand and deliver!'). It expresses 1st person and 3rd person commands by means of the verb 'let' ('let me be!', 'let us live!', 'let it be!', 'let them eat cake!'). E.g.

> (1st pl.) *audiāmus* 'let us listen'; *interficiāmus* 'let us kill'; *eāmus* 'let's go'

> (2nd s./pl.) *accipiās* 'please welcome', 'welcome!', 'see that you welcome' (often used in poetry)

> (3rd s./pl.) *fīat* 'let there become' 'may there be' (cf. *fīat lūx* 'let there be light' (Genesis))

Cf. phrases very often used in English: *habeās corpus* 'you must/please produce the person'; *caueat ēmptor* 'let the buyer beware'; *stet* 'let it stand'.

Notes

1   The negative for jussives is *nē*, e.g. *nē ueniant* 'let them not come'.

2   When a jussive subjunctive occurs in a question, it is known as 'deliberative' (from *dēlīberō* 1 'I weigh carefully, consider'), e.g.

> *quid scrībam*? 'What am I to write?' (Plautus)

> *utrum Karthāgō dīruātur* … ? 'Should Carthage be destroyed … ?' (Cicero)

> *quid ego faciam*? *maneam aut abeam*? 'What should (shall) I do? Should (shall) I stay, or leave?' (Plautus)

The negative here is *nōn*.

In deliberative questions, the imperfect subjunctive indicates potential past time, e.g.

> '*nōn ego illī argentum redderem*?' '*nōn redderēs.*' 'Shouldn't I have paid the money to him?' 'You shouldn't have paid it.' (Plautus)

EXERCISES

1 *Translate*:

(a) abeās.   (b)   commorēmur.

(c) maneāmus.   (d)   nē querātur.

(e) nē praemium requīrant.   (f)   nē frūstrā moriāmur.

(g) ueniat.   (h)   abeāmus.

(i) quid dīcerem?   (j)   quid dīcam?

(k) quid faceret?

2 *Translate these sentences*:

(a) moriāmur et in media arma ruāmus. (Virgil)

(b) uiuāmus, mea Lesbia, atque amēmus. (Catullus)

(c) nē difficilia optēmus. (Cicero)

(d) cautus sīs, mī Tīrō. (Cicero)

(e) faciāmus hominem ad imāginem et similitūdinem nostram et praesit
piscibus maris … (Genesis)

(f) et dīxit Deus: 'fiat lūx!' et lūx facta est. (Genesis)

(g) dīxit quoque Deus: 'fīat firmāmentum in mediō aquārum et dīuidat aquās
ab aquīs.' (Genesis)

(h) sapiās, uīna liquēs, et spatiō breuī spem longam resecēs. (Horace)

(i) quid faciat?[1] pugnet?[1] uincētur fēmina pugnāns.
clāmet?[1] at in dextrā quī uetet, ēnsis erat. (Ovid)

(j) haec cum uidērem, quid agerem, iūdicēs? (Cicero)

1. The subject of the verbs *faciat, pugnet, clāmet* is 'she', i.e. Lucretia (see **3B**).

ruō 3 I rush
optō 1 I wish for
caut-us a um careful (perf. participle of
   caueō)
imāgō imāgin-is 3f. image
similitūdō similitūdin-is 3f. likeness
piscis pisc-is 3m. fish
firmāment-um ī 2n. prop, firmament
dīuīdō 3 I divide

sapiō 3/4 I am sensible
uīn-um ī 2n. wine
liquō 1 I strain
spati-um ī 2n. space, distance
resecō 1 I cut back, prune
dextr-a ae 1f. right hand
quī + subj. expressing purpose
ēnsis ēns-is 3m. sword

158   **Subjunctives expressing wishes and possibility**

There are two other independent uses of the subjunctive.

1   **Expressing wishes**

This usage is often marked by *utinam* (negative *utinam nē*). The tenses are used as for conditions (see **S2(c)**).

Present is used to express a wish for the FUTURE, e.g.

> *ualeant cīuēs meī*! 'may my fellow-citizens fare well!' (Cicero)

Imperfect is used to express a wish for the PRESENT (see also note), e.g.

> *illud utinam nē uērē scrīberem* 'would that I were not writing this in all truth' (Cicero)

Pluperfect is used to express a regret about what happened (or did not happen) in the PAST, e.g.

> *utinam susceptus nōn essem* 'I wish I'd never been reared!' (Cicero)

NB Imperfect subjunctive, as with conditionals and jussives, sometimes refers to the past (see **144**[3], **157**[2]).

2   **Expressing possibility – the 'potential' subjunctive (cf. 143)**

The range of expressions covers much of what is expressed in English by 'may/ might', 'can/could', 'should' and 'would'. In 1st s. we have

> *uelim* 'I would like'
>
> *nōlim* 'I would not like'
>
> *mālim* 'I would prefer'

These are commonly followed by another subjunctive, e.g.

> *uelim adsīs* 'I should like you to be here'

Other 1st s. expressions are

> *ausim* 'I would dare' (from *audeō*; normal subjunctive *audeam*)
>
> *possim* 'I would be able'

(Note the imperfect *uellem* 'I would have wished' etc.)

2nd s. is used in 'generalising' statements, e.g.

> (present) *haud inueniās* 'you (= one) may scarcely find'
>
> (imperfect) *crēderēs* 'you (= one) would have believed'

3rd s. expressions include, e.g.

> (present) *dīcat aliquis* 'someone may say' (Livy) (see **171**)
>
> (imperfect) *quis arbitrārētur* 'who would have thought …?' (Cicero)

EXERCISE

Translate:

(a) uellem mē ad cēnam inuitāssēs.[1] (Cicero)

(b) putārēsne umquam accidere posse ut mihi uerba dēessent? (Cicero)

(c) utinam populus Rōmānus ūnam ceruīcem[2] habēret. (Caligula)

1. *inuītō* 1 I invite.
2. *ceruīx ceruīc-is* 3f. neck.

159 **Impersonal verbs: active**

These impersonal verbs appear *only in the 3rd person singular active*, but in any tense (present, future, imperfect, perfect etc.), in indicative or subjunctive. They also possess an infinitive form, so that they can appear in accusative and infinitive constructions.

You have already met (**88.5**) *licet licēre licuit* (or *licitum est*) 'it is permitted to X (dat.) to Y (inf.)', e.g.

> *illīs licuit exīre* 'it was permitted to them to leave', 'they were allowed to leave', and
>
> *placet placēre placuit* (or *placitum est*) 'it is pleasing to X (dat.) to Y (inf.)'; 'X (dat.) votes to Y (inf.)', e.g.
>
> *mihi placēbit sequī* 'it will be pleasing for me to follow', 'I shall vote to follow'
>
> *negat sibi placuisse hoc dīcere* 'he denies that it was pleasing (lit. 'it to have been pleasing') to him to say this', 'he denies that he voted to say this'

and (**4B(iii)**) *oportet oportēre oportuit* 'it is right/proper for X (acc.) to Y (inf.)', 'X should/ought', e.g.

> *mē oportuit abīre* 'it was right for me to leave', 'I ought to have left'

Now learn the following, some of which take a slightly different construction:

> *decet decēre decuit* 'it is fitting for X (acc.) to Y (inf.)'
>
> *dēdecet dēdecēre dēdecuit* 'it is unseemly for X (acc.) to Y (inf.)'
>
> *paenitet paenitēre paenituit* 'it repents X (acc.) of Y (gen.)' *or* 'it repents X (acc.) to Y (inf.)' (i.e. 'X regrets / is dissatisfied with Y')
>
> *miseret miserēre miseruit* 'it moves X (acc.) to pity at/for Y (gen.)'
>
> *pudet pudēre puduit* 'it moves X (acc.) to shame for Y (gen.)' (i.e. 'X is ashamed at/for Y')
>
> *libet libēre libuit* (or *libitum est*) 'it is pleasing/agreeable for X (dat.) to Y (inf.)', 'X chooses to'

Examples of these are:

> *uōs decēbit nihil dīcere* 'it will be fitting for you to say nothing'

> *tē dēdecet audīre* 'it is unseemly for you to hear'

> *eōs paenituit illīus uerbī* 'it repented them of that word', 'they regretted that word'

> *tē paenitēbit hoc facere* 'it will repent you to do this', 'you will repent/regret doing this'

> *hominēs miseruit poenae* 'it moved the men to pity at the punishment', 'the men were moved to pity / felt sorry at the punishment'

> *mē eius miseret* 'it moves me to pity for him', 'I feel sorry for him'

> *miseret tē aliōrum, tuī tē nec miseret nec pudet* 'you feel sorry for others, but for yourself you have neither pity nor shame' (Plautus)

> *libet mihi tē accusāre* 'it is pleasing to me to accuse you', 'I want to accuse you', 'I choose to accuse you'

NB Differentiate *licet* 'it is permitted' (cf. licence) from *libet* 'it is agreeable' (cf. libidinous; *ad lib.* = *ad libitum* 'to the point that pleases').

EXERCISES

1 *Translate into English*:

(a) mē decet hanc sententiam dīcere.

(a) abīre tē oportēbat.

(b) lēgātīs placuit studium coniūrātiōnis simulāre.

(c) Lentulum illīus iūris iūrandī paenitēbit.

(d) omnibus licet spem habēre.

(e) nōn omnibus eadem placent. (Pliny)

2 *Translate into Latin*:

(a) I regret my enthusiasm for the conspiracy.

(b) Catiline decided to leave Rome.

(c) You may complain.

(d) You (*pl.*) ought to hand yourselves over to the consul.

(e) It is fitting for a man to die in battle.

160   **Impersonal verbs: passive**

Remember that some verbs govern a dative or ablative instead of a direct object in the acusative. Such verbs can be passive ONLY as *in the 3rd person singular*, impersonally, e.g.

mihi parcēbātur lit. 'it was being spared to me', i.e. 'I was being spared', 'clemency was being extended to me'

eīs nocētur lit. 'it is being harmed to them', i.e. 'they are being harmed', 'harm is being done to them'

eī nōn crēdētur lit. 'it will not be trusted to him', i.e. 'he will not be trusted', 'there will be no trust extended to him'

Hint: when a verb controlling the dative appears in the *passive*, LOOK FOR THE DATIVE TO BE THE SUBJECT IN YOUR ENGLISH VERSION, e.g., *mihi ignōtum est* lit. 'it has been forgiven to me' i.e., 'I have been forgiven'.

Notes

1 Note the common impersonal passive idiom with verbs of 'going' and 'coming' to denote general movement, e.g.

ītur lit. 'it is being gone', i.e. 'people are going'

itum est lit. 'it was gone', i.e. 'people went'

uentum est lit. 'it has been come', i.e. 'there has been an arrival'

2 There is a passive impersonal *infinitive*, for use in accusative and infinitive constructions, e.g.

dīxit mīlitibus imperārī lit. 'he said <u>it to be being ordered</u> to the soldiers', i.e. 'he said that orders were being given to the soldiers', 'he said that the soldiers were being given their orders'

nescit fēminae ignōtum esse lit. 'he does not know <u>it to have been forgiven</u> to the woman', i.e. 'he does not know that the woman was forgiven'

See **156** for futures, where *fore ut* is always used.

3 The *agent* (person by whom the action of the passive verb is done) is expressed by *ā/ab* + abl., e.g.

<u>*ā mīlitibus*</u> *mihi crēditum est* 'I was believed <u>by the soldiers</u>'

EXERCISES

1 *Translate into English*:

(a) concurritur. (Horace)

(b) diū pugnātum est.

(c) ad forum uentum est.

(d) ītur ad arma.

(e) tibi nōn crēditum est.

237

(f) ā nōbīs nōn parcētur labōrī.[1] (Cicero)

(g) ā coniūrātōribus cīuitātī nocēbitur.

(h) nōbīs imperātum est, ut in proelium inīrēmus.

(i) cibus, somnus,[2] libīdō – per hunc circulum[3] curritur.[4] (Seneca)

1. *labor labōr-is* 3m. work, toil.
2. *somn-us ī* 2m. sleep.
3. *circul-us ī* 2m. unending cycle.
4. *currō* 3 I run, continue, go on.

2 *Translate into Latin*:

(a) Fighting is going on.

(b) There was a rush.

(c) You (*s.*) will not be spared.

(d) Catiline was not believed by Cicero.

(e) An instruction had been given to Lentulus.

161   **Numerals: cardinal 11–90 and ordinal 1st–10th**

Cardinal

11	XI	úndecim
12	XII	duódecim
13	XIII	trédecim
14	XIV	quattuórdecim
15	XV	quíndecim
16	XVI	sédecim
17	XVII	septéndecim
18	XVIII	duodēuigíntī
19	XIX	ūndēuigíntī
20	XX	uīgíntī
30	XXX	trīgíntā
40	XL	quādrāgíntā
50	L	quīnquāgíntā
60	LX	sexāgíntā
70	LXX	septuāgíntā
80	LXXX	octōgíntā
90	XC	nōnāgíntā

Ordinal

1st	prī́mus (prī́or)
2nd	secúndus (álter)
3rd	tértius
4th	quā́rtus
5th	quī́ntus
6th	séxtus
7th	séptimus
8th	octā́uus
9th	nṓnus
10th	décimus

Notes

1 Ordinals decline like *mult-us a um.*

2 See **54** for cardinals 1–10, 100–1,000.

EXERCISES

1 *Translate these phrases*: septimus fīlius; mīlites trēdecim; hōrā tertiā; trīgintā gladiī; rēx octāuus; undēuigintī exempla; quīntus pōns; nōnāgintā cīuēs.

2 *Translate into Latin* (*and give the Roman numeral for the cardinal numbers*): twenty soldiers; seventy men; the third consulship; ninety women; the fourth slave; eighteen battles; the first citizen; fifty ships.

English–Latin

*Reread the text of **5C(iii)**, then translate this passage into Latin*:

Cicero was seized by great anxiety.[1] He therefore spoke to himself as follows: 'You should realise[2] that you have saved the state from danger. Do not hesitate to demand the death penalty from the conspirators. If they are spared [3, 4] by you, the state will be harmed.[3] If Roman citizens are killed[4] on the say-so of a consul, this death penalty will be a burden on you. Nevertheless, you ought to be bold. I think that you won't regret[5] this boldness. For you will have saved the state.'

1. Turn the sentence into the active, with 'anxiety' as subject, 'Cicero' as object.
2. Use jussive subjunctive.
3. Remember that *noceō/parcō* take dative, so you must use impersonal passives here ('they' and 'the state' will be dative; 'by you' *ā* + abl.).
4. Use future perfect tense.
5. Use *fore ut* + subjunctive.

239

Section 5D

Grammar and exercises for 5D

162   **Further uses of the gerundive**

With any tense of *sum*, carrying the idea of obligation, duty, necessity

(i)   personally, e.g.

> *mīlitēs erant <u>reuocandī</u>* 'the soldiers were <u>to be called back</u>', 'had to be recalled', 'needed to be recalled'

(ii) impersonally, in the neuter singular, e.g.

> *<u>prōuidendum</u> est* 'it is <u>to be taken care about</u>', 'care needs to be taken'

> *<u>eundum</u> est* 'it is <u>to be gone</u>', 'one must go'

Notes

1   The impersonal construction is very common with verbs which do not take a direct object in the accusative. These cannot be used personally in the passive, so appear in the passive impersonally with a number of adjustments (cf. **160**), e.g.

> *parcendum est fēminae* 'it is to be spared to the woman', 'the woman must be spared' (*parcō* takes the dat.)

Deponents also are used thus, e.g.

> *ūtendum est sapientiā* 'one should use wisdom' (*ūtor* takes the abl.)

2   'By' a person is normally expressed by a *plain dative* with gerundives, e.g. *omnia sunt paranda <u>Caesarī</u>* 'everything is to be prepared by <u>Caesar</u>'. But where the verb in gerundive form normally takes the dative, *ā/ab* + abl. is used instead, e.g. *parcendum est fēminae ā mē* 'the woman must be spared by me', 'I must spare the woman.'

EXERCISES

1   *Form the gerundive of the following intransitive verbs and translate (using neuter singular, and translating 'it must be —ed'):* commoror, prōgredior, eō, ūtor, parcō, obstō, pāreō, fruor (*optional:* perueniō, praecipiō, nītor, profugiō, accēdō, festīnō, cūnctor, noceō).

2   *Translate:*

    (a) mihi prōuidendum est.

    (b) nōbīs prōgrediendum erat.

    (c) tibi eundum erit.

(d) dēlenda est Karthāgō.

(e) arx capienda erat.

(f) dolor augendus nōn est.

(g) supplicium sūmendum erit.

(h) supplicēs trādendī nōn sunt.

(i) ā tē cīuibus parcendum est.

(j) cīuibus ā mē nocendum nōn erat.

(k) moriendum est omnibus. (Cicero)

(l) nīl sine ratiōne faciendum est. (Seneca)

(m) ōrandum est ut sit mēns[1] sāna[2] in corpore sānō. (Juvenal)

(n) nūllī enim nisi audītūrō dīcendum est. (Seneca)

1. *mēns ment-is* 3f. mind.
2. *sān-us a um* healthy.

3 *Give the Latin for*:

(a) I must go away.

(b) Cicero will have to take care.

(c) We had to go forward.

(d) Our fatherland must be preserved.

(e) The conspirators must be punished.

(f) We must not harm our fatherland.

(g) Cicero should spare no conspirator.

163   ***timeō, metuō, uereor* 'I am afraid to/that/lest'**

These 'verbs of fearing' can take an infinitive or subjunctive construction.

They take an *infinitive* construction when English does, e.g.

> *timeō īre* 'I am afraid to go'
>
> *ueritī sunt dīcere* 'they were afraid to say'

They take a *subjunctive* construction with *nē* (negative *ut* or *nē nōn*) when the meaning is 'fear that/lest'. One would expect a subjunctive here: the speaker is uncertain about what will happen (cf. **143**). E.g.

> *uereor nē Caesar mox redeat* 'I am afraid that/lest Caesar will soon return'
>
> The negative of this is expressed by *nē … nōn*, e.g. *metuimus nē Cicerō satis praesidī nōn habeat* 'we fear that Cicero does not have enough of a guard'
>
> The negative can also be expressed by plain *ut*: *timent ut ad patriam ueniant* 'they are afraid that they will not reach their fatherland'

Observe that

> fearing + *nē* = 'fear that/lest' (i.e. what you want *not* to happen may happen)
>
> fearing + *ut/nē nōn* = 'fear that … NOT' (i.e. what you want to happen may *not*)

Notes

1 The subjunctive is controlled by rules of sequence (see **A–G Intro.(a)**).

2 Any verb of effort or precaution (i.e. which expresses the idea of apprehension, worry, danger or anxiety) can use this construction, e.g.

> *prōuidendum est nē populō Rōmānō dēsīs* 'care must be taken lest you fail the Roman people'

3 As with purpose clauses, any reference to the subject of the main verb inside the clause will be reflexive; cf. **150**[1].

EXERCISES

1 *Translate*:

(a) uereor nē urbs incendātur.

(b) prōuidendum est nē hostēs in urbem ingrediantur.

(c) perīculum est nē supplex captus interficiātur.

(d) Cicerō metuēbat ut satis seuērus esse uidērētur.

(e) omnēs ōrdinēs ueritī sunt nē hostēs impiī urbem caperent.

(f) cūra erat nē uirginēs Vestālēs agitārentur.

(g) tibi haec omnia dīcere uereor.

(h) multī cīuēs timēbant nē cōnsul satis īrātus nōn esset.

(i) ante senectūtem[1] cūrāuī ut[2] bene uīuerem, in senectūte[1] ut[2] bene moriar. bene autem morī est libenter[3] morī. (Seneca)

1. *senectūs senectūt-is* 3f. old age.
2. *ut.* Is the construction 'fearing'?
3. *libenter* willingly.

2 *Give the Latin for*:

(a) I am afraid that I will see the flight of the citizens.

(b) Everyone was afraid to speak.

(c) Cicero feared that the Senate would not be strict enough.

(d) A suppliant does not fear his enemies.

(e) There is anxiety in case children are killed.

(f) There was a danger of the city being destroyed.

EITHER

Reading exercise / Test exercise

Caesar, advancing against the Gallic tribe the Nervii, has pitched camp on the other side of a river-valley from them. As the work of building proceeds, the Nervii launch an unexpected attack.

Caesarī omnia ūnō tempore erant agenda: uexillum prōpōnendum, quod erat īnsigne cum ad arma concurrī oportēret; signum tubā dandum; ab opere reuocandī mīlitēs; quī paulō longius aggeris petendī causā prōcesserant arcessendī; aciēs īnstruenda; mīlitēs cohortandī; signum dandum. quārum rērum magnam partem temporis breuitās et successus hostium   5
impediēbat … Caesar, necessāriīs rēbus imperātīs, ad cohortandōs mīlitēs quam in partem fors obtulit dēcucurrit et ad legiōnem decimam dēuēnit. (Caesar, *Dē Bellō Gallicō* 2.20.1–2 and 2.21.1)

Caesarī [hold until solved by *agenda*]	*prōcēdō* 3 *prōcessī* I advance
uexill-um ī 2n. flag	*aciēs aciē-ī* 5f. battle-line
prōpōnendum [supply *erat* – watch out for suppression of verb 'to be' throughout this passage with gerundives]	*īnstruō* 3 I draw up
	breuitās breuitāt-is 3f. shortness
	success-us ūs 4m. coming up close, approach
īnsigne īnsign-is 3n. mark	*necessāri-us a um* necessary
concurrī [see **160²**]	*fors fort-is* 3f. fortune, luck
tub-a ae 1f. trumpet	*offerō offerre obtulī* I bring
opus oper-is 3n. the work of building a camp	*dēcurrō* 3 *dēcucurrī* I run down
	legiō legiōn-is 3f. legion
agger agger-is 3m. material for an earthwork	*dēueniō* 4 *dēuēnī* I come down

OR

English–Latin

1 *Translate into Latin (refer back to **145.1** for the grammar of consecutive* quī *clauses)*:

(a) The suppliant stretches forth his hands towards the sort of people who are compassionate.

(b) Lentulus is the sort of man everyone fears.

(c) He is the sort who performs wicked acts.

(d) There is no one who doesn't desire the harmony of all the sections of society.

(e) I fear the sort of man who is always complaining.

OR

2 *Reread the text of **5D(iv)**, then translate this passage into Latin:*

Conscript fathers, you must[1] take care, lest you fail the Roman people. I, the consul, am prepared to[2] defend the safety of the state. All ranks are in agreement. There is not a slave who[3] is not prepared to[2] defend the state. Our land herself stretches forth to you suppliant hands. You must protect[4] our land. All are afraid that other conspirators may destroy our freedom. You must[1] take care that this cannot happen ever again.

1. Use impersonal gerundive (n.) + dat. of 'you'.
2. *parātus ad* + gerundive construction.
3. Use subjunctive.
4. Use gerundive in nom. with 'land', dat. of 'you'.

Section 5E

Grammar and exercises for 5E

164 **Summary of participles**

(a) Present participles, '—ing': 1st conj. *-āns* (*-ant-*), 2nd conj. *-ēns* (*-ent-*), 3rd conj. *-ēns* (*-ent-*), 4th conj. and 3rd/4th conj. *-iēns* (*-ient-*); cf. **122**

(b) Future participles, 'about to —': stem of perfect participle + *-ūrus -ūra -ūrum*; cf. **81**

(c) Perfect participles (deponent) 'having —ed': stem of perfect participle + *-us -a -um*; (others) 'having been —ed'; cf. **77**, **119**

All are adjectives, and agree with the person or thing they describe.

NB Only active verbs which take an object in the *accusative* have a passive participle used as an adjective. For example, *uentus* and *imperātus* are impossible in that form because both come from verbs which are intransitive: *ueniō* takes *ad* + acc., and *imperō* takes a dative. These forms exist only in the impersonal perfect passive, e.g. *uentum est* lit. 'it has been come', i.e. 'people have come'; *imperātum est* lit. 'it has been ordered', i.e. 'orders have been given'. You will have noticed that the 4th p.p. of intransitive verbs is always given in the *-um* form.

EXERCISES

1 *Translate the participles in this list; say whether they are deponent or passive*: commorātus, coctus, mortuus, ūsus, datus, adiūtus, agitātus, lātus, gestus, cognitus, cōnātus, secūtus, intellēctus, locūtus, exortus, prōmissus, sūmptus, frāctus, mōtus (*optional*: portātus, pollicitus, inuentus, hortātus, nūntiātus, minātus, necātus, reductus, perfectus, uocātus, amplexus, arbitrātus, seruātus, īnstructus, dispositus, ueritus, tēnsus, obsessus, questus).

2 *Translate these sentences*:

(a) Lentulus tenebrās cōnspicātus nihilōminus negāuit sē mortem timēre.

(b) cēterī custōdēs ā cōnsulibus dispositōs sequēbantur.

(c) cōnsul sēcum multa locūtus supplicium sūmere cōnstituerat.

(d) Celer ā senātū missus in agrō Pīcēnō erat.

(e) agmen ā cōnsule īnstructum Catilīna uīdit.

(f) Catilīnae montibus et cōpiīs hostium clausō[1] fuga erat nūlla.

1. *claudō* 3 *clausī clausus* I shut in, cut off.

3 *Translate into Latin using perfect participles passive to translate 'when' and
   'as' clauses. NB None of these sentences calls for the ablative absolute.*

(a) When they had captured the soldier, the guards killed him.

(b) After the column had been seen, Catiline hurried towards it.

(c) When the guards had been set Cicero gave them instructions.

(d) The appearance of the column as it had been drawn up was not worthy of
     the commander.

(e) Catiline's soldiers advanced, using weapons previously[1] captured.

1. Leave out 'previously'.

165   ***dum, antequam/priusquam***

1 *dum* + indicative 'while'

dum takes the *present* indicative where 'while' means 'at one point during', e.g.

> *dum Cicerō haec loquitur, Catilīna abiit* '(At one point) while
> Cicero was speaking, Catiline left'

But *imperfect* indicative is used where the 'while' clause covers the whole period
described by the main verb, e.g.

> *dum Cicerō sequēbatur, Catilīna fugiēbat* 'while Cicero was
> following, Catiline was fleeing'

2 *dum* 'until'

dum + indicative indicates the idea of time only, e.g.
> *manē dum redierō* 'wait until I get back' (note fut. perf.!)

dum + subjunctive indicates anticipation or intention, e.g.
> *manē dum redeam* 'wait <u>for me</u> to come back'

cf. *manēbat dum Catilīna castra mouēret* (subjunctive) 'he was waiting <u>for</u>
Catiline <u>to move</u> camp'; contrast *mānsit dum Catilīna castra mōuit* (indicative)
'he waited until Catiline (actually) <u>moved</u> camp'

3 *antequam/priusquam* 'before'

antequam and *priusquam* work rather like *dum*: indicative expresses purely time,
subjunctive anticipation or intention, e.g.

> with indicative: *antequam <u>abiit</u>, epistolam scrīpsit* 'before <u>he left</u>,
> he wrote a letter'

> with subjunctive: *Catilīna abiit antequam legiōnēs Rōmānae
> <u>peruenīrent</u>* 'Catiline left before the Roman legions <u>should arrive</u>'

NB *ante-* and *prius-* are often split from *quam*, e.g. *ante uēnī quam uir* 'I arrived
before the man' (Ovid).

246

4 *dum* (*dummodo*, *modo*) + subjunctive

A specialised meaning *of dum* is 'provided that', 'on condition that', e.g.

> *omnia faciam dum amīcus fīās* 'I will do anything provided you
> become my friend'

166   ***utpote quī* (*quae quod*) + subjunctive**

utpote reinforces the causal sense *of quī*, i.e. 'as is natural for one who'. The verb
is subjunctive. Cf. *quippe quī* **145.2.** E.g.

> *miser sum*, *utpote quem Cynthia amet* 'I am wretched, as is natural
> for one whom Cynthia loves'

NB *ut quī* is also used in this way.

EXERCISES

EITHER

Translate into English:

(a) dum senātus rem cōnsīderābat, Catilīna legiōnēs suās īnstruēbat.

(b) Catilīna exspectābat, dum sociī cōnsilia Rōmae perficerent.

(c) Catilīna, antequam in Galliam īret, nouās cōpiās ex urbe exspectābat.

(d) dum Catilīna prope Pistōriam manet, Rōmae Cicerōnī sē coniūrātōrēs
     trādidērunt.

(e) cōnsul laetus est, dum salua sit rēs pūblica.

(f) tē omnēs amant mulierēs, quī sīs tam pulcher. (Plautus)

OR

Translate into Latin:

(a) While this was happening at Rome, Catiline spoke to his soldiers.

(b) He said, 'I shall wait until our friends arrive.'

(c) 'Provided they are safe, our plans can be completed.'

(d) 'I must relate certain matters to Lentulus, before I depart for Gaul.'

(e) But all the time Catiline was speaking, the consul was preparing war.

Reading exercise/Test exercise

*Note especially in reading this passage (i) the use of the participle in Latin, where
a clause or other formulation would be needed in English; (ii) that accusative
future and perfect participles may actually be infinitives without* esse *and form
part of an indirect statement.*

L. Tarquinius, another captured Catilinarian, gives information to the Senate, similar to that of Volturcius.

post eum diem quīdam L. Tarquinius ad senātum adductus erat, quem ad Catilīnam proficīscentem ex itinere retractum aiēbant. is cum sē dīceret indicātūrum dē coniūrātiōne, sī fidēs pūblica data esset, iussus ā cōnsule quae scīret ēdīcere, eadem ferē quae Volturcius dē parātīs incendiīs, dē caede bonōrum, dē itinere hostium senātum docet; praetereā sē missum quī Catilīnae nūntiāret nē eum   5
Lentulus et Cethēgus aliīque ex coniūrātiōne dēprehēnsī terrērent, eōque magis properāret ad urbem adcēdere, quō et cēterōrum animōs reficeret et illī facilius ē perīculō ēriperentur. (Sallust, *Catiline* 48.3–4)

post (+ acc.) after	*dē parātīs incendiīs* [see **119** note]
addūcō 3 *addūxī adductus* I bring (to)	*doceō* 2 I inform X (acc.) of Y (acc.) 5
retrahō 3 *retrāxī retractus* I drag back	*quī ... nūntiāret* [expresses purpose]
aiō 3 I say	*dēprehendō* 3 *dēprehendī dēprehēnsus*
indicō 1 I make a declaration, give information	I capture [tr. *aliī ... dēprehēnsī* 'the capture of the others ...' – what does it mean literally?]
fidēs pūblica (5f. + 1/2 adj.) public pledge (of impunity or protection)	*terreō* 2 I frighten
ēdīcō 3 I declare	*eō magis* 'by that much the more'
eadem ... quae 'the same ... as'	*adcēdere = accēdere*
ferē almost	*reficiō* 3/4 I revive, restore

OR

English–Latin

Reread the text of 5E(ii), then translate this passage into Latin:

While at Rome this punishment was being exacted[1] from Lentulus, Catiline drew up his forces. He was waiting until[2] troops should be sent from his allies. But after it was reported that Lentulus was dead and the conspiracy revealed, he started to make[3] his way through the mountains. The consul Antonius, sent by the senate with the purpose of[4] defeating him in battle, pursued him. Metellus also moved his camp from Picenum, to obstruct Catiline as he hurried towards Transalpine Gaul. After Catiline saw that he was shut in by mountains and enemy troops, he decided to join battle as soon as possible with Antonius, in order to give more[5] hope to his soldiers.

1. Use *dum* + present indicative.
2. Use *dum* + imperfect subjunctive.
3. Use historic infinitive.
4. Either *eō cōnsiliō ut* or *quī* + subjunctive.
5. *quō* + comparative adjective + subjunctive.

Section 5F

Grammar and exercises for 5F

167 Perfect subjunctive active

	1	2	3
1st s.	amā́u-eri-m (amā́rim etc.)	habú-eri-m	dī́x-eri-m
2nd s.	amā́u-erī-s	habú-erī-s	dī́x-erī-s
3rd s.	amā́u-eri-t	habú-eri-t	dī́x-eri-t
1st pl.	amāu-erí-mus	habu-erí-mus	dīx-erí-mus
2nd pl.	amāu-erí-tis	habu-erí-tis	dīx-erí-tis
3rd pl.	amā́u-eri-nt	habú-eri-nt	dī́x-eri-nt

	4	3/4
1st s.	audī́u-eri-m (audíerim etc.)	cḗp-eri-m
2nd s.	audī́u-erī-s	cḗp-erī-s
3rd s.	audī́u-eri-t	cḗp-eri-t
1st pl.	audīu-erí-mus	cēp-erí-mus
2nd pl.	audīu-erí-tis	cēp-erí-tis
3rd pl.	audī́u-eri-nt	cḗp-eri-nt

Notes

1 The perfect subjunctive active is formed by taking the stem of the 3rd p.p. and adding *-erim -erīs -erit -erīmus -erītis -erint*. Observe that, in this respect, it is *almost identical* in form to the future perfect (see **140**). (The only difference is that the future perfect has the 1st s. in *-erō* and usually a short *i* at *-eris, -erimus, -eritis*.) Note the normal active personal endings (*-m, -s, -t, -mus, -tis, -nt*).

2 Note that in 1st and 4th conj. the forms *amā-rim* etc. and *audi-erim* etc. are common. Cf. *dēlēu-erim* and *dēlē-rim*.

168 Perfect subjunctive deponent

	1	2	3
1st s.	minā́t-us a um sim	pollícit-us a um sim	locū́t-us a um sim
2nd s.	minā́t-us a um sīs	pollícit-us a um sīs	locū́t-us a um sīs
3rd s.	minā́t-us a um sit	pollícit-us a um sit	locū́t-us a um sit
1st pl.	minā́t-ī ae a sī́mus	pollícit-ī ae a sī́mus	locū́t-ī ae a sī́mus
2nd pl.	minā́t-ī ae a sī́tis	pollícit-ī ae a sī́tis	locū́t-ī ae a sī́tis
3rd pl.	minā́t-ī ae a sint	pollícit-ī ae a sint	locū́t-ī ae a sint

	4	3/4
1st s.	mentít-us a um sim	prōgréss-us a um sim
2nd s.	mentít-us a um sīs	prōgréss-us a um sīs
3rd s.	mentít-us a um sit	prōgréss-us a um sit
1st pl.	mentít-ī ae a sīmus	prōgréss-ī ae a sīmus
2nd pl.	mentít-ī ae a sītis	prōgréss-ī ae a sītis
3rd pl.	mentít-ī ae a sint	prōgréss-ī ae a sint

Note

The perfect subjunctive deponent is formed by taking the stem of the perfect participle, adding the appropriate endings *-us -a -um* etc. to agree with the subject, and adding *sim sīs sit sīmus sītis sint*, the present subjunctive of *sum*.

169 **Perfect subjunctive passive**

	1	2	3	4	3/4
1st s.	amát-us sim	hábit-us sim	díct-us sim	audít-us sim	cápt-us sim
2nd s.	amát-us sīs	hábit-us sīs	díct-us sīs	audít-us sīs	cápt-us sīs
3rd s.	amát-us sit	hábit-us sit	díct-us sit	audít-us sit	cápt-us sit
1st pl.	amát-ī sīmus	hábit-ī sīmus	díct-ī sīmus	audít-ī sīmus	cápt-ī sīmus
2nd pl.	amát-ī sītis	hábit-ī sītis	díct-ī sītis	audít-ī sītis	cápt-ī sītis
3rd pl.	amát-ī sint	hábit-ī sint	díct-ī sint	audít-ī sint	cápt-ī sint

NB The endings *-us a um* and *-i ae a* apply as above

NB For formation of perfect subjunctive passive, see note on deponent (above) **168**.

Summary

Perfect active subjunctive: 3rd p. pl. in *-erim -erīs -erit -erīmus -erītis -erint*.

Perfect deponent/passive subjunctive: perfect participle + *sim sīs sit sīmus sītis sint*.

EXERCISES

1 *Form and conjugate the perfect subjunctive of these verbs (form passive only when requested):* dispōnō (*passive*), cohortor, peruenniō, occupō, pūniō (*passive*), moueō, ūtor, cōnficiō, uereor, sūmō (*passive*) (*optional*: portō, oblīuīscor, eō, possum, ferō (*passive*), audeō, cōnsīdō, īnstruō (*passive*), persequor, aduocō (*passive*)).

2 *Pick out the perfect subjunctives in this list, detailing tense and mood (i.e. indicative or subjunctive) of the others:* frēgistī, curāuerīs, mōueris, āfueram, ēgisset, īnstrūxerō, sūmpserim, properāuit, adlocūtus sit, ūsus esset, praebuerit, rogāuerint, arbitrātus erit, iussī sītis, nōluimus, mīseritis, dūxerīmus, conuocāta sit, interfectus erit, petīta sīs (*optional*: uīceram, uīnxerīs, secūtae sīmus, passa est, prohibitus sit, conuocāuerītis, temptāuerimus, impedīuissem, cōnsiderāuimus, exorta essem, uīsum sit, collocāuerim, questus erō, oppresserīmus).

170   **Use of perfect subjunctive**

The perfect subjunctive is used in certain constructions already met, in accordance with the usual rules of sequence of tenses (see **R3** note 4), e.g.

(a) Subordinate clauses in indirect speech, **147**

(b) Result clauses, *tam* (etc.) … *ut* + subj. '(so) … that', **149**, e.g. *potest fierī <u>ut</u> īrātus <u>dīxerit</u>* 'it may be <u>that he spoke</u> in anger' (Cicero)

(c) *cum* + subj. 'since', 'although' **126**, **146** (but not usually 'when')

(d) *quī* + *subj.* in generic or causal sense, **145**

(e) Fearing clauses (*timeō* (etc.) *nē*), **163**

In these cases it should be translated as a plain past ('I —ed') or perfect ('I have —ed'), whichever fits better.

171   **Perfect subjunctive: independent usages**

The use of the present subjunctive in an imperative or potential sense has already been met (**152** and **158**). The perfect subjunctive is also used in these senses, e.g.

(a) Jussive: *nē petīuerīs* 'do not seek' (= *nōlī petere*)

(b) Potential: *dīxerit aliquis* 'someone may say'; *errāuerim fortasse* 'I may/could perhaps have been wrong'.

EXERCISES

EITHER

1 *Translate into English*:

(a) tū nē quaesierīs ... (Horace)

(b) nūllam aciem, nūllum proelium timuerīs. (Livy)

(c) nē hostibus cesserīs.

(d) nūllī inuīderīs.

(e) nē restiterīs.

(f) quis tibi hoc dīxerit?

OR

2 *Translate into Latin (using* nē + *perfect subjunctive for prohibitions)*:

(a) Do not be daring.

(b) Do not reveal this plan.

(c) Do not give yourself up.

(d) Do not harm the state.

(e) Do not kill the consul.

(f) Someone may assert.

172   **Indirect (reported) questions**

You have already met indirect statements ('I say *that*': **98–9**, **148**) and indirect commands ('I tell/urge/persuade etc. someone *to*': **136**). Consider the following examples:

(a) *rogō quid faciās* 'I ask what you are doing'.

(b) *nescīuit cūr uēnisset* 'he did not know why he had come'.

(c) *quaerō quō itūrus sīs* 'I am enquiring to where you are about to go'.

All these report direct questions: (a) 'What are you doing?' (b) 'Why have you come?' etc. Quite simply, Latin reports these questions in exactly the same way that English does, except that the verb is in the *subjunctive*. All you have to do is to translate the subjunctive *as if it were the identical tense of the indicative*.

Notes

1 *num* (or *an*) in indirect questions mean 'if', 'whether'; *num quis* means 'if anyone' (cf. *nē quis, sī quis* **136**[3], **145**[2], **144**[1]; forms **14**).

2 *necne* in indirect questions means 'or not'.

3 As with indirect statements and commands, references to the subject of the main verb are reflexive, e.g.

> *Caesar mīlitēs rogāuit utrum sē audīre possent necne* 'Caesar asked the soldiers whether they could hear him (= Caesar) or not'

4   Where Latin uses future participle + *sim/essem* to express the future, you should translate this into a simpler future in English, e.g.

> *Strobīlus nescīuit ubi aulam cēlātūrus esset* 'Strobilus did not know where he was about to hide the pot', i.e. 'would hide the pot' (see **81**)

EXERCISES

1   *Translate these sentences*:

(a) omnēs rogant num seruōs accēperit Catilīna.

(b) nescit cōnsul utrum ad urbem an ad Galliam Catilīna itūrus sit.

(c) Metellus sciēbat quō Catilīna prōgressūrus esset.

(d) nēmo scit quot mīlitēs habuerit Mānlius.

(e) nesciō quantam praedam Catilīna adeptus sit.

(f) cīuēs rogant num cōnsul coniūrātōrēs pūnīre cōnstituerit.

(g) quis rogāuit utrum ignāuus esset Lentulus necne?

(h) Sallustius nārrat quālis Tulliānī faciēs fuerit.

(i) omnēs scīmus quot legiōnēs Catilīna īnstrūxerit.

(j) cōnsulēs rogāuērunt num cōpiae Catilīnae magnae futūrae essent.

(k) scīre uelim utrum Catilīna an cōnsul uictūrus sit.

(l) rogāuī utrum Catilīna ipse suōs mīlitēs in proelium dūxisset necne.

EITHER

Translate these sentences:

(a) scrībis tē uelle scīre quī sit status[1] reī pūblicae. (Cicero)

(b) quid faciendum sit, ā faciente discendum[2] est. (Seneca)

(c) cōnsīderābimus quid fēcerit, quid faciat, quid factūrus sit. (Cicero)

(d) uīuam an[3] moriar, nūlla est in mē metus.[4] (Ennius)

(e) nihil est difficilius quam quid deceat uidēre. (Cicero)

---

1. *stat-us ūs* 4m. situation.
2. *discō* 3 I learn.
3. *an* or (note that there is no preceding *utrum*).
4. *metus* (unusually) is f. here.

OR

3 *Translate into Latin (see **R3** note 4 for strict rules)*:

(a) I would like to tell you why you have been called together.

(b) You all know how idle Lentulus has been.

(c) Do not tell me how many enemies are pursuing us.

(d) I urge you to remember how much hope you have placed in this battle.

(e) Someone may ask why we are fighting.

173 **Conditional clauses: 'if X had happened, Y would have happened'**

Where a *sī* ('if') clause uses the pluperfect subjunctive and the main clause uses a pluperfect subjunctive, the meaning is 'if X had happened, Y would have happened' (cf. **144**), e.g.

> *sī Catilīnam uīdissem, fūgissem* 'if I had seen Catiline, I would have fled'
>
> *sī effūgissent, Rōma dēlēta esset* 'if they had escaped, Rome would have been destroyed'

Notes

1 This meaning is sometimes expressed by imperfect subjunctives (see **144**[3]).

2 Mixtures of the set formulae are also possible, e.g. *sī hoc fēcissem, laetus essem* 'If I had done this, I would (now) be happy.'

EXERCISES

EITHER

1 *Translate into English*:

(a) nisi Lentulus ignāuus fuisset, rēs pūblica magnō in perīculō fuisset.

(b) sī coniūrātōrēs dīuitiās habuissent, Catilīnae sē numquam adiūnxissent.

(c) Catilīnae mīlitēs, nisi eōs necessitūdō pugnāre coēgisset, effugere cōnātī essent.

(d) uīcisset Catilīna, nisi Fortūna eī inuīdisset.

(e) sī Catilīnae satis frūmentī fuisset, in montibus manēre cōnstituisset.

OR

2 *Translate into Latin*:

(a) You would all have lived your life in exile, if I had not made this plan.

(b) If Lentulus had been brave, our danger would not now be so great.[1]

(c) If you had possessed wealth, you would now be fighting against me.[1]

(d) Catiline would have gone into exile, if he had foreseen the idleness of Lentulus.

(e) If Catiline had not made a speech, his soldiers would not have realised how much danger there was.

1. Use *sī* + plupf. subj., impf. subj.

174   ***quōminus, quīn*** + subjunctive

1   *quōminus* (= *quō minus*, 'so that … not') is used after verbs of preventing, hindering, restraining, obstructing, and is an extension of the purpose or result clause constructions already met (**149**, **155**). The best translation in these circumstances is usually 'from —ing', e.g.

> *mē impedit quōminus eam* 'he hinders me so that I cannot go / from going'
>
> *eīs obstitit quōminus īrent* 'he stood in their way so that they could not go', 'he opposed their departure'
>
> *nāuēs uentō tenēbantur quōminus in portum uenīre possent* 'the ships were prevented by the wind from coming (= 'so that they could not come') into the harbour'

NB See further Reference Grammar **S2(f)**.

2   *quīn* (*quī nē* 'how not?') is generally found in a negative context and has a number of usages of deliberative, consecutive and indirect force using the subjunctive:

(a) After negative expressions of preventing, e.g. *nīl tē impedit quīn eās* 'nothing prevents you from going / so that you cannot go'

(b) Meaning 'but that', 'without', 'that not' in negative contexts, e.g. *numquam eum uideō quīn rīdeam* 'I never see him but that I laugh / without laughing', *numquam ēgressus sum quīn uidērer* 'I never went out but that I was seen / without being seen'; *nēmo tam sapiēns est quīn erret* 'no one is so wise but that he makes a mistake / that he does not make a mistake'

Note also the expressions *facere nōn possum quīn* 'I cannot do (a thing) but that', 'I cannot help —ing'; *fierī nōn potest quīn* 'it cannot come about but that …', 'it is impossible that … not'; *nōn multum abest quīn* 'it is not far from being the case that …'

(c) In certain negative expressions of doubting meaning '(but) that', e.g. *dubium nōn est quīn* 'there is no doubt (but) that …'; *nōn dubitō quīn* 'I do not doubt (but) that …'; *dubitārī nōn potest quīn* 'it cannot be doubted (but) that'.

Examine the following examples:

> *nōn dubium erat quīn Catilīna uincerētur* 'there was no doubt that Catiline was being defeated'

> *nēmo dubitābit quīn Lentulus ignāuus fuerit* 'no one will doubt that Lentulus was a coward'
>
> *nēmo est quīn sciat* 'everyone knows'
>
> *fierī nōn potest quīn rēs pūblica salua sit* 'it is impossible that the state will not be safe'
>
> *Catilīna facere nōn poterat quīn frūstrā loquerētur* 'Catiline could not help speaking to no purpose'

NB See further Reference Grammar **Q2(a)**, **S2(a) 3(i)–(iv)**, **S2(e)**.

EXERCISES

EITHER

1 *Translate into English*:

(a) impedior quōminus tibi nārrem quid Catilīna dīxerit.

(b) nec aetās impedit quōminus et cēterārum rērum et in prīmīs agrī colendī studia teneāmus. (Cicero)

(c) nōn dubium est quīn Catilīna coniūrātor fuerit.

(d) quīn loquar, numquam mē potes dēterrēre.[1] (Plautus)

(e) dubitārī nōn potest quīn Fortūna Catilīnae inuīderit.

(f) quis dubitet quīn in uirtūte dīuītiae sint? (Cicero)

(g) nēmo est tam senex quī sē annum nōn putet posse uīuere. (Cicero)

(h) nōn potest iūcundē[2] uīuī nisi cum uirtūte uīuātur. (Cicero)

1. *dēterreō* 2 I frighten off, prevent.
2. *iūcundē* happily.

OR

2 *Translate into Latin* (*see note above for references to Reference Grammar discussions*):

(a) Nothing stops you from speaking.[1]

(b) There is no doubt that[2] this is true.

(c) Catiline was prevented from[3] leaving the mountains.

(d) I am being held back by necessity from following the rest of the army.[4]

(e) There was no doubt that Catiline was forced to fight.

1. *quōminus* or *quīn*.
2. *quīn*.
3. *nē* or *quōminus*.
4. 'I hold back' = *teneō* 2; *nē* or *quōminus*.

EITHER

Reading exercise / Test exercise

In indirect speech there are three basic constructions: (i) statements are expressed by acc. + inf.; (ii) commands by ut/nē *+ subjunctive; (iii) indirect questions by a question word + subjunctive. As you know, subordinate clauses within it also have subjunctive verbs. You need also to know that in extended passages, indirect commands are often represented by subjunctive* alone. *In reading, the most important thing is to be aware when such an extended passage begins: once the fact of indirect speech is spotted, the next thing is to remember that the tense of the introductory verb will affect the tense of all subjunctives.*

Caesar has just won a battle at the river Arar against one canton (pāg-us ī *2m.*) *of the migrating Helvetii. They send him an embassy, headed by Divico.*

is ita cum Caesare ēgit: sī pācem populus Rōmānus cum Heluetiīs faceret, in eam partem itūrōs atque ibi futūrōs ubi eōs Caesar cōnstituisset atque esse uoluisset; sīn bellō persequī perseuērāret, reminīscerētur et ueteris incommodī et prīstinae uirtūtis Heluetiōrum. quod imprōuīsō ūnum pāgum adortus esset, cum eī quī flūmen trānsīssent suīs auxilium ferre nōn possent, nē ob eam rem aut suae   5 magnopere uirtūtī tribueret aut ipsōs dēspiceret. sē ita ā patribus māiōribusque suīs didicisse, ut magis uirtūte quam dolō contenderent aut īnsidiīs nīterentur. quārē nē committeret ut is locus ubi cōnstitissent ex calamitāte populī Rōmānī et internetiōne exercitūs nōmen caperet aut memoriam prōderet.

(Caesar, *Dē Bellō Gallicō* 1, 13.3–7)

is = Diuicō
agō 3 ēgī I deal, do business [indirect speech begins after the colon]
faceret [indirect: it represents either *faciat* ('were to make') or *faciet* ('is going to make')]
itūrōs, futūrōs sc. *esse*: 'they would go … and stay' [both refer to the Helvetii]
cōnstituō 3 cōnstituī I place, put
sīn but if
perseuērāret [indirect: represents either *perseuēret* ('were to continue') or *perseuērābit* ('is going to continue')]
perseuērō 1 I continue
reminīscerētur [indirect command]
reminīscor 3 dep. I remember (+ gen.)

incommod-um ī 2n. misfortune [inflicted by the Helvetii upon L. Cassius in 107]
prīstin-us a um former
quod 'as for the fact that' [the reported speech continues]
imprōuīsō unexpectedly
adorior 4 dep. *adortus* I attack   5
flūmen flūmin-is 3n. river
trānseō trānsīre trānsiī I cross
nē [introduces an indirect command, negative]
suae [hold until solved]
tribuō 3 I attribute [i.e. 'it', 'the fact that' – the *quod* clause is the object of this verb]
ipsōs [i.e. the Helvetii]
dēspiciō 3/4 I look down on

sē [i.e. the Helvetii]
discō 3 *didicī* I learn
contendō 3 I struggle, fight
quārē therefore
nē [introduces another negative
    indirect command]
committeret [tr. 'act in such a way']

cōnsistō 3 *cōnstitī* I stop
interneciō internecion-is 3f. killing,
    slaughter   10
memori-a ae 1f. remembrance, record
prōdō 3 I hand down, transmit;
    produce

NB For rules governing *conditions* in indirect speech, see Reference Grammar
R4(b).

OR

English–Latin

*Reread the text of **5F(i)**, then translate this passage into Latin:*

'You can see, soldiers, in what danger our affairs are. Two armies prevent us from
leaving these mountains without a battle. If we had not relied upon Lentulus, we
would have already escaped. Now, however, we must fight, for our fatherland,
for our liberty and for our lives. Do not be[1] cowards. If we win[2] there is no doubt
that[3] safety is ours. If we yield[2] through fear, nothing will stop us from[4] being
butchered.'

1. *nē* + perfect subjunctive.
2. Use future perfect.
3. *quīn* + subjunctive.
4. *quōminus* + subjunctive or *quīn* + subjunctive.

Grammar and exercises for 5G

175   **Gerunds: -*nd*- forms, '–ing'**

We have already seen that verbs can form adjectives (i.e. participles and gerundives), when they act like adjectives agreeing with nouns or pronouns, e.g.

> *nāue <u>captā</u> nautae effūgērunt* 'with the ship captured, the sailors fled'

> *hic homo <u>monendus</u> est* 'this man is to be / must be warned'.

Verbs can also form nouns. As such, verbs take the form of the *infinitive*, or the *gerund*, which has exactly the same forms as the neuters of the *gerundive* (see **151**). The declension is as follows (acc. to abl. as for 2n. nouns):

	1 'loving'	2 'having'	3 'speaking'
nom.	amā́-re	habḗ-re	dī́c-e-re
acc.	amá-nd-um	habé-nd-um	dīc-é-nd-um
	amā́-re	habḗ-re	dī́c-e-re
gen.	amá-nd-ī	habé-nd-ī	dīc-é-nd-ī
dat.	amá-nd-ō	habé-nd-ō	dīc-é-nd-ō
abl.	amá-nd-ō	habé-nd-ō	dīc-é-nd-ō

	4 'hearing'	3/4 'capturing'
nom.	audī́-re	cáp-e-re
acc.	audi-é-nd-um	capi-é-nd-um
	audī́-re	cáp-e-re
gen.	audi-é-nd-ī	capi-é-nd-ī
dat.	audi-é-nd-ō	capi-é-nd-ō
abl.	audi-é-nd-ō	capi-é-nd-ō

Deponents have exactly the same forms and *active* meaning, i.e. *mina-nd-um* 'threatening', *pollice-nd-um* 'promising', *loqu-e-nd-um* 'speaking', *menti-e-nd-um* 'lying', *prōgredi-e-nd-um* 'advancing'.

Usages

1 The infinitive is used as a noun-gerund in e.g. *dulce est amāre* 'it is sweet <u>to make love</u>', 'love-making is pleasant'. Here *amāre* is noun-subject. Cf. *cupiō succurrere* 'I desire <u>to help</u>', 'I like <u>helping</u>'. Here the infinitive is a noun-object. With prepositions, the *-nd-* form is used, e.g. *ad amandum* 'with a view to loving'.

2 *ad* + acc. 'for the purpose of', e.g. *ad dīcendum* 'for the purpose of speaking', 'with a view to speaking'. The gerund may take an object, e.g. *ad nāuem capiendum* 'to capture the ship'. In this, and similar cases, Latin often writes 'to the ship to-be-captured', i.e. turning the gerund into a gerundive, to agree with the noun, i.e. *ad nāuem capiendam.* This is called 'gerundival attraction'. See note 3 below for another example, and cf. **152.2** (gerundives).

3 *causā/grātiā* + gen. 'for the sake of', 'for the purpose of', e.g. *dīcendī causā* 'for the sake of speaking' (note word-order); *habendī grātiā* 'for the sake of having', 'in order to have'. 'For the sake of capturing the ships' could be *nāuēs capiendī causā* or (with gerundival attraction) *nāuium capiendārum causā.* See note 2 above.

4 In the abl., e.g. *dīcendō* 'by speaking', *omittendō* 'by omitting' (cf. *innuendō* 'by hinting'), e.g. *ūnus homō nōbīs cūnctandō restituit rem* 'one man (i.e. Q. Fabius Maximus Cunctator) restored our fortunes by delaying' (Ennius).

NB Remember the irregular gerunds *eund-um* 'going' (*eō*), *oriund-um* 'rising' (*orior*). *Faciundum* 'making', 'doing', *gerundum* 'doing' etc. are also found, for *faciendum/gerendum.* The key vowel was originally *-u-*.

EXERCISES

1 *Form, translate and decline the gerunds of the following verbs:* exorior, dormiō, petō, nōscō, fugiō, commoror, teneō, eō (*optional:* uoluō, uulnerō, occidō, uersor, reperiō, agō, gerō, taceō).

2 *Translate into English:*

   (a) ad ūtendum.

   (b) eundī causā.

   (c) discēdendō.

   (d) resistendī grātiā.

   (e) ad uulnerandum.

   (f) uidendō.

   (g) uoluendī causā.

3 *Translate into Latin for* (*using gerunds*):

(a) To wound.

(b) For the purpose of delaying.

(c) By holding.

(d) For the sake of arising.

(e) To assist.

(f) Of seeking.

(g) In doing.

4 *Translate these sentences or phrases saying whether gerund or gerundive is being used*:

(a) ad mīlitēs uulnerandōs.

(b) mihi eundum est.

(c) prōgrediendī causā.

(d) mīlitibus nōminandīs.

(e) fortiter resistendō.

(f) ad corpora uoluenda.

(g) sauciīs ab integrīs succurrendum erat.

(h) coniūrātōrēs cōnsul praetōribus pūniendōs trādidit.

(i) discēdendī grātiā.

(j) ad exercitum īnstruendum.

(k) hominis mēns[1] discendō[2] alitur[3] et cōgitandō. (Cicero)

(l) nihil tam difficile est quīn quaerendō inuestīgārī[4] possit. (Terence)

1. *mēns ment-is* 3f. mind.
2. *discō* 3 I learn.
3. *alitur* 'is fed', 'grows'.
4. *inuestīgō* 1 I trace out.

176   ***quisque* and *quisquam***

quisque means 'each and every', 'everyone'. It is often used with the superlative, e.g. *optimus quisque* 'each and every best (male)', 'all the best men'; *pessima quaeque* 'each and every most wicked woman', 'all the most wicked women'.

quisquam means 'anyone', 'any' and is normally found in negative contexts, e.g. *nec quisquam* 'and not anyone', 'and no one'.

quisque and *quisquam* decline like *quis* (**29**) + *-que/-quam*. Note that the neuter of *quisquam* is *quicquam* and the neuter of *quisque* is *quidque* or *quodque*.

177   ***uterque***

uterque means 'both', 'each (of two)' and declines as follows:

	s.		
	m.	f.	n.
nom.	utér-que	útr-a-que	utr-úm-que
acc.	utr-úm-que	utr-ám-que	utr-úm-que
gen.	←——— utr-īús-que ———→		
dat.	←——— utr-īús-que ———→		
abl.	utr-ó̄-que	utr-ā̆-que	utr-ó̄-que

	pl.		
	m.	f.	n.
nom.	utr-ī́-que	utr-aé-que	útr-a-que
acc.	utr-ó̄s-que	utr-ā̆s-que	útr-a-que
gen.	utr-ōrúm-que	utr-ārúm-que	utr-ōrúm-que
dat.	←——— utr-ī́s-que ———→		
abl.	←——— utr-ī́s-que ———→		

Cf. *alter, nūllus, tōtus, ūnus, sōlus* etc., which also decline exactly like *mult-us a um* except for the gen. s. in *-īus* and the dat. s. in *-ī*.

178   **4th declension neuter *corn-ū ūs*: 'horn', 'wing of army'**

	s.	pl.
nom./voc.	córnū	córnu-a
acc.	córnū	córnu-a
gen.	córnū-s	córnu-um
dat.	córnū	córn-ibus
abl.	córnū	córn-ibus

NB The only other noun of this type you are likely to meet is *genū* 'knee' (cf. 'genuflect', to bend the knee).

EXERCISES

EITHER

1 *Translate into English*:

(a) pessimus quisque coniūrātiōnī ignōscit.

(b) stultissimus quisque haec intellegere potest.

(c) nec quisquam hoc dīcere ausus est.

(d) interdīcitque[1] omnibus nē quemquam interficiant. (Caesar)

(e) in omnī arte[2] optimum quidque rārissimum[3] est. (Cicero)

(f) remedia utrīusque fortūnae. (Title of a book by the fourteenth-century Italian Petrarch)

(g) tū mihi uidēris utrumque factūrus. (Cicero)

(h) aut enim nēmo aut, sī quisquam, ille sapiēns[4] fuit. (Cicero)

(i) prō sē quisque ad populum loquēbatur. (Cicero)

(j) … nec quisquam ex agmine tantō audet adīre uirum. (Virgil)

1. *interdīcō* 3 (+ dat.) I forbid.
2. *ars art-is* 3f. art.
3. *rār-us a um* rare.
4. *sapiēns sapient-is* wise.

OR

2 *Translate into Latin*:

(a) All the best men resist their enemies.

(b) Nor did the commander send anyone wounded into battle.

(c) The commander of each of the two armies encouraged his soldiers.

(d) It is not possible to say anything good.[1]

(e) Petreius encouraged each individual.

(f) By relating each man's deeds he encouraged the soldiers.

1. 'good': genitive; cf. *quid negōtī*.

179   **Further comparative clauses**

1 *atque/ac*

atque/ac is used after adjectives or adverbs which express 'likeness' or 'unlikeness', such as *īdem* 'the same', *alius* 'different', 'other', *aliter* 'differently', *contrā* 'opposite', 'contrary', *par* 'equal', *pariter* 'equally', *perinde* 'in like manner', *similis* 'like', 'similar', e.g.

> iussērunt simulācrum Iouis, <u>contrā atque anteā fuerat</u>, ad orientem conuertere 'they ordered (them) to turn the statue of Jupiter towards the East, <u>contrary to what it had been before</u>'
> <u>perinde</u> ēgit <u>ac dīxit</u> 'he acted <u>just as he said</u>'

2 Correlatives

You have already met *ut* meaning 'as', which acts as a correlative to *sīc* or *ita* 'thus', e.g. *ut tū imperās, sīc/ita ego faciō* 'as you order, so I do'. In the same way, *tam* 'so' is answered by *quam* 'as', e.g.

> *tam beātus erat ille quam miser ego* 'he was as (lit. so) happy as I unhappy'

tot 'so many' is answered by *quot* 'as many', e.g.

> *tot uirī sunt quot fēminae* 'so many men there are, as many (as) (there are) women', 'there are as many men as women'

Cf. *tantus* ('so great') … *quantus* ('as great', 'as'); *tālis* ('of such a sort') … *quālis* ('of which sort', 'as'), e.g.

> *tanta sapientia eī inest quanta uīs* 'there is so great wisdom in him as great (as there is) force', 'he is as much brain as brawn'

> *tālem uirtūtem praebēbat quālem Horātius* 'he showed bravery of such a sort as the sort (which) Horatius (showed)'

3 Unreal comparisons

quasi, uelut, tamquam mean 'as if', 'as though' and (with or without *sī* added) take a *subjunctive* where the comparison is unreal or hypothetical. Constructions under **179.1** add *sī*, e.g.

> *ita sē gerit quasi stultus sit* 'he is behaving as though he were a fool' (but he is not)

> *perinde agit ac sī hostis sit* 'he acts just as though he were an enemy' (but is not)

EXERCISES

1 *Translate into English*:
   (a) Catilīna aliter ac Petrēius ratus erat agēbat.
   (b) tam ignāuus erat Gabīnius quam Lentulus.
   (c) perinde atque eī imperātum erat, sīc Mānlius ēgit.
   (d) rēs gestae sunt contrā atque exspectāuerat Petrēius.
   (e) loquitur quasi stultus sit.
2 *Translate these sentences*:
   (a) nihil est hominī tam timendum quam inuidia. (Cicero)
   (b) nihil est tam fallāx quam uīta hūmāna, nihil tam īnsidiōsum. (Seneca)

(c) quot hominēs, tot sententiae. (Terence)

(d) plērīque habēre amīcum tālem uolunt, quālēs ipsī esse nōn possunt. (Cicero)

(e) paruī sīc iacent, tamquam omnīnō sine animō sint. (Cicero)

inuidi-a ae 1f. envy, hatred	*īnsidiōs-us a um* dangerous
fallāx fallāc-is deceitful	*paruī* = babies
hūmān-us a um human	*omnīnō* altogether, completely

OPTIONAL

3 *Translate into Latin (using comparative clauses):*

(a) This man is as good as that man.

(b) My son is acting against my wishes.

(c) You are the sort of person that your father was.

(d) He is acting differently from the way he was told to.

(e) I will act in accordance with your commands.

(f) He was walking as though he had been wounded.

EITHER

Reading exercises / Test exercises

1 *The speaker is Cato the Censor (234–149). He is talking about old age with Gaius Laelius (b. 186) and Publius Scipio Africanus (Minor) (c. 185–129), who are pictured as young men at the time of the conversation. His particular theme here is what can be done to overcome what are normally seen as the peculiar drawbacks of old age.*

resistendum, Laelī et Scīpiō, senectūtī est eiusque uitia dīligentiā compēnsanda sunt, pugnandum tamquam contrā morbum sīc contrā senectūtem, habenda ratiō ualētūdinis, ūtendum exercitātiōnibus modicīs, tantum cibī et pōtiōnis adhibendum, ut reficiantur uīrēs, nōn opprimantur. nec uērō corporī sōlum subueniendum est, sed mentī atque animō multō magis; nam haec   5
quoque, nisi tamquam lūminī oleum īnstillēs, exstinguuntur senectūte. et corpora quidem exercitātiōnum dēfatīgātiōne ingrauēscunt, animī autem sē exercendō leuantur. nam quōs ait Caecilius 'cōmicōs stultōs senēs', hōs significat crēdulōs oblīuiōsōs dissolūtōs, quae uitia sunt nōn senectūtis, sed inertis ignāuae somniculōsae senectūtis. ut petulantia, ut libīdō magis est   10
adulēscentium quam senum, nec tamen omnium adulēscentium, sed nōn probōrum, sīc ista senīlis stultitia, quae dēlīrātiō appellārī solet, senum leuium est, nōn omnium. (Cicero, *Dē Senectūte (Catō Māior)* 35–6)

senectūs senectūt-is 3f. old age

uiti-um ī 2n. fault, shortcoming

compēnsō 1 I balance

pugnandum sc. *est* [note the ellipse
of *est*, which is understood from
the previous part of the sentence
resistendum … est (also in line 2:
habenda; line 3: *ūtendum*; line 4:
adhibendum)]

tamquam just as, as though

morb-us ī 2m. disease

ratiō ratiōn-is 3f. method, regimen

ualētūdō ualētūdin-is 3f. health

exercitātiō exercitātiōn-is 3f. exercise

modic-us a um moderate

pōtiō pōtiōn-is 3f. drink

adhibeō 2 I use

reficiō 3/4 I refresh

5   *corporī* [hold until solved, reading as
a phrase with *sōlum*]

subueniō 4 (+ dat.) I help

mēns ment-is 3f. mind

lūmen lūmin-is 3n. light

ole-um ī 2n. oil

īnstillō 1 I drop X (acc.) into Y (dat.)
[note mood of *īnstillēs*: subjunctive
expressing generalised 2nd s. (see
158.2)]

exstinguō 3 I quench, put out

quidem indeed [emphasising *corpora*]

dēfatīgātiō dēfatīgātiōn-is 3f.
exhaustion, weariness

ingrauēscō 3 I grow heavier
(i.e. stiffer)

exerceō 2 I train, exercise

leuō 1 I relieve [the prevalent
metaphor centres on the stems
grau- 'heavy', *leu-* 'light']

ait '(he) calls'

Caecilius = C. Statius, an early
Roman comic poet

cōmic-us a um comic

significō 1 I mean

crēdul-us a um credulous   **10**

oblīuiōs-us a um forgetful

dissolūt-us a um slack

iners inert-is idle

somniculōs-us a um drowsy

ut [hold until solved]

petulanti-a ae 1f. impudence,
waywardness

adulēscēns adulēscent-is 3m. youth

prob-us a um honest, upright

senīl-is e of old men

stultiti-a ae 1f. foolishness

dēlīrātiō dēlīrātiōn-is 3f. dementia,
dotage, madness

leu-is e frivolous, weak

2   *The rape of Ceres' daughter Proserpina. She is picking flowers with her
girlfriends. Her uncle, the god of the Underworld, Pluto, sees her, falls in love
with her and snatches her off to Hades. Suspension of adjective in the first half
of the line is particularly noticeable in this piece. (See* **180.4.3** *and* **186** *for the
metre.)*

> fīlia, cōnsuētīs ut erat comitāta puellīs,
>   errābat nūdō per sua prāta pede,
> ualle sub umbrōsā locus est aspergine multā
>   ūuidus ex altō dēsilientis aquae.
> tot fuerant illīc, quot habet nātūra, colōrēs,   5
>   pictaque dissimilī flōre nitēbat humus,
> quam simul aspexit, 'comitēs, accēdite', dīxit
>   'et mēcum plēnōs flōre referte sinūs!'

praeda puellārīs animōs prōlectat inānis,
    et nōn sentītur sēdulitāte labor.   **10**

Proserpina wanders off, by chance not followed by any of her friends.
hanc uidet et uīsam patruus uēlōciter aufert,
    rēgnaque caeruleīs in sua portat equīs,
illa quidem clāmābat, 'iō, cārissima māter,
    auferor!' ipsa suōs abscideratque sinūs:
panditur intereā Dītī uia, namque diurnum   **15**
    lūmen inassuētī uix patiuntur equī.
at chorus aequālis, cumulātae flōre ministrae,
    'Persephonē', clāmant 'ad tua dōna uenī!'
ut clāmāta silet, montīs ululātibus implent,
    et feriunt maestā pectora nūda manū.   **20**

(Ovid, *Fastī* 4.425–34 and 445–54)

cōnsuētīs [hold until solved]
cōnsuēt-us a um usual
comitō 1 I accompany
errō 1 I wander
nūdō [hold until solved]
nūd-us a um naked
prāt-a ōrum 2n. pl. meadows
uallis uall-is 3f. valley
umbrōs-us a um shady
aspergō aspergin-is 3f. spray
ūuid-us a um wet [read *aspergine*
    multā ūuidus as one phrase]
alt-um ī 2n. high place
dēsiliō 4 I leap down [read *ex altō*
    dēsilientis aquae as one phrase,
    dependent on *aspergine*]
5   *tot ... quot* as many ... as
color colōr-is 3m. colour
picta [hold until solved]
pingō 3 *pīnxī pictus* I paint
dissimil-is e diverse
flōs flōr-is 3m. flower
niteō 2 I shine
humus [remember this is f.]
simul as soon as
aspiciō 3/4 *aspexī* I spot
plēnōs [hold until solved: *plēnus* takes
    gen. or abl. when it means 'full of']

referō referre I bring back
sin-us ūs 4m. fold of garment,
    bosom
puellār-is e girlish
prōlectō 1 I entice away
inān-is e vain, empty
sentītur [passive: await subject]   **10**
sēdulitās sēdulitāt-is 3f. earnest
    application, concentration
uīsam [refers to Proserpina]
patru-us 2m. uncle
uēlōciter swiftly
rēgna [hold until solved]
rēgn-um ī 2n. kingdom, realm
caeruleīs [hold until solved]
caerule-us a um dark
portat sc. 'her'
quidem indeed
iō help!
cār-us a um dear
suōs [hold until solved]
abscindō 3 *abscidī* I tear apart
-que 'even'
panditur [passive: await subject]   **15**
pandō 3 I open
Dīs Dīt-is 3m. Hades, Pluto [*Dītī* =
    dative of agent, 'by']
namque for in fact

267

diurn-us a um of the day [don't stop reading at the line-end]

lūmen lūmin-is 3n. light

inassuētī [hold until solved]

inassuēt-us a um unaccustomed

uix with difficulty

chor-us ī 2m. group

aequāl-is e of the same age

cumulō 1 I load

ministr-a ae 1f. attendant

cumulātae ... ministrae [in apposition to *chorus aequālis*]

Persephonē [vocative]

dōn-um ī 2n. gift

sileō 2 I am silent

ululāt-us ūs 4m. cry, wail

impleō 2 I fill X (acc.) with Y (abl.)

maestā [hold until solved]   **20**

maest-us a um sad

pectus pector-is 3n. breast

OR

English–Latin

Reread the text of 5G(iii) and then translate this passage into Latin:

When the fighting[1] was finished, you would have seen many corpses in the place. It was also possible to see[2] how much daring[1] there had been in Catiline and in his army. Each man had fallen in the place which he had seized by fighting. Nor had anyone run away. Catiline, who had run into the middle of the enemy for the purpose of dying quickly, was found far from his own men. He still retained the ferocity of expression[3] he had had[3] when[4] alive. But the victory was not a joyful event for the Romans. All the best men had died or been wounded seriously. Those who had come out for the purpose of stripping corpses found not only enemies, but also friends and relatives as they turned over the cadavers. There were both joy and sorrow in the camp that night.

1. Do not use a gerund here, but a noun.
2. Use *uidērī poterat* (lit. 'it could be seen').
3. Do not forget to insert a *quī* clause here, though English neglects it.
4. Not needed: use adj. alone, agreeing with subj.

Grammar and exercises for 6A

180   **Roman poetry**

1 Introduction

Consider the following lines from Pope's *Epistle to a Lady* (1735):

> Pleasures the Sex, as Children Birds, pursue,
> Still out of Reach, but never out of View

Put bluntly, it means 'The (female) sex pursues pleasures as children pursue birds; the pleasures remain out of reach, but never out of view.' The utterance is different from prose in a number of important ways:

(a) It is in metre.

(b) The word-order is different from prose.

(c) It is very compressed ('pursue' serves for both limbs of the first line).

(d) It is cleverly balanced (e.g. the balance of 'Pleasures [object] the Sex [subject] as Children [subject] Birds [object]').

(e) The image is striking: women pursuing pleasure as children pursue birds.

Until one gets used to it, reading this sort of poetry, even in English, is quite hard work. Balance, compression, striking word-order and powerful imagery are all features of Latin poetry too, and since Latin is an inflected language, the dislocation of expected symmetry by means of calculated asymmetry (= *uariātiō*) can be that much more violent. But no less important to a Roman poet is balance. Consider the following haunting lines from Virgil:

> *tum pinguēs agnī, et tum mollissima uīna,*
> *tum somnī dulcēs, dēnsaeque in montibus umbrae*

> 'then fat the lambs, and then most sweet the wine,
> then sleep (is) sweet, and deep on the mountains (are) the shadows'

Observe the compression (no verbs), and the balance with variety. Of the four *cōla* (limbs), three start with *tum*, but not the fourth; the first line runs adjective–noun, adjective–noun; the second runs noun–adjective, adjective(prepositional phrase)–noun. The metre adds to the effect by being slow and heavy, and allowing, unusually, two adjacent vowels (*agnī et*) their full value. (Note that in line 2 *dēnsaeque in* the *-e* of *-que* is, as normally, lost before the following *i-*.)

The word-order of the above example is not, however, difficult. Generally, Roman poets do not go in for extremes of word-order (or hyperbaton, 'leapfrog', as the technical term is). Here is an example of an extreme word-order from that most arch and sophisticated of poets, Ovid:

sī quis quī quid agam forte requīrat erit

'If there will perhaps be anyone who asks what I am doing'
(Natural order would be *sī quis forte erit quī requīrat quid agam.*)

One can compare the strained balance of the Ovid with e.g. Sidney's

Vertue, beautie and speeche did strike, wound, charme
My heart, eyes, ears, with wonder, love, delight.

In both English and Latin there is a limit to how much one can take of this sort of thing.

(See further L. P. Wilkinson, *Golden Latin Artistry*, Cambridge, 1963, Chapter 8. Bristol Classical Press reprint 1985.)

2 Rhetorical features of Latin prose and poetry

Here are the technical terms, with examples, for some of the most important figures of Latin writing:

(a) Ellipse (sometimes called by its Greek term *apo koinou*): a figure in which a word or words needed to complete the sense are understood from another part of the sentence, e.g.

Player King (*Hamlet* III.ii):
[thirty years have passed]
Since love our hearts and Hymen did our hands
Unite

i.e. 'since love (united) our hearts'.

(b) Antithesis: a figure in which ideas are sharply contrasted by the use of words of opposite or very different meaning, e.g.

Pope (*Epistle to Dr Arbuthnot*) on the danger of flatterers:
Of all mad Creatures, if the Learn'd are right,
It is the Slaver kills, and not the Bite.

'Slaver' and 'Bite' are in antithesis.

(c) Asyndeton: a figure in which conjunctions are missed out, to give an effect of speed and economy, e.g.

Rochester (*The Imperfect Enjoyment*):
With arms, legs, lips close clinging to embrace.

(d) Chiasmus: a figure in which corresponding parts of a sentence are placed criss-cross (a-b-b-a), e.g.

Shakespeare, *Sonnet* 154:
Love's fire heats water, water cools not love.
a   b   b   a

Pope (*On Women*):
A Fop their Passion, but their Prize, a Sot.
a   b   b   a

(e) The golden line: term applied to a line in Latin poetry which consists of two adjectives and two nouns with a verb in between, in the pattern a b (verb) A B, e.g.

> *impiaque aeternam timuērunt saecula noctem*
> a   b   (verb) A   B

'and the unholy ages feared the everlasting night'.

A 'silver' line takes the order a b (verb) B A.

(f) Tricolon: a group consisting of three equivalent units, e.g. 'I came, I saw, I conquered', 'with arms, legs, lips'. Frequently, these units increase in length ('ascending tricolon'), e.g. 'Friends, Romans, countrymen'. (Cf. tetracolon – four units.)

(g) Anaphora: a figure in which a word (or words) is repeated in successive clauses or phrases (usually at the start of the clause or phrase), e.g.

Shakespeare, *Richard II* II.ii:

> With mine own tears I wash away my balm,
> With mine own hands I give away my crown
> With mine own tongue deny my sacred state.

(h) Assonance: similarity of vowel sounds of words near each other, e.g.

Thomas Gray:

> Along the h<u>ea</u>th and n<u>ea</u>r his favourite tr<u>ee</u>.

(i) Alliteration: any repetition of the same sounds or syllables (especially the beginnings of words) of two or more words close to each other, e.g.

> <u>L</u>ow <u>l</u>ies the <u>l</u>evel <u>l</u>ake.

(j) Hyperbaton: a figure in which the natural word-order is upset, e.g.

Milton (translating Horace's *rīdentem dīcere uērum quid uetat?*):

> Laughing to teach the truth, what hinders?

i.e. 'What hinders one-who-is-laughing from teaching the truth?'
The Latin word-order, however, is normal.

3 Poetic word-order

Adjectives and nouns

One of the most frequent word-orders in poetry is adjective, then something else, then the noun with which the adjective agrees, e.g.

> *Lāuīnaque uēnit lītora* 'and he came to the Lavinian shores'
> *altae moenia Rōmae* 'the walls of high Rome'
> *Trōiānō ā sanguine* 'from Trojan blood'
> *Rōmānam condere gentem* 'to found the Roman race'
> *quem dās fīnem?* 'what end do you give?'
> *noua pectore uersat cōnsilia* 'she turned over new plans in her heart'

Here is a double example:

> *saeuae memorem Iūnōnis ob īram* 'on account of the unforgetting anger of savage Juno'

The best tactic to adopt is to register the adjective and *move on*: concentrate your attention on nouns and verbs first and foremost, and try to solve them as you come to them. This will lay clear the bare bones of the sentence. You can then reread, concentrating on the adjectives and seeing where they fit. Thus a first reading should concentrate on the underlined words:

> *ingentia <u>cernēs</u> <u>moenia</u> surgentemque nouae <u>Karthāginis arcem</u>.*
> '(something about "large") you will see the walls and (something about "rising" and "new") the citadel of Carthage'.

Then reread, concentrating on *ingentia*, *surgentem* and *nouae*, seeing where they agree:

> 'you will see the *huge* walls and *arising* the citadel of *new* Carthage'.

NB When adjectives precede and are separated from their nouns in prose, the effect is to emphasise strongly one element or the other (usually the first).

EXERCISE

Translate the following (adjectives underlined):

(a) <u>Tyriam</u> quī aduēneris urbem.

(b) templum Iūnōnī <u>ingēns.</u>

(c) uidet <u>Īliacās</u> ex ōrdine pugnās.

(d) bellaque iam fāmā <u>tōtam uulgāta</u> per urbem.

(e) feret <u>haec aliquam</u> tibi fama salūtem.

(f) animum pictūrā pāscit <u>inānī</u>.

(g) <u>ardentīsque</u> āuertit equōs.

(h) iuuat īre et <u>Dōrica</u> castra / <u>dēsertōsque</u> uidēre locōs.

(i) <u>summā</u> dēcurrit ab arce.

(j) <u>tacitae</u> per <u>amīca</u> silentia lūnae.

Tyri-us a um Carthaginian
quī aduēneris 'since you have come to'
Iūnō Iūnōn-is 3f. the goddess Juno
Īliac-us a um of Troy, Trojan
fām-a ae 1f. rumour

uulgāt-us a um spread
aliquam (acc. s. f.) some
fām-a ae 1f. reputation
pictūr-a ae 1f. scene
pāscō 3 I feed
inān-is e illusory

ardēns ardent-is fiery
āuertō 3 I turn aside
equ-us ī 2m. horse
iuuat it gives pleasure
Dōric-us a um Greek
dēsert-us a um abandoned
summ-us a um top (of)

dēcurrō 3 I run down
arx arc-is 3f. citadel
tacit-us a um quiet
amīc-us a um friendly
silenti-a ōrum 2n. pl. silences
lūn-a ae 1f. moon

Verbs

It is extremely common for verbs to come early in the sentence, sometimes well before the quoted subject. So you must hang on to the person of the verb and wait for a subject to appear, e.g.

> *obstipuit prīmō aspectū Sīdōnia Dīdō* 'he/she/it fell silent at the first look' – ah, that is 'Carthaginian Dido fell silent...'
> *conticuēre omnēs* 'they fell silent' – ah, 'everyone fell silent'

NB Verb–subject is also a common order in prose.

Word-groups

We have 'phrased' together words that can usefully be taken in groups together, e.g.

> *tālibus⌐ ōrantem⌐ ⌐dictīs ārāsque ⌐tenentem*
> *audiit Omnipotēns*
>
> 'the one begging (*acc.*) with such words and holding (*acc.*) the altars the All-powerful (*i.e. Jupiter*) heard'

Delayed introductory word

Conjunctions like *cum, dum, ubi, sī, sed, et* are often held back in the sentence (as in prose: see **126⁴**), e.g.

> *namque sub ingentī lūstrat dum singula templō* 'for while he surveys individual items under the great temple'
>
> *magnum rēginae sed enim miserātus amōrem* 'but pitying the queen's great love'

4 Latin metre

Latin metre is more complex than English because in Latin metre *every syllable counts* (cf. English, where metre depends largely on stress).

For the purpose of metre, every syllable in Latin counted as either *heavy* (–) or *light* (∪). Heavy syllables may be compared to longer notes in music, light to shorter.

273

Heavy and light syllables

Here are some basic rules:

(a) A syllable is *heavy* if its vowel is pronounced *long*, e.g. *pōnō, īrātō*.

(b) A syllable is *heavy* if the vowel is followed by two consonants or a double consonant (*x, z*), e.g. *ingentēs* .

> Word division makes no difference, e.g. *et* is 'light', but *et fugit* would make *et* heavy, because the *t* is followed by an *f*, making two consonants.

(c) A syllable is *heavy* if it contains a diphthong, e.g. *aedēs*. (cf. note 1 below).

(d) A syllable is *light* if it contains a short vowel followed by only one consonant (or none), e.g. *et omnibus*. Contrast *et ueniō*

Elision

If a word ends in a vowel or in *-m*, and the next word begins with a vowel (or *h*), the final vowel or *-m* syllable is 'elided' ('crushed out of existence') and does not count for the purposes of the metre, e.g.

> eg[o] et tū
> uirtūt[em] et
> c[um] habeās

Notes

1 The 'heaviness' or 'lightness' of a vowel *has no effect on its natural pronunciation.* Thus the *et* of *et fugit* may count as heavy for the purposes of scansion, but it would not be pronounced *ēt* as a consequence. To help you to see the difference between *vowel length* and *syllable quantity* we have continued to mark long vowels (immediately above the letter), as well as setting out the metrical pattern (above the line), e.g. *corripuēre* indicates that the first vowel (*-o-*) is pronounced *short*, but belongs in a *heavy* syllable (because followed by two consonants *-rr-*); the fourth vowel, however (*-ē-*), is pronounced *long* (the syllable will therefore be *heavy*).

2 Verse was read with the *normal* word stress (see p. xv). Do not allow the rhythmic stress of the metre to distort the natural stress of the words.

The hexameter: Virgil's metre

The hexameter has six feet, consisting of a mixture of dactyls (— ∪ ∪) and spondees (– –), on the following pattern:

1	2	3	4	5	6
– ∪∪	– ∪∪	– ∪∪	– ∪∪	– ∪∪	– ∪
– –	– –	– –	– –	(– –)	

In the 'Additional readings' for Section 5 (*TV* p. 312), you will find a passage of Virgil. Here are the first three lines of that first Virgil passage scanned for you:

$$\text{Corripu}\,|\,\text{ēre}\;\;\text{ui}\,|\,\text{[am] intere}\,|\,\text{ā, quā}\,|\,\text{sēmita}\,|\,\text{mōnstrat}$$

$$\text{iamqu[e]}\;\;\text{asc}\,|\,\text{endēb}\,|\,\text{ant}\;\;\text{coll}\,|\,\text{em,}\;\;\text{quī}\,|\,\text{plūrimus}\,|\,\text{urbī}$$

$$\text{imminet}\,|\,\text{aduers}\,|\,\text{āsqu[e]}\;\;\text{asp}\,|\,\text{ectat}\,|\,\text{dēsuper}\,|\,\text{arcēs.}$$

Notes

1 Foot 5 is usually a dactyl, very occasionally a spondee.

2 The line usually has a word-division (*caesūra*, lit. 'cutting') in the middle of the third foot or the fourth. E.g. the *caesura* in the above examples is after *intereā* (4th foot), *ascendēbant*, *aduersāsqu(e)* (3rd foot).

181   ***Hendecasyllables*** **(= 'eleven syllables')**

The first five poems of Catullus (**6A(i)–(v)**) which you read make use of the following new metrical elements:

⌣ = *anceps* ('doubtful', 'two-edged')

– ⌣ ⌣ – ⌣ – = *choriambocretic*   (*choriamb* – ⌣ ⌣ – blended together with *cretic* – ⌣ –)

⌣ – ⌣ = *bacchiac*

The poems scan as follows:

⌣ ⌣ | – ⌣ ⌣ – ⌣ – | ⌣ – ⌣

i.e. two *anceps*, *choriambocretic*, *bacchiac*, e.g.

$$\text{cēnāb}\,|\,\text{is}\;\;\text{bene}\quad\text{mī}\;\;\text{Fabul}\,|\,l\,\text{[e] apud}\quad\text{mē}$$

EXERCISE

Using the above scheme, scan any one of the five poems in this metre, adding the correct word stress (see rule, p. xv). Then read it aloud, thinking through the meaning as you read.

NB Remember to check for elision.

182 ***Scazon*** **('limping iambics')**

Poem **6A(vi)** makes use of the following metrical elements:

$$\cup = anceps \text{ (doubtful syllable)}$$
$$- \cup - = cretic$$

(The combination *anceps* + *cretic* is known as an iambic 'measure'.) The poem scans as follows:

$$\cup - \cup - \,|\, \cup - \cup - \,|\, \cup - - \cup$$

i.e. two iambic measures + ∪ ‑‑ ∪ , e.g.

$$\breve{u} - \quad \cup \, \acute{-} \,|\, \acute{u} \cup - \,|\, \cup - \acute{u} \cup$$
$$miser \quad Catull|e \quad d\bar{e}sin\bar{a}s| \quad inept\bar{i}re$$

The metre is called 'limping iambics' because it seems to limp to a close. The sprightly iambics of the first two measures are rounded off not by a third, but by the 'limping' ∪ ‑‑ ∪.

EXERCISE

Using the above scheme, scan **6A(vi)**, adding the correct word stress (see rule, p. xv). Then read it aloud, thinking through the meaning as you read.

NB Remember to check for elision.

183 **Sapphics**

Poem **6A(vii)** is made up of stanzas in *Sapphic* metre, so named after the seventh-century Greek poetess from Lesbos, Sappho, who specialised in them. Sapphics use the following metrical elements, all of which you have already met:

$$- \cup - = cretic$$
$$\cup = anceps \text{ (doubtful syllable)}$$
$$- \cup \cup - \cup - = choriambocretic \text{ (see } \mathbf{181})$$
$$- \cup \cup - = choriamb$$

Sapphics scan as follows:

First three lines: $- \cup - | \underline{\cup} | - \cup \cup - \cup - | \underline{\cup}$
Last line: $- \cup \cup - | \underline{\cup}$

i.e. *cretic*, *anceps*, *choriambocretic*, *anceps* (× 3), *choriamb*, *anceps*, e.g.

$$F\bar{u}r[\bar{\imath}] \;\; et \;\; Aur\big|\bar{e}l\big|\bar{\imath} \;\; com\bar{\imath}t\bar{e}s \;\; Catull\big|\bar{\imath}...$$

$$t\bar{u}nd\breve{\imath}t\breve{u}r \;\Big|\; \bar{u}nd\bar{a}$$

EXERCISE

Using the above scheme, scan poem **6A(vii)**, adding the correct word stress (see rule, p. xv). Then read it aloud, thinking through the meaning as you read.

NB Remember to check for elision.

Grammar and exercises for 6D

See pp. 273–4 for the principles of Latin metre, and pp. 274–5 for the basic rules of the hexameter.

184   **The hexameter in Lucretius**

The metre is used by both Lucretius and Virgil (see pp. 274–5), but Lucretius is in some ways less strict. Lucretius for instance allows elision of *-s* to produce a light syllable, e.g.

$$\overset{\smile}{min}\Big|\overset{-\ \smile}{ori}\overset{-}{bu'}\ \ \overset{\prime}{n}\Big|\overset{-}{ostris} \text{ (for } \overset{\smile}{min}\Big|\overset{-\ \smile}{ori}\overset{\prime}{bus}\ \ \overset{-}{n}\Big|\overset{-}{ostris})$$

Here are the first three lines of the Lucretius passage scanned for you:

$$\overset{-\ \smile\ \smile}{praetere}\Big|\overset{-}{a}\ \overset{\prime}{cael}\Big|\overset{-}{i}\ \ \overset{\smile\ \smile}{rati}\Big|\overset{-}{ones}\Big|\overset{\prime}{ordine}\Big|\overset{-}{certo}$$

$$\overset{-\ \smile\ \smile}{et\ uari}\Big|[a]\ \ \overset{-}{annor}\Big|\overset{\prime}{um}\ \ \overset{-}{cern}\Big|\overset{\prime}{ebant}\Big|\overset{\smile\ \smile}{tempora}\Big|\overset{\prime}{uerti}$$

$$\overset{-}{nec}\ \ \overset{\smile\ \smile}{poter}\Big|\overset{-}{ant}\ \ \overset{\smile\ \smile}{quibus}\Big|\overset{-}{id}\ fier\Big|et\ \ \overset{\smile\ \smile}{cogn}\Big|\overset{\prime}{oscere}\Big|\overset{-}{causis.}$$

NB The caesura (see above p. 275, note 2) comes after *caelī*, *annōrum*, *id* (3rd foot).

185   **Archilochean**

The metre Horace uses in *Odes* 4.7 is called Archilochean, after the seventh-century BC poet Archilochus of Paros. The scheme is a couplet, made up as follows:

(a) hexameter (see above pp. 274–5)

(b) half-hexameter, with dactyls ($-\smile\smile$) only: $-\smile\smile \mid -\smile\smile \mid \underset{\smile}{\smile}$.

E.g.

$$\overset{-\ \ -}{diffug}\Big|\overset{\prime\ \smile}{ere}\ \ \overset{\smile}{niu}\Big|\overset{-}{es,}\ \ \overset{\smile\ \smile}{rede}\Big|\overset{-}{unt}\ \ \overset{-}{iam}\Big|\overset{\prime\ \smile\ \smile}{gramina}\Big|\overset{\prime\ \ -}{campis}$$

$$\overset{-\ \ \smile\ \smile}{arborib}\Big|\overset{\prime\ \ \smile}{usque}\ \ \overset{\smile}{com}\Big|\overset{-}{ae}$$

6D(iv) Elegiac couplet

The metre used by Martial, Crotti (*Text and vocabulary* p. 310) and Ovid in *Fastī* (p. 266ff.) and *Amōrēs* 1.5 is the elegiac couplet. It consists of a *hexameter* (see above p. 274), followed by a *pentameter*, the scheme of which is:

$$- \cup\cup \mid - \cup\cup \mid - \parallel - \cup\cup \mid - \cup\cup \mid \cup$$

E.g.

$$\bar{a}dp\check{o}s\check{u}\mid\bar{\imath} \quad m\check{e}d\check{\imath}\mid\bar{o}\parallel m\acute{e}mbr\check{a} \quad l\check{e}\check{u}\mid\acute{a}nd\check{a} \quad t\check{o}r\mid\bar{o}$$

There is always a caesura (see p. 275, note 2) in the place marked by ‖ in the example and the scheme.

> ### EXERCISE
>
> *Scan the lines which you have translated in each section, taking care to watch for elisions. Mark foot divisions with |. Mark caesuras in hexameters* and *in pentameters with ‖. Add the correct word stress (see rule, p. xv). Read each piece aloud, thinking through the meaning as you read.*

Reference Grammar

The Reference Grammar pulls together the Running Grammar sections, and adds to them features of the language which did not seem immediately appropriate for a beginner dealing with the basics. For further reading, both on grammar and on the historical and social linguistic background, we recommend:

James Clackson and Geoffrey Horrocks, *The Blackwell History of the Latin Language*, Malden, Oxford and Victoria 2007

B. L. Gildersleeve and Gonzalez Lodge, *Latin Grammar*, rev. edn, London 1895 (Bristol Classical Press reprint 1997)

L. R. Palmer, *The Latin Language*, London 1954

Jacob Wackernagel, *Lectures on Syntax*, tr. D. R. Langslow, Oxford 2009

Michael Weiss, *Outline of the Historical and Comparative Grammar of Latin*, Ann Arbor and New York 2009

E. C. Woodcock, *A New Latin Syntax*, London 1959 (Bristol Classical Press reprint 1985)

A Introduction: some key notions and the verb-system

(a)   An opening statement about the categories of the verb in Latin

The verb in Latin comprises two kinds of form, FINITE and NON-FINITE.

FINITE and NON-FINITE forms *differ essentially* in that FINITE forms denote (and usually mark in their ending) the person and number of the subject ('I walk, they run' etc.). NON-FINITE forms do not ('walking', 'to run' etc.).

Nearly all FINITE and some NON-FINITE forms *have in common* that they inflect for

voice (active vs. passive)

tense (present, future, perfect).

The NON-FINITE forms are the following:

participle

infinitive

gerund

gerundive

supine

The FINITE forms are the following:

> indicative
>
> imperative
>
> subjunctive

(b) Verbs and objects: transitive and intransitive

Only transitive verbs make a personal passive (*pórtor* 'I am carried', *portáris* 'you are carried', etc.): the passive of intransitive verbs is limited to the 3rd s. and is impersonal (*éī pārḗtur* lit. 'to him it is obeyed', i.e. 'he is obeyed'; *ad pórtam aduénitur* lit. 'it is come to the gate, there is a coming to the gate', i.e. 'people (unspecified) come to the gate'.

(c) Forms: the system of stems, moods and tenses

Any Latin verb (with very few exceptions) makes a full conjugation (illustrated in the table below for the 2nd s. of *hábe-ō* 'I have, hold' in the active) based on *two stems*, the 'present' stem (or *īnfectum*, or 'imperfective' – not to be confused with the present tense) and the 'perfect' stem (or *perfectum*, or 'perfective' – not to be confused with the perfect tense). On each stem, a Latin verb makes *three tenses* (past, present, future) *of the indicative*, and *two tenses* (past, present) *of the subjunctive*.

This simple but powerful generalisation about the Latin verb-system goes back at least as far as the (first-century BC) work *On the Latin Language* by Varro, a friend of Cicero's. Note e.g. that the 'past' tense formed on the 'present' stem is what we call the imperfect, while the 'past' of the 'perfect' stem is what we know as the pluperfect. Note also the absence (except in special circumstances, see p. 293 below) of a future subjunctive! We shall come to the main *use* of the perfect as a past tense under 'Meaning' (below (e)).

Tenses	Made on the 'present' stem *habe-*:		Made on the 'perfect' stem *habu-*:	
	of the INDICATIVE	of the SUBJUNCTIVE	of the INDICATIVE	of the SUBJUNCTIVE
Denoting past time	IMPERFECT *habḗ-bās*	IMPERFECT *habḗ-rēs*	PLUPERFECT *habú-erās*	PLUPERFECT *habu-íssēs*
Denoting present time	PRESENT *hábē-s*	PRESENT *hábe-ās*	PERFECT *habu-ístī*	PERFECT *habú-eris*
Denoting future time	FUTURE *habḗ-bis*		FUTURE PERFECT *habú-eris*	

Notes

1   The perfect (active) stem of *hábeō* is *habu-*. In many forms of this system, it is enlarged with the addition of *-is-*, e.g. in the perfect active infinitive *habuísse*, composed of *habu-* + *-is-* + the active infinitive ending *-se*; or in the pluperfect subjunctive *habuíssēs*, composed of *habu-* + *-is-* + the 'past' subjunctive marker *-sē-* + 2nd s. ending *-s*. But other parts of the perfect system are based on *habu-* + *-er-*, e.g. the pluperfect indicative *habú-er-am* and the future perfect *habú-er-ō*. What is going on? The reason is that in early Latin, before a vowel, the *-is-* element turned regularly into *-er-*. In other words, *habú-er-am* was once **habu-is-ā-m*, and *habú-er-ō* was once **habu-is-ō*. This *-is-* to *-er-* sound change occurs quite frequently, and explains also for example why the genitive of *cinis* 'ash' is *cíneris*, and why the city of the people called *Falíscī* is *Falériī*.

2   The 2nd s. is used for illustration in the table above because the original length (or quantity) of the vowel before the ending (long or short) is preserved in a final syllable only before *-s*. Before any other final consonant, e.g. 1st s. *-m*, 3rd s. *-t*, 3rd pl. *-nt*, 1st s. passive *-r*, original long vowels were regularly shortened (before the classical period): hence, for example, imperfect *habébăm*, *habébăt*, with short *ă*, versus *habébās* with long *ā* (originally the same long *ā* as that of the pluperfect indicative; cf. the note on p. 297 below). So, for the original length of the vowel in a verbal ending or suffix, look at the 2nd s. or the 1st or 2nd pl. (*habḗbā-s*, *habḗbā̠-mus*, *habḗbā̠-tis*; *hábēs*, *habḗmus*, *habḗtis*). Knowing the length of vowels in endings and suffixes is essential for: (a) scansion, (b) placing the accent on the correct syllable when reading a word aloud (contrast e.g. *audímus* with *dícimus*), and (c) helping you to learn the forms of the verb that belong together with greater ease and understanding (e.g. *audīs*, *audíre*, *audírem* all on the same (present) stem with long *ī*).

(d)   Forms: keys in the 'principal parts'

In books aimed at describing and teaching Latin, verbs are presented not as single forms, but as small sets of forms called 'principal parts', which between them allow the correct prediction of every grammatical form of the verb, active and (where appropriate) passive. In most traditional grammar-books and dictionaries, active verbs generally have four principal parts, deponents have three, as follows:

> 1(+2):   *hábe-ō*, *habḗ-re* (active), *pollíce-or*, *pollicḗ-rī* (deponent): the first two principal parts give the ('present') stem of forms of the present, future and imperfect indicative, the present and imperfect subjunctive, the present participle (active), the imperative, and the gerund(ive).

> 2:   *habḗ-re* (active), *pollicḗ-rī* (deponent): the second principal part (present infinitive active) in particular gives the key (in the vowel before the infinitive ending) to the correct conjugation (2nd conj. verb stems end in *-ē-*, *habḗ-re*, stem *habē-*; 1st conj. in *-ā-*, e.g. *amā-*; 3rd in *-e-*, which often becomes *-i-*, e.g. stem *díce-/dící-*; 4th in *-ī-*, e.g. *audī-*).

3: *hábu-ī* (active), *pollícit-us sum* (deponent): the third principal part (the 1st s. perfect active indicative) gives the 'perfect' stem (*habu-*, *pollicit-*), which is the key to all the *active* forms of the perfect, pluperfect and future perfect indicative and of the perfect and pluperfect subjunctive.

4: *hábit-um* (active only): the fourth principal part (traditionally the supine in *-um*, but see note below) contains the stem of the perfect (passive) participle (in a sense, for active verbs a third stem *hábit-*, alongside *habē-* and *habu-*). This holds the key to all the perfect *passive* forms of active verbs, and the future participle (the basis of the future infinitive active), as well as all nominal (noun) forms derived from the verb, including the supine (the basis of the future infinitive passive).

Note

In this course, in place of the traditional second principal part (pres. inf.), we give only the number of the conjugation to which the verb belongs (e.g. *dícō* 3, *iáciō* 3/4, *pollíceor* 2); we print the second principal part only if it is irregular (e.g. *férō, férre*). We give the fourth principal part of transitive active verbs (= the third principal part of deponents) in the form of the perfect participle (ending in *-us*), e.g. *amátus* (*ámō*), *proféctus* (*profícīscor*). All other verbs have the 4th p.p. printed in the n.s. (*-um*), e.g. *cúrsum* (*cúrrō*). Where neither supine nor perfect participle is attested, we print a dash (—) in the last p.p. position. (On the form and function of the supine, the traditional 4th p.p. of active verbs, see **A7** below.)

(e)   Meaning: time and type of action

With Varro's insight about the two stems and three tenses of the Latin verb (in the table in (c) above), compare this statement of Seneca's (first century AD) about time: *témpus tríbus pártibus cōnstat* ('consists of' + abl.): *praetéritō, praesénte, futūrō*. The <u>time</u> of the action of a verb, however, is not the whole story of its meaning. In English, for example, *I held* and *I was holding* both clearly refer to past time, but *I was holding* is certainly durative in meaning (the holding occupying a stretch of time), while *I held* carries no such implication and its type of action is often called 'simple' past. Again, *I have held* contains some reference to an action in past time, but is also, perhaps mainly, a statement of the present completeness of the action of holding. So in Latin, too, the meaning of the verb is in a sense two-dimensional, comprising both time (past, present, future) and type of action (unspecified or 'simple', durative or ongoing, completed). As the table below shows, within this two-dimensional view of the system, three tenses of the Latin verb (present, future and perfect) have more than one meaning. *Note especially the two very different meanings of the Latin perfect.* The discussion below the table spells out these meanings, and a few special uses of the tenses, one by one.

Time & Type Latin and English	SIMPLE TYPE	DURATIVE TYPE	COMPLETED TYPE
PAST TIME	*PERFECT *habu-istī* 'you held'	IMPERFECT *habḗ-bās* 'you were holding'	PLUPERFECT *habú-erās* 'you had held'
PRESENT TIME	PRESENT *hábē-s* 'you hold'	'you are holding'	*PERFECT *habu-istī* 'you have held'
FUTURE TIME	FUTURE *habḗ-bis* 'you will hold'	'you will be holding'	FUTURE PERFECT *habú-eris* 'you will have held'

Present tense (*simple or durative present*)

The Latin present may have durative meaning, 'I am —ing', or it may mean simply 'I —', 'I do —'. An important type of durative use of the present is with an adverb or adverbial phrase of time, when it means 'I have —ed and still am —ing', e.g. *sexāgíntā ánnōs uíuō* 'I have been living for sixty years (and still am)'. In other contexts, the present can acquire additional meanings such as 'I begin to —', 'I can —', 'I try to —'.

The Latin present tense can also be used where one would naturally expect a (simple) past tense. It makes the action more vivid. This usage is called the 'historic' present.

Imperfect tense (*durative past*)

The Latin imperfect is a durative past tense, i.e. meaning usually 'I was —ing', 'used to —', 'kept on —ing'. It may sometimes have a modal nuance and mean 'I tried to —', 'began to —'. Occasionally, it may be translated as if it were a simple past, 'I —ed', since English does not always pay as close attention to the durative aspect of the verb as does Latin.

Future tense (*simple or durative future*)

Like the present, the Latin future may be either simple ('I shall —') or durative ('I shall be —ing').

Perfect tense (*simple past or completed present*)

The Latin perfect means either 'I —ed', 'I did —' (simple past) or 'I have —ed', 'I have done with —ing' (completed present). The latter use is sometimes referred to as 'the perfect with *have*', or 'the resultative perfect'. It is seen most strikingly in the (very few) verbs with perfect forms that bear present meaning: *nṓuī* ('I have got to know', 'I have recognised' and hence) 'I know', *mémini* ('I have called to mind' and hence) 'I remember'. (This state of affairs exists because the Latin perfect is the result of the falling together of two prehistoric tenses, the old perfect (I have held) and the old simple past, or 'aorist' (I held).) The meaning of the Latin perfect has consequences for the sequence of tenses of the subjunctive ((**f**) below).

Pluperfect tense (*completed past*)

The Latin pluperfect means 'I had —ed', 'I had been —ing', 'I finished —ing'.

Future perfect tense (*completed future*)

The Latin future perfect means (literally) 'I shall have —ed'. Frequently, however, especially in *if* or *when* clauses envisaging completed future actions, it is best translated in idiomatic English with a perfect with *have* or with a present, e.g. *póstquam líbrum lḗgerō* 'after I have read the book ...', *sī uénerit* 'if he comes ...'.

(f) A central syntactic rule: sequence of tenses of the subjunctive

When the main verb of a sentence is PRESENT, FUTURE, FUTURE PERFECT or PERFECT WITH *HAVE* (i.e. meaning 'have —ed'), the sequence is said to be 'primary' (or 'present'), and subordinate subjunctives in that sentence can only be present, perfect or future participle + *sim*. When the main verb of a sentence is IMPERFECT, PERFECT (simple past, i.e. 'I —ed') or PLUPERFECT, the sequence is termed 'secondary' (or 'historic'), and subordinate subjunctives can only be imperfect, pluperfect or future participle + *éssem* (or *fórem*). (For an important exception in result clauses, see **149.**)

A1 Active forms: personal endings: s. *-ō/-m -s -t*, pl. *-mus -tis -nt*

Present indicative active: 'I —', 'I am —ing', 'I do —'
Key: A E I Ī I

	1st conjugation 'I love'	2nd conjugation 'I have'	3rd conjugation 'I say'
1st s.	ámō	hábeō	díco
2nd s.	ámās	hábēs	dícis
3rd s.	ámat	hábet	dícit
1st pl.	amā́mus	habḗmus	dícimus
2nd pl.	amā́tis	habḗtis	dícitis
3rd pl.	ámant	hábent	dícunt

	4th conjugation 'I hear'	3rd/4th conjugation 'I capture'
1st s.	aúdiō	cápiō
2nd s.	aúdīs	cápis
3rd s.	aúdit	cápit
1st pl.	audī́mus	cápimus
2nd pl.	audī́tis	cápitis
3rd pl.	aúdiunt	cápiunt

Present participle active: '–ing'

Key: -NT-

1 'loving' ámāns (amánt-)	2 'having' hábēns (habént-)	3 'saying' dī́cēns (dīcént-)

4 'hearing' aúdiēns (audiént-)	3/4 'capturing' cápiēns (capiént-)

Pattern of declension

	s. m./f.	n.	pl. m./f.	n.
nom.	ámāns	ámāns	amā́ntēs	amántia
acc.	amántem	ámāns	amántīs (amántēs)	amántia
gen.	←amántis→		←amántium (amántum)→	
dat.	←amántī→		←amántibus→	
abl.	←amánte (amántī)→		←amántibus→	

Notes

1 Form: in the nom. s., note the effect of the rule that a vowel is always long (remains long or is lengthened) before *ns*.

2 Meaning/use: note that, like any Latin adjective, the participle can be used as a noun to denote a man/woman/thing who/which carries out the action of the verb. So, e.g. *ámāns* 'lover', very close in meaning to *amā́tor*; *cūrántes* 'the ones treating (the patient)', close in meaning to *mḗdicī* 'doctors'.

Present infinitive active: 'to —'

Key: -ĀRE -ĒRE -ERE -ĪRE -ERE

1	*2*	*3*	*4*	*3/4*
'to love'	'to have'	'to say'	'to hear'	'to capture'
amā́re	habḗre	dī́cere	audī́re	cápere

Gerund: '(the act of) —ing' (a noun, NB: contrast the participle, basically an adjective)

Key: INF., or -ND-

1	*2*	*3*
'(*the act of*) loving'	'(*the act of*) having'	'(*the act of*) saying'
amā́re, amánd-um ī 2n.	habḗre, habénd-um ī 2n.	dī́cere, dīcénd-um ī 2n.

4	*3/4*
'(*the act of*) hearing'	'(*the act of*) capturing'
audī́re, audiénd-um ī 2n.	cápere, capiénd-um ī 2n.

Notes

1 The gerund is a NOUN, in contrast with the participle, which is essentially an ADJECTIVE. This distinction is especially important for speakers of English, in which gerund and present participle are identical in form (—*ing*). Can you identify the two very different meanings of each of the following English sentences, and for each meaning say whether the first word (*flying*, *visiting*) is gerund or participle? *Flying planes used to be dangerous. Visiting relatives can be a nuisance.*

2 The gerund is always based on the present stem (which is why it is included here, in **A1**).

3 The present infinitive form often functions as a noun, in the nominative or accusative, e.g. *errā́re hūmā́num est* 'to err (i.e. the act of erring) is human', *uītḗmus errā́re* 'let us avoid erring'. The gerund itself has no nominative, and its accusative is used only after prepositions, e.g. *ad beā́te uīuéndum* 'with a view to living happily' – in effect, the infinitive supplies these missing forms of the gerund.

Present imperative active: '—!'

Key: Ā Ē E/I Ī E/I

	1 'love!'	*2* 'have!'	*3* 'demand!'	*4* 'hear!'	*3/4* 'capture!'
2nd s.	ámā	hábē	pósce[1]	aúdī	cápe
2nd pl.	amā́te	habḗte	póscite	audī́te	cápite

1 We use *poscō* here because *dīcō* has an irregular s. imperative.

Note

This imperative is sometimes called the 'first' imperative, to distinguish it from the 'second', future, imperative (below, A2 note 1).

Present subjunctive active: 'I —', 'I may —', 'I would —'

Key: E A

	1	*2*	*3*	*4*	*3/4*
1st s.	ámem	hábeam	dī́cam	aúdiam	cápiam
2nd s.	ámēs	hábeās	dī́cās	aúdiās	cápiās
3rd s.	ámet	hábeat	dī́cat	aúdiat	cápiat
1st pl.	amḗmus	habeā́mus	dīcā́mus	audiā́mus	capiā́mus
2nd pl.	amḗtis	habeā́tis	dīcā́tis	audiā́tis	capiā́tis
3rd pl.	áment	hábeant	dī́cant	aúdiant	cápiant

A2 Future active: 1st s. ending *-ō* (1, 2) but *-am* (3, 4, 3/4)

Future indicative active : 'I shall/will —', 'I shall/will be —ing'

Key: ĀBI ĒBI E IE IE

	1	2	3	4	3/4
	'I shall love'	*'I shall have'*	*'I shall say'*	*'I shall hear'*	*'I shall capture'*
1st s.	amábō	habébō	dícam	aúdiam	cápiam
2nd s.	amábis	habébis	dícēs	aúdiēs	cápiēs
3rd s.	amábit	habébit	dícet	aúdiet	cápiet
1st pl.	amábimus	habébimus	dīcémus	audiémus	capiémus
2nd pl.	amábitis	habébitis	dīcétis	audiétis	capiétis
3rd pl.	amábunt	habébunt	dícent	aúdient	cápient

Future participle active: 'about to —', 'on the point of —ing', 'with a view to —ing'

Key: perf. part. stem + -ŪR-US A UM

1	2	3
'about to love'	*'about to have'*	*'about to say'*
amātúr-us a um	habitúr-us a um	dictúr-us a um

4	3/4
'about to hear'	*'about to capture'*
audītúr-us a um	captúr-us a um

Note

-úr-us a um declines like *lóngus*, **J1(a)**.

Future infinitive active: 'to be about to —'

Key: perf. part. stem + -ŪR-US A UM + ESSE

1	2	3
'to be about to love'	*'to be about to have'*	*'to be about to say'*
amātúr-us a um ésse	habitúr-us a um ésse	dictúr-us a um ésse

4	3/4
'to be about to hear'	*'to be about to capture'*
audītúr-us a um ésse	captúr-us a um ésse

NB *-úr-us a um* declines like *lóngus*, **J1(a)**.

Notes

1 An artificial (periphrastic) 'future' subjunctive active is formed of the future participle + *sim sīs sit / éssem éssēs ésset* (sometimes *fórem fórēs fóret*), according to the rule for the sequence of tenses of the subjunctive (see **A Intro.(f)** above). This periphrastic future subjunctive is used almost exclusively in indirect questions, e.g. *nésciō* (pres., therefore primary sequence) *quándo hoc confectŭrus sit / nesciébam* (impf., therefore secondary sequence) *quándo hoc confectŭrus ésset* 'I do not/did not know when he will/would finish this'.

2 The future (or 'second') imperative ('(then) —!') is formed by adding *-tō* (2nd and 3rd s.), *-tóte* (2nd pl.), *-ntō* (3rd pl.) to the present stem (e.g. 2nd or 3rd s. *amătō, habétō, póscitō, audítō, cápitō*). It expresses an order which is not to be obeyed immediately, e.g. *laédere hanc cauétō* '(then) take care (in future) not to rub her up the wrong way' (Catullus). It is therefore common after an *if* or *when* clause referring to future time, e.g. *sī ā mē díligī uīs, lítterās ad me míttitō* 'if you wish to be loved by me, (then) send me letters' (Cicero).

Note that the common verb *scíō* 'I know' makes only a future imperative, *scítō, scitóte* (there is no pres. imper. **sci, *scite*).

A3 Imperfect active: personal endings as for the present except 1st s. *-m*

Imperfect indicative active: 'I was —ing', 'I used to —', 'I began —ing'
Key: ĀBA ĒBA

	1	*2*	*3*
	'I was loving'	'I was having'	'I was saying'
1st s.	amắbam	habébam	dīcébam
2nd s.	amắbās	habébās	dīcébās
3rd s.	amắbat	habébat	dīcébat
1st pl.	amābắmus	habēbắmus	dīcēbắmus
2nd pl.	amābắtis	habēbắtis	dīcēbắtis
3rd pl.	amắbant	habébant	dīcébant

293

	4 'I was hearing'	3/4 'I was capturing'
1st s.	audiēbam	capiēbam
2nd s.	audiēbās	capiēbās
3rd s.	audiēbat	capiēbat
1st pl.	audiēbāmus	capiēbāmus
2nd pl.	audiēbātis	capiēbātis
3rd pl.	audiēbant	capiēbant

Note

The 4th conj. forms *audībam*, *audībās* etc. are sometimes found in early Latin, and occasionally in classical Latin poetry.

Imperfect subjunctive active: 'I was —ing', 'I might —', 'I would —'

Key: present infinitive active + endings.
(This key is purely accidental, but it works! Note, however, that the *e* before the ending is long, except, as usual ((c) note 2 above), in 1st and 3rd s. and 3rd pl.)

	1	2	3	4	3/4
1st s.	amārem	habērem	dīcerem	audīrem	cáperem
2nd s.	amārēs	habērēs	dīcerēs	audīrēs	cáperēs
3rd s.	amāret	habēret	dīceret	audīret	cáperet
1st pl.	amārēmus	habērēmus	dīcerēmus	audīrēmus	caperēmus
2nd pl.	amārētis	habērētis	dīcerētis	audīrētis	caperētis
3rd pl.	amārent	habērent	dīcerent	audīrent	cáperent

Note

The imperfect has *only* the indicative and the subjunctive: there is no imperfect participle, imperative or infinitive.

A4 Perfect active: personal endings: s. *-ī, -istī, -it*, pl. *-imus, -istis, -ērunt/-ēre*

Perfect indicative active: 'I —ed', 'I have —ed'

Key: perf. stem + Ī ISTĪ etc.

	1 'I loved', 'I have loved'	2 'I had', 'I have had'	3 'I said', 'I have said'
1st s.	amā́ui	hábuī	dī́xī
2nd s.	amāuístī (amā́stī)	habuístī	dīxístī (dī́xtī)
3rd s.	amā́uit	hábuit	dī́xit
1st pl.	amā́uimus	habúimus	dī́ximus
2nd pl.	amāuístis (amā́stis)	habuístis	dīxístis
3rd pl.	amāué̄runt (amāué̄re/ amā́runt)	habué̄runt (habué̄re)	dīxé̄runt (dīxé̄re)

	4 'I heard', 'I have heard'	3/4 'I captured', 'I have captured'
1st s.	audī́uī	cḗpī
2nd s.	audīuístī (audiístī/ audī́stī)	cēpístī
3rd s.	audī́uit	cḗpit
1st pl.	audī́uimus	cḗpimus
2nd pl.	audīuístis (audī́stis)	cēpístis
3rd pl.	audīuḗrunt (audīué̄re/ audié̄runt/audié̄re)	cēpé̄runt (cēpé̄re)

Notes

1   The endings are of course added to the perfect stem. Note the presence of the *-is-* (commented on above) in the 2nd person endings, s. *-is-tī* pl. *-is-tis*.

2   In the 3rd pl., in addition to regular *-ērunt* and archaic/poetic *-ēre*, there is also *-ĕrunt* (with short ĕ), rare in literary Latin (only eight times in Plautus, once in Terence) but common in the spoken language (and continued in the Romance languages, e.g. Ital. *dissero* 'they said' < L. *dīxĕ́runt*).

Perfect infinitive active: 'to have —ed'

Key: perf. stem + -ISSE

1	*2*	*3*
'to have loved'	'to have had'	'to have said'
amāuísse (amásse)	habuísse	dīxísse

4	*3/4*	
'to have heard'	'to have captured'	
audīuísse (audísse)	cēpísse	

Notes

1 On the *-is-* extension of the perfect stem, see p. 285 note 1 above. The *-se* that follows is the marker of infinitive active, originally identical with that of the present infinitive, still seen in *es-se* 'to be', though the present infinitive ending is usually *-re* (*amá-re*, *habé-re*, etc.), the s of *-se* having become *r* regularly between vowels.

2 There is no regular perfect participle active except in deponents (see **C4** below). Note, however, *cēnátus* 'having dined', *iūrátus* 'having sworn'.

3 A 'perfect imperative' (perfect in form, that is) is found only for *méminī* 'I remember' (perfect in form, present in meaning; see **F1(a)** below).

Perfect subjunctive active: 'I —ed', 'I have —ed'

Key: perf. stem + -ERIM, -ERĪS etc.

	1	*2*	*3*
1st s.	amáuerim (amárim *etc.*)	habúerim	díxerim
2nd s.	amáuerīs	habúerīs	díxerīs
3rd s.	amáuerit	habúerit	díxerit
1st pl.	amāuerímus	habuerímus	dīxerímus
2nd pl.	amāuerítis	habuerítis	dīxerítis
3rd pl.	amáuerint	habúerint	díxerint

	4	*3/4*
1st s.	audíuerim (audíerim *etc.*)	céperim
2nd s.	audíuerīs	céperīs
3rd s.	audíuerit	céperit
1st pl.	audīuerímus	cēperímus
2nd pl.	audīuerítis	cēperítis
3rd pl.	audíuerint	céperint

Note

On the -*er*- extension of the perfect stem, see p. 285 note 1 above. The long
-*ī*- that follows is an old marker of another mood called 'optative': in Latin, the
prehistoric optative and subjunctive fell together in one mood, which we call
'subjunctive'.

A5 Pluperfect active

Pluperfect indicative active: 'I had —ed'

Key: perf. stem + -ER-AM, -ER-ĀS *etc.*

	1	*2*	*3*
	'I had loved'	'I had had'	'I had said'
1st s.	amāueram (amáram *etc.*)	habúeram	díxeram
2nd s.	amáuerās	habúerās	díxerās
3rd s.	amáuerat	habúerat	díxerat
1st pl.	amāuerámus	habuerámus	dīxerámus
2nd pl.	amāuerátis	habuerátis	dīxerátis
3rd pl.	amáuerant	habúerant	díxerant

	4	*3/4*
	'I had heard'	'I had captured'
1st s.	audíueram (audíeram *etc.*)	céperam
2nd s.	audíuerās	céperās
3rd s.	audíuerat	céperat
1st pl.	audīuerámus	cēperámus
2nd pl.	audīuerátis	cēperátis
3rd pl.	audíuerant	céperant

Note

On the -*er*- extension of the perfect stem, see p. 285 note 1 above. The long -*ā*-
that follows is probably an old marker of past time (the pluperfect, remember, is
the past of the perfect system), just like the -*ā*- in the imperfect, the past of the
present system (cf. (c) and the table on p. 284 above).

Pluperfect subjunctive active: 'I had —ed', 'I would have —ed'

Key: perf. stem +-ISSEM -ISSĒS *etc.*

	1	2	3
1st s.	amāuíssem (amássem *etc.*)	habuíssem	dīxíssem
2nd s.	amāuíssēs	habuíssēs	dīxíssēs
3rd s.	amāuísset	habuísset	dīxísset
1st pl.	amāuissḗmus	habuissḗmus	dīxissḗmus
2nd pl.	amāuissḗtis	habuissḗtis	dīxissḗtis
3rd pl.	amāuíssent	habuíssent	dīxíssent

	4	3/4
1st s.	audīuíssem (audíssem *etc.*)	cēpíssem
2nd s.	audīuíssēs	cēpíssēs
3rd s.	audīuísset	cēpísset
1st pl.	audīuissḗmus	cēpissḗmus
2nd pl.	audīuissḗtis	cēpissḗtis
3rd pl.	audīuíssent	cēpíssent

Notes

1 On the *-is-* extension of the perfect stem, see p. 285 note 1 above. The *-sē-* that follows is the marker of past subjunctive, originally identical with that of the imperfect subjunctive, still seen in *és-sē-s* from *es-se* 'to be', though the imperfect subjunctive suffix is usually *-rē-* (*amā́-rē-s, habḗ-rē-s,* etc.), the *s* of *-sē-* having become *r* regularly between vowels.

2 Like the imperfect, the pluperfect has *only* the indicative and the subjunctive: there is no pluperfect participle, imperative or infinitive.

A6 Future perfect active

Future perfect indicative active: 'I shall have —ed'

Key: perf. stem +-ERŌ, -ERIS etc.

	1	2	3
	'I shall have loved'	*'I shall have had'*	*'I shall have said'*
1st s.	amā́uerō (amā́rō *etc.*)	habúerō	dī́xerō
2nd s.	amā́ueris	habúeris	dī́xeris
3rd s.	amā́uerit	habúerit	dī́xerit
1st pl.	amāuérimus	habuérimus	dīxérimus
2nd pl.	amāuéritis	habuéritis	dīxéritis
3rd pl.	amā́uerint	habúerint	dī́xerint

	4	3/4
	'I shall have heard'	'I shall have captured'
1st s.	audíuerō (audíerō etc.)	cḗperō
2nd s.	audíueris	cḗperis
3rd s.	audíuerit	cḗperit
1st pl.	audīuérimus	cēpérimus
2nd pl.	audīuéritis	cēpéritis
3rd pl.	audíuerint	cḗperint

Notes

1 On the *-er-* extension of the perfect stem, see p. 285 note 1 above. The short *-i-* that follows in this future of the perfect system is an old subjunctive marker (originally *-e-*), in origin identical with the *-i-* of the future of the present system in *-b-is*, *-b-it*, *-b-imus*, *-b-itis* (**A2** above).

2 There is no future perfect participle, imperative, infinitive or subjunctive.

A7 Supine

Key: perf. part. stem + -UM

1	2	3	4	3/4
'to love'	'to have'	'to say'	'to hear'	'to capture'
amātum	hábitum	díctum	audītum	cáptum

Notes

1 The stem is identical with that of the perfect participle. The form is identical with acc. s. of 4th decl. nouns – indeed, the supine (like the infinitive) is in origin a case-form of an action noun ('loving', 'having', 'saying', etc.). Note that some deponents also make a supine, e.g. *quéstum* 'to complain' from *quéror*, *quérī*.

2 The supine in *-um* always has active meaning. It is found above all after verbs of motion or implied motion (sending, etc.) to express the purpose of the person(s) moving or moved. So, e.g. *lēgātī ab Rōmā uēnḗrunt quéstum iniúriās* 'envoys came from around Rome to complain about the treatment they had suffered' (Livy); *lēgắtōs ad Caésarem míttunt rogắtum auxílium* 'they send envoys to Caesar *to ask for* help' (Caesar).

3 The supine in *-um* is regularly used to form the 'future infinitive passive' (**B2** below).

4   There is also the 'second' supine in -*u*, originally the ablative or dative of the same action-noun. This supine occurs especially with evaluative adjectives meaning 'good', 'pleasant', 'easy', 'useful' and their opposites, e.g. *óptimum fáctū* 'the best thing *to do*', *mīrắbile díctū* 'wonderful *to tell*', *intelléctū difficilis* 'difficult *to understand*', *lépida memorắtuī* (NB with a clear dative ending) 'things pleasant *to relate*' (Plautus).

B Passive

B1 Present passive: personal endings: s. *-r, -rís* (or *-re*), *-tur*, pl. *-mur, -minī, -ntur*

Present indicative passive: 'I am (being) —ed'

Key: A E I Ī I

	1 '*I am (being) loved*'	2 '*I am (being) held*'	3 '*I am (being) said*'
1st s.	ámor	hábeor	dícor
2nd s.	amáris (amáre)	habéris (habére)	díceris (dícere)
3rd s.	amátur	habétur	dícitur
1st pl.	amámur	habémur	dícimur
2nd pl.	amáminī	habéminī	dícíminī
3rd pl.	amántur	habéntur	dīcúntur

	4 '*I am (being) heard*'	3/4 '*I am (being) captured*'
1st s.	aúdior	cápior
2nd s.	audíris (audíre)	cáperis (cápere)
3rd s.	audítur	cápitur
1st pl.	audímur	cápimur
2nd pl.	audíminī	capíminī
3rd pl.	audiúntur	capiúntur

Present infinitive passive: 'to be —ed'

Key: -ĀRĪ -ĒRĪ -Ī -ĪRĪ -Ī

1 '*to be loved*'	2 '*to be held*'	3 '*to be said*'	4 '*to be heard*'	3/4 '*to be captured*'
amárī	habérī	dícī	audírī	cápī

Present imperative passive: 'be —ed!'

Key: -RE -MINĪ

	1	*2*	*3*	*4*	*3/4*
	'be loved!'	*'be held!'*	*'be said!'*	*'be heard!'*	*'be captured!'*
2nd s.	amā́re	habḗre	dī́cere	audī́re	cápere
2nd pl.	amā́minī	habḗminī	dīcíminī	audī́minī	capíminī

Gerundive: 'to be —ed', 'requiring, needing to be —ed', 'must be —ed'

Key: -ND-

1	*2*	*3*
'to be loved'	*'to be held'*	*'to be said'*
amánd-us a um	habénd-us a um	dīcénd-us a um
4	*3/4*	
'to be heard'	*'to be captured'*	
audiénd-us a um	capiénd-us a um	

Notes

Pattern of declension

See *lóng-us a um* (**J1(a)**).

1 Like the gerund, the gerundive is based always on the present stem (and so is presented here with the present passive).

2 A few verbs retain the old form of the gerundive in -*únd*-, e.g. *eúndum*, *oriúndum*, *gerúndus*.

3 The gerundive is an ADJECTIVE, in which the meaning of the verb is in the PASSIVE. (Contrast the gerund **A1** above), a NOUN with the meaning of the verb in the ACTIVE.) The gerundive's basic meaning is simply 'being —ed', 'who/which is (to be) —ed'. When it is used PREDICATIVELY, however (i.e. in the NOMINATIVE or, in indirect speech, the accusative), it usually has an additional modal nuance of obligation, 'requiring to be —ed', 'who/which must be —ed'. Compare *árcis piándae caúsā* 'for the sake of the citadel being purified' (neutral passive) with *arx est piánda* 'the citadel is (requiring) to be purified' (with a clear sense of obligation).

Present subjunctive passive: 'I may be –ed', 'I would be –ed', '(that) I am –ed'

Key: Ē EĀ Ā IĀ IĀ (1st conj. Ē, everywhere else Ā)

	1	2	3
1st s.	ámer	hábear	dícar
2nd s.	améris (amére)	habeáris (habeáre)	dīcáris (dīcáre)
3rd s.	amétur	habeátur	dīcátur
1st pl.	amémur	habeámur	dīcámur
2nd pl.	amémīnī	habeámīnī	dīcámīnī
3rd pl.	améntur	habeántur	dīcántur

	4	3/4
1st s.	aúdiar	cápiar
2nd s.	audiáris (audiáre)	capiáris (capiáre)
3rd s.	audiátur	capiátur
1st pl.	audiámur	capiámur
2nd pl.	audiámīnī	capiámīnī
3rd pl.	audiántur	capiántur

B2 Future passive

Future indicative passive : 'I shall be –ed'

Key: ĀBI ĒBI E IE IE

	1	2	3
	'I shall be loved'	*'I shall be held'*	*'I shall be said'*
1st s.	amábor	habébor	dícar
2nd s.	amáberis (amábere)	habéberis (habébere)	dīcéris (dīcére)
3rd s.	amábitur	habébitur	dīcétur
1st pl.	amábimur	habébimur	dīcémur
2nd pl.	amābímīnī	habēbímīnī	dīcémīnī
3rd pl.	amābúntur	habēbúntur	dīcéntur

	4 '*I shall be heard*'	*3/4* '*I shall be captured*'
1st s.	aúdiar	cápiar
2nd s.	audiḗris (audiḗre)	capiḗris (capiḗre)
3rd s.	audiḗtur	capiḗtur
1st pl.	audiḗmur	capiḗmur
2nd pl.	audiḗminī	capiḗminī
3rd pl.	audiéntur	capiéntur

Form traditionally described as 'future infinitive passive'

Key: perf. part. stem + -UM -ĪRĪ

1 '*that there is a* *movement to love*' amắtum[1] ī́rī	*2* '*that there is a* *movement to have*' hábitum[1] ī́rī	*3* '*that there is a* *movement to say*' díctum[1] ī́rī
4 '*that there is a* *movement to hear*' audī́tum ī́rī	*3/4* '*that there is a* *movement to capture*' cáptum ī́rī	

Notes

1 The so-called 'future infinitive passive' is used only in indirect statement (acc. + inf.): hence the use of 'that' in the translations in the table above.

2 This fixed, unchanging periphrastic form comprises the supine in -*um* (**A7** above) + the present passive infinitive of *éō, ī́re* 'to go': hence the cumbersome literal translation in the table above. The simpler literal translation of e.g. *asseuḗrat/asseuērắuit úrbem cáptum ī́rī* 'She declares/declared the city to be about to be captured' comes out in natural English of course as 'She declares/declared that the city will/would be captured.'

3 The future (or 'second') imperative passive s. is formed as for the active (**A2** note 2 above), but with -*r* added at the end, e.g. 2nd/3rd s. *amắtor* 'be loved / let her be loved', 3rd pl. *amántor* 'let them be loved'. There is, however, no 2nd pl. form.

4 There is no future passive participle, or future passive subjunctive.

B3 Imperfect passive

Imperfect indicative passive: 'I was (being) —ed'

Key: ĀBA ĒBA

	1	*2*	*3*
	'*I was (being) loved*'	'*I was (being) held*'	'*I was (being) said*'
1st s.	amā́bar	habḗbar	dīcḗbar
2nd s.	amābā́ris (amābā́re)	habēbā́ris (habēbā́re)	dīcēbā́ris (dīcēbā́re)
3rd s.	amābā́tur	habēbā́tur	dīcēbā́tur
1st pl.	amābā́mur	habēbā́mur	dīcēbā́mur
2nd pl.	amābā́minī	habēbā́minī	dīcēbā́minī
3rd pl.	amābántur	habēbántur	dīcēbántur

	4	*3/4*
	'*I was (being) heard*'	'*I was (being) captured*'
1st s.	audiḗbar	capiḗbar
2nd s.	audiēbā́ris (audiēbā́re)	capiēbā́ris (capiēbā́re)
3rd s.	audiēbā́tur	capiēbā́tur
1st pl.	audiēbā́mur	capiēbā́mur
2nd pl.	audiēbā́minī	capiēbā́minī
3rd pl.	audiēbántur	capiēbántur

Note

There are no imperfect passive participles, imperatives or infinitives.

Imperfect subjunctive passive: 'I was being —ed', 'I might be —ed', 'I would be —ed'

Key: active infinitive + endings

	1	*2*	*3*
1st s.	amā́rer	habḗrer	dī́cerer
2nd s.	amārḗris (amārḗre)	habērḗris (habērḗre)	dīcerḗris (dīcerḗre)
3rd s.	amārḗtur	habērḗtur	dīcerḗtur
1st pl.	amārḗmur	habērḗmur	dīcerḗmur
2nd pl.	amārḗminī	habērḗminī	dīcerḗminī
3rd pl.	amāréntur	habēréntur	dīceréntur

	4	3/4
1st s.	audī́rer	cáperer
2nd s.	audīréris (audīrére)	caperéris (caperére)
3rd s.	audīrḗtur	caperéntur
1st pl.	audīrḗmur	caperḗmur
2nd pl.	audīrḗminī	caperḗminī
3rd pl.	audīréntur	caperḗtur

B4 Perfect passive

Perfect indicative passive: 'I was —ed', 'I have been —ed'

Key: perfect participle + SUM

	1 '*I was loved*', '*I have been loved*'	2 '*I was held*', '*I have been held*'	3 '*I was said*', '*I have been said*'
1st s.	amā́tus a um sum	hábitus a um sum	díctus a um sum
2nd s.	amā́tus a um es	hábitus a um es	díctus a um es
3rd s.	amā́tus a um est	hábitus a um est	díctus a um est
1st pl.	amā́tī ae a súmus	hábitī ae a súmus	díctī ae a súmus
2nd pl.	amā́tī ae a éstis	hábitī ae a éstis	díctī ae a éstis
3rd pl.	amā́tī ae a sunt	hábitī ae a sunt	díctī ae a sunt

	4 '*I was heard*', '*I have been heard*'	3/4 '*I was captured*', '*I have been captured*'
1st s.	audī́tus a um sum	cáptus a um sum
2nd s.	audī́tus a um es	cáptus a um es
3rd s.	audī́tus a um est	cáptus a um est
1st pl.	audī́tī ac a súmus	cáptī ae a súmus
2nd pl.	audī́tī ae a éstis	cáptī ae a éstis
3rd pl.	audī́tī ae a sunt	cáptī ae a sunt

Note

The participle here is always in the nom., s. or pl., m., f. or n., in agreement with the subject. This point applies equally to all the passive forms of the perfect system (and of course to the perfect system of the deponents).

Perfect participle passive: 'having been —ed'

Key: perf. part. ending in -US -A -UM

1	2	3
'having been loved'	'having been held'	'having been said'
amãt-us a um	hábit-us a um	díct-us a um

4	3/4	
'having been heard'	'having been captured'	
audĩt-us a um	cápt-us a um	

Notes

1 The perfect participle is one of the forms built on the stem of the fourth
   principal part (the 'third' stem). It ends in *-us a um*, and declines like *longus*
   (**J1(a)**).

2 The perfect participle is the basis of all the forms of the passive of the perfect
   system as a whole, i.e. the pluperfect and future perfect, as well as the perfect.

Perfect infinitive passive: 'to have been —ed'

Key: perf. part. ending in -US -A -UM + ESSE

1	2	3
'to have been loved'	'to have been held'	'to have been said'
amãt-us a um ésse	hábit-us a um ésse	díct-us a um ésse

4	3/4	
'to have been heard'	'to have been captured'	
audĩt-us a um ésse	cápt-us a um ésse	

Note

The perfect participle here may be either nom. or acc., depending on the
construction of the inf.

Perfect subjunctive passive: 'I was —ed', 'I have been —ed'

Key: perf. part. + SIM

	1	2	3
1st s.	amā́tus a um sim	hábitus a um sim	díctus a um sim
2nd s.	amā́tus a um sīs	hábitus a um sīs	díctus a um sīs
3rd s.	amā́tus a um sit	hábitus a um sit	díctus a um sit
1st pl.	amā́tī ae a sī́mus	hábitī ae a sī́mus	díctī ae a sī́mus
2nd pl.	amā́tī ae a sī́tis	hábitī ae a sī́tis	díctī ae a sī́tis
3rd pl.	amā́tī ae a sint	hábitī ae a sint	díctī ae a sint

	4	3/4
1st s.	audī́tus a um sim	cáptus a um sim
2nd s.	audī́tus a um sīs	cáptus a um sīs
3rd s.	audī́tus a um sit	cáptus a um sit
1st pl.	audī́tī ae a sī́mus	cáptī ae a sī́mus
2nd pl.	audī́tī ae a sī́tis	cáptī ae a sī́tis
3rd pl.	audī́tī ae a sint	cáptī ae a sint

B5 Pluperfect passive

Pluperfect indicative passive: 'I had been —ed'

Key: perf. part. + ERAM

	1 *'I had been loved'*	2 *'I had been held'*	3 *'I had been said'*
1st s.	amā́tus a um éram	hábitus a um éram	díctus a um éram
2nd s.	amā́tus a um érās	hábitus a um érās	díctus a um érās
3rd s.	amā́tus a um érat	hábitus a um érat	díctus a um érat
1st pl.	amā́tī ae a erā́mus	hábitī ae a erā́mus	díctī ae a erā́mus
2nd pl.	amā́tī ae a erā́tis	hábitī ae a erā́tis	díctī ae a erā́tis
3rd pl.	amā́tī ae a érant	hábitī ae a érant	díctī ae a érant

	4	*3/4*
	'I had been heard'	'I had been captured'
1st s.	audītus a um éram	cáptus a um éram
2nd s.	audītus a um érās	cáptus a um érās
3rd s.	audītus a um érat	cáptus a um érat
1st pl.	audītī ae a erámus	cáptī ae a erámus
2nd pl.	audītī ae a erátis	cáptī ae a erátis
3rd pl.	audītī ae a érant	cáptī ae a érant

Pluperfect subjunctive passive: 'I had been —ed', 'I would have been —ed'

Key: perf. part. + ESSEM

	1	*2*	*3*
1st s.	amátus a um éssem	hábitus a um éssem	díctus a um éssem
2nd s.	amátus a um éssēs	hábitus a um éssēs	díctus a um éssēs
3rd s.	amátus a um ésset	hábitus a um ésset	díctus a um ésset
1st pl.	amátī ae a essémus	hábitī ae a essémus	díctī ae a essémus
2nd pl.	amátī ae a essétis	hábitī ae a essétis	díctī ae a essétis
3rd pl.	amátī ae a éssent	hábitī ae a éssent	díctī ae a éssent

	4	*3/4*
1st s.	audītus a um éssem	cáptus a um éssem
2nd s.	audītus a um éssēs	cáptus a um éssēs
3rd s.	audītus a um ésset	cáptus a um ésset
1st pl.	audītī ae a essémus	cáptī ae a essémus
2nd pl.	audītī ae a essétis	cáptī ae a essétis
3rd pl.	audītī ae a éssent	cáptī ae a éssent

B6 Future perfect passive

Future perfect indicative passive: 'I shall have been —ed'

Key: perf. part. + ERŌ

	1 '*I shall have been loved*'	*2* '*I shall have been held*'	*3* '*I shall have been said*'
1st s.	amátus a um érō	hábitus a um érō	díctus a um érō
2nd s.	amátus a um éris	hábitus a um éris	díctus a um éris
3rd s.	amátus a um érit	hábitus a um érit	díctus a um érit
1st pl.	amátī ae a érimus	hábitī ae a érimus	díctī ae a érimus
2nd pl.	amátī ae a éritis	hábitī ae a éritis	díctī ae a éritis
3rd pl.	amátī ae a érunt	hábitī ae a érunt	díctī ae a érunt

	4 '*I shall have been heard*'	*3/4* '*I shall have been captured*'
1st s.	audítus a um érō	cáptus a um érō
2nd s.	audítus a um éris	cáptus a um éris
3rd s.	audítus a um érit	cáptus a um érit
1st pl.	audítī ae a érimus	cáptī ae a érimus
2nd pl.	audítī ae a éritis	cáptī ae a éritis
3rd pl.	audítī ae a érunt	cáptī ae a érunt

C Deponent forms: personal endings: s. *-r -ris* (or *-re*) *-tur*, pl. *-mur -minī -ntur*

Deponent verbs generally show *passive* forms (i.e. exactly the same forms as the passive of regular *-ō*, *-s*, *-t* verbs) but with *active* meaning. Note, however, that they make a present active participle in *-ns* (*-nt-*), a future active participle in *-ūrus a um*, and an active gerund (in *-ndum*), and that, if they make a gerundive (in *-ndus*), it remains *passive* in meaning.

C1 Present deponent

Present indicative deponent: 'I —', 'I am —ing', 'I do —'

Key: as for passive, but active in meaning

	1 'I threaten'	2 'I promise'	3 'I speak'
1st s.	mínor	pollíceor	lóquor
2nd s.	mináris (mináre)	pollicéris (pollicére)	lóqueris (lóquere)
3rd s.	minátur	pollicétur	lóquitur
1st pl.	minámur	pollicémur	lóquimur
2nd pl.	minámini	pollicémini	loquímini
3rd pl.	minántur	pollicéntur	loquúntur

	4 'I lie'	3/4 'I advance'
1st s.	méntior	prōgrédior
2nd s.	mentíris (mentíre)	prōgréderis (prōgrédere)
3rd s.	mentítur	prōgréditur
1st pl.	mentímur	prōgrédimur
2nd pl.	mentímini	prōgredímini
3rd pl.	mentiúntur	prōgrediúntur

Present participle deponent: '—ing'

Key: as for active (exactly like **A1** above; and active in meaning)

1 'threatening' mínāns (minánt-)	2 'promising' póllicēns (pollicént-)	3 'speaking' lóquēns (loquént-)

4	3/4
'lying'	*'advancing'*
méntiēns (mentiént-)	prōgrédiēns (prōgrediént-)

Note

The present participle deponent is *active* in form as well as active in meaning.

Present infinitive deponent: 'to —'

Key: as for passive (but active in meaning)

1	2	3	4	3/4
'to threaten'	*'to promise'*	*'to speak'*	*'to lie'*	*'to advance'*
minā́rī	pollicḗrī	lóquī	mentī́rī	prógredī

Present imperative deponent: '—!'

Key: as for passive (but active in meaning)

	1	2	3	4	3/4
	'threaten!'	*'promise!'*	*'speak!'*	*'lie!'*	*'advance!'*
2nd s.	minā́re	pollicḗre	lóquere	mentī́re	prōgrédere
2nd pl.	minā́minī	pollicḗminī	loquíminī	mentī́minī	prōgredíminī

Gerundive: 'to be —ed', 'requiring, needing to be —ed', 'must be —ed' (see 151 footnote)

Key: as for passive (and remaining *passive* in meaning)

1	2	3
'to be encouraged'	*'to be promised'*	*'to be spoken'*
hortánd-us a um	pollicénd-us a um	loquénd-us a um

4	3/4
'to be lied'	*'to be advanced'*
mentiénd-us a um	aggrediénd-us a um

Notes

1 For declension, see *lóng-us* (**J1(a)**).

2 *órior* 'rise' retains the old gerundive form *oriúndum*.

Gerund: '(the act of) —ing'

Key: as above (and remaining active in meaning)

1	*2*	*3*
'(*the act of*) *threatening*'	'(*the act of*) *promising*'	'(*the act of*) *speaking*'
minā́rī, minánd-um ī 2n.	pollicḗrī, pollicénd-um ī 2n.	lóquī, loquénd-um ī 2n.
4	*3/4*	
'(*the act of*) *lying*'	'(*the act of*) *advancing*'	
mentī́rī, mentiénd-um ī 2n.	prṓgredī, prōgrediénd-um ī 2n.	

Present subjunctive deponent: 'I —', 'I may —', 'I would —'

Key: INF, or -ND-, as for passive (but active in meaning)

	1	*2*	*3*
1st s.	míner	pollícear	lóquar
2nd s.	minḗris (minḗre)	polliceā́ris (polliceā́re)	loquā́ris (loquā́re)
3rd s.	minḗtur	polliceā́tur	loquā́tur
1st pl.	minḗmur	polliceā́mur	loquā́mur
2nd pl.	minḗminī	polliceā́minī	loquā́minī
3rd pl.	minéntur	polliceántur	loquántur

	4	*3/4*
1st s.	méntiar	prṓgrédiar
2nd s.	mentiā́ris (mentiā́re)	prōgrediā́ris (prōgrediā́re)
3rd s.	mentiā́tur	prōgrediā́tur
1st pl.	mentiā́mur	prōgrediā́mur
2nd pl.	mentiā́minī	prōgrediā́minī
3rd pl.	mentiántur	prōgrediántur

C2 Future deponent

Future indicative deponent: 'I shall —', 'I shall be —ing'

Key: as for passive (but active in meaning)

	1 *'I shall threaten'*	2 *'I shall promise'*	3 *'I shall speak'*
1st s.	minábor	pollicébor	lóquar
2nd s.	mináberis (minábere)	pollicéberis (pollicébere)	loquéris (loquére)
3rd s.	minábitur	pollicébitur	loquétur
1st pl.	minábimur	pollicébimur	loquémur
2nd pl.	minābíminī	pollicēbíminī	loquémini
3rd pl.	minābúntur	pollicēbúntur	loquéntur

	4 *'I shall lie'*	3/4 *'I shall advance'*
1st s.	méntiar (*rarely* mentíbor)	prōgrédiar
2nd s.	mentiéris (mentiére)	prōgrediéris (progrediére)
3rd s.	mentiétur	prōgrediétur
1st pl.	mentiémur	prōgrediémur
2nd pl.	mentiémini	prōgrediémini
3rd pl.	mentiéntur	prōgrediéntur

Future participle deponent: 'about to —', 'on the point of —ing', 'with a view to —ing'

Key: as for active verbs (perf. part. stem + *-ūr-us -a -um*) and active in meaning

	1 *'about to threaten'*	2 *'about to promise'*	3 *'about to speak'*
	minātúr-us a um	pollicitúr-us a um	locūtúr-us a um

	4 *'about to lie'*	3/4 *'about to advance'*
	mentītúr-us a um	prōgressúr-us a um

Note

The future participle deponent is *active* in form as well as active in meaning.

Future infinitive deponent 'to be about to'

Key: as for active (perf. part. stem + *-ūr-us -a -um* + *ésse*) and active in meaning

1	*2*	*3*
'to be about to threaten' minātū́r-us a um ésse	*'to be about to promise'* pollicitū́r-us a um ésse	*'to be about to speak'* locūtū́r-us a um ésse

4	*3/4*	
'to be about to lie' mentītū́r-us a um ésse	*'to be about to advance'* prōgressū́r-us a um ésse	

Notes

1 The future infinitive deponent is *active* in form as well as active in meaning. Deponent verbs do not make a future passive infinitive (cf. **B2** with notes 1 and 2 above), but they do make a supine in *-um* with active meaning (cf. **A7** above).

2 For the 'future' subjunctive (exactly as in active verbs), see **A2** note 1.

3 The future (or 'second') imperative of deponent verbs is passive in form but active in meaning, e.g. *ū́titor* 'then use' (see **A2** note 2 and **B2** note 3 above).

C3 Imperfect deponent

Imperfect indicative deponent: 'I was −ing', 'I used to −', 'I began −ing'

Key: as for passive (but active in meaning)

	1	*2*	*3*
	'I was threatening'	*'I was promising'*	*'I was speaking'*
1st s.	minā́bar	pollicḗbar	loquḗbar
2nd s.	minābā́ris (minābā́re)	pollicēbā́ris (pollicēbā́re)	loquēbā́ris (loquēbā́re)
3rd s.	minābā́tur	pollicēbā́tur	loquēbā́tur
1st pl.	minābā́mur	pollicēbā́mur	loquēbā́mur
2nd pl.	minābā́minī	pollicēbā́minī	loquēbā́minī
3rd pl.	minābā́ntur	pollicēbā́ntur	loquēbā́tur

	4 'I was lying'	*3/4* 'I was advancing'
1st s.	mentiḗbar	prōgrediḗbar
2nd s.	mentiēbā́ris (mentiēbā́re)	prōgrediēbā́ris (prōgrediēbā́re)
3rd s.	mentiēbā́tur	prōgrediēbā́tur
1st pl.	mentiēbā́mur	prōgrediēbā́mur
2nd pl.	mentiēbā́minī	prōgrediēbā́minī
3rd pl.	mentiēbā́ntur	prōgrediēbā́ntur

Note

No participles, infinitives or imperatives.

Imperfect subjunctive deponent: 'I was —ing', 'I might —', 'I would —'

Key: as for passive (but active in meaning)

	1	*2*	*3*
1st s.	minā́rer	pollicḗrer	lóquerer
2nd s.	minārḗris (minārḗre)	pollicērḗris (pollicērḗre)	loquerḗris (loquerḗre)
3rd s.	minārḗtur	pollicērḗtur	loquerḗtur
1st pl.	minārḗmur	pollicērḗmur	loquerḗmur
2nd pl.	minārḗminī	pollicērḗminī	loquerḗminī
3rd pl.	minārḗntur	pollicērḗntur	loquerḗntur

	4	*3/4*
1st s.	mentī́rer	prōgréderer
2nd s.	mentīrḗris (mentīrḗre)	prōgrederḗris (prōgrederḗre)
3rd s.	mentīrḗtur	prōgrederḗtur
1st pl.	mentīrḗmur	prōgrederḗmur
2nd pl.	mentīrḗminī	prōgrederḗminī
3rd pl.	mentīrḗntur	prōgrederḗntur

Note

The imperfect has *only* the indicative and the subjunctive: there is no imperfect participle, imperative or infinitive.

C4 Perfect deponent

See the notes under **B4** above.

Perfect indicative deponent: 'I —ed', 'I have —ed'

Key: as for passive (but active in meaning)

	1 '*I threatened*', '*I have threatened*'	*2* '*I promised*', '*I have promised*'	*3* '*I spoke*', *I have spoken*'
1st s.	minātus a um sum	pollícitus a um sum	locútus a um sum
2nd s.	minātus a um es	pollícitus a um es	locútus a um es
3rd s.	minātus a um est	pollícitus a um est	locútus a um est
1st pl.	minātī ae a súmus	pollícitī ae a súmus	locútī ae a súmus
2nd pl.	minātī ae a éstis	pollícitī ae a éstis	locútī ae a éstis
3rd pl.	minātī ae a sunt	pollícitī ae a sunt	locútī ae a sunt

	4 '*I lied*', '*I have lied*'	*3/4* '*I advanced*', '*I have advanced*'
1st s.	mentít-us a um sum	prōgréss-us a um sum
2nd s.	mentít-us a um es	prōgréss-us a um es
3rd s.	mentít-us a um est	prōgréss-us a um est
1st pl.	mentít-ī ae a súmus	prōgréss-ī ae a súmus
2nd pl.	mentít-ī ae a éstis	prōgréss-ī ae a éstis
3rd pl.	mentít-ī ae a sunt	prōgréss-ī ae a sunt

Perfect participle deponent: 'having —ed'

Key: as for passive (but usually (see note 2 below) active in meaning)

1 '*having threatened*' minát-us a um	*2* '*having promised*' pollícit-us a um	*3* '*having spoken*' locút-us a um

4 '*having lied*' mentít-us a um	*3/4* '*having advanced*' prōgréss-us a um

Notes

1 The perfect participle of many deponents is used to mean '—ing' (i.e. as a present participle): e.g. *rátus* 'thinking', *uéritus* 'fearing', *arbitrātus* 'thinking' etc.

2 Many deponents have a *passive* as well as an active meaning in the perfect participle: e.g. *pollícitus* 'having promised' or 'having *been* promised'.

Perfect infinitive deponent: 'to have —ed'

Key: as for passive (but active in meaning)

1	2	3
'to have threatened'	'to have promised'	'to have spoken'
minắt-us a um ésse	pollícit-us a um ésse	locūt-us a um ésse

4	3/4
'to have lied'	'to have advanced'
mentīt-us a um ésse	prōgréss-us a um ésse

Note

There are no deponents with a perfect imperative.

Perfect subjunctive deponent: 'I —ed', 'I have —ed'

Key: as for passive (but active in meaning)

	1	2	3
1st s.	minắtus a um sim	pollícitus a um sim	locūtus a um sim
2nd s.	minắtus a um sīs	pollícitus a um sīs	locūtus a um sīs
3rd s.	minắtus a um sit	pollícitus a um sit	locūtus a um sit
1st pl.	minắtī ae a sīmus	pollícitī ae a sīmus	locūtī ae a sīmus
2nd pl.	minắtī ae a sītis	pollícitī ae a sītis	locūtī ae a sītis
3rd pl.	minắtī ae a sint	pollícitī ae a sint	locūtī ae a sint

	4	3/4
1st s.	mentītus a um sim	prōgréssus a um sim
2nd s.	mentītus a um sīs	prōgréssus a um sīs
3rd s.	mentītus a um sit	prōgréssus a um sit
1st pl.	mentītī ae a sīmus	prōgréssī ae a sīmus
2nd pl.	mentītī ae a sītis	prōgréssī ae a sītis
3rd pl.	mentītī ae a sint	prōgréssī ae a sint

C5 Pluperfect deponent

Pluperfect indicative deponent: 'I had –ed'

Key: as for passive (but active in meaning)

	'I had threatened' *1*	'I had promised' *2*	'I had spoken' *3*
1st s.	minátus a um éram	pollícitus a um éram	locútus a um éram
2nd s.	minátus a um érās	pollícitus a um érās	locútus a um érās
3rd s.	minátus a um érat	pollícitus a um érat	locútus a um érat
1st pl.	mináti ae a erámus	pollíciti ae a erámus	locúti ae a erámus
2nd pl.	mináti ae a erátis	pollíciti ae a erátis	locúti ae a erátis
3rd pl.	mináti ae a érant	pollíciti ae a érant	locúti ae a érant

	4 'I had lied'	*3/4* 'I had advanced'
1st s.	mentítus a um éram	prōgréssus a um éram
2nd s.	mentítus a um érās	prōgréssus a um érās
3rd s.	mentítus a um érat	prōgréssus a um érat
1st pl.	mentíti ae a erámus	prōgréssi ae a erámus
2nd pl.	mentíti ae a erátis	prōgréssi ae a erátis
3rd pl.	mentíti ae a érant	prōgréssi ae a érant

Note

Like the imperfect, the pluperfect has *only* the indicative and the subjunctive: there is no pluperfect participle, imperative or infinitive.

Pluperfect subjunctive deponent: 'I had –ed', 'I would have –ed'

Key: as for passive (but active in meaning)

	1	*2*	*3*
1st s.	minátus a um éssem	pollícitus a um éssem	locútus a um éssem
2nd s.	minátus a um éssēs	pollícitus a um éssēs	locútus a um éssēs
3rd s.	minátus a um ésset	pollícitus a um ésset	locútus a um ésset
1st pl.	mináti ae a essémus	pollíciti ae a essémus	locúti ae a essémus
2nd pl.	mináti ae a essétis	pollíciti ae a essétis	locúti ae a essétis
3rd pl.	mináti ae a éssent	pollíciti ae a éssent	locúti ae a éssent

	4	3/4
1st s.	mentítus a um éssem	prōgréssus a um éssem
2nd s.	mentítus a um éssēs	prōgréssus a um éssēs
3rd s.	mentítus a um ésset	prōgréssus a um ésset
1st pl.	mentítī ae a essḗmus	prōgréssī ae a essḗmus
2nd pl.	mentítī ae a essḗtis	prōgréssī ae a essḗtis
3rd pl.	mentítī ae a éssent	prōgréssī ae a éssent

C6 Future perfect deponent

Future perfect indicative deponent: 'I shall have –ed'

Key: as for passive (but active in meaning)

	1	2	3
	'I shall have threatened'	*'I shall have promised'*	*'I shall have spoken'*
1st s.	minấtus a um érō	pollícitus a um érō	locútus a um érō
2nd s.	minấtus a um éris	pollícitus a um éris	locútus a um éris
3rd s.	minấtus a um érit	pollícitus a um érit	locútus a um érit
1st pl.	minấtī ae a érimus	pollícitī ae a érimus	locútī ae a érimus
2nd pl.	minấtī ae a éritis	pollícitī ae a éritis	locútī ae a éritis
3rd pl.	minấtī ae a érunt	pollícitī ae a érunt	locútī ae a érunt

	4	3/4
	'I shall have lied'	*'I shall have advanced'*
1st s.	mentítus a um érō	prōgréssus a um érō
2nd s.	mentítus a um éris	prōgréssus a um éris
3rd s.	mentítus a um érit	prōgréssus a um érit
1st pl.	mentítī ae a érimus	prōgréssī ae a érimus
2nd pl.	mentítī ae a éritis	prōgréssī ae a éritis
3rd pl.	mentítī ae a érunt	prōgréssī ae a érunt

Note

There is no future perfect participle, infinitive, imperative or subjunctive.

D Semi-deponents

Some verbs in Latin have present, future and imperfect tenses (i.e. their present system) in ACTIVE forms, but perfect, pluperfect and future perfect tenses (i.e. their perfect system) in DEPONENT forms. Meaning is NOT affected by this alternation of form. E.g.

aúdeō 2 aús-us	'I dare'
aúdeō	'I dare'
audébō	'I shall dare'
audébam	'I was daring'
aúsus sum	'I have dared'
aúsus éram	'I had dared'
aúsus éro	'I shall have dared'
fío fierī fáctus	'I become', 'I am made', 'I am done'
fíō	'I become'
fíam	'I shall become'
fíēbam	'I was becoming'
fáctus sum	'I became'
fáctus éram	'I had become'
fáctus érō	'I shall have become'

Note the irregular conjugation of *fīō*:

1st s.	fíō
2nd s.	fīs
3rd s.	fit
1st pl.	—[1]
2nd pl.	—[1]
3rd pl.	fíunt

1 *fímus* and *fítis* are not found.

Notes

1 Semi-deponents have past participles with *active* meaning, just like full deponents, e.g. *aúsus* 'having dared', *fáctus* 'having been made', 'having become'.

2 Similar verbs are *gaúdeō 2 gāuísus* 'I rejoice', *sóleō 2 sólitus* 'I am accustomed'; *fídō 3 físus* 'I trust'.

3 *aúdeō* has a regular subjunctive *aúdeam -ās* etc. and a form *aúsim* used only as a potential, meaning 'I would dare'. Cf. *uélim* 'I would like'. See **153.2**.

E Irregular verbs

E1 Irregular verbs: *sum*

sum ésse futŭr-us 'I am'

	Present	*Future*	*Imperfect*
	Indicative 'I am'	*Indicative 'I shall be'*	*Indicative 'I was'*
1st s.	sum	érō	éram
2nd s.	es	éris	érās
3rd s.	est	érit	érat
1st pl.	súmus	érimus	erắmus
2nd pl.	éstis	éritis	erắtis
3rd pl.	sunt	érunt	érant

Infinitive 'to be'	*Infinitive 'to be about to be'*
ésse	futŭr-us a um esse (*or* fóre)
	Participle 'about to be'
	futŭr-us a um

Imperative 'be!'	*Imperative*
2nd s. es	*2nd/3rd s.* éstō '*be!*' '*let him be!*'
2nd pl. éste	*2nd pl.* estŏte '*be!*'
	3rd pl. súntō '*let them be!*'

	Subjunctive	*Subjunctive*
1st s.	sim	éssem (*sometimes* fórem fórēs *etc.*)
2nd s.	sīs	éssēs
3rd s.	sit	ésset
1st pl.	sĭmus	essémus
2nd pl.	sĭtis	essétis
3rd pl.	sint	éssent

Notes

1 The verb 'to be' in classical Latin has no present participle!

2 The imperfect subjunctive is 'regular' in that it appears to comprise the present infinitive + endings. This is a feature of all 'irregular' verbs.

3 All perfect forms are made regularly on the stem of *fú-ī*.

E2 Irregular verbs: *férō*

Active

férō férre túlī lătus 'I bear', 'I carry', 'I endure', 'I lead'

	Present Indicative 'I carry'	Future Indicative 'I shall carry'	Imperfect Indicative 'I was carrying'
1st s.	férō	féram	ferébam
2nd s.	fers	férēs	ferébās
3rd s.	fert	féret	ferébat
1st pl.	férimus	ferēmus	ferēbắmus
2nd pl.	fértis	ferétis	ferēbátis
3rd pl.	férunt	férent	ferébant

Infinitive 'to carry'
férre

Imperative 'carry!'
2nd s. fer
2nd pl. férte

Participle 'carrying'
férēns (ferént-)

	Subjunctive		Subjunctive
1st s.	féram		férrem
2nd s.	férās		férrēs
3rd s.	férat		férret
1st pl.	ferắmus		ferrḗmus
2nd pl.	ferắtis		ferrḗtis
3rd pl.	férant		férrent

Passive

	Present Indicative 'I am being carried'	Future Indicative 'I shall be carried'	Imperfect Indicative 'I was (being) carried'
1st s.	féror	férar	ferébar
2nd s.	férris	ferḗris (ferére)	ferēbắris (ferēbắre)
3rd s.	fértur	ferétur	ferēbắtur
1st pl.	férimur	ferḗmur	ferēbắmur
2nd pl.	feríminī	ferḗminī	ferēbắminī
3rd pl.	ferúntur	feréntur	ferēbántur

Infinitive
'to be carried'
férrī

Imperative
'be carried!'
2nd s. férre
2nd pl. feríminī

	Subjunctive	*Subjunctive*
1st s.	férar	férrer
2nd s.	ferǎris (ferǎre)	ferrěris (ferrěre)
3rd s.	ferǎtur	ferrětur
1st pl.	ferǎmur	ferrěmur
2nd pl.	ferǎminī	ferrěminī
3rd pl.	ferántur	ferréntur

Notes

1 The active infinitive *férre* is by regular sound-change from **fer-se* (for *-se* as the original ending of active infinitive, cf. **A4** perf. inf. note 1); compare the infinitives *uélle*, *nólle*, *mǎlle* from **uel-se*, etc. (**E5** note 3 below).

2 All perfect active forms are made regularly on the stem of *túl-ī*; all perfect passive forms are made regularly with the perfect passive participle *lǎt-us*.

E3 Irregular verbs: *póssum*

	Póssum pósse pótuī 'I can', 'I am able'		
	Present	*Future*	*Imperfect*
	Indicative 'I can'	*Indicative 'I shall be able'*	*Indicative 'I was able'*
1st s.	póssum	póterō	póteram
2nd s.	pótes	póteris	póterās
3rd s.	pótest	póterit	póterat
1st pl.	póssumus	potérimus	poterǎmus
2nd pl.	potéstis	potéritis	poterǎtis
3rd pl.	póssunt	póterunt	póterant

Infinitive 'to be able'
pósse

	Subjunctive	*Subjunctive*
1st s.	póssim	póssem
2nd s.	póssīs	póssēs
3rd s.	póssit	pósset
1st pl.	possímus	possḗmus
2nd pl.	possítis	possḗtis
3rd pl.	póssint	póssent

Notes

1 The form *pótēns* (*potent-*), which perhaps looks like a present participle of *póssum*, is in fact never so used: it is an adjective meaning 'powerful, able'.

2 All perfect forms of *póssum* are made regularly on the stem of *pótu-ī*.

E4 Irregular verbs: *éō*

Active

éō, íre, ī(u)ī 'I go'

	Present	*Future*	*Imperfect*
	Indicative 'I go'	*Indicative 'I shall go'*	*Indicative 'I was going'*
1st s.	éō	íbō	íbam
2nd s.	īs	íbis	íbās
3rd s.	it	íbit	íbat
1st pl.	ímus	íbimus	ībámus
2nd pl.	ítis	íbitis	ībátis
3rd pl.	éunt	íbunt	íbant

Infinitive 'to go'   *Infinitive 'to be about to go'*
íre   itúr-us a um ésse

Imperative 'go!'
2nd s. ī
2nd pl. íte

Participle 'going'   *Participle 'about to go'*
íēns (eúnt-is)   itúr-us a um

Gerund 'to go',
'*(the act of) going*'
íre, eúnd-um ī 2n.

	Subjunctive		*Subjunctive*
1st s.	éam		írem
2nd s.	éās		írēs
3rd s.	éat		íret
1st pl.	eā́mus		īrḗmus
2nd pl.	eā́tis		īrḗtis
3rd pl.	éant		írent

Passive (used in compounds)

	Present
	Indicative 'I am approached'
1st s.	ádeor
2nd s.	adī́ris (adī́re)
3rd s.	adī́tur
1st pl.	adī́mur
2nd pl.	adī́minī
3rd pl.	adeúntur

Note

All perfect active forms are made regularly on the stem of *i-ī/ī̆u-ī*; all perfect passive forms (especially of compounds) are made regularly with the stem *it-* (the stem of the supine *ítum* and of the future participle *itū́rus*).

E5 Irregular verbs: *uólō, nṓlō, mā́lō*

uólō uélle uóluī 'I wish'

nṓlō nṓlle nṓluī 'I am unwilling', 'I refuse'

mā́lō mā́lle mā́luī 'I prefer'

Note that *nṓlō* and *mā́lō* are in origin compounds of *uólō*, from **ne-uólō* 'I do not wish' and **mag(i)s-uólō* 'I wish rather', respectively. All three are formed regularly in the present system as third conjugation verbs except in the following forms:

	Present Indicative 'I wish'	Present Indicative 'I refuse'	Present Indicative 'I prefer'
1st s.	uólō	nṓlō	mā́lō
2nd s.	uīs	nōn uīs	mā́uīs
3rd s.	uult	nōn uult	mā́uult
1st pl.	uólumus	nṓlumus	mā́lumus
2nd pl.	uúltis	nōn uúltis	māuúltis
3rd pl.	uólunt	nṓlunt	mā́lunt

	Infinitive 'to wish'	Infinitive 'to refuse'	Infinitive 'to prefer'
	uélle	nṓlle	mā́lle

Imperative 'do not (wish)!'
2nd s. nṓlī
2nd pl. nōlī́te

	Present Subjunctive	Present Subjunctive	Present Subjunctive
1st s.	uélim	nṓlim	mā́lim
2nd s.	uélīs	nṓlīs	mā́līs
3rd s.	uélit	nṓlit	mā́lit
1st pl.	uelī́mus	nōlī́mus	mālī́mus
2nd pl.	uelī́tis	nōlī́tis	mālī́tis
3rd pl.	uélint	nṓlint	mā́lint

	Imperfect Subjunctive	Imperfect Subjunctive	Imperfect Subjunctive
1st s.	uéllem	nṓllem	mā́llem
2nd s.	uéllēs etc.	nṓllēs etc.	mā́llēs etc.

Notes

1 2nd s. *uīs* is the result of a curious remodelling. The original form became regularly *uel*, which survives as a conjunction meaning 'or'.

2 *uólō* and *mā́lō* have no imperative forms attested.

3 The three infinitives, all in *-lle*, go back to *-uel-se* and reflect the regular assimilation of *-ls-* to *-ll-* between vowels. For *-se* as the original ending of active infinitive, cf. *és-se* and **A4** perf. inf. note 1 above, and compare the infinitive *férre* (**E2** note 1 above).

4 On the forms of the imperfect subjunctive, cf. **E1** note 2 above.

F Defective and impersonal verbs

F1 Defective verbs

These verbs are so called because they lack certain forms (Latin *dēfícere* 'to be lacking').

(a) ***coépī, mémínī, ṓdī***

cóepī 'I have begun' (generally), *mémínī* 'I remember' and *ṓdī* 'I hate' (always) have only perfect-stem *forms*. Note that *mémínī* and *ṓdī* are present in meaning.

	Indicative	
Perfect	coépī '*I began*'	mémínī '*I remember*'
Future perfect	coéperō '*I shall have begun*'	memínerō '*I shall remember*'
Pluperfect	coéperam '*I had begun*'	memíneram '*I remembered*'
Perfect	ṓdī '*I hate*'	
Future perfect	ṓderō '*I shall hate*'	
Pluperfect	ṓderam '*I hated*'	
	Infinitive, imperative, participles	
Perfect infinitive	coepísse '*to have begun*'	meminísse '*to remember*'
Future infinitive	coeptū́r-us a um esse '*to be about to begin*'	none
Imperative	none	2nd s. meméntō ⎫ '*remember!*' 2nd pl. mementṓte ⎭
Perfect participle	coépt-us a um '*having begun*', '*having been begun*'	none
Future participle	coeptū́r-us a um '*about to begin*'	none
Perfect infinitive	ṓdísse '*to hate*'	
Future infinitive	ōsū́r-us a um esse '*to be about to hate*'	
Imperative	none	
Perfect participle	ṓs-us a um '*hating*'	
Future participle	ōsū́r-us a um '*about to hate*'	
	Subjunctive	
Perfect	coéperim	memínerim	ṓderim
Pluperfect	coepíssem	meminíssem	ōdíssem

Notes

1 On the meaning of *ṓs-us a um*, the perf. part. of *ṓdī*, cf. **C4** note 1 above.

2 *nṓscō* 'I get to know' has a perfect form *nṓuī,* meaning 'I have got to know', i.e. 'I know' (in effect, with present meaning). Thus *nṓuerō* (often 'contracted' to *nṓrō*) 'I shall know', *nṓueram* (often *nṓram*) 'I used to know, I knew', *nōuísse* (often *nṓsse*) 'to know'.

(b)   *áiō*

	Present indicative 'I say'	Imperfect indicative 'I said', 'I was saying'
1st s.	áiō	aiḗbam
2nd s.	áis	aiḗbās *etc.*
3rd s.	áit	
1st pl.	—	
2nd pl.	—	
3rd pl.	áiunt	

Note

There is also (rarely) the present subjunctive 3rd s. *áiat* and 3rd pl. *áiant*, and the present participle *áiēns* (*aient-*).

(c)   *ínquam* 'I say'

	Present indicative 'I say'	Future indicative 'I will say'	Imperfect indicative 'I was saying', 'I said'
1st s.	ínquam	—	—
2nd s.	ínquis	ínquiēs	—
3rd s.	ínquit	ínquiet	inquiḗbat
1st pl.	ínquimus	—	—
2nd pl.	ínquitis	—	—
3rd pl.	ínquiunt	—	—

Notes

1 Note also esp. perfect 3rd s. *ínquit*, 2nd s. *inquīsti*; and imper. *ínque*, future imper. *ínquitō*.

2 *ínquam* is used only to introduce direct speech.

F2 Impersonal verbs

These verbs have only the third person singular in each tense, an infinitive and a gerund:

opórtet 'it is right for (the *accusative*) to (*infinitive*)'

décet 'it is fitting for (the *accusative*) to (*infinitive*)'

dēdecet 'it is unseemly for (the *accusative*) to (*infinitive*)'

míseret 'it moves (the *accusative*) to pity for/at (the *genitive*)', 'X (acc.) is sorry for Y (gen.)'

paénitet 'it repents (the *accusative*) of (the *genitive*)', 'X (acc.) regrets Y (gen.)'

píget 'it vexes (the *accusative*) at (the *genitive*)', 'X (acc.) is sick of Y (gen.)'

púdet 'it moves (the *accusative*) to shame at (the *genitive*)', 'X (acc.) feels shame at Y (gen.)'

taédet 'it wearies (the *accusative*) at (the *genitive*)', 'X (acc.) is tired of Y (gen.)'

líbet 'it is agreeable to (the *dative*) to (*infinitive*)', 'X (dat.) chooses to Y (inf.)'

lícet 'it is permitted to (the *dative*) to (*infinitive*)' (also with *ut* + subj.)

plácet 'it is pleasing to (the *dative*) to (*infinitive*)', 'X (dat.) decides to Y (inf.)'

Note the principal parts: they are all regular 2nd conj., e.g. opórtet oportḗre opórtuit. líbet, lícet and plácet are also commonly used in the passive perfect, líbitum est 'it pleased', lícitum est 'it was allowed', plácitum est 'it was decided'.

The following impersonal verbs are followed by *ut* + subjunctive or accusative and infinitive constructions:

áccidit 'it happens (that)' (*ut* + subj.)

appā́ret 'it is evident (that)' (*ut* + subj. or acc. + inf.)

cṓnstat 'it is agreed (that)' (acc. + inf.)

rḗfert
interest } 'it is important (that)' (acc. + inf. or *ut* + subj.)

Note

'It is of importance to me, you etc.' méā, túā, súā, nóstrā, uéstrā rḗfert or interest (i.e. the f. abl. s. of the possessive adjective, as if in agreement with rē of rḗfert!).

Both *réfert* and *ínterest* take this curious construction; *ínterest* may alternatively take a genitive of the person(s) concerned, e.g. *ínterest ómnium* 'it is in the interests of all' (Cicero).

Verbs which do not control an object in the accusative cannot be turned into the passive directly, and have to adopt an impersonal 3rd s. form, e.g.

> *ítur* lit. 'it is being gone', i.e. 'people are going'
>
> *uéntum est* lit. 'it has been come', i.e. 'there has been an arrival', 'people have come'
>
> *míhi nōn créditur* lit. 'it is not being believed to me', 'credence is not being given to me', i.e. 'I am not believed'
>
> *éīs parcēbātur* lit. 'it was being spared to them', 'clemency was being extended to them', i.e. 'they were being spared'

Note in these instances that the agents (the people doing the coming, going, believing, sparing etc.) are not specified.

G Principal parts of irregular verbs

This list contains the principal parts of all irregular verbs met in the course together with a few important additions. Verbs are listed without their prefixes (e.g. for *inuéniō* see under *uéniō*). There are two exceptions:

(a) Where a verb is normally found only with a prefix, e.g. *cōnflígō*.

(b) Where a verb has been met in the course only with a prefix.

The Total Learning Vocabulary (p. 409) contains the principal parts of all compound irregular verbs learned. Note that where a verb has no perfect participle, the future participle appears where that exists.

ábeō see *éō*

abíciō see *iáciō*

ábsum see *sum*

accḗdō see *cḗdō*

áccidit see *cádō*

accípiō see *cápiō*

áddō see *dō*

ádeō see *éō*

ádferō see *férō*

adgrédior see *grádior*

ádsum see *sum*

accúmbō 3 *accúbuī accúbitum* I lie at table

adipíscor 3 dep. *adéptus* I get, gain, acquire

adiúngō see *iúngō*

ádloquor see *lóquor*

adórior see *órior*

ágō 3 *ḗgī ā́ctus* (compounds *-igō* 3 *-ḗgī -ā́ctus*) I do, act; drive, lead, direct; spend, pass; discuss

áiō (no inf., perf. or perf. part.) I say

álō 3 *áluī áltus* I feed, nourish, rear; support, strengthen

āmíttō see *míttō*

animaduértō see *uértō*

apériō 4 *apéruī apértus* I open; reveal

arcéssō 3 *arcessī́uī arcessī́tus* I summon

ā́rdeō 2 *ā́rsī ārsū́rus* I burn; am in love

árguō 3 *árguī argū́tus* I charge; make clear, prove

aspíciō 3/4 *aspéxī aspéctus* I look upon

attríbuō see *tríbuō*

aúdeō 2 semi-dep. *aúsus* I dare

aúferō auférre ábstulī ablā́tus I take away

aúgeō 2 *aúxī aúctus* I increase

bíbō 3 *bíbī* — (*pṓtus* used as perf. part; *pōtū́rus* as fut. part.) I drink

cádō 3 *cécidī cā́sum* (compounds *-cidō* 3 *-cidī -cā́sus*) I fall; die

caédō 3 *cécī́dī caésus* (compounds *-cī́dō* 3 *-cī́dī -cī́sus*) I cut (down); flog, beat; kill

cánō 3 *cécinī* — (compounds *-cinō*) I sing; play

cápiō 3/4 *cḗpī cáptus* (compounds *-cípiō* 3/4 *-cēpī -céptus*) I take, capture

cárpō 3 *cárpsī cárptus* (compounds *-cérpō* 3 *-cérpsī -cérptus*) I pluck

cáueō 2 *cā́uī caútus* I am wary

cḗdō 3 *céssī céssum* I yield; go

cérnō 3 *crḗuī crḗtus* I decide; see

cíngō 3 *cī́nxī cī́nctus* I gird; surround

circúmeō see *éō*

circumsédeō see *sédeō*

claúdō 3 *claúsī claúsus* (compounds *-clū́dō* 3 *-clū́sī -clū́sus*) I shut

coépī coepísse coéptus I have begun

cognōscō see *nōscō*

cōgō 3 *coḗgī coáctus* I force, compel, gather

cólō 3 *cóluī cúltus* I worship; cultivate, till; inhabit

cólligō see *légō*

commíttō see *míttō*

commóueō see *móueō*

compléctor 3 dep. *compléxus* I embrace

cómpleō 2 *compléuī complétus* I fill up; accomplish

comprehéndō see *prehéndō*

concídō see *cádō*

concúrrō see *cúrrō*

concútiō 3/4 *concússī concússus* (see *quátiō*) I shake violently; disturb, alarm

cóndō see *dō*

cōnfíciō see *fáciō*

cōnfíteor see *fáteor*

cōnflígō 3 *cōnflíxī cōnflíctus* I fight

cōnfódiō see *fódiō*

coníciō see *iáciō*

coniúngō see *iúngō*

cōnsídō 3 *cōnsḗdī* — I settle down; encamp

cōnsístō 3 *cōnstitī* — (see *sístō*) I stop; stand my ground

cōnspíciō 3/4 *cōnspéxī cōnspéctus* I catch sight of; observe, gaze on

cốnsulō 3 *cōnsúluī cōnsúltus* I consult

conuéllō see *uéllō*

conuéniō see *uéniō*

cóquō 3 *cóxī cóctus* I cook

crḗdō 3 *crḗdidī crḗditum* I believe (in); entrust

crépō 1 *crépuī crépitus* I rattle

crḗscō 3 *crḗuī crḗtum* (= sprung from) I grow (intrans.)

cúbō 1 *cúbuī cúbitum* I lie; sleep; recline at table

cúpiō 3/4 *cupíuī cupítus* I desire, yearn for; want desperately

cúrrō 3 *cucúrrī cúrsum* (compounds often have perf. -*cúrrī*) I run

dēcípiō see *cápiō*

dḗdō see *dō*

dēféndō 3 *dēféndī dēfḗnsus* I defend

dḗférō see *férō*

dḗfúngor see *fúngor*

déleō 2 *dēlḗuī dēlḗtus* I destroy

dēprehéndō see *prehéndō*

dḗscéndō see *scándō*

dḗserō see *sérō*

dḗspuō see *spúō*

dḗsum see *sum*

dī́cō 3 *dī́xī díctus* I speak, say

diffī́dō see *fī́dō*

dīmíttō see *míttō*

díscḗdō see *cḗdō*

díscō 3 *dídicī* — I learn

dispṓnō see *pṓnō*

dī́uidō 3 *dīuī́sī dīuī́sus* I divide

dṓ 1 *dédī dátus* (compounds -*dō* 3 -*didī* -*ditus*) I give

dóceō 2 *dócuī dóctus* I teach

dū́cō 3 *dū́xī dúctus* I lead; think, consider

édō ḗsse ḗdī ḗsus (3rd s. pres. *ēst*) I eat

effíciō see *fáciō*

effúgiō see *fúgiō*

ēgrédior see *grádior*

ḗíciō see *iáciō*

émō 3 *ḗmī ḗmptus* (compounds -*imō* 3 - *ḗmī* -*ḗmptus*) I buy

éō ī́re íī ítum I go/come

ērípiō see *rápiō*

excḗdō see *cḗdō*

excípiō see *cápiō*

éxeō see *éō*

exórior see *órior*

expéllō see *péllō*

exstínguō 3 *exstī́nxī exstínctus* I extinguish

fáciō 3/4 *fḗcī fáctus* (most compounds -*fíciō* 3/4 -*fḗcī* -*féctus*) I make; do

fállō 3 *feféllī fálsus* I deceive

fáteor 2 dep. *fássus* (compounds *-fíteor* 2 dep. *-féssus*)
  I acknowledge

fáueō 2 *fắuī faútum* I am favourable to

fériō 4 (*percússī percússus*) I strike; beat; kill

férō férre túlī lătus I bear; lead

férueō 2 *féruī* (or *férbuī*) — I boil

fīdō 3 semi-dep. *fīsus* I trust

fīgō 3 *fīxī fīxus* I fix

findō 3 *fídī físsus* I cleave, split

fíngō 3 *fínxī fíctus* I make up, fabricate

fíō fíerī fáctus semi-dep. I become; am done, am made

fléctō 3 *fléxi fléxus* I bend

fléō 2 *flḗuī flḗtum* I weep

flúō 3 *flúxī* — I flow

fódiō 3/4 *fŏdī fóssus* I dig

frángō 3 *frḗgī frắctus* (compounds *-fríngō* 3 *-frḗgī -frắctus*) I break

frúor 3 dep. *frŭctus* I enjoy

fúgiō 3/4 *fŭgī fugitŭrus* I escape, run off, flee

fúlgeō 2 *fúlsī* — I shine

fúndō 3 *fŭdī fŭsus* I pour; rout

fúngor 3 dep. *fŭnctus* I perform, discharge

gaúdeō 2 semi-dep. *gāuīsus* I am glad, rejoice

gérō 3 *géssī géstus* I do, conduct

gígnō 3 *génuī génitus* I beget, produce

grádior 3/4 dep. *gréssus* (compounds *-grédior* 3/4 *-gréssus*) I step, walk, go

haéreō 2 *haésī haésum* I stick

haúriō 4 *haúsī haústus* I drain, draw

iáciō 3/4 *iḗcī iáctus* (compounds *-íciō* 3/4 *-iḗcī -iéctus*) I throw

ignōscō 3 *ignŏuī ignŏtus* I forgive (+ dat.) (see also *nŏscō*)

impōnō see *pŏnō*

incéndō 3 *incéndī incénsus* I set fire to; burn

indúlgeō 2 *indúlsī* — I yield, give myself up to

índuō 3 *índuī indŭtus* I put on

íneō see *éō*

ingrédior see *grádior*

ínquam no inf. *ínquiī* — I say

īnspíciō 3/4 *īnspéxī īnspéctus* I look into, inspect, examine

īnstítuō see *státuō*

ínstō see *stō*

ínstruō see *strúō*

ínsum see *sum*

intellégō see *légō*

interfíciō see *fáciō*

inuắdō see *uắdō*

inuéniō see *uéniō*

inuídeō see *uídeō*

īrắscor 3 dep. *īrắtus* I grow angry

irrídeō see *rídeō*

iúbeō 2 *iússī iússus* I order, command

iúngō 3 *iúnxī iúnctus* I yoke; join

iúuō 1 *iúuī iútus* I help; delight, please

lắbor 3 dep. *lắpsus* I slip, glide, fall down; make a mistake

lacéssō 3 *lacessíuī lacessítus* I provoke

laédō 3 *laésī laésus* (compounds *-lídō* 3 *-lísī -lísus*) I harm

láuō 1 *lắuī lauắtus/laútus/lótus* I wash

légō 3 *légī léctus* (compounds *-ligō* 3 *-légī -léctus*) I read; gather; choose

líbet 2 *líbuit* or *líbitum est* it pleases

lícet 3 *lícuit* or *lícitum est* it is permitted

lóquor 3 dep. *locútus* I speak, say

lúdō 3 *lúsī lúsum* I play

mắlō mắlle mắluī — I prefer

máneō 2 *mắnsī mắnsum* I remain, wait

méminī meminísse (perfect form) I remember

métuō 3 *métuī metútus* I fear

mínuō 3 *mínuī minútus* I lessen

mísceō 2 *míscuī míxtus* or *místus* I mix

míttō 3 *mísī míssus* I send; throw

mórdeō 2 *momórdī mórsus* I bite

mórior 3/4 dep. *mórtuus* I die, am dying

móueō 2 *móuī mótus* I move; remove; cause, begin

nancíscor 3 dep. *náctus* or *nắnctus* I gain

náscor 3 dep. *nātus* I am born

néctō 3 *néxī néxus* I link together

neglégō see *légō*

néqueō see *quéō*

nītor 3 dep. *nīxus* or *nīsus* I lean on; strive, exert myself

nṓlō nṓlle nṓluī — I refuse, am unwilling

nṓscō 3 *nṓuī nṓtus* (compounds: some have perf. part, -*nitus*, e.g.
    cógnitus from *cognṓscō*) I get to know (perfect tenses = 'I know' etc.)

nūbō 3 *nūpsī nūptus* I marry (of a bride; + dat. of man)

oblīuīscor 3 dep. *oblĭtus* I forget

óbstō see *stō*

óccidō see *cádō*

occīdō see *caédō*

occúrrō see *cúrrō*

ṓdī ōdísse ṓsus (perfect participle = 'hating') I hate

offéndō 3 *offéndī offḗnsus* I meet with; offend

omíttō see *míttō*

ópprimō see *prémō*

órior 4 dep. *órtus* (note pres. *órĕris, órĭtur, órĭmur*, fut. part. *oritŭrus*;
    gerundive *oriúndum*; compound *adórior* has 4th conj. present) I rise;
    spring from, originate

osténdō 3 *osténdī ostḗnsus* or *osténtus* I show, reveal

pacīscor 3 dep. *páctus* I make an agreement

pándō 3 *pándī pássus* I spread out, extend; throw open, disclose

párcō 3 *pepércī* or *pársī parsŭrus* (compounds -*pércō* 3 -*pérsī*) I spare

páriō 3/4 *péperī pártus* (fut. part. *paritŭrus*; compounds -*périō* 4
-*perī* -*pértus*) I bring forth, bear, produce; obtain, acquire

patefáciō see *fáciō*

pátior 3/4 dep. *pássus* (compounds -*pétior* 3/4 dep. -*péssus*) I
    endure, suffer; allow

péllo 3 *pépulī púlsus* (compounds -*péllō* 3 -*pulī púlsus*) I push,
    drive back

péndeō 2 *pepéndī* — (compounds: perf. -*péndī*) I hang (intrans.)

percéllō 3 *pérculī percúlsus* I strike down; unnerve, scare

pérdō see *dō*

péreō see *éō*

pérferō see *férō*

perficiō see faciō

pérgō 3 *perrḗxī perrḗctum* (see *régō*) I go on, go ahead, continue

pérlegō see *légō*

perscrī́bō see *scrī́bō*

pérsequor see *séquor*

persuádeō see *suádeō*

peruéniō see *uéniō*

pétō 3 *petī́uī petī́tus* I beg; seek; proposition, court; attack, make for; stand for (public office)

píget 2 *píguit* or *pígitum est* it vexes

píngō 3 *pī́nxī píctus* I paint

plaúdō 3 *plaúsī plaúsus* (compounds sometimes *-plṓdō* 3 *-plṓsī -plṓsus*) I clap

pṓnō 3 *pósuī pósitus* I place, position, put; lay aside

póscō 3 *popóscī* — I demand

possídeō see *sédeō*

póssum pósse pótuī — I am able, can; am powerful, have power

pṓtō 1 *pōtā́uī pṓtus* ('having drunk', see *bíbō*) I drink

praecípiō see *cápiō*

praefíciō see *fáciō*

prehéndō 3 *prehéndī prehḗnsus* I lay hold of

prémō 3 *préssī préssus* (compounds *-primō* 3 *-préssī -préssus*) I press; oppress

procúmbō 3 *procúbuī procúbitum* I collapse

prōfúgiō see *fúgiō*

prōgrédior see *grádior*

prōíciō see *iáciō*

prōmíttō see *míttō*

prōpṓnō see *pṓnō*

proficī́scor 3 dep. *proféctus* I set out

prōspíciō 3/4 *prōspéxī prōspéctus* I look out (on); foresee

prōtégō see *tégō*

prōuídeō see *uídeō*

púdet 2 *púduit* or *púditum est* it shames

quaérō 3 *quaesī́uī quaesī́tus* (compounds *-quī́rō* 3 *-quīsī́uī -quīsī́tus*) I seek, look for; ask

quátiō 3/4 — *quássus* (compounds *-cútiō* 3/4 *-cússī -cússus*) I shake (trans.)

quéō quíre quíuī I am able

quéror 3 dep. *quéstus* I complain

quiĕ́scō 3 *quiĕ́uī quiĕ́tus* I rest

rắdō 3 *rắsī rắsus* I scrape, shave

rápiō 3/4 *rápuī ráptus* (compounds *-rípiō* 3/4 *-rípuī -réptus*) I snatch, seize, carry away, plunder

recípiō see *cápiō*

réddō see *dō*

rédeō see *éō*

rédimō see *émō*

redŭ́cō see *dŭ́cō*

régō 3 *rĕ́xī rĕ́ctus* (compounds *-rigō* 3 *-rĕ́xī -rĕ́ctus*: except *pérgō*, *súrgō*, q.v.) I keep straight, rule

relínquō 3 *relĭ́quī relíctus* I leave, abandon

remáneō see *máneō*

remíttō see *míttō*

réor 2 dep. *rátus* I think, believe, suppose

repéllō see *péllō*

repériō 3 *répperī repértus* I find

rĕ́pō 3 *rĕ́psī* — I creep

réprimō see *prémō* 3

requiĕ́scō see *quiĕ́scō*

requĭ́rō see *quaérō*

resístō 3 *réstitī* — (see *sístō*) I resist

respíciō 3/4 *respéxī respéctus* I look round (back) at, turn my gaze upon; reflect upon; care for

respóndeō 2 *respóndī respŏ́nsum* I reply

retíneō see *téneō*

rétrahō see *tráhō*

reuértor see *uértō*

rĭ́deō 2 *rĭ́sī rĭ́sus* I smile, laugh

rúmpō 3 *rŭ́pī rúptus* I break

rúō 3 *rúī rŭ́tus* (fut. part. *ruitŭ́rus*; compounds have perf. part. *-rŭtus*) I rush; fall

scándō 3 *scándī scánsum* (compounds *-scéndō* 3 *-scéndī -scĕ́nsus*) I climb *scíndō* 3 *scídī scíssus* I tear, cut

scrī́bō 3 *scrī́psī scrī́ptus* I write

sécō 1 *sécuī séctus* I cut

sédeō 2 *sḗdī séssum* (some compounds *-sídeō* 2 *-sḗdī -séssus*) I sit

séntiō 4 *sḗnsī sḗnsus* I feel; understand; perceive, realise

sepéliō 4 *sepelī́uī sepúltus* I bury

séquor 3 dep. *secū́tus* I follow

sérō 3 — — (compounds *-serō* 3 *-séruī -sértus*) I put in rows

sī́dō 3 *sī́dī* — (compounds have perf. and perf. part. of *sédeō*: *-sḗdī -séssus*) I settle (intrans.)

sínō 3 *sī́uī sítus* (compounds drop *-u-* in perf., e.g. *dḗsinō* 3 *dḗsiī*) I allow

sístō 3 *stítī* (or *stétī*) *státus* (compounds all intransitive, with no perf. part.: cf. *cōnsístō*, *resístō*) I set; stay

sóleō 2 semi-dep. *sólitus* I am accustomed, am used

sóluō 3 *sóluī solū́tus* I release, undo; pay

spárgō 3 *spársī spársus* (compounds *-spérgō* 3 *-spérsī -spérsus*) I scatter, sprinkle

spérnō 3 *sprḗuī sprḗtus* I reject, despise

spúō 3 *spúī spū́tum* I spit

státuō 3 *státuī statū́tus* (compounds *-stítuō* 3 *-stítuī -stítū́tus*) I set up, settle

stérnō 3 *strā́uī strā́tus* I throw on the ground, strew

stō 1 *stétī státum* (most compounds *-stō* 3 *-stítī* with fut. part. *-statū́rus*, but no perf. part.) I stand

stríngō 3 *strínxī stríctus* I draw; strip; graze

strúō 3 *strū́xī strū́ctus* I heap up, build

suádeō 2 *suā́sī suā́sum* I recommend

succúrrō see *cúrrō*

suḗscō 3 *suḗuī suḗtus* I accustom myself

sum ésse fúī futū́rus I am

sū́mō 3 *sū́mpsī sū́mptus* I take; consume

súrgō 3 *surrḗxī surrḗctum* (see *régō*) I rise, arise, get up

suscípiō see *cápiō*

sustíneō see *téneō*

taédet 2 *taésum est* it wearies

tángō 3 *tétigī tā́ctus* (compounds *-tíngō* 3 *-tigī -tā́ctus*) I touch, lay hands on

tégō 3 *tḗxī tḗctus* I cover

témnō 3 *-témpsi -témptus* (compounds *-temnō* 3) I despise

téndō 3 *teténdī téntus* or *tḗnsus* (compounds *-téndo* 3 *-téndī -téntus*) I stretch (out); offer; direct; travel; strive, fight

téneō 2 *ténuī téntus* (compounds *-tíneō* 2 *-tínuī -téntus*) I hold

térō 3 *trĭ́uī trĭ́tus* I rub

tóllō 3 *sústulī sublắtus* I lift, remove, take away

tóndeō 2 *totóndī tṓnsus* I shear

trắdō see *dō*

tráhō 3 *trắxī tráctus* I drag

trắnseō see *éō*

tríbuō 3 *tríbuī tribŭ́tus* I assign, grant

túeor 2 dep. *túitus* or *tŭ́tus* I look after, protect; look at

túndō 3 *tutudī tŭ́sus* or *tŭ́nsus* (compounds *-túndō* 3 *-tudī -tŭ́sus/-tŭ́nsus*) I beat, strike, pound

uắdō 3 —— (compounds *-uắdō* 3 *-uắsī -uắsus*) I go

uéhō 3 *uéxī uéctus* I carry

uéllō 3 *uéllī* or *uúlsī uúlsus* I pull, pluck

uéniō 4 *uḗnī uéntum* I come, arrive

uértō 3 *uértī uérsus* I turn (trans.)

uétō 1 *uétuī uétitus* I forbid

uídeō 2 *uĭ́dī uĭ́sus* I see (passive: 'I seem')

uínciō 4 *uĭ́nxī uĭ́nctus* I bind

uíncō 3 *uĭ́cī uíctus* I conquer

uĭ́sō 3 *uĭ́sī* — I visit

uĭ́uō 3 *uĭ́xī uĭ́ctum* I am alive, live

ulcĭ́scor 3 dep. *últus* I avenge myself on, avenge

uólō uélle uóluī — I wish, want

uóluō 3 *uóluī uolŭ́tus* I roll, turn over (trans.)

ŭ́rō 3 *ússī ústus* I burn

ŭ́tor 3 dep. *ŭ́sus* I use, make use of; adopt

H–I Nouns, pronominal nouns/adjectives

H1 Nouns: first declension

séru-a ae 1f. 'slave-woman'

	s.	pl.
nom./voc.	sérua	séruae
acc.	séruam	séruās
gen.	séruae (seruā́ī)	seruā́rum
dat.	séruae	séruīs
abl.	séruā	séruīs

Notes

1 1st decl. nouns are feminine except for a few masculines, e.g. *agrícola* 'farmer', *naúta* 'sailor', *scrība* 'scribe', men's names such as *Numa*, and a few other names, e.g. *Hadria* the Adriatic sea.

2 The alternative gen. sg. ending *-ā́ī* is archaic and poetic.

3 *fília* 'daughter' and *déa* 'goddess' have dat./abl. pl. in *-ā́bus*, i.e. *fīliā́bus*, *deā́bus* (to avoid confusion with the dat./abl. pl. of *fílius* and *déus*).

H2 Nouns: second declension

(a) *séru-us ī* 2m. 'male slave'

	s.	pl.
nom.	séruus	séruī
voc.	sérue	séruī
acc.	séruum	séruōs
gen.	séruī	seruṓrum
dat.	séruō	séruīs
abl.	séruō	séruīs

Notes

1 Virtually all 2nd decl. nouns are masculine. An important because common exception is *húm-us ī f.* 'ground'.

2 Originally, this type declined nom. *-os* acc. *-om* (and type **(f)** below *-om -om*). These nom. and acc. forms are often found in inscriptions and Early Latin, and, if the stem ended in *-u-* (as in *seruos*), still in the early Empire. The gen. pl. sometimes ends in plain *-um* rather than *-ṓrum* (cf. **H2(d)** *uir* and **(e)** *deus* below).

(b) *púer púerī* 2m. 'boy'

	s.	pl.
nom./voc.	púer	púerī
acc.	púerum	púeros
gen.	púerī	puerórum
dat.	púerō	púerīs
abl.	púero	púerīs

(c) *cúlter cúltr-ī* 2m. 'knife'

	s.	pl.
nom./voc.	cúlter	cúltrī
acc.	cúltrum	cúltrōs
gen.	cúltrī	cultrórum
dat.	cúltrō	cúltrīs
abl.	cúltrō	cúltrīs

(d) *uir uír-ī* 2m. 'man'

	s.	pl.
nom./voc.	uir	uírī
acc.	uírum	uírōs
gen.	uírī	uirórum (uírum – *cf.* déus)
dat.	uírō	uírīs
abl.	uírō	uírīs

(e) *dé-us ī* 2m. 'god'

	s.	pl.
nom./voc.	déus	dī (déī, díī)
acc.	déum	déōs
gen.	déī	deórum (déum)
dat.	déō	dīs
abl.	déō	dīs

(f) **(NB neuter) *sómni-um ī* 2n. 'dream'**

	s.	*pl.*
nom./voc.	sómnium	sómnia
acc.	sómnium	sómnia
gen.	sómnī (*or* sómniī)	somniṓrum
dat.	sómniō	sómniīs
abl.	sómniō	sómniīs

H3 Nouns: third declension

(a) **(Consonant stem) *fūr fǔr-is* 3m. 'thief'**

	s.	*pl.*
nom./voc.	fūr	fǔrēs
acc.	fǔrem	fǔrēs
gen.	fǔris	fǔrum
dat.	fǔrī	fǔribus
abl.	fǔre	fǔribus

NB Monosyllables with *two* consonants at the end of the stem have genitive plural in *-ium*, e.g. *mṓns mónt-is* 'mountain', gen. pl. *móntium*. Such nouns are in fact old *i*-stems.

(b) **(*i*-stem) *aédis aéd-is* 3f. 'temple'; pl. 'temples' or 'house'**

	s.	*pl.*
nom./voc.	aédis	aédēs
acc.	aédem	aédīs (aédēs)
gen.	aédis	aédium
dat.	aédī	aédibus
abl.	aéde (aédī)	aédibus

Note

Historically, the *-i-* was wholly dominant, cf. the declension of *túrris* 'tower': *túrris túrrim túrris túrrī túrrī*.

(c) **(Neuter consonant stem) _nṓmen nṓmin-is_ 3n. 'name'**

	s.	pl.
nom./voc.	nṓmen	nṓmina
acc.	nṓmen	nṓmina
gen.	nṓminis	nṓminum
dat.	nṓminī	nōmínibus
abl.	nṓmine	nōmínibus

(d) **(Neuter consonant stem) _ónus óner-is_ 3n. 'load, burden'**

	s.	pl.
nom./voc.	ónus	ónera
acc.	ónus	ónera
gen.	óneris	ónerum
dat.	ónerī	onéribus
abl.	ónere	onéribus

Note

The original stem was _onos-_ nom. acc. s. alternating with _ones-_ in all other forms. The _-o-_ became _-u-_ in the final syllable in nom. s. (_onus_), and the _-s-_ became _-r-_ between vowels (a far-reaching and characteristic sound-change of Latin), i.e. *_onesis_→_óneris_.

(e) **(Neuter _i_-stem) nouns in _-al -ar -re_ and _-le_: _máre már-is_ 3n. 'sea'**

	s.	pl.
nom./voc.	máre	mária
acc.	máre	mária
gen.	máris	márium (márum _is found_)
dat.	márī	máribus
abl.	márī (máre _is found_)	máribus

Note

Cf. _ánimal_ 'animal', _cálcar_ 'spur' and _cubíle_ 'couch'.

(f)   **Four irregular 3rd declension nouns: *Iūppiter, bōs, uīs, nēmo***

Iúppiter Ióu-is 3m. 'Jupiter'

nom./voc.	Iúppiter
acc.	Ióuem
gen.	Ióuis
dat.	Ióuī
abl.	Ióue

---

bōs bóu-is 3m. 'ox' *3f.* 'cow'

	s.	*pl.*
nom./voc.	bōs	bóuēs
acc.	bóuem	bóuēs
gen.	bóuis	bóum
dat.	bóuī	bṓbus (bū́bus)
abl.	bóue	bṓbus (bū́bus)

---

uīs 3f. (s.) force', *(pl.)* 'strength'

	s.	*pl.*
nom./voc.	uīs	uī́rēs
acc.	uim	uī́rēs
gen.	—	uī́rium
dat.	—	uī́ribus
abl.	uī	uī́ribus

---

nḗmo 3 m.f. 'no one', 'none', 'no' (pronoun)

	s.
nom./voc.	nḗmo
acc.	nḗminem
gen.	nūllī́us (*this form and the abl.* nū́llō *being supplied by the adjective* nū́llus '*not any(one), no(one)*')
dat.	nḗminī
abl.	nū́llō

Notes

1 Consonant- and *i*-stem nouns can be masculine, feminine or neuter. The following clues can help:

> *Masculine*: nouns ending in -*ōs*, -*ō*, -*or*, -*er* (main exceptions: *dōs* 'dowry', f.; *ōs ṓris* 'mouth', n.; *árbor* 'tree', f.)

Feminine: nouns ending in -*x*, -*ās*, -*dō*, -*gō*, -*iō*, -*ūs* (if polysyllabic), -*ns* (main exceptions: *dux* 'leader', m.; *fās* 'right', n.; *órdō* 'rank', m.; *mōns* 'mountain', *pōns* 'bridge', *fōns* 'fountain'; *dēns* 'tooth', all m.)

Neuter: nouns ending in -*us*, -*ūs* (if monosyllabic), -*en*, -*al*, -*ar*, -*re*, -*le*

2 Finding the nominative can be difficult with such nouns. Note the following clues:

(i) gen. s. ending in -*cis*, -*gis*: nominative in -*x* (e.g. *pắcis*→*pāx*)

(ii) gen. s. ending in -*tis*, -*dis*: nominative in -*s* (e.g. *uirtŭtis*→*uírtūs*)

(iii) gen. s. ending in -*pis*: nominative in -*ps* (e.g. *prĭncipis*→*prĭnceps*)

(iv) gen. s. ending in -*ris*: nominative in -*s*, -*r* (e.g. *témporis*→*témpus*, *mătris*→*mắter*)

(v) gen. s. ending in -*lis*: nominative in -*l* (e.g. *sólis*→*sōl*)

3 As a general rule: (a) nouns with the *same* number of syllables in the nominative singular as in the genitive singular (parisyllabic) have genitive plurals in -*ium*, e.g. *cĭuis*, gen. s. *cĭuis*, gen. pl. *cĭuium*. These are *i*-stem. (b) Nouns with *more* syllables in the genitive singular than in the nominative singular (imparisyllabic) have gen. pl. in -*um*, e.g. *uírtūs*, gen. s. *uirtŭtis*, gen. pl. *uirtŭtum*. These are consonant stem.

The major exceptions to (a) are *cánis cán-is* m. or f. 'dog', *iúuenis iúuen-is* m. 'young man', *sénex sén-is* m. 'old man', *sḗdēs sḗd-is* f. 'abode', *páter pátr-is* m. 'father', *mắter mắtr-is* f. 'mother', *fráter frắtr-is* m. 'brother', *accípiter accípitr-is* m. 'hawk', all of which have gen. pl. in -*um*. The rule for major exceptions to (b) is given in the note under *fūr* (**H3(a)** above).

H4 Nouns: fourth declension

(a)   *mán-us ūs* 4f. 'hand'

	s.	pl.
nom./voc.	mánus	mánūs
acc.	mánum	mánūs
gen.	mánūs	mánuum
dat.	mánuī	mánibus
abl.	mánū	mánibus (mánubus))
		mánibus

(b) **(Neuter)** *córn-ū ūs* 4n. 'horn', 'wing of army'

	s.	*pl.*
nom./voc.	córnū	córnua
acc.	córnū	córnua
gen.	córnūs	córnuum
dat.	córnū	córnibus
abl.	córnū	córnibus

(c) **(Irregular)** *dómus* 4f. 'house'

	s.	*pl.*
nom./voc.	dómus	dómūs
acc.	dómum	dómūs *or* dómōs
gen.	dómūs *or* dómī	domṓrum *or* dómuum
dat.	dómuī *or* dómō	dómibus
abl.	dómō	dómibus

Notes

1 In spite of the fact that the model noun *mánus* is f. (not to mention *dómus*), most 4th decl. nouns are *masculine*. Other common feminines include *pórticus* 'porch', *tríbus* 'tribe' and *Idūs* (pl.) 'the Ides'.

2 In early Latin the gen. s. is sometimes in -*ī* as in the second declension in nouns other than *dómus* (e.g. *senā́tī* gen. of *senā́tus* 'senate'). Note that all the 'irregular' forms of *dómus* show second declension endings.

3 Note that the dat. s. is usually in -*uī* for m. and f. nouns, -*ō* for neuters, but that occasionally m. and f. nouns have dat. s. -*ū*.

H5 Nouns: fifth declension

rēs ré-ī 5 f. 'thing', 'matter', 'business', 'affair'

	s.	*pl.*
nom./voc.	rēs	rēs
acc.	rem	rēs
gen.	ré-ī (rē)	rḗrum
dat.	ré-ī (rē)	rḗbus
abl.	rē	rḗbus

Note 5th decl. nouns are all feminine, except *diēs* 'day', which is usually m. (f. when it means the goddess *Diēs*, or an appointed day), and its compound *merídiēs* 'midday', 'south' is always m.

H6 Greek declensions

Roman poets often use the Greek forms of Greek nouns, especially for names. For the most part, only nom., acc. and gen. s., nom. and acc. pl. are found. The other cases have the normal Latin forms. Here are some examples (with the Greek endings in italic).

1st declension *Aené-ās ae* m. 'Aeneas', *Priámid-ēs ae* m. 'son of Priam', *Eurýdic-ē ēs* f. 'Eurydice'

nom.	Aené-*ās*	Priámid-*ēs*	Eurýdic-*ē*
voc.	Aené-*ā*	Priámid-*ē*	Eurýdic-*ē*
acc.	Aené-*ān*	Priámid-*ēn*	Eurýdic-*ēn*
gen.	Aené-ae	Priámid-ae	Eurýdic-*ēs*
dat.	Aené-ae	Priámid-ae	Eurýdic-ae
abl.	Aené-ā	Priámid-ē (-ā)	Eurýdic-ē

Notes

1 The pl. of such nouns is as for *séru-a*, except that nouns in *-dēs* have gen. pl. in *-um*, e.g. *Aenéad-um* 'of the followers of Aeneas'.

2 The Latin form of names like *Eurýdicē* is often found, e.g. *Cýbel-a Cýbel-am* etc. 'Cybele'.

2nd declension *Dél-os ī* f. 'Delos', *Péli-on ī* n. 'Pelion'

nom./voc.	Dél-*os*	Péli-*on*
acc.	Dél-*on*	Péli-*on*
gen.	Dēl-ī	Péli-ī
dat./abl.	Dél-ō	Péli-ō

3rd declension *crátēr crātér-os/crātér-is* m. 'mixing-bowl'

	s.	*pl.*
nom./voc.	crátēr	crātér-es
acc.	crātér-*a*/-em	crātér-*as*
gen.	crātér-*os*/-is	crātér-um
dat.	crātér-ī	crātér-ibus
abl.	crātér-e	crātér-ibus

Note

Other 3rd declension Greek forms are e.g. 'hero' m.: nom. *hḗrōs*, acc. *hērṓ-a*; 'Orpheus' m.: nom. *Órpheus*, voc. *Órpheu*, acc. *Órphea*, gen. *Órpheos*; 'Paris' m.: nom. *Páris*, voc. *Pári*, acc. *Párin/Párida*, gen. *Páridos*; 'Socrates' m.: nom. *Sṓcratēs*, voc. *Sṓcratē*, acc. *Sṓcratem*.

I1 Personal pronouns

(a) *égo* 'I', *tū* 'you (s.)'; *nōs* 'we', *uōs* 'you' (pl.)

pl.	*s.*	*pl.*	*s.*	*pl.*
nom.	égo 'I'	nōs 'we'	tū 'you'	uōs 'you'
acc.	mē	nōs	tē	uōs
gen.	méī	nóstrum/nóstrī	túī	uéstrum/uéstrī
dat.	míhi (mī)	nṓbīs	tíbi	uṓbīs
abl.	mē	nṓbīs	tē	uṓbīs

(b) Reflexive pronoun *sē* 'himself,' 'herself', 'itself', 'themselves'

s./pl.	
nom.	—
acc.	sē (sḗsē)
gen.	súī
dat.	síbi
abl.	sē (sḗsē)

Notes

1 Possessive adjectives based on personal pronouns are:

> mé-us a um 'my', 'mine' ⎫ declining like *lóng-us a um* **J1 (a)** (*but*
> tú-us a um 'your', 'yours' ⎭ note *mī* voc. s. m. of *mé-us*)

> nóster nóstr-a um 'our', 'ours' ⎫ declining like *púlcher púlchr-a*
> uéster uéstr-a um 'your', 'yours' ⎭ *um* **J1 (b)**

> sú-us a um 'his', 'hers', 'its', 'theirs' (reflexive – i.e. the 'he', 'she',
> 'it', 'them' being referred to are the same person as the subject of
> the clause in which they stand, but see 'reflexives' in the Index of
> Grammar for five important exceptions)

These usually follow their noun (unless emphatic). But *mī* (voc. s. of *méus*) usually precedes.

2 *cum* 'with' *follows* the ablative of these pronouns, forming with each a single word, *mécum, técum, sécum, nóbīscum, uóbīscum* (cf. **I3** note 1 below).

I2 Demonstrative pronouns

(a)   ***is éa id*** 'that', 'those', 'that person', 'he', 'she', 'it'

	s.			pl.		
	m.	*f.*	*n.*	*m.*	*f.*	*n.*
nom.	is	éa	id	éī (íī)	éae	éa
acc.	éum	éam	id	éōs	éās	éa
gen.	←——— éius ——→			eórum	eárum	eórum
dat.	←——— éī ——→			←——— éīs (íīs) ———→		
abl.	éō	éā	éō	←——— éīs (íīs) ———→		

Compare the definitive pronoun *ídem éadem ídem* 'the same':

	s.			pl.		
	m.	*f.*	*n.*	*m.*	*f.*	*n.*
nom.	ídem	éadem	ídem	eídem (ídem)	eaédem	éadem
acc.	eúndem	eándem	ídem	eósdem	eásdem	éadem
gen.	←———— eiúsdem ——→			eōrúndem	eārúndem	eōrúndem
dat.	←———— eídem ——→			←——— eísdem (ísdem) ———→		
abl.	eódem	eádem	eódem	←——— eísdem (ísdem) ———→		

(b)   ***hic haec hoc*** **'this', 'this person', 'this thing', 'the latter'; pl. 'these'**

	s.			pl.		
	m.	f.	n.	m.	f.	n.
nom.	hic	haec	hoc	hī	hae	haec
acc.	hunc	hanc	hoc	hōs	hās	haec
gen.	←—— húius ——→			hŏrum	hărum	hŏrum
dat.	←—— huic ——→			←—— hĭs ——→		
abl.	hōc	hāc	hōc	←—— hĭs ——→		

Note

The strengthened forms *huiúsce*, *hŏsce*, *hăsce* and *hĭsce* are reasonably common. The final *-ce* in these is an old deictic particle meaning 'here' (seen also in *écce* 'look here!', and <u>*cĕdo*</u> 'give here!'). A trace of *-ce* survives in those forms of *hic haec hoc* ending in *-c*.

(c)   ***ille ílla íllud*** **'that', 'that person', 'that thing', 'the former'; pl. 'those'**

	s.			pl.		
	m.	f.	n.	m.	f.	n.
nom.	ílle	ílla	íllud	íllī	íllae	ílla
acc.	íllum	íllam	íllud	íllōs	íllās	ílla
gen.	←—— illíus ——→			illŏrum	illárum	illŏrum
dat.	←—— íllī ——→			←—— íllīs ——→		
abl.	íllō	íllā	íllō	←—— íllīs ——→		

(d)   ***íste ísta ístud*** **'that (of yours)'**

	s.			pl.		
	m.	f.	n.	m.	f.	n.
nom.	íste	ísta	ístud	ístī	ístae	ísta
acc.	ístum	ístam	ístud	ístōs	ístās	ísta
gen.	←—— istíus ——→			istŏrum	istárum	istŏrum
dat.	←—— ístī ——→			←—— ístīs ——→		
abl.	ístō	ísta	ístō	←—— ístīs ——→		

(e) *ípse ípsa ípsum* 'very', 'actual', 'self'

	s.			pl.		
	m.	*f.*	*n.*	*m.*	*f.*	*n.*
nom.	ípse	ípsa	ípsum	ípsī	ípsae	ípsa
acc.	ípsum	ípsam	ípsum	ípsōs	ípsās	ípsa
gen.	←——— ipsī́us ———→			ipsṓrum	ipsā́rum	ipsṓrum
dat.	←——— ípsī ———→			←——— ípsīs ———→		
abl.	ípsō	ípsā	ípsō	←——— ípsīs ———→		

13 Relative pronoun

quī quae quod 'who', 'which', 'what'

	s.			pl.		
	m.	*f.*	*n.*	*m.*	*f.*	*n.*
nom.	quī	quae	quod	quī	quae	quae
acc.	quem	quam	quod	quōs	quās	quae
gen.	←——— cúius ———→			quṓrum	quā́rum	quṓrum
dat.	←——— cui ———→			←——— quíbus (quīs) ———→		
abl.	quō	quā	quō	←——— quíbus (quīs) ———→		

Notes

1 *quṓcum, quā́cum, quibū́scum* 'with whom/which'.

2 *quī* as an old abl. form is found mostly in the word *quī́cum* 'with whom', where it is m. f. or n. s., and even occasionally pl.

14 Interrogative (indefinite) pronoun/adjective

quis/quī, quae/quis, quid/quod 'who?', 'which?', 'what?'

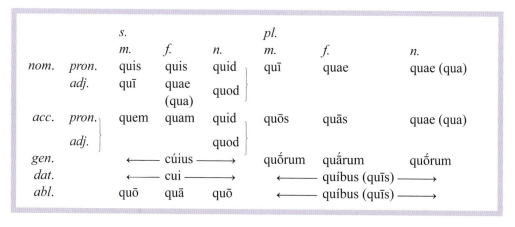

		s.			pl.		
		m.	*f.*	*n.*	*m.*	*f.*	*n.*
nom.	*pron.*	quis	quis	quid	quī	quae	quae (qua)
	adj.	quī	quae (qua)	quod			
acc.	*pron.*	quem	quam	quid	quōs	quās	quae (qua)
	adj.			quod			
gen.		←——— cúius ———→			quṓrum	quā́rum	quṓrum
dat.		←——— cui ———→			←——— quíbus (quīs) ———→		
abl.		quō	quā	quō	←——— quíbus (quīs) ———→		

Notes

1   After *sī*, *nē*, *nísi*, *num*, the meaning of *quis* (indefinite) is 'any', 'anyone', and nom. s. f. and n. pl. nom./acc. are always *qua*.

2   *quis* is quite often used for *quī* (adj.), e.g. *quis... púer*? 'What boy?' (Horace). Cf. *áliquis* **I5(b)** note 2 below.

3   *quī*, an old ablative form, as an interrogative means 'how?', e.g. *quī fit, Maecḗnas?* 'How does it come about, Maecenas?' (Horace).

I5 Compound pronouns

(a)   *quídam quaédam quóddam* 'a', 'a certain'

	s.		
	m.	*f.*	*n.*
nom.	quídam	quáedam	quóddam (quíddam)
acc.	quéndam	quándam	quóddam (quíddam)
gen.	←—— cuiúsdam ——→		
dat.	←—— cúidam ——→		
abl.	quódam	quádam	quódam

	pl.		
	m.	*f.*	*n.*
nom.	quídam	quaédam	quaédam
acc.	quósdam	quásdam	quaédam
gen.	quōrúndam	quārúndam	quōrúndam
dat.	←—— quíbusdam ——→		
abl.	←—— quíbusdam ——→		

(b)   *áliquis áliqua áliquid* 'someone' and *áliquī áliqua áliquod* 'some'

	áliquis 'someone'			*áliquī* 'some' (adj.)		
	m.	*f.*	*n.*	*m.*	*f.*	*n.*
nom.	áliquis	áliqua	áliquid	áliquī	áliqua	áliquod
acc.	áliquem	áliquam	áliquid	áliquam	áliquam	áliquod
gen.	←— alicúius —→			←— alicúius —→		
dat.	←— álicui —→			←— álicui —→		
abl.	áliquō	áliquā	áliquō	áliquō	áliquā	áliquō

Notes

1 The pl. is the same as for *ali-* + *qui* (**I4** above), except that the n. pl. is *áliqua.*

2 *áliquis* is quite often used for *áliquī* (adj.), e.g. *num ígitur <u>áliquis dólor</u> in córpore est* 'Surely there isn't <u>any pain</u> in your body?' (Cicero). Cf. *quis*, **I4** note 2.

(c)   **Other compound pronouns and pronoun-adjectives**

(i) *quísque quaéque quódque* 'everyone', 'everything', 'each and every'. *quísque* is very often used to mean 'every(one)', e.g. *súa <u>cuíque</u> natiōnī relígiō est, nóstra nōbīs* '<u>every</u> nation has its own religion, and we have ours' (Cicero). Its placement immediately after a form of *súus* is very common. Note also superlative + *quísque*, e.g. *óptimus quísque* 'all the best men' and *quótus quísque* 'how few!'

(ii) *quísquam quídquam/quícquam* 'anyone', 'anything'. *quísquam* is normally found in negative contexts (or in questions where a negative is implied, e.g. *quid <u>quísquam</u> suspicārī áliud pótest?* 'What else can <u>anyone</u> suspect?' (Cicero)).

(iii) *quísquis* 'whoever'; *quídquid* or *quícquid* 'whatever'; *quīcúmque quaecúmque quodcúmque* 'whoever', 'whatever'. *quísquis* and *quīcúmque* are used to introduce relative clauses; e.g. *férreus est, heu, heu, <u>quísquis</u> in úrbe mánet* 'anyone who stays in Rome (oh dear, oh dear) is made of iron' (Tibullus); *dī tíbi dent <u>quaecúmque</u> óptēs* 'may the gods give you <u>whatever</u> (things) you desire' (Plautus).

(iv) *écquis* 'anyone?', *écquid* 'anything?', adj. *écquī écqua/écquae écquod* 'any?' *écquis* introduces questions and means 'Is there anyone (who)?', e.g. *heus, <u>écquis</u> hīc est?* 'Hey, is there <u>anyone</u> here?' (Plautus).

Note

Compounds of *quis* decline like *quis* (**I4** above). Compounds of *quī* decline like *quī* (**I3** above). But not all forms are found in all of these pronouns/adjectives.

16 Special pronoun-adjectives

(a)   *álius ália áliud* 'other', 'another'

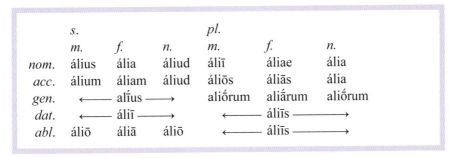

	s.			pl.		
	m.	*f.*	*n.*	*m.*	*f.*	*n.*
nom.	álius	ália	áliud	áliī	áliae	ália
acc.	álium	áliam	áliud	áliōs	áliās	ália
gen.	←——— alíus ———→			aliṓrum	aliā́rum	aliṓrum
dat.	←——— álī ———→			←——— álīs ———→		
abl.	áliō	áliā	áliō	←——— álīs ———→		

Note

Genitive and dative s. are not common, and occasionally the 2nd decl. forms (gen. s. m./n. *álī* f. *áliae*; dat. s. m. *áliō* f. *áliae*) are found. *alteríus* (gen. s. of *álter*) is also used for gen. s.

(b)   *núll-us a um* 'no (one)', 'not any', 'no man'

	s.			pl.		
	m.	*f.*	*n.*	*m.*	*f.*	*n.*
nom.	núllus	núlla	núllum	núllī	núllae	núlla
acc.	núllum	núllam	núllum	núllōs	núllās	núlla
gen.	←——— nūllíus ———→			nūllṓrum	nūllā́rum	nūllṓrum
dat.	←——— núllī ———→			←——— núllīs ———→		
abl.	núllō	núllā	núllō	←——— núllīs ———→		

(c)   *álter álter-a álter-um* 'one (of two)', 'the one ... the other'

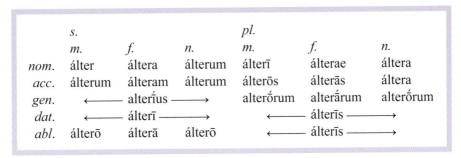

	s.			pl.		
	m.	*f.*	*n.*	*m.*	*f.*	*n.*
nom.	álter	áltera	álterum	álterī	álterae	áltera
acc.	álterum	álteram	álterum	álterōs	álterās	áltera
gen.	←——— alteríus ———→			alterṓrum	alterā́rum	alterṓrum
dat.	←——— álterī ———→			←——— álterīs ———→		
abl.	álterō	álterā	álterō	←——— álterīs ———→		

(d) *utérque útraque utrúmque* 'both', 'each (of two)'

	s.			pl.		
	m.	*f.*	*n.*	*m.*	*f.*	*n.*
nom.	utérque	útraque	utrúmque	utríque	utraéque	útraque
acc.	utrúmque	utrámque	utrúmque	utrósque	utrásque	útraque
gen.	←——— utríúsque ———→			utrōrúmque	utrārúmque	utrōrúmque
dat.	←——— utríque ———→			←——— utrísque ———→		
abl.	utróque	útráque	utróque	←——— utrísque ———→		

Note

The most characteristic feature of the declension of all the pronouns/adjectives above (**I2–I6**) is the gen. s. in -*íus* and dat. s. in -*ī* alongside mainly second declension endings. The following special pronoun-adjectives also decline like *lóng-us a um* elsewhere, but have gen. s. in -*íus* and dat. s. in -*ī*: *ún-us a um* 'one', *sól-us a um* 'alone', *tốt-us a um* 'the whole', *úll-us a um* 'any', *úter útr-a um* 'which of two?', 'whichever of two', *neúter neútr-a um* 'neither'.

I7 Numerals

Cardinal						Ordinal[1]	
			m.	*f.*	*n.*		
1	I		únus	úna	únum[2]	*1st*	prímus (príor)
2	II	*nom.*	dúo	dúae	dúo	*2nd*	secúndus (álter)
		acc.	dúōs/dúo	dúās	dúo		
		gen.	duốrum	duárum	duốrum		
		dat./ abl.	duốbus	duábus	duốbus		
			m./f.	*n.*			
3	III	*nom.*	trēs	tría		*3rd*	tértius
		acc.	trēs (trīs)	tría			
		gen.	← tríum →				
		dat.	← tríbus →				
		abl.	← tríbus →				
4	IV/IIII		quáttuor			*4th*	quártus
5	V		quínque			*5th*	quíntus
6	VI		sex			*6th*	séxtus
7	VII		séptem			*7th*	séptimus
8	VIII		óctō			*8th*	octáuus
9	IX/VIIII		nóuem			*9th*	nốnus

10	X	décem	10th	décimus
11	XI	úndecim	11th	ūndécimus
12	XII	duódecim	12th	duodécimus
13	XIII	trḗdecim	13th	tértius décimus
14	XIV	quattuórdecim	14th	quā́rtus décimus
15	XV	quíndecim	15th	quíntus décimus
16	XVI	sḗdecim	16th	séxtus décimus
17	XVII	septéndecim	17th	séptimus décimus
18	XVIII	duodēuīgíntī	18th	duodēuīcénsimus
19	XIX	ūndēuīgíntī	19th	ūndēuīcénsimus
20	XX	uīgíntī	20th	uīcénsimus
30	XXX	trīgíntā	30th	trīcénsimus
40	XL	quādrāgíntā	40th	quādrāgénsimus
50	L	quīnquāgíntā	50th	quīnquāgénsimus
60	LX	sexāgíntā	60th	sexāgénsimus
70	LXX	septuāgíntā	70th	septuāgénsimus
80	LXXX	octōgíntā	80th	octōgénsimus
90	XC	nōnāgíntā	90th	nōnāgénsimus
100	C	céntum	100th	centénsimus
200	CC	ducént-ī ae a (*like pl. of lóng-us*)	200th	ducenténsimus
300	CCC	trecént-ī ae a	300th	trēcenténsimus
400	CD	quadringént-ī ae e	400th	quadringenténsimus
500	D	quīngént-ī ae a	500th	quīngenténsimus
1,000	M	mílle (*indecl. adj.*) *pl.* mília *gen.* mílium *dat./abl.* mílibus (*see note 1*)	1,000th	mīllénsimus

1 The ordinal numerals all decline like *lóng-us a um*.
2 *únus* declines like *tótus*, i.e. with gen. s. ūnī́us, dat. s. únī; in the pl. únī, únae, úna, it declines like the pl. of *lóngus* (**I6(d)** note).

Notes

1 Normally, *mílle* is used as an indeclinable adjective and *mília* as a noun (i.e. with the noun it is describing in the gen. pl.), e.g.

> *mílle mílitēs* = one thousand soldiers
>
> *dúo mília mílitum* = two thousand(s) (of) soldiers
>
> *tría mília mílitum* = three thousand(s) (of) soldiers etc.

2 Latin has three other sets of numerals. One (the distributives) answers the question 'how many each?', e.g. *síngul-ī ae a* 'one each', then *-nī*, e.g. *bín-ī ae a* 'two each' (these are adjectives). A second (the numeral adverbs) answers the question 'how many times?', e.g. *sémel* 'once', *bis* 'twice', *ter* 'three times', *quáter*, then *-iēns*, e.g. *míliēns* 'a thousand times'. The third (multiplicative adjectives) answers the question 'of how many parts?', 'how many-fold?', e.g. *tríplex tríplic-is* 'threefold'.

3 The ending *-énsimus* was, after the Augustan period, often written *-ésimus*.

J–K Adjectives, adverbs and prepositions

Introduction

(a) Adjectives agree with the word they describe in *gender* (m., f. or n.), *case* (nom., acc., gen., dat., abl.) and *number* (s. or pl.). Thus, an adjective which is genitive plural masculine can agree only with a noun which is genitive plural masculine.

(b) Any adjective may function as a noun, its meaning then depending on its gender, m. 'man', f. 'woman', n. 'thing'. So, e.g.

> *bónī* (nom. pl. m.) 'good *men*'
>
> *bónae* (nom. pl. f.) 'good *women*'
>
> *bóna* (nom. pl. n.) 'good *things*', 'goods'
>
> *fugiéntēs* (nom. pl. m. or f.) '*people* as they are fleeing'
>
> *rogántī* (dat. s. m. or f.) 'to the *person* asking'
>
> *mors málum est* 'death is a bad *thing*'

Some adjectives are especially common used as nouns or, in the case of e.g. *hic, ílle, is* (etc.), pronouns. Note the common use of *uétus* 'old' for 'old man', *paúper* 'poor' for 'poor man', *díues* 'rich' for 'rich man'.

(c) Occasionally, a Latin adjective, esp. one denoting rank ordering or relative quantity (e.g. *prímus, sólus, tótus*) or attitude of mind or manner (e.g. *laétus* 'happy', *inuítus* 'unwilling'), is best translated in English as an adverb (e.g. *uir laétus ábiit* 'the man went away happily'). Adjectives denoting position (e.g. *súmmus, médius, próximus*) often call for a noun in English (e.g. *súmmō mónte* 'at the top of the mountain').

J1 Adjectives: first/second declension

(a) *lóng-us a um 'long'*

	s.			pl.		
	m.	*f.*	*n.*	*m.*	*f.*	*n.*
nom.	lóngus	lónga	lóngum	lóngī	lóngae	lónga
voc.	lónge	lóngá	lóngum	lóngī	lóngae	lónge
acc.	lóngum	lóngam	lóngum	lóngōs	lóngās	lónga
gen.	lóngī	lóngae	lóngī	longṓrum	longā́rum	longṓrum
dat.	lóngō	lóngae	lóngō	⟵ lóngīs ⟶		
abl.	lóngō	lóngā	lóngō	⟵ lóngīs ⟶		

(b) *púlcher púlchr-a um 'beautiful', 'handsome'*

	s.			pl.		
	m.	*f.*	*n.*	*m.*	*f.*	*n.*
nom./voc	púlcher	púlchra	púlchrum	púlchrī	púlchrae	púlchra
acc.	púlchrum	púlchram	púlchrum	púlchrōs	púlchrās	púlchra
gen.	púlchrī	púlchrae	púlchrī	pulchrṓrum	pulchrā́rum	pulchrṓrum
dat.	púlchrō	púlchrae	púlchrō	⟵ púlchrīs ⟶		
abl.	púlchrō	púlchrā	púlchrō	⟵ púlchrīs ⟶		

(c) *míser míser-a míser-um 'unhappy'*

	s.			pl.		
	m.	*f.*	*n.*	*m.*	*f.*	*n.*
nom./voc	míser	mísera	míserum	míserī	míserae	mísera
acc.	míserum	míseram	míserum	míserōs	míserās	mísera
gen.	miserī	míserae	miserī	miserṓrum	miserā́rum	miserṓrum
dat.	míserō	míserae	míserō	⟵ míserīs ⟶		
abl.	míserō	míserā	míserō	⟵ míserīs ⟶		

Note

Nearly all adjectives in *-er a um* are type (b), i.e. without the *-e-* in declension. Three other important examples of type (c) are *ásper* 'rough', *līber* 'free', *prósper* 'prosperous'; also all compound adjectives in *-fer* and *-ger* 'bearing X'.

J2 Adjectives: third declension

(a)   *ómnis ómne* 'all', 'every'

	s. m./f.	n.	pl. m./f.	n.
nom.	ómnis	ómne	ómnēs	ómnia
acc.	ómnem	ómne	ómnīs (ómnēs)	ómnia
gen.	← ómnis →		← ómnium →	
dat.	← ómnī →		← ómnibus →	
abl.	← ómnī →		← ómnibus →	

(b)   *ingēns ingēns (ingént-)* 'huge'

	s. m./f.	n.	pl. m./f.	n.
nom.	íngēns	íngēns	ingéntēs	ingéntia
acc.	ingéntem	íngēns	ingéntīs (ingéntēs)	ingéntia
gen.	← ingéntis →		← ingéntium →	
dat.	← ingéntī →		← ingéntibus →	
abl.	← ingéntī →		← ingéntibus →	

(c)   *céler céler-is céler-e* 'swift', 'fast'

	s. m.	f.	n.	pl. m./f.	n.
nom.	céler	céleris	célere	célerēs	celéria
acc.	célerem	célerem	célere	célerīs (célerēs)	celéria
gen.	← céleris →		← celérium →	
dat.	← célerī →		← celéribus →	
abl.	← célerī →		← celéribus →	

(d)   *ácer ácris ácre* 'keen', 'sharp'

	s. m.	f.	n.	pl. m./f.	n.
nom.	ácer	ácris	ácre	ácrēs	ácria
acc.	ácrem	ácrem	ácre	ácrīs (ácrēs)	ácria
gen.	← ácris →		← ácrium →	
dat.	← ácrī →		← ácribus →	
abl.	← ácrī →		← ácribus →	

Note

All these are *i*-stems.

(e) **Consonant-stem adjectives: *dīues* and *paúper***

	s.		*pl.*	
	m/f.	*n.*	*m/f.*	*n.*
nom.	dīues (dīs)	dīues (dīte)	dīuitēs (dītēs)	dīuita (dītia)
acc.	dīuitem (dītem)	dīues (dīte)	dīuites (dītēs)	dīuita (dītia)
gen.	← dīuitis (dītis) →		← dīuitum (dītium) →	
dat.	← dīuite (dītī) →		← dīuítibus (dītibus) →	
abl.	← dīuitī (dītī) →		← dīuítibus (dītibus) →	

	s.		*pl.*	
	m/f.	*n.*	*m/f.*	*n.*
nom.	paúper	paúper	paúperēs	paúpera
acc.	paúperem	paúper	paúperēs	paúpera
gen.	← paúperis →		← paúperum →	
dat.	← paúperī →		← paupéribus →	
abl.	← paúpere →		← paupéribus →	

Notes

1 *dīues* has also a set of contracted *i*-stem forms (in brackets), which are commonly used. Both *dīues* and *paúper* are often used as nouns (see **47** and **J Intro.(b)** above).

2 Other important consonant-stem adjectives include: *caélebs caélib-is* 'unmarried', *cómpos cómpot-is* 'possessing', *ínops ínop-is* 'poor' (abl. s. -*ī*), *mémor mémor-is* 'mindful' (abl. s. -*ī*), *párticeps partícip-is* 'sharing', *sóspes sóspit-is* 'safe', *supérstes supérstit-is* 'surviving', *uétus uéter-is* 'old'.

J3 Comparative and superlative adjectives

These are formed as follows:

> Comparatives ('more —', 'rather —', 'quite —'): gen. s. stem + -*ior* (neuter -*ius*)

> Superlatives ('very —', '—est', 'most —', 'extremely —'): gen. s. stem + -*íssimus*, or nom. s. + -*rimus* (in the case of adjectives which end in -*er* in the nominative, e.g. *púlcher* → (comparative) *púlchrior* → (superlative) *pulchérrimus*)

Note also the irregular superlative, gen. s. stem + -*limus*, of six adjectives in -*ilis*, viz. *fácilis* 'easy', *diffícilis* 'difficult', *símilis* 'similar', *dissímilis* 'dissimilar', *grácilis* 'slender', *húmilis* 'lowly': e.g. *facíl-limus*.

The declension of comparative and superlative forms is as follows:

(a)   **Comparative adjectives: *lóngior lóngius* 'longer'**

	s.		pl.	
	m./f.	*n.*	*m./f.*	*n.*
nom.	lóngior	lóngius	longiṓrēs	longiṓra
acc.	longiṓrem	lóngius	longiṓrēs	longiṓra
gen.	← longiṓris →		← longiṓrum →	
dat.	← longiṓrī →		← longiṓribus →	
abl.	← longiṓre →		← longiṓribus →	

Note

These adjectives are *consonant stems* (cf. *dĩues*, *paúper*, **J2(e)** above).

(b)   **Superlative adjectives: *longíssimus a um* 'longest' (sometimes -*íssumus*)**

	s.		
	m.	*f.*	*n.*
nom.	longíssimus	longíssima	longíssimum
acc.	longíssimum	longíssimam	longíssimum
gen.	longíssimī	longĩssimae	longíssimī
dat.	longíssimō	longíssimae	longíssimō
abl.	longíssimō	longíssimā	longíssimō

	pl.		
	m.	*f.*	*n.*
nom.	longíssimī	longíssimae	longíssima
acc.	longíssimōs	longíssimās	longíssima
gen.	longissimṓrum	longissimā́rum	longissimṓrum
dat.	← longíssimīs →		
abl.	← longíssimīs →		

(c) Irregular comparatives and superlatives: *bónus, málus, múltus, mágnus, páruus*

bón-us a um	mélior (meliṓr-is)	óptim-us a um	'good', 'better', 'best' (*cf. ameliorate, optimise*)
mál-us a um	pḗior (pēiṓr-is)	péssim-us a um	'bad', 'worse', 'worst' (*cf. pejorative, pessimist*)
múlt-us a um	plūs (plŭ́r-is)	plŭ́rim-us a um	'much', 'more', 'most' (*cf. plus* (+))
mágn-us a um	mā́ior (māiṓr-is)	máxim-us a um	'big', 'bigger', 'biggest' (*cf. major, maximise*)
páru-us a um	mínor (minṓr-is)	minim-us a um	'small/few', 'smaller/fewer/ less', 'smallest/fewest/least' (*cf. minor, minimise*)

Note

These all decline quite regularly (see (a) *lóngior* and (b) *longíssimus* above) except *plūs*:

	s. (plūs *here* = *noun*)	pl. m./f.	n.
nom.	plūs	plŭ́rēs	plŭ́ra
acc.	plūs	plŭ́rīs (plŭ́rēs)	plŭ́ra
gen.	plŭ́ris	← plŭ́rium →	
dat.	–	← plŭ́ribus →	
abl.	plŭ́re	← plŭ́ribus →	

Note

plūs functions either as the comparative of the adverb *múltum* 'much', or as a neuter noun taking its complement in the gen. (e.g. *plūs uī́nī* 'more wine'), while the plural *plŭ́rēs, plŭ́ra* is the comparative of the plural adj. *múlt-ī ae a* (the adj. *múltus* 'much' in the s. has no true comparative).

J4 Adverbs

(a) Regular and irregular positive adverbs

1 Regular adverbs

Regular adverbs in English are made by adding '-ly' to the adjective (e.g. slow-ly, quick-ly, passionate-ly). In Latin, adverbs (which, unlike adjectives, never change in form) are also regularly formed from adjectives as follows:

Adverbs based on 1st/2nd declension adjectives: add *-ē* to the stem, e.g. *stúltus → stúltē* 'foolishly'; *míser → miserē* 'unhappily'; *púlcher → púlchrē* 'beautifully'. A few end in *-ō*, e.g. *crébrō* 'frequently', *contínuō* 'immediately', *méritō* 'deservedly', *cértō* 'for a fact', *tū́tō* 'safely', and a very few are made with the third declension ending *-iter*, e.g. *hūmā́nus → hūmā́niter* 'gently', *álius → áliter* 'otherwise'.

Adverbs based on 3rd declension adjectives: add *-iter* to the stem, e.g. *céler → celériter* 'swiftly', *fórtis → fórtiter* 'bravely'; *-iter* appears as *-ter* in *audácter* 'boldly' ← *aúdāx* and after stems in *-(n)t-*, e.g. *díligénter* ← *díligēns* 'careful'. Note the important exception *fácile* 'easily'.

2   **Irregular adverbs**

bónus → béne 'well'

páruus → paúlum '(a) little', 'slightly'

múltus → múltum 'much'

mágnus → magnópere 'greatly'

Note

The meaning of *lóngē* (regularly formed from *lóngus* 'long') is 'far'.

(b)   **Regular comparative and superlative adverbs 'more −ly' 'most −ly'**

Comparative and superlative adverbs are formed from the comparative and superlative adjectives.

	'foolishly'	*'more foolishly'*	*'most foolishly'*
Adjective	stúlt-us	stúlt-<u>ior</u>	stultíssim-<u>us</u>
Adverb	stúlt-ē	stúlt-<u>ius</u>	stultíssim-<u>ē</u>
	'quickly'	*'more quickly'*	*'most quickly'*
Adjective	céler	celér-<u>ior</u>	celérrim-<u>us</u>
Adverb	celér-iter	celér-<u>ius</u>	celérrim-<u>ē</u>

Note

The comparative adverb has the same form as the neuter of the comparative adjective.

(c)   **Irregular comparative and superlative adverbs**

Most of these are only irregular in so far as the corresponding adjective has irregular comparative and superlative forms. If you already know the adjective forms, most of these adverbs are formed quite regularly from the adjective.

béne	'well'	mélius	'better'	óptimē	'best'
mále	'badly'	pĕius	'worse'	péssimē	'worst'; 'very badly'
paúlum	'a little'	mínus	'less'	mínimē	'very little'; 'no'
múltum	'much'	plūs	'more'	plūrimum	'most'; 'a lot',
magnópere	'greatly'	mágis	'more'	máximē	'very much'; 'most'; 'yes'

Note

Check *mágis* (contrast the n. adj. *mãius*) and *plūs* (probably from earlier **plou-is*, with the same ending as *mágis*); on *plūs*, cf. **J3(c)** note above.

J5 'Comparative' constructions

(a)   **Comparative**

1   *quam* means 'than' when it is used with a comparative, e.g. *tū sắnior es quam égo* 'you are saner than I'. Cf. *mắlo pắcem quam béllum* 'I prefer peace to war' (*mắlō = mágis uólō* 'I want X more than Y'). Observe that the two things compared are in the same case, e.g. *mãiŏrem hábeō líbrum quam túum* (*líbrum*) 'I have a larger book than yours.'

2   But Latin can also compare two items by dropping *quam* and putting the item compared in the ablative, e.g.

> *tū mē sắnior es* 'you are saner <u>than I</u>'
>
> *quis sapiéntior <u>sapiénte</u> est*? 'who is wiser <u>than the wise</u>?'

3   Note the use of the comparative + *quam quī* + subjunctive in the idiom 'too — to do something', e.g.

> *sapiéntior est quam quī hoc fáciat* '(lit.) he is wiser than one who would do that', i.e. 'he is too wise to do that'

4   Note the correlative use of the ablative of the measure of difference (see **L(f)3(iv)**) with comparative adjectives or adverbs in sentences meaning 'the more … the more …', e.g.

> *quō própius éa conténtiō accĕdit … éō clắrius id perīculum appắret* '<u>the closer</u> that fight comes, <u>the more clearly</u> that danger appears' (Caelius)
>
> *tántō bréuius ómne quántō fēlīcius témpus* '<u>the happier</u> a period (is), <u>the shorter</u> it (is)' (or 'seems to be') (Pliny) (lit. '<u>by so much shorter</u> every (time is), <u>by how much the happier</u> the time (is)', i.e. 'time flies when you're having fun').

(b)   **Superlative**

quam with the superlative means 'as — as possible', e.g.

> *cḗnam quam máximam hábeō* 'I have the largest dinner possible'

This usage applies equally to adverbs, e.g.

> *quam celérrimē* 'as fast as possible'

(c)   **Other 'comparative' constructions**

1   *átque/ac*

átque/ac is used after adjectives or adverbs which express 'likeness' or 'unlikeness', such as *ídem* 'the same', *álius* 'different', 'other', *áliter* 'differently', *cóntrā* 'opposite', 'contrary', *par* 'equal', *páriter* 'equally', *perínde* 'in like manner', *símilis* 'like', 'similar'. E.g.

> *iussḗrunt simulắcrum Ióuis, <u>cóntrā átque ánteā fúerat</u>, ad oriéntem conuértere* 'they ordered (them) to turn the statue of Jupiter towards the East, <u>contrary to what it had been before</u>' (Cicero).

> *<u>perínde</u> ēgit <u>ac dīxit</u>* 'He acted <u>just as he said</u>'.

2   **Correlatives**

ut meaning 'as' acts as a 'correlative' to *sīc* or *íta* 'thus', e.g. *ut tū ímperās, sīc / íta égo fáciō* 'as you order, so I do'. In the same way, *tam* 'so' is answered by *quam* 'as', e.g.

> *tam beắtus érat ílle quam míser égo* 'he was as (lit. so) happy as I unhappy'

tot 'so many' is answered by *quot* 'as many', e.g.

> *tot uírī sunt quot fḗminae* 'so many men there are as many (as) (there are) women', 'there are as many men as women'

Cf. *tántus* 'so great'… *quántus* 'as great', 'as'; *tắlis* 'of such a sort'… *quắlis* 'of which sort', 'as', e.g.

> *tánta sapiéntia éī ínest quánta uīs* 'there is so great wisdom in him as great (as there is) force', 'he has as much brain as brawn'

> *tắlem uirtū́tem praebḗbat quắlem Horắtius* 'he showed bravery of such a sort as the sort (which) Horatius (showed)'

See **J5(a)4** above for other correlative usages.

3   **Unreal comparisons**

quási, uélut, támquam mean 'as if', 'as though' and (with or without *sī* added) take a *subjunctive* where the comparison is unreal or hypothetical. Constructions under **J5(c)1** add *sī*. E.g.

íta sē gérit quási stúltus sit 'he is behaving as though he were a fool' (but he is not).

perínde ágit ac sī hóstis sit 'he acts just as though he were an enemy' (but he is not).

Note

támquam, quási, uélut, sícut and *ut* are all used with nouns to express 'like', 'as it were', e.g. *mónte dēcúrrēns uélut ámnis* '*like a river* as it runs down from the mountain' (Horace – speaking of Pindar).

K List of prepositions

This list is in alphabetical order and contains the most important prepositions (some of which have not been met in the course).

ā, ab or *abs* (+ abl.) away from; by; on the side of

ábsque (+ abl.) = *sine*

ad (+ acc.) towards; at, near; for the purpose of; note *úsque ad* right up to

aduérsum/aduérsus (+ acc.) opposite to; against

ánte (+ acc.) before, in front of

ápud (+ acc.) at the house of, in the hands of, in the works of; among

círcum/círcā/círciter (+ acc.) around, about

cis/cítrā (+ acc.) this side of

clam (+ acc./abl.) unknown to

cóntrā (+ acc.) against

córam (+ abl.) in the presence of

cum (+ abl.) with

dē (+ abl.) about, concerning; from; down from

ē, ex (+ abl.) out of, from; in accordance with; after

érgā (+ acc.) towards

éxtrā (+ acc.) outside

in (+ acc.) into, onto; against; (+ abl.) in, on

ínfrā (+ acc.) below

ínter (+ acc.) among; between

íntrā (+ acc.) within

iúxtā (+ acc.) close to, near

ob (+ acc.) on account of, because of; before, so as to obstruct

pénes (+ acc.) with, in the possession of

per (+ acc.) through, by; in the name of, by the aid of

post (+ acc.) behind, after

prae (+ abl.) before; in comparison with; for, as a result of

praéter (+ acc.) past; beyond; except

prō (+ abl.) for, in return for; on behalf of; in front of; instead of; in accordance with

própe (+ acc.) near

própter (+ acc.) on account of

secúndum (+ acc.) behind; along; after; according to

síne (+ abl.) without

sub, súbter (+ acc.) under, beneath; just after, just before; (+ abl.) beneath, under; at

súper (+ acc.) over, above; beyond;
  (+ abl.) over, above; about,
  concerning
súprā (+ acc.) above
ténus (+ gen./abl.) as far as (placed
  after the word it governs)

trāns (+ acc.) across
uérsus, *uérsum* (+ acc.) towards, in
  the direction of (placed *after* the
  word it governs)
últrā (+ acc.) beyond
úsque (+ acc.) all the way to

Note also the abl. nouns *caúsā* and *grătiā* (+ gen.), placed *after* the word they govern, meaning 'for the sake of, 'for the purpose of'.

When prepositions are followed by the noun they govern, their accent is determined by treating the two words as one, e.g. *ápud* (natural accent) and *apúd mē* (as though it were *apudmē*).

L–V Constructions

Introduction

(a)   Simple sentences

Simple sentences may be classified into four categories:

1   *Statements (including exclamations)*: e.g. *Caésar ábit* 'Caesar leaves', *quam trístis est* 'how sad he is!'

'Potential' statements ('would', 'should', 'could') are expressed by the subjunctive, e.g. *uélim* 'I should wish', *dícat/díxerit áliquis* 'someone would/may say', as are 'generalising' statements, e.g. *haud inuéniās* 'you (i.e. one) would not find', *créderēs* 'you would have believed'.

2   *Questions*: e.g. *abísne?* 'are you leaving?' (*-ne* turns a statement into a question), *quis ábit* 'who is leaving?'

Double questions are asked with *útrum … an*, e.g. *útrum ábīs an mánēs?* 'are you going or staying?' *útrum* is often omitted (in direct and indirect speech), e.g. *ábīs an mánēs? ánnōn* means 'or not' in direct speech; in indirect speech, 'or not' is *nécne*.

an is very flexible. It can introduce a plain question (like *-ne*), or mean 'whether' or 'or'. *num* means 'surely not?', inviting the answer 'no' (*num* means 'if, whether' in indirect questions, e.g. *rógō num ábeās* 'I ask whether you depart'); *nónne* means 'surely?', inviting the answer 'yes'; *écquis* means 'anyone' in a question, e.g. *écquis ábit?* 'is anyone leaving?' (see above **I5(c) (iv)** and note).

'Deliberative' questions take the form 'what am I to', 'should I —?' and are expressed by the subjunctive, e.g. *quid fáciam* 'what am I to do?' *quid fácerem* 'what was I to do?'

3   *Commands*: e.g. *ábī!* 'leave!'; *nólī abíre* 'don't leave!'

nē + perfect subjunctive also expresses prohibitions, e.g. *nē trānsíerīs* 'do not cross'; *nē* + present subjunctive is used in general prohibitions, e.g. *nē pétās* 'you (i.e. one) should not seek'; *nē* + imperative is common in poetry, e.g. *nē fúgite hospítium* 'do not shun our hospitality' (Virgil).

Jussives ('let us', 'let him', 'let them') are expressed by the subjunctive (present), e.g. *abeámus* 'let us leave', *fíat* 'let there be'.

'Polite' subjunctives can be used to express 'please', e.g. *ábeās* 'kindly leave' (poetic), or general precepts, e.g. *sápiās* 'you (i.e. one) should be wise'. Often commands are made more polite by the use of *fac, uídē* 'see to it (that)', *cáuē* 'take care (not to)', *uélim* 'I would like (X to)' with subjunctive, e.g. *fac míhi scríbās* 'make sure you write to me'.

4 *Wishes*: e.g. *uólō abíre* 'I want to leave'. The subjunctive is also used to express wishes, e.g. *uáleant cíuēs* 'may the citizens flourish'. Sometimes *útinam* (negative *útinam nē*) precedes the wish, e.g. *útinam nē hoc scrīpsíssēs* 'would you had not written this'.

uólō or *uélim* + subjunctive sometimes combine, e.g. *uólō tū hoc fácias* 'I wish (that) you would do this'.

Note

In general, the tenses are used as in subjunctive conditionals (see **S2(c)**), present referring to a wish for the future, imperfect to a wish for the present, pluperfect to a wish for the past.

(b) **Agreement**

1 A verb agrees with its subject in number and person, e.g.

   Caésar ádest

ádest is third person, singular, because *Caésar* (subject) is third person, singular.

2 An adjective agrees with the word it describes in number, gender and case, e.g.

   fḗminam trístem uídeō 'I see the unhappy woman'

fḗminam is accusative, singular, feminine, so *trístem* is accusative, singular, feminine (see **J Intro.**).

Notes

1 The verb 'to be' is often omitted in sentences, e.g. *níhil bónum nísi quod honéstum* 'nothing [is] good except what is honourable'.

2 A singular subject will sometimes take a plural verb, if the subject implies 'a number of people', e.g. *pars mílitum cáptī sunt* 'part of the soldiers was captured', 'some soldiers were captured'. Likewise, a list of subjects can be taken all together and the verb be singular, or the verb be singular because the last in the list is singular. Where there are both masculine and feminine subjects described by one adjective, the adjective will tend to agree with the masculine.

3 More information may be added about a noun or pronoun by further nouns or pronouns in the same case, e.g. *thēsáurus Dēmaénetī, áuī Eucliṓnis* 'the treasure of Demaenetus, grandfather of Euclio'. *áuī* is genitive, because it refers to *Dēmaénetī*: it is said to be 'in apposition' to *Dēmaénetī*.

(c) **Sequence of tenses**

Primary sequence means that the main verb is present, future, future perfect, or perfect with 'have' (e.g. 'I have loved', not 'I loved'). In these cases, subjunctives used in subordinate clauses are restricted to the present, perfect and future participle + *sim*.

Secondary or *historic sequence* means that the main verb is imperfect, perfect without 'have' (e.g. 'I loved') or pluperfect. In these cases, subjunctives used in subordinate clauses are restricted to imperfect, pluperfect and future participle + *éssem*.

L The cases

(a)   Nominative

The nominative case is used for:

1   The *subject* of a sentence or clause, e.g. *Eúcliō aúlam pórtat* 'Euclio carries the pot' (note that the subject of an indirect statement goes into the accusative – see **R1**).

2   The *complement*, especially with the verbs 'to be', 'to become' and the like, e.g. *Eúcliō sénex est* 'Euclio is an old man'; *Caésar cónsul fit* 'Caesar becomes consul'.

(b)   Vocative

The vocative case is used to indicate *the person or thing addressed*, e.g. *(ō) Eúcliō, cūr aúlam pórtās?* 'Euclio, why are you carrying a pot?'; *et tū, Brūte?* 'you too, Brutus?'

(c)   Accusative

The accusative case limits or defines. It is used in a number of ways.

1   For the *direct object* of a verb, e.g. *Eúcliō aúlam pórtat* 'Euclio carries a pot'.

Some verbs take a double accusative. Some examples are:

   dóceō 'I teach X (acc.) Y (acc.)'

   rógō 'I ask X (acc.) for Y (acc.)'; cf. *ōrō* 'I beg X (acc.) for Y (acc.)'

   cḗlō 'I hide X (acc.) from Y (acc.)'

E.g. *Eúcliō Lycṓnidem prūdéntiam dócet* 'Euclio teaches Lyconides wisdom'; *mē cōnsília cḗlat* 'he hides his plans from me'.

The 'cognate' accusative expresses the same idea as the verb, e.g. *uíam it* 'he travels on a road'; *lū́dum lū́dit* 'he plays a game'.

2   To express *motion towards*, often with *ad* or *in*, e.g.

   Eúcliō ad aédīs uénit 'Euclio comes to the house'

   Rṓmam éunt 'they go to Rome'

3   To express *time throughout which*, e.g.

   trēs díēs 'for three days'

4   To express *extent of space and its measurement*, e.g.

   tría mī́lia pássuum ambulāuḗrunt 'they walked for three miles'

   céntum pédēs áltus 'one hundred feet high'

5   To express the idea '*in respect of*', e.g.

   pédēs trémit 'he trembles in (respect of) his feet'

   míhi símilis fáciem 'like me in (respect of) his face'

This is very common in poetry.

6 To express an *adverbial idea* (always in the neuter), e.g.

> *dúlce* 'sweetly'
>
> *quid?* 'to what extent?' or 'why?'
>
> *múltum* 'much'

7 To express *exclamations*, e.g.

> *mē míserum!* 'unhappy me!'

(d) **Genitive**

The genitive often defines or completes the meaning of a noun. Its translation in English involves most often 'of'. Note, however, the various relationships that 'of' can indicate.

1 *Possession*, author or source ('belonging to', 'written by', 'derived from'), e.g.

> <u>*Eucliōnis*</u> *aédēs* 'the house <u>of Euclio</u>'
>
> <u>*Vérgilī*</u> *líber* 'a book <u>of Virgil</u>' (i.e. written by Virgil)

Note that possession of a characteristic is indicated by the genitive in the following idiom:

> <u>*stúltī*</u> *est haec dícere* 'it is <u>(the mark) of a fool</u> to say this'

2 *Part of a whole*, e.g.

> *mágna pars <u>cíuium</u>* 'a great part <u>of the citizens</u>'

Cf. *nímis* 'too much', *sátis* 'enough', *párum* 'too little', *áliquid* 'some', *quid?* 'what (amount)?', *plūs* as a <u>noun</u> 'more': all take the 'partitive' genitive.

3 *Description of content or material* ('consisting of', 'containing'), e.g.

> *pōculum <u>áquae</u>* 'a cup <u>of water</u>'

4 *Description of quality or character* (always an adjective + noun phrase), e.g.

> *uir <u>mágnae sapiéntiae</u>* 'a man <u>of great wisdom</u>'

5 *Value*, e.g.

> *hómo <u>níhilī</u>* 'a fellow <u>of nothing</u>', i.e. 'of no worth'
>
> *fémina <u>plúrimī</u>* 'a woman of <u>very much (worth)</u>'

6 *Subjective and objective genitives.* Consider the ambiguity of *ámor pátris* 'the love of the father' – does it mean 'the love which the father shows' (i.e. 'father loves' – father is subject, so 'of the father' is subjective genitive) or 'the love which is shown to the father' (i.e. someone loves father, father is the object, and so 'of the father' is objective genitive)? The context will tell you, but you must be aware of both possibilities. Note that *méī, túī, súī, nóstrī, uéstrī* (**11(a)**) are *objective* genitives, i.e. *ámor nóstrī* can only mean 'love which is shown to us', not 'love which we feel'.

7 Many *verbs and adjectives* control the genitive case, especially words involving:

> remembering and forgetting (*mémini̯, oblīui̯scor*)
>
> pitying (*míseret*)
>
> losing or lacking (*égeō*) (also with abl.)
>
> filling (*plḗnus*) (also with abl.)

e.g.

> *uerbṓrum oblīui̯scor* 'I forget <u>the words</u>'
>
> *mē míseret <u>túī</u>* 'I feel pity <u>for you</u>'
>
> *cíbī́ égeō* 'I need <u>food</u>'
>
> *plḗnus <u>áquae</u>* 'full <u>of water</u>'

8 *símilis* 'like', 'resembling' takes the genitive or dative, e.g.

> *uir <u>méī</u> símilis* 'a man like <u>me</u>'.

(e) Dative

The dative case is best dealt with in two parts.

1 People in the dative

The common idea here is that the person in the dative will be interested or involved in the action, often to her/his advantage or disadvantage. The action, in other words, has some consequence for the person in the dative. Often 'to', 'for' or 'from' will translate it adequately. In this sense, the dative case is used in the following ways.

(i) To indicate the indirect object of the sentence – that is, the person *to whom* something is given, told, said, promised, shown, e.g.

> *aúlam <u>tíbi</u> dō* 'I give <u>you</u> (= to you) the pot'
>
> *fắbulām <u>míhi</u> nắrrā!* 'tell <u>me</u> (= to me) the story'
>
> *quid <u>Caésarī</u> dīxístī?* 'what did you say <u>to Caesar</u>?'

(ii) To indicate the person *to whose advantage or disadvantage* something is done, e.g.

> *béne est <u>míhi</u>* 'it's fine <u>for me</u>'
>
> *aúrum <u>míhi</u> aúfert* 'he takes the gold <u>from me</u>'

(iii) To indicate possession, with the verb 'to be', e.g.

> *est <u>míhi</u> pecū́nia* 'there is money <u>to me</u>', '<u>I</u> have money'. See also **88.1**.

(iv) (With the perfect passive or gerundive) to indicate the agent, showing *by whom* something is done, e.g.

> *haec míhi dícta sunt* 'these things have been said <u>by me</u>'
>
> *hoc míhi faciéndum est* 'this is to be done <u>by me</u>'
>
> (The dative of agent is most frequent with the gerundive.)

(v) To indicate the person *interested* in the action (only personal pronouns, especially in lively, colloquial discourse), e.g.

> *quid míhi Célsus ágit?* 'what is Celsus doing? <u>It interests me</u> / <u>I should like to know</u> / <u>please tell me</u>' (Horace).

(vi) To indicate the person judging, *in whose eyes* something is the case, e.g.

> *Quíntia fōrmósa est múltīs* 'Quintia is beautiful <u>to many</u> / <u>in the eyes of many</u>' (Catullus).

(vii) With certain verbs, and adjectives. Examples of verbs are:

crḗdō 'I believe'	*párcō* 'I spare'
fáueō 'I favour'	*pắreō* 'I obey'
fīdō 'I trust'	*persuắdeō* 'I persuade'
ignṓscō 'I pardon'	*pláceō* 'I please'
ímperō 'I order'	*resístō* 'I resist'
inuídeō 'I envy'	*subuéniō* 'I come to help'
īrắscor 'I am angry at'	
mínor 'I threaten'	
nóceō 'I harm'	

Many compound verbs, especially those compounded with *ob-*, *sub-*, *prae-*, *bene-*, *male-*, *satis-*, also take the dative.

Adjectives denoting nearness, likeness, helpfulness, kindness, trust etc., or which imply advantage or disadvantage, take the dative, e.g.

> *próximus éī* 'near(est) <u>(to) him</u>'
>
> *Caésarī símilis* 'resembling <u>Caesar</u>'
>
> *míhi útilis* 'useful <u>to me</u>'

2   **Nouns (often abstract) in the dative (the 'predicative' dative)**

Nouns in the dative usually show that which a thing *serves for*, or what its *purpose is*, e.g.

> *ódiō sum Rōmắnīs* 'I serve <u>*for a hatred*</u> to the Romans', i.e. 'I am hated by the Romans'
>
> *uoluptắtī sum éi* 'I serve <u>*for a pleasure*</u> to him/her'
>
> *mīlitēs auxíliō mīsit* 'he sent the soldiers to serve <u>*for assistance*</u>, i.e. to be a help'

(f)   Ablative

The ablative case has four basic usages. 'By', 'with', 'from', 'in' are often used to translate it effectively in English.

1   The 'true' ablative (Latin *ablấtus* 'carried away') denoting separation *from* or *away from*, e.g.

> *ex úrbe* 'out of the city'
>
> *nắtus Ióue* 'born from Jupiter'
>
> *dominātiốne līberấtus* 'freed from tyranny'

Under this heading belongs the ablative of comparison (lit. 'starting from a point of comparison with'), e.g.

> *quid móllius úndā*? 'what is softer than water?'

2   The 'locative/temporal ablative' denoting place/time *in*, *on*, or *at* which, e.g.

> *in úrbe* 'in the city'
>
> *térrā maríque* 'on land and sea'
>
> *déxtrā* 'on the right'
>
> *tríbus hốrīs* '(with)in three hours'
>
> *íllō díē* 'on that day'

3   The 'instrumental' ablative (by means of which), e.g.

(i)   Of agent (*by whom* a thing is done): *ab hīs laudắtur* 'he is praised by these people'.

(ii)   Of instrument or means (*by which* something is carried out): *sáxīs sē deféndunt* 'they defend themselves with rocks'.

(iii) Of cause (why something happens): *amốre périit* 'he died (because) of love'.

(iv) Of measure of difference: *tū mūltō áltior es* 'you are much taller' (lit. 'taller by much'). Note *éō* 'by so much', *quō* 'by how much', *tántō* 'by so much', *quántō* 'by how much', *paúlō* 'by a little', *hōc* 'by this amount', *aliquántō* 'by a certain amount'. See **J5(a)4**.

(v)   Of price (cf. genitive of value at **L(d)5**): *múltō aúrō hanc aúlam ếmī* 'I bought this pot at a price of much gold'; cf. *mágnō* 'at a high price', *páruō* 'at a small price', *uĩlī* 'at a cheap price'.

(vi) Of respect: *uir pietắte gráuis* 'a man serious in respect of his piety' (Virgil). (This may also be classified as a *locative* ablative.)

4 The 'accompanying' ablative (with which), e.g.

   (i) Of manner (how something is done): *súmmā (cum) celeritā́te uénit* 'he came <u>with very great speed</u>'.

   (ii) Of description: *uir mágnā uirtū́te* 'a man <u>(with) of great bravery</u>'.

   (iii) The ablative absolute, e.g. *tē dúce uincḗmus* '<u>with you as leader</u>, we shall win' (this shows the *accompanying* circumstances). Cf. **P** note 3.

5 Many verbs and some adjectives are followed by the ablative case. Some examples of verbs are:

fúngor 'I perform'	*dṓnō* 'I present X (acc.) with Y
frúor 'I enjoy'	(abl.)'
útor 'I use'	*abúndō* 'I abound in'
pótior 'I take possession of'	*ópus est* 'there is a need of X (abl.)
(alternatively + gen.)	to Y (dat.), i.e. Y needs X'

Adjectives followed by the ablative include:

dígn-us a um 'worthy of'	*plḗn-us a um* 'full of (alternatively
frḗt-us a um 'relying on'	+ gen.)

6 Note the following adverbs and phrases, all of which can be explained in terms of one of the uses of the ablative set out above:

siléntiō 'in silence'	*uī* 'by force'
iū́re 'rightly'	*nā́tū māíor* 'older' (lit. 'greater *in*
mṓre māiṓrum 'in the fashion of	*respect of* birth')
our ancestors'	*aéquō ánimō* 'with equanimity'
méā spónte 'on my own initiative'	*bónā fídē* 'in good faith'
ū́sū 'in practice'	*méā senténtiā* 'in my opinion'
fórte 'by chance'	*méā caúsā* 'for my sake'

(g)   **Locative**

The locative is the remnant of an old case. It is used to express 'at' with names of towns and one-town islands. By the classical period, in the singular it has the same form as the genitive in the first and second declensions (*-ae* and *-ī*), as the dative in the third declension (where *-ī* tends to replace earlier *-e*); in the plural of all declensions it is identical with the dative-ablative (*-īs*, *-ibus*). So, e.g.

>   1st decl. s. *Rṓmae* 'at Rome'
>
>   2nd decl. s. *Corínthī* 'at Corinth', *Dḗlī* 'on Delos'
>
>   1st decl. pl. *Athḗnīs* 'at Athens'
>
>   3rd decl. s. *Carthā́ginī* 'at Carthage' (for earlier *Karthagine*)
>
>   3rd decl. pl. *Sárdibus* 'at Sardes'

Note also the following special usages:

dómī 'at home'
húmī 'on the ground'
rū́rī 'in the country' (tending to replace earlier *rū́re*)
béllī 'at war'
mīlítiae 'on military service'

ánimī 'in the mind'
lū́cī 'at dawn' (alternating with *lū́ce*)
témperī (or *témpore*) 'at the right time'

Notes

1 The Latin locative is often the source of Romance place-names, e.g. Italian *Firenze* 'Florence' < Latin *Floréntiae*, French *Aix* < Latin *Áquīs* (lit. 'at the waters').

2 The names of towns and one-town islands have the additional peculiarity that the case-relations 'to, into' are often expressed by the plain accusative and '(away) from' by the plain ablative, i.e. without a preposition, e.g.

Rṓmam 'to Rome'
Rṓmā 'from Rome'
Syrācū́sās 'to Syracuse'

M The infinitive

The infinitive combines properties of the verb and the noun. It acts as a verb in that it can be active or passive, it can show present, future or past tense and it can govern a case-form of a noun or pronoun. The infinitive can also act as a noun (always neuter) in that it can be the (nominative) subject or (accusative) object of a verb.

(a)   **As a noun (= the missing cases of the gerund)**

The infinitive often acts as a nominative or accusative gerund, e.g.

hūmā́num est errā́re 'to err is human', 'error is human'
errā́re málum dū́cimus 'we consider error (lit. 'to do wrong') wicked'

(b)   **As a verb (prolative infinitive)**

The infinitive is used in Latin (as in English) as the complement of certain verbs, e.g. *póssum* 'I am able to', *débeō* 'I ought to', *uólō* 'I wish to', *cṓnor* 'I try to', *incípiō* 'I begin to', *dúbitō* 'I hesitate to', *sóleō* 'I am accustomed to', etc.

It is common with verbs of being said or thought, e.g.

dī́citur málus ésse 'he is said to be wicked'
uidḗtur bónus ésse 'he seems to be good'

(c) **Indirect speech**

The verb of indirect statements (see **R1**) is in the infinitive, e.g.

> *pútō tē abiísse* 'I think that you have gone away' (lit. 'I think you to
> have gone away')

(d) **Historic infinitive**

The 'historic' infinitive is used to describe vividly an action which would
normally be in imperfect past tense of the indicative, e.g.

> *multī séquī, fúgere, occídī, cápī* 'many were following, fleeing,
> being killed and captured'

N Gerund

A gerund is a neuter noun, formed from a verb, with exactly the same form
as the neuter s. of the gerundive (see **O**), e.g. *amánd-um ī* 2n. 'love', 'loving'.
All such gerunds end in *-ndum*, e.g. *monéndum, capiéndum, regéndum* etc. This
form is *never* nominative, and even the accusative is used normally only after a
preposition (the direct accusative being supplied by the infinitive; see **M** above).
It is most commonly used with a preposition or defining noun, e.g.

> *ad regéndum* 'with a view to ruling, in order to rule'
>
> *ars dīcéndī* 'the art of speaking'
>
> *regéndī grátiā* 'for the sake of ruling'
>
> *capiéndī caúsā* 'for the sake of taking, in order to take'

It can take an object, e.g. *naúīs capiéndī caúsā* 'to capture the ships', lit. 'for the
sake of capturing (gen.) the ships (acc.)' (though classical writers usually express
this by noun + gerundive + *caúsā* – *naúium capiendárum caúsā* lit. 'for the sake
of the ships being captured' (all gen.), see **O** note 3). The gerund can stand on its
own in the dative and ablative, e.g.

> *docéndō et discéndō* 'by teaching and learning'
>
> *óperam legéndō dat* 'he pays attention to reading'

O Gerundive

The gerundive is a passive adjective, based on a verb, ending in *-nd-us a um*,
meaning 'being —ed', 'to be —ed', and in the nominative 'requiring to be —ed',
'needing to be —ed', 'that must be —ed' (cf. **B1** above and notes), e.g

> *captíuōs necándōs trádidit* 'he handed over the captives to be slain'
>
> *Rōma līberánda est* 'Rome is to be freed', 'Rome must be freed',
> 'Rome needs to be freed'

Notes

1 The gerundive usually has its agent (if s/he is expressed) in the *dative*, e.g.

> *Rṓma Brū́tō līberánda est* 'Rome must be freed by Brutus'.

However, verbs which in the active take a dative object have their agent expressed after the gerundive by means of the usual passive construction, i.e. *ā/ab* + abl., e.g. *míhi parcéndum est ā tē* lit. 'it is to be spared to me by you', i.e. 'you must spare me'.

2 Where a verb is intransitive, the gerundive becomes impersonal and therefore neuter s., e.g.

> *eúndum est míhi* 'it is to be gone by me', 'I must go'

3 In cases where a gerundive + noun, translated literally, sound odd, turn the phrase round into an active form, e.g.

> *ad mī́litēs capiéndōs* (lit.) 'with a view to the soldiers being captured' → 'with a view to capturing the soldiers'
>
> *in līberándā pátriā* (lit.) 'in the fatherland being freed' → 'in freeing the fatherland'
>
> *rḗgī creándō* 'for a king being made' → 'for making a king'

(See **N** above for this construction expressed (rarely) by the gerund.)

P Participles

There are three tenses of the participle in Latin:

(a) The present participle active (see **A1**), meaning '—ing', 'while —ing' (used also by deponent verbs)

(b) The future participle active (see **A2**), meaning 'about to —', 'on the point of —ing', 'with a view to —ing' (used also by deponent verbs)

(c) The perfect participle active (used only by deponent verbs), 'having —ed' (sometimes just '—ing': see also **C4** note 2 for passive meaning in some deponent verbs) and, much more frequent, the perfect participle passive (used by transitive active verbs) meaning 'having been —ed' (see **C4**, **B4**)

Participles are adjectives and agree in case, number and gender with the noun or pronoun to which they refer. Sometimes they are used as attributive adjectives, to describe or modify a noun, e.g. *áqua féruēns* 'boiling water'. But their commonest use is predicative, e.g. *Plátō scrī́bēns est mórtuus* 'Plato died *while writing*' (Cicero). (Contrast the attributive adjective *noster* in *Plátō nóster est mórtuus* '*our* Plato has died'. See under 'Predicative' in the Glossary of Grammatical Terms, p. xxii.)

Notes

1 A participle standing on its own either is an adjective functioning as a noun (**J Intro.(b)** above) and means 'a/the man/woman/thing —ing' etc., e.g.

> *moritū̆rī* '(masculine plurals) about to die', 'those about to die'

or agrees with a noun or pronoun left out, and refers to a person already mentioned, e.g.

> *rogántī respóndit* 'to (him) as he was asking he replied', 'he replied to his question'.

2 Participles indicate the *time* of the action in relation to the adjoining verb, i.e. a present participle indicates the action is going on *at the same time as the verb*, a future participle that it will happen *after the verb*, a perfect participle that it has happened *before the verb*.

3 Participles, especially present active and perfect passive, are often used with a noun or pronoun in the ablative (*ablative absolute*) to form an accompaniment to the action of a clause, e.g.

> *Cethḗgus, recitā̆tīs lítterīs, repénte contícuit* 'when the letter had been read out (lit. '(with) the letter having been read out'), Cethegus suddenly fell silent' (Cicero)

Cf. *tē dúce* 'under your leadership', lit. '(with) you as leader' (**L(f)3(iii)**).

4 The relationship between verb and participle can be more than merely temporal and suggest cause, concession or condition, e.g.

> *tímeō Dánaōs et dṓna feréntīs* 'I fear the Greeks, even though bringing gifts'

> *nōn míhi nísi admónitō uēnísset in méntem* 'it wouldn't have entered my head if I hadn't been reminded' (Cicero)

5 The passive participle often expresses not the thing or person acted on, but the very act itself, e.g.

> *uiolā̆tī hóspitēs, lēgā̆tī necā̆tī, fā̆na uexā̆ta hanc tántam effēcḗrunt uāstitā̆tem* lit. 'violated guests, slaughtered ambassadors, ravaged shrines brought about this so great devastation', but better 'the violation of guests, the slaughter of ambassadors, the destruction of shrines …' etc.

Q1 Relative clauses: *quī* + indicative

A relative clause, introduced in Latin by some form of the relative pronoun *quī quae quod* 'who', 'which', 'what', 'that' (see **I4**) is an adjectival clause which describes a noun, e.g.

> 'The girls <u>who are present</u>'
> 'The book <u>which I gave you</u> is very old'

The word to which the relative pronoun refers is called the antecedent. In the above examples, the antecedent of 'who' is 'the girls', and the antecedent of 'which' is 'the book'.

The relative gets its *gender* (m., f. or n.) and its number (s. or pl.) from the *antecedent*; it gets its *case* from its *function* within the relative clause. Observe the following examples:

> *ámō puéllās <u>quae ádsunt</u>* 'I like the girls <u>who are present</u>'

quae: feminine, plural (because 'girls' is the antecedent); nominative, because 'who' is the subject of 'are present'.

> *úbi est fráter méus, <u>quem uidḗre nōn póssum</u>* 'where is my brother, <u>whom I cannot see?</u>'

quem: masculine, singular (because 'brother' is the antecedent); accusative, because 'whom' is the object of 'I cannot see'.

> *ábest rēx <u>cúius mílitēs ádsunt</u>* 'the king, <u>whose soldiers are present,</u> is absent'

cúius: masculine, singular (antecedent 'king'); genitive, because 'whose' means 'of whom', 'belonging to whom', so genitive of possession.

> *púerī <u>quíbus pecúniam dédī</u> effūgḗrunt* 'the boys <u>to whom I gave the money</u> have run off'

quíbus: masculine, plural (antecedent 'boys'); dative, because I gave the money *to* them.

> *úbi est sáxum <u>quō percússus sum</u>* 'where is the rock <u>by which I was hit?</u>'

quō: neuter, singular (antecedent 'rock'); ablative, because it was the instrument by which I was hit.

Notes

1 The so-called 'connecting' relative in Latin joins a sentence closely to the previous one. The connecting relative in effect comprises a conjunction ('and', 'but') and a demonstrative pronoun. So, e.g.

> *Caésar mílitēs mīsit. quōs úbi mīsit …* 'Caesar sent the soldiers. Whom when he had sent …', i.e. '<u>And/But</u> when he had sent <u>them</u> …'

2 Observe the following idioms:

> *mílitēs quōs habébat óptimōs mísit* 'he sent the soldiers whom best he had', i.e. 'he sent the best soldiers he had'

> *quā es prūdéntiā, níhil tē effúgiet* lit. 'with what wisdom you are, nothing will escape you' i.e. 'such is your wisdom …'

Q2 Relative clauses: *quī* + subjunctive

When a relative clause 'hides' a clause of result, purpose, cause or concession, the verb is subjunctive.

(a) *Hidden result clause*, often called 'generic' (*quī* does service for *tális ut* 'of such a kind that' or the like), e.g.

> *is est quī paupéribus nóceat* 'he is the sort of person who harms the poor'

> *sunt quī pútent* 'there are people (of the sort) who think …'

> *némō est quī hoc fáciat* 'there is no one who does this'

> *némō est quīn próbet* 'there is no one who does not approve' (note that here *quīn = ut nōn*)

NB *est quī, sunt quī*, when they refer to a definite antecedent, take the indicative, e.g. *múltī sunt quī pútant* 'there are many who think …'

(b) *Hidden purpose* (*quī* does service for *ut is* 'in order that he' or the like), e.g.

> *mílitēs mísit quī hóstīs circúmdarent* 'he sent soldiers who would / to surround the enemy'

(c) *Hidden cause* (*quī* does service for *cum is* 'since he' or the like), e.g.

> *ámō tē quī mē ámēs* 'I love you who (i.e. because you) love me'

These clauses often occur with *útpote quī* or *quíppe quī*.

(d) *Hidden concession* (*quī* does service for *quamquam* 'although' or the like), e.g.

> *Vérrēs, quī uísus múltis diébus nōn ésset, támen sē in cōnspéctum dédit* 'Verres, who had not been seen for many days, nevertheless presented himself to view', i.e. 'Verres, *although* he …' (concessive)

Notes

Observe the following idioms:

1 *dígnus est quī ímperet* 'he is worthy to govern'.

2 *quō* + comparative + subjunctive indicates purpose, e.g. *quō celérius effúgiat* 'in order that he may escape more quickly'. To put this another way, if the focus of a purpose cause is a comparative adverb or adjective, *ut* is replaced by *quō*.

3 *mãíor est quam quem uíncere póssim* 'he is greater than one whom I can defeat', 'he is too great for me to defeat'.

R Indirect speech

When words are not quoted 'direct', i.e. verbatim, but given in reported form (e.g. 'he claimed that she was gone', 'we told him to leave at once', 'she asked where they were'), Latin

(a) uses the accusative and infinitive to express indirect statements

(b) uses *ut/nē* + subjunctive (sometimes plain infinitive) to express indirect commands

(c) uses question word + subjunctive to express indirect questions

(d) puts all subordinate verbs into the subjunctive (except that after *dum* in the sense 'at one point while' the verb occasionally remains indicative)

(e) makes all references to the speaker reflexive

R1 Indirect statements

When you come across a verb of saying, thinking, reporting etc., or even a noun implying these actions (e.g. *nũntius*), be ready for an accusative and infinitive construction. This reports what is being said or thought, e.g.

> *Caésar díxit hóstīs appropinquãre* 'Caesar said *the enemy to be approaching*', i.e. 'that the enemy were approaching'.

> *pũtō tē púlchrum fuísse* 'I consider <u>you to have been handsome</u>', i.e. 'that you were handsome'.

> *spérõ tē mox discessũrum ésse* 'I hope <u>you to be about to go soon</u>', i.e. 'that you will go soon'.

Notes

1 Observe that the subject of the indirect statement is in the accusative, and the verb in the infinitive. The tense of the infinitive reflects the relation in time between the reported action and the verb of saying/thinking: perfect = before, present = contemporary with, future = after.

2 Note how *English* changes in response to the tense of the introductory verb of saying or thinking, e.g.

> *Caésar dícit hóstīs appropinquãre* lit. 'Caesar says the enemy to be approaching', 'that the enemy *are* approaching'

> *Caésar díxit hóstīs appropinquãre* 'Caesar said the enemy to be approaching', 'that the enemy *were* approaching'

3 *négō* means 'I say that … NOT'. In a sentence of this kind, the negative is always transferred to the verb of saying, i.e. *négō* is always used, and not *dícō … non …*

> *negā́uit cóquum málum ésse* 'he denied the cook to be wicked', 'he *said* that the cook was *not* wicked'

4 A reflexive refers to the subject of the main verb, e.g.

> *Caésar dī́xit sē discessū́rum ésse* 'Caesar said that he (i.e. Caesar) would leave'

cf. *Caésar dī́xit éum discessū́rum* 'Caesar said that he (someone else) would leave'

Note that *sē* and the other personal pronouns tend to come second in the clause unless emphatic.

5 *esse* is sometimes dropped from the infinitive (see the second example in 4 above).

6 *fóre ut* + subjunctive 'that it should come about that' is often used in indirect statements to get round the need for a future passive infinitive.

7 Remember to start your translation into English with the word 'THAT' – a word which does not appear in the Latin in these constructions at all.

R2 Indirect commands

Indirect commands are signposted by a word of ordering, persuading, commanding etc. followed by *ut* or *nē*. The verb is in the subjunctive – present in primary sequence, imperfect in secondary. So, e.g.

> *míhi ímperat/imperā́uit ut ábeam/abī́rem* 'he orders/ordered me that I should go / to go away'

> *éōs hortā́tī sunt / hortántur nē trī́stēs éssent/sint* 'they urged/urge them that they should not be / not to be unhappy'

Notes

1 Observe *nē … quis* 'that no one' (see **I4** for declension of *quis* indefinite), *nē … ū́llus* 'that not any', *nē … úmquam* 'that never'.

2 References in the indirect command to the subject of the ordering verb are reflexive, e.g.

> *Caésar mīlítibus imperā́uit ut síbi pārḗrent* 'Caesar ordered the soldiers to obey him (i.e. Caesar)' (*éī* would refer to someone other than Caesar)

3 Some verbs take an infinitive construction as in English, esp. *iúbeō* 'I order' and *uétō* 'I forbid', 'order not to', e.g.

> *iússit mē abī́re* 'he ordered me to leave'

> *éōs prṓgredī uétuit* 'he forbade them / told them not to advance'

4 In extended indirect speech, commands are sometimes introduced without *ut*, with just the plain subjunctive.

R3 Indirect questions

In classical Latin, the verb in an indirect question is in the *subjunctive*. The rules are complex (see below), but the simplest thing to do is to translate the subjunctive as if it were the closest corresponding tense in the indicative, e.g.

rógat <u>cūr uḗnerīs</u> 'he asks <u>why you have come</u>'

nescîuit <u>quid fácerēs</u> 'he did not know <u>what you were doing</u>'

petḗbam quid <u>dictū́rus ésset</u> 'I was asking <u>what he was about to say</u> / <u>would say</u>'

Notes

1 *num* and *an* in an indirect question mean 'if', 'whether', *num quis* means 'if/whether anyone' (cf. *nē quis, sī quis, nísi quis*).

2 *útrum … nécne* in an indirect question means 'whether … or not'.

3 References to the subject of the verb of asking (etc.) will be reflexive, e.g.

Caésar rogắuit cūr ómnēs sē timḗrent 'Caesar asked why everyone feared him (i.e. Caesar)'

4 Here are some examples from which you can deduce the chart, given below. They give the full picture of the exact relationship between the sequence, tense of verb and subjunctive required.

Main verb primary	Question word	Subjunctive	Main verb primary	Question word	Subjunctive
rógo	cūr	uḗnerit	I ask	why	he came / has come / was coming / had come
rógō	cūr	uéniat	I ask	why	he is coming
rógō	cūr	uentū́rus sit	I ask	why	he will come / he is going to come
Main verb secondary	Question word	Subjunctive	Main verb secondary	Question word	Subjunctive
rogắuī	cūr	uēnísset	I asked	why	he had come
rogắuī	cūr	uenī́ret	I asked	why	he was coming
rogắuī	cūr	uentū́rus ésset	I asked	why	he would come / he was going to come

Summary chart

	Question refers to		
	Present	*Future*	*Past*
Introductory verb primary (e.g. *rógo* 'I ask')	Pres. subj. 'is —ing'	Fut. part. + *sim* 'will —', 'is going to —'	Perf. subj. '—ed', 'has —ed', 'was —ing', 'had —ed'
Introductory verb secondary (e.g. *rogáui* 'I asked')	Impf. subj. 'was —ing'	Fut. part. + *éssem* 'would —', 'was going to —'	Plupf. subj. 'had —ed', 'had been —ing'

R4 Subjunctives in indirect speech

(a) All subordinate clauses in indirect speech (except occasionally *dum* in the sense 'at one point while') have their verbs in the subjunctive. The subjunctives follow the rule of sequence, i.e.

> Primary main verb: subjunctives used are present (referring to present and future time) and perfect (referring to past time)

> Secondary main verb: subjunctives used are imperfect (referring to present and future time) and pluperfect (referring to past time)

Occasionally future time will be referred to by means of the future participle + *sim* (primary) or + *éssem* (*fórem*) (secondary). See **142** note.

(b) Conditional sentences in indirect speech have a subjunctive in the *sī/nísi* clause ('protasis'), and an accusative + infinitive in the main clause ('apodosis'). The rules of sequence for the subjunctives are the same as those in **R4(a)** above. Note that only context will allow you to distinguish between a future indicative condition and a subjunctive condition referring to the future, e.g. (he said that) *sī pácem pópulus Rōmánus cum Heluétiīs fáceret, in éam pártem itū́rōs* could represent (direct speech) *either*:

(1) *sī pácem ... fáciat, in éam pártem eámus* 'if (the Roman people) were to make peace (with the Helvetii), we would go to that side ...'; present subjunctive (referring to the future)

or

(2) *sī pácem ... fáciet, in éam pártem íbimus* 'if (the Roman people) is going to make peace (with the Helvetii), we shall go to that side ...'; future indicative.

In the other subjunctive conditions (imperfect and pluperfect), 'would be —ing' and 'would have —ed' (the apodosis) are both represented by future participle + *fuísse*. E.g. *uidḗmur quiētū́rī fuísse, nísi essḗmus lacessī́tī* 'it seems we would have kept quiet, had we not been provoked' (Cicero) (representing direct speech *sī* + pluperfect subjunctive, pluperfect subjunctive).

S The subjunctive

The subjunctive originally expressed the will, desire or hope *on the part of the speaker* that something should be (e.g. *uíuat rēx* 'may the king live' – this is the *speaker's* desire rather than the king's). It is used in main clauses and subordinate clauses. In subordinate clauses in classical Latin it is often used merely as a conventional way of signalling subordination, and does not carry its original force (so e.g. in indirect questions, see **R3**).

S1 Main clauses

(Cf. **L–V Intro.**)

(a) **As an imperative**

Expresses an order, or prohibition, e.g.

> *nē trānsíerīs* 'do not cross'

or the jussive subjunctive 'let us/him' etc., e.g.

> *eámus* 'let us go'
>
> *amḗmus* 'let us make love'

(b) **'Deliberative' subjunctive**

In English this takes the form 'what am I to?', e.g.

> *quid fáciam* 'what am I to do?'

(c) **Wishes**

Examples:

> *sīs félix* 'may you be happy'
>
> *uólō tū scríbās* 'I want you to write'

or, with *útinam* 'O that!':

> *útinam adéssēs* 'O that you were present!'

(See **L–V Intro.(a)4**)

(d)   **Conditional/potential**

Examples:

> *uélim* 'I should like to'
>
> $\left.\begin{array}{l} \textit{díxerit} \\ \textit{dícat} \end{array}\right\}$ *áliquis* 'someone might / would say'
>
> *sī adfuísset, uīdísset* 'if he had been there, he would have seen'

S2 Subordinate clauses

The subjunctive may be found in a number of clauses already dealt with elsewhere, i.e. indirect commands, indirect questions and subordinate clauses in indirect speech (on all of which see **R2**, **R3** and **R4**), relative clauses (see **Q2**), temporal clauses (see **T**), causal clauses (**U**) and concessive clauses (**V**).

(a)   **Result (or consecutive) clauses: 'so ... that', 'so ... as to'**

1 The 'that' clause is expressed by *ut* + subjunctive (negative *nōn*). The subjunctive is normally present, imperfect or perfect.

2 There are a number of different words for 'so'. These include: *ádeō, íta, tam, sīc, éō.*

Note also *tántus* 'so great', *tot* 'so many', *tális* 'of such a sort', e.g.

> *tántum est perículum ut némō uénerit* 'so great is the danger that no one has come'
>
> *tam fórtis érat ut uíncī nōn pósset* 'he was so brave that he could not be defeated'
>
> *íta ágere dēbémus ut ómnēs nōs laúdent* 'we ought so to act that all praise us'

3 Consecutive constructions are also used in the following idioms:

(i) *tántum ábest ut ... ut* 'X is so far from (*ut*) ... THAT' (*ut* consecutive); *fácere nōn póssum quīn* 'I cannot do (a thing) but that ...', 'I cannot help —ing'; *fierī nōn pótest quīn* 'it cannot come about but that ... not'.

(ii) *quī* + subjunctive can mean 'of such a kind that' (generic), when it is followed by a consecutive construction, e.g. *nōn sum <u>is quī</u> quiéscere <u>póssim</u>* 'I am not the <u>sort of person who can</u> keep quiet.'

> Cf. *némō est quīn próbet* 'there is no one of the sort who does not approve' (Cicero) (*quīn = quī nōn*).

(iii) *áccidit ut (nōn)* + subjunctive 'it happens that …'; *perficiō/efficiō/fáciō ut (nōn)* 'I bring it about that …'; *nōn múltum ábest quīn* 'it is not far from being the case that …'

(iv) *númquam accédō quīn ábeam dóctior* 'I never approach (you) <u>without going away</u> more learned' (Cicero).

(b)   **Purpose (or final) clauses: 'in order to/that', 'to'**

Purpose clauses are commonly expressed by *ut* (negative *nē*) + subjunctive. The subjunctive is present in primary sequence, imperfect in secondary. E.g.

> *uénio ut uídeam* '<u>I come in order to</u> / <u>to</u> / <u>in order that I may see</u>'
>
> *uḗnī ut uidḗrem* 'I came <u>in order (etc.) to see</u>'

Note that *nē quis* = 'that no one' (see **14** for declension of *quis* indefinite), *nē úmquam* 'that never', *nē úllus* 'that not … any', 'lest any'.

Notes

1 *quī* + subjunctive (**Q2(b)** above) frequently expresses purpose, especially with verbs of movement, e.g.

> *legátōs mísit quī pácem péterent* 'they sent ambassadors <u>who should seek</u> / <u>to seek</u> peace'

2 References back in the purpose clause to the subject of the main verb are expressed by the reflexive, e.g.

> *Caésar uénit ut mílitēs sē uidérent* 'Caesar arrived so that his soldiers should see <u>him</u> (i.e. Caesar)'

3 *quō* + subjunctive expresses purpose when there is a comparative in the purpose clause, e.g.

> *quō celérius effúgiat* 'so that he may escape more quickly'

4 *perficiō/efficiō/fáciō ut* (neg. *nē*) + subjunctive ('I bring it about that') may express purpose, as well as result (see **S2(a)3(iii)**).

5 Observe how many ways there are of expressing purpose in Latin:

(i)   ut/nē + subjunctive ⎤
                    ⎥(see above)
(ii) *quī* + subjunctive ⎦

(iii) *ad* + gerund/gerundive 'with a view to —ing'

(iv) *caúsā* + gerund/gerundive (see **N, O**)

(v) The supine (see **A7** for formation): used especially with verbs of motion, e.g. *mílitēs mísit pácem petítum* 'he sent soldiers <u>to seek</u> peace'

(c)   **Conditional sentences**

The 'if' clause of a conditional sentence is often called the 'protasis', the main clause the 'apodosis'.

1   **Indicative**

Where a conditional sentence uses an indicative in both clauses, translate normally, e.g.

> *sī tū sápiēns es, égo stúltus* 'if you are wise, I am a fool'

(See, however, note 1 below.)
Note that English is less accurate about future and future perfects than Latin, e.g.

> *sī puélla discédet, laetus érō* 'if the girl departs (lit. 'will depart') I shall be delighted'

> *sī hoc féceris, habébō grátiam* 'if you do this (lit. 'will have done this') I shall be grateful'

2   **Subjunctive**

Where a conditional sentence has the subjunctive in both clauses, translate with 'would', 'should', 'were', as follows:

(i)   Present subjunctive (refers to future time) 'If X were to happen, Y would happen'

(ii) Imperfect subjunctive (refers to present time) 'If X were now happening, Y would be happening'

(iii) Pluperfect subjunctive (refers to past time) 'If X had happened, Y would have happened'

e.g.

> *sī puélla discédat, laétus sim* 'if the girl were to depart, I would be delighted'

> *sī puélla discéderet, laétus éssem* 'if the girl were (now) departing, I would (now) be happy'

> *sī puélla discessísset, laétus fuíssem* 'if the girl had departed, I would have been delighted'

Notes

1 Latin sometimes mixes indicatives and subjunctives in conditional sentences. Generally speaking, such conditions should be treated on the 'would/should' pattern, e.g.

> *pōns íter paéne hóstibus dédit, nísi únus uir fuísset* 'the bridge almost gave the enemy a way across (and would have done), if there had not been one man' (Livy)

2 The indicative is normal in the main clause (apodosis) of a condition usually calling for the subjunctive where it involves the ideas of possibility (e.g. *póssum*) or obligation (e.g. *débeō* or gerundive), e.g.

> *nísi fēlícitās in socórdiam uertísset, exúere íugum <u>potuére</u>* (for *potuíssent*) 'if their success had not turned to sloth, <u>they would have been able</u> to throw off the yoke' (Tacitus)
>
> *sī únum díem morátī essétis, <u>moriéndum</u> ómnibus <u>fúit</u>* (for *fuisset*) 'if you had delayed for one day, you <u>would</u> all <u>have had to die</u>' (Livy)

3 The imperfect subjunctive can be used (vividly) to refer to past time, e.g.

> *uidérēs* 'you would have seen'

4 *nísi*, *nī* and *sī nōn* all mean 'if ... not', 'unless'

5 *sī/nísi quis* means 'if/unless *anyone*' (see **I4** for declension of *quis* indefinite). Cf. *sī/nísi quándō* 'if/unless at any time'

6 *síue ... síue* (*seu ... seu*) means 'whether ... or' and introduces alternative conditions, e.g.

> *síue haec uéra síue fálsa sunt, proficíscar* 'whether these things are false or true, I shall set out'

7 For conditional sentences in indirect speech, see **R4(b)**.

(d)   **Verbs of fearing**

uéreor/tímeō meaning 'I fear *to*' take the infinitive as in English.

uéreor/tímeō meaning 'I fear *that/lest*' take the subjunctive, and are introduced by *nē* ('that', 'lest'), *ut* ('that ... not') or *nē ... nōn* ('that ... not'). The subjunctive follows normal rules of sequence, e.g.

> *tímeō nē uéniat* 'I fear lest he come', in natural English 'I fear he will come'
>
> *timébam nē uēnísset* 'I was afraid that he had come'

NB As in purpose clauses, any reference back from the *nē/ut/nē nōn* clause to the subject of the main verb will be reflexive.

(e)   **Verbs of doubting**

nōn dúbitō 'I do not doubt', *nōn dúbium est* 'there is no doubt' and similar negative expressions of doubting are followed by *quīn* + subjunctive, e.g.

> *nōn dúbium est quīn érrēs* 'there is no doubt that you are wrong'

Notes

1 The last example amounts to an indirect question (see above **R3**), since it in effect reports the question 'Are you not wrong?' *quīn* is composed from *quī* (old abl. of *quī quae quod*: **I3** note 2 and **I4** note 3) and the negative *-ne*. The original meaning (common in Plautus) is 'how not?', 'why not?'

2 The affirmative version of the last example (even more clearly an indirect question) is *dúbitō an* + subj. 'I doubt whether …'

(f)   **Verbs of hindering, preventing, forbidding**

Verbs like *impédiō* 'I hinder', *dētérreō* 'I deter', *prohíbeō* 'I prevent', *óbstō* 'I stand in the way of (X doing something)' are followed by *nē* or *quóminus* with the subjunctive, or, if they are negated, by *quóminus* or *quīn* + subjunctive.
  Compare then e.g.

> *tē impédiam <u>nē/quóminus</u> ábeās* 'I shall prevent you from leaving'

with

> *tē <u>nōn</u> impédiam <u>quóminus/quīn</u> ábeās* 'I shall <u>not</u> prevent you from leaving'

NB After *prohíbeō*, the infinitive or accusative and infinitive is common, e.g. *prohíbeō tē abíre* 'I prevent you from going'.

(g)   **'Provided that'**

dum, dúmmodo, módo can mean 'provided that' (negative in all instances *nē*), when the verb is subjunctive, e.g.

> *óderint dum métuant* 'let them hate, provided that they fear' (Accius
>   – Roman tragedian: a favourite quotation of Caligula)

T Temporal clauses

Temporal adverbial clauses indicate the time at/during/after (etc.) which something takes place, e.g. 'when', 'as soon as', 'after', 'while', 'until', 'whenever', etc.

(a) *úbi, ut* ('when'), *póstquam* 'after', *símulac, quam prímum* ('as soon as') take the indicative.

Note that when Latin uses the perfect indicative, English frequently translates with the pluperfect, e.g.

> *úbi Caésar peruénit* 'when Caesar arrived / had arrived'

(b) *dum, dónec* 'while' take the indicative, e.g.

> *dum uíuō, spérō* 'while I live, I hope'

Note that when 'while' means 'at one point when', the indicative is *always present even when referring to past time*, e.g.

> *dum lóquor, hómo intrắuit* 'while I was speaking, the fellow entered'

(c) *dum, dỗnec* 'until' and *ántequam, priúsquam* 'before' take

1 the indicative when the clause conveys nothing but the idea of pure time, e.g. *manḗbat dum Caésar peruḗnit* 'he waited until Caesar arrived'

2 the subjunctive when the action is expected or waited for or intention is being expressed, e.g. *manḗbat dum Caésar uenȋret* lit. 'he waited until Caesar should come', 'he waited for Caesar to come' (seeing Caesar is part of his purpose); *ábiit priúsquam Caésar éum uidḗret* 'he left before Caesar should see him' (his purpose was not being seen by Caesar)

(d) *cum* 'when' takes

1 the indicative when referring to present or future time, e.g. *cum uidḗbis, tum sciḗs* 'when you (will) see, then you will know'

2 the subjunctive (pluperfect or imperfect) when referring to past time, e.g. *cum haec dīxísset, ábiit* 'when he had said this, he left'

(e) An exception to **T(d)2** is that *cum* takes the indicative when referring to the past in the following circumstances:

1 when it expresses pure time, e.g. *cum égo Rỗmae éram, tū Londíniī érās* '(at the time) when I was at Rome, you were in London'

2 when it means 'whenever', in which case present time is conveyed by the perfect, past time by the pluperfect, e.g. *cum mē uȋderat, laetābắtur* 'whenever he saw me, he rejoiced'

3 in so-called 'inverted' *cum*, where (as in English) the main action is conveyed in the *cum*/when clause, e.g. *abȋbam cum nŭntius peruḗnit* 'I was going away when a messenger arrived'

U Causal clauses: 'because', 'since'

The causal conjunctions *quod, quía, quóniam, quándō* all mean 'because' or 'since', and their verbs take the indicative when the speaker/author is vouching for the reason, e.g.

> *ádsunt quod offícium sequúntur* 'they are present because they follow their duty' (that is the speaker's explanation)

ádsunt quod offícium sequắntur, with the verb of the *quod* clause in the subjunctive, would mean 'they are present <u>on the grounds</u> that (i.e. as they or a third party allege) they follow their duty': this is in effect indirect/reported speech.

cum 'since' nearly always takes the subjunctive. After certain verbs, however, including *laúdō* 'I praise', *dóleō* 'I grieve', *gaúdeō* 'I rejoice', it can take the indicative, e.g.

> *dóleō cum aéger es* 'I grieve because you are ill'

Notes

1 *quī* + subjunctive can denote cause (**Q2(c)** above), e.g.

> *ámō tē quī mē ámēs* 'I love you who (= because you) love me'

quī in such utterances is often strengthened by being preceded by *quíppe*, *útpote* or *ut*.

2 Causal clauses are often signposted or picked up by *éō* or *idcírcō* 'for the following reason, for the reason just given'.

V Concessive clauses

These are introduced by *étsī*, *etiámsī* 'even if', *quámquam*, *quámuīs* 'although', or *quī* + subjunctive. The first two, *étsī* and *etiámsī*, in fact introduce conditional clauses (note the *-si*) and so take either indicative or subjunctive according to the type of condition/concession being conveyed. Compare e.g.

> *etiámsī tácent, sátis dícunt* 'though they are silent, they say enough'
>
> *etiámsī táceant, sátis dícant* 'though they were to be silent, they would say enough'

Of the second pair, *quámquam* 'although' takes the indicative, while *quámuīs* 'however' takes the subjunctive, e.g.

> *quámquam inimícus es* 'although you are hostile'
>
> *quámuīs inimícus sīs* 'however hostile you may be'

Finally, the relative *quī* 'who' can be used with concessive force (**Q2(d)** above), in which case it takes the subjunctive, e.g.

> *égo quī fórtis sim támen fúgiam* 'I, who am brave, nevertheless will flee' i.e. 'I, though brave …'

Note

The impersonal verb *lícet* 'it is allowed' is quite often followed by a subjunctive verb and functions in effect as a concessive conjunction, 'though', e.g. *frémant ómnēs lícet, dícam quod séntiō*. 'Though they may all make a commotion, I will say what I think' (Cicero).

W Word-order

(a) Emphasis and scene-setting

1 *Caésar in Gálliam conténdit* 'Caesar marched into Gaul' may be called for convenience the 'normal' or 'narrative' order of that sentence in Latin. An 'emphatic' order would be *in Gálliam Caésar conténdit* 'it was into Gaul that Caesar marched' (answering the question 'Where was Caesar marching?'), or *conténdit in Gálliam Caésar* (answering the question 'What was it that Caesar was doing concerning Gaul?'). Putting the verb first is common in vivid or excited narrative, when we want to know at once what is happening, or when there is no stated subject to the verb, so that the verbal ending is the only clue to it.

Observe how 'emphasis' affects the position of 'attributive' adjectives, normally placed *after* the noun (e.g. *uir bónus* 'good man'). They come first when they define it (emphatically) rather than merely add a description, e.g. *útram túnicam mấuīs – álbam an purpúream? purpúream túnicam mãlō* 'Which tunic do you prefer – the white or the purple?' 'The <u>purple</u> tunic is the one I prefer.'

2 *Gállia est ómnis dĩuĩsa in pártīs trēs* 'As for Gaul, the whole of it, it is divided into parts – how many? – Well, *three* actually.' Caesar 'sets the scene' – we are talking about the whole of Gaul – and leaves to the end the real importance of what he is to say: that it is divided into *three* parts. Observe how he continues: *quắrum ũnam íncolunt Bélgae, áliam Aquitắnī*, 'of which, well, we have one part lived in by – Belgians – and another by – Aquitanians'. Again, Caesar sets the scene and then gives the really important information: it was Belgians and Aquitanians who lived in two of the parts.

English also uses 'scene-setting' word-order to emphasise in this way, e.g. '*Talent*, Mr. Micawber *has*; *capital*, Mr. Micawber *hasn't*' (Dickens).

(b) Shadowing

1 Latin tends to alternate emphatic and unemphatic words or phrases within the sentence. In the example of the coloured tunics given above, the word *purpúream* in the answer is emphatic, and the word *túnicam* – less necessary, since we already know that tunics are what is being discussed – carries less emphasis. It may be helpful to think metaphorically of *túnicam* being cast into the shadow by the emphatic *purpúream* which precedes it.

2 Certain classes of words tend to be placed in the shadow of the first important word in the sentence or clause (regardless of whether they are connected with it grammatically or logically). These are: (i) particles like *énim, aútem*, which connect the sentence they occur in with what precedes; (ii) unemphatic personal and demonstrative pronouns like *mē, tíbi, éum, nōs*, even the nominatives *égo*,

tu, ílle when unstressed, e.g.: *hīs míhi rébus, Scípiō, léuis est senéctūs* (Cicero) 'it is because of these things, Scipio, that old age is no burden for me' (note here that unstressed *míhi* attaches itself to the emphatic demonstrative *hīs* even at the cost of interrupting the grammatically connected words *hīs* and *rébus*). (iii) The verb, when unemphatic, often gravitates to a position just after the first emphatic word: this happens especially with forms of *ésse* in auxiliary function or otherwise unstressed, e.g. *in Gálliam est Caésar proféctus* 'it was for Gaul that Caesar set out'.

3   Adverbial phrases may be 'shadowed' (or 'sandwiched') between two grammatically connected words when they are logically connected with the enclosing phrase, e.g.: *mágnā in hāc rē prūdéntiā ūténdum est* 'great prudence must be used in this matter' (*in hāc rē* limits the application of the prudence to *this matter*); *clārṓrum uirṓrum post mórtem honṓrēs pérmanent* 'the honours paid to great men remain after death' (*post mórtem* warns us in good time that we are thinking of a special kind of honour – the sort that may be paid after death).

(c)   **Some consequences of emphasis, scene-setting and shadowing**

1   The normal place for subordinating conjunctions is at the beginning of their clause, but when other words in the clause are used for 'scene-setting' (as often in temporal or conditional clauses), the conjunction often ends up immediately before the verb: *Caésar in Gálliam cum contendísset* 'when Caesar had marched into Gaul'.

2   In accusative and infinitive constructions, if there is no other word with more emphasis, the infinitive often comes at the very beginning, being often followed immediately by an unemphatic pronoun subject: (*díxit míhi Caésar*) *uélle sē cōnsulátum pétere* 'Caesar told me he wanted to stand for the consulship.' On the other hand, if one of the other words is emphatic, it will naturally come first (the unemphatic pronoun remaining in second place): (*díxit míhi Caésar*) *cōnsulátum sē uélle pétere* 'Caesar told me that it was the <u>consulship</u> he wanted to stand for.' When it is discovered for the first time that Britain is an island, Tacitus reports the event as follows: *hanc ṓram nouíssimī máris tunc prímum Rōmṓna clássis circumuécta ínsulam ésse Británniam adfirmấuit,* 'that was the first time a Roman fleet had rounded this shore of the furthest sea, and this confirmed that Britain was an <u>island</u>' – i.e. 'it was an <u>island</u> that Britain was'.

Appendix: The Latin language[1]

A brief history of the Latin language

The beginnings

Latin is an Indo-European (IE) language, that is one of the many languages belonging to the IE family, whose members extended already in ancient or medieval times from the Atlantic coasts of Europe (e.g. Old Irish) to India (e.g. Sanskrit, the 'Latin' of India) and Chinese Turkestan (an IE language called Tocharian). Even in Europe itself, these languages constitute several different groups: Hellenic, represented by the numerous dialects of ancient Greek; Italic, comprising Latin and its closest relatives in central Italy, notably Faliscan (the dialect of Falerii), Umbrian and Oscan (the language of the Samnites); Germanic, including Icelandic, English, Dutch, German, the Scandinavian languages, and Gothic; and Celtic, including Irish, Welsh, Cornish, Breton, and extinct languages (such as Old Gaulish) spoken on the continent of Europe (see schema below). Latin is in the unique position of being not only a member of the Italic group but also the ancestor of the very important surviving group of

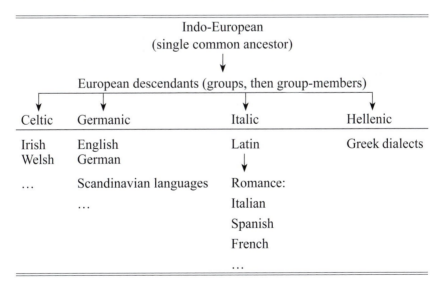

Indo-European
(single common ancestor)
↓
European descendants (groups, then group-members)

Celtic	Germanic	Italic	Hellenic
Irish	English	Latin	Greek dialects
Welsh	German	↓	
…	Scandinavian languages	Romance:	
	…	Italian	
		Spanish	
		French	
		…	

1 On the subjects touched on in this Appendix, see the books listed on p. 283 above, especially those by Clackson and Horrocks, Palmer, Wackernagel, and Weiss. Many of the examples in the section on Latin and the Romance languages are drawn gratefully from Weiss.

European languages that we call 'Romance' (including Portuguese, Spanish, French, Italian, Rumanian), which developed during the later Roman Empire and subsequently. In the early years of the Roman Republic, say around 500 BC, Latin, the dialect of Rome, was just one of many languages spoken in Italy (some of them IE, whether members of the Italic branch or like Greek and Messapic belonging to other IE groups, others non-IE, most famously Etruscan). By the fourth century BC, however, the energy of the Romans had reduced most of their neighbours to the status of subject allies, with the result that their languages, known to us mainly from inscriptions (also from testimonia and from isolated words taken into Latin), were gradually replaced by Latin in the course of the last three centuries BC and died out completely in the early Empire.

Early Latin

Our evidence for very early Latin, from before the end of the third century BC, when a substantial literary record begins with the plays of Plautus, consists of (a) later quotations, often modernised or garbled, of earlier, sometimes much earlier texts, religious, legal or (from the middle of the third century) literary, and (b) inscriptions, contemporary documents inscribed on metal, stone or clay. Our oldest surviving Latin inscriptions date from the seventh, sixth and fifth centuries BC. They comprise a handful of short and in various ways controversial inscriptions. Probably the earliest, and certainly the most famous, is that scratched on a golden brooch from a tomb in Praeneste (from before 600 BC): MANIOS MED FHE:FHAKED NVMASIOI (that is to say, in classical Latin: *Mănius mē fēcit Numériō* 'Manius made me for Numerius').[2] In the roughly four centuries between the inscribing of this brooch and the plays of Plautus (*c.* 254–184 BC), fundamental and far-reaching changes took place in the Latin language, as even these four seventh-century forms show: the endings *-os* and *-oi* became *-us* and *-ō* (see **H2(a)** note 2); *-d* dropped at the end of a word after a long vowel, so that *med* became *mē* (cf. the early Latin ablative singular forms *Gnaiuod* (classical *Gnaeō*), *sententiad* (classical *sententiā*)); the reduplicated perfect that we seem to see in *fhefhaked* was lost altogether in favour of the long-vowel type seen in classical *fēcit*; and single intervocalic *-s-* (as in *Numásioi*) became *-r-* regularly in all words with very few exceptions, a change called 'rhotacism', one of the most important sound-changes giving Latin its characteristic appearance (see **H3(d)** note). Other early inscriptions show other inherited sounds which have changed and become obscured by the classical period: so, for example, the diphthongs which have regularly merged with the long vowels by the first century at the latest (e.g. early *quei, sei, oinom, abdoucit* become classical *quī, sī, ūnum, abdūcit*); until about

---

2 This inscription has been often challenged as a forgery. The balance of probability is now in favour of its authenticity, but, whether it is genuine or not, the linguistic lessons it encapsulates are not affected (i.e. if it is a forgery, then its forger knew his Very Early Latin very well, probably better than anyone at that point in the nineteenth century when the brooch was supposedly unearthed!).

150 BC, the second declension distinguished gen. s. *-ī* from nom. pl. *-ei* (cf. the early dat./abl. pl. *-eis*); by well before Cicero was born (in 106 BC), nom. pl. and gen. s. were indistinguishable, as *-ī* (cf. classical dat./abl. pl. *-īs*). Another set of sound-changes characteristic of Latin arose from the accent in early Latin. While classical Latin limits the position of the accent to the second or third syllable from the end of the word, early Latin put a strong stress on the first syllable of all words, as a result of which the vowels and diphthongs in the syllables immediately after this accent were reduced (or 'weakened'). These weakened vowels survived the later shift in the position of the accent and are still seen particularly clearly in compound words, notably verbs prefixed with prepositions (e.g. early *cápiō*: *éncapiō > éncipiō* → classical *cápiō*: *incípiō*; similarly, *sēdeō*: *obsídeō*; *aéstimō*: *exístimō*; *caédō*: *incídō*; *claúdō*: *inclúdō*), or adjectives with the negative prefix *in-* (e.g. *áptus*: *inéptus*; *árma*: *inérmis*; *aéquus*: *iníquus*).

The Empire

By the end of the Republic, Roman rule extended to territories almost completely encircling the Mediterranean, and including all the islands. In the eastern Mediterranean, Greek had been long established as the second language of the users of a great variety of tongues, but in the West Latin had no such competition, and passed with surprising rapidity from being a *lingua franca* to being adopted as the language of the country in the Iberian peninsula and Gaul. The conquest by the emperor Claudius in the first century AD introduced Latin to Britain but, as in other peripheral parts of the Empire, it did not long survive the collapse of central authority in the Western Empire in the fifth century.

The Middle Ages

From this point the history of Latin divides into two. (1) In the older Roman territories of Italy, Spain and Gaul, where Latin had ousted the native languages, it gradually developed in its spoken form into the various Romance languages. (2) As the medium of Western Christianity it persisted, primarily as a *written* language of liturgy and administration, throughout the old Roman lands and wherever Christianity became established, on the borders of the Empire as in Britain, or beyond them as in Germany and Scandinavia and among some of the Western Slavs. This Christian Latin, though subject to local influences on vocabulary and idiom, was transmitted by education (i.e. it was a learned language rather than a native language), and each generation of students learned it consciously – and more or less painfully! – in an almost unchanging form. Within educated communities such as monasteries and, later, universities, Latin became a spoken language also, as well as being the normal medium of teaching and writing on serious and technical subjects such as grammar, rhetoric, logic, mathematics, law, medicine, theology and history (though in Britain both Celtic and Anglo-Saxon, and in parts of Scandinavia, the vernacular languages were cultivated in written form for learned purposes earlier than elsewhere). As the context of medieval Latin was first and foremost a religious one, the language of St Jerome's late fourth-century revision of previous Latin translations of the Bible (which became the core of the Vulgate version) was immensely influential, and sanctified late popular usages such as a simple sentence structure, changes in the use of cases and the subjunctive, and the abandonment of the accusative and infinitive construction in reported speech. At the same time, the ancient practice, more appropriate to native speakers than to learners, of confining literary study to the poets, especially Virgil, was continued – albeit not without Christian misgivings about their pagan subject-matter – and thus constructions proper to verse found their way into medieval prose works.

The renascences

As the standard and even the continued existence of this medieval Christian Latin depended on the efficiency of educational institutions, it fluctuated with the stability and prosperity of a given region, and its history is marked by a series of renascences following periods of declining standards. One such was the Carolingian Renascence under the patronage of the Emperor Charlemagne, *c.* 800 AD, who summoned to his court Alcuin of York to advise him and direct a reform of clerical education, and who made provision for cathedral and monastic schools. A good many classical Latin authors would have been lost to us if their works had not been collected and recopied at this time. A similar renascence took place in the twelfth century, more concerned with creation than conservation, and associated with a greater emphasis on secular learning and the first universities with their devotion to dialectic and professional training in medicine and law. The renascence to which the title 'the Renaissance' is normally applied began about 1300 in northern Italy and at the papal court at Avignon. It was characterised by an eagerness to search out, copy and edit new texts, and by an admiration for the style and a sympathetic appreciation of the virtues of writers of the classical period, above all of Cicero, and it marked the beginning of the end of the Middle Ages, which is unfairly stigmatised as a period of barbarism and ignorance.

Latin and the Romance languages

Evolution

It is common to speak of Latin as a 'dead' language, in the sense that there are no native speakers of the language of Plautus or Cicero or Augustine or Cassiodorus. A better term for it is 'corpus' language, in that we have a large corpus, or collection, of written utterances by native speakers representing a great range of times, places and socio-economic circumstances, one variety of which – classical Latin – has been selected, cultivated, preserved and transmitted over the centuries as a learned language in parallel with the Romance languages, native languages acquired by babies and toddlers. In a very important sense, however, Latin is no more a dead language than, say, Old French or even nineteenth-century Spanish, in that it is continued in the Romance languages in an unbroken series of natural transmissions from parent to child, from the last native speakers of a language we would recognise as Latin to the present generation of Romance speakers. (All languages are corpus languages for periods without access to native speakers. Even living languages, such as twenty-first-century British English, are increasingly studied through very large electronic corpora without recourse to interviews with native speakers.)

The basic questions concerning the differentiation of the Romance languages from Latin – how? when? where? – are delicate and controversial. On what may fairly be called a standard view, until about AD 800 'Latin' referred to a great range of both written and spoken forms of the language, including varieties (especially spoken) that departed considerably from educated standards of correctness. Only in the ninth century AD (the first surviving document dates from 842) did the first attempts at writing the spoken forms continuously reveal that these had come to be perceived as different languages from Latin.

Wherever Latin had become the ordinary language, by late classical times its differing local development created dialects distinct in small ways from their neighbours, and, as new states came into being after the Dark Ages, in each a particular dialect, usually associated with the seat of government, acquired prestige; as the size of states increased, these prestige dialects took the first steps towards becoming national languages.

Thus, in addition to the well-known modern national languages of French, Spanish, Portuguese, Italian and all their dialects, the Romance group includes languages such as Provençal and Catalan, reflecting cultural or former political units, as well as the Romance dialects spoken in the Alpine regions (Rhaeto-Romance) and the various islands (Sardinia, Corsica, the Balearic Islands).

Far to the east lies Romanian, first recorded in the sixteenth century, whose survival is something of a mystery in view of the late foundation and short-lived existence of the Roman province of Dacia. Dalmatian, formerly spoken in former Yugoslavia, died out about a century ago. Since the Middle Ages trade and colonisation have carried Romance languages all over the world, so that Portuguese became established in Brazil, Africa and the Far East; Spanish in Mexico and the rest of South America (hence the term 'Latin America'); and French in North America and Africa.

Variety

While all these languages have developed from roughly the same starting-point that we refer to, however loosely, as 'Latin', they have not all diverged from Latin to the same degree but have evolved each in its own characteristic fashion. At one extreme, French looks really very different from Latin, while, at the other end, Sardinian is remarkably conservative. The regional diversification of Latin certainly began long before our earliest written records of Romance, and was clear both in speech and in writing long before the fall of the Empire in the West. Of the many factors affecting the features of regional varieties, the most important include (for a given area) the length of time for which Latin was spoken, the status it enjoyed and the uses to which it was put, and the nature and intensity of the contact between Latin and other languages (e.g. with Celtic and, later, Germanic languages in France, with the pre-Roman Iberian languages and, later, with Arabic in Spain, with Magyar and Bulgarian in Romania).

Characteristics

We normally work backwards from the (attested or surviving) members of a language family in order to reconstruct their (unrecorded) common ancestor. So, for example, we have no documents in Indo-European, but we confidently reconstruct this prehistoric language in considerable detail by reasoning from systematic comparisons between the oldest surviving 'daughter' languages, Hittite, Greek, Sanskrit, Iranian, Latin etc.

If (ignoring our Latin documents) we apply this 'comparative method' to the Romance languages, we find ourselves reconstructing a language different in important respects from classical Latin. We certainly reconstruct a Latin of sorts, but a form of the language reflecting a more popular and less literary, colloquial style, unhappily called 'Vulgar' Latin (from the Latin *sérmō uulgáris*, the Latin of the *uúlgus*, the common people, or the Latin spoken *uūlgō*, in common parlance everyday Latin). While most of the detail is peculiar to each language and dialect, some general statements about the nature of the evolution from Latin to Romance can be made. A fascinating aspect of these changes, which is becoming increasingly apparent as linguistic studies progress, is the extent to which Romance forms, structures and usages are anticipated, foreshadowed in late (and even not so late!) Latin.

Nouns and adjectives

(A)   All the languages (with the limited exceptions of Old French and Romanian) abandoned all case-distinctions, reducing the noun to two forms, a singular and a plural, and retaining the Latin accusative forms as the base forms (plus a few odd remnants). (1) The singular continues the Latin accusative singular minus the *-m* (which was already weak, probably only a nasalisation, in many varieties of ancient Latin), e.g. Italian *notte* is clearly not from nom. *nox* but from acc. *noctem*; cf. the nasals at the end of French *rien* 'nothing' < Latin *rem* 'thing'; Spanish *quien*, Portuguese *quem* 'who' < Latin *quem* 'whom'. (2) The Romance plural continues either the Latin accusative plural (so in Fr., Sp., Port.: e.g. Fr. *murs* < Lat. *mūrōs*; Sp. *coronas* < Lat. *corōnās*; Sp. *anos* < Lat. *annōs*) or the Latin nominative plural (so in Ital. Rom.: e.g. Ital. *corone* < Lat. *corōnae*; Ital. *anni* < Lat. *annī*).

(B)   The three gender classes of Latin were reduced to two by the loss of the neuter, with neuter nouns generally becoming masculine (as already in first-century and even Republican Latin, e.g. *balneus* for *balneum* 'bath' in Petronius and in Pompeiian graffiti; *collus* for *collum* 'neck' in Republican authors including Varro).

(C) The five Latin declensions were reduced to three. Fifth declension nouns were transferred to the first declension (e.g. Romance words for 'ice', Old Italian *ghiaccia* etc., reflect not classical Latin *glaciēs* but rather *glacia; cf. already classical Latin 1st decl. *māteria* tending to replace 5th decl. *māteriēs*); and fourth declension nouns were transferred to the second, with a few retentions, esp. of feminine 4th decl. nouns (e.g. the standard Italian for 'hands' is *mani*, though some dialects have plural *le mano* < Lat. *illae manūs*; note that Lat. *manum* retains its feminine gender in most Romance languages, Ital. *la mano*, Fr. *la main*, Sp. *la mano*, etc.

(D) The synthetic forms of the comparative of regular adjectives and adverbs were systematically replaced by combining *plūs* (Ital., Fr.) or *magis* (Sp., Port., Rom.) with the positive grade, e.g. Lat. *calidior* → Ital. *più caldo*, Fr. *plus chaud*, Sp. *más caliénte* (the superlative being marked by the addition of the definite article, Fr. *le plus chaud*, etc.); compare already in pre-classical Latin e.g. *plūs miser* in Ennius, *magis fidēlis* in Plautus. A few irregular comparatives survive, e.g. Lat. *meliōrem* 'better' > Ital. *migliore*, Fr. *meilleur*, Sp. *mejor*; Latin *māiorem* 'bigger' > Ital. *maggiore*, Sp. *mayor*. In place of the inflected adverb, e.g. *lentē*, the Romance languages formed phrases with the Latin ablative *mente* (lit. 'with a — mind'), e.g. *lentā mente* → Ital., Sp. *lentamente*, Fr. *lentement*.

(E) The indefinite and definite articles were introduced and grammaticalised (i.e. made standard, obligatory features of Romance grammar), based on forms of Latin *ūnus* 'one' and *ille* 'that', respectively. So, e.g. Lat. *ūnus homo* 'one fellow' > Ital. *un uomo* 'a man'; Lat. *ūnum hominem* > Fr. *un homme*; Lat. *illum hominem* > Fr. *l'homme*; Lat. *illī/illōs hominēs* > Ital. *gli uomini*, Fr. *les hommes*; Sp. *el* < Lat. nom. *ille*, Ital. *il* < dat. *illī*, Ital. *lo* < acc. *illum*.

(F) The insubstantial demonstratives *is* and *hic* disappeared, their functions being taken by *ipse*, *iste*, and compounds of these with *ecce*. So, e.g. from *ipse*, *ipsum*: Sp. *ese* 'this', Ital. *esso* 'it'; from *iste*: Sp. *este* 'this'; from *ecc(u) istu(m)/iste*: Ital. *questo*, Fr. *ce*, *cet*, Old Sp. *aqueste*. Note also the combination *ecce/eccu/accu* + various forms of *ille* > Fr. *celui*, *ceux*, *celle(s)*, Ital. *quel*, *quello*, etc., Sp. *aquel*, *aquella*, etc. (Note that we find various combinations of *ecce* + *iste* or *ille* already in Plautus.)

Verbs

(A) The four (and a half!) Latin conjugations of the present were reduced everywhere, but in different ways in different Romance languages: to four in Romanian, to three in Spanish, Portuguese and Italian (1st vs. 2nd + 3rd vs. 4th), to two in French (1st vs. the rest).

(B) The whole synthetic passive was lost and replaced by (a) the reflexive pronoun *se* + the active (e.g. Lat. *appellātur* → *se appellat* (already in

Latin) → Fr. *il s'appelle*), or (b) a new phrasal passive comprising the perfect participle passive + *esse*. So, e.g. Lat. *amātur* → Ital. *è amato*, Fr. *il est aimé* (or, one could say, the Latin perfect passive *amātus est* was reinterpreted as present). All deponents were eliminated or replaced by forms with active endings.

(C)   The synthetic future and (except in Portuguese) the pluperfect indicative disappeared; the future perfect survived only in Spanish and Portuguese. Furthermore, in Western Romance, the imperfect subjunctive was lost and replaced by the pluperfect subjunctive, e.g. Lat. *cantāuisset/cantāsset* > e.g. Ital. *cantasse*, Fr. *il chantât*. Romanian used the pluperfect subjunctive to replace the lost pluperfect indicative, e.g. Rom. *jurasem* continues Lat. *iūrāssem* in form, but *iūrāueram* in meaning.

(D)   The Latin synthetic future (in *-bō -bis -bit* and *-am -ēs -et*) was replaced nearly everywhere in Romance by a combination of the present infinitive of the main verb followed by *habeō* in the sense 'I have to / I ought to'. The combination was at first periphrastic but soon grammaticalised and rendered synthetic: e.g. Lat. *cantāre habet* (and this *is* attested in late Latin) > Ital. *canterà*, Fr. *il chantera*. (Other Romance future constructions include *dēbeō* + inf. in Sardinian, and *uolō* + inf. in Romanian with the verb 'to wish' as in other Balkan languages, including modern Greek.)

(E)   Beside the Latin synthetic perfect (which became the Romance preterite), a new periphrastic perfect was formed with the present of *habēre* or *tenēre* (in intransitive verbs, sometimes with *esse*) + the perfect participle, e.g. Latin *cantātum habet* (and again, this is well attested in late Latin) > Ital. *ha cantato*, Fr. *il a chanté*. In parallel with this, a new pluperfect was created using the imperfect of the auxiliary verb, e.g. Lat. *habēbat cantātum* > Fr. *il avait chanté*.

(F)   The other notable Romance creation was the conditional, formed like the new future (D above) but with the imperfect or (in Italian) the perfect of *habeō* added to the infinitive, e.g. *cantāre-habēbat/habuit* → Fr. *il chanterait*, Ital. *canterebbe*; a parallel past conditional was then formed from the conditional of *habeō* plus the past participle, e.g. Fr. *il aurait chanté*.

(G)   The future participle (in *-urus*) did not survive, and the present participle (in *-nt-*), except in other, mainly adjectival, uses (e.g. Sp. *caliente* 'hot', Fr. *pendant* 'during'), was generally replaced by the ablative of the gerund, e.g. Lat. *cantandō* > Ital. *cantando*, Sp. *cantando*, Fr. *chantant*. (This use of the gerund can be seen already in first-century literary authors, including Livy.)

Vocabulary

The Latin words that survived into Romance are often not among those used by classical literary authors. This is for a variety of reasons: the classical word may have been monosyllabic or otherwise physically too slight to survive sound-change, or it may have been irregular in its declension/conjugation, or it may simply have gone out of fashion generally or at that particular social level. Often a monosyllabic or irregular word was either extended with a prefix or suffix or replaced altogether by a longer synonym or near-synonym of a common regular type. (I say 'synonym or near-synonym', but note that the replacement word often undergoes a slight change of meaning.)

So, for example, the monosyllabic and irregular *edō* 'eat' came to be replaced by *comedō* 'eat up' (Sp. *comer*) or *mandūcō* 'chew' (Fr. *manger*, Ital. *mangiare*); *ferre* 'to bring' by 1st conj. *portāre* 'carry' or *leuāre* 'lift'; *eō*, *īre* 'to go' by e.g. *uādō* (Fr. *je vais*, Ital. *vado*) or *ambulāre* (Fr. *aller*); *ōs* (*ōris*) 'mouth' by *bucca* 'cheek, gob' (Fr. *bouche*, Ital. *bocca*); *apis* 'bee', *auris* 'ear' and *auis* 'bird' by what were originally their diminutives, *apicella* (Fr. *abeille*), *ōricula* (Fr. *oreille*) and *aucellus* (Ital. *uccello*).

Other lexical choices characteristic of Vulgar Latin and Roman and affecting 'core' vocabulary include the replacement of e.g. *ignis* 'fire' by *focus* 'hearth' (Fr. *feu*, etc.); *magnus* 'great' by *grandis* (Fr. *grand*, etc.); *equus* 'horse' by *caballus* 'nag, workhorse' (Fr. *cheval*, etc.); *breuis* 'short' by *curtus* 'cut short' (Fr. *court*, etc.); *pulcher* 'beautiful' by *bellus* 'pretty' (Fr. *beau*, etc.) or *fōrmōsus* 'shapely' (Sp. *hermoso*, etc.); and *domus* 'house' by *casa* 'hut' (Ital. *casa*, etc.) or *mānsiō* 'dwelling' (Fr. *maison*).

However, as Romance languages never lost the sense of being connected in some way with Latin, they continued to draw new vocabulary from 'school' or 'book' Latin, and from one another, as they developed into cultivated literary languages in the course of the Middle Ages. These later acquisitions can often be recognised because they are closer in form to their Latin source than the words that have shared the whole development of their particular Romance language (compare, e.g., Fr. *sûreté* and *sécurité* both from Lat. *sēcūritātem*, or Fr. *épice* 'spice' and *espèce* 'species' both from Lat. *speciem*, the first in each case by sound-change through Vulgar Latin, the second by later borrowing from medieval Latin).

The Latin element in English[3]

First–fourth centuries AD

The Romans attempted the conquest of Britain unsuccessfully under Julius Caesar in 55 BC, and successfully under the emperor Claudius in AD 43, after which they remained in control of Britain (but not of Ireland) until about the end of the fourth century. During this period at least the town-dwelling Britons

---

3 This subject (and others touched on in this Appendix) is very well treated by J. G. F. Powell, *Introduction to Philology for the Classical Teacher* (Cambridge 1988).

became familiar with Latin, and many Latin words were taken over into their own language and survive to the present day in its descendant, Welsh. At this time the Angles and Saxons, Germanic tribes speaking a language that was to be the ancestor of English, were still on the Continent, living along the North Sea coast of the present Netherlands, though some had already been brought into Britain by the Romans to act as a coastal defence force against other Germanic raiders. Some Latin words had been adopted by the Germanic peoples generally, in the context of trade and service with the Roman army on the Continent, and so were already part of their language when the Angles and Saxons began in the fifth century to migrate to Britain and settle there. Some of these words were in fact Greek in origin but were already naturalised in Latin. A number of modern English words have survived from this early period, absorbed partly on the Continent and partly during the Anglo-Saxons' first century in Britain.

We have: ark (*arca*, chest; also the surname Arkwright), bishop (*episcopus*), butter (*būtyrum*), candle (*candēla*), chalk (*calc-em*), cheap (*caupō*; place-names Cheapside, Chipping- 'market'; surname Chap-man 'trader'), cheese (*cāseus*), Chester (*castra*; and names in -caster, -cester, -chester), church (*kyriakon*), copper (*cuprum*), coulter (*culter*), devil (*diabolus*), dish (*discus*), fever (*febris*), inch (*uncia*), kiln (*culīna*), kitchen (*coquīna*), line (*līnea*), mallow (*malua*), mile (*mīlle passūs*), mill (*molīnum*), mint (coinage, *monēta*), mint (herb, *menta*), -monger, as fish-monger (*mangō*), pitch (tar, *picem*), purple (*purpura*), pillow (*puluīnus*), pile (as in pile-driver, *pīlum*), pin (*penna*), pine (tree, *pīnus*), port (*portus*), post (*postis*), priest (*presbyter*), plant (*planta*), pit (*puteus*), pound (weight, *pondō*), sack (*saccus*), sickle (*secula*), street (*strāta uia*), shrive (*scrībere*), shrine (*scrīnium*), tile (*tēgula*), toll (tax, *telōnium*), turtle-dove (*turtur*), wall (*uallum*), wine (*uīnum*).

Many others have fallen out of use in the course of time while others survive in dialect, such as *sikker* (*sēcūrus*) 'certain' (later taken over in its French form as sure, and then again from Old French or Latin as secure), *neep* (*nāpus*) 'turnip', *soutar* (*sūtor*) 'shoemaker' (and as a surname). Others have undergone a change of meaning which obscures the relationship, such as shambles (*scamellum*, originally 'butcher's stall'), pine (*poena*, originally 'punish', 'torment').

Fifth–sixth centuries AD

A little later, the English acquired more Latin words of a very similar kind from British speakers. This was in the period immediately after the settlement and before their conversion to Christianity in the seventh century had made any of them familiar with Latin as a written language. Examples include: anchor (*anchora*), cat (*cattus*), chervil (*cerefolium*), chest (*cista*), cowl (*cucullus*), fork (*furca*), minster (*monastērium*), monk (*monachus*), mortar (pestle and mortar, *mortārium*), mussel (*musculus*), nun (*nonna*), provost (*praepositus*), punt (*pontō*), relic (*reliquiae*), Saturday (*Saturnus*; the other days of the week were given Germanic names on the pattern of the Latin ones), stop (up) (*stuppāre*, from *stuppa* 'tow'), strap (*stroppus*), trivet (*tripodem*), trout (*tructa*).

A few others are now archaic or poetical, or of historical interest only: so, e.g. cockle (weed, *cocculus*), kirtle (tunic, *curtus*), lave (*lauāre*), soler (*sōlārium*; the sunny room or parlour in a medieval castle, now reintroduced in its Latin form in a new context).

Seventh–tenth centuries AD

During the remaining centuries before the Norman Conquest of 1066, many new Latin words appeared in English books but the majority of them were only superficially anglicised and never became widely used. Their survival rate is accordingly low. Some examples are: alms (*eleemosyna*), altar (*altāre*), apostle (*apostolus*), arch- (*archi-*), balsam (*balsamum*), beet (*bēta*), camel (*camēlus*), cole-wort, kale (*caulis*), cook (*coquus*), cope (garment, *cap(p)a*), creed (*crēdō*), idol (*īdōlum*), lily (*līlium*), martyr (*martyr*), mass (service, *missa*), offer (*offerre*), paradise (*paradīsus*), plaster (medical, *(em)plastrum*), part (*partem*), pope (*papa*), psalm (*psalmus*), purse (*bursa*), school (*schola*), spend (*(e)xpendere*), title (*titulus*), and perhaps verse (*uersus*).

In some cases where the word has survived the original meaning is no longer current: so, e.g. prime and noon (*prīma* and *nōna hōra*) originally denoted the first and ninth hours of the monastic day, and scuttle (*scutella*, diminutive of *scūtum* 'shield') originally meant 'dish', 'platter'.

Some members of this late pre-Conquest group are more likely to have been borrowed a second time from French than to have survived from earlier times, and this was certainly the case with many of the Latin loan-words found in Anglo-Saxon, when the modern forms show that they were lost and re-acquired in this way. So, e.g. Anglo-Saxon *mentel* from Latin *mantellum* 'cloak' was lost, but re-acquired from Old French *mantel*, whence English *mantle* and modern French *manteau*.

7 Eleventh–fifteenth centuries and after

It is noteworthy that the Norman Conquest did not herald an immediate influx of French words, rather the most prolific period of borrowing was right at the end of the Norman period, in the fourteenth and fifteenth centuries, as part and parcel of the establishment and spread of English as a literary language. From the Conquest to the Renaissance, a very large number of words of ultimately Latin origin found their way into Middle English, but almost invariably they did so either through French or with the same modifications of endings as similar words had undergone in French, so that direct borrowings from Latin are hard to identify.

From the sixteenth century this type of borrowing (from French or Latin) continues, but now we start to find a substantial number of words coming into English as unmodified Latin and retaining such features as Latin plural formations. The largest number of this last type came in during the sixteenth and seventeenth centuries with a sharp decline thereafter, except in the terminologies of the natural sciences. A few examples from each century will illustrate the fully Latin appearance of this type of loanword.

Sixteenth century: alias, arbiter, area, circus, compendium, decorum, delirium, exit, genius, ignoramus, interim, interregnum, medium, peninsula, radius, species

Seventeenth century: affidavit, agenda, census, complex, curriculum, fulcrum, honorarium, lens, pendulum, premium, rabies, series, specimen, squalor, tedium

Eighteenth century: alibi, bonus, deficit, inertia, insomnia, propaganda, ultimatum, via

Nineteenth century: aquarium, consensus, omnibus, referendum.

Total Latin–English Learning vocabulary

Note

This vocabulary contains all the words in the Learning Vocabularies which appear in the *Text and Vocabulary* volume, together with words learned in this *Grammar and Exercises* volume, which are referred to by subsection number, printed in bold. Words which appear in sections of *Text and Vocabulary* in forms significantly different from the basic form are also entered, with a reference to the basic form, e.g. *ablāt-*: see *auferō*; *cuius* gen. s. of *quī/quis*.

A

ā/ab (+ abl.) away from 1D; by (usually a person, after passive verbs) 4D(i)

abeō abīre abiī abitum I go/come away 1C

abiciō 3/4 *abiēcī abiectus* I throw down, throw away 4F(i)

ablāt-: see *auferō*

absēns absent-is absent, away 4C(ii)

abstul-: see *auferō*

absum abesse āfuī āfutūrus I am away from, am absent 4C(i); I am distant 5E(ii)

ac (or *atque*) and 2A

    aliter ac otherwise than

    alius ac different from

    contrā ac contrary to what

    īdem ac the same as

    par ac equivalent to

    pariter ac equally as

    perinde ac in like manner as, just as

    similis ac similar to (see **179.1**)

accēdō 3 *accessī accessum* I approach, reach 4E(iii)

access-: see *accēdō*

accidit 3 *accidit* — (*ut* / *ut nōn* + subj.) it happens (that / that not) 4F(i)

accipiō 3/4 *accēpī acceptus* I receive, welcome; learn; obtain 2E; sustain, meet with 4E(ii)

accūsō 1 I accuse X (acc.) of Y (gen.) 4A(iii)

ācer ācr-is e keen, sharp, hot 53

acerb-us a um bitter 5D(ii)

aci-ēs ēī 5f. battle-line; sharp edge, point; keenness (of sight) 5G(i)

āct-: see *agō*

ad (+ acc.) towards; at 1A; for the purpose of 4F(i); *usque ad* right up to 6A(iv)

addō 3 *addidī additus* I add; increase 5F(i)

adeō adīre adiī aditum I go/come to, approach 1C

adeō to such an extent 5A(i)

adept-: see *adipīscor*

adferō adferre attulī allātus (or *afferō* etc.) I bring to 5C(iii)

adgredior (*aggredior*) 3/4dep. *adgressus* (*aggressus*) I go up to 2B; attack 4E(i)

adhūc up to now 6B(ii)

adipīscor 3dep. *adeptus* I get, gain, acquire 2B

adiungō 3 *adiūnxī adiūnctus* I join X (acc.) to Y (dat.) 5A(ii)

adloquor (*alloquor*) 3dep. *adlocūtus* (*allocūtus*) I address 2B

adorior 4dep. *adortus* I attack, rise up against 6C(ii)

adsum adesse adfuī adfutūrus I am present, am at hand 2D; (+ dat.) I am present with 3D(iv)

aduers-us a um hostile; opposite; unfavourable 5F(i); in front (i.e. facing the enemy) 5G(iii)

aduertō: see *animaduertō*

adulēscēns adulēscent-is 3m. youth 6B(viii)

aduocō 1 I summon 5F(i)

aedifici-um ī 2n. building 3D(v)

aedificō 1 I build 3B(i)

aedis aed-is 3f. temple; pl. *aed-ēs aed-ium* house 1B

aeger aegr-a um ill 5G(i)

aegrē with difficulty 6D(iv)

Aenē-as ae 1m. (acc. *Aenēan*) Aeneas 3A(ii)

aequor aequor-is 3n. plain; sea 6A(vii)

aequ-us a um fair, balanced, equal 1G; level; calm; impartial 3D(ii)

aes aer-is 3n. bronze 5A(ii)

    aes aliēn-um aer-is aliēn-ī 3n. + 1/2adj. debt (lit. 'someone else's bronze') 5A(ii)

aestimō 1 I value; estimate 6A(iv)

aetās aetāt-is 3f. age; lifetime; generation 5A(ii)

afferō see *adferō*

affirmō 1 I state strongly, assert 4A(iii)

age come! 1G

ager agr-ī 2m. land, field, territory 2B

aggredior: see *adgredior*

agitō 1 I stir up, incite (*agō* + *-it-*) 5A(i)

agmen agmin-is 3n. column 5E(ii)

agō 3 *ēgī āctus* I do, act 2B; drive, lead, direct 4F(ii); spend, pass 5F(ii); (*dē* + abl.) discuss 6C(iii)

    grātiās agō (+ dat.) I thank 2D

Agrigentīn-us ī 2m. person from Agrigentum 4A(i)

aiō irr. I say 6B(iv)

aliās at another time **102**

alibī somewhere else **102**

alicubī somewhere **102**

aliēn-us a um someone else's 5A(ii)

    aes aliēn-um aer-is aliēn-ī debt (lit. 'someone else's bronze') 5A(ii)

aliquandō at some time 6B(viii)

aliquantō to some extent **102**

aliquī aliqua aliquod some (adj.) **102**

aliquis aliqua aliquid someone (pron.) **102**

aliquot several 5A(ii)

aliter ac otherwise than **179.1**

ali-us a ud other 3A(i), 4B(iii) (see **102**)
    (two different cases in same clause = 'different … different': see **102**)

aliī … aliī some… others **102**
    alius ac other than **179.1**

alloquor: see *adloquor*

alō 3 *aluī altus* I feed, nourish, rear; support; strengthen 6B(iv)

alter alter-a um one (or other) of two 2A (see **62**)

alt-us a um high; deep 6A(vii)

amb-ō ae ō both 2E (declined as *duo*, see **54**)

amīciti-a ae 1f. friendship 6B(vii)

amīc-us a um friendly 3D(i)

amīc-us ī 2m. friend, ally 3D(i)

āmittō 3 *āmīsī āmissus* I lose 1F

amō 1 I love, like 1B

amor amōr-is 3m. love 3B(ii); pl. girl-friend, sexual intercourse 6A(i)

amplexor 1dep. I embrace 2E

amplius more than 5G(i)

ampl-us a um large, great 5B(i)

an = *-ne* = ? (in direct questions); whether, if (in indirect questions: + subj. = *num*) 6D(iii)

    utrum … an = double question, i.e. A or B? (negative *annōn*) 5D(i)

    utrum … an (+ subj.) whether … or (indirect question: negative *necne*) **172**

anim-a ae 1f. soul, life, breath 5G(iii)

animaduertō (or *animum aduertō*) 3 *animaduertī animaduersus* I observe, take note of 6B(i)

animum aduertō = *animaduertō* 6C(ii)

anim-us ī 2m. mind, spirit, heart 1E

annōn or not? (see *an* or *utrum*) 5D(i)

ann-us ī 2m. year 3A(ii)

ante (+ acc.) before, in front of 2D; (adv.) earlier, before 4E(ii)

anteā before 4G(i)

antequam before **165**

aperiō 4 *aperuī apertus* I open; reveal 5B(ii)

appellō 1 I name, call; address 5G(i)

appropinquō 1 (+ dat.) I approach 6C(ii)

apud (+ acc.) at the house of, in the hands of, in the works of 1F; among 4A(i)

aqu-a ae 1f. water 1C

ār-a ae 1f. altar 5D(iv)

arbiter arbitr-ī 2m. judge 3A(i)

arbitror 1dep. I think, consider; give judgment 2C

arbor arbor-is 3f. tree 6D(iii)

arcessō 3 *arcessīuī arcessītus* I summon 5D(i)

ārdeō 2 *ārsī ārsum* I burn; am in love 6C(i)

argent-um ī 2n. silver; silver-plate; money 4C(i)

arm-a ōrum 2n. pl. arms; armed men 5A(i)

armāt-us a um armed 5A(iii)

ars art-is 3f. skill, art, accomplishment 6D(ii)

arx arc-is 3f. citadel 5D(i)

Asi-a ae 1f. Asia Minor 4B(i)

asper asper-a um harsh, cruel, dangerous 3A(ii); rough 5E(ii)

aspici-ō 3/4 *aspexī aspectus* I look upon 4H

at but 2A

atque (or *ac*) and, also 2A (see *ac* for list of comparative expressions learned in **179.1**)

atrōx atrōc-is fierce, unrelenting 6B(vii)

attribuō 3 *attribuī attribūtus* I assign, give 5D(i)

attul-i-: see *adferō*

auctōritās auctōritāt-is 3f. weight, authority 5B(i)

audāci-a ae 1f. boldness, cockiness 1G

audācter boldly (from *audāx*) 3B(i)

audāx audāc-is brave, bold, resolute 1F

audeō 2 semi-dep. *ausus* I dare 2E (see **76**)

audiō 4 I hear, listen to 1D

auferō auferre abstulī ablātus I take away X (acc.) from Y (dat.) 1F

augeō 2 *auxī auctus* I increase (trans.) 5D(iv)

aul-a ae 1f. pot 1A (NB the normal classical Latin form is *olla*, while *aula* generally means 'court' or 'palace')

aure-us a um golden 2D

aur-um ī 2n. gold 1A

aus-: see *audeō*

aut or 1F

aut … aut either … or 4D(ii)

autem but, however (2nd word) 1A

autumn-us ī 2m. autumn, fall 6D(ii)

au-us ī 2m. grandfather 3B(i)

auxiliō est (it) is of help to X (dat.), X (nom.) helps Y (dat.) 3D(v)

auxili-um ī 2n. help, aid 3D(v)

B

bell-um ī 2n. war: *bellum gerō* I wage war 3A(ii)

bell-us a um pretty, beautiful 6B(ii)

bene well, thoroughly, rightly 1E; good! fine! 2A (see **79**)

benīgn-us a um kind, favourable 3B(ii)

bibō 3 *bibī* — I drink 4B(iii)

bon-a ōrum 2n. pl. goods 5F(ii)

bon-us a um good, brave, fit, honest 1E

breu-is e short, brief 3A(i)

breuī (sc. *tempore*) shortly, soon 5C(i)

C

cadō 3 *cecidī cāsum* I fall; die 5G(ii)

caedēs caed-is 3f. slaughter, carnage 5B(iii)

caedō 3 *cecīdī caesus* I cut (down); flog, beat; kill 4B(iv)

caelest-is e in the heavens 6D(iii)

cael-um ī 2n. sky, heaven 6D(i)

caes-: see *caedō*

calamitās calamitāt-is 3f. disaster, calamity 4B(i)

camp-us ī 2m. field, plain 6D(iii)

candid-us a um white; bright, beautiful 6A(vi)

capiō 3/4 *cēpī captus* I take, capture 2A

caput capit-is 3n. head; source 2B

carcer carcer-is 3m. prison; barrier 5E(i)

Carthāgō Carthāgin-is 3f. Carthage 3A(ii)

castīgō 1 I rebuke, chasten 2D

castr-a ōrum 2n. pl. camp 2B

cās-us ūs 4m. outcome; event, occurrence; disaster, death

cāsū by accident; by chance 6B(viii)

caueō 2 *cāuī cautus* I am wary 2B

caus-a ae 1f. case; reason 4F(i); cause 4G(ii)

causā (+ gen. – which precedes it) for the sake of **152.2**

411

cecid-: see *cadō*

cēdō 3 *cessī cessum* I yield; go 5F(i)

celer celer-is e swift 2A

celeritās celeritāt-is 3f. speed 4B(iv)

celeriter quickly (from *celer*) 3B(ii)

celerrimē very quickly (from *celer*: see **87**) 3C(ii)

cēlō 1 I hide 1A

cēn-a ae 1f. dinner 1F

cēn-ō 1 I dine 3C(i)

centum 100 54

centuriō centuriōn-is 3m. centurion 5G(i)

cēp-: see *capiō*

certē without doubt 1G

certior fīō (*fierī factus*) I am informed 6B(i)

certiōrem faciō (3/4 *fēcī*) I inform X (acc.) 6B(i)

certō for a fact 1G

certō 1 I struggle, fight; vie 5F(i)

cert-us a um sure, certain 5B(ii)

cess-: see *cēdō*

cēter-ī ae a the rest, the others 4B(i)

cib-us ī 2m. food 4E(i)

circiter (adv.) about 5E(ii)

circum (+ acc.) around 4C(ii)

circumeō circumīre circumiī circumitum I go around 4C(ii)

circumsedeō 2 *circumsēdī circumsessus* I besiege, blockade 6B(ii)

citō quickly 2C

cīuis cīu-is 3m. and f. citizen 1F

cīuitās cīuitāt-is 3f. state 4G(ii)

clam secretly 1B

clāmitō 1 I keep on shouting (*clāmō* + *-it-*) 4G(i)

clāmō 1 I shout 1A

clāmor clāmōr-is 3m. shout; outcry; noise 4A(iv)

clār-us a um famous, well-known 4B(i); clear 6B(vi)

classis class-is 3f. fleet 4D(i)

Cleomenēs Cleomen-is 3m. Cleomenes 4E(i)

coēg-: see *cōgō*

coepī (perfect form: past participle active/passive *coeptus*) I began 4B(ii)

cōgitō 1 I ponder, reflect, consider 1C

cognit-: see *cognōscō*

cognōscō 3 *cognōuī cognitus* I get to know, examine 2B (perf. tense = 'I know',

plupf. = 'I knew', fut. perf. = 'I shall know')

cōgō 3 *coēgī coāctus* I force, compel; gather 4H

cohors cohort-is 3f. governor's retinue; cohort 4D(i)

cohortor 1dep. I encourage 5C(ii)

collēg-a ae 1m. colleague 6B(iv)

colligō 3 *collēgī collēctus* I collect, gather; gain, acquire 4C(ii)

collocō 1 I place, station 5A(iii)

coll-um ī 2n. neck 6D(iv)

colō 3 *coluī cultus* I worship; cultivate, till; inhabit 4A(ii)

com-a ae 1f. hair; foliage 6D(iii)

comes comit-is 3m. companion, friend; (pl.) retinue 4B(i)

committō 3 *commīsī commissus* I commit 4H

commod-us a um satisfactory, convenient 6B(i)

commoror 1dep. I delay, wait 4E(iii)

commoueō 2 *commōuī commōtus* I move; remove; excite, disturb 4C(ii)

commūn-is e shared in, common, universal 5D(ii)

comparō 1 I prepare, provide, get ready, get 4B(iii)

complector 3dep. *complexus* I embrace 6B(iii)

complūr-ēs complūr-ium several 6B(iii)

concidō 3 *concidī* — I fall, collapse; am killed 4F(i)

concordi-a ae 1f. harmony 5D(iii)

concurrō 3 *concurrī concursum* I run together 4B(iv)

condemnō 1 I condemn X (acc.) for Y (gen.) 6B(i)

condiciō condiciōn-is 3f. condition, term 6B(vi)

condiciōnem (*condiciōnēs*) *ferre* to make terms 6B(vi)

cond-ō 3 *condid-ī conditus* I found 3A(ii)

cōnfect-: see *cōnficiō*

cōnficiō 3/4 *cōnfēcī cōnfectus* I finish 5C(iii); weaken 6C(iii)

cōnfirmō 1 I state clearly, confirm 4A(iii)

cōnfiteor 2dep. *cōnfessus* I confess, acknowledge 4G(i)

cōnflagrō 1 I burn (intrans.) 4E(ii)

coniciō 3/4 *coniēcī coniectus* I throw 4A(iv)

coniūnx coniug-is 3f. wife; 3m. husband 3B(ii)

coniūrātiō coniūrātiōn-is 3f. conspiracy 5A(i)

coniūrātor coniūrātōr-is 3m. conspirator 5A(i)

cōnor 1dep. I try 2C

cōnscrīptī: patrēs cōnscrīptī = senators 5D(ii)

cōnseruō 1 I keep safe, preserve 5D(ii)

cōnsīderō 1 I consider, ponder 5B(ii)

cōnsīdō 3 *cōnsēdī* — I settle down; encamp 5E(ii)

cōnsili-um ī 2n. plan; advice; judgement 1E

cōnsistō 3 *cōnstitī* — I stop, stand my ground 6C(ii)

cōnspicor 1dep. I catch sight of 2E

cōnstit-: see *cōnsistō*

cōnstituō 3 *cōnstituī cōnstitūtus* I decide 4C(i)

cōnsul cōnsul-is 3m. consul 3D(iv)

cōnsulāt-us ūs 4m. consulship 5A(i)

continenti-a ae 1f. self-control, restraint 1G

contiō contiōn-is 3f. meeting, assembly 5F(i)

contrā (+ acc.) against 4H
    contrā ac contrary to what 5G **179.1**

cōnūbi-um ī 2n. marriage 3B(ii)

conuell-ō 3 *conuellī conuulsus* I tear away 4H

conueniō 4 *conuēnī conuentum* (*ad*) I meet (at) 4B(iii)

conuīui-um ī 2n. party 4B(iii)

conuocō 1 I summon, call together 5A(iii)

cōpi-a ae 1f. multitude, crowd 5E(ii)

cōpi-ae ārum 1f. pl. troops 5E(ii)

coqu-ō 3 *coxī coctus* I cook 1F; **83**

coqu-us ī 2m. cook 1A

corn-ū ūs 4n. wing (of army); horn 5G(i)

corōn-a ae 1f. garland 1A

corpus corpor-is 3n. body 3D(iii)

cotīdiē daily 4D(ii)

crēber crēbr-a um frequent; thick, close 6B(ii)

crēdō 3 *crēdidī crēditum/us* I believe in (+ dat.); entrust X (acc.) to Y (dat.) 1G

crūdēl-is e cruel 5D(i)

cui dat. s. of *quī/quis*

cuidam dat. s. of *quīdam*

cuiquam dat. of *quisquam*

cuius gen. s. of *quī/quis*

cuiusdam gen. s. of *quīdam*

culp-a ae 1f. fault; blame (often of sexual misconduct) 6A(vii)

culter cultr-ī 2m. knife **28**

cum (+ abl.) with 2A; (+ subj.) when; since; although 4E(iii)
    cum semel as soon as 6A(iv)
    cum ... tum both ... and 5D(ii)

cūnctor 1dep. I delay; hesitate (+ inf.) 5C(i)

cūnct-us a um all, the whole of 6D(iii)

cupiditās cupiditāt-is 3f. lust, greed, desire 4B(ii)

cupiō 3/4 *cupīuī cupītus* I desire, yearn for; want desperately 4B(i)

cūr why? 1A

cūr-a ae 1f. care; worry, concern 1B

cūrō 1 I look after, care for 1B; see to the —ing of X (acc. + gerundive) 4H; am in command 5G(i)

curs-us ūs 4m. running; course; direction; voyage 6C(ii)

custōs custōd-is 3m. and f. guardian 3B(i)

D

dat-: see *dō*

dē (+ abl.) about, concerning 2A; from, down from 4F(i)

de-a ae 1f. goddess 3A(i)

dēbeō 2 I ought (+ inf.); owe 2D

decem ten **54**

dēcēp-: see *dēcipiō*

decet 2 it befits X (acc.) to Y (inf.) 5C(iii) and **159**

decim-us a um tenth **161**

dēcipiō 3/4 *dēcēpī dēceptus* I deceive 2A

decus decor-is 3n. honour; beauty 5F(i)

ded-: see *dō*

dēdecet 2 it is unseemly for X (acc.) to Y (inf.) **161**

dēdecorī est it is a disgrace for X (dat.) 5C(iii)

dēdō 3 *dēdidī dēditus* I hand over, surrender 3D(iv)

dēdūcō 3 *dēdūxī dēductus* I lead away, lead down 2B

dēess-: see *dēsum*

dēfendō 3 *dēfendī dēfēnsus* I defend 2C

dēferō dēferre dētulī dēlātus I report, bring news of; accuse, denounce; transfer 4A(iii)

dēfu-: see *dēsum*

dein = *deinde* 6A(iv)

deinde then, next 1A

dēlāt-: see *dēferō*

dēleō 2 *dēlēuī dēlētus* I destroy 2D

dēnique finally; in a word 4E(i)

dēscendō 3 *dēscendī dēscēnsum* I descend 6C(iv)

dēsum dēesse dēfuī dēfutūrus I am missing, am lacking; fail; abandon (+ dat.) 4D(ii)

dētul-: see *dēferō*

de-us ī 2m. god 1B (see **16**)

dexter dextr-a um right; favourable 5G(i)

dextr-a ae 1f. right hand 5F(i)

dī nom. pl. of *deus*

dīc imperative s. of *dīcō* 1D

dīcō 3 *dīxī dictus* I speak, say 1D

diēs diē-ī 5m. and f. day 2B

in *diēs* day by day 3C(i)

difficil-is e difficult 2A

diffīdō 3semi-dep. *diffīsus* (+ dat.) I distrust 6C(iii)

dignitās dignitāt-is 3f. distinction, position; honour; rank, high office 4H

dign-us a um worthy; (+ abl.) worthy of 4H

dīligēns dīligent-is careful, diligent 3C(i)

dīligenti-a ae 1f. care, diligence 5D(iii)

dīmicō 1 I fight 6B(vi)

dīmittō 3 *dīmīsī dīmissus* I send away 5B(i)

discēdō 3 *discessī discessum* I depart; (*in sententiam* + gen.) go over to X's view 5E(i)

discordi-a ae 1f. discord, strife, quarrel (with capital letter, the goddess Discord) 3A(i)

dispōnō 3 *disposuī dispositus* I set, place (in different places) 5E(i)

diū for a long time 3D(v)
   comp. *diūtius* 3D(v)
   superl. *diūtissimē* 3D(v)

dīuers-us a um different 5A(iii)

dīues dīuit-is rich (as noun 3m. rich man) 1D, **47**

dīuiti-ae ārum 1f. pl. riches 5F(i)

diūtius any longer 3D(v) (see *diū*)

dīu-us ī 2m. god 6D(i)

dō 1 *dedī datus* I give 1B; *operam dō* I pay attention to X (dat.) 1E

doct-us a um skilled in X (abl.); learned 5A(ii)

doleō 2 I suffer pain, grieve 6A(vi)

dolor dolōr-is 3m. pain, anguish 5D(i)

dol-us ī 2m. trick, fraud, deception 2E

domī at home 1D

domin-us ī 2m. master 1C

domō from home 2A

domum to home, homewards 1D

domum dūcō I take home, marry 1D

dom-us ūs 4f. (irr.) house, home **56**

dōnō 1 I give 6A(i)

dōn-um ī 2n. gift, offering 4H

dormiō 4 I sleep 1F

dōs dōt-is 3f. dowry 1E

dubitō 1 I doubt; hesitate (+ inf.) 6B(vi)

dubi-us a um doubtful **174.2**

dūc imperative s. of *dūcō* **37**

ducent-ī ae a 200 **54**

dūcō 3 *dūxī ductus* I lead 1D; think, consider 6B(vii)

dulc-is e sweet 5D(iii)

dum (+ indic.) while 2A; (+indic./subj.) until; (+ subj.) provided that (also *dummodo, modo*) **165.4**

duo duae duo two **54**

duodecim twelve 5B(iii)

duodēuīgintī eighteen **161**

dūx-: see *dūcō*

dux duc-is 3m. leader 3A(ii)

E

ē (+ abl.) out of, from (also *ex*) 1C
ea nom. s. f. or nom./acc. pl. n. of *is*
eā abl. s. f. of *is*
eadem nom. s. f. or nom./acc. pl. n. of *īdem*
eādem abl. s. f. of *īdem*
eae nom. pl. f. of *is*
eam acc. s. f. of *is*
eandem acc. s. f. of *īdem*
eārum gen. pl. f. of *īdem*
eās acc. pl. f. of *is*
eāsdem acc. pl. f. of *īdem*
ēbri-us a um drunk 4D(i)
ecce look! see! 2A
ēducō 1 I raise, educate 3C(i)
efficiō 3/4 *effēcī effectus* I bring about (*ut* +
    subj.); cause, make; complete 5A(i)
effugiō 3/4 *effūgī* — I escape 4B(iii)
ēg-: see *agō*
egeō 2 *eguī* — I lack, need, am in want of
    (+ abl. or gen.) 4E(i)
ego I 1A
ēgredior 3/4dep. *ēgressus* I go/come
    out 2B
ēgregi-us a um outstanding, excellent 6B(iii)
ēgress-: see *ēgredior*
eī dat. s. or nom. pl. m. of *is*
eīs dat./abl. pl. of *is*
eius gen. s. of *is*
enim for (2nd word) 1A
eō īre iuī or *iī itum* I go/come 1C
eō to that place 5C(i) *quō* + comparative ...
    eō + comparative 'the more X ... the
    more Y' 6B(vi)
eōdem abl. s. m. or n. of *īdem*
eōrum gen. pl. of *is*
eōs acc. pl. m. of *is*
eōsdem acc. pl. m. of *īdem*
epul-ae ārum 1f. pl. meal, feast 3C(i)

eques equit-is 3m. horseman; pl. cavalry
    3D(iv); 'knight' (member of the
    Roman business class) 4G(ii)
equitāt-us ūs 4m. cavalry 6C(ii)
equus ī 2m. horse 3A(i)
ergō therefore 2D
ēripiō 3/4 *ēripuī ēreptus* I snatch away,
    rescue X (acc.) from Y (dat.) 5C(iii)
errō 1 I am wrong; wander 6B(vii)
et and; also, too; even Intro.; *et ... et*
    both ... and 1E
etiam still, even, as well; actually, then!, yes
    indeed 2C
    nōn sōlum (or *nōn modo*) ... *sed etiam*
        not only ... but also 4F(ii)
    etiam atque etiam again and again 6B(vii)
etsī although, even though, even if 6C(iii)
Eucliō Eucliōn-is 3m. Euclio Intro.
ex (or *ē*) (+ abl.) out of, from 1C
excēdō 3 *excessī excessum* I depart, go out;
    surpass 6C(ii)
excipiō 3/4 *excēpī exceptus* I sustain,
    receive; welcome; catch; make an
    exception of 6C(ii)
excōgitō 1 I think up, devise 4C(ii)
excūsō 1 I excuse 6B(i)
exempl-um ī 2n. copy; example 5C(i)
exeō exīre exiī exitum I go/come out, leave 1C
exercit-us ūs 4m. army 2A
exi-: see *exeō*
exīstimō 1 I think, consider 5B(i)
exiti-um ī 2n. death, destruction **15**
exorior 4dep. *exortus* I arise 5C(ii)
explicō 1 I tell, explain 1B
expugnō 1 I storm 4A(i)
exsili-um ī 2n. exile 5F(ii)
exspectō 1 I await, wait for 4D(i)
extrēm-us a um furthest 6A(vii)

F

fābul-a ae 1f. story; play 6B(i)
fac imperative s. of *faciō* 37
facēti-ae ārum 1f. pl. wit 6A(ii)
faciēs faci-ēī 5f. appearance; face 5E(i)
facil-is e easy 1F
facinus facinor-is 3n. deed; crime;
    endeavour 1E
faciō 3/4 *fēcī factus* I make, do 1E

certiōrem faciō I inform X (acc.) 6B(i)
faciō ut (+ subj.) I bring it about that (cf.
    efficiō/perficiō ut) 6C(i)
fact-: see *fīō*
fact-um ī 2n. deed 4H
fām-a ae 1f. rumour, report; reputation 4A(i)
famili-a ae 1f. household Intro.
fān-um ī 2n. shrine 1G

fās n. indecl. right 4H

fāt-um ī 2n. fate 3A(ii)

fēc-: see *faciō*

fēmin-a ae 1f. woman 1D

fer imperative s. of *ferō* **37**

ferē almost 6B(iv)

feriō 4 I strike; beat; kill (perfect active and
    passive tenses supplied by *percussī*
    percussus – perf. and perf. part. of
    percutiō 3/4) 4D(ii)

ferō ferre tulī lātus I bear; lead 1E
    mē ferō I betake myself, charge 3B(i)
    condiciōnem (condiciōnēs) ferre to make
    terms 6B(vi)

ferōci-a ae 1f. fierceness 5G(iii)

ferōx ferōc-is fierce 3A(ii)

ferr-um ī 2n. sword; iron 3C(iii)

festīnō 1 I hurry 4B(iii)

fidēs fid-ēī 5f. loyalty, honour; trust, faith;
    promise; protection 6B(viii)

fid-us a um faithful, loyal 6B(viii)

fīli-a ae 1f. daughter Intro.

fīli-us ī 2m. son 1D

fingō 3 *fīnxī fictus* I make up, fabricate 6B(ii)

fīō fierī factus I become; am done, am made
    (passive of *faciō*) 2D (see **76**)
    certior fīō I am informed 6B(i)

flamm-a ae 1f. flame 6D(i)

fleō 2 *flēuī flētum* I weep 6C(iv)

flūmen flūmin-is 3n. river 3B(i)

fore = futūrum esse to be about to be **97**
    fore ut (+ subj.) that it will/would turn
    out that … **156**

fōrm-a ae 1f. shape, looks; beauty 2C

fōrmōs-us a um handsome, graceful, shapely
    3A(i)

fors f. chance (only nom. and abl. *forte* by
    chance) 3C(i)

fortasse perhaps 6B(viii)

forte by chance, perchance 6B(i)

fort-is e brave, courageous; strong 2A

fortūn-a ae 1f. fortune, luck; pl. wealth
    5B(ii)

fortūnāt-us a um fortunate, lucky in X (abl.)
    5A(ii)

for-um ī 2n. forum, marketplace 2D

frangō 3 *frēgī frāctus* I break 5B(iii)

frāter frātr-is 3m. brother 1D

frīgus frīgor-is 3n. cold; pl. cold spells
    6D(ii)

frūment-um ī 2n. corn 5F(i)

fruor 3dep. *frūctus* I enjoy (+ abl.)
    4B(i)

frūstrā in vain 5A(iii)

fu-: see *sum*

fug-a ae 1f. flight 5D(i)

fugiō 3/4 *fūgī fugitum* I escape, run off, flee
    1F

fugō 1 I put to flight 6D(ii)

fulgeō 2 *fulsī* — I shine 6A(vi)

fundāment-um ī 2n. foundation 3B(i)

fūr fūr-is 3m. thief 1B

furor furōr-is 3m. rage, fury; madness
    4F(ii)

futūr-us a um future, to come, destined to be
    3A(ii)

G

gaudi-um ī 2n. joy 5G(iii)

gēns gent-is 3f. race; tribe; clan; family;
    people 3A(ii)

genus gener-is 3n. family; stock; tribe 4C(i);
    type, kind 5D(ii)

gerō 3 *gessī gestus* I do, conduct 2D
    bellum gerō I wage war 2D

gladi-us ī 2m. sword 3C(ii)

glōri-a ae 1f. glory, renown, fame 4E(iii)

gradior 3/4dep. *gressus* I step, walk, go (cf.
    compounds in *-gredior*) 6A(vii)

Graec-ī ōrum 2m. pl. the Greeks 3A(ii)

Graec-us a um Greek 4B(i)

grāti-a ae 1f. friendship 3B(ii)

grātiā (+ gen. – placed after the noun it
    qualifies) for the sake of **152.2**

grāti-ae ārum 1f. pl. thanks, recompense
    2D
    grātiās agō (+ dat.) I give thanks
    2D

grāt-us a um pleasing (to X dat.) 5A(i)

grauid-us a um pregnant 3B(i)

grau-is e serious, important, weighty; heavy
    4E(ii)

grauitās grauitāt-is 3f. seriousness; solemnity;
    importance, authority 4B(iii)

H

habeō 2 I have 1A; hold, regard 1D
 negōtium habeō I conduct business 1F
 ōrātiōnem habeō I make a speech 5F(i)
habitō 1 I dwell Intro.
hāc this way 2E
Hannibal Hannibal-is 3m. Hannibal (son of
 Hamilcar, leader of the Carthaginians)
 3D(i)
harēn-a ae 1f. sand 6A(v)
haud not 2C
Helen-a ae 1f. Helen 3A(ii)
hic haec hoc this; this person, thing; pl.
 these; (as pron.) this man/woman/
 thing; he/she/it 2C (see **63**)
hīc here 2A

hinc from here 2C **63.3**
hodiē today 1E
homo homin-is 3m. human, man, fellow 1E
honest-us a um honourable 3C(i)
honor honōr-is 3m. respect 1B
hōr-a ae 1f. hour 2D
hortor 1dep. I urge, encourage 2B
hospes hospit-is 3m. host; friend; guest;
 connection 4B(i)
hostis host-is 3m. enemy 2B
hūc (to) here 2E
hūmān-us a um human 4H
hum-us ī 2f. ground 5E(i)
 humī on the ground (locative) 5E(i)
 humum to the ground 5E(i)

I

ī imperative s. of *eō* **37**
i-: see *eō*
iaceō 2 I lie 4D(i)
iactō 1 I discuss; throw; boast; toss about
 6B(ii)
iam now, by now, already; presently 2C
iānu-a ae 1f. door 3A(i)
ibi there 2D
idcircō for this/that reason, therefore 5D(i)
īdem eadem idem the same 3C(iii) (see **86**)
 īdem ac the same as **179.1**
idōne-us a um suitable (for), qualified (for)
 (+ dat.) 5B(i)
igitur therefore 1A
ignāui-a ae 1f. laziness; cowardice 5F(i)
ignāu-us a um lazy; cowardly 5F(i)
ignis ign-is 3m. fire 1C
ignōscō 3 *ignōuī ignōtum* I forgive (+ dat.)
 4G(i)
Īli-um ī 2n. Ilium, Troy 3A(ii)
ille ill-a illud that; pl. those; (as pron.) that man/
 women/thing; he/she/it 2C (see **64**)
illīc there **64**
illinc from there **64**
illūc to there **64**
imāgō imāgin-is 3f. appearance; ghost; idea
 3B(ii); image, statue 4H
imitor 1dep. I imitate 6B(viii)
immō more precisely, i.e. no *or* yes (a strong
 agreement or disagreement with what
 precedes) 2D

immortāl-is e immortal 4G(i)
impedīment-um ī 2n. hindrance 3D(v)
 impedīmentō (maximō) sum (+ dat.) I am
 a (very great) hindrance (to) 3D(v)
 (see **88**)
impediō 4 I prevent, impede, hinder 5A(iii)
imperātor imperātōr-is 3m. general;
 commander; ruler; leader 3D(ii)
imperi-um ī 2n. command, order; empire
 3B(i); power, authority; dominion
 5D(ii)
imperō 1 I give orders (to), command (+
 dat.: often followed by *ut/ nē* + subj.
 'to / not to') 3D(iii)
impetrō 1 I obtain by request 6C(iii)
impet-us ūs 4m. attack 4A(i)
 impetum faciō I make an attack 4A(i)
impiger impigr-a um energetic 3C(iii)
impi-us a um with no respect for gods,
 parents or fatherland 5D(iv)
impōnō 3 *imposuī impositus* I put X (acc.)
 on Y (dat.) 6D(ii)
in (+ acc.) into, onto; (+ abl.) in, on 1A; (+
 acc.) against 2D
 in diēs day by day, as the days go by 3C(i)
incendi-um ī 2n. fire 4E(ii)
incendō 3 *incendī incēnsus* I set fire to; burn
 (trans.) 4E(ii)
incert-us a um uncertain 6B(ii)
inde thence, from there; for that reason;
 from that time 3C(iii)

ineō inīre iniui or *iniī initum* I enter, go in 1F

inerm-is e unarmed 6C(ii)

īnfest-us a um hostile; at the ready; indicating attack 6C(ii)

īnflammāt-us a um inflamed, on fire 4C(i)

ingeni-um ī 2n. talent, ability **15**

ingēns ingent-is huge, large, lavish 1F

ingredior 3/4dep. *ingressus* I enter 2E

inimīc-us a um hostile, enemy 4G(ii)

innocēns innocent-is guiltless 4A(iii)

inquam I say (*inquis, inquit; inquiunt*) 2D

īnsidi-ae ārum 1f. pl. trap, ambush 5A(iii)

īnspiciō 3/4 *īnspexī īnspectus* I look into, inspect, examine 2B

īnstituō 3 *īnstituī īnstitūtus* I begin; construct; resolve 6C(iii)

īnstō 1 *īnstitī* — I press upon; urge; pursue; am at hand, approach; strive after 5G(ii)

īnstruō 3 *īnstrūxī īnstrūctus* I draw up; prepare, equip 4H

īnsum inesse īnfuī īnfutūrus I am in (+ dat.) 5A(i)

integer integr-a um whole, untouched 5G(ii)

intellegō 3 *intellēxī intellēctus* I perceive, understand, comprehend, grasp 4B(iii)

inter (+ acc.) among; between 4B(iii)

intereā meanwhile 4A(i)

interficiō 3/4 *interfēcī interfectus* I kill, murder 3B(i)

intrō 1 I enter 1A

intrō (adv.) inside 2E

inueniō 4 *inuēnī inuentum* I find 1F

inuideō 2 *inuīdī inuīsum* I envy, begrudge (+ dat.) 5F(ii)

inuitō 1 I invite 4B(iii)

inuīt-us a um unwilling 6A(vi)

inuocō 1 I invoke, call upon 3B(ii)

ioc-us ī 2m. joke, joking, fun 6A(ii)

Iou-: see *Iuppiter*

ipse ipsa ipsum very, actual, self **103**

īrāscor 3dep. *īrātus* I grow angry with X (dat.) 2C

īrāt-us a um angry 2C

irrīdeō 2 *irrīsī irrīsus* I laugh at, mock 1E

is ea id that; he/she/it **70**

iste ista istud that over there/of yours (used especially when referring to opponents at a trial) 4A(iii) (see **91**)

it-: see *eō*

ita so, thus; yes 1D

Ītali-a ae 1f. Italy 3A(ii)

itaque and so, therefore 5A(iii)

item likewise 5C(i)

iter itiner-is 3n. journey, route 5E(ii)

iterum again 2A

iubeō 2 *iussī iussus* I order, command, tell 1D

iūcund-us a um pleasant 5D(iii)

iūdex iūdic-is 3m. judge 4A(ii)

iūdici-um ī 2n. judgement 3A(i)

iūdicō 1 I judge 3A(i)

Iūnō Iūnōn-is 3f. Juno, wife of Jupiter, goddess of marriage 3A(i)

Iuppiter Iou-is 3m. Jupiter, Jove (King of the Gods) 2A

iūs iūr-is 3n. rights, law, privilege, justice 3D(iii)

iūs iūrand-um iūr-is iūrand-ī 3n. oath 3D(iii)

iuss-: see *iubeō*

iussū by the order of X (gen.) 5C(iii)

iuuenis iuuen-is 3m. young man 1G

iuuō 1 *iūuī iūtus* I help; delight, please 6A(iii)

L

labor labōr-is 3m. toil, hard work; trouble 5D(iv)

lābor 3dep. *lāpsus* I slip, glide, fall down; make a mistake 6D(ii)

lacert-us ī 2m. arm, upper arm 6D(iv)

laedō 3 *laesī laesus* I harm 6A(iii)

laetiti-a ae 1f. merriment, festivity, joy 4B(iii)

laet-us a um joyful, happy 3B(i)

Lampsacēn-us ī 2m. person from Lampsacum 4B(i)

lān-a ae 1f. wool 3C(i)

Lar Lar-is 3m. Lar, household god 1A

latebr-ae ārum 1f. pl. hiding-place, lair 6D(iv)

Latīn-us a um Latin 5A(ii)

418

latrō latrōn-is 3m. robber, bandit 5G(i)

latus later-is 3n. side; flank 5G(ii)

Lāuīni-um ī 2n. Lavinium 3A(ii)

lect-us ī 2m. couch, bed 2B

lēgāt-us ī 2m. ambassador, official 2B;
    commander 5G(i)

legiō legiōn-is 3f. legion 5E(ii)

legō 3 *lēgī lēctus* I read 3C **83**

lepōs lepōr-is 3m. charm 6A(ii)

lēx lēg-is 3f. law 4A(iv)

līber līber-a um free 4F(i)

līber-ī ōrum 2m. pl. children 3B(ii)

līberō 1 I free, release 4D(i)

lībertās lībertāt-is 3f. freedom, liberty 4G(i)

libet 2 (perf. *libuit* or *libitum est*) it pleases
    X (dat.) to Y (inf.), X chooses to Y
    159

libīdō libīdin-is 3f. lust, desire 3C(ii)

licet 2 *licuit* it is permitted to X (dat.) to Y
    (inf.) 3D(v)

līctor līctōr-is 3m, magistrate's attendant,
    lictor 4F(i)

lingu-a ae 1f. tongue; language 6A(v)

litter-ae ārum 1f. pl. letter 4C(i); literature
    5A(ii)

lītus lītor-is 3n. shore 4E(i)

loc-us ī 2m. place; pl. *loc-a ōrum* 2n. region
    4A(iii)

locūt-: see *loquor*

longē far 3D(iii) (see **79**)

long-us a um long, lengthy 2A

loquor 3dep. *locūtus* I am speaking,
    say 2B

lūct-us ūs 4m. grief, mourning 5G(iii)

lūc-us ī 2m. grove, wood 3B(ii)

lūdō 3 *lūsī lūsum* I play 6A(iii)

lūmen lūmin-is 3n. light; pl. eyes
    6D(ii)

lūn-a ae 1f. moon 2A

lūx lūc-is 3f. light 5D(i)

M

maest-us a um sad 3C(iii)

magis more 3C(iii) (see **87**)

magistrāt-us ūs 4m. magistrate, state official
    4A(iii)

magnopere greatly **79**

magn-us a um great, large 1D

māior māius gen. *māiōr-is* greater, bigger **74**

mālō mālle māluī I prefer (X *quam* Y) 2A

mal-um ī 2n. trouble, evil 2E

māl-um ī 2n. apple 3A(i)

mal-us a um bad, evil, wicked 1C

mandō 1 I entrust X (acc.) to Y (dat.) 5A(i);
    order X (dat.) (to / not to: *ut/nē* +
    subj.) 6B(iii)

maneō 2 *mānsī mānsum* I remain, wait 1C

manifest-us a um in the open; obvious, clear;
    caught in the act 5B(ii)

man-us ūs 4f. hand 2A; band 5B(iii)

mare mar-is 3n. sea (abl. *marī*) 4E(ii)

Mars Mart-is 3m. the god Mars 3B(i)

mātrimōni-um ī 2n. marriage 3A(i)

mātrōn-a ae 1f. wife, mother; lady 5A(ii)

maximē very greatly; most of all (from
    magnus: see **87**) 3C(iii)

maxim-us a um very great, biggest **74**

mē acc. or abl. of *ego* 1A

mēcum with/to me (myself) (= *mē* + *cum*);
    pl. *nōbīscum* 2C

meditor 1dep. I think 3A(i)

medi-us a um middle (of) 4F(ii)

melior melius gen. *meliōr-is* better **74**

melius (adv.) better **87**

membr-um ī 2n. limb 6A(iii)

meminī (perfect form) I remember 5F(i)

memor memor-is remembering X (gen.);
    mindful of X (gen.) 5D(iv)

memori-a ae 1f. remembering, memory,
    recollection; record 6B(i)

mendāx mendāc-is lying, untruthful 2A

mēns ment-is 3f. mind, purpose 3D(i)

mentiō mentiōn-is 3f. mention 4E(iii)

mentior 4dep. I lie, deceive 2B

Mercuri-us ī 2m. Mercury, messenger of
    Jupiter 3A(i)

mer-us a um unmixed, pure 6A(i)

met-us ūs 4m. fear, terror 4E(iii)

me-us a um my, mine 1B (vocative s. m.
    mī: **17A**)

mī = *mihi* (dat. s. of *ego*) 6A(iv)

mī voc. s. m. of *meus* **17A**

mihi dat. s. of *ego*

mīlēs mīlit-is 3m. soldier 2C

mīlia mīl-ium 3n. pl. thousands (see *mīlle*) **54**

mīlitār-is e military 5C(ii)

mīlle 1,000 (pl. *mīlia*) **54**

min-ae ārum 1f. pl. threats 3C(ii)

Mineru-a ae 1f. Minerva, goddess of crafts and wisdom 3A(i)

minimē very little; no **87**

minim-us a um smallest, fewest, least **74**

minor 1dep. I threaten (+ dat.) 2B

minor minus gen. *minōr-is* smaller, fewer, less **74**

minus (adv.) less **87**

mīr-us a um amazing, wonderful 6B(v)

mīs-: see *mittō*

miser miser-a um miserable, unhappy, wretched 1C

miserand-us a um to be pitied 5D(i)

miseret 2 it moves X (acc.) to pity for Y (gen.) **159**

misericors misericord-is compassionate 5D(i)

miss-: see *mittō*

mittō 3 *mīsī missus* I send 1F; throw 6C(ii)

modest-us a um chaste, modest, discreet 5A(ii)

modo now 2A; only 4F(ii)

  nōn modo … sed etiam not only … but also (also *nōn sōlum … sed etiam*) 4F(ii)

modo … modo at one time … at another 5E(ii)

mod-us ī 2m. way, fashion, manner 4C(ii)

moenia moen-ium 3n. pl. walls, ramparts 3A(ii)

moneō 2 I advise, warn 1C

mōns mont-is 3m. mountain 5A(i)

mor-a ae 1f. delay 4G(i)

mōre in the manner of, like (+ gen.) 5F(ii)

morior 3/4dep. *mortuus* I die 3C(ii)

mors mort-is 3f. death 2E

mortāl-is is 3m. (or *mortāl-is e* adj.) mortal 3A(ii)

mōs mōr-is 3m. way, habit, custom; pl. character 2C

mōt-: see *moueō*

moueō 2 *mōuī mōtus* I remove X (acc.) from Y (abl.); move **83**; cause, begin 5A(i)

mox soon 2A

mulier mulier-is 3f. woman, wife 2C

multitūdō multitūdin-is 3f. mob, crowd, number 4E(ii)

multō (by) much, far 3A(ii)

multum (adv.) much **79**

mult-us a um much, many 1B

mūnus mūner-is 3n. gift; duty 6A(ii)

mūr-us ī 2m. wall 3B(i)

mūtō 1 I change, alter, exchange 6A(ii)

N

nam for 1A

nārrō 1 I tell, relate X (acc.) to Y (dat.) 5A(i)

nāscor 3dep. *nātus* I am born 3B(i)

nātūr-a ae 1f. nature 5B(i)

nāt-us a um born of/from (abl.) 4C(i)

nāuigō 1 I sail 4E(i)

nāuis nāu-is 3f. ship 4D(i)

naut-a ae 1m. sailor 4D(i)

-ne (added to the first word of a sentence) = ? 1E

nē (+ subj.) not to, that X should not **136**; lest, in order that not, in order not to **150**; that, lest **163**; (+ perf subj.) don't **170**

nē … quidem not even (emphasising the word in between) 6B(iii)

nē quis that no one **136**; in order that no one **150**

nec and … not; neither; nor (= *neque*) 1D

necesse est it is necessary for X (dat.) to Y (inf.) 3D(iv)

necessitūdō necessitūdin-is 3f. necessity 5F(ii)

necō 1 I kill 2C

nefāri-us a um wicked, vile, criminal 4D(ii)

neglegenti-a ae 1f. carelessness 4G(i)

neglegō 3 *neglēxī neglēctus* I ignore, overlook, neglect 4B(ii)

negō 1 I deny, say that X is not the case (acc. + inf.) 4A(iii)

negōti-um ī 2n. business, work, duty 4A(ii)

  negōtium habeō I do business 1F

quid negōtī? what (of) business/problem/
   trouble? 1F

nēmo nēmin-is 3m. no one, nobody 3C(iii)
   (see **86**)

neque and... not; neither; nor (also *nec*) 1C

nēquiti-a ae 1f. wickedness 4E(ii)

nesciō 4 I do not know 2B

nesci-us a um knowing nothing, ignorant
   (of: gen.) 2C

neu = *nēue* 6C(iv)

nēue (+ subj.) and (that X) should not, and
   not to 4F(i)

niger nigr-a um black 2A

nihil (indecl. n.) nothing 1E

nihilī of no worth/value 2C

nihilōminus nevertheless 5C(iii)

nīl = *nihil* nothing 1F

nimis too much of X (gen.) 1D

nisi unless, if... not; except 2C

nītor 3dep. *nīsus* or *nīxus* I lean on (+ abl.);
   strive, exert myself 4E(i)

nix niu-is 3f. snow 6D(i)

nōbil-is e renowned, distinguished;
   well-born, noble 4B(i)

noceō 2 I harm (+ dat.) 5C(iii)

noctū by night 6C(iii)

nōlī (+ inf.) do not **59**

nōlō nōlle nōluī I refuse, am unwilling (+
   inf.) 2A (see **52**)

nōmen nōmin-is 3n. name 1D

nōminō 1 I name 5G(i)

nōn no(t) 1A

nōnāgintā 90 5C **161**

nōndum not yet 5B(ii)

nōnne surely not, doesn't/don't? 3C(i)
   (see **85**)

nōn nūll-ī ae a some 6B(vii)

nōn-us a um ninth **161**

nōs we **43**

nōscō 3 *nōuī nōtus* I get to know (perfect
   tenses = I know etc.) 5B(i)

noster nostr-a um our 2A

nōt-us a um known, well-known
   5B(i)

nōu-: see *nōscō*

nou-us a um new 3B(i)

nox noct-is 3f. night 2A

noxi-us a um guilty; harmful 3C(iii)

nūdō 1 I strip 4F(ii)

nūd-us a um naked 6D(iii)

nūll-us a um no, none 1B (gen. s. *nūllīus*;
   dat. s. *nūllī*) (see **62**)

   nōn nūll-ī ae a some 6B(vii)

num surely... not? **93**; (+ subj.) whether
   (indirect question) **172**

numer-us ī 2m. number 4D(ii)

numquam never 1C

nunc now 1A

nūntiō 1 I announce 2A

nūnti-us ī 2m. messenger; message; news
   3C(iii)

nūpti-ae ārum 1f. pl. marriage-rites 1E

O

ō (+ voc.) O (addressing some one) 2B

ob (+ acc.) on account of, because of
   3A(ii)

obdūrō 1 I am firm, hold out, persist 6A(vi)

oblīuīscor 3dep. *oblītus* I forget 2B; (+ gen.
   of person) 5D(iv)

obscūr-us a um dark; obscure; mean, ignoble
   6D(ii)

obsecrō 1 I beg, beseech 4B(iv)

obsess-: see *obsideō*

obsideō 2 *ōbsēdī obsessus* I besiege 5B(iii)

obstō 1 *obstitī obstātum* I stand in the way
   of, obstruct (+ dat.) 3D(iv)

occāsiō occāsiōn-is 3f. opportunity 5E(ii)

occidī I'm done for! 1E

occidō 3 *occidī occāsum* I fall, die 5G(iii);
   set 6A(iv)

occīdō 3 *occīdī occīsus* I kill 3A(ii)

occupō 1 I seize 5C(iii)

occurrō 3 *occurrī occursum* I run to meet,
   meet; attack (+ dat.) 6C(iv)

octāu-us a um eighth **161**

octō eight **54**

octōgintā eighty **161**

ocul-us ī 2m. eye 1C

odiō est (he/it/she) is hateful to X (dat.), X
   (dat.) hates Y (nom.) 3D(v)

offendō 3 *offendī offēnsus* I meet with;
   offend 6B(ii)

offici-um ī 2n. duty, job 2A

omittō 3 *omīsī omissus* I give up; let fall;
 omit, leave aside 5G(ii)
omnīnō altogether, completely 6B(i)
omn-is e all, every; n. pl. *omnia* everything 1F
onerī est it is a burden to X (dat.) 5C(iii)
onus oner-is 3n. load, burden 1E
oper-a ae 1f. attention 1E; service 5A(iii)
 operam dō 1 *dedī datus* (+dat.) I pay
 attention to 1E
opēs op-um 3f. pl. resources; wealth (s. *ops*
 op-is 3f. help, aid) 5B(ii)
opīnor 1dep. I think 2B
oportet 2 it is right/fitting for X (acc.) to Y (inf.),
 X (acc.) ought to Y (inf.) 4B(iii) (see **159**)
oppid-um ī 2n. town 2A
opportūn-us a um strategic, suitable,
 favourable 5A(iii)
oppress-: see *opprimō*
opprimō 3 *oppressī oppressus* I surprise;
 catch; crush 2C; press down on 3C(ii)

P

paene almost 5D(iv)
paenitet 2 X (acc.) regrets Y (gen.) **159**
palam openly 6B(ii)
pandō 3 *pandī passus* I spread out, extend;
 throw open, disclose 6D(i)
par par-is equal
 par ac equivalent to *pariter ac* equally as
 (see **179.1**)
parcō 3 *pepercī parsum* I spare (+ dat.) 4B(iv)
parēns parent-is 3m. father, parent; f.
 mother 5B(iii)
pāreō 2 I obey (+ dat.) 3D(iv)
pariō 3/4 *peperī partus* I bring forth, bear,
 produce; obtain, acquire 6B(vii)
Paris Parid-is 3m. Paris 3A(i)
parō 1 I prepare, get ready; provide, obtain;
 I am about (to) 3D(i)
pars part-is 3f. part; faction, party
 3D(v); side 6B(vi) *aliī … pars* (or
 pars … pars) some … others **102**
paru-us a um small 3A **74**
pāstor pāstor-is shepherd 3A(i)
patefaciō 3/4 *patefēcī patefactus* I reveal,
 expose, throw open 5C(iii)
pater patr-is 3m. father 1D; senator
 patrēs = fathers of the city 3B(ii)
 patrēs cōnscrīptī = senators 5D(ii)

optimē (adv.) best **87**
optim-us a um best 1D (see **74**)
opus oper-is 3n. job, work, task 2B;
 fortification 6C(iii)
opus est (+ abl.) there is need of 5F(ii)
ōrāc(u)l-um ī 2n. oracle 6A(v)
ōrātiō ōrātiōn-is 3f. speech 5F(i)
 ōrātiōnem habeō I make a speech 5F(i)
ōrdō ōrdin-is 3m. rank (i.e. section of
 society or line of soldiers) 5D(ii);
 order 6D(i)
orior 4dep. *ortus* I arise, begin; spring from,
 originate 3B(ii)
ōrō 1 I beg, pray 4B(iv)
ōs ōr-is 3n. face; mouth 4F(ii)
ostendō 3 *ostendī ostēnsus* or *ostentus* I
 show, reveal 1G
ōtiōs-us a um at leisure 6A(iii)
ōti-um ī 2n. cessation of conflict; leisure,
 inactivity 3D(iii)

patior 3/4 *passus* endure, suffer;
 allow 2E
patri-a ae 1f. fatherland 5D(ii)
pauc-ī ae a a few, a small number of
 5B(i)
paulātim little by little, gradually
 5G(ii)
paulō slightly (cf. *multō*) 4E(i)
paulum a little, slightly **79**
pauper pauper-is 3m. f. poor man/woman
 1D; (adj.) poor **47**
pāx pāc-is 3f. peace 4B(i)
pecūni-a ae 1f. money 1D
pēior pēius gen. *pēiōr-is* worse **74**
peper-: see *pariō*
per (+ acc.) through, by 2C; in the name of
 4G(i)
percuss-: see *feriō*
perdō 3 *perdidī perditus* I lose; destroy
 6B(ii)
pereō perīre periī peritum I perish, die
 6A(vi)
perfēc-: ⎫
perfect-: ⎭ see *perficiō*
perferō perferre pertulī perlātus I endure
 (to the end); complete; carry to;
 announce 6A(vi)

422

perficiō 3/4 *perfēcī perfectus* I finish, complete, carry out 2B; *perficiō ut/ut nōn* (+ subj.) I bring it about that/that not 4F(ii)

pergō 3 *perrēxī perrēctum* I proceed, continue 2A

perīcul-um ī 2n. danger **15**

peri -: see *pereō*

periī I'm lost 1E

perinde ac in like manner as, just as **179.1**

perit-: see *pereō*

perlegō 3 *perlēgī perlēctus* I read through, peruse 4C(i)

perscrībō 3 *perscrīpsī perscrīptus* I write in detail 6B(i)

persequor 3dep. *persecūtus* I pursue, follow after 5F(i)

persuādeō 2 *persuāsī persuāsum* I persuade X (dat.) ('that/that not', 'to /not to' *ut/ nē* + subj.) 4F(i)

perueniō 4 *peruēnī peruentum* I reach, arrive at, come to (*ad* + acc.) 4A(i)

pēs ped-is 3m. foot 4F(i)

pessimē worst, very badly **87**

pessim-us a um worst **74**

petō 3 *petīuī petītus* I beg **136**; seek 4G(i); proposition, court; attack, make for 5A(ii); stand for (public office) 5A(iii)

Phaedr-a ae 1f. Phaedra Intro.

pietās pietāt-is 3f. respect for the gods (also for family, home and native land) 6D(i)

pīl-um ī 2n. heavy javelin 5G(ii)

pīrāt-a ae 1m. pirate 4D(i)

placet 2 it pleases X (dat.) to Y (inf.); X (dat.) decides to Y (inf.) 3D(i)

plānē clearly 2C

plān-us a um level, flat; plain, distinct 6D(iv)

plēn-us a um full (of) (+ gen. or abl.) 1A

plērīque plēraeque plēraque the majority of 5B(i)

plūrēs plūr-ium more **74**

plūrimum (adv.) most, a lot **87**

plūrim-us a um most, very much **74**

plūs plūr-is 3n. more X (gen.) 3A(i) (see **74**)

pōcul-um ī 2n. cup 4C(i)

poen-a ae 1f. penalty 5C(iii)

polliceor 2dep. I promise 2B

pōnō 3 *posuī positus* I set up, place, position, put 3A(ii); lay aside (= *dēpōnō*) 6D(iv)

pōns pont-is 3m. bridge 5C(ii)

popul-us ī 2m. people 3B(ii)

porrō besides, moreover 5C(iii)

port-a ae 1f. gate 3A(ii)

pōrtō 1 I carry 1A

port-us ūs 4m. harbour 4D(i)

poscō 3 *poposcī —* I demand 1E

posit-: see *pōnō*

possideō 2 *possēdī possessus* I have, hold, possess 1B

possum posse potuī I am able, can 2A; am powerful, have power (+ adv.) 4E(iii)

post (adv.) later, afterwards; (+ acc.) after, behind 2D

posteā afterwards 4A(ii)

postquam (conjunction + indicative) after 5A(iii)

postrēmō finally 4C(ii)

postrēm-us a um last 4E(i)

postulō 1 I demand **136**

posu-: see *pōnō*

pot-: see *possum*

potenti-a ae 1f. power 5F(i)

potior 4dep. I control (+ gen.) 6B(vi); gain control of (+ abl.) 6C(iii)

potius rather 3B(ii)

potu-: see *possum*

praebeō 2 I show, display; *mē praebeō* I show myself to be X (acc. adj./noun) 5C(iii); provide, offer 6D(iv)

praecept-: see *praecipiō*

praecipiō 3/4 *praecēpī praeceptus* I instruct, give orders to X (dat.) (to / not to Y: *ut/nē* + subj.) 5B(ii)

praeclār-us a um very famous, outstanding, brilliant 4D(ii)

praed-a ae 1f. booty 2B

praedō praedōn-is 3m. pirate; robber 4D(i)

praefect-us ī 2m. captain, prefect; (adj.) in charge of (+ dat.) 4D(i)

praeficiō 3/4 *praefēcī praefectus* I put X (acc.) in charge of Y (dat.) 5G(i)

praemi-um ī 2n. prize, reward 5B(ii)
praesēns praesent-is present 6B(iii)
praesidi-um ī 2n. protection, defence, guard
    4G(i)
praesum praeesse praefuī praefutūrus I am
    in charge of (+ dat.) **83**
praatereā besides, moreover 4A(iv)
praetereō praeterīre praeteriī praeteritus I
    pass by; neglect, omit 6A(vii)
praetor praetōr-is 3m. praetor (Roman state
    official) 4B(iv)
prec-ēs um 3f. pl. (occasionally *prex prec-is*
    3f.) prayer(s) 3C(ii)
precor 1dep. I pray, beg 2B
premō 3 *pressī pressus* I press; oppress
    6D(iv)
preti-um ī 2n. price, value, reward 3C(ii)
prīmō at first 4A(iv)
prīmum (adv.) first
    ubi prīmum as soon as 5B(i)
    quam prīmum as soon as possible 5E(ii)
prīm-us a um first 3D(iv) *in prīmīs*
    especially 5A(i)
prīnceps prīncip-is 3m. leader, chieftain;
    (adj.) first 4E(i)
prīstin-us a um former; original 5G(ii)
prius (adv.) before, earlier; first 5A(iii)
priusquam (conjunction) before **165**
prō (+ abl.) for, in return for; on behalf of;
    in front of 2E; instead of 5B(ii); in
    accordance with 5G(i)
prōcurrō 3 *prōcucurrī prōcursum* I run
    forward, advance 6C(i)
proeli-um ī 2n. battle 2B
proficīscor 3dep. *profectus* I set out 2B
profugiō 3/4 *profūgī* — I escape, flee away
    4F(ii)

prōgredior 3/4 dep. *prōgressus* I advance 2B
prohibeō 2 I prevent, hinder, keep X (acc.)
    from Y (abl. / *ā(ab)* + abl.) 5A(iii)
prōiciō 3/4 *prōiēcī prōiectus* I throw down
    6C(iv)
prōmittō 3 *prōmīsī prōmissus* I promise 1E
prope (adv.) almost; (+ acc.) near 4B(i)
properō 1 I hurry, make haste 5E(ii)
propius nearer 5C(i)
prōpōnō 3 *prōposuī prōpositus* I set before;
    imagine; offer 5D(i)
propter (+ acc.) on account of 2E
prōteg-ō 3 *prōtexī prōtectus* I protect 3D(v)
prōuideō 2 *prōuīdī prōuīsus* I take care of
    (that: often followed by *nē* + subj.)
    5D(ii)
prōuinci-a ae 1f. province 4C(ii)
proxim-us a um nearest, next 4F(i)
pudet 2 X (acc.) is ashamed at/for Y (gen.)
    159
pudīciti-a ae 1f. chastity 3C(iii)
pudor pudōr-is 3m. modesty, sense of shame
    6D(iv)
puell-a ae 1f. girl 1D
puer puer-ī 2m. boy 3B(i) (see **28**); slave
    3D(v)
pugn-a ae 1f. battle, fight 5E(ii)
pugnō 1 I fight 2B
pugn-us ī 2m. fist 4A(i)
pulcher pulchr-a um beautiful 1D; (sup.)
    pulcherrim-us a um **73**; (comp.)
    pulchrior pulchriōr-is **72**
pulchritūdō pulchritūdin-is 3f. beauty
    3A(i)
pūniō 4 I punish 5C(iii)
pūtid- us a um rotten 2E
putō 1 I think 4A(iii)

Q

quā where **139**
quadrāgintā forty **161**
quadringent- ī ae a 400 **154**
quaerō 3 *quaesīuī quaesītus* I seek, look for;
    ask 4G(i)
quāl-is e what sort of 6B(iii)
    tālis … quālis of such a kind as **179.2**
quam how! (+ adj. or adv.); (after comp.)
    than 2C

tam … quam as … as **179.2**
    (+ superl. adv.) as … as possible 5B(ii)
    quam prīmum as soon as possible 5E(ii)
quamquam although 2E
quamuīs (+ subj.) although **146**; (+ adj.)
    however, ever such a 5A(i)
quandō since, when 2C
quantī: *tantī … quantī* of as much value …
    as **69**

quantum as much as 5D(iii)

quant-us a um how much, how great 5F(i)

    tantus ... quantus as much ... as **179.2**

quārē why? 1B; therefore 6A(ii)

quārt-us a um fourth **161**

quasi as if, like 1E

quattuor four **54**

quattuordecim 14 **161**

-que (added to the end of the word) and 1D

quemadmodum how 6B(i)

queror 3dep. *questus* I complain 5B(i)

quī quae quod which? what? **29**; who, which **106**; (+ subj.) since (also with *quippe*) **145**; (+ subj.) in order that/to **150**

quia because 2A

quīcumque quaecumque quodcumque whoever, whatever 6A(vii)

quid what? 1C; why? 4A(ii)

    quid cōnsilī? what (of) plan? 1E

    quid negōtī? what (of) business? what problem? what trouble? 1F

quīdam quaedam quid-/quod-dam a, a certain, some 4A(i)

quidem indeed (places emphasis on the preceding word) 6B(viii)

    nē ... quidem not even (emphasising the enclosed word) 6B(iii)

quiēs quiēt-is 3f. sleep, rest 6A(iii)

quīn (+ subj.) from —ing; that ... not; (but) that **174**

quīndecim fifteen **161**

quīngent-ī ae a 500 **54**

quīnquāgintā fifty **161**

quīnt-us a um fifth 4E(i)

quippe quī (*quae quod*) inasmuch as he/she/it **145.2**

quis quid who?, what? **29**

quis qua quid (after *sī, nisi, nē, num*) anyone, anything **136**, **144**

quisquam quicquam (after negatives) anyone **176**

quisque quaeque quodque (*quidque*) each **176**

quisquis quidquid (or *quicquid*) whoever, whatever 6B(v)

quō to where? 1E; whither, to where 4E(ii); (see also **139** for *quō* as abl. s. of *quī, quae, quod*)

    quō + comp. + subj. in order that ... more **155**

    quō + comp ... *eō* + comp. the more ... the more 6B(vi)

quōcumque (to) wherever 5F(i)

quod because 1B

quod sī but if 6B(vii)

quōminus (+ subj.) so that ... not; from —ing **174**

quoque also 1A

quot how many 5F(i) *tot ... quot* as many as **179.2**

R

rapiō 3/4 *rapuī raptus* I seize, snatch away, carry away, plunder 3B(ii)

ratiō ratiōn-is 3f. plan, method; reason; count, list; calculation 4C(ii)

recēp-: see *recipiō*

recipiō 3/4 *recēpī receptus* I welcome, receive, take in 4B(ii); *mē recipiō* I retreat 6C(iii)

recordor 1dep. I remember 2B

reddō 3 *reddidī redditus* I return, give back 1G

redeō redīre rediī reditum I return (intrans.) 1C

redūcō 3 *redūxī reductus* I lead back 4E(iii)

rēgīn-a ae 1f. queen 4H

rēgnō 1 I reign, rule 3A(ii)

rēgn-um ī 2n. kingdom 3B(i)

relict-: see *relinquō*

religiō religiōn-is 3f. sense of reverence, religious scruples 4H

religiōs-us a um sacred, revered, holy, awesome 4A(ii)

relinquō 3 *relīquī relictus* I leave, abandon 3A(ii)

reliqu-us a um remaining, left 4E(ii)

remaneō 2 *remānsī remānsum* I remain 6C(iii)

remittō 3 *remīsī remissus* I send back; remit 6C(iii)

reor 2dep. *ratus* I think, believe, suppose 5G(ii)

repellō 3 *reppulī repulsus* I drive back, drive out 4A(i)

repente suddenly 4A(i)

reperiō 4 *repperī repertus* I find 4A(iii)

reprimō 3 *repressī repressus* I hold back, check 6C(ii)

requīrō 3 *requīsīuī requīsītus* I seek out; ask for 5B(i)

rēs re-ī 5f. thing, matter, business; property; affair 2B

   rēs pūblic-a re-ī pūblic-ae 5f. and 1/2adj. state, republic 4H

resistō 3 *restitī* — I resist (+ dat.); stand back; halt, pause 5G(ii)

respiciō 3/4 *respexī respectus* I look round (back) at, turn my gaze upon; reflect upon; care for 6C(i)

respondeō 2 *respondī respōnsum* I reply 2B

retineō 2 *retinuī retentus* I hold back, detain, restrain; maintain 4B(ii)

reuertor 3 dep. *reuersus* I return 6C(iv)

reuocō 1 I call back 4C(ii)

rēx rēg-is 3m. king 2A

rīp-a ae 1f. bank 6D(ii)

rogō 1 I ask 1C

Rōm-a ae 1f. Rome 3A(ii) (*Rōmae*, locative, at Rome 3C(ii))

Rōmān-us a um Roman 3A(ii)

Rōmul-us ī 2m. Romulus 3B(i)

rūmor rūmōr-is 3m. rumour, (piece of) gossip, unfavourable report 6A(iv)

S

sacer sacr-a um holy, sacred 4A(iii)

sacerdōs sacerdōt-is 3m. or f. priest, priestess 4A(iii)

sacr-a ōrum 2n. pl. rites 4A(iii)

saepe often 3D(iv)

saeu-us a um wild; angry 2B

saltem at least 6B(vii)

saluē welcome! 1E

salūs salūt-is 3f. safety 4F(i)

   salūtem dīcīt (*S.* or *S.D.* at a letter-head) 'he greets' (+ dat.) 6B(i)

   salūtī est (it/he/she) is a source of salvation to X (dat.), X (nom.) saves Y (dat.) 3D(iv)

salūt-ō 1 I greet 2D

salu-us a um safe 1C

sānct-us a um holy 4H

sanguis sanguin-is 3m. blood 4F(i)

sapienti-a ae 1f. wisdom, intelligence 2A

satis enough (of) (+ gen.) 1D

sauci-us a um wounded 5G(ii)

scaen-a ae 1f. stage 1A

scelest-us a um criminal, wicked 2C

scelus sceler-is 3n. crime, villainy; criminal, villain 1E

sciō 4 I know 1F

scrībō scrībere scrīpsī scrīptus I write **83**

sē himself, herself, itself/themselves **80**

sēcum with/to himself/herself 1E

secund-us a um second **161**

secūris secūr-is 3f. axe 4D(ii)

secūt-: see *sequor*

sed but 1A

sēdecim sixteen **161**

sēd-ēs is 3f. base, foundation 4H

semel once 6A(iv)

   cum semel as soon as 6A(iv)

semper always 1A

senāt-us ūs 4m. senate 3D(v)

senex sen-is 3m. old man 1B

sēns-: see *sentiō*

sententi-a ae 1f. opinion; judgement; sentence; maxim 5C(iii)

sentiō 4 *sēnsī sēnsus* I feel; understand; perceive, realise 4A(ii)

septem seven **54**

septendecim seventeen **161**

septim-us a um seventh **161**

septuāgintā seventy **161**

sepulc(h)r-um ī 2n. tomb 6A(v)

sequor 3 dep. *secūtus* I follow 2B

sermō sermōn-is 3m. conversation, discussion 4B(iii)

seru-a ae 1f. slave-woman Intro.

serui-ō 4 I serve (+ dat.) 3D(ii)

seruō 1 I save, keep 1C; keep safe, preserve
     4C(i)

seru-us ī 2m. slave 1A

sēsē = *sē* 5C(ii)

seu (or *sīue*) ... *seu* (or *sīue*) whether ... or
     6A(vii)

seuēr-us a um strict, stern 3C(i)

sex six **54**

sexāgintā sixty **161**

sext-us a um sixth **161**

sī if 1A

     sī + pres. subj., pres. subj. if X were to
          happen, Y would happen **144**

     sī + impf. subj., impf subj. if X were
          happening (now), Y would be
          happening (sometimes: if X had
          happened, Y would have happened)
          144

     sī + plupf. subj., plupf. subj. if X had
          happened, Y would have happened **173**

     quod sī but if 6B(vii)

sīc thus, so 2A

Sicili-a ae 1f. Sicily 4C(ii)

sīcutī (or *sīcut*) (just) as 5C(ii)

sīdus sīder-is 3n. star 6A(v)

sign-um ī 2n. seal, signal, sign 2D; statue
     4A(iii); standard; trumpet-call 5G(i)

silu-a ae 1f. wood 6D(ii)

sim pres. subj. of *sum*

simil-is e resembling, like (+ gen. or dat.) 2A

similis ac similar to **179.1**

simul at the same time 4B(iii); together
     6A(vii); = *simulatque* as soon as
     6B(iv)

simulācr-um ī 2n. image, copy 4A(i)

simulatque (or *simulac* or *simul*) as soon as
     6B(iv)

simulō 1 I feign 5B(ii)

sīn but if 6B(viii)

sine (+ abl.) without 2D; *sine dubiō* without
     doubt, certainly 2D

singul-ī ae a individual, one by one 6D(iv)

sinister sinistr-a um left; unfavourable
     5G(i)

sinō 3 *sīuī situs* I allow, permit 2C

sīue (or *seu*) ... *sīue* (or *seu*) whether ... or
     6A(vii)

soci-us ī 2m. ally, friend 4H

sodāl-is is 3m. friend 6A(ii)

sōl sōl-is 3m. sun 2A

soleō 2semi-dep. *solitus* I am accustomed,
     am used (+ inf.) 4A(iii)

solit-: see *soleō*

sollicitō 1 I bother, worry 2E; stir up, arouse;
     incite to revolt 5B(i)

sōlum (adv. of *sōlus*) only 4B(iii) *nōn*
     sōlum ... *sed etiam* not only ... but
     also 4F(ii)

soluō 3 *soluī solūtus* I release, undo 2D

sōl-us a um (gen. s. *sōlīus*: dat. s. *sōlī*) alone
     4B(iii); lonely 6D(ii)

somni-um ī 2n. dream 1B

somn-us ī 2m. sleep 6A(iii)

soror sorōr-is 3f. sister 1D

spati-um ī 2n. space; time 6B(vi)

spectācul-um ī 2n. public entertainment,
     show 3B(ii)

spērō 1 I hope; expect 5E(ii)

spēs spē-ī 5f. hope(s); expectation 5B(i)

Staphyl-a ae 1f. Staphyla Intro.

statim at once 1C

stet-: see *stō*

stō 1 *stetī statum* I stand 1C

studi-um ī 2n. enthusiasm, zeal 5B(ii)

stultē stupidly 4C(ii)

stult-us a um stupid, foolish 2A

suāu-is e sweet, pleasant, delightful 6B(i)

sub (+ abl.) beneath, under 1A

subitō suddenly 2D

sublāt-: see *tollō*

subsidi-um ī 2n. reserve; help 5G(i)

succurrō 3 *succurrī succursum* I run to help,
     assist (+ dat.) 5G(ii)

sum esse fuī futūrus I am Intro.

summ-us a um highest, top of 1G
     summum supplicium the death penalty
     4G(ii)

sūmō 3 *sūmpsī sūmptus* I take; put on; eat
     supplicium sūmō (*dē* + abl.) I exact the
     penalty (from) 5D(i)

sūmpt-: see *sūmō*

super (adv.) more than enough; above, over;
     (prep. + acc./abl.) over, above; (+
     abl.) about 6A(v)

superb-us a um proud, haughty, arrogant 6D(ii)

superior superiōr-is higher; earlier 6C(iv)

supplex supplic-is (adj.) suppliant (also as noun) 5D(iv)

supplici-um ī 2n. punishment

    summum supplicium the death penalty 4G(ii)

    supplicium sūmō (*dē* + abl.) I exact the penalty (from) 5D(i)

supplicō 1 I make prayers (to) 1B; (+ dat.) 3D(i)

taceō 2 I am silent 1C

tacit-us a um silent 2D

tāct-: see *tangō*

tāl-is e of such a kind 4H

    tālis… quālis of such a kind as **179.2**

tam so 2A

    tam … quam as … as **179.2**

tamen however, but (second word) 1B

tamquam as though **179.3**

tandem at length 1B

tangō 3 *tetigī tāctus* I touch, lay hands on 1G

tantī … quantī of as much value … as **69**

tant-us a um so great, so much, so important 3D(v)

    tantus … quantus as much … as **179.2**

tard-us a um slow 4E(ii)

tē you (s.) 1A

tēcum with/to you(rself); pl. *uōbīscum* 2C

tegō 3 *tēxī tēctus* I cover 5G(iii)

tēl-um ī 2n. weapon 5A(iii)

templ-um ī 2n. temple 4A(i)

temptō 1 I try, test, attempt; attack 5E(ii)

tempus tempor-is 3n. time 2D

tendō 3 *tetendī tēnsus* or *tentus* I stretch (out); offer; direct; travel 5D(iv); strive, fight 5G(ii)

tenebr-ae ārum 1f. pl. shadows, darkness 6D(ii)

teneō 2 *tenuī tentus* I hold 3C(ii)

terg-um ī 2n. back (6C(ii))

terr-a ae 1f. land 3A(i)

terreō 2 I frighten 6B(viii)

terribil-is e dreadful, frightening 5E(i)

terti-us a um third **161**

testis test-is 3m. witness 4F(i)

tetig-: see *tangō*

surgō 3 *surrēxī surrēctum* I rise, arise, get up 6D(ii)

suscipi-ō 3/4 *suscēpī susceptus* I undertake 4H

suspicor 1dep. I suspect 2D

sustineo 2 *sustinuī sustentus* I withstand; support 6C(ii)

sustul-: see *tollō*

su-us a um his, hers/their(s) 3B(i) and **80**

Syrācūsān-us ī 2m. person from Syracuse, Syracusan 4A(iv)

thalam-us ī 2m. chamber, bedchamber 6D(iv)

thēsaur-us ī 2m. treasure 1B

timeō 2 I fear, am afraid of 1A; (*nē* + subj.) am afraid that/lest **163**

timid-us a um frightened, fearful 5C(ii)

timor timōr-is 3m. fear 6B(vi)

tollō 3 *sustulī sublātus* I lift, remove, take away 4A(iii)

tor-us ī 2m. couch, bed 6D(iv)

tot so many 4E(iii)

    tot … quot as many … as **179.2**

tōt-us a um (gen. s. *tōtīus*; dat. s. *tōtī*) whole, complete 4A(i)

trādō 3 *trādidī trāditus* I hand over 5C(ii)

trāns (+ acc.) across 6A(vii)

trānseō trānsīre trānsiī trānsitus I cross 3B(i)

trecent-ī ae a 300 **54**

trēdecim thirteen **161**

trēs tri-a three **54**

trīgintā thirty **161**

trīst-is e sad, gloomy, unhappy 1F

Trōiān-ī ōrum 2m. pl. the Trojans 3A(ii)

Trōiān-us a um Trojan 3A(ii)

trucīdō 1 I butcher 5F(ii)

tū you (s.) 1A

tueor 2dep. *tuitus* or *tūtus* I look after, protect; look at 6B(viii)

tul-: see *ferō*

tum then 1D

    cum … tum both … and 5D(ii)

tunic-a ae 1f tunic 6D(iv)

turb-a ae 1f. crowd, mob 1F

turp-is e disgusting, filthy, outrageous, ugly 4B(i)

tūt-us a um safe 4G(i)

U

tu-us a um your(s) (s.) 1C

uacu-us a um empty; free (from: + abl. or *ā* (*ab*) + abl.) 6B(vii)

ualdē very much, strongly 6B(v)

ualē goodbye! 1D

ualeō 2 I am strong; am well, am powerful; am able (cf. *ualē* = 'Farewell!' 'Goodbye!') 6A(vii)

uari-us a um diverse, various 3B(ii)

ubi where (at)? 1E; when? 1F

  ubi primum as soon as 5B(i)

ubicumque wherever 6B(vii)

-ue (added onto the end of a word: cf. *-ne* and *-que*) or 6A(vii)

uehemēns uehement-is impetuous, violent 5D(i)

uehementer strongly 4F(i)

uel ... uel either ... or 5A (ii)

  uel even 5D(iv)

uelim pres. subj. of *uolō*

uellem impf. subj. of *uolō*

uelut as, just as 5C(ii)

ueniō 4 *uēnī uentum* I come 3A(i)

uent-: see *ueniō*

uent-us ī 2m. wind 6D(i)

Venus Vener-is 3f. Venus, goddess of love 3A(i)

uerber uerber-is 3n. blow; whip 4F(i)

uerberō 1 I flog, beat 1C

uerb-um ī 2n. word 2A

uereor 2 dep. I fear, am afraid 5D(ii) (*nē* + subj. that/lest **163**)

uerit-: see *uereor*

uērō indeed 2D

Verrēs Verr-is 3m. Verres 4A(i)

uersor 1dep. I am occupied; stay, dwell; am in a certain condition 5G(ii)

uers-us ūs 4m. verse; pl. poetry 5A(ii)

uertō 3 *uertī uersus* I turn (trans.) 6C(ii)

uērum but 2D

uēr-us a um true 1G

Vestāl-is e Vestal (belonging to the goddess Vesta) 5D(i)

uester uestr-a um your(s) (pl.) 2A

uestis uest-is 3f. clothes, clothing, dress 4D(ii)

uetō 1 *uetuī uetitus* I forbid 4A(iv)

uetus ueter-is (like *dīues* **47**) old; long-established 5A(i)

uexō 1 I annoy, trouble, worry 1C

ui-a ae 1f. way, road 2A

uīc-: see *uincō*

uīcīn-us ī 2m. neighbour 1C

uict-: see *uincō*

uictor uictōr-is 3m. victor 3C(i)

uictōri-a ae 1f. victory 2A

uideō 2 *uīdī uīsus* I see 1B

uideor 2dep. *uīsus* I seem 2C; passive I am seen **121**

uīgintī twenty **161**

uinciō 4 *uīnxī uīnctus* I bind 2A

uincō 3 *uīcī uictus* I conquer 2D

uinc(u)l-um ī 2n. chain, bond 4F(ii)

uīn-um ī 2n. wine 6A(i)

uir uir-ī 2m. man, husband 1D

uīr-ēs ium (pl. of *uīs*) strength, military forces 3D(iv)

uirgō uirgin-is 3f. unmarried woman 3B(ii)

uirtūs uirtūt-is 3f. manliness, courage; goodness 1G; virtue 3D(iii)

uīs-: see *uideō/uideor*

uīs 2nd s. of *uolō*

uīs irr. force, violence (acc. *uim*; abl. *uī*); pl. *uīr-ēs ium* 3f. strength; military forces 3D(iv)

uīt-a ae 1f. life 2E

uīuō 3 *uīxī uīctum* I am alive, live 3C(i)

uīu-us a um alive, living 5G(iii)

ūll-us a um (gen. s. *ūllīus*; dat. s. *ūllī*) any (cf. *nūllus* **62**) 4B(i)

ultim-us a um furthest; last; greatest 6A(vii)

umbr-a ae 1f. shadow, darkness; shade, ghost 6D(ii)

umer-us ī 2m. shoulder 6D(ii)

umquam ever 3A(ii)

und-a ae 1f. water, wave 6D(ii)

unde from where, whence 5G(ii)

undecim eleven **161**

undēuīgintī nineteen **161**

unguent-um ī 2n. ointment 1B

ūniuers-us a um all together; whole, entire 6C(ii)

ūn-us a um (gen. s. *ūnīus*; dat. s. *ūnī*) one **54**

uōbīscum with you (pl.) 2C

uocō 1 I call 1A

uolō uelle uoluī I wish, want 1E

uoluntās uoluntāt-is 3f. will, wish 5D(ii)

uoluō 3 *uoluī uolūtus* I roll, turn over (trans.) 5G(iii)

uoluptās uoluptāt-is 3f. agreeable experience, pleasure, desire 2D

uōs you (pl.) **43**

uōt-um ī 2n. vow, prayer 6D(i)

uōx uōc-is 3f. voice; word 2E

urbs urb-is 3f. city 2D

ūs-: see *ūtor*

usque continually, without a break 6A(iv)

    usque ad (+ acc.) right up to 6A(iv)

ut (+ indic.) how! 1C; (+ indic.) as, when 1D; (+ subj.) to …, that … should 4F(i) (**136**); (+ subj.) that (after *accidit, perficiō* etc.) **137.**; (+ subj.) that (result) **149**; (+ subj.) in order to/ that (purpose) **150**; (+subj.) that … not (after verbs of fearing) **163**

uterque utraque utrumque each of two, both **177**

utī = *ut* 5B(ii)

utinam I wish that **158.1**

ūtor 3dep. *ūsus* I use, make use of; adopt (+ abl.) 4B(i)

utpote (*quī quae quod*) as is natural (for one who) (+ subj.) **166**

utrimque on both sides 5C(ii)

utrum … an (double question) X or Y? (negative *annōn* = or not?) 5D(i); (+ subj.) whether … or (indirect question) (negative *necne* = or not) 5D(i)

uulnerō 1 I wound 5G(iii)

uulnus uulner-is 3n. wound 3C(iii)

uult 3rd s. of *uolō*

uultis 2nd pl. of *uolō*

uult-us ūs 4m. face, expression 5G(iii)

uxor uxōr-is 3f. wife 1D

Total English–Latin vocabulary for exercises

Note

This vocabulary is compiled specifically for the English–Latin exercises in the Grammar and contains only those words and forms required to complete these successfully.

A

a(n): simply use noun; see also 'a certain'

abandon *relinquō* 3

able, be *possum posse potuī*

about to: use future participle

absence, in X's absence: use *absēns absent-is* agreeing with X

absent (use with noun to tr. 'in X's absence') *absēns absent-is*

accordance: in accordance with *perinde ac* (+ indic.)

account (noun) *ratiō ratiōn-is* 3f.; I make an account *ratiōnem habeō*

accuse *accūsō* 1

accustomed, be *soleō* 2 semi-dep. *solitus*

a certain *quīdam quaedam quoddam*; see **92**

achieve one's object *rem perficiō* 3/4 *perfēcī perfectus*

act (verb) *agō* 3 *ēgī*; *faciō* 3/4 *fēcī*; (noun) *facinus facinor-is* 3n.

actual *ipse ipsa ipsum*

address *adloquor* 3 dep. *adlocūtus*

Aeneas *Aenē-ās ae* 1m

advance *prōgredior* 3/4 dep. *prōgressus*

advantage: to X's advantage: use dat. of X

affair(s) *rēs rē-ī* 5f.

affirm *affirmō* 1

afraid

  be ... (of) *timeō* 2

  be ... (that) *uereor* 2

  dep. *ueritus*

  nē + subj.; *timeō* 2

  nē + subj.; *metuō* 3

  metuī nē + subj.

  (*ut* + subj. that ... not)

  be ... to: as above, but + inf.

after (conjunction) *postquam* + perf. indicative; if a deponent verb, use perfect participle; (preposition) *post* + acc.; (adverb) afterwards *post*

again *iterum*; (= after this) *posthāc*

against *in* (+ acc), *ad* (+ acc.)

against: fighting against *cum* + abl.

against (= contrary to what) *contrā ac* (+ indic.)

agreement, be in *cōnsentiō* 4 *cōnsēnsī cōnsēnsus*

aid *oper-a ae* 1f.; *auxili-um ī* 2n.

Alcumena *Alcumēn-a ae* 1f.

alive, be *uīuō* 3

alive *uīu-us a um*

all *omn-is e*

all the best men *optimus quisque*

all the time = while *dum* + same tense as main verb

Allobroges *Allobrog-ēs um* 3m. pl.

allow *sinō* 3 *sīuī*

allowed, X is *licet* 2 (X dat. *licet* + inf.)

ally *soci-us ī* 2m.

alone *sōl-us a um*

already *iam*

also *quoque*; *etiam*; *et*; not only ... but also
    nōn solum ... sed etiam

although *quamquam*; or use abl. abs. with
    present/perfect participle; *cum* +
    subj.; *quamuīs* + subj.

always *semper*

am: see 'be'

ambassador *lēgāt-us ī* 2m.

amid: use abl. (of attendant circumstances);
    or *inter* (+ acc.)

Amphitruo *Amphitruō Amphitruōn-is* 3m.

and *et*; *atque/ac*

angry *īrāt-us a um*; grow angry *īrāscor*
    3 dep.

announce *nūntiō* 1

Antonius *Antōni-us ī* 2m.

anxiety *cūr-a ae* 1f.
    anxiety in case *cūra nē* + subj.

anyone (after negatives) *quisquam*

anything (after negatives) *quicquam* (= *quid*
    + *quam*)

appear *uideor* 2 dep.; *appāreō* 2

appearance *faciēs, faci-ēī* 5f.

approach *adeō adīre*; *adgredior* 3/4 dep.
    (both use *ad* + acc.)

are: see 'be'

arise *exorior* 4 dep. *exortus* (gerund
    exoriundum)

armed men *arm-a ōrum* 2n. pl.; *armāt-ī*
    ōrum 2m. pl.

army *exercit-us ūs* 4m.

arrive (at) *peruentō* 4 *peruēnī peruentum ad*
    (+ acc.) (except names of towns and
    one-town islands; there acc. only)

as: see 'consider'
    as much as: see 'worth
        as much as'
    as (e.g. as you ought) *ut* (+ indic.); just as
        ita ... ut
    as X ... as Y *tam* (+ adj.) ... *quam*
    as soon as possible *quam prīmum*
    as (time): use abl. abs. with present
        participle or any case of present
        participle, depending on construction
        of sentence
    as follows *sīc*
    as though *tamquam* (+ subj.)
    as well *quoque*

ask *quaerō* 3 *quaesīuī quaesītus*

ask for *rogō* 1 (+ acc.)

asleep, be *dormiō* 4

assert *affirmō* 1

assist *succurrō* 3 (+ dat.)

at: in time phrases use abl. alone
    at home *domī*
    at once *statim*
    at the house of *apud* (+ acc.)
    at the same time *simul*

attack *adgredior* 3 dep. *aggressus*; *petō* 3
    petīuī pētītus

attempt *cōnor* 1 dep.

attention, pay *operām dō* 1 (to X dat.)

away from *ā* (*ab*) (+ abl.)

axe *secūris secūr-is* 3f.

B

back, be = come back *redeō redīre*

bad *mal-us a um*

base *sēdēs sēd-is* 3f.

battle *proeli-um ī* 2n.

be *sum esse*
    be accustomed *soleō* 2 semi-dep. *solitus*
        sum
    be missing *dēsum dēesse dēfuī*

bear *ferō ferre*

beast, wild beast *bēsti-a ae* 1f.

beat *uerberō* 1; *caedō* 3 *cecīdī caesus*

beautiful *pulcher pulchra pulchrum*

beauty *pulchritūdō pulchritūdin-is* 3f.

because *quod, quia* (+ indic); occasionally
    use abl. abs.
    because of *propter* (+ acc); *ob* (+ acc.)

become *fīō fierī factus sum*
    become acquainted with *cognōscō* 3 *cognōuī*

bedroom *cubicul-um ī* 2n.

before (when the action of the main clause is
    conditional on the completion of the
    'before' clause) *antequam* + subj.

beg *precor* 1 dep.; *ōrō* 1; *obsecrō* 1

believe *crēdō* 3 *crēdidī crēditum* (+ dat.); in
    passive used impersonally: X (dat.)
    is believed Y (*ā* + abl.)

belonging to X: use dat. or gen. of X

beseech *ōrō* 1; *obsecrō* 1

besiege *obsideō* 2 *obsēdī obsessus*

best *optimus a um*

 all the best men *optimus quisque*

bestow *dō dare*

betake oneself *sē ferō* (*tulī lātus*)

better *meli-or meli-us*

 I'd better = *mihi melius est* + inf.

big *ingēns ingent-is*

black *niger nigr-a um*

blame *castīgō* 1

bold *audāx audāc-is*

boldly *audācter*

boldness *audāci-a ae* 1f.

booty *praed-a ae* 1f.

bore: X is a … to: X (nom.) *taediō est* to Y (dat.)

born (of) *nāt-us a um* (+ abl. of origin)

both … and *et … et*

bother *sollicitō* 1

boy *puer puer-ī* 2m.

brave *fort-is e*

break *frangō* 3 *frēgī frāctus*

bring *portō* 1; *ferō ferre*

 bring to land (of a ship) *appellō* 3 *appulī appulsus*

 bring with *addūcō* 3 *addūxī adductus*

brother *frāter frātr-is* 3m.

Brutus *Brūt-us i* 2m.

build *aedificō* 1

building *aedifici-um ī* 2n.

burden *onus oner-is* 3n.

 be a … on *onerī esse*: X (nom.) is a burden on Y (dat.)

burdensome, X is … to Y: X (nom.) *onerī est* to Y (dat.)

burn (intrans.) *cōnflagrō* 1

burn (trans.) *incendō* 3 *incendī incēnsus*

business *negōti-um ī* 2n.; *rēs rē-ī* 5f.

 do business: see 'do'

but *sed* (1st word); *autem* (2nd word); *tamen* (usu. 2nd word); (= except) *nisi*

butcher *trucīdō* 1

by *ā* or *ab* + abl. (often after passive verbs); by —ing abl. of gerund.

C

cadaver *cadāuer cadāuer-is* 3n.

call *uocō* 1

call back *reuocō* 1

called: use *nōmine* (abl. of *nōmen*)

call together *conuocō* 1

calm *aequō animō*

camp *castr-a ōrum* 2n. pl.

can *possum posse*

captain *praefect-us ī* 2m.

capture *capiō* 3/4 *cēpī captus*

care for *cūrō* 1

care, take *prōuideō* 2

carry *portō* 1; *ferō ferre tulī*

Carthage *Carthāg-ō in-is* 3f.

cast lots *sortior* 4 dep.

catch sight of *cōnspicor* 1 dep.

Catiline *Catilīn-a ae* 1m.

certain (= a) *quīdam quaedam quoddam*

certainly *certē*

chain *uinc(u)l-um ī* 2n.

change (intransitive) *sē mutāre*

chap: omit or use *uir uir-ī* 2m.; *homo homin-is* 3m.

charge, be in … of *praesum praeesse* (+ dat.)

character *mōr-ēs um* 3m. pl.

chastity *pudīciti-a ae* 1f.

cheer up *bonum animum habeō* 2

children *līber-ī ōrum* 2m. pl.

Chrysalus *Chrȳsal-us ī* 2m.

Cicero *Cicerō Cicerōn-is* 3m.

citizen *cīuis cīu-is* 3m.

city *urbs urb-is* 3f. (city of X: put X in same case as *urbs*)

claim *arguō* 3 *arguī*

clearly *plānē*

Cleomenes *Cleomen-ēs Cleomen-is* 3m.

clever *doct-us a um*

collect *colligō* 3 *collēgī*

column *agmen agmin-is* 3n.

come *eō īre iī itum*; *ueniō* 4 *uēnī uentum*

 come out *exeō exīre*; *ēgredior* 3/4 dep.

 come to *adeō adīre adiī aditum*

 come up to *accēdō* 3 *accessī accessum*

command (noun) *imperi-um ī* 2n.; (vb) *iubeō* 2; *imperō* 1 commander *imperātor imperātōr-is* 3m.; *dux duc-is* 3m.

commit *commutō* 3 *commīsī commissus*

compassionate *misericors misericord-is* (3 adj.)

compel *cōgō* 3 *coēgī coāctus*

complain *queror* 3 dep. *questus*

complete *perficiō* 3/4 *perfēcī perfectus*; *cōnficiō* 3/4 *cōnfēcī cōnfectus*

concerning *dē* (+ abl.)

confirm *cōnfirmō* 1

conquer *uincō* 3 *uīcī*

conscript *cōnscrīpt-us a um*

consider (X as Y) *habeō* 2 (X acc., Y acc.); *arbitror* 1 dep. (same construction)

conspiracy *coniūrātiō coniūrātiōn-is* 3f.

conspirator *coniūrātor coniūrātōr-is* 3m.

constellation *sign-um ī* 2n.

consul *cōnsul cōnsul-is* 3m.

consulship *cōnsulāt-us ūs* 4m. stand for consulship *cōnsulātum petō* (3)

continue *pergō* 3

contrary: see 'on the contrary'

conversation *sermō sermōn-is* 3m.

cook (noun) *coqu-us ī* 2m.; (vb) *coquō* 3

corpse *corpus corpor-is* 3n.; *cadāuer cadāuer-is* 3n.

could: see 'can'

courage *uirtūs uirtūt-is* 3f.

coward(ly) *ignāu-us a um*: for 'coward' use as noun

crime *scelus sceler-is* 3n.

criminal *scelest-us ī* 2m.

cross *crux cruc-is* 3f.

cross *transeō transīre*

crowd *turb-a ae* 1f.; *multitūdō multitūdin-is* 3f.

cup *pōcul-um ī* 2n.

Curius *Cūri-us ī* 2m.

custom *mōs mōr-is* 3m.

cut (vb) *caedō* 3 *cecīdī*

D

danger *perīcul-um ī* 2n.

  danger of X happening *perīculum nē* + subj.

dare *audeō* 2

daring (adj.) *audāx audāc-is*; (noun) *audāci-a ae* 1f.

daughter *fīli-a ae* 1f.

day *di-ēs diēī* 5m.

dead *mortu-us a um*

dear me = *mē miserum/miseram*

death *mors mort-is* 3f.

  death penalty *summ-um supplici-um ī* 2n.

deceive *dēcipiō* 3/4 *dēcēpī dēceptus*

decide *placet* 2 *placuit*: X (dat.) decides to Y (inf.); *cōnstituō* 3 *cōnstituī cōnstitūtus* (to: infinitive)

declare *affirmō* 1

deed *facinus facinor-is* 3n.; (= something already done) *fact-um ī* 2n.

defeat *uincō* 3 *uīcī*

defend *dēfendō* 3 *dēfendī dēfēnsus*

defendant: use *iste ista istum* (see **91**)

delay (vb) *moror* (1 dep.); *commoror* (1 dep.); (noun) *mor-a ae* 1f.

Demaenetus *Dēmaenet-us ī* 2m.

demand *poscō* 3; *postulō* 1

depart (= set out) *proficīscor* 3 dep. *profectus*

  depart for *proficīscor ad* (+ acc.)

desire (vb) *cupiō* 4

destined to be *futūr-us a um*

destroy *dēleō* 2 *dēlēuī*

destruction *exiti-um ī* 2n.

devise *excōgitō* 1

die *morior* 3/4 dep. *mortuus*; (= fall in battle) *occidō* 3 *occidī occāsum*

differently from *aliter ac* (+ indic.)

difficult *difficil-is e*

dignity *dignitās dignitāt-is* 3f.

dinner *cēn-a ae* 1f

Diodorus *Diodōr-us ī* 2m.

disadvantage, to X's: use dat. of X

disbelieve: use *nōn crēdō* 3

disembark *in terram exeō* (*exīre exiī exitum*)

disregard (for) *neglegenti-a ae* 1f. (+ gen.)

disturb *commoueō* 2 *commōuī*

do *faciō* 3/4 *fēcī factus*; *agō* 3 *ēgī āctus*; *gerō* 3 *gessī gestus*

  do business *negōtium agō* (3) or *gerō* (3)

done for, I'm *periī*

don't/do not (as command) *nōlī/nōlīte* + inf.; *nē* + perfect subj.

door *iānu-a ae* 1f.

doubt: use adj. *dubi-us a um* (rephrase 'there's no doubt', as 'it is not doubtful'); without doubt *sine dubiō*

there is no … that *nōn dubium est quīn* + subj. (see **174** for sequence)

dowry *dōs dōt-is* 3f.

drag back *retrahō* 3 *retrāxī retractus*

draw *ferō ferre*

draw up *īnstruō* 3 *īnstrūxī īnstrūctus*

drink *bibō* 3 *bibī*

drive back *repellō* 3 *reppulī*

drunk *ēbri-us a um*

duty *offici-um ī* 2n.

dwell *habitō* 1

E

each (man, woman, thing) *quisque quaeque quidque*

each individual *ūnus quisque*

each (of two) *uterque utraque utrumque*

easily *facile*; more easily *facilius*

easy *facil-is e*

eight *octō*

elect *creō* 1

embark *in nāuem ingredior* 3/4 *ingressus*

embrace *complector* 3 dep. *complexus*; *amplexor* 1 dep.

encourage *hortor* 1 dep.; X (acc.) to Y (*ut* + subj. – neg. *nē*: see **136** for rules of sequence); (troops) *cohortor* 1 dep. (with acc. or *ut* + subj.)

endure *ferō ferre, patior* 3/4 *passus* endure, suffer; allow

enemy *hostis host-is* 3m.

enjoin *iubeō* 2 (X acc. to Y inf.)

enjoy *fruor* 3 dep. *frūctus* (+ abl.)

enough *satis* (+ gen.); or qualifying an adj.

enter *intrō* 1; *ingredior* 3/4 dep.

enthusiasm *studi-um ī* 2n.

enthusiasm for + gen.

entrust *mandō* 1 (X acc. to Y dat.)

-er: use comparative adj.

escape *fugiō* 3/4; *profugiō* 3/4 *profūgī*

-est: use superlative adj.

estimate *coniciō* 3/4 *coniēcī coniectus*

Euclio *Eucliō Eucliōn-is* 3m.

even *etiam*

event *rēs re-ī* 5f.

ever *umquam*

every *omn-is e*

everything: use n. pl. of *omnis* or *omnis* + *rēs*

everyone: use m. pl. of *omnis*

evil *mal-us a um*

exact (the penalty) *supplicium sūmō* 3

examine *īnspiciō* 3/4 *īnspexī īnspectus*

excellence *uirtūs uirtūt-is* 3f.

excellent *optim-us a um*

except *nisi*

execute *necō* 1

exile *exsili-um ī* 2n.

expression *uult-us ūs* 4m.

extent, to such an *adeō*

extremely: use superlative adj. or adv. or *summ-us a um* with a noun in abl. (e.g. 'extremely beautiful' = 'of very great beauty' abl.)

eye *ocul-us ī* 2m.

F

fail *dēsum dēesse dēfuī* + dat.

fall (often = die) *cadō* 3 *cecidī cāsum*; *occidō* 3 *occidī occāsum*

family *famili-a ae* 1f.; *genus gener-is* 3n.

far from *longē ā* (*ab*) + abl.

fate *fat-um -ī* 2n.

father *pater patr-is* 3m.

fatherland *patri-a ae* 1f.

fear (vb) *timeō* 2; *uereor* 2 dep.; that … not *ut* + subj.; (noun) *timor timōr-is* 3m.; *met-us ūs* 4m.

feign *simulō* 1

fellow *uir -ī* 2m.; (slang) *homo homin-is* 3m.

ferocious *ferōx ferōc-is*

ferocity *ferōci-a ae* 1f.

field *ager agr-ī* 2m.

fight *pugnō* 1; *certō* 1; fight a war *bellum gerō*

fighting *pugn-a ae* 1f; *proeli-um ī* 2n.; in 'fighting is going on' use impersonal passive of *pugnō* 1

finally *postrēmō*; *tandem* (= at length)

find *inueniō* 4 *inuēnī inuentus*; *reperiō* 4 *repperī repertus* (= something that was mislaid or lost)

find out *cognōscō* 3 *cognōuī cognitus*

finish *cōnficio* 3/4 *cōnfēcī cōnfectus*

fire (noun) *ignis ign-is* 3m.; *incendi-um ī* 2n.; (vb = set alight) *accendō* 3 *accendī accēnsus*

fist *pugn-us ī* 2m.

fitting, it is *decet* (for X acc. to Y inf.)

flat-fish *mūrēn-a ae* 1f

flight *fug-a ae* 1f.

follow *sequor* 3 dep.

food *cib-us ī* 2m.

fool (noun) *stult-us ī* 2m.; (vb) *dēcipiō* 3/4 *dēcēpī dēceptus*

for: use dat.; (= because) *nam* (1st word), *enim* (2nd word); (= on behalf of) *prō* (+ abl.); for the sake of *causā* (+ gen.), *grātiā* (+ gen.) – placed after the noun or phrase they qualify

forbid *uetō* 1 *uetuī uetitus*

force *cōgō* 3 *coēgī coāctus* (X acc. to Y inf.)

forces *cōpi-ae ārum* 1f. pl.; *exercit-us ūs* 4m.

foresee *prōuideō* 2 *prōuidī prōuīsus*

forget *oblīuīscor* 3 dep. *oblītus*

forum *for-um ī* 2n.

found *condō* 3/4 *condidī conditus*

foundations *fundāment-a ōrum* 2n. pl.

free (vb) *līberō* 1

freedom *lībertās lībertāt-is* 3f.

friend *amīc-us ī* 2m.; *comes comit-is* 3m.

friendly *amīc-us a um*

from (= away) *ā (ab)* + abl. or (= out of) *ē (ex)* + abl.; (= because of) use abl. of cause

full (of) *plēn-us a um* (+ gen.)

Fulvia *Fului-a ae* 1f.

future *futūr-us a um*

G

Gabinius *Gabīni-us ī* 2m.

gain *adipīscor* 3 dep. *adeptus*

garland *corōn-a ae* 1f.

Gaul *Galli-a ae* 1f.

  Transalpine Gaul *Galli-a Trānsalpīn-a Galli-ae Trānsalpīn-ae* 1f.

Gavius *Gaui-us ī* 2m.

general *dux duc-is* 3m.

get in X's way *obstō* 1 (+ dat.)

get ready (trans.) *comparō* 1; *parō* 1

gift *dōn-um ī* 1n.

girl *puell-a ae* 1f.

give *dō dare dedī* (X acc. to Y dat.)

  give back *reddō* 3 *reddidī redditus*

  give oneself up *sē trādere* (*trādidī trāditus*) (the pronoun will change with the person: *mē trādō, tē trādis* etc.)

  give orders *iubeō* 2 (+ acc); *imperō* 1 (+ dat.)

  give orders (that) *imperō ut* + subj.

gladly *laet-us a um*

go *eō īre iī itum*

  go around *circum-eo -īre -iī -itum*

go away *abeō abīre abiī abitum*; *ēgredior* 3/4 dep. *ēgressus* (gerundives *abeundum, ēgrediendum*)

go back *redeō redīre*

go forward *prōgredior* 3/4 *prōgressus*

go in *ineō inīre*; *ingredior* 3/4 dep.

go out *exeō exīre exiī*; *ēgredior* (3/4 dep.)

go on *pergō* 3

go to *accēdō* 3 *accessī accessum*

going to —: use future participle

god *de-us ī* 2m. (pl. *dī*: see **16**); household god *Lar Lar-is* 3m.

goddess *de-a ae* 1f.

gold *aur-um ī* 2n.

golden *aure-us a um*

good *bon-us a um*

good! *bene*

goodbye! *uale*

great *magn-us a um*; greatest, very great *maxim-us a um, summ-us a um*; so great *tant-us a um*

greater *māior māius*

greed *cupiditās cupiditāt-is* 3f; greed for X: use *cupiditās* + gen.

Greek *Graec-us a um*

grove *lūc-us ūs* 4m.

H

hand *man-us ūs* 4f.

hand over *trādō* 3 *trādidī trāditus*

Hannibal *Hannibal -is* 3m.

happen *fīō fierī factus*; or use passive of *gerō* 3 *gessī gestus*

    it happens that *accidit* (3 *accidit*) *ut* + subj.

harbour *port-us ūs* 4m.

harm *noceō* 2 *nocuī nocitum* (+ dat.); in the passive use impersonally: X (dat.) is harmed by Y (*ā* + abl.)

harmful *noxi-us a um*

harmony *concordi-a ae* 1f.

has: see 'have'

Hasdrubal *Hasdrubal -is* 3m.

hated, X is … by Y: X (nom.) *odiō est* to Y (dat.)

have *habeō* 2; or use *sum* + dat. of person who has, nom. of thing/person possessed; I have —ed: use perfect tense

have/had to X: use gerundive of the X with *sum* (have to) *eram* (had to). The person who 'has to' is in the dat. when the verb is intransitive.

he: use verb in 3rd person singular; in indirect statement (acc. + inf.) use *sē* if it refers to subject of introductory verb, *eum* if to a different person

head, be at the … of *praesum praeesse* (+ dat.)

hear (of) *audiō* 4

help, be a help to X *auxiliō esse* (X dat.)

her: use parts of *ea*

here *hīc*; (= to here) *hūc*

hers: use gen. of *haec*, *illa* or *ea*

herself *sē* (pronoun); *ips-e a um* (adj.)

hesitate *cūnctor* 1 dep. (to: inf.)

hide *cēlō* 1

highest *summ-us a um*

him: use *hic*, *ille* or *is*; in law-court speeches *iste* is often used when 'him' = 'the defendant'

grow angry *īrāscor* 3 dep. *īrātus*

guarantor *cognitor cognitōr-is* 3m.

guard, guardian *custōs custōd-is* 3m.

himself (acc.) *sē* (gen.) *suī* (dat.) *sibi* (abl.) *sē*; (speaks) to himself *sēcum*

hinder, be a hindrance to X *impedīmentō esse* (X dat.)

his: where it refers to the subject and there is no emphasis, use noun alone: where it refers to someone other than the subject, use gen. of *hic*, *ille* or *is*; if referring to subject with some emphasis use *su-us a um*

hold *teneō* 2

    hold back *reprimō* 3 *repressī repressus*; *teneō* 2 *tenuī tentus*; *retineō* 2 *retinuī retentus*; X (acc.) from doing Y: *quōminus* or *nē* + subj.

home (= to home) *domum*; (= at home) *domī*; (= from home) *domō*

honour (noun) *honor honōr-is* 3m.

hope *spēs spē-ī* 3f.

horse *equ-us ī* 2m.

hospitable *hospitāl-is e*

hour *hōr-a ae* 1f.

house *aed-ēs ium* 3f. pl.; *dom-us ūs* 4f. (irr. see **56**); in the house *domī*; from the house *domō*

household *famili-a ae* 1f.

    household god *Lar Lar-is* 3m.

how! *ut* (+ indic); how the matter stands: see stands; how (qualifying an adjective) *quam*: may introduce indirect question (followed by subj. verb)

    how many *quot* (introducing direct or indirect question: ind. questions have subj. verb)

    how much *quant-us a um* (introduces both direct and indirect questions: ind. questions have subj. verb)

however *tamen* (usu. 2nd word); *autem* (2nd word) or *sed* (1st word)

huge *ingēns ingent-is*

hurry *properō* 1

husband *uir uir-ī* 2m.

I

I *ego* (only when emphatic: otherwise use
  1st s. of verb only)
idle *ignāu-us a um*
idleness *ignāui-a ae* 1f.
if *sī*; (very occasionally use abl. abs.); if …
  not *nisi*
ignorant of *nesci-us a um* + gen.
important, such an *tant-us a um*
in *in* (+ abl.)
  in case *nē* + subj.
  in order (not) to *ut* + subj., negative *nē*; see
    150 for rules of sequence
  in order to … more *quō* + comp. adj./adv.
    + subj. (see **155**)
  in X place: often just abl. without *in*.
    Some towns have a special locative
    (see under name of town)
  in X's praetorship/consulship etc.: plain abl.
    name + abl. of *praetor*, *cōnsul* etc.
  in X time: plain abl.
  in X way *ita*; *sīc*; or a phrase in abl. with
    mod-us ī 2m.

in —ing: abl. of gerund
inasmuch as *quippe quī* + subj.
indeed *uērō*
individual: each individual *ūnus quisque*
inflamed *īnflammāt-us a um*
innocent *innocēns innocent-is*
inside (= to inside) *intrō*
instruct *praecipiō* 3/4 *praecēpī praeceptus*
  X dat. to / not to do Y (*ut/nē* + subj.;
    see **136** for rules of sequence)
instruction: in 'an instruction has been
  given' use impersonal passive of
  praecipiō 3/4 *praecēpī praeceptus*:
  give the instructions: see 'instruct'
intend(ing) to: use future participle
intention *mēns ment-is* 3f.
into *in* + acc.
invite (someone to something) *uocō* 1 (to: *ad*
  + acc.); *inuītō* 1 (X acc. to Y *ad* + acc.)
is: see 'be'
it: use 3rd person singular of verb
Italy *Ītali-a ae* 1f.

J

join *adiungō* 3 *adiūnxī adiūnctus* (transitive)
  (X acc. to Y dat.)
  join someone or something: *sē adiungere*
    (+ dat.)
  join battle with *proelium committō*
    3 *commīsī commissus cum*
    + abl.

joy *laetiti-a ae* 1f; *gaudi-um ī* 2n.
joyful *laet-us a um* (X was not a joyful
  event: use adj. on its own, or with
  rēs)
judge *iūdex iūdic-is* 3m.
Jupiter *Iuppiter Iou-is* 3m.
just as (… so) *ut* (… *ita*)

K

keep *seruō*, *adseruō* 1
  kept —ing: use imperfect tense
  keep quiet *taceō* 2
  keep shouting *clāmitō* 1
kill *necō* 1; *interficiō* 3/4 *interfēcī*
  interfectus

kindly *benīgne*
king *rēx rēg-is* 3m.
know *sciō* 4; *cognōuī cognitus*; (=
  understand) *intellegō* 3 *intellēxī*
  intellēctus
known: well known *clār-us a um*

L

lack *egeō* 2 *eguī* (+ abl.)
lad: use adj. in appropriate case of masculine
  (alternatively *homo homin-is* 3m.;
  puer puer-ī 2m.)
Lampsacum, people of *Lampsacēn-ī ōrum*
  2m. pl.
land *terr-a ae* 1f.; (= native land) *patri-a*
  ae 1f.

Lar *Lar Lar-is* 3m.
large *ingēns ingent-is*; *magn-us a um*
later *post*
laugh *rīdeō* 2 *rīsī rīsus*
law *lēx lēg-is* 3f.
lead *dūcō* 3 *dūxī*
leader (= general) *dux duc-is* 3m.; *prīnceps*
  prīncip-is 3m.

438

leadership, under X's: use abl. of name and
abl. of *dux duc-is* 3m.

learn *cognōscō* 3 *cognōuī cognitus*

leave

(= go away) *abeō abīre*

(= abandon) *relinquō* 3 *relīquī*

(= go out) *ēgredior* 3/4 dep.
ēgressus

leisure *ōti-um ī* 2n.

Lentulus *Lentul-us ī* 2m.

lest (esp. after verbs of fearing or
apprehension) *nē* + subj.

let (X ... do Y, or X be done): use 3rd s./pl.
subj. present; let ... not *nē* + perf.
subj. 3rd s./pl.

letter *litter-ae ārum* 1f. pl.

liberty *lībertās lībertāt-is* 3f.

lictor *līctor līctōr-is* 3m.

lie *mentior* 4 dep.

life *uīt-a ae* 1f.

like (adj.) *simil-is e* (+ dat. or gen.); (vb) X
likes: X (dat.) *placet*; (vb) *uolō uelle
uoluī* (only in potential subj. usages:
e.g. 'I would like')

Lilybaeum *Lilybae-um ī* 2m.; locative *Lilybaeī*;
use acc. for 'to', abl. for 'from'

listen *audiō* 4

live *uīuō* 3 *uīxī uīctum* (no past participle)
live one's life *aetātem agō* (3 *ēgī
āctus*)

long *long-us a um*

look after *cūrō* 1

looks *fōrm-a ae* 1f.

lot, a ... of: use *mult-us a um*

love (vb) *amō* 1

lover *amātor amātōr-is* 3m.

Lucretia *Lucrēti-a ae* 1f.

lust *cupiditās cupiditāt-is* 3f.; *libīdō
libīdinis* 3f.

lying *mendāx mendāc-is*

M

madness *īnsani-ā ae* 1f.

magistrate *magistrāt-us ūs* 4m.

make *faciō* 3/4 *fēcī factus*
make a speech *ōrātiōnem habeō* 2
make love to *amō* 1
make plans *cōnsilium capiō* (3/4 *cēpī captus*)
make one's way *iter faciō* 3/4

man: old man, see 'old': *uir uir-ī* 2m.; in
military contexts, use *mīlitēs* for 'men'
(= human being) *homo homin-is* 3m.

manage to *perficiō* (3/4 *perfēcī perfectus*) *ut*
+ subj.; *efficiō* (3/4 *effēcī effectus*) *ut*
+ subj. (rules of sequence in **135**)

many *mult-ī ae a* (pl.)

marriage *cōnūbi-um ī* 2n.

married *nūpt-us a um*

marry *in mātrimōnium dūcō* (3 *dūxī ductus*)
(X acc.)

massive *ingēns ingent-is*

master *domin-us ī* 2m.

matter *rēs rē-ī* 5f.

may ('X may do Y'): X (dat.) *licet* + inf.;
sometimes occurs in subordinate
clauses – check the construction; in
main clause, 'someone may —', use
perfect subjunctive (potential)

mean *dīcō* 3 *dīxī dictus*

meanwhile *intereā*

mention *loquor* 3 dep. *loquī locūtus*

Mercury *Mercuri-us ī* 2m.

merriment *laetiti-a ae* 1f.

message *nūnti-us ī* 2m.

Messana *Messān-a ae* 1f.

Metellus *Metell-us ī* 2m.

middle (of) *medi-us a um*

mind *anim-us ī* 2m.

missing, be *dēsum dēesse dēfuī*

money *pecūni-a ae* 1f.

moon *lūn-a ae* 1f.

more: normally use comparative form of adj.
or adv.
more (adv.) *magis*
more (s.) *plūs* (+ gen.); (pl.) *plūrēs plūra*
(3rd decl. adjective)

mountain *mōns mont-is* 3m.

move (= upset) *commoueō* 2 *commōuī
commōtus*; (= physically move)
moueō 2 *mōuī mōtus*

much (adj.) *mult-us a um*; too much *nimis*
(+ gen.); much (adv.) = (by) far
multō

murder *necō* 1

N

must: X (dat.) *necesse est* Y (inf.); often use
gerundive (X must do Y = Y nom.).
Must be done, gerundive agreeing
with Y, by X (dat.). With intransitive

name (noun) *nōmen nōmin-is* 3n.; (vb) name
X as Y *nōminō* 1 X (acc.) Y (acc.)
necessity *necessitūdō necessitūdin-is* 3f.
neighbour *uīcīn-us ī* 2m.
neighbouring *uīcīn-us a um*
never *numquam*
nevertheless *tamen* (2nd word);
nihilōminus
new *nou-us a um*
new man *nouus homo*
next (= and then) *deinde*
nigh, be *adsum adesse*
night *nox noct-is* 3f.
no/none (of) (adj.) *nūll-us a um*

verbs X must Y = Y (nom. n.
gerundive) + *est* X (dat.)
my *me-us a um* (voc. s. m. *mī*)
myself: use part of *ego*

no! *immō*
no one *nēmō nēmin-is* 3m.; after *nē* use *quis*
there is no one who … *nēmō est quī* … +
subj. (generic)
noble *nōbil-is e*
nobles *nōbil-ēs ium* 3m. pl.
nor *neque, nec*
not *nōn*
not to (indirect command) *nē* + subj.
and not to *nēue* + subj.
not yet *nōndum*
nothing *nihil, nīl*
now *nunc*
number *numer-us ī* 2m.

O

O! *ō* (followed by voc. in direct address,
acc. if an exclamation)
oar *rēm-us ī* 2m.
oath *iūs iūrand-um iūr-is iūrand-ī* 3n.
obey *pāreō* 2 (+ dat.)
object: see 'achieve one's object'
obstruct *obsistō* 3 *obstitī* + dat.
obtain *adipīscor* 3 dep. *adeptus*
obviously *plānē*
of: use gen. to denote possession, source;
use abl. or gen. in descriptions
(e.g. a man of great courage)
often *saepe*
old: old man *senex sen-is* 3m.
on: in a time phrase, use abl.
on account of *propter* (+ acc); *ob*
(+ acc.)
on the point of: use future participle
on the contrary *immō; minimē*
on the say so (of) *iussū* (+ gen.)
once X had been —ed: use abl. abs.

one *ūn-us a um* (like *nūllus*, **62**)
one of *ūnus ē* (*ex*) + abl.
only *sōlum*; not only … but also *nōn*
sōlum … sed etiam
onto *in* (+ acc.)
or *aut* (where two things: either … or *aut* …
aut)
ordain *dēcernō* 3
order, give an … to *iubeō* 2 *iussī iussus* (+
acc.); *imperō* 1 (+ dat.)
order X to Y *iubeō* (+ acc. + inf.); *imperō*
(X dat. *ut* + subj.); (noun) *imperi-um*
ī 2n.
other *alius aliud* (gen./dat. s. *alī-us alī-ī*)
ought *dēbeō* 2; X ought to Y: X (acc.)
oportet + inf.
our *noster nostr-a um*
out of *ē* (*ex*) + abl.
over (of time): use plain acc.
own, his: use *su-us a um* if it refers to the
subject of the verb

P

part *pars part-is* 3f.
party *conuīui-um ī* 2n.

patron *patrōn-us ī* 2n.
peace *pāx pāc-is* 3f.

penalty *supplici-um ī* 2n.

    exact the penalty *supplicium sūmō* (3) *dē* (+ abl.)

people: use *homo homin-is* 3m. in pl., or pl. of adjective on its own; (= nation) *popul-us ī* 2m.

perform (an act) *committō* 3 *commīsī commissus*

person: use m. of adj. or pronoun

persuade *persuādeō* 2 *persuāsī persuāsum*; persuade … X (dat.) to Y (*ut* + subj. – negative *nē*)

Petreius *Petrēi-us ī* 2m.

Philodamus *Philodām-us ī* 2m.

Picenum *ager Pīcēn-us, agr-ī Pīcēn-ī* 2m.

pirate *pīrāt-a ae* 1m.; *praedō praedōn-is* 3m.; (adj.) *pīrātic-us a um*

place (noun) *loc-us ī* 2m.

    in X's place *in locum* (+ gen.)

place (vb) *pōnō* 3 *posuī positus*; *collocō* 1

plan *cōnsili-um ī* 2n.

    plans, make *cōnsilium capiō* 3/4

pleasure *uoluptās uoluptāt-is* 3f; X is a pleasure to Y: X (nom.) *uoluptātī est* Y (dat.)

poetry *uers-ūs uum* 4m. pl.

    write poetry *uersūs facere*

ponder *cōnsīderō* 1; *excōgitō* 1

poor, poor man *pauper pauper-is* 3m. or adj.; (= unhappy) *miser miser-a um*

possess *habeō* 2

possible, it is *potest* (often uses a passive inf.)

pot *aul-a ae* 1f. (the usual classical Latin form is *olla*; *aula* usually means 'court', 'palace')

pour scorn on *irrīdeō* 2 *irrīsī irrīsus*

power *imperi-um ī* 2n.

praetorship, in X's …: use abl. of name and abl. of *praetor praetōr-is* 3m.

pray (to), supplicate *supplicō* 1 (+ dat.); *precor* 1 dep.

prayers *prec-ēs um* 3f. pl.

prefer *mālō mālle māluī*; prefer X to Y *mālō* X (acc.) *quam* Y (acc.)

prepare *parō* 1 prepared to *parāt-us a um ad* (+ acc.) (with a gerundive phrase)

present, be *adsum adesse adfuī* (with: + dat.)

preserve *cōnseruō* 1

pretty *pulcher pulchr-a um*

prevent *prohibeō* 2 (X acc. from doing Y inf.); *impediō* 4 (X acc. from doing Y: *nē* or *quōminus* if *impediō* positive, *quīn* or *quōminus* if *impediō* negative)

priest *sacerdōs sacerdōt-is* 3m.

priesthood *sacerdōti-um ī* 2n.

promise *polliceor* 2 dep.

protect *dēfendō* 3 *dēfendī dēfēnsus*

protection *praesidi-um ī* 2n.

provided that *dum* (*dummodo*) + subj.

province *prōuinci-a ae* 1f.

punish *pūniō* 4

punishment *supplici-um ī* 2n.

    exact punishment from *supplicium sūmō* (3) *dē* + abl.

purpose, with the … of *ut* + subj.; *quī* + subj.: *ut* is in this case often preceded by *eō cōnsiliō*; for the purpose of —ing *grātiā* or *causā* + gen. gerund/gerundive phrase (e.g. *resistendī causā* for the purpose of resisting): note they are post-positions (i.e. come after the word they govern)

pursue *sequor* 3 dep. *secūtus*; *persequor* 3 dep. *persecūtus*

put up *pōnō* 3 *posuī*

Q

qualities *uirtūt-ēs um* 3f. pl.

queen *rēgīn-a ae* 1f.

quick *celer celer-is e*

quickly *celeriter*

quiet, keep *taceō* 2

R

Raecius *Raeci-us ī* 2m.

rank *ōrdō ōrdin-is* 3m.

rather than *potius quam*

    rather X: use comparative adjective

read *legō* 3 *lēgī lēctus*

    read through *perlegō* 3 *perlēgī perlēctus*

ready, get (trans.) *comparō* 1; *parō* 1

realise *sentiō* 4 *sēnsī sēnsus*

rebuke *castīgō* 1

recall *recordor* 1 dep.

refer *referō referre*

refuse *nōlō nōlle nōluī*; (= say no) *negō* 1

regret X (acc.) *paenitet*; I regret X *mē*
paenitet + gen.

relate *nārrō* 1

relative (= blood-kin) *cognāt-us ī* 2m.

rely upon *nītor* 3 dep. *nīsus/nīxus* (+ abl.)

remember *recordor* 1 dep.; *meminī*
meminisse (perfect form, present
meaning)

remove X's Y, Y from X *auferō* (Y acc. X
dat.)

remove *tollō* 3 *sustulī sublātus*; *auferō*
auferre abstulī ablātus

reply *respondeō* 2 *respondī*

report (= denounce) *dēferō* irr. 3 *dēferre*
dētulī; (= announce) *nūntiō* 1

rescue *ēripiō* 3/4 *ēripuī ēreptus* (X acc. from
Y dat.)

resist *resistō* 3 *restitī* — (+ dat.)

resolute *audāx audāc-is*

resources *op-ēs um* 3f. pl.

respect *honor honōr-is* 3m.

rest (of) *cēter-us a um*; *reliqu-us a um*

retain *retineō* 2 *retinuī retentus*

return (= go back) *redeō redīre rediī*;
regredior 3/4 *regressus*; (= give
back) *reddō* 3 *reddidī redditus*

reveal *aperiō* 4 *aperuī apertus*; *patefaciō*
3/4 *patefēcī patefactus*

reward *praemi-um ī* 2n.

rich (man) *dīues dīuit-is* 3m.; or adj.

Roman *Rōmān-us a um* (for 'a Roman',
'Romans' use m. forms as nouns)

Rome *Rōm-a ae* 1f.; locative *Rōmae*; for 'to'
use acc; for 'from' use abl.

rotten *pūtid-us a um*

Rubrius *Rubri-us ī* 2m.

run

run away *fugiō* 3/4 *fūgī*

run into *incurrō* (3 *incurrī incursum*) *in*
+ acc.

run together *concurrō* 2 *concurrī*

rush: in 'there was a rush' use impersonal
passive of *concurrō* 3 *concurrī*
concursum

S

safe (= saved) *salu-us a um*

safety *salūs salūt-is* 3f.

sail *nāuigō* 1

sailor *naut-a ae* 1m.

sake, for the ... of *causā* (+ gen.); *grātiā*
(+ gen.) – placed after the noun
or phrase they qualify; for the
sake of —ing *causā/grātiā* + gen.
gerund/gerundive phrase (place
causā/grātiā after noun or phrase it
governs)

same *īdem eadem idem*
at the same time *simul*

Sanga *Sang-a ae* 1m.

save (= keep safe) *seruō* 1; save X from
Y *ēripiō* 3/4 *ēripuī ēreptus* (X acc.
from Y dat.)

say *dīcō* 3 *dīxī dictus*
introducing direct speech *inquam inquis*
inquit 3rd pl. *inquiunt*
say ... not *negō* 1 (often with acc. + inf.)
say so, on the ... of *iussū* + gen.

scene *tumult-us ūs* 4m.

scorn: see 'pour scorn on'

scoundrel *scelest-us a um* – use as a noun

sea *mare mar-is* 3n; abl. *marī* = by sea

section of society *ōrdō ōrdin-is* 3m.

see *uideō* 2 *uīdī uīsus*

seek *petō* 3; *quaerō* 3
seek out *requīrō* 3 *requīsīuī requīsītus*

seem *uideor* 2 pass. *uīsus*

seize *occupō* 1

self-control *continenti-a ae* 1f.

senate *senāt-us ūs* 4m.

send *mittō* 3 *mīsī missus* (X acc. to Y *ad* +
acc.)

send away *dīmittō* 3 *dīmīsī dīmissus*

seriously *grauiter*

seriousness *grauitās grauitāt-is* 3f.

Sertorius, of *Sertōriān-us a um*

Servilius *Seruīli-us ī* 2m.

set *occidō* 3 (intrans.)

set out *proficīscor* 3 *profectus*
set (a trap) *īnsidiās parō* 1 for X (dat.)
set free *līberō* 1
set (guards) *dispōnō* 3 *disposuī dispositus*

set on fire *incendō* 3 *incendī incēnsus*

shall: use future tense

shall have: use future perf. tense

shame *pudor pudōr-is* 3m.

shape *fōrm-a ae* 1f.

she: use 3rd s. of verb; for emphasis use *illa* or *haec*

ship *nāuis nāu-is* 3f.

shore *lītus lītor-is* 3n.

should *dēbeō* 2; occasionally subj. alone is used (jussive): e.g. 'X should do Y'; gerundive is also used to express 'should' as obligation, X (dat.) should do Y (n. gerundive + *est*). Where 'should' occurs in subordinate clauses check whether the conjunction takes a subj.; if so, then nothing else is required to express 'should' (e.g. until troops should be sent ... *dum* + subj.)

shout *clāmō* 1

   keep shouting *clāmitō* 1

shrine *fān-um ī* 2n.

shut in *claudō* 3 *claudī clausus*

Sicily *Sicili-a ae* 1f.

signal *sign-um ī* 2n.

silent, be *taceō* 2

silently *tacit-us a um*

silver *argent-um ī* 2n.

since *cum* + subj.

slave *seru-us ī* 2m.

slave-girl/woman *seru-a ae* 1f.

sleep *dormiō* 4

small *paru-us a um*; very small *minim-us a um*

snatch (away) *rapiō* 3/4 *rapuī raptus*

so X (adj./adv.) *tam*

   so = to such an extent *adeō*

   so as to / so that (purpose = in order that) *ut* + subj. (negative *nē*); see **150** for rules of sequence

   so as to ... more —ly / so that ... more —ly (purpose) *quo* + comp. adverb + subj.; see **150** for rules of sequence

   so great *tant-us a um*

society, section of *ōrdō ōrdin-is* 3m.

soldier *mīlēs mīlit-is* 3m.

someone *aliquis*

son *fīli-us ī* 2m. (voc. s. *fīlī*)

soon *mox*; *iam*

sorrow *lūct-us ūs* 4m.

sort (of person/people who) *is quī* + subj. (generic); sort of person that *tālis... quālis*

Sosia *Sōsi-a ae* 1m.

source, X is a ... of pleasure to Y: X (nom.) *uoluptātī est* Y (dat.)

spare *parcō* 3 *pepercī parsum* (+ dat.); in passive used impersonally, X (dat.) will be spared (3rd s.) by Y *a* (*ab*) + abl.

speak *dīcō* 3 *dīxī dictus*; *loquor* 3 dep. *locūtus*

   speak to (= address) *alloquor* 3 dep. *allocūtus*

speech, make a *ōrātiōnem habeō* 2

spirits *anim-us ī* 2m. (often plural in this sense)

spot *loc-us ī* 2m.; pl. *loc-a ōrum* 2n.

spouse *coniūnx coniug-is* 3m./f.

stage *scaen-a ae* 1f.

stand *stō* 1 *stetī status*; how the matter stands *ita ... ut rēs est*

   stand in X's way *obstō* 1 *obstitī* (+ dat.)

   stand for consulship *cōnsulātum pētō* (3 *petīuī petītus*)

Staphyla *Staphyl-a ae* 1f.

star *sign-um ī* 2n.

start *coepī coepisse* (past tenses only). Occasionally 'started to' can be expressed by either (a) historic infinitive or (b) imperfect indicative

state (strongly) *affirmō* 1; *dīcō* 3 *dīxī dictus*

state (noun) *rēs pūblic-a rē-ī pūblic-ae* 5f. + 1/2f. adj.; *cīuitās cīuitāt-is* 3f.

station *collocō* 1; *pōnō* 3 *posuī positus*

statue *simulācr-um ī* 2n.

stay *maneō* 2 *mānsī mānsum*

stop *prohibeō* 2 (X acc. from doing Y inf.); *impediō* 4 (X acc. from doing Y: *quōminus* or *nē* when *impediō* positive; *quōminus* or *quīn* when negative)

story *fām-a ae* 1f. 'The story is that...' *fāma est* followed by acc. + inf.; tell a story – use *rēs* or n. of *hic*

strategic *opportūn-us a um*

street *ui-a ae* 1f.
stretch forth *tendō* 3 *tetendī tēnsus*
strict *seuēr-us a um*
strike *feriō* 4
strip *nūdō* 1; (= rob corpses) *spoliō* 1
stupid *stult-us a um*
substitute *substituō* 3 *substituī substitūtus*
succeed *rem bene gerō* 3 *gessī gestus*
such, to such an extent *adeō*
   such an important *tant-us a um*
suddenly *subitō*
suffer *patior* 3/4 dep. *passus*

summon *uocō* 1; *arcessō* 3 *arcessīuī arcessītus*
suppliant *supplex supplic-is* (adj.); also used as a noun
supporter *soci-us ī* 2m.
surely? *nōnne*; surely not? *num*; surely *certē*
suspect *suspicor* 1 dep.
swift *celer celer-is e*
sword *ferr-um ī* 2n.
Syracusans *Syrācūsān-ī ōrum* 2m. pl.
Syracuse *Syrācūs-ae ārum* 1f. pl.; locative *Syrācūsīs*

T

take (= capture) *capiō* 3/4 *cēpī captus*; (= lead off) *dēdūcō* 3 *dēdūxī dēductus*
take away *auferō auferre abstulī ablātus*; *tollō* 3 *sustulī sublātus*
take care lest/that *prōuideō* 2 *prōuīdī prōuīsus nē* + subj.
take X from Y: *auferō* X (acc.) from Y (dat.)
talk *loquor* 3 dep. *locūtus*
Tarquinius *Tarquini-us ī* 2m.
task *opus oper-is* 3n.
tear away *conuellō* 3 *conuellī conuulsus*
Teleboans *Tēlebo-ae ārum* 1m. (pl.)
tell *loquor* 3 dep. *locūtus*; *dīcō* 3 *dīxī dictus*; (= relate) *nārrō* 1 (X acc. to Y dat.); (= order) *iubeō* 2 *iussī iussus*
temple *templ-um ī* 2n.
than *quam*; or use abl. of comparison
that *ille illa illud*; *is ea id*
that (conjunction): use acc. + inf. construction after verbs of saying thinking, perceiving; *ut* + subj. after verbs of command (neg. *nē*); so... that (as a result) *ut* + subj.; see **149**
the: simply use noun
their: referring to the subject, use noun alone
them: use pl. of *hic ille* or *is*
then (= next) *deinde*; (= at that point) *tum*
Theomnastus *Theomnāst-us ī* 2m.
there *ibi*
there is *est*
there are *sunt*
there was *erat, fuit* or *factus est*
therefore *igitur* (2nd word)

these: see 'this'
they: use 3rd pl. verb
thief *fūr fūr-is* 3m.
thing *rēs rē-ī* 5f.; or use neut. adj.
think *opīnor* 1 dep.; *arbitror* 1 dep.; *putō* 1; think X (to be) Y: *habeō/arbitror* X (acc.) Y (acc.)
thirty *trīgintā*
this *hic haec hoc*; sometimes possible to use part of *quī quae quod* at beginning of sentence
those: see 'that'
thousand *mīlle* pl. *mīlia* (='thousands of' + gen.)
threaten *minor* 1 dep. (+ dat.); threaten X with Y: *minor* X (dat.) Y (acc.)
threats *min-ae ārum* 1f. pl.
three *trēs tri-um*
three hundred *trecent-ī ae a*
through *per* (+ acc.); of extent of time use acc. alone; = because of: use abl. of cause
throughout: use abl. of place (where the noun has an adjective); or *per* (+ acc.)
throw *coniciō* 3/4 *coniēcī coniectus*
thus *sīc*; *ita*
time *tempus tempor-is* 3n.
to (motion) *ad* (+ acc.), *in* (+ acc.); (gainer) plain dative
  to X (vb): after *uolō, nōlō, mālō* use infinitive; prefer X to Y: see 'prefer'
  to (as in: order X to – indirect command) *ut* + subj.; see also 'manage to'

to: where this indicates purpose use *ut/
ne* (not to) + subj. For sequence see
150. In some cases it is possible to
use *quī* + subj., see **150**; also *ad* +
gerundive + noun (acc.); or *ad* +
gerund (acc.)

to such an extent (... that ...) *adeō...
(ut* + subj.)

today *hodiē*

too much *nimis* (+ gen.)

top *summ-us a um*

touch *tangō 3 tetigī tāctus*

towards *ad* (+ acc.)

town *oppid-um ī* 2n.

Transalpine Gaul *Galli-ae Transalpin-ae*
1f.

trap, set a *īnsidiās parō* 1 (for X
dat.)

treasure *thēsaur-us ī* 2m.

trick *dol-us ī* 2m.

troops *cōpi-ae ārum* lf. pl.

trouble *mal-um ī* 2n.

Troy *Trōi-a ae* lf.

true *uēr-us a um*

truly *uērō*

truth, in *uērō*

try *cōnor* 1 dep.

turn, do a good *bene faciō* 3/4 (+ dat.)

turn over (trans.) *uoluō 3 uoluī uolūtus*

twins *gemin-ī ōrum* 2m. pl.

two *du-o ae o*

two hundred *ducent-ī ae a*

U

Umbrenus *Umbrēn-us ī* 2m.

understand *intellegō 3 intellēxī*

unhappy *miser miser-a um*

unless *nisi*

unmarried girl *uirgō uirgin-is* 3f.

until (with idea of purpose) *dum* + subj.

up, what's...?: see 'what'

upbraid *castīgō* 1

urge *cohortor* 1 dep. (X acc. to Y: *ut* +
subj.)

us: see 'we'

use *ūtor* 3 dep. *ūsus* ('using' = *ūs-us a um*)
used to —: use imperfect indicative

utmost *summ-us a um*

V

various *dīuers-us a um*

Verres *Verrēs Verr-is* 3m.

very: use superlative form of adj. or adv. as
appropriate

very quickly: use superlative adverb (from
celer); or abl. phrase of manner,
summā celeritāte

via *per* (+ acc.)

victor *uictor uictōr-is* 3m.

victory *uictōri-a ae* lf.

view, in my *ut opīnor*

vile *turp-is e*

visit *uīsō* 3

voice *uōx uōc-is* 3f.

W

wage (war) (*bellum*) *gerō 3 gessī gestus*;
(*bellum*) *faciō* 3/4

wait *exspectō* 1; *maneō 2 mānsī mānsum*

wall *mur-us ī* 2m.

walls *moen-ia ium* 3m. pl.

want *uolō uelle uoluī*; not want *nōlō nōlle
nōluī*

war *bell-um ī* 2n.

was/were —ing: use imperfect indicative

watch *īnspiciō 3/4 īnspexī īnspectus*

water *aqu-a ae* lf.

way (= habit, custom) *mōs mōr-is* 3m.; (=
manner) *mod-us ī* 2m.; (= journey)
iter itiner-is 3n.

make one's way *iter faciō* 3/4
ways *mōr-ēs um* 3m. pl.

we *nōs* (if emphatic: otherwise, use plain 1st
person pl.)

wealth *dīuiti-ae ārum* 2f. pl.

weapon *tēl-um ī* 2n.

weight (= authority or influence) *auctōritās
auctōritāt-is* 3f.

well known *clār-us a um*

were to ... in conditional sentences: pres.
subj.

what? *quid?*; or use appropriate form of the
adjective *quī?*

what X? *quid* + gen.

what's up? *quid negōtī est?*

what a *ō* + acc. of exclamation

when *ubi* (+ perf. indic.); with deponent
verbs, use past participle; *cum* +
plupf. subj. or use abl. abs.

where *ubi*

where to? *quō*

which?: use appropriate form of *quī* to agree
with noun

which: use nom. of *quī quae quod*; or
use a part. agreeing with the noun
described

while *dum* + present indicative (when the
main clause interrupts the action of
the *dum* clause); or use abl. abs. with
pres. part.

who? *quis*

who *quī quae quod*; see **106–7, 145**; **150**

whole (of) *tōt-us a um* (gen. s. *tōtīus*, dat.
s. *tōtī*)

whom?: use acc. s./pl. m./f. of *quis* as
appropriate

whom: see 'who' (use acc. s. or pl.)

whose?: use gen. s./pl. of *quis* as appropriate

whose: use gen. s. or pl. of *quī quae quod*;
or dat. (with parts of *esse*)

why? *cūr*; *quārē*; in indirect questions
followed by subj. verb

wicked *mal-us a um*; *scelest-us a um*

wife *uxor uxōr-is* 3f.

wild beast *bēsti-a ae* lf.

will: use fut. tense

will have: use fut. perf. tense

win *uincō* 3 *uīcī uictus*

wisdom *sapienti-a ae* lf.

wish *uolō uelle uoluī*; not wish *nōlō nōlle
nōluī*

with (= accompanied by) *cum* (+ abl.);
(= by means of, or describing
circumstances) plain abl.; with X
—ing – use abl. abs. with pres. part.

without *sine* (+ abl.); without doubt *sine
dubiō*

woman *fēmin-a ae* 1f; *mulier mulier-is* 3f.

worry *cūr-a ae* lf.

worse *pēior us*

worship *colō* 3 *coluī cultus*

worth as much as *tantī … quantī …* ; of no
worth *nihilī*

worthy (of) *dign-us a um* (+ abl.)

would: use fut. inf. (in acc. + inf.
construction – 'that' clause – in
secondary sequence); in conditional
sentences use subj. (see rules in **144**,
173); in purpose clauses: use correct
sequence (impf. subj. see **150**); I
would like = *uelim* (pres. subj. –
potential)

would be: in indirect statement past
sequence use supine + *īrī* (e.g.
captum īrī would be captured) or *fore
ut* + subj. (pres. for primary, impf.
for secondary sequence)

would have: in conditional sentences use
plupf. subj. or impf. subj.

wound *uulnerō* 1

wretched *miser miser-a um*

write (poetry) *faciō* (*uersūs* 4m. pl.)

Y

year *ann-us ī* 2m.

ye gods! *prō dī immortālēs!*

yes *ita*

yet *tamen* (2nd word in clause)

yield *cēdō* 3 *cessī cessum* (to X dat.)

you (s.) *tū*, (pl.) *uōs* (only if emphatic: if not,
use 2nd person s./pl. of verb)

young man *iuuenis iuuen-is* 3m.

your *tu-us a um* (when 'you' is one person);
uester uestr-a um when 'you'
is pl.

yourself: use part of *tū*

yourselves *uōs*

youth *iuuenis iuuen-is is* 3m.

Index of grammar

Numbers alone refer to Sections 1–6 in this volume (adscript numbers refer to numbered definitions and superscript numbers to notes within those, e.g. 48.1, 89⁶). Letters A–W (with numbers/letters following) refer to the Reference Grammar (pp. 283–396). Page numbers are given for grammar which occurs outside these parts. For a simplified definition of terms, see the Glossary of Grammatical Terms, pp. xvii–xxiv.

Table 1.1 Active verbs

	Indicative	Infinitive	Imperative	Subjunctive	Participles
Present	*amō, habeō*, 2, 3; *dīcō*, 24; *audiō*, 25; *capiō*, 33	41	*amō*, 1; *habeō* 2; *dīcō*, 24; *audiō*, 25; *capiō* 36; irr., 37	129	122
Future	50	97	A2 note 1	172⁴, A2 note 2, L–V Intro.(c)	81–3
Imperfect	89			132	
Perfect	65	95		167	
Future perfect	140				
Pluperfect	104			123	

Table 1.2 Deponents

	Indicative	Infinitive	Imperative	Subjunctive	Participles
Present	58	58	58	130	122
Future	68	97	A2 note 1	172[4], A2 note 2, L–V Intro.(c)	81
Imperfect	90			133	
Perfect	75	96		168	77
Future perfect	141				
Pluperfect	105			124	

Table 1.3 Passive

	Indicative	Infinitive	Imperative	Subjunctive	Participles
Present	112	118	117	131	
Future	113	118	B2 note		
Imperfect	114			134	
Perfect	115	118		169	82–3, 119
Future perfect	142				
Pluperfect	116		125		
Gerundive				151